This book is due for return on or before the last date shown below.

The Routledge Companion to Alternative Organization

Despite the Great Recession, slightly different forms of global capitalism are still portrayed as the only game in town by the vast majority of people in power in the world today. Unbridled growth, trade liberalization and competition are advocated as the only or best ways of organizing the contemporary world. Unemployment, yawning gaps between rich and poor, political disengagement and environmental devastation are too often seen as acceptable 'side effects' of the dominance of neo-liberalism.

But the reality is that capitalism has always been contested and that people have created many other ways of providing for themselves. This book explores economic and organizational possibilities which extend far beyond the narrow imagination of economists and organizational theorists. Chapters on co-operatives, community currencies, the transition movement, scrounging, co-housing and much more paint a rich picture of the ways in which another world is not only possible, but is already taking shape. The aim of this companion is to move beyond complaining about the present and into exploring this diversity of organizational possibilities. Our starting point is a critical analysis of contemporary global capitalism and is merely the opening for thinking about organizing as a form of politics by other means, and one that can be driven by the values of solidarity, freedom and responsibility.

This comprehensive companion, with an international cast of contributors, gives voice to forms of organizing which remain unrepresented or marginalized in organizational studies and conventional politics, yet which offer more promising grounds for social and environmental justice. It is a valuable resource for students, activists and researchers interested in alternative approaches to economy and society in a variety of disciplinary and interdisciplinary fields.

Martin Parker is Professor at the School of Management, University of Leicester, UK.

George Cheney is Professor of Communication Studies and Coordinator of Doctoral Education in Communication and Information at Kent State University, Ohio, USA.

Valérie Fournier is Senior Lecturer in Organization Studies at Leicester University, UK.

Chris Land is Senior Lecturer in Work and Organization at the University of Essex, UK.

Routledge Companions in Business, Management and Accounting

Routledge Companions in Business, Management and Accounting are similar to what some publishers call 'handbooks' i.e. prestige reference works providing an overview of a whole subject area or sub-discipline, and which survey the state of the discipline including emerging and cutting edge areas. These books provide a comprehensive, up-to-date, definitive work of reference which can be cited as an authoritative source on the subject.

One of the key aspects of the *Routledge Companions in Business, Management and Accounting* series is their international scope and relevance. Edited by an array of well regarded scholars, these volumes also benefit from teams of contributors which reflect an international range of perspectives.

Individually, *Routledge Companions in Business, Management and Accounting* provide an impactful one-stop-shop resource for each theme covered, whilst collectively they represent a comprehensive learning and research resource for researchers and postgraduates and practitioners.

Published titles in this series include:

The Routledge Companion to Fair Value and Financial Reporting
Edited by Peter Walton

The Routledge Companion to Nonprofit Marketing
Edited by Adrian Sargeant and Walter Wymer Jr

The Routledge Companion to Accounting History
Edited by John Richard Edwards, Stephen P. Walker

The Routledge Companion to Creativity
Edited by Tudor Rickards, Mark A. Runco, Susan Moger

The Routledge Companion to Strategic Human Resource Management
Edited by John Storey, Patrick M. Wright, David Ulrich

The Routledge Companion to International Business Coaching
Edited by Michel Moral, Geoffrey Abbott

The Routledge Companion to Organizational Change
Edited by David M. Boje, Bernard Burnes and John Hassard

The Routledge Companion to Cost Management
Edited by Falconer Mitchell, Hanne Nørreklit and Morten Jakobsen

The Routledge Companion to Digital Consumption
Edited by Russell W. Belk and Rosa Llamas

The Routledge Companion to Identity and Consumption
Edited by Ayalla A. Ruvio and Russell W. Belk

The Routledge Companion to Public-Private Partnerships
Edited by Piet de Vries and Etienne B. Yehoue

The Routledge Companion to Alternative Organization

Edited by Martin Parker, George Cheney,
Valérie Fournier and Chris Land

Routledge
Taylor & Francis Group

LONDON AND NEW YORK

First published 2014
by Routledge
2 Park Square, Milton Park, Abingdon, Oxon OX14 4RN

and by Routledge
711 Third Avenue, New York, NY 10017

Routledge is an imprint of the Taylor & Francis Group, an informa business

British Library Cataloguing in Publication Data
A catalogue record for this book is available from the British Library

Library of Congress Cataloging in Publication Data
A catalog record for this book has been requested

ISBN: 978–0–415–78226–5 (hbk)
ISBN: 978–0–203–72535–1 (ebk)

Typeset in Bembo
by Refinecatch Limited, Bungay, Suffolk

Printed and bound in Great Britain by
TJ International Ltd, Padstow, Cornwall

Contents

Contents

List of figures

List of tables

Author biographies

Maurizio Atzeni is Marie Curie Research Fellow at the University of Loughborough (UK) and at the Conicet's Centro de Investigaciones Laborales (CEIL) based in Buenos Aires. He has published widely on the issues of trade unionism in Argentina, on mobilization theory and collective action, and on workers' self-management. Recent books include *Workplace Conflict: Mobilization and Solidarity in Argentina* and the edited *Alternative Work Organizations*, both published with Palgrave. He is currently involved in an EU-sponsored project on workers' organization and collective action among informal workers in the city of Buenos Aires.

Molly Scott Cato is Professor of Strategy and Sustainability at Roehampton University and has worked for several years as a green economist. Her latest book, *The Bioregional Economy: Land, Liberty and the Pursuit of Happiness* (Routledge, 2012), develops ideas for a new model of stable and sustainable economic life. In 2009, she published *Green Economics: An Introduction to Theory, Policy and Practice* and she has also written widely on themes concerned with mutualism, social enterprise, policy responses to climate change, banking and finance, and local economies. Molly is an active member of the Green Party, the party's national speaker on economics, and leader of the Green group on Stroud District Council. She works with Transition Stroud and was involved in the launch of a local currency in Stroud in 2009. She is also a Director of Stroud Common Wealth.

George Cheney (PhD, Purdue University, 1985) is Professor of Communication Studies and Coordinator of Doctoral Education in Communication and Information at Kent State University, Ohio, USA. He is an associate investigator with the Ohio Employee Ownership Center, also at Kent State. Previously, George held faculty appointments at the universities of Illinois at Urbana-Champaign, Colorado at Boulder, Montana-Missoula, Utah, and Texas at Austin. George has lectured, taught, conducted research, and consulted extensively in Europe, Latin America and New Zealand (where he has served as an adjunct professor at the University of Waikato in Hamilton since 1998). His teaching and research interests include: identity at work and in organizations, employee participation and workplace democracy, globalization and consumerism, professional ethics and corporate social responsibility, transparency in theory and practice, and discourses of peace and war. George has worked with organizations in all three major sectors. Working solo or collaboratively, George has published 10 books and more than 100 articles, chapters and reviews. George has followed the Mondragon cooperatives since 1992, publishing an award-winning book, *Values at Work* (Cornell University Press, 1999, 2002), as well as a series of articles on the cooperatives' encounters with market globalization and their efforts to revitalize practices associated with their core values of participation, equality and solidarity (especially in collaboration with the LANKI institute for cooperative studies at Mondragon). Currently, George is building on that work as well as collaborating on cooperative projects in several parts of the US. As an engaged scholar and citizen, George is committed to service learning, community-based research, and the practical contributions of the social sciences and the humanities in addressing social, economic and political problems.

Leanne Cutcher is an Associate Professor in the Discipline of Work and Organizational Studies in the School of Business at the University of Sydney, Australia. Her research explores the interconnections between production, consumption and reproduction processes. This has led to an exploration of how issues of gender, race, space and age impact on organizational, employee and consumer identity. The research sites for much of this work have been credit unions.

Karen Dale is Senior Lecturer in the Department of Organisation, Work and Technology at Lancaster University, UK. She has also worked for the universities of Warwick, Essex and Leicester. Before becoming an academic, Karen worked in the NHS and local government – where she became acutely aware of the significance of gender and reproductive labour – and later worked in policy development and as a Women's Equality Officer trying, in some small way, to address these issues. Karen has also written about embodiment and organizations, most extensively in *Anatomising Embodiment and Organisation Theory* (Palgrave, 2001), and about architecture, space and social materiality as related to organization studies, including *The Spaces of Organisation and the Organisation of Space: Power, Identity and Materiality at Work* with Gibson Burrell (Palgrave, 2008).

Massimo De Angelis is Professor of Political Economy at the University of East London. He is author of *The Beginning of History* (Pluto, 2007) and editor of the web journal *The Commoner*, which he founded in 2001. His research interests and publications span from the critique of economic discourse to a social conflict-based theory of capitalist systems. Over the last ten years he has been working on a theoretical framework to understand the role of commons within capitalism and their potential for radical emancipation. His scientific research is interwoven with practical work in rural areas of the Italian Apennines, where he is among the founders and promoters of an association that aims at catalyzing activities such as community gardening, theatre labs and participative methods of territorial governance.

Jeff Ferrell is Professor of Sociology at Texas Christian University, USA, and Visiting Professor of Criminology at the University of Kent, UK. He is author of the books *Crimes of Style*; *Tearing Down the Streets*; *Empire of Scrounge*; and, with Keith Hayward and Jock Young, *Cultural Criminology: An Invitation* (winner of the 2009 Distinguished Book Award from the American Society of Criminology's Division of International Criminology). He is co-editor of the books *Cultural Criminology*; *Ethnography at the Edge*; *Making Trouble*; *Cultural Criminology Unleashed*; and *Cultural Criminology: Theories of Crime*. Jeff Ferrell is founding and current editor of the NYU Press book series *Alternative Criminology*, and one of the founding editors of the journal *Crime, Media, Culture* (winner of the ALPSP 2006 Charlesworth Award for Best New Journal). In 1998, he received the Critical Criminologist of the Year Award from the Critical Criminology Division of the American Society of Criminology.

Nicolas Fischer is a tenured researcher at the French National Centre for Scientific Research (CNRS), appointed at the Centre de recherches sociologiques sur le droit et les institutions pénales (CESDIP), at the University of Versailles Saint-Quentin in Guyancourt. His research focuses on immigration policies and immigration control in Europe, the sociology of confinement institutions and the sociology of law and the state. He completed his PhD on the history and ethnography of immigration detention facilities at the Institut d'Etudes Politiques de Paris in 2007. His current research focuses on the independent control of confinement devices and the 'transparency' of contemporary repressive practices.

Valérie Fournier is Senior Lecturer in Organization Studies at Leicester University. Her research interests range from Critical Management Studies to alternative organizations and economies. Her recent work has explored ideas of utopia, degrowth and communal organizing. She is currently working on the commons as a mode of organizing, as well as on the implications of permaculture for understanding our relationships with the environment and the idea of sustainability.

Shiv Ganesh (PhD, Purdue University, 2000) is a Professor at Massey University's School of Communication, Journalism and Marketing. Shiv studies substantive issues that arise from the intersection of communication processes with globalization, civil society organizing and digital technologies. He is currently leading a funded project that traces how emerging and established forms of social justice organizing intersect in volatile technological environments. His work has appeared in such outlets as *Communication Monographs, Communication Theory, Human Relations, Management Communication Quarterly, Organization Studies*, and *Work, Employment & Society*. Shiv's writing has also won several awards; most recently, his work with Heather Zoller on dialogue, activism and social change won an outstanding article of the year award from the National Communication Association in the USA. In 2012 he received the International Communication Association's Frederic Jablin Award for Outstanding Contributions to the field of Organizational Communication. He was also editor-in-chief of the *Journal of International and Intercultural Communication* from 2010 to 2013.

David Harvie teaches finance and political economy at the University of Leicester School of Management, where he is a member of the Centre for Philosophy and Political Economy. He is also a member of The Free Association writing collective (www.freelyassociating.org) and an editor of *Turbulence: Ideas for Movement* (www.turbulence.org.uk). As well as commons, David has written on globalization, social movements and the political economy of education. Many of his writings can be downloaded from http://www2.le.ac.uk/departments/management/people/dharvie or from http://leicester.academia.edu/DavidHarvie. He can be contacted at d.harvie@le.ac.uk.

Josiah Heyman is Professor of Anthropology and Chair of the Department of Anthropology and Sociology at University of Texas El Paso. His work focuses on borders, states, power, public issues and engaged social sciences. He is the author or editor of three books and over seventy scholarly articles, book chapters and essays. His most recent publications are "Culture Theory and the US–Mexico Border," *in A Companion to Border Studies* (Wiley-Blackwell, 2012) and (with John Symons) "Borders" in *A Companion to Moral Anthropology* (Wiley-Blackwell, 2012). He has also participated in numerous community initiatives addressing public policies and human rights at the US–Mexico border, and is currently working with community organizations on detailed policy language concerning human rights performance of so-called border security agencies to be included in possible immigration reform legislation. He can be contacted at jmheyman@utep.edu.

Donald E. Janzen's educational background consists of BS and MS degrees in physics from the University of Louisville, and MA and PhD degrees in anthropology from the University of Michigan. As an anthropologist, he first specialized in archaeology and conducted extensive excavations at the Pleasant Hill Shaker Village in Kentucky. He continued with investigations at the White Water Shaker Village in Ohio and the West Union Shaker Village in western Indiana. For the past thirty-five years he has been visiting both historic and contemporary cooperating communities in the United States as a cultural anthropologist. He recently donated over 12,000 digital images, from the 225 communities he has visited, to the Center for Communal Studies at the University of Southern Indiana. He is a Charter Member of the Communal Studies Association and served as its Executive Secretary for thirteen years.

Kelum Jayasinghe is a Reader in Accounting. He joined the Essex Business School at the University of Essex in September 2008, having previously held positions at the University of Wales (Aberystwyth), the University of Bradford (UK) and the University of Colombo (Sri Lanka). He has produced a number of research papers from his research projects and has publications in the *Accounting, Auditing and Accountability Journal* (AAAJ), *Critical Perspectives on Accounting* (CPA), *Qualitative Research in Accounting and Management* (QRAM), the *International Journal of Critical Accounting* (IJCA), and the *International Journal of Entrepreneurial Behaviour and Research* (IJRBR).

Jennifer Keahey has worked in Africa, Asia, Europe and North America as a practitioner and as a scholar. She holds a BA in Anthropology and French, an MA in International Development and Social Change, and, in spring 2013, received a PhD in Sociology from Colorado State University where she was closely involved with the Center for Fair & Alternative Trade (CFAT). For her dissertation research, Dr Keahey collaborated with a team of scholars and practitioners to design and implement a participatory commodity networking research programme in South Africa's Rooibos tea sector. Her broader research interests include political economy, development, inequality and sustainable social change, with particular expertise in alternative standards and certifications. In August 2013, Dr Keahey joined Arizona State University West's School of Social and Behavioral Sciences, where she works as an Assistant Professor of Sociology and remains affiliated with CFAT as a Research Associate.

Chris Land is a Senior Lecturer in Work and Organisation at the University of Essex. His research encompasses a range of topics from social movement organizing and the idea of community in organization studies, to the concept of value and the relationship between economic value and non-economic values, for example, ethics and aesthetics. He is currently working to combine these themes in an analysis of the shifting ideological formations of contemporary capitalism as it struggles to respond to an onslaught of crises – ecological, financial and human – that challenge its basic legitimacy as a mode of organization.

Docey Lewis has worked for thirty-five years in over forty countries as a textile designer and business adviser for commercial, fair trade and international development projects. She began her career in San Francisco as a weaver and yarn designer, developing fabrics for fashion and interiors. In the 1980s, Docey founded IMA Designs, a weaving factory and commercial design studio in the Philippines with a focus on natural fibre wall coverings. Now based in New Harmony, Indiana, Docey and her son Owen are partners in a textile and paper workshop in Nepal. Docey is a consultant for 3form, Inc's *Full Circle* product line and has been Senior Textile Consultant to Aid to Artisans (ATA) since 1988, most recently working on organic cotton in Senegal. She has served on ATA's board as well as on those of Vital Edge Aid and the HandEye Fund.

Geoff Lightfoot is Senior Lecturer in Entrepreneurship and Accounting at the University of Leicester, where he is also a member of the Centre for Philosophy and Political Economy. His research is wide-ranging but recently his primary focus has been on the historical development of the academic discipline of finance since the 1950s and the practical application of financial instruments in different aspects of social and economic life. The two overlap, and a particular interest has been how the academic community of finance scholars became so entwined with financial institutions that the opportunity for any meaningful scholarly critique was lost. Alongside this, he has examined the monopoly profits and egregious behaviour of academic publishers, and the sociological precursors to contemporary theorizations of entrepreneurship.

James Loucky is Professor of Anthropology at Western Washington University, where teaching and research revolve around migration, human rights, borders, and family and community well-being throughout the Americas. He has worked closely with Maya communities in Guatemala and Los Angeles, and with other Latino groups across North America. His authored or co-edited works include *Humane Migration: Establishing Legitimacy and Rights for Displaced People* (Kumarian, 2012), *Mesoamerican/North American Partnerships for Community Wellbeing* (Practicing Anthropology 34, 2012), *Immigration in America Today: An Encyclopedia* (Greenwood, 2006), and *The Maya Diaspora: Guatemalan Roots, New American Lives* (Temple, 2000). He can be reached at James.Loucky@wwu.edu.

Seonaidh McDonald is a Reader in Sustainable Behaviours at Aberdeen Business School, Robert Gordon University. Her research interests centre on sustainable consumption, and she has investigated individual behaviour and decision-making processes across a wide range of issues, including waste, travel, domestic appliances, food, household goods and energy. She also has a strong interest in qualitative research methods and how these are used within management research.

Marianne Maeckelbergh is Lecturer in Cultural Anthropology and Development Sociology at Leiden University, the Netherlands. She is the author of *The Will of the Many: How the Alterglobalisation Movement is Changing the Face of Democracy* (Pluto, 2009) and has been active in grass-roots social movements since the early 1990s.

Peter Mason is CEO of the Credit Union Foundation Australia in Sydney, Australia. His work includes managing credit union development projects in the Asia Pacific region. He is also completing his PhD at Deakin University, Melbourne, where he is undertaking research relating to social capital development within credit unions and their associated communities in the Solomon Islands, Cambodia and Timor Leste.

Pete North is Reader in Alternative Economies in the Department of Geography and Planning at the University of Liverpool. He gained his BA in History and Politics in 1984. After a few years working for the Departments of Employment, Trade and Industry, and Environment, he gained his MA in Peace Studies from the University of Bradford (1993) and his PhD from the School for Advanced Urban Studies at the University of Bristol (1997). He joined the University of Liverpool in 2002. His research focuses on social movements that organize broadly against globalization and for localization, and that develop alternatives to capitalism, in particular alternative currencies. He is interested in thinking about links between economies, livelihoods and environments that are not exploitative and which provide an alternative to forms of growth and development that may not be sustainable in the long term, given the need to avoid dangerous climate change.

Martin Parker works at the School of Management, University of Leicester. He writes about culture, ethics and politics, and is particularly interested in alternative forms of organizing. Recent work includes *The Dictionary of Alternatives* (Zed, 2007, with Fournier and Reedy), and *Alternative Business: Outlaws, Crime and Culture* (Routledge, 2012). He also writes about angels, the circus, shipping containers and skyscrapers.

Joshua M. Pearce received his PhD in Materials Engineering from Pennsylvania State University. He then developed the first Sustainability Program in the Pennsylvania State System of Higher Education as an Assistant Professor of Physics at Clarion University of Pennsylvania and helped develop the Applied Sustainability Graduate Program while at Queen's University, Canada. He is currently an Associate Professor, cross-appointed in the Department of Materials Science & Engineering, and in the Department of Electrical & Computer Engineering at the Michigan Technological University where he runs the Open Sustainability Technology Research Group. His research concentrates on the use of open-source appropriate technology to find collaborative solutions to problems in sustainability and poverty reduction. His research spans areas of electronic device physics, materials engineering of solar photovoltaic cells and 3-D printing, but also includes applied sustainability and energy policy.

Donald E. Pitzer is Professor Emeritus of History and Director Emeritus of the Center for Communal Studies at the University of Southern Indiana. He earned a bachelor's degree at Wittenberg University, his master's and PhD in history from The Ohio State University, and was a scholar-in-residence at Harvard. He is a founder and first president of the Communal Studies Association and the International Communal Studies Association. He was CSA executive director from 1976 to 1993. Starting with the historic Harmonist and Owenite communal groups of New Harmony, Indiana, he has visited and researched communes and intentional communities worldwide, and taught, lectured and published widely. His theory of developmental communalism goes beyond examining individual communities. It emphasizes why whole movements adopt communal living as a method of social reform and helps explain how the evolution of their alternative organization relates to the endurance and success of both the movements and their intentional communities.

Laura T. Raynolds is a Professor of Sociology and the Co-Director of the Center for Fair & Alternative Trade (CFAT) at Colorado State University. She holds a PhD in Development Sociology from Cornell University. Her research focuses on globalization, international development, food and agriculture, gendered labour forces, and fair and alternative trade. Laura Raynolds is co-editor and a lead author of *Fair Trade: The Challenges of Transforming Globalization*, as well as the author of over thirty-five articles and book chapters on related themes. She has received grants for her groundbreaking research from the National Science Foundation, Ford Foundation, US Agency for International Development, and the John D. & Catherine T. MacArthur Foundation. Dr Raynolds is currently working on a field-based study of Fair Trade-certified flower production in Ecuador.

Alf Rehn is Chair of Management and Organization at Åbo Akademi University, Finland. His research has dealt with subjects as varied as creativity, haute cuisine, project management, popular culture, philosophy, boredom, innovation and luxury, and has despite this published in a series of books and a large number of articles. He is a devoted fan of Ethel Merman and the divine Patsy Cline. See www.alfrehn.com.

Ned Rossiter is an Australian media theorist and author of *Organized Networks: Media Theory, Creative Labour, New Institutions* (2006). He was based in Perth, Melbourne, Northern Ireland, Beijing, Shanghai and Ningbo before taking up an appointment as Professor of Communication in 2011 in the School of Humanities and Communication Arts at the University of Western Sydney where he is also a member of the Institute for Culture and Society. Ned is also an Honorary Research Fellow at the Centre for Creative Industries, Peking University.

The Trapese Collective are Kim Bryan, Paul Chatterton and Alice Cutler. Trapese have been designing and delivering popular education workshops since 2005, when they were first active in promoting alternatives against the Group of Eight summit at Gleneagles. Trapese have run summer schools and workshops that provide tools, ideas and skills in active campaigning and building alternatives to capitalism. They have written a book with Pluto Press called *Do It Yourself, a Handbook for Changing our World*. See www.trapese.org.

Dennis Thomas is a Professor of Economics in the School of Management and Business at Aberystwyth University, with his teaching specialisms covering microeconomics and game theory and industrial organization and policy. He has published widely and extensively in internationally recognized journals and his recent research activities have seen an increasing inter-disciplinary focus covering corporate governance, entrepreneurship and accounting practices and structural change in not-for-profit organizations.

Marcelo Vieta (PhD, Social and Political Thought, York University) was born in Quilmes, Argentina, and grew up in Canada. He is a Postdoctoral Fellow at the Social Economy Centre, Ontario Institute for Studies in Education at the University of Toronto (OISE/UofT). He is also a Research Fellow at the European Research Institute on Cooperative and Social Enterprises (EURICSE) in Trento, Italy, where he also completed a one-year Postdoctoral Research Fellowship in January 2013. In addition, he is Research Associate at York University's Center for Research on Latin America and the Caribbean (CERLAC) and sits on the board of the Canadian Association for Studies in Co-operation (CASC). In recent years, Marcelo has been researching and publishing on the historical conditions, the political economic contexts and the lived experiences of the worker-recuperated enterprises of Argentina; the social and solidarity economies of Latin America; and the cooperative movements of Italy and Canada.

Tom Webb is a political economist who has had a varied career as a welfare worker, an adviser to two Canadian cabinet ministers and the Prime Minister, a consultant, a senior manager in a large cooperative and Director of a University Extension Department. He oversaw the creation of the English-speaking world's only masters-level cooperative management degree located in a business school. He has more than thirty-five years' involvement with cooperatives and credit unions as a board member, manager and consultant. Tom Webb has been a speaker at cooperative events in Canada, the United States, the United Kingdom, Australia and New Zealand. He is now Adjunct Professor at Saint Mary's University and was a key organizer of

Imagine 2012: The International Conference on Co-operative Economics. He is currently engaged as a speaker, consultant and writer as well as teaching in the Co-operative Management Education Program.

Colin C. Williams is Professor of Public Policy in the Management School at the University of Sheffield in the United Kingdom. His research interests include the informal economy, work organization and the future of work, subjects on which he has published some twenty monographs and 270 journal articles over the past twenty-five years. His recent books include *The Role of the Informal Sector in Post-Soviet Economies* (Routledge, 2013), *Informal Work in Developed Nations* (Routledge, 2010), *Rethinking the Future of Work: Directions and Visions* (Palgrave Macmillan, 2007), *The Hidden Enterprise Culture* (Edward Elgar, 2006), *A Commodified World? Mapping the Limits of Capitalism* (Zed, 2005) and *Cash-in-Hand Work* (Palgrave Macmillan, 2004).

Rachel Wright-Summerton is a founding member and archivist of the Padanaram Settlement, begun in 1966 by her father, Daniel Wright, near Bedford, Indiana. She is an adjunct Professor of Education at Ivy Tech State Community College in Bloomington, Indiana where she has taught for ten years. She graduated from Indiana University with a BS in Elementary Education and an MS in Educational Psychology and School Administration. Within the community, she was a teacher and administrator of Padanaram Village School for twenty-five years. She was also a business manager in the compost company, an arm of the lumber business. A member of the board of advisers of the Center for Communal Studies at the University of Southern Indiana, Rachel has been published in *Shared Visions, Shared Lives* (1996); *Communal Societies: Journal of the Communal Studies Association,* and elsewhere. She recently published a poetry memoir and is working on a history of her community.

Soenke Zehle is Lecturer in Media Art and Design and has a long-time involvement in the collaborative conceptualization and implementation of net.cultural projects. Soenke Zehle co-initiated and currently works as Managing Director of xm:lab – Experimental Media Lab at the Academy of Fine Arts Saar, Saarbrücken, Germany. For projects and publications see xmlab.org.

Heather Zoller (PhD, Purdue) is a Professor in the Department of Communication at the University of Cincinnati. Her research focuses on organizing and the politics of public health. Topics include health activism and corporate issues management; dialogue, participation and community organizing; and occupational and environmental health. Her research appears in journals such as *Communication Theory, Communication Monographs, Journal of Applied Communication Research* and *New Solutions: A Journal of Environmental and Occupational Health Policy.* She is co-editor of the book *Emerging Perspectives in Health Communication: Meaning, Culture & Power.*

Preface

Alternatives are vital to our survival

Vandana Shiva

Corporate globalization has brought the planet, and the lives of millions of people on it, to the brink. Climate catastrophes are already killing hundreds of thousands. The 2013 climate disaster in my region of the Himalaya has killed 20,000 people. A few years ago the floods in the Indus killed 10,000. Climate extremes are an environmental externality of a fossil fuel based, capital driven economy. We must find alternatives both because oil is running out, and because climate chaos has become a major threat to our survival.

As this book shows, the primacy given to corporations and their rights, over the rights of nature and the rights of people, is leading to ecological destruction on the one hand, and to the privatization of vital resources and the commons on the other. Water is being privatized, seeds are being privatized, even the air and atmosphere are being privatized through emissions trading. If the corporations had not been stopped at Rio+20, they would have imposed on the world an economy where even nature's ecological functions and services would be financialized and privatized.

There are many false constructions and myths that have allowed a socially and ecological destructive model to dominate, and to spread the illusion of TINA, that There Is No Alternative. This is not true. There many alternatives, alternatives that are both ecologically sustainable and respect nature's rights, are socially just and respect human rights. Indeed, these alternatives have become a survival imperative for all of us. Alternatives are the dominant system in peasant and tribal societies. They are also the emerging systems in parts of the industrialized world facing economic and financial collapse. In Greece, Italy, Spain unemployed youth are returning to the land, creating new economies based on cooperation and exchange, like those documented in this book.

'Seed' and 'Food' are the new colonies that multinational corporations are trying to carve out for themselves through genetically modified organisms, patents, seed laws, and free trade agreements. Indeed, corporations which recognize the power of the alternatives people are shaping are now seeking to criminalize alternatives, whether it be the proposed EC law on Seed, or free trade agreements trying to destroy cooperatives and public procurement, while insisting that they own the intellectual property of the Seed.

Yet Seed and Food are also the domains where movements are reclaiming the commons, the dignity of labour, co-operation, a sense of place, and membership in the Earth Community.

The myth is that industrial farming based on chemicals and genetics feeds the world. The reality is that it is only 28 percent of the food supply. In fact, 72 percent of the food that is eaten comes from small farms. Yet while supplying a quarter of the food, corporate driven industrial agriculture is responsible for 75 percent of the ecological destruction on the planet. To protect the earth, generate creative and meaningful work, and provide more and better food, alternatives are vital. As this book shows, the seeds of these alternatives are being sown everywhere, and form a vital part of the contest between an ecocidal and genocidal system, and alternative ideas which are attempting to create Earth Democracy to protect the freedom of humans and all species.

Section 1
Introduction

Advanced capitalism

Its promise and failings

Isn't capitalism the best and only imaginable way of organising our economy? It may have a few unfortunate but inevitable consequences and run into a few crises, but with a bit of fine-tuning, we are told, it constitutes the apotheosis of human history. After all, hasn't the fall of the Berlin Wall clearly demonstrated that alternatives to capitalism are not viable? That we have run out of alternatives? And with the unprecedented level of wealth, innovation and individual freedom that capitalism has granted us in its short history, why should we want anything else? Why is this book about 'alternatives' even necessary?

With what has been called advanced, corporate, consumer, neo-liberal or global capitalism, we seem to have reached a stage where it is easier to imagine the end of the world than the end of capitalism (Fisher, 2009). Obviously in this book we disagree, and our aim is to demonstrate that there are many alternative points of departure for imagining and practising organisation.

But in order to make space for these alternatives, our aim in these first three chapters is to put capitalism in its place, to show that it is just one among many ways of organising. We need to persuade you that there is a problem, and that there are alternatives. And we start this journey by attempting to define what capitalism is, and what consequences it has for our lives.

What is capitalism?

Capitalism is difficult to define not only because it has taken and continues to take many different forms, but also because it is not really a thing that one can point to, but more a set of social and economic relations. At its most basic level, capitalism is an economic system whereby capital is invested in order to make more capital; in other words, capitalism is a process through which capital gets accumulated (Harvey, 2011). There are various ways of accumulating capital, but since the first industrial revolution of the late eighteenth century in Europe, the dominant way has been through production. Here capital is put to work by hiring labour to produce goods that are sold on the market for a profit.

In order to illustrate the various elements and sets of relations that go into the making of capitalism, let's take the example of this book. Ironically, this book is a capitalist product, but what does this mean?

This book has been produced by a private publishing company, Routledge, itself owned by Taylor & Francis, itself merged with Informa plc. Informa plc is a multinational company with operations in 40 countries and has developed through the acquisition of 'brands' in the world of publishing, conferences and exhibitions. In 2010 the group reported a total turnover of £1,226.5 million, an operating profit of £164 million and after-tax profits of £98.9 million (Informa plc, 2011: 9). On its website, Informa plc boasts its 'strong track record of creating value from organic growth and acquisitions'. But we need to be clear about what sort of value we are talking about here. Value refers to profit that can be distributed to shareholders in the form of dividends, or return on investment. On this count, Informa has indeed created much value; in 2010, its academic publishing produced a net profit margin of 27.6 per cent (Informa plc, 2011), well above the average for non-publishing sectors (Harvie *et al.*, 2012). In order to produce 'value' or profit, Routledge/Informa plc assembled sufficient capital, in the forms of office space, computers, paper, desks and so on; it also hired labour (maybe a lot of which was subcontracted) to manage the relations with the writers, proof read, design, print and market the book. The aim of the whole process is to sell the book on the market for a profit. Ironically, the authors of the book won't get paid, because most of us are paid by universities, and this will help Informa to make greater profits.

There are various points worthy of note about this process. First, the book, or copyright on the book, is the property of Routledge/Informa (i.e. the owner of capital) rather than of the people who worked on its production (be it the academics who wrote the chapters for 'free', or the people hired or subcontacted by Informa to format, print and distribute the book). Second, the book is only of value to Routledge to the extent that it can be sold on the market for a profit. So what matters here is what the book can be exchanged for in the market (exchange value) rather the value the book may have to users (use value). Commodities such as this book are only a means to the end of capital accumulation or the pursuit of profit. So the content or quality of the book only matter to the extent that they confer exchange value.

This brief example serves to highlight some of the main principles of capitalism which we will explore in the next section.

Principles of capitalism

Private appropriation of the means of production and the division between capital and labour

One fundamental element of capitalism is the division between capital and labour, and the private appropriation of the means of production (capital) by a particular class (capitalists). The means of production refers to all the resources necessary for production: land, buildings, machinery, raw material and so on. These means of production can only produce wealth if they are put to work, and for this, capital requires a sufficient reserve of labour having the requisite qualities in terms of skills or flexibility, and willing to work for a wage (Harvey, 2011). While we now tend to take waged labour for granted, this has not always been the case (and is still not the case everywhere). The right conditions had to be created for the emergence of this sort of work.

Before the emergence of capitalism in Western Europe, most people produced what they consumed by possessing or having access to means of production (a small plot of land or access to common land on which they could grow food, raise animals, gather wood and so on). This was largely a rural subsistence economy where most people produced essentially for their own needs, selling whatever surplus they made on the market to buy the commodities they couldn't produce themselves. The dispossession of the mass from direct access to the means of production was therefore essential to create a reserve of labour power that capitalists could hire. Small peasants were expropriated from access to common land through processes of enclosure, or driven off the land by more competitive and larger commercial farms, and formed a landless proletariat who had no choice but to sell their labour for a wage. This process of expropriation of the mass from access to the means of production (what is referred to as primitive accumulation by Marxist theorists) is what made it possible for industrial capitalism to develop in Britain in the late eighteenth century (Harvey, 2003). But it is still ongoing in many parts of the world. In developing countries, peasants or small producers are being deprived of the means through which they provided for themselves and are being pushed into a global reserve of relatively cheap labour available for hire in capitalist production (Harvey, 2011).

So capitalism is based on the division between the owners of the means of production, and workers who, not having access to means of production, have to sell their labour to ensure their livelihood.[1] The relationships between these two classes are marked by conflict and power inequality. In order to maximise profit, capitalists will seek to maximise the surplus value[2] they can extract from labour by increasing its productivity or decreasing its cost (Wright, 2010). Thus the relationship between capital and labour is hierarchical in the sense not only that labour relinquishes the goods and services it produces for capitalists (e.g. this book is the property of Routledge/Informa), but also in the sense that while in the hire of capital, labour subjects itself to its rules. And as we'll see later in this chapter, capitalist firms have deployed various techniques to increase control over labour and lower its cost.

One final point worth mentioning about labour is its changing composition. At least in Western societies, contemporary capitalism relies less and less on the making of things, on factory work, and increasingly on 'immaterial labour', i.e. the kind of labour that relies on abilities such as language, creativity, knowledge or affect to produce the informational and cultural content of commodities (Lazzarato, 1996; Weidner, 2009). Of course things are still being made, but manufacturing has tended to be delocalised to developing economies, in particular China and South East Asia, where labour is cheaper. And the value of these commodities rests more on their branding, their symbolic value, than on their functionality. For example, while Nike shoes are still being physically produced in China, most of their surplus value is created by marketing teams in the West who, through branding, sell an image or lifestyle rather than a pair of shoes (Klein, 2000).

Free market

A second feature of capitalism is its reliance on the market as the main coordinating mechanism. A central motif of neo-liberal economics is the notion that the free market is the most efficient way of allocating resources, of organising the economy, and of harmonising competing interests. Adam Smith's (1776) famous metaphor of the 'invisible hand'[3] has been deployed to suggest that, in a free market, all individuals and firms freely and rationally pursue their own interest in maximising their gain by engaging in voluntary exchange with each other, and that, in this process, the interests of all parties are reconciled. For example, it is in the interests of profit-seeking capitalists to produce what consumers want, at a price they are willing to pay. If they start producing poor-quality products, or charging too much, then they will be driven out of the market by better quality or cheaper producers.[4] Similarly, if labour collectively organise in a country or industry to demand high wages, producers will delocalise somewhere with cheaper labour, bringing down wages (through unemployment) in the original place to levels that the market can bear. Another example is the trickle-down effect where the market will eventually distribute the increasing wealth of a rich minority to the majority: as the rich spend their wealth on new products and services, they create employment opportunities for the majority. On this view, it is only by opening themselves up to the free market that developing countries will grow and the poor will prosper.

So free market competition channels the self-interests of buyers, consumers and workers towards mutually desirable ends such as better products, lower costs, profitable enterprise or job opportunities. If producers are left free to produce, consumers free to choose, and workers free to sell their labour, the market will reach an equilibrium that will serve the interests of all. As such, the market is supposedly self-regulating and should be left to its own devices, free of government intervention. However, the issue of government (lack of) intervention is a moot point in the history and theory of capitalism. Even neo-liberal economists would agree that, at a minimum, states need to create and enforce contract and private property law (Wright, 2010). And, as we will see in Chapter 2, in many countries the state has played, and continues to play, an important role in creating the right conditions for capitalist development, or regulating the operation of the market and curbing its excesses. Indeed, all successful capitalist economies, including the UK and the USA, the supposed champions of the free market, have built their economic strengths on the back of government interventions, including protectionism, subsidies to help their nascent industries, or investment in infrastructure such as roads, rail or airports (Chang, 2010). States have also intervened, to different degrees, in mediating the relationships between capital and labour, and in setting limits on what can be bought and sold on the market (Chang, 2010). In many countries, the state bans or at least restricts the trading of organs, weapons, drugs, pornography and so on. Finally, the incapacity of markets to regulate themselves was vividly illustrated with the 2008 financial crisis where even the most neo-liberal governments had to bail out banks and industries 'too big to fail' to the tune of hundreds of billions of dollars to save the economy from collapsing.

All this suggests that the notion of the free market is a rather elusive one and seems to correspond more to a myth than a reality. Indeed, as Polanyi (1944) and many others since have demonstrated (e.g. Callon, 1998; Patel, 2009) markets are socially constructed and have no independent existence, therefore they cannot be set free. Nonetheless, the idea of the market as some sort of natural force outside human control is a way of thinking which informs a great deal of commentary, even when actual state and corporate policies indicate precisely the opposite.

Profit motive

If the idea of the 'free' market and the division between capital and labour constitute necessary conditions for the development of capitalism, then the profit motive constitutes its driving force. Indeed, what makes capitalism so creative and dynamic is the continuous search for profitable opportunities (Harvey, 2003; Wright, 2010).

Of course, the pursuit of wealth is not new to capitalism; pharaohs, pirates, merchants and kings all tried to accumulate wealth too. But what is new about capitalism is that the production process is organised around this principle of wealth accumulation; so goods and services are not produced for their intrinsic value or for their immediate consumption, but for their ability to be exchanged for a profit (Harvey, 2011). The production of goods and services is a means to an end. This, in turn, has several implications.

First, things which may have use value but cannot be traded on the market for a profit will be of little interest to capitalists (e.g. providing food, medicine or education for people who have no money). However, capitalism has been particularly creative in transforming what appear to be unprofitable activities into lucrative investment opportunities (e.g. education, organic farming, fair trade and micro-finance, to mention only a few examples, some of which we cover in this book).

A second implication of the profit motive is that in order to be traded for a profit, goods and services need to be priced against each other, they need to be made commensurable. As De Angelis and Harvie (2009) note, 'Things, services, goods only become commodities if they can be commensurated [. . .]. Otherwise they remain many tonnes of wheat or barrels of oils [. . .]', or this book just remains a book. To be sold, the book must have a price. Measures that allow for commensuration are therefore essential to capitalism. Monetisation, attaching a price tag or exchange value to materials or labour, enables the abstraction of all goods and services into tradable equivalents. There are various theories about how this exchange value is set, from Marxist theories stressing the abstract labour embodied in goods to neo-liberal economic theories stressing the role of supply and demand. But what is important for our purpose is that capitalism transforms everything it touches into a system of equivalence whereby commodities, goods or services, acquire a price, an exchange value, on the basis of which they can be traded and profit can be realised (De Angelis and Harvie, 2009; Fisher, 2009).

Capitalist dynamics

These three principles of capitalism taken together – i.e. the search for profitable investment in a competitive market through hiring waged labour – have certain implications for the conduct of economic activities and point to particular dynamics of capital accumulation.

Efficiency

Since profits cannot (always) be obtained by simply charging more money for things, they depend on producing more efficiently: on producing more (things, value) for less (inputs), or maximising the output to input ratio. Capitalist firms will try to squeeze as much surplus value out of labour and other resources as possible, through (for example) work intensification or cost reduction. As Weber (1978) noted, this makes some forms of means/ends calculation and rational accounting systems essential to capitalist enterprise and the pursuit of profit (see Jayasinghe and Thomas, this volume).

Management knowledge and practice has developed around this question of rationalisation, and includes many efficiency-increasing technologies and innovations designed to reduce the cost of labour and increase its productivity (Harvey, 2011; Wright, 2010). Among the most notable of these rationalising technologies was Taylor's 'scientific management' and the subsequent development of the assembly line by Henry Ford. Through careful observation and measurement, a particular task can be divided into various components, timed, formalised and standardised. As a result, jobs can be designed so as to require less skill and to maximise productivity.

In contemporary capitalism, this process of rationalisation, or means/ends calculation, is not confined to the assembly line and the production of things but has been extended to knowledge or immaterial work. The figure of the call centre worker is emblematic here of how the delivery or 'knowledge' work can be divided up, measured and controlled (Taylor and Baynes, 2005). And a similar process of quantification and control has occurred with professional labour. Doctors, teachers, probation officers find their labour increasingly subject to performance measures, standardisation and audit (de Angelis and Harvie, 2009).

The deregulation and flexibilisation of labour markets has also provided more cost-effective ways of hiring, firing and deploying labour according to needs (Cooper, 2008; Felsted and Jewson, 1999; McDowell and Christopherson, 2009). Another strategy for reducing labour cost is delocalisation. Over the last couple of decades at least, many Western organisations have delocalised production to developing countries offering cheaper labour; China has become the 'workshop of the world' and India the 'office of the world' on the ground of their cheap labour and low levels of taxation and regulation (Chang, 2010). For example, much of the labour used in the publishing industry to format, proofread, print, market or distribute books and journals is increasingly outsourced to low-cost economies (Dahlman and Huws, 2007).

Market expansion and growth

Another obvious way to increase profit is to sell more things. Finding new markets has been central to capitalist expansion. As local or national markets get saturated, capitalist firms have to expand further afield. So, for example, nineteenth-century cotton mill owners in Manchester sold their fabric to India, US farmers sell corn to Mexico, Nestlé sells its infant formula in developing countries and so on.

But selling more things is not just about finding new markets for a particular product, first because the market might eventually become saturated, and second because a profitable market will attract competitors which in turn will make the rate of profit fall (Wright, 2010). It also requires constantly inventing or finding more things to sell. This may be through making improvements in existing products (producing safer, faster or greener cars, healthier burgers . . .), inventing new products (televisions, phones, anti-depressants, e-book readers . . .), or selling things that previously were not for sale but were common property (e.g. drinking water, health, education, genes . . .). In its search for more and more things that can be exchanged on the market for profit, capitalism has managed to transform goods that were outside market relations into commodities that can be sold for a profit (Fisher, 2009; Harvey, 2003, 2011; Patel, 2009), a point we will explore later.

The relentless innovation of capitalist firms in designing and selling new products goes hand in hand with relentless consumption. It has become a truism to claim that we live in an increasingly commodified world, that more and more of our lives is mediated by the market (Patel, 2009). An increasing proportion of the goods and services we rely on for survival or pleasure (e.g. food, water, child care, sports and leisure, and so on) are acquired on the market for a price, rather than through self-provisioning or a mutual network of exchange with friends or family.

In order to pay our way through all this consumption, we are increasingly reliant on waged labour, and debt. If mass consumption is essential to capital accumulation, so is the provision of credit to sustain consumption (Harvey, 2011). Indeed, there is a whole credit industry which since the 1980s has been able to develop with fewer and fewer regulatory restrictions to provide consumer credit for everything from cars to education, toys, houses or holidays, including to poorer and poorer sections of society as we saw recently with sub-prime mortgages (Potts, 2011). The provision of credit is not only essential to underwrite consumption, it also provides another avenue for profitable capital investment as capital invests in capital itself (Harvey, 2011).[5]

In short, capitalism and its quest for accumulation rests on producing, selling and consuming ever more. It relies on and requires endless growth. The centrality of growth to capitalist economies is evident both at firm and national levels. Growth in GDP is considered as the holy grail of economic policy by most national governments and international institutions from the World Bank to the European Central Bank (Harvie *et al.*, 2009; Wright, 2010). Growth has become the fetish of capitalism and is supposed not only to deliver increased profit for capitalist firms, but also jobs, prosperity and better lives for all (Hamilton, 2003).

The growth imperative is also evident at the level of firms where the profit motive encourages expansion. The continuous need to accumulate capital means that capitalist firms have a tendency to grow larger and larger, both through internal growth and through acquisition (to paraphrase Informa). For example, through the sorts of mergers and acquisitions Informa has engaged in, the global market for academic publishing has become dominated by just a few key players (Beverungen *et al.*, 2012). More generally, the history of capitalism since the nineteenth century has been the history of the increasing concentration of capital around a decreasing number of multinational corporations that have acquired enormous power not only within their particular industries but also over governments (Barnet and Muller, 1974; Foster *et al.*, 2011). Some corporations have become so large that their sales far exceed the GDP of some countries. Of the 100 largest economies in the world in 2000, 51 were corporations and 49 were countries (based on comparison of corporate sales and countries' GDPs) (Anderson and Cavanagh, 2000).

Producing capitalist subjects

Capitalism not only signals a great transformation in the mode of production, but also in individuals' subjectivity: the way people understand themselves, and relate to each other. Capitalism requires and produces certain types of human beings: 'free' autonomous agents maximising their own utility through both work and consumption, or *homo economicus*. Indeed, the two figures of the freely choosing consumer and the self-investing flexible worker are central motifs of contemporary capitalism (Burkitt, 2008).

As mentioned earlier, increased labour flexibility is an important cost-reduction strategy for contemporary organisations. Individual workers may be redeployed across different jobs or functions of an organisation, across different locations, or simply dismissed. Demand for ever-increasing flexibility in the labour market means that individual workers constantly have to restyle, retrain themselves, to invest in themselves to remain employable (Burkitt, 2008). These investment decisions do not take place solely in the workplace or even in education, but embrace all of social life (Grey, 1994; Rose; 1989; Weidner, 2009, Cremin, 2011). For example, Grey (1994) illustrates how accountants invest in their appearance or in building appropriate social networks in order to advance their career. Similarly, students may take on extra-curricular activities to build their CV. The self becomes an enterprise, a project to be managed in order to maximise returns (in terms of salary, career prospects and so on).

In short, modern capitalism constitutes subjects as free autonomous, rational, utility-maximising agents in at least two ways: as consumers freely choosing on the market, and as workers personally managing their employment prospects (Burkitt, 2008; Du Gay, 1995). Both contribute to the individualisation of selves living more and more isolated from each other. As Margaret Thatcher famously proclaimed, 'there is no such thing as society', only free individuals responsible for their own success and failures.

And indeed, who wouldn't like to think of themselves as 'free', as able to do what they wanted free of interference from government, bureaucracy, trade unions, god, or the force of tradition? The market leaves us free to choose between all sorts of products and services to consume, job opportunities to apply for, or even better, free to set up our own business, to become the next Mark Zuckerberg or Richard Branson. This freedom to become what we want constitutes one of the greatest appeals of capitalism. The strength of market capitalism is not only its supposed economic superiority or 'efficiency', but also as Hayek (1944), Friedman (1962) or Nozick (1974) have argued (albeit in different ways) its close association with individual freedom, at least a certain kind of freedom. But as we shall see in the next section, efficiency, growth and freedom, the hallmarks of capitalism, are all contested ideas.

The dark side of capitalism

There is no doubt that capitalism, in its short history, has produced unprecedented levels of growth and wealth. Some of us have standards of living which are higher than ever. We can buy an ever-growing range of products and services, we are free to roam the world in search of better jobs, better holidays, we can live longer, and we have access to ever-increasing knowledge (Harvey, 2011; Wright, 2010). But the increased wealth, freedom and choice that some of us have acquired have come at a cost: environmental degradation, spiralling poverty among many, a crisis in public health, violence, alienation, anxieties and insecurity. The aim of the last section of this chapter is to examine the cost of capitalism by questioning the conceptions of freedom, efficiency and growth it relies on.

Freedom and atomisation

Flexible labour markets and boundaryless careers may create new opportunities to free oneself from the shackles and routines of predictable careers in bureaucratic organisations, but as Sennett (1998, 2008) has argued, it can also have ravaging effects on psychological well-being. The demand for flexibility in working lives, and consequently social lives, leads to the erosion of stable social networks and coherent life narratives. Individuals become atomised, uprooted from networks of social relations and solidarity, and their life experience reduced to a succession of present moments (Fisher, 2009).

And insofar as we take solace from alienating work in consumption, this only exacerbates feelings of insecurity and anxiety. Consumption leaves us with an insatiable desire for more. But beyond a certain level of material wealth, more does not equate to happiness but to rising rates of depression and anxiety (Wilkinson and Pickett, 2010). The notion of Affluenza suggests that increasing consumption and wealth leave us with feelings of emptiness (James, 2007; Layard, 2005). The competitive drive for money, status and material things leads to anomie, alienation and addiction, while undermining our capacity to build connections with others. For example, James (2008) reports spiralling levels of mental disorders in Anglo-Saxon societies which he attributes to the more advanced forms of neo-liberal forms of capitalism, or 'selfish capitalism', prevalent in these countries. So capitalist subjects may be free, but this freedom comes at the cost of atomisation, alienation and increased psychological disorders.

In addition, we can question the way in which freedom is constituted and distributed by capitalism. The neo-liberal conceptualisation of freedom in terms of individuals' ability to compete freely on the labour market, and to exercise consumer choice, provides a very partial and restrictive vision of freedom. As we will show in Chapter 3, this is a negative conception that defines freedom in terms of the absence of interference or coercion in our actions (Berlin, 1969; Macpherson, 1973). And, of course, in this sense the market leaves us free, within legal constraints. But as many feminists (Hirschmann, 2003) and others (Macpherson, 1973) have argued, this negative view of freedom means very little if we do not consider the unequal power relations that prevent some of us from exercising 'choice' in the market; so women may be free to participate in the labour market, but this ignores the social and power relations that place them in the position of the 'carer' or homemaker and severely constrain their choice (see Dale's chapter in this volume). Similarly, deregulated, flexible, free labour markets may make workers free to move between jobs, but for many this freedom may be limited to poorly paid, casual employment. Freedom within the world of work is also severely restricted; an important part of the employment contract is that employees agree to do what they are told (even though this may leave room for various degrees of self-determination) (Wright, 2010). And as Macpherson (1973) argued, in a capitalist society, most of us are coerced to get into waged labour to survive. All of these examples suggest that the negative conception of freedom might be very restrictive, and undermine our ability to make autonomous choices. A positive conception of freedom would instead emphasise our capacity to be self-directed, not only to choose between existing options, but to exercise choice about the ends we want to pursue (Berlin, 1969). The difference between these two conceptions of freedom can be illustrated with consumer choice. The free market, by removing trade barriers, has made us freer as consumers to choose between different products from different parts of the world. However, the wide range of products we can buy tends to be based on a restricted number of key ingredients, and is produced and distributed by a decreasing number of powerful multinational companies and retail chains that control what we can – and cannot – consume (Gabriel and Lang, 1995; Klein, 2000; Schor, 1998). While we may be free to buy strawberries at Christmas in the UK, our freedom to buy more local food products, or to have some autonomy in the kind of food we put in our mouth, not to mention to have access to some affordable land to grow our own food, is far more limited.

So the extension of the free market and negative freedom has to be set against the erosion of positive freedom, and in particular the freedom to participate in the decisions affecting our lives (Bauman, 1988, 2007). The increasing power of multinational corporations is seriously eroding democracy, placing decision-making further and further away from the communities affected by these decisions, or from democratically elected governments. As we saw earlier, the largest multinational corporations have annual sales that exceed the budgets of many states, giving them enormous powers over countries with little resources. Under pressure from institutions promoting free trade globally (i.e. the World Bank, World Trade Organization, International Monetary Fund), national states have had to abdicate their power to regulate (the labour market, environmental protection, financial markets) to multinational corporations (Korton, 1995; Sklair, 2002). This corporate takeover is not confined to small and weak economies; through lobbying and close alliances between governments and corporate representatives, corporations have been able to buy government in the global North too (Korten, 1995; Monbiot, 2000; Stiglitz, 2011).

Efficiency and externality

As we saw earlier, one way to accumulate capital is to increase efficiency; that is, to maximise the output to input ratio. But efficiency depends very much on what we have decided to count as output and input. In a capitalist economy, what counts as cost or input is what we have to pay for in the market. But the market fails to take into account all the actual costs of producing things. It misses what has no exchange value; for example, the pollution created in producing things that the producers don't have to clean. These 'hidden' costs are referred to as externalities; they are costs that neither the producer nor the consumer has to bear, but are pushed to another party (Patel, 2009).

Environmental damage constitutes one of the main externalities of capitalism, a cost passed on to local communities having, for example, to live in despoiled environments, or to humanity as a whole, including future generations. Indeed, it seems perfectly rational for profit-maximising companies to dump the cost of waste or pollution somewhere else if they are allowed to do so (Wright, 2010). But this continuous search for profitable opportunities is rapidly destroying the environment on which we (and corporations) rely for survival (see Cato, this volume).

Ever-increasing levels of production and consumption are leaving ever-larger ecological footprints in the forms of waste and pollution. As production is delocalised in search of cheaper costs, goods have to travel further and further away, generating (mostly uncounted) environmental costs in the forms of CO_2 emission (Jackson, 2009). The increasing consumption of packaged food, electrical goods, mobile phones, holidays, cars and so on also produces increasingly unmanageable amounts of waste (Ferrell, this volume and 2005; Rogers 2005). Much of the (toxic) waste and pollution generated by consumption in Western societies is exported to developing countries in the global South (Lazaroff, 2002; Weber *et al.*, 2008).

To sum up, capitalism may be producing lots of cheap goods, but it can only do so because it fails to account for much of the cost of production and consumption on the environment, cost that has to be borne mostly by the most disenfranchised, and will have to be borne by future generations.

Another way of increasing efficiency and externalising cost is to appropriate resources for free. Capitalist firms seeking to maximise profits have a strong incentive to appropriate resources that are 'free' in the sense that they stand outside the market and hence have no price tag (Wright, 2010). This process of appropriation, the enclosure of common or public resources, or what Harvey (2003) refers to as accumulation by dispossession, has been central to the accumulation of wealth (in the hands of a few) and has taken various forms throughout the history of capitalism.

We have already seen that the enclosure of common land was essential to the early stage of capitalist development. But this process of enclosure is ongoing; all over the world, peasants and indigenous populations continue to be expelled from land and deprived of access to natural resources through legal and illegal means (Harvey, 2011). As a result, the increasing mass of the dispossessed have to rely on market exchange and sell their labour to capitalist firms, often working for less than subsistence wages in sweatshop conditions (Bakan, 2004; Klein, 2000; *New Internationalist*, 2004).

In its neo-liberal phase, global capitalism has sought to appropriate more and more of our common wealth (see De Angelis and Harvie, this volume). To mention just a few examples, in urban centres throughout the world, the most disadvantaged are being expropriated (through, for example, rising property taxes and rents, or violence) to make space for real estate developments (Harvey, 2011). Free public spaces in cities are sold to private developers and transformed into spaces of consumption such as corporate coffee chains, bars and restaurants, shopping malls or executive flats (Minton, 2009). Corporations have been engaged in a relentless plunder of collectively owned resources, from publicly funded medical knowledge, to software innovation, the airwaves, the public domain of creative works, biodiversity, genetic commons or indigenous people's knowledge (Bollier, 2003; Nonini, 2006; Scharper and Cunningham, 2006; Shiva, 1997).

The publishing industry with which we started this chapter has also been particularly adept at appropriating public resources for private profits. Academic publishers have been able to reap well-above-average profits of 30 to 40 per cent through a process of double appropriation: they appropriate the intellectual property rights for the knowledge produced by writers paid by public funds, and sell this knowledge back to universities. Thus publishers don't bear the cost of the work that goes into publishing but rely on 'free work'; the work of writing, editing and peer-reviewing is done by academics often paid for by public funding (Beverungen *et al.*, 2012).

As the above examples suggest, capitalist firms' ability to reduce costs does not mean that costs disappear, but mainly that they have been externalised, placed outside the market (Patel, 2010). Costs are pushed down through some people being dispossessed: of land, knowledge, seeds, access to free drinking water, dwelling, health or subsistence wages. The logic of capital is simple. If profits aren't being made because something is cheap, free or unneeded, then there is an opportunity for profits to be made.

Inequality

Unsurprisingly, considering that wealth is at least partly accumulated through dispossession, global capitalism has led to increased inequality (Harvey, 2011; Wilkinson and Pickett, 2010; Wright, 2010). Far from the trickle-down effects that would have supposedly lifted the poor out of poverty, it has created a trickling-up effect leading to the increased concentration of wealth in the hands of a few, a trend aptly captured by the slogan of the Occupy movement 'We are the 99%'.

There is plenty of evidence suggesting that developmental programmes designed to bring the benefits of global capitalism to the poor by extending free trade and deregulating global markets have mainly benefited Northern multinational corporations (de la Barra, 2006; Klein, 2000; Korten, 1995; *New Internationalist*, 2004; Sklair, 2002). For example, a report from the United Nation Development Programme (UNDP) (2006) showed that the poorest 20 per cent of the planet accounted for 1.1 per cent of world income in 2006 against 2.3 per cent in 1970; the richest 20 per cent (mainly living in the North) accounted for 86 per cent of the world income against 70 per cent in 1970.

And growing inequalities are also evident within 'advanced' economies in the global North. For example, the wealthiest 1 per cent of US citizens controlled 40 per cent of American wealth in 2011, and took in nearly a quarter of the nation's yearly income; 25 years earlier, the corresponding figures were 33 per cent and 12 per cent (Stiglitz, 2011). These increasing inequalities are not only a worrying trend in themselves, but are also associated with a wide range of heath, psychological and social problems (Wilkinson and Pickett, 2010). Growing inequalities increase the importance of social status and competition in the way people assess themselves and each other; this in turn creates the conditions for divisive social relations, the erosion of community life, and trust; it makes for poor mental and physical health, educational performance and social mobility, as well as increased violence. And, as Wilkinson and Pickett's (2010) study of health inequalities in different countries demonstrates, it is not just those at the bottom who suffer, but the vast majority of the population.

'Uneconomic' growth

Considering the environmental, health and social costs of contemporary capitalism, it seems sensible to question the rationality of its endless pursuit of growth, or growth fetish (Hamilton, 2003, 2010). As we saw earlier, growth in production and consumption is essential to capitalism; growth (in GDP, GDP per capita, or in companies' turnover) is taken as the main indicator of economic wealth and the main target of economic and business policies (Harvie *et al.*, 2009). But this equates commodity production with well-being and fails to take into account the conditions of production (e.g. working hours, dangerous work, poverty wages), its hidden costs (e.g. stress, anxiety, environmental destruction) or the distribution of wealth (Chang, 2010; Harvie *et al.*, 2009).

As early as 1972, a Club of Rome report recognised that there were natural 'Limits to Growth' (Meadows *et al.*, 1972): the earth has finite resources and a limited ability to support growth and absorb pollution. It seems that we have already exceeded these ecological limits. According to the Global Footprint Network's calculations, in 2012 the demands we made on the Earth's biocapacity (to absorb waste and regenerate renewable resources) was the equivalent of 1.5 planets. This means that it took the Earth one year and six months to regenerate what we used in a year. The calculations also suggest that if current population and consumption trends continue, by the 2030s we will need the equivalent of two Earths (Global Footprint Network website, 2012).

So the demand for growth starts to appear 'uneconomic' (Daly, 2007). It makes us worse off by using up our natural capital and resources, while providing no benefits to human well-being and welfare. Not only do measures of growth fail to take into account the damaging effects of production and consumption (e.g. on the environment, our health or quality of life), but they also count as positive the whole industries that have emerged to deal with these effects (e.g. pharmaceutical industry, waste management). Thus we arrive at the absurd situation where, for example, the more ill, obese, diabetic or depressed we get, the more remedies the pharmaceutical industry can sell us, and the more the economy will grow. Similarly, a whole industry has sprung up to clean up our waste and pollution, again contributing to economic growth (*The Economist*, 2009; Porter, 2002; Rogers, 2005; Royle, 2005).

Recent books such as *The Spirit Level* (Wilkinson and Pickett, 2010), *Prosperity without Growth* (Jackson, 2009) or *Mismeasuring our Lives: Why the GDP Doesn't Add Up* (Stiglitz *et al.*, 2010) have all denounced this focus on growth as the ultimate end. And many have proposed alternative measures of economic well-being that would take a variety of additional factors into account, such as literacy, average life expectancy, equality, working time or pollution (see Harvie *et al.* (2009) or Jackson (2009) for an overview). Behind these alternative proposals lies a fundamental question about what counts as prosperity or well-being, and whether capitalism and its obsessive pursuit of economic growth provides the best answer. We think it doesn't, hence this book of alternatives.

Conclusion

From this inevitably brief discussion, capitalism emerges as an enormously powerful force that extends its tentacles to more and more of the globe, and more and more of our lives. It produces not only goods and services but also the sorts of subjects who will buy these goods (the desiring consumers), the sorts of subjects who will produce these goods and services (free labour), and the credit necessary for their purchase. Capitalism has become so powerful that it has colonised our imagination, leading to a monoculture where capitalism appears as the only realistic option (Fisher, 2009; Michaels, 2011), as if there were no alternatives. Indeed, following one of its deepest crises in 2008, many people seem to assume that we should be working our way back to business as usual. Shortly after being bailed out with public funds, banks resumed paying gigantic bonuses; and government leaders across Europe have been busy placing their economies under increased market discipline, squeezing public services and further liberalising labour markets.

Yet there are many cracks. As illustrated in this chapter, capitalism is in many ways dysfunctional and produces many irrationalities; it makes some of us sicker, some of us poorer, and it relies on natural resources which, through its own plundering, are rapidly being eroded.

Moreover, capitalism relies on our own complicity (Fisher, 2009); it relies on us getting into debt, buying things, working for a wage. But what happens when some of us stop behaving like *homo economicus*, when some us stop buying so much, or labouring for a wage, and if instead we start collectively re-appropriating various means of production, if we start producing for ourselves rather than for capitalist enterprises, if we start sharing or giving our labour, goods, services outside of the 'free market'? As we explore in the next chapter of this book, many throughout history have expressed their discontent with capitalism, and have forged relations of production and exchange that do not follow the logic of capital accumulation. It is by looking at the cracks and gaps within capitalism that we begin to see that alternatives already exist, and that many of the resources and ideas we need are already available to us.

Notes

1   In contemporary capitalism, class relations have become more complex, through both the development of the 'middle classes' and the democratisation of shareholding through, for example, pension funds. However, the division between capital and labour remains fundamental to the understanding of class relations (see e.g. Wright (2005) for a discussion of contemporary class structure).

2   Surplus value refers to the value created by labour that exceeds the cost of hiring it.

3   The significance of the 'invisible hand' in the work of Adam Smith is more the making of twentieth-century neo-liberal economists than of Smith himself, since the famous metaphor appears only once in the *Wealth of the Nations*, and three times altogether in all of Smith's work (Werhane, 1991).

4   This reasoning of course ignores the fact that producers may collude and agree on price that they can force on consumers; it also ignores the fact that consumers do not always have perfect information to compare prices or services across producers, or that producers may acquire monopoly over particular markets.

5   As Marx predicted, if rates of profit fall in the productive sphere, capital will look to financial investment for better returns:

> More capital is accumulated than can be invested in production, and for example lies fallow in the form of money in the bank. This results in loans abroad, etc, in short speculative investment.
>
> *(Marx, 1969: 484)*

And just as capitalism has been particularly creative in the productive sphere, so it has in the financial spheres. Debt has become a commodity; for example, with Collateral Debt Obligations (CDOs), mortgages are bundled together and securitised to be traded on financial markets (Lanchester, 2010). The same thing could be said of micro-finance, initially created by not-for-profit organisations as a means to help the poor but increasingly becoming a way through which commercial banks can squeeze profits out of the poor (e.g. Bateman, 2010; and see Chapter 3, this volume). Indeed, in its search for profitable investment, capital has increasingly looked to usurious lending, fuelling housing bubbles, and creating growing levels of debt among consumers and governments in the process (Harvey, 2011; Potts, 2011).

References

Anderson, S. and Cavanagh, J. (2000) *Top 2000: The Rise of Corporate Global Power.* Washington, DC: Institute for Policy Studies.

Bakan, J. (2004) *The Corporation.* London: Free Press.

Barnett, R. and Muller, J. (1974) *Global Reach.* New York: Simon and Schuster.

Bateman, M. (2010) *Why Micro-Finance Doesn't Work?* London: Zed Books.

Bauman, Z. (1988) *Freedom.* Milton Keynes: Open University Press.

Bauman, Z. (2007) Collateral casualties of consumerism, *Journal of Consumer Culture*, 7(1):25–56.

Berlin, I. (1969) *Two Concepts of Liberty.* Oxford: Clarendon Press.

Beverungen, A., Böhm, S. and Land, C. (2012) The poverty of journal publishing, *Organization*, 19(6): 929–938.

Bollier, D. (2003) *Silent Theft: The Private Plunder of our Common Wealth*. London: Routledge.

Burkitt, I. (2008) Subjectivity, self and everyday life in contemporary capitalism, *Subjectivity*, 23: 236–245.

Callon, M. (ed.) (1998) *The Laws of Markets*. Oxford: Blackwell.

Chang, H-J. (2010) *23 Things They Don't Tell You About Capitalism*. London: Penguin.

Cooper, M. (2008) The inequality of security: Winners and losers in the risk society, *Human Relations*, 61(9): 1229–1228.

Cremin, C. (2011) *Capitalism's New Clothes*. London: Pluto Press.

Dahlmann, S. and Huws, U. (2007) Sunset in the West: Outsourcing editorial work from the UK to India – A case study of the impact on workers, *Work Organization, Labour and Globalisation*, 1(1): 59–75.

Daly, H. (2007) 'Ecological economics: The concept of scale and its relation to allocation, distribution, and uneconomic growth'. In H. Daly, *Ecological Economics and Sustainable Development: Selected Essays of Herman Daly*: 82–103. Cheltenham, Edward Elgar.

De Angelis, M. and Harvie, D. (2009) Cognitive capitalism and the rat-race: How capital measures immaterial labour in British universities, *Historical Materialism*, 17: 3–30.

De la Barra, X. (2006) Who owes and who pays? The accumulated debt of neoliberalism, *Critical Sociology*, 32(1): 125–161.

Du Gay, P. (1995) *Consumption and Identity at Work*. London: Sage.

Felsted, A. and Jewson, N. (eds) (1999) *Global Trends in Flexible Labour*. London: Macmillan.

Fisher, M. (2009) *Capitalist Realism: Is There No Alternative?* Winchester: O Books.

Foster, J.B., McChesney, R.W. and Jonna, R.J. (2011) Monopoly and competition in the twenty-first century, *Monthly Review*, 62: 13–19.

Friedman, M. (1962) *Capitalism and Freedom*. Chicago: University of Chicago Press.

Gabriel, Y. and Lang, T. (1995) *The Unmanageable Consumer: Contemporary Consumption and its Fragmentation*. London: Sage.

Global Footprint Network website, www.footprintnetwork.org/en/index.php/GFN/page/at_a_glance/ (accessed 22 October 2012).

Grey, C. (1994) Career as a project of the self, *Sociology*, 28(2): 479–497.

Hamilton, C. (2003) *Growth Fetish*. Sydney: Allen & Unwin.

Hamilton, C. (2010) *Requiem for a Species: Why we Resist the Truth About Climate Change*. London: Routledge.

Harvey, D. (2003) *The New Imperialism*. Oxford: Oxford University Press.

Harvey, D. (2011) *The Enigma of Capital and the Crisis of Capitalism*. London: Profile Books.

Harvie, D., Lightfoot, G., Lilley, S. and Weir, K. (2012) What are we to do with feral publishers, *Organization*, 19(6): 905–914.

Harvie, D., Slater, G., Philip, B. and Wheatley, D. (2009) Economic well-being and British regions: The problem with GDP per capita, *Review of Social Economy*, 67(4): 483–505.

Hayek, F. (1944) *The Road to Serfdom*. Chicago: University of Chicago Press.

Hirschmann, N. (2003) *The Subject of Liberty: Toward a Feminist Theory of Freedom*. Princeton: Princeton University Press.

Informa plc (2011) *Informa plc Annual Report & Financial Statements for the Year Ended 31 December 2010*. Zug, Switzerland: Informa plc.

Jackson, T. (2009) *Prosperity Without Growth: Economics for a Finite Planet*. London: Earthscan.

James, O. (2007) *Affluenza: How to Be Successful and Stay Sane*. London: Vermillion.

James, O. (2008) *The Selfish Capitalist*. London: Vermillion.

Kanter, R.M. (1990) *When Giants Learn to Dance*. London: Free Press.

Klein, N. (2000) *No Logo*. London: Flamingo.

Korten, D. (1995) *When Corporations Rule the World*. West Hartford, CT: Kumarian Press.

Lanchester, J. (2010) *Whoops!: Why Everyone Owes Everyone and No One can Pay*. London: Allen Lane.

Layard, R. (2005) *Happiness*. New York: Penguin.

Lazaroff, C. (2002) High-tech U.S. trash floods Asia, *Environment News Service*. Available online at www.ens-newswire.com/ens/feb2002/2002-02-26-07.asp (accessed 16 March 2012).

Lazzarato, M. (1996) 'Immaterial labour'. In M. Hardt and P. Virno (eds), *Radical Thought in Italy: A Potential Politics*: 133–147. Minneapolis: University of Minnesota Press.

Macpherson, C.B. (1973) *Democratic Theory: Essays in Retrieval*. Oxford: Clarendon Press.

McDowell, L. and Christopherson, S. (2009) Transforming work: New forms of employment and their regulation, *Cambridge Journal of Regions, Economy and Society*, 2: 335–342.

Marx, K. (1969) *Theories of Surplus Value*, Part II. London: Lawrence and Wishart.

Meadows, D.H., Meadows, D.L., Randers, J. and Behrens, W. (1972) *The Limits to Growth*. New York: Universe Books.

Michaels, F. S. (2011) *Monoculture: How One Story is Changing Everything*. Kamloops, BC: Red Clover Press.

Minton, A. (2009) *Ground Control*. London: Penguin.

Monbiot, G. (2000) *The Captive State*. London: Macmillan.

New Internationalist (2004) Issue 374 on 'The Free Trade Game'. Available online at www.newint.org/issue374/contents.htm (accessed 20 March 2012).

Nonini, D. (2006) Introduction: The global idea of the 'common', *Social Analysis*, 50(3): 164–177.

Nozick, R. (1974) *Anarchy, State and Utopia*. New York: Basic Books.

Patel, R. (2009) *The Value of Nothing*. London: Portobello Books.

Polanyi, K. (1944) *The Great Transformation*. New York: Rinehart.

Porter, R. (2002) *The Economics of Waste*. Washington, DC: Resource for the Future.

Potts, N. (2011) Marx and the crisis, *Class and Capital*, 35(3): 455–473.

Rogers, H. (2005) *Gone Tomorrow: The Hidden Life of Garbage*. New York: New Press.

Rose, M. (1989) *Governing the Soul: The Shaping of Private Life*. London: Routledge.

Royte, E. (2005) *Garbage Land*. New York: Back Bay Books.

Scharper, S.B. and Cunningham, H. (2006) The genetic commons: Resting the neo-liberal enclosure of life, *Social Analysis*, 50(3): 195–202.

Schor, J. (1998) Tackling turbo consumption, *Cultural Studies*, 22(5):588–598.

Schwartzman, K.C. (1998) Globalisation and democracy, *Annual Review of Sociology*, 24: 159–181.

Sennett, R. (1998) *The Corrosion of Character: The Personal Consequences of Work in New Capitalism*. London: Norton.

Sennett, R. (2008) *The Culture of the New Capitalism*. New Haven, CT: Yale University Press.

Shiva, V. (1997) *Biopiracy: The Plunder of Nature and Knowledge*. Cambridge, MA: South End Press.

Sklair, L. (2002) *Globalization: Capitalism and its Alternatives*. Oxford: Oxford University Press.

Smith, A. (1776) *The Wealth of nations*. London: Methuen & Co., Ltd.

Stiglitz, J. (2011) Of the 1%, by the 1%, for the 1%. *Vanity Fair*. Available online at www.vanityfair.com/society/features/2011/05/top-one-percent-201105 (accessed 15 February 2012).

Stiglitz, J., Sen, A. and Fitoussi, J. P. (2010) *Mismeasuring our Lives: Why the GDP Doesn't Add Up*. New York: The New Press.

Taylor, P. and Bain, P. (2005) 'India calling to the far away towns': The call centre labour process and globalization, *Work, Employment & Society*, 19(2): 262–282.

The Economist (2009) Special Report on Waste, 26 February.

United Nation Development Programme, United Nation Environment Programme, World Bank and World Research Institute (2000) A guide to world resources 2000–2001. Washington: World Research Institute. Available online at www.wri.org/publication/world-resources-2000-2001-people-and-ecosystems-fraying-web-life (accessed 16 February 2012).

UNDP (2006) *Human Development Report 2006*. New York: United Nations.

Weber, C., Peters, G., Guan, D. and Hubacek, K. (2008) The contribution of Chinese exports to climate change, *Energy Policy*, 36(9): 3572–3577.

Weber, M. (1978) *Economy and Society*. Berkeley: University of California Press.

Weidner, J.R. (2009) Governmentality, capitalism, and subjectivity, *Global Society*, 23(4): 387–411.

Werhane, P. (1991) *Adam Smith and his Legacy for Modern Capitalism*. Oxford: Oxford University Press.

Wilkinson, R. and Pickett, K. (2010) *The Spirit Level*. London: Bloomsbury Press.

World Bank Development Indicators (2008) Washington, DC: World Bank.

Wright, E. (ed.) (2005) *Approaches to Class Analysis*. Cambridge: Cambridge University Press.

Wright, E. (2010) *Envisioning Real Utopias*. London: Verso.

2

Alternatives
Past, present and prospective

'The idea that nothing else is possible is the last weapon that they have. One of the remarkable things about this present historical moment is that they're hardly arguing that capitalism is a good system anymore. What they're saying is that it is the only possible system. Almost all the old arguments – a rising tide lifts all boats, even the poor's lives are improving, capitalism is an engine of technological development, that capitalism creates democracy – those arguments have been obviously proved false. The only line that they have now is "nothing else is possible that wouldn't make things even worse". So the only way they can maintain that is to nip any alternatives in the bud.'

David Graeber on State Repression, interview conducted in Berlin, 30 May 2012: http://www.youtube.com/watch?v=eAzUQlSR6NQ&feature=share

As a system of social organization, capitalism clearly has many negative consequences (see Chapter 1). Irreversible environmental degradation, increasing economic inequality, and a stunting of human growth and diversity are all well-recognized results of the capitalist imperative to endless accumulation for its own sake. Despite this, the doctrine that capitalism is the only game in town can leave people with the sense that 'it is easier to imagine the end of the world than to imagine the end of capitalism' (Jameson, 2003: 76). In two decades we have travelled a long way from those heady days when, in the aftermath of the collapse of the Soviet bloc and the fall of the Berlin wall, Francis Fukuyama (1992) could pronounce the 'end of history' and suggest that liberal capitalism is the best of all possible systems, in this, the best of all possible worlds. Even so, a resigned 'nothing else is possible that wouldn't make things even worse' has the power to forestall a discussion of alternatives and to grant capitalism a privileged position at the centre of social, political and economic debate. In Margaret Thatcher's famous words, 'there is no alternative,' a sentiment often reduced to the simple 'TINA'.

In this book we question this 'capitalocentric' logic that posits capitalism as the only option but in this chapter we want to go a little further and ask how far we should consider capitalism to be a coherent and relatively unified system at all (Gibson-Graham, 2006). Instead of taking capitalism as a necessary starting point for political or economic analysis, we want to de-centre capitalism, recognizing that it is a partial, incomplete and contradictory system, or rather 'systems', as there are many varieties of capitalism both historically and today. It is only through theoretical suturing that these differences and absences can be integrated into a single, unified system. In reality, capitalism is partial, fragmented, and has always existed alongside, or even dependent upon, non-capitalist alternatives, as, for example, in the unpaid domestic labour of women supporting men who earn a 'family wage' (Dalla Costa and James, 1975; Dale, this volume). In this chapter we outline some of these differences and alternatives, starting with varieties of capitalism in the first part and then moving on to consider the range of non-capitalist forms of production, distribution, exchange and consumption that exist alongside these capitalisms. Throughout, our concern is to challenge the 'capitalist realism' (Fisher, 2007) that limits our organizational imagination by insisting that 'there is no alternative' to capitalism and deriding those who seek better systems of organizing by labelling them as fantasists. Instead we want to demonstrate the sheer variety of non-capitalist organizational forms that exist both today and historically. Against a simple logic of commodification and the capitalist colonization of the world with a single, coherent logic, we suggest that variety and difference, not capitalist identity, is the norm (Gibson-Graham, 2006).

By showing how even apparently capitalist forms of organizing are dependent upon non-capitalism, we want to show those who proclaim capitalism as the one and only possible way of organizing to be the true fantasists. This is not to say that all of these non-capitalist alternatives are desirable. Many of the examples we consider – unpaid domestic labour, slavery and enclosure – are part and parcel of capitalist social and economic reproduction, even if they themselves are non-capitalist in the strict sense. In the final parts of this chapter we therefore overview, all too briefly, a range of non-capitalist forms of organizing, contemporary and historical, that suggest forms of organization with potential for more radical, social transformation. The following chapter works through the kinds of values that these progressive alternatives work with, and towards, and hence also considers what we have excluded. The main sections of the book – Chapters 4 through 23 – are dedicated to in-depth, detailed discussions of what we consider to be the most important examples of progressive alternatives today. In Chapter 24 we return to this question of how far alternative forms of organization might hold out a radical potential for deep-rooted, socio-economic change, or whether these seemingly non-capitalist alternatives can exist alongside capitalist forms without disrupting them, or even strengthening them. But before we ask whether capitalism will always recuperate even the most radical organizational gesture, we should first ask how stable, solid and uniform 'capitalism' really is.

Putting 'capitalism' in its place

Boltanski and Chiapello (2005: 4) offer a minimal definition of capitalism as 'an imperative to unlimited accumulation of capital by formally peaceful means' (see also Harvey (2011) and Chapter 1 of this book). Leaving aside the often bloody and violent reality of capitalist accumulation, particularly when it comes to securing the raw materials like oil that advanced capitalist economies remain dependent upon (Retort, 2005), this minimal formula provides a simple and straightforward definition of capitalism. Following Marx's (1976) analysis in Volume 1 of *Capital*, money is capital insofar as it is invested in order to increase its magnitude. There are, however, many ways in which capitalist systems can be organized to realize this growth and to generate an economic surplus. 'While capitalism is defined by the accumulation of capital, the social relations of capitalism may take many institutional forms' (Jackson and Deeg, 2006: 10). In short, capitalism is more a goal than a system of social organization, and accumulation can be realized in a number of ways.

To be a little more precise, in Chapter 1 we added two other defining features of capitalism to this underlying profit motive: first, the separation of capital and labour, with ownership and control of the means of production – factories, machines, raw materials, etc. – resting ultimately with capital (Gibson-Graham, 2006: xxiv); second, trade through formally 'free' markets. Within these rather broad limits there are a range of different institutional forms and social relationships that capitalism can take. While neo-classical economics assumes that markets are a natural mechanism for organizing exchange, and that other social institutions, even the nation state, are a hindrance to the operation of pure markets, in reality even markets and private property are organized and regulated by social institutions, including the discipline of economics itself (MacKenzie *et al.*, 2007) and other human and technological intermediaries that enable markets to perform 'freely' (Callon *et al.*, 2007). Even nations that promote neo-liberal economic doctrines of deregulation still have to ensure that markets are managed so as to work in the way they are naturally supposed to, but also to limit the chaos that uncontrolled free trade would wreak. As an example of the latter, consider legislation and taxation around drugs and alcohol. In the USA, addictive narcotics like cocaine and heroin are tightly controlled by legislation and policing and are not deemed appropriate for governance by free markets and open trade; otherwise large companies already involved in the intoxication business, for example, Phillip Morris or Diageo, would doubtless have subsidiaries operating in the lucrative crack-cocaine and crystal meth markets (Parker 2012). As well as constraining the boundaries within which free enterprise reigns, governments must also ensure that 'free' markets are regulated so that they function correctly and in accordance with economic doctrine and the need for a degree of social stability. In the UK, the Conservative government of the 1980s and 1990s pursued a neo-liberal economic policy of privatization and de-regulation, passing more legislation in order to realize this 'de-regulation', and deploying state-controlled, police power in order to break organized labour and ensure the 'free' functioning of markets.

Given that markets are themselves social institutions, and that all forms of economic activity need institutionalization and regulation in some form, researchers have sought to map out the different 'varieties of capitalism' (Hall and Soskice, 2001). Although there have been many comparative approaches to the analysis of the specific institutional forms taken by contemporary capitalism, the key dimensions revolve around finance, corporate governance, employment relations, the welfare state and innovation systems (Jackson and Deeg, 2006). To give a few examples, the financing of capitalist investment can flow primarily from established banks, as is the case in Japan, or from markets, as is more common in the USA. This can have significant implications for investment as banks are more likely to invest for long-term capital growth but be relatively risk averse, while stock markets are more likely to be concerned with short-term gain but have a much higher risk tolerance. In this way, the institutional forms through which finance capital flows will shape the innovation climate and have impacts on the kinds of businesses that are funded, the strategic horizon of senior management, and the stability of the labour market.

A second major line of differentiation in varieties of capitalism is the regulation of the capital/labour relationship. In a classic study of national variations in approaches to employee relations, Colin Crouch (1993) suggested three main frameworks: a conflictual approach, as exemplified by France and Italy, in which antagonisms between employers and employees were openly recognized and collective bargaining conducted within an adversarial climate; a pluralist approach, as exemplified in the UK, in which difference was recognized but assumed to be amenable to negotiation and reconciliation through collective bargaining between employees' and employers' representatives; and, finally, the corporatist approach taken in countries like Sweden and Germany, in which a tripartite bargaining process is conducted between employees, employers and the government. Which of these approaches is taken can have a profound influence on the process and outcome of collective bargaining over pay and conditions, impacting upon economic inequality, competitiveness and employment security.

In addition to finance and the employment relationship, different models of capitalism can vary in their mechanisms of corporate governance: whether the costs of skill creation are met by employers or central government education planning; how work itself is organized according to different production models, from large-scale, standardized manufacturing systems to more flexible forms of distributed, networked production; how national innovation systems function and the role of state-sponsored research and development; and, finally, to the functioning of the welfare state (Jackson and Deeg, 2006). Taking these last two examples, both demonstrate clearly the continued importance of the nation state in capitalism. Indeed, varieties of capitalism are often referred to in terms of ideal-type nations, from Japanese systems, to Mediterranean, Anglo-Saxon (US and UK), German or Nordic systems. Far from the neo-liberal dogma, shared by left and right alike, that the nation state is powerless in the face of footloose capital and corporate power, it remains a key force in shaping economic and social relations.

The key point here is that while these various models for organizing production, distribution, exchange and consumption all have some basic features in common, they are also very different. To emphasize only the shared features and suggest they are all forms of 'capitalism' is to construct an abstract theoretical category that subordinates difference to identity. It is only by neglecting this variety that we could possibly say 'capitalism' is the only game in town, because capitalism seems to mean many things.

Non-commodified, non-capitalist relations

As we have seen, capitalism is subject to significant variation within the parameters of a basic definition in terms of accumulation for its own sake and the use of waged labour. Perhaps more importantly, even within this minimal definition the argument that capitalism has colonized or commodified the world is overstated (Williams, 2005, and this volume). If we step out of a capitalocentric world view to examine the full length and heterogeneity of the global value chains that make up the world economy, we can see an enormous variety of non-capitalist forms of organization. Not all of these should be seen as positive, and many would fail to meet the criteria of an 'alternative' as we propose them in this book (see e.g. the section on microfinance in Chapter 3), but they are important to take into account as they offer crucial evidence against the too readily taken-for-granted assumptions that the world has been commodified, globalized, or even McDonaldized in the image of capitalist organization (Ritzer, 2013).

Non-capitalist work 1: slavery

To start with, consider the central role accorded to waged labour in capitalist production. As Karl Marx (1976), and before him Adam Smith (1976) and David Ricardo (1971) recognized, waged labour lies at the heart of capitalist production. The capitalist system of production depends on a formally free labourer for two reasons. Economically, it is the wage–labour relation that enables the specifically capitalist production of surplus value, which results from the possibility of an employee producing more value for their employer than is necessary to compensate their wages (Marx, 1976; Braverman, 1974). On the other hand, the formal 'freedom' to choose an employer, and the idea that the worker 'owns' their own labour power in some sense, even if they are forced to sell this labour power in order to secure the basic means of existence, is an indispensable part of the political and ideological legitimation of capitalism. At its most simple, this formal freedom differentiates the capitalist worker from the feudal peasant or the slave but even today slavery is commonplace. By some accounts there are more people working in slavery today than at any time in history: up to 27 million (Bales and Cornell, 2008: 8). While concentrated in India, Pakistan and Nepal (ibid.) slavery exists around the world, from those held against their will, trafficked and forced to work as prostitutes in the sex trade, to imprisoned Chinese political dissidents forced to work in labour camps, without pay, to produce cheap commodities both for domestic consumption and export (Bonded Slaves, 2012).

Certainly slavery has changed its face. At the most basic level, it is now illegal in most places, even where the practice of slavery is common. In Pakistan, for example, where bonded labour is an essential mainstay of the domestic brick manufactories, slavery is technically illegal but labourers are indebted by borrowing money, for example, for marriage, from the brick-kiln owners for whom they then have to work to pay off the debt, a process that is often unending and spans generations, bringing an entire family under the owner's control. While this could be thought of as a form of pay – given that money is paid up front – the reality of the experience is clearly one of enslavement, with little hope of ever paying off the debt-bond, and very real risks of violent reprisal if the bonded employees run away (Bonded Slaves, 2012). On the other hand, the simple fact of slavery continuing, even in so-called advanced economies (Bales and Cornell, 2008), shows that capitalism is quite readily able to sit alongside non-commodified forms of labour and exchange. The stronger case can also be made, however, that capitalism in any form is dependent upon other forms of organizing for its very existence. To take perhaps the most obvious example of this, we now turn to consider domestic labour.

Non-capitalist work 2: domestic labour

In many places, today and historically, it has been the unpaid housework of women that enables capitalist production. Without the 'free' labourer discussed above, capitalism proper does not exist, and yet this labourer is a product of non-commodified processes of social reproduction, taking place mainly in the home. As Mariarosa Dalla Costa and Selma James wrote in the 1970s:

> Serving men and children in wageless isolation had hidden that we were serving capital. Now we know that we are not only indispensable to capitalist production in those countries where we are 45% of their waged labour force. We are always their indispensable workforce, at home, cleaning, washing and ironing; making, disciplining and bringing up babies; servicing men physically, sexually and emotionally.
>
> *(Dalla Costa and James, 1975: 3)*

Although for some relatively affluent, dual-income families in the more privileged sectors of advanced capitalist economies, this work has become commodified through paid childcare and domestic labour, for many it remains unpaid and primarily the responsibility of women, suggesting a non-capitalist system of social organization that nevertheless serves the interests of capital. Where this work is commodified, the isolation that Dalla Costa and James refer to means that domestic labour is one of the main spaces of slavery in the advanced capitalist societies (Bales and Cornell, 2008) and, even where legitimate, depends upon immigrant labour undertaken in isolation from other domestic workers and in the private spaces of the employer's own home, rather than a quasi-public workplace like a factory, office or call centre (Ehrenreich and Hochschild, 2003). When women travel to work as domestic servants, for example, from Guatemala to the United States, they often leave other women at home – mothers and grandmothers – to care for their own children while they are paid to care for the children of another family (Heyman *et al.*, this volume). The unpaid labour of care provided in Guatemala thus frees one woman to take on the domestic work of another, who can work as if they were a man who is cared for and free of domestic responsibilities (cf. Acker, 1990). In a longer or shorter chain, then, non-capitalist forms of domestic labour create the conditions of possibility for capitalism to exist. In the framework of this book, we can see these forms of non-commodified labour as simultaneously alternatives to, and a part of, a broader capitalist system of social organization. Alternative insofar as they do not fit within the characteristic model of accumulation for its own sake, waged labour, and hierarchical relations of control (leaving aside the patriarchal organization of the home for the moment). Capitalist insofar as without these modes of social reproduction, capitalism would lack its basic raw material: labour.

Non-capitalism and enclosure: primitive accumulation

While 'free' labour should be understood as a necessary condition of capitalist production, it is not a sufficient condition. For the capitalist relation to be produced there must be free labourers – free to enter into a waged-labour contract, and free from any alternative other than to sell their labour power for a wage in order to survive – but there must also be those who own the capital needed to productively employ them – machinery and raw materials – and who can collectively claim ownership of the means of subsistence, which are sold back to workers in exchange for the money they earn as wages. Labour, raw materials and private ownership of the means of subsistence are thus the preconditions of capitalist production but are not in themselves initially the product of capitalism. Just as capitalism needs non-capitalist relations to reproduce labour power, so it depends upon some previous form of accumulation in order to create owners of capital who can employ labour. Marx (1976) referred to this as the 'so called primitive accumulation', noting that it was dependent upon a range of practices that preceded capitalism but which were a necessary precondition for it. To give just one example, the 'enclosure' of common land upon which the peasantry had some rights to hunt, graze their livestock or collect firewood was a form of privatization that not only put large areas of land under private ownership, thereby allowing for a more massified model of agricultural production and the use of waged labour on farms. It also dispossessed peasants from their livelihoods, forcing them into the industrializing cities to search for paid work. Finally, it created a market for agricultural products where none had been before, as peasants who previously had grown what they needed for their own consumption now had to use their wages to buy basic necessities (see De Angelis and Harvie, this volume).

While Marx understood primitive accumulation as a pre-capitalist form, contemporary theorists have suggested that this process is ongoing and at work alongside capitalism proper (De Angelis, 2006). In Brazil, for example, the logging or clearance of rain forests for beef production can be understood as a form of modern-day, capitalist enclosure that brings new sources of raw material into production. With technological innovation in oil and gas, practices like fracking or the extraction of oil from tar sands bring new parts of the natural environment into the circuits of capitalist production, with new forms of property rights being claimed upon them. Less tangibly, the internet has become a virtual space subject to processes of enclosure. For example, Facebook and Google maintain the appearance of an informational commons, as they are free to use, but effectively commodify the information and audiences generated by the sites' users to sell to advertisers and market researchers (Fuchs, 2012; Rossiter and Zehle, this volume). Other high-tech, clearly capitalist examples of enclosure and primitive accumulation include the ongoing battles over Intellectual Property Rights (IPR) and Digital Rights Management (DRM) in the cultural industries, where ownership of the basic resources of collective cultural reproduction are claimed for ever-longer periods by companies who can profit from them directly or trade them as basic commodities (Hesmondhalgh, 2013). With biotechnology companies even patenting genes – the most basic codes of biological reproduction – it is not going too far to say that life itself is currently subject to forms of enclosure and primitive accumulation (De Angelis, 2006).

If capitalism is understood as the conjunction of a profit motive, waged labour and the private ownership of capital, then the ongoing rounds of primitive accumulation identified above suggest that non-capitalist forms of production exist alongside, and closely interwoven with, capitalist forms of production. If we add the conventionally accepted idea that exchange under capitalism, whether of wage labour or of goods, should be formally free, then the idea that capitalism is the only game in the global village quickly disappears. Whether their primary cause or not, contestation over access to oil and other strategic resources has been a central feature of many recent wars (Harvey, 2003; Retort, 2005). Despite a reigning ideology in which 'free' markets prevail and the state is impotent and withering away, military expenditure remains high or increasing in all advanced capitalist countries and the close relationship between national interest and corporate interest has meant that companies from the USA have been the main beneficiaries when their government has gone to war in oil-rich countries like Iraq (Harvey, 2003). In this sense, and against its own dominant ideology and hegemonic representation, capitalism remains dependent upon very basic processes of expropriation through violence, rather than formally free trade and, in its drive to increase profits, continually expands the sphere of production to bring more of the globe and of life under the rule of private property and accumulation.

Although the alternatives we have considered so far are not capitalism per se, they clearly serve capital and the accumulation process, so in the most limited, minimal definition might be considered capitalist. The danger of viewing them in this way is that it runs the risk of reproducing a capitalocentric world view in which even slavery or theft can be deemed 'capitalist' in some sense. Politically, it may be more efficacious to focus on difference and multiplicity and to acknowledge that even capitalist organization is dependent upon non-capitalist forms of organization for its own, ongoing reproduction. In this sense we are suggesting that rather than there being no alternative to capitalism, the reality is that even capitalism is dependent upon non-capitalism: its constitutive other, or outside. But this is not a book about slavery and theft. In the next chapter we will outline some principles according to which we might separate these practices from what we are identifying as constructive, progressive alternatives to capitalism. The bulk of this book is then given over to a detailed account of a range of vibrant, viable, non-capitalist practices that embody politically radical and socially progressive values. Two tasks remain for this chapter, however. First, to assess the evidence that capitalist forms of organization are growing in significance; and second, to prefigure some of the sheer diversity of alternatives to capitalism that exist both in the past and today.

The commodification thesis: is capitalism spreading?

It remains for us to ask whether the processes we have identified so far are compatible with the oft-articulated insight that even if capitalism is not the only game in town, it is progressively becoming more dominant, and that the processes of primitive accumulation and slavery, that we have been considering so far in this chapter, are merely the cutting edge along which capitalism is expanding to dominate more and more of life, dragging commodification and capitalist relations proper in its wake. This thesis, commonly referred to as the commodification thesis, has recently been articulated very clearly by Paul Adler when he claims that:

> The commodity form progressively takes over more spheres of activity such as food production and preparation, childcare and education, healthcare, and culture. In this process, traditional forms of community – with both their attractive features and their features inimical to women's freedom and to creative individual flourishing – are swept away, as gift exchange and traditional fealty are replaced by the cash nexus and instrumental association.
>
> *(Adler, 2009: 69)*

Against this we can examine the empirical evidence behind this all too common assertion. Based on a comprehensive analysis of the evidence for a range of non-commodified forms of work, ranging from unpaid, domestic work, through non-monetized forms of exchange, to monetized forms of exchange undertaken without expectation of profit, Colin Williams has argued that 'the populations of the advanced economies now spend the same amount of time engaged in non-exchanged work as they do in paid formal employment' (Williams, 2005: 32). Within this category of 'non-exchanged work', Williams includes:

- Subsistence work, which is undertaken without monetary reward for one's own or one's family's benefit, for example, housework, DIY, gardening, etc.;
- Non-monetized exchange, where goods and services are provided to others for free. This category would include anything from informal arrangements like helping the neighbours out with childcare, to formal volunteering through organized charities, etc.;
- Not-for-profit monetized exchanges, for example, working for a wage at an NGO or other not-for-profit organization.

The data that Williams (2005, and this volume) reviews suggest that not only does non-commodified labour remain a significant part of 'working' life in advanced capitalist economies, but according to some evidence it is actually growing as a proportion of all work undertaken in those economies. As he summarizes the situation for subsistence work alone:

> subsistence work still occupies about half of people's total work time and can be valued as equivalent to between 65 and 122 per cent of GDP in the UK . . . similar estimates are reached about its size elsewhere in the advanced economies.
>
> *(Williams, 2005: 46)*

There may be a number of reasons for non-capitalist forms of work and organization to be growing. On the one hand, as Williams notes, in some European countries, the hours of formal paid work have been decreasing so that even if people are spending less time on non-commodified work, that proportion of their work is not declining as fast as their paid work (Williams, 2005: 44). On the other hand, we can also see the emergence of new forms of unpaid work. To take one of the better known examples, the development of free and open-source software is mainly coded by unpaid workers and the final product is distributed freely and for no monetary profit. The motivations of free and open-source software producers have been extensively debated, with some focusing on the intrinsic rewards of community member-ship and puzzle solving (von Hippel, 2005) and others emphasizing the indirect benefits that can accrue to producers such as enhanced employability, making open-source coding a kind of unpaid internship in software design and programming (Lerner and Tirole, 2001). In either case the economic significance should not be underestimated. Open-source systems like Linux have moved into the mainstream in recent years, with laptops on sale in supermarkets proudly displaying a 'designed for Linux' sticker, where the 'designed for Windows' slogan used to appear. Even the mainstream software architecture of the internet is open-source. Apache is an open-source server software that was designed and 'patched' by those running servers in the early years of the internet. It remains the mainstay of the internet, accounting for somewhere in the region of 70 per cent of websites on the internet (von Hippel, 2007: 4). As chapters 13 and 21 suggest, the free software movement can be understood as part of a wider development of a post-industrial gift economy. Against the dominant capitalist ideology of ever-deepening commodification, an ideology that is shared by capitalism's apologists and its most vociferous critics, the emergence of new forms of sharing in the very heartlands of capitalist expansion demonstrate its potential to give birth to, or at least create the conditions of possibility for the emergence of, alternative forms of social and economic organization.

Contesting capitalism: active alternatives past, present and prospective

So far this chapter has argued for the need to de-centre capitalism and recognize its plurality and coexistence alongside a range of non-capitalist forms. In one sense we might consider these to be 'alternatives' in that they clearly diverge from the central organizational principles of capitalism laid out in Chapter 1, even if they are not something we would necessarily think of as politically desirable and progressive. As we examine developments like open-source software gift economies, however, it becomes clear that at least some of these forms of organi-zation embody quite distinct ethical values, modes of subjectivization and political potentials. In some accounts, this ability to foster alternatives in the high-tech heartlands of capitalist innovation suggests a version of the classical Marxist thesis that capitalism will produce its own gravediggers, not in the form of an insurrectionary proletariat but rather as collaborative communities of dot.communists effectuating a kind of radical democracy as an outgrowth and overcoming of capitalism's contradictions (Hecksher and Adler, 2006; Hardt and Negri, 1999). Historically, however, most progressive, democratic alternatives to capitalism have grown in opposition to the dominant social order. Even if that order is, to some degree, a necessary condition for the alternatives that grow up to oppose or overcome it, it is not a sufficient condition and cannot fully explain those alternatives.

For that we need to also account for active human agency, a resilient desire for more participative and egalitarian forms of social organization, and the positive creativity of resist-ance, which does not merely refuse authority but even in the organization of opposition prefigures other possible worlds that will instantiate the values driving resistance (see also Chapter 23). Historically and today there are many such alternatives, some mythologized and romanticized, some ambivalent, and many unsuccessful. Throughout this book we examine a wide range of these, focusing particularly on recent or current examples. In the final chapter we consider further the question of when an alternative might be considered successful and whether these alternatives might collectively inaugurate a new social and political-economic order. For now, however, it is worth briefly reviewing a few key historical and contemporary 'alternatives' that are not included in this book. There are many of them, and if you want to know more, have a look at a whole dictionary full (Parker *et al.*, 2007). We present a few here – The Diggers, pirates and Kibbutizim – to illustrate that that the activities documented in this book are part of a long and diverse tradition.

Digging for victory

'On Sunday 1 April [in 1649] . . . a group of poor men (described as labourers in a legal action three months later) collected on St George's Hill in the [English parish of Walton-on-Thames, just outside London] and began to dig the waste land there' (Hill, 1972: 110). The group, who became known as 'The Diggers' or 'True Levellers', grew in number, causing agitation to the local landowners who saw this as a challenge to their position, even though the land was not cultivated. After being moved on to Cobham Heath, a few miles away, The Diggers were finally driven from the area, and their colony burned, within one year of first breaking the ground (Hill, 1972: 113). In one sense this occupation, which Hill argues was not restricted to the St George's Hill Diggers but was spread around the country before being crushed by Cromwell's armies, was a response to the poverty in England at the time. After the English Civil War, the disarray in the country meant that food was in short supply and crime was ever-present. Despite this, and even though the Parliamentarians in the Civil War had sought to abolish Monarchy and Feudalism, the local landowners and lords held on to the right to prevent the use of the common land in such a way that would benefit the poor. The Diggers' attempts at cultivating the commons were thus an effort to provide food for themselves when none was otherwise available. For the landowners this was a threat to their power, derived from a monopolistic control over agricultural land, and threatened to destroy the value of their land by bringing more land into agricultural use. The Diggers went further, however, and their most famous member, Gerard Winstanley, wrote during the winter of 1649 to 1650 that:

> He that works for another, either for wages or to pay him rent, works unrighteously . . . but they that are resolved to work and eat together, making the earth a common treasury, doth join hands with Christ to lift up the creation from bondage, and restores all things from the curse.
>
> *(Winstanley, quoted in Hill, 1972: 129)*

More than just a pragmatic attempt at self-provenance, or even a struggle against the dominant social order, The Diggers were actively seeking to make an earthly paradise, held in common by all, regardless of class or lineage, and to organize according to principles of collectivity and community without hierarchy or private property.

The example of The Diggers may seem like a fairly marginal curiosity from a short and turbulent period in English history, but this was a time when the Protestant faith in Europe was coming to the end of the Reformation period, which gave rise to the 'Protestant Ethic of Capitalism' that Weber (2001) so famously documented. While drawing upon similar religious inspirations, the ethic that Winstanley articulated for The Diggers contested the very ideas of work as employment for a Master, and we can understand it as part of a challenge to the emerging foundations of capitalism in the country that would arguably become the cradle of industrial capitalism.

Pirates

The democratic ideals of The Diggers were not restricted to the radical factions of the English Civil War. Just a few years later, these same principles took float in the Golden Age of piracy, conventionally understood as stretching from around 1690 to 1720 (Land, 2007: 171). Although the historical record of piracy in this period is rather thin, and mostly gleaned from the (at least partially fictitious) work of Captain Johnson and British Royal Naval records (themselves hardly scientifically objective and disinterested), there is some evidence to suggest that the English, French, Dutch and Spanish pirates operating in and around the North Atlantic in this period had some quite 'alternative' and democratic organizational principles of their own (Rediker, 2004). As with The Diggers, desperation was often the driving force behind the revolt and mutiny that would turn a crew to pirating, but once cut free from their owners and captain, and operating outside the law, pirates developed at least some relatively progressive organizational politics. They arguably had one of the earliest forms of workers' representation with the Quartermaster, the captain's second in command, standing for the interests of the crew in the distribution of plunder and other decisions. They had a relatively well-developed form of workplace democracy, with the captain elected by the crew and subject to recall if they were unhappy with his leadership. They also had a rudimentary form of industrial injury compensation scheme and organizational principles that prefigured the French Revolution's triad '*Liberté, Égalité, Fraternité*'.

Although it is perhaps stretching things to suggest that the 'Golden Age' pirates of the early eighteenth century were proto-anarchists, or even communists, searching for utopian organizational forms (Parker, 2009), they do at least show us that other principles of organizing were possible then, even on the mercantile and naval ships that went on to provide the model for industrial discipline and organization in the factories of the industrial revolution (Rediker, 2004).

Kibbutz

Jumping forward a couple of centuries, and in quite a different political and religious context, similar principles underpin the Israeli Kibbutzim: community-owned factories, collectively run by the workers, which provided the industrial power that kick-started the state of Israel and continue, on a much smaller scale, into the present day. Although Kibbutzim are often involved in quite traditional forms of heavy industry, and subject to the pressures of competing in international markets for their products, they maintain quite distinct organizational structures that are explicitly socialist in orientation, incorporating features such as 'socialised labour, accumulation and distribution by collective consent and the eradication of class and social inequality' (Warhurst, 1996a: 5). The Kibbutz is thus a 'democratic, egalitarian and voluntary gemeinschaft-type society' in which the governance of its industry is managed democratically by the whole community, which 'exercises usufruct rights, controlling the means of production and appropriating all surplus labour and value'(ibid.). While Warhurst's account of the Kibbutz suggests that a strongly gendered division of labour persists in these organizations, with men taking on the high-prestige, often physically demanding work of controlling the manufacturing plant, these organizations clearly challenge conventional capitalist practices. In refusing to separate ownership and control from labour, by enacting a radical form of collective ownership and accountability, and by reintegrating work and life via the wider social organization of the community (Warhurst, 1996a, 1996b, 1998), the Kibbutzim carry on, with variations and differences, some of the non-capitalist principles put to work by The Diggers in the seventeenth century and the radical pirate communities of the early eighteenth century.

The central chapters of this book, from Chapter 4 to 23, review a range of other, mostly contemporary alternatives, all drawing in some ways upon these radical traditions. They challenge the hegemonic idea that there is only one way to organize and show instead a range of organizational forms. Some of these can exist comfortably alongside the range of capitalist organizations populating today's global economies. Others represent a more radical challenge to the principles of capitalist organization identified in Chapter 1. In Chapter 3 we therefore turn to consider in more detail the kinds of principles underpinning the radical, and we would argue progressive, forms of organization represented by The Diggers, Golden Age pirates and Kibbutzim as well as cooperatives, communes, local exchange trading systems, localism, anarchism, community currencies, industrial democracy, partnerships, open-source, degrowth, collectivism, worker self-management, intentional communities, bartering, autonomism, ecology, feminism, gift exchange, fair trade, social economy, Occupy, small states, community currencies, bioregionalism, self-provisioning, syndicalism, slow food, transition towns, time banks, gift relations, social accounting, the commons, recycling, permaculture, appropriate technology, city-state, communitarianism, credit unions, eco-villages, consumer co-ops, trade unions, socialism, mutualism, microfinance, fair trade, Islamic finance, garden city, utopias, and all the other forms of alternative organizing past and present which could have made these twenty chapters into 200.

References

Acker, J. (1990) 'Hierarchies, jobs, bodies: A theory of gendered organizations', *Gender and Society*, 4(2): 139–158.

Adler, P. (2009) 'Marx and organization studies today', in P. Adler (ed.) *The Oxford Handbook of Sociology and Organization Studies: Classical Foundations*. Oxford: Oxford University Press.

Bales, K. and Cornell, B. (2008) *Slavery Today*. Toronto: Groundwork Books.

Boltanski, L. and Chiapello, E. (2005) *The New Spirit of Capitalism*. London: Verso.

'Bonded Slaves' (2012) *Slavery: A 21st Century Evil*, Al Jazeera documentary. Available online at www.aljazeera.com/programmes/slaverya21stcenturyevil/2011/10/20111010144417942321.html (accessed 14 May 2013).

Braverman, H. (1974) *Labor and Monopoly Capital*. New York: Monthly Review Press.

Callon, M., Millo, Y. and Muniesa, F. (eds) (2007) *Market Devices*. Oxford: Blackwell.

Crouch, C. (1993) *Industrial Relations and European State Traditions*. Oxford: Clarendon Press.

Dalla Costa, M. and James, S. (1975) *The Power of Women and the Subversion of the Community*, 3rd edn. Bristol: Falling Wall Press.

De Angelis, M. (2006) *The Beginning of History: Value Struggles and Global Capital*. London: Pluto Press.

Ehrenreich, and Hochschild, A.R. (2003) *Global Woman: Nannies, Maids and Sex Workers in the New Economy*. London: Granta Books.

Fisher, M. (2007) *Capitalist Realism*. London: Zero Books.

Fuchs, C. (2012) 'The political economy of privacy on Facebook', *Television & New Media*, 13(2): 139–159.

Fukuyama, F. (1992) *The End of History and the Last Man*. Harmondsworth: Penguin.

Gibson-Graham, J.K. (2006) *A Post-Capitalist Politics*. Minneapolis: Minnesota University Press.

Hall, P. and Soskice, D. (eds) (2001) *Varieties of Capitalism. The Institutional Foundations of Comparative Advantage*. Oxford: Oxford University Press.

Hardt, M. and Negri, A. (1999) *Empire*. Cambridge, MA: Harvard University Press.

Harvey, D. (2003) *The New Imperialism*. Oxford: Oxford University Press.

Heckscher, C. and Adler, P.S. (2006) *The Firm as a Collaborative Community: Reconstructing Trust in the Knowledge Economy*. New York: Oxford University Press.

Hesmondhalgh, D. (2013) *The Cultural Industries*, 2nd edn. London: Sage.

Jackson, G. and Deeg, R. (2006) 'How Many Varieties of Capitalism? Comparing the Comparative Institutional Analyses of Capitalist Diversity', Max-Plank-Institut für Gesselschaftforschung Discussion Paper, No. 06/2. http://hdl.handle.net/10419/19930.

Jameson, F. (2003) 'Future city', *New Left Review*, 21: 65–79.

Land, C. (2007) 'Flying the black flag: Revolt, revolution and the social organization of piracy in the "golden age"', *Management and Organizational History*, 2(2): 169–192.

Lerner, J. and Tirole, J. (2001) 'The open source movement: Key research questions', *European Economic Review*, 45(4–6): 819–826.

MacKenzie, D., Muniesa F. and Siu, L. (eds) (2007) *Do Economists Make Markets? On the Performativity of Economics*. Princeton: Princeton University Press.

Marx, K. (1976) *Capital*, Volume 1. London: Penguin.

Parker, M. (2009) 'Pirates, merchants and anarchists: Representations of international business', *Management and Organizational History*, 4(2): 167–185.

Parker, M. (2012) *Alternative Business: Outlaws, Crime and Culture*. London: Routledge.

Parker, M., Fournier, V. and Reedy P. (2007) *The Dictionary of Alternatives*. London: Zed Books.

Rediker, M. (2004) *Villains of All Nations: Atlantic Pirates in the Golden Age*. London: Verso.

Retort (2005) *Afflicted Powers: Capital And Spectacle In A New Age Of War*. London: Verso.

Ricardo, D. (1971) *On the Principles of Political Economy and Taxation*. Harmondsworth: Penguin.

Ritzer, G. (2013) *The McDonaldization of Society*, 7th edn. Thousand Oaks, CA: Sage.

Smith, A. (1976) *An Inquiry into the Nature and Causes of the Wealth of Nations*. Oxford: Clarendon Press.

von Hippel, E. (2005) *Democratizing Innovation*. Cambridge, MA: MIT Press.

von Hippel, E. (2007) 'Horizontal innovation networks – by and for users', *Industrial and Corporate Change*, 16(2): 293–315.

Warhurst, C. (1996a) 'High society in a workers' society: Work, community and Kibbutz', *Sociology*, 30(1): 1–19.

Warhurst, C. (1996b) 'The management of production and the changing character of the Kibbutz as a mode of production', *Economic and Industrial Democracy*, 17: 419–445.

Warhurst, C. (1998) 'Recognizing the possible: The organization and control of a socialist labor process', *Administrative Science Quarterly*, 43(2): 470–497.

Weber, M. (2001) *The Protestant Ethic and the Spirit of Capitalism*. London: Routledge.

Williams, C. (2005) *A Commodified World? Mapping the Limits of Capitalism*. London: Zed Books.

3
Imagining alternatives
(with Geoff Lightfoot)

Introduction

It is fairly easy to point to the problems of the present, and suggest that we need new forms of organizing, as we did in Chapter 1. What is much harder is to systematically imagine what those alternatives might look like, to turn opposition and analysis into proposals. Colin Ward once suggested that anarchist organizations should be voluntary, functional, temporary and small (1966: 387). While this is a provocative beginning, it shows the problem with any attempt to state general principles as if they were truths. 'Functional' for whom? Could a temporary organization administer justice, or make computers? How small should an organization be, or how big can it get before we split it in two? Is slavery an alternative to capitalism? Is piracy, or the Kibbutz, or digging unused land for food? At some point, being critical of other people, economic ideas and institutions must turn into a strategy of providing suggestions, resources and models, but these themselves must be criticized. This is a really important point, because we wouldn't want any readers of this book to think that what we are calling 'alternatives' are somehow new, pure or uncontroversial.

This is not a worked-out manifesto for a utopia which could be inaugurated tomorrow. As Chapter 2 showed, the world is more complex than that, with different histories and spaces running parallel to the rise of different capitalisms. Neither do we believe that there will be another world one day in which all our problems will be solved once its logic is explained, or humans can become innocent again, or a prophet will turn up with some instructions. As the chapters that follow this one clearly show, all forms of organizing are 'political', which is another way of saying that they are contested. They have upsides and downsides, and it simply isn't possible to say that there are some arrangements that are unambiguously good, and others that are unambiguously bad. Markets can be hugely helpful forms of reward and distribution in some circumstances, and communes can be oppressive and narrow places which crush individuals. Hierarchies of authority can be helpful, too, on occasion, particularly for making quick decisions, while democratic and popular education could easily reproduce sexist and racist ideas. The key issue that we want to bring out in the book is an awareness of the consequences of particular forms, and to always understand that there are other ways of doing things. We have choices, individually and collectively, and we must never assume that 'there is no alternative' because of certain immutable laws of markets or organizing (Clegg, 1990: 58; Fisher, 2007).

This book is an attempt to articulate some general principles which might guide thinking about alternatives to globalizing capitalism and market managerialism at the present time, so it is incumbent on us to say just what we are 'for' and not just moan about what we are 'against' (Parker, 2002a). Consequently, this chapter outlines some key principles which seem to tie together the chapters which follow, and which might be read as a sort of manifesto for defining 'the alternative'. That is to say, it describes what we have decided to put in this book, and what to exclude on the grounds that it doesn't fit with our definition of what counts as sufficiently different from the present. In broad terms, we will suggest three principles which we have been guided by – autonomy, solidarity and responsibility – and that we think any reflection on the politics of organizing needs to deal with. To summarize very briefly, we wish to encourage forms of organizing which respect personal autonomy, but within a framework of cooperation, and which are attentive to the sorts of futures they will produce. This is a simple statement to make, almost a vacuous one, but it actually produces some complex outcomes, because gaining agreement on any of these ideas is very tricky indeed.

Before we do that, however, we want to show how these arguments about defining what lies inside and outside 'alternative' might work by using the example of microfinance. This is a method of providing capital for small businesses which seems to be both a way of contesting the power of big banks and big business, and also an example of the way in which global and financialized capitalism can seek profits from some rather unlikely sources. So, why haven't we included a chapter on it here?

Contesting microfinance (by Geoff Lightfoot)

Microfinance seemed to offer so much to so many and still holds a lingering promise of cost-free or even profitable poverty alleviation. Its modern development is typically traced back to Muhammad Yunus in Bangladesh in the 1970s. He described his experience of lending a small sum of money (around $27.00) to a group of women which enabled them to buy stock for their business of making bamboo furniture. The group was able to repay his money in full and make a small profit which, had they financed their borrowing from the local money-lender, would have been swallowed up by the interest on the loan. Such a tale, on its own, seems heart-warming but scarcely noteworthy as a global alternative. However, Yunus made the radical claim that the model was scalable: it could grow from an individual providing funds out of their own pocket to a professionally organized institution. Yunus demonstrated this by starting a project borrowing money from state and commercial banks to lend onwards to the poor. The project grew to include 28,000 lenders by 1982 and in 1983 was reformed as the Grameen Bank. By 2011, the Bank had 8.4 million members (borrowers) with over 75 billion Bangladeshi Taka (just under $1 billion) in outstanding loans (Grameen Bank, 2012). This market – of tiny loans at reasonable interest rates – had been overlooked by traditional banks because the transaction costs (of arranging loans and monitoring repayment), coupled with a perception that the poor were more likely to default on their loans, suggested that such operations would always be loss-making. Yunus's insight was that targeted loans, primarily to groups of women, could actually achieve repayment rates that were higher than those for other borrowers and that this would make the model sustainable. Thus, a microfinance bank could be self-financing and, by dispersing money to the entrepreneurially minded poor, could help people to work their own way out of poverty. And, by directing loans to women, the project would help empower many who had been doubly disadvantaged – the female poor in a patriarchal society.

At this point, microfinance starts to look very interesting to a number of different parties. First, it appeals to charities, governments and other non-governmental organizations as a possible way of addressing poverty and hardship. It is particularly appealing, perhaps, because it brings the promise of seriously addressing poverty without spending money. As a consequence, governments in many less-developed countries, where poverty is widespread but government funds to address it are limited, have attempted to develop microfinance networks. It also has a strong ideological appeal – rather than creating a benefit or dependency culture, individuals assisted by microfinance appear to be self-reliant and entrepreneurial. Thus, many international bodies, such as the World Bank and the International Monetary Fund, have become interested.

The second strong appeal comes with the suggestion that repayment rates are very high. High repayment rates minimize the risk and, if the returns are high enough, become potentially interesting investment opportunities. Of course, economic theory suggests that there is a correlation between risk and return – low-risk investments deliver a much lower return than high-risk – so when an investment promises high returns with low risks, investors pile in. As a consequence, there has been a wave of commercialization of microfinance which has seen both indigenous commercial banks enter the microfinance market and a surge in capital from global financial markets being directed into microfinance institutions. This increase has been strongly promoted by the World Bank through its International Finance Corporation, whose mission is 'Private Sector Solutions for Development' and which had, in 2012, a $2 billion microfinance investment portfolio (World Bank, 2012). Indeed, the World Bank and other international finance institutions, as Bateman and Chang (2009) note, have forcefully argued that private sector, profit-oriented businesses are the *only* viable long-term solution for the microfinance sector.

The demands of private capital have, unsurprisingly, caused conflicts with the goals of poverty alleviation or empowerment. Arvelo *et al.* (2008) inadvertently give an insight into how the giant investment bank Morgan Stanley assesses microfinance investments: great detail in how to evaluate risk and return but at no point considering the mission of those institutions funded. Yunus himself argued (2008: 6) that 'when institutions with a social mission move towards a commercial mission, the commercial mission will take over and the social mission will get lost'. This is perhaps most clearly evidenced by Rosenberg (2007: 4) who argued that the financial success of Compartamos in Mexico came from 'the very high profitability of the institution based on interest rates that were around 85% per year plus a 15% government tax'. These rates are often defended on the grounds that they 'are far below what poor people routinely pay to village money-lenders and other informal sources' (CGAP, 2006) or that the marginal utility to the poor is far higher than for other borrowers.

Whether justified by comparison with money-lenders or not, we can see that commercial microfinance results in higher interest charges to the poor than other borrowers. The possibilities of poverty reduction through commercial microfinance seem very distant indeed. But it would be a mistake to simply suggest that non-commercial microfinance would work much better. Milford Bateman's (2010) comprehensive critique argues that microfinance creates barriers to successful development by directing labour to marginal enterprises that do not have the potential for generating sustainable growth and diverting funds away from institutions that more effectively promote development. Adopting a wider perspective, he suggests that countries which have strong microfinance networks have remained resolutely poor, while growth in rapidly developing economies owes little or nothing to microfinance. Ultimately, for Bateman, microfinance works to maintain poverty rather than resolve it.

Bateman's bleak conclusion is not unwarranted and leads to the question as to whether there is anything that can be salvaged from microfinance. Possibly not, if we look at the effects in general terms. Once sucked into the maelstrom of global finance, with the demands of ever-increasing profitability, microfinance will inevitably work to suck money from some of the poorest people in the world to deliver it to some of the richest. But at a micro-level, as Yunus's original tale demonstrated, small interventions make a difference in everyday lives and if microfinance is to deliver any hope, it has to remain local and essentially charitable.

The means and ends of organizing

As we have just seen, it isn't always easy to decide what is 'alternative'. There are almost certainly many people who would disagree with the analysis of microfinance which Geoff Lightfoot provides above, but in this book we eventually decided that microfinance simply wasn't alternative enough. What seems to have happened in this area, as Muhammad Yunus suggested, is that the goal of poverty reduction has become displaced by a business logic, the logic of capitalism. Even if we discount this form of economic determinism, another possible explanation is that, as the sociologist Robert Michels suggested with his phrase the 'iron law of oligarchy', those who become powerful within an organization are often motivated by self-enhancement, self-preservation and the consolidation of power (Georgiou, 1981). This means that organizations often just keep on doing whatever it is that they do, like zombies that move but have no consciousness or heart. As Cheney (2002) notes, organizations don't self-destruct, regardless of whether their ends have been corrupted, or their means are still appropriate.

This means that we always need to be wary about organizing, even organizing that looks like it is 'alternative', such as microfinance (though see the chapters on complementary currencies and credit unions in this volume). Part of the problem here rests on making some judgements about the inseparability of means and ends. That is to say, is it enough to decide that a particular form of organizing aims at an end that we deem to be 'good'? We might well say that it is, and consequently that certain ends justify almost any means. So, if a big bank is making money, but people are being lifted out of poverty, then we might be satisfied. Or, if a very hierarchical form of managerialism is being used in a company that manufactures organic foods, then we could agree that this is still a good organization. Of course we can also play these arguments in reverse, and suggest that the means are the evidence that we should use in our judgements. So if an organization was cooperatively owned, but engaged in a particularly cruel form of factory farming, we could perhaps discount the means in some way. Or perhaps we could imagine a form of community currency being used to exclude 'outsiders' from engaging in certain kinds of financial transactions. In these cases, it might be that our care for animals, or for certain sorts of humans, means that the ownership of the organization or the origin of the medium of exchange is pretty irrelevant to our final judgements.

As should be pretty clear, the distinctions we are making here are very troublesome, and could well create some rather paradoxical outcomes. In fact, we believe that any argument about a separation between means and ends should be treated with extreme scepticism, because we do not think you can make a judgement about one in isolation from the other. The distinction between the two often makes us assume that we have no choice but to use particular methods, or to attempt to achieve particular goals. Max Weber captured the difference rather nicely in terms of his distinction between the instrumentally rational action which in modern times he saw as characteristic of bureaucratic organizations (*zweckrational*) and value-rational action which was aimed at a particular ethical, political or spiritual goal (*wertrational*) (Weber, 1922). But though they may seem different, the key issue for Weber is that they are both 'rational' in the sense that they are explanations that can be used to justify forms of action and organization. So the question is not whether one way of thinking is irrational, or less rational, because every form of life is underpinned by a certain sort of rationality. We can't simply disentangle the question of how something is done from the broader issue of why it should be done, and neither do noble ends justify the use of any means necessary.

Take, for example, the question of the university. Can we detach 'how' something is being taught from why it is being taught? Many policy makers and students might argue that the university should be relevant to the economy, which seems to be a way of saying that it should prepare students for jobs. In which case, the university is merely a means to get a degree certificate. But it is very difficult to argue that the end of certifying potential employees is the *only* purpose of the university, simply because the means are crucial in order to achieve the end. The process of learning is what we learn, and the certificate you get when you leave states that you have undergone that process, not simply that you have learnt certain facts and can repeat them when poked. Hypnosis or smart drugs would be more effective if this was the case, and we wouldn't bother with books like this one, and Informa would have nothing to sell. Indeed, in some sense the educational means are the end, unless we argue that a university is only there to award degree certificates in return for money. To use a different example, we sometimes walk because we want to get to somewhere in particular, but we also go for walks because we like walking, and it makes us fitter, and we can talk with our friends and see interesting things. Which is the means and which is the end?

Think about the idea of making a decision. Within conventional organizations, decisions are made by those with power and status. We could say that a decision is a means to an end, and having 'managers' to make those decisions is a means that ensures that getting to the end is more speedy and efficient. Perhaps, but as many anarchists, feminists and socialists have argued, we could treat a collective form of decision making as an end in itself, as an art of cooperating, and not simply a means to some end (Lovink and Scholz, 2007). If the intention of the organization's members is to take decisions slowly and democratically, then the very process of organizing in a particular way becomes its own reward, as well as a process by which other goals might be achieved. As Maeckelbergh's chapter later in this volume on the alter-globalization movement shows, such organizing is 'prefigurative', in the sense that it attempts to bring into being new forms of social relationships. A distinction between means and end, cause and effect, which seems quite secure in common sense begins to look rather suspicious, and politically loaded, in the context of alternative organization.

So we are suspicious of arguments which suggest that any means are acceptable to achieve certain ends, just as we are about suggestions that only certain means are 'efficient' or justifiable. Allowing big financial institutions to make money from the poor is a useful example, because excluding microfinance from this book is not to say that we are against poverty reduction, simply that we do not think that any means are justifiable. (And in any case, there might be better means than these.) The whole point of a book like this is to show that we can, and should, treat all arguments about means and ends as political ones. We should always be suspicious if someone tells us that there is no alternative, no choice, and that we should be 'realistic'. The end point of many arguments against change is that things have to be like this because of 'the market', or 'the bottom line', or 'human nature' which, as we showed in Chapter 1, are usually assertions that suit pro-capitalists. In fact, we think that almost no particular forms of human organizing are inevitable, and that there are always choices about means, ends and the relations between them. For example, if we imagine the university as a mechanism for producing the future, then perhaps it can produce different futures, and different sorts of people to inhabit those futures? The only other position is that history has ended and there are no alternatives, in which case books like this are exercises in futility. The attitude of cynical fatalism which this requires is one we do not share.

Three principles

However, opening up the politics and possibilities of organizing like this doesn't solve our problems. It makes things much more difficult because we can longer admit to any arguments about inevitability, and instead have to justify our individual and collective choices on the basis of what forms of rationality we wish to encourage. These will have to be reasons which encompass both means and ends, both processes and purposes, and rest upon some sort of idea about the kinds of society and people we wish to encourage. This means that visions of a better form of social order, ideas about utopia if you will (Parker, 2002b; Parker *et al.*, 2007), are central to the judgements we might make concerning what is alternative and what is mainstream, about the difference between finance and microfinance, fair exchange and appropriation. We should not assume that we will ever know the 'one best way' to organize (to borrow Frederick Taylor's term), and might instead encourage debate about ideas that are different to the way that we do things now – whether old, new, marginal, hidden, possible or imaginary.

Having said that, it seems fair to try to explain the general principles that we think tie together the ideas and practices in this book because we are not suggesting that 'anything goes'. As we noted in the previous chapter, there are many 'alternatives' to the present, including fascism, feudalism and slavery, but we are not advocating any of these here. So what are the themes that bring together the twenty substantive chapters in this book? As we noted briefly above, we think there are three broad orientations, values, logics or principles at work here – autonomy, solidarity and responsibility – and in this section we will explore them in a bit more detail.

First, we think that any alternative worth exploring must be able to protect some fairly conventional notions of individual autonomy, that is to say, to respect ourselves. This is not a controversial or novel idea, but one that underpins most conservative, liberal and libertarian political philosophy (Mill, 1859; Nozick, 1974). Words like liberty, diversity, dignity and difference are more often honoured in the breach rather than the observance but still gesture towards the radical proposal that individual freedoms really do matter. When we feel that we have been forced to do something that we don't want to do we are diminished in an important way, and any social system which relies on coercion, of an economic, ideological or physical form, is not one which we can support easily. This means that we do think that individuals should have choices about some of the most important ways in which they live their lives. If there is no autonomy within a given social system, only rules, then we are justified in calling it totalitarian, uniform and intolerant of difference. For most of the readers of this book, this will be an easy principle to establish, because (as we argued in Chapter 1) it underlies so much of the ideology which supports neo-liberal capitalism, and yet we also want to argue that it contains a radical core which must lie at the heart of any robust 'alternative'.

Our second principle reverses the assumptions of the first, and begins with the collective, and our duties to others. This could be variously underpinned with forms of communist, socialist and communitarian thought, as well as virtue ethics, and insists that we are social creatures who are necessarily reliant on others (MacIntyre, 1981; Marx and Engels, 1848/1967; Mulhall and Swift, 1992). This means that words like solidarity, cooperation, community and equality become both descriptions of the way that human beings are, and prescriptions for the way that they should be. On their own, human beings are vulnerable and powerless, victims of nature and circumstance. Collectively – bound together by language, culture and organization – they become powerful, and capable of turning the world to their purposes. Perhaps even more important than this is the way in which we humans actually make each other, providing the meanings and care which allow us to recognize ourselves as ourselves. In the most general sense, this is what 'social construction' means (Berger and Luckmann, 1967), the making of the human through and with other humans in such a way that it becomes impossible to imagine even being human without some conception of a society to be oriented to.

Let's pause a moment before thinking about the third principle, because it's fairly clear that one and two are at best in tension with one another, at worst contradictory. How can we be both true to ourselves, and at the same time orient ourselves to the collective? How can we value freedom, but then give it up to the group? Our answer to these problems is that we need to understand both principles as co-produced. For example, when we speak of being free, we usually mean 'free to', in the sense of being free to be able to exercise choices about where to go, who to vote for, what to buy and so on. This is precisely the idea of liberty that we are very often encouraged to imagine as being the pre-eminent principle around which our lives *should* be organized within a consumer society. But a moment's thought also allows us to see that 'freedom to' is only possible if we also experience 'freedom from'. As the political philosopher, Isaiah Berlin, put it, 'positive' and 'negative' liberty are not the same things, even if they appear to be aimed at the same goals (1969). The individual freedom to be who we want to be rests on our freedoms from hunger, dislocation, violence and so on which can only be pursued collectively. We, as individuals, can only exercise our autonomy within some sort of collective agreement, a social contract if you like, which provides us with a shelter against events. So 'freedom' is an entirely abstract concept unless it is embedded within some sort of institution. Otherwise, we might as well talk about being free to starve or pay high interest rates on loans, or at liberty to become a refugee or political prisoner. This is what liberalism so often misses. In its entirely credible and modern defence of individual autonomy against despotic exercises of power it tends to have an allergic reaction towards the institutions which are needed to ensure that we can eat well and sleep safely in our beds.

The reverse is also true of course. As the history of the twentieth century showed very clearly, just because a social system claims to be collective (whether communist, nationalist, capitalist or national socialist) it doesn't mean that it is. Even if it is supported by a majority, there might be compelling reasons not to support certain dominant norms, to stand out against the mass (Arendt, 1963). Often enough, loud claims to be representing others are actually providing a warrant for the powerful to do what they want. The suggestion that individual preferences should always be dissolved in the collective, and that any dissent from the dominant line is heretical, is one that we find in a wide variety of flavours. Liberty is usually suppressed in the name of a greater good – 'the corporation', 'the people', 'the state', 'the nation' – but what is common is that it requires conformity, fear, exile or death to enforce it. There is not such merit in being collective that the destruction of all liberties is necessary in order to achieve it. Indeed, as Zygmunt Bauman has argued, the impulse to create the perfect collectivity is itself something to be distrusted (1989, 2007). The idea of creating the ideal human within the ideal city is one that requires that people and things which don't fit are 'weeded' out, and that all the contradictions and politics of real people in real places are reduced to a 'year zero' from which we can begin again. It is because of such assumptions – often enough wielded by feudal kings, generals and bishops – that assertions of individual liberty matter.

That being said, the dichotomy between the individual and society is not quite so straightforward or dramatic because it is also often mediated by some sort of identity as a member of a group, class or category *within* or *between* wider societies (Jenkins, 2008). When organizing happens on this level – social movements, women's groups, indigenous organizations, social class-based politics – it is often protecting a form of collective autonomy against perceived repression or ignorance. The politics of identity insists on the importance of some forms of collective distinction and on the 'right' to express them. Here we can see many practical examples of how a certain sort of individual difference becomes aligned with a cooperative strategy, and consequently a form of distinctiveness can be articulated as the precondition for a form of solidarity. When a group of vegetarians establishes their own co-operative, or the Somali migrants in an Italian city establish self-help groups, they are making an identity claim. We can be 'different together', a position which appears to dissolve a clear distinction between liberalism and communitarianism, between the demand for freedom and the embracing of a collectivity. This is not the same as insisting on radical autonomy, but neither is it necessarily a form of totalitarianism. As with many matters, the messy reality of actual organizing is rarely as simple as theoretical distinctions would suggest.

In any case, even if we acknowledge that our two first principles do embody a profound contradiction, does this matter? Contradiction is not something to be feared or eliminated by arguments in books. Instead it is a lived reality for people who take on the responsibilities of reflexive organizing, as they juggle mixed motives and outcomes individually and collectively. The tensions between being free, making enough money, having an impact, worrying about the future, or whatever, are not ones which will go away by making theoretical gestures. Indeed, if there were no tensions or conflicts in a particular set of ideas it would be difficult to understand it as living thought. If we already have all the answers, if we already know the one best way to do things, then there would be little point in a book like this, and no way to understand what a word like 'politics' might mean.

Our third principle is a little easier, however, in the sense that it presents a more direct challenge to the externalizing tendencies of capitalism which we discussed in Chapter 1. We think that any alternative worth the name must have a responsibility to the future – to the conditions for our individual and collective flourishing. This will involve words which are used often nowadays, but not always taken very seriously as practices, such as sustainability, accountability, stewarding, development and progress. The economic and organizational structures of the present tend not to encourage such responsibilities, instead treating people and planet as resources which can be used for short-term gain by a few. In large part these are matters which bear upon questions of climate change, environmental degradation and loss of biodiversity, but not exclusively. The conditions for our individual and collective flourishing are also institutional and cultural, and hence any responsibility to the future must also have regard to the sorts of people we create, and the sorts of organizational arrangements they make, and that make them. This means, for example, being attentive to what technologies do to us and for us (in Chapter 21); what sorts of assumptions about democracy and hierarchy we embed into our workplaces (in Chapter 4); or how the architecture of our dwellings separates home from work, or women from men (in Chapter 8). We take 'responsibility' to be a term which presses us to think about all sorts of consequences, which encourages us to respond to the 'long future', and not insulate ourselves with the usual arguments which merely end up displacing problems to some other place and some other time. As the Great Law of the Iroquois Confederacy was supposed to have it – 'In every deliberation, we must consider the impact of our decisions on the next seven generations'.

What we have here, then, are three principles which we require of alternatives, three responsibilities which must be negotiated and understood – to ourselves, to others and to our future. All three are elements of what we believe to be alternative and any one in isolation is insufficient. An organization which only defends individual liberty will not be able to coordinate very much, but an organization which only demands collective loyalty must necessarily expel disagreement. And, since we don't know, and probably won't agree on, what the future should look like then the balance between individualism and collectivism will also be written across our futures. These three cannot be treated as matters that can ever be solved for once and for all, but rather as concerns that must be raised, and addressed, in the certain knowledge that there will always be disagreements. Too much concern for ourselves ends up as possessive individualism and selfishness; too much direction from others and bending to the collective will is a form of coercion; and too many promises about the ideal future neglect the mucky problems of the present. In this book, evidence of all three is required before we deem something to be 'alternative'.

Prefigurative politics

Thinking about these three dimensions makes organization into a series of choices and encourages us to see that there is always another way of getting things done. It problematizes the relationship between means and ends, often making means into ends themselves. Rather than believing that 'we have no alternative', we become able to see that 'organizing' is an open process, and become more able to understand and debate the values which underpin particular institutions and ways of doing things.

Another implication of this is to think of organizing as a kind of politics made durable. Our current versions of markets, management, hierarchy, leaders, employees, consumption and so on constitute a particular set of political assumptions. These aren't necessary and inevitable arrangements, dictated by the structure of our monkey genetics, or the calculus of the invisible hand of the market. Rather than seeing organizing as a technical matter, something to be left to experts with MBAs perhaps, we can understand it as a way of working through the complex ways of being human with other humans and hence a responsibility and possibility for all of us. This is what we might call 'reflexive organizing', a form of working which deliberately and continually reflects on how people and things are being put together. For example, if we claim that democracy – the rule of the people – is a value that we care about then we might reasonably ask just why so many decisions in workplaces are taken autocratically, by a small minority. Arguments from expertise or efficiency might work in particular cases – such as when a doctor uses their expertise to diagnose a medical problem, or something has to be done quickly – but this is not the case in many situations. Why assume that all forms of organization need a class of people called 'managers', and that these people should be paid so much more than the workers? Why are these managers appointed, and not elected? Why assume that the people who work for a company will be different to the people who own it? Why not have workers or trade union representatives sitting on boards of directors? Why do shareholders have votes, but not employees, members of local communities, customers and so on?

Once these sorts of questions and many others are opened up, it is difficult to get them back in the box. The answers become prefigurative of a certain attitude, a constitutive politics in themselves. This is to stress the open-ended quality of organizing and the importance of thinking about organizational processes as part of thinking through the recognition of individual autonomy, the encouragement of solidarity, and taking responsibility for the future. As we explored above, how we reach decisions can be as important as the decisions themselves. This is a really important shift, because it moves us away from thinking that organizing is what happens *after* decisions have been taken, and that it can be left to other people. In a society with a complex division of labour, professional politicians and policy makers, global supply chains and gigantic corporations, it is not surprising that we should believe this. Most often, the responsibility does not seem to be ours when we swipe a credit card, buy some shoes or tick a box on a ballot paper. We make a choice, and someone else organizes things for us. In this book, we are proposing that organizing is a decision too, a decision which prefigures and shapes what follows.

In some rather important ways, we also think that these principles press us to think locally, to think small (Schumacher, 1973) because any meaningful use of words like difference, community, sustainability and so on must refer to a particular group of people with names and faces. Otherwise the words are merely hopeful labels with no referent to the times and places where we live our lives. One of the features of the 'there is no alternative' argument is to point to forces outside the local which constrain decision making. 'If it was up to me . . .', 'in an ideal world . . .', 'if we don't do this . . .', are all phrases which deny local agency and point to a framework which means that things just have to be like they are. Other people and things – 'head office', 'the market', 'the customer' – can be given the responsibility for the maintenance of the social order. But this buck passing has a cost in terms of the way that it prevents us from thinking that these responsibilities are ours, and that we can imagine different ways that things can be done. That is why many of our alternatives confront us with the local, with what is in front of our noses, because it is there that we spend most of our lives. That being said, small isn't always beautiful, particularly when it comes to the avoidance of insularity and the building of (real and metaphorical) bridges, but it is less likely to do as much damage. In other words, we don't have to assume that organizations must grow and become big, because in taking our three responsibilities seriously we might decide that local works better.

The rest of the book

Not that any of this is easy, because simply imagining that the world could be different merely builds castles in the air. This is not a utopian book, in the sense of putting forward some images of what a perfect world might look like. It's more like a recipe book, in which the chapters function to provide some ideas and inspiration by documenting the history, current state and future possibilities of alternatives to market managerial capitalism. With a recipe book, you are not told what to make, but are encouraged to think that you don't need to keep on eating Chicken McNuggets. Other ideas are available.

The following twenty chapters explore these ideas in terms of three issues – how this affects conceptions of work and labour, exchange and consumption, and the sorts of resources required to re-imagine organizing in different ways. We have divided the book into these sections because we believe that it broadly reflects the sorts of questions that are raised by reflexive organizing. How shall we work and make a living? What shall we buy and sell? How shall we deal with the people and things that we organize? None of the chapters in each of the sections represents a final or settled answer, rather an attempt to open up questions which many people in the societies of the global North do not even see to be questions. In the final chapter, Chapter 24, we return to the broader idea of change, and to what extent we should be pessimistic about the idea that 'another world is possible', to quote the slogan of the World Social Forum (McNally, 2005). Obviously we can't be that pessimistic, otherwise we would not have put this book together, but we do think we need to acknowledge the forces and interests ranged against change. This book will not change the world, but the ideas and practices within it, if taken seriously and not dismissed as 'mere idealism', might.

References

Arendt, H. (1963/1994) *Eichmann in Jerusalem: A Report on the Banality of Evil*. London: Penguin.

Arvelo, M., Bell, J-L., Novak, C., Rose, J. and Venugopal, S. (2008) 'Morgan Stanley's Approach to Assessing Credit Risks in the Microfinance Industry', *Journal of Applied Corporate Finance*, 20:1, 124–134.

Bateman, M. (2010) *Why Doesn't Microfinance Work?* London: Zed Books.

Bateman, M. and Chang, H-J. (2009) 'The Microfinance Illusion'. Available online at www.microfinancetransparency.com/evidence/PDF/App.3%20Chang%20Bateman%20article.pdf

Bauman, Z. (1989) *Modernity and the Holocaust*. Cambridge: Polity.

Bauman, Z. (2007) *Liquid Times*. Cambridge: Polity.

Berger, P. and Luckmann, T. (1967) *The Social Construction of Reality*. Harmondsworth: Penguin.

Berlin, I. (1969) *Two Concepts of Liberty*. Oxford: Clarendon Press.

CGAP (2006) 'Why Do MFIs Charge High Interest Rates?' Available online at http://www.cgap.org/about/faq/why-do-mfis-charge-high-interest-rates (accessed 13 March 2013).

Cheney, G. (2002) *Values at Work*. Ithaca, NY: Cornell University Press.

Clegg, S. (1990) *Modern Organizations*. London: Sage.

Fisher, M. (2007) *Capitalist Realism*. Winchester: Zero Books.

Georgiou, P. (1981) 'The Goal Paradigm and Notes toward a Counter-paradigm', in M. Zey-Ferrell and M. Aiken (eds) *Complex Organizations: Critical Perspectives*. Glenview, IL: Scott Foresman, 69–88.

Grameen Bank (2012) 'Annual Report'. Available online at www.grameen.com/index.php?option=com_content&task=view&id=1150&Itemid=983 (accessed 13 March 2013).

Jenkins, R. (2008) *Social Identity*. London: Taylor and Francis.

Lovink, G. and Scholz, T. (2007) *The Art of Free Cooperation*. Brooklyn, NY: Autonomedia.

Macintyre, A. (1981) *After Virtue*. London: Duckworth.

Marx, K. and Engels, F. (1967) *The Communist Manifesto*. Harmondsworth: Penguin.

McNally, D. (2005) *Another World is Possible*. Winnipeg: Arbeiter Ring Publishing.

Mill, J.S. (1859/2005) *On Liberty*. New York: Cosimo Classics.

Mulhall, S. and Swift, A. (1992) *Liberals and Communitarians*. Oxford: Blackwell.

Nozick, R. (1974) *Anarchy, State and Utopia*. New York: Basic Books.

Parker, M. (2002a) *Against Management*. Cambridge: Polity.

Parker, M. (ed.) (2002b) *Utopia and Organization*. Oxford: Blackwell.

Parker, M., Fournier, V. and Reedy, P. (2007) *The Dictionary of Alternatives: Utopia and Organization*. London: Zed Books.

Rosenberg, R. (2007) 'CGAP Reflections on the Compartamos Initial Public Offering: A Case Study on Microfinance Interest Rates and Profits'. Available online at http://edu.care.org/Documents/CGAP%20Reflections%20on%20the%20Compartamos%20Initial%20Public%20Offering—%20A%20Case%20Study%20on%20Microfinance%20Interest%20Rates%20and%20Profits.pdf (accessed 13 May 2013).

Schumacher, E. (1973/1993) *Small is Beautiful*. London: Vintage.

Ward, C. (1996) 'The Organization of Anarchy', in L. Krimerman and L. Perry (eds) *Patterns of Anarchy*. New York: Anchor Books, 386–396.

Weber, M. (1922/1978) *Economy and Society: Volume 1*. Berkeley: University of California Press.

World Bank (2012) 'Microfinance and Financial Inclusion'. Available online at http://go.worldbank.org/XZS4R3M2S0 (accessed 13 March 2013).

Yunus, M. (2008) 'Is it Fair to do Business with the Poor?' *Geneva Papers on Inclusiveness*. Geneva: World Microfinance Forum.

Section 2
Work and labour

In this section, we focus on work and labour practices in their full array of actual possibilities and try to expand the range of imagined options, especially with respect to the parameters suggested by prevailing market forms and contemporary frames of human activity. Within this section, we have urged authors to consider a common set of questions, such as: What counts as labour? And, how do we count it? What counts as production? And, how do we value it? What sorts of relations are implied or achievable within various arrangements of work practices and structures of organizations?

This collection of chapters is fundamentally about the relationship between the material world and the cultural world. We think that making things is impossible to separate from questions of social solidarity and relationship. We are always making things together. In this regard, all of the authors represented in this section are travelling the same broad path that would reconnect work, and therefore economy, with profoundly cultural concerns. They are re-embedding the economy, insisting that it is always social, and that 'markets' are made.

The chapters collected here also display a common interest in *boundaries*. This is true in multiple ways. First, these chapters challenge the notion that roles in labour and organizational contexts are completely defined and fully realized in the contemporary economy. Second, these chapters move us toward the edges of what contemporary capitalism would regard as value-able, and perhaps into some areas where value – in the sense of commensuration – is refused. Third, the authors writing here urge us to reconsider the separations and relationships between spheres – the domains of human interests before they are institutionalized in the senses to which we are all accustomed. Fourth, these chapters are animated by the idea of the a priori worth of the human person and that those currently marginalized in the global economy deserve some sort of place at the table and a voice in our decisions. Fifth, these chapters recognize that forms of organizing are being transfigured through a variety of group and network forms, obviously catalysed to a great extent by technology. Finally, these chapters move us toward a much broader concern for the situatedness of work, labour and organizing in an interconnected and environmentally disturbed world.

Chapter 4, by Atzeni and Vieta, treats the practices of self-management, particularly in *empresas recuperadas* (recuperated enterprises) in Argentina. Since the virtual collapse of the Argentine economy in 2001, a great deal of experimentation with worker takeovers and conversions of urban and rural enterprises has occurred. A decade of observation and assessment on this important set of cases offers one of the world's great records of achievements and challenges in worker self-government (or *auto-gestión*). At the same time, the authors look toward how self-governance and suspicion of managerialism, including the transformation of a traditional capitalist firm, may become a more broadly utilized model for attaining economic justice and democratic revival.

Chapter 5, by Webb and Cheney, focuses on worker co-operatives but more in the context of the broader co-operative movement. If the previous chapter was about control, then this chapter is about ownership, although it is practically difficult to disentangle the two. Beginning with a section on the history, types and principles of worker, and other forms of co-operatives, the authors move into a series of organizational challenges, including questions of membership, size and involvement. Co-operatives, like many forms of organization, must contend with the practical meaning of 'the degeneration thesis'. Three avenues for further consideration of the relationship between worker co-operatives and the market are featured: the development of genuinely co-operative capital, the reinvention of participation, and the embrace of larger environmental alongside community-building concerns.

Chapter 6, by Pitzer, reviews the long-standing tradition of communal living and intentional communities, in various parts of the world. The hallmarks of these social experiments are regard for well-being and some sense of being different from the world outside. However, cases differ according to focus on questions of solidarity, security or wider action. Featuring two cases in the US and one in Senegal, Pitzer reveals the important organizational dynamics of communities that, in the terms of the sociology of religion, must constantly reflect on the boundaries between them and the larger economy and society. This is true, of course, regardless of these communities' religious, spiritual or secular foundations. The lessons here for many other types of value-driven organization in terms of their opposition to and relationship with the mainstream are important, as well as their commitments to collective control and/or ownership.

Chapter 7, by Williams, offers a nuanced discussion of two terms that are often either conflated or whose interactions are neglected: '(non-)commodified' and '(non-)monetized' labour. Using a variety of existing and suggested examples, Williams confronts us with a diverse range of possibilities for treating work in the realm of profit (or not) and incorporating it into economic exchange (or not). At the same time, Williams blurs the boundaries between different forms of activity and exchange in observing the many types of labour practices that can make up a person's day. Williams' framework and essential message are full of hope as well as possibility as he 'puts capitalism in its place' and shows just how much of what we do lies outside the terms of capital.

Chapter 8, by Dale, more than any other chapter in this volume, deals with the organization of the family. On one level, this discussion speaks to the kind of division of spheres that Weber and others charted in the nineteenth century; at the same time, Dale speaks of the many influences brought to bear in the social and material construction of the household in industrialized society. Dale's reflections on the household unit and its operation are historically informed and yet serve to expand our vision of contemporary 'domesticity'. The two forward-looking cases of the socialization of domestic labour and the co-housing model are both very instructive for community-building and building collectives and resiliency within what would otherwise be atomized relationships and networks.

Chapter 9, by Heyman, Fischer and Loucky, is, in a sense, about organizing the impossible, but directly confronts questions of space and place which are often simply assumed. International migration, including the fuzzy boundary between voluntary and non-voluntary forms, is a neglected topic in the academic and even the practical worlds of organizations – that is, outside the specific missions and domains of concerned NGOs. With the realm of displaced and often extremely distressed or oppressed persons, the meaning of 'alternative organizing' takes on a more poignant and more urgent character than we are often led to consider. As the authors explain, at issue for many immigrants and immigrant groups, especially the dispossessed, are basic human dignity and well-being as guaranteed by governments, protecting persons from violence and repression from any source, and ensuring a degree of autonomy in the labour practices of refugee camps.

Chapter 10, by Rossiter and Zehle, is also fundamentally concerned with social movements and agency – in this case as they are being reconfigured by technology and 'the politics of anonymity'. Working within the realm of virtual collaboration, the authors consider deeply how the nature of codes, protocols and standards affects the very means of communicating and organizing. Thus, what may sometimes appear as an ever-expanding system can, in fact, become quite controlled. Within such a dynamic and seemingly boundaryless context for organizing, what looks like an anarchistic and lateralist set of relations, there are both challenges and advantages to social change agents. Regardless, the meaning of anonymity for collective agency is key to understanding this historical moment and the possibilities for leveraging societal transformation to produce forms of work and labour which are like the ones described in these chapters.

4

Between class and the market

Self-management in theory and in the practice of worker-recuperated enterprises in Argentina

Maurizio Atzeni and Marcelo Vieta

Introduction

In mainstream organizational and economic theory, and more broadly amongst business leaders, managers, and within news media punditry, there is widespread scepticism about the possibility of workers' self-management, workers' direct democratic control of production and its administration. Business gurus and management practitioners dismiss the idea of collective democratic management as either totally unrealistic, inefficient, or as a direct threat to the stability of business, the economy, and society at large. Often brought up is the 'inefficiency' of democracy on shop floors when returns must be maximized. This is the old productivity vs. democracy debate in theories of the labour-managed firm (e.g. Hansmann, 1996; Jensen and Meckling, 1976; Ward, 1958). They also find fundamentally inconceivable the idea that a profitable business can be run without the existence of 'strategic' leaderships, vertical chains of command and centralized decision making. 'How can you make it without leaders?' they ask. Leadership is the 'keyword', the pivotal concept for those interested in the study or practice of management, witnessed in the tonnes of paper used to write about it.

Echoing this position, mainstream economic and organization theories have also rarely considered different ways of organizing production and its supervision based on alternative sets of values and aims. And when they do, workers' participation is inevitably viewed not as a way of empowering workers for its own sake but, again, through instrumental lenses highlighting its potential for reducing labour and supervision costs, increasing returns on investment and, ultimately, maximizing profits (Cheney et al., 2011). It is true that attention has been given to ' "the social side of the enterprise" – to the dignity, rights, and full engagement of a person at work' (215) through emphasis on democracy, participation and empowerment. Enterprises increasingly involve workers in quality circles, work teams, job enrichment plans, quality of work–life programs, employee stock ownership plans and the like (Cheney et al., 1998; 53–59). However, even in the few cases in which such practices can be considered as genuine, it is questionable as to what extent a real democracy in workplaces can be achieved in a social system based on private property and in which organizations are structured to fit the common profit maximization model.

Despite the existence of cultural prejudices and structural obstacles to workers' self-management, historical recurrences of cases and events in which workers have taken direct democratic control of production and its administration prove that self-management can be a real, democratic and empowering organizational alternative to the authoritarian, top-down and elitist structure of a traditional capitalist organization. Indeed, history shows that workers' self-management is one of the viable and available options for organizing workplaces, and possibly the organizational structure *par excellence* for a more inclusive and equitable society.

This chapter analyses the theoretical challenges and empirical underpinnings of workers' self-management. The first part of the chapter theorizes self-management as *rooted in class-based actions and struggle*. The concept and practices of self-management are, we assert, structurally embedded within and generated by the same economic system to which it suggests an alternative. That is, self-management most often emerges from the struggles and contradictions inherent in the labour process within capitalism. More specifically, practices of self-management are rooted in the spontaneous, 'bottom-up' and direct actions of workers struggling to go beyond the typically exploitative, and authoritarian nature of the capitalist workplace. *Self-management is also characteristically transformative.* It both prefigures alternative forms of organizing work that are infinitely more democratic and humane than those proffered by the investor-owned and capital-managed firm, and fundamentally changes the values, attitudes and behaviours of its protagonists as they transition from managed employees to self-managed workers. We also analyse the constraints and opportunities for workers' self-management as an alternative organizational form in the light of market competition.

In order to illustrate these three points, in the second part of the chapter the theory of self-management touches down on the contemporary empirical evidence provided by Argentina's *empresas recuperadas por sus trabajadores* (worker-recuperated enterprises, or ERTs) – over 200 formerly investor- or privately owned firms in trouble that were converted to worker cooperatives by their employees, especially in the last 15 years or so, and coinciding with Argentina's socio-economic crisis of 2001 to 2002. We end the chapter by briefly comparing and contrasting Argentina's ERTs to other historical cases of workplace takeovers and self-management, suggesting that the neo-liberal brand of capitalism has brought with it unique challenges and opportunities for new experiments with workers' self-management.

Theoretical foundations

The roots of self-management in spontaneous and self-directed workers' struggles

The organization of work and the decision-making process in traditional capitalist businesses are typically hierarchical and undemocratic, although this authoritarian, management-led work environment is considered, even in the most advanced democratic societies, not just 'fair' with respect to the capitalist's property rights, but also 'necessary' for 'efficient' production. This conviction and the corresponding prejudice regarding any other, more democratic and alternative forms of work organization are, in turn, essential to the ideological reproduction of capitalism in society. Indeed, even the traditional working class, as Marx (1976) pointed out, 'by education, tradition and habit looks at the requirements of this mode of production as self-evident natural laws' (899).

Despite these material and ideological obstacles, self-management has been one of the ways in which workers have attempted to go beyond capitalist forms of organization. An historical overview of self-management puts into relief the different ways it has been taken up by workers, reflected in the variety of origins and contexts, the relevance of external obstacles, and the influence of internal contradictions in the development and establishment of self-management. The emergence of self-management, for instance, has often coincided with periods of economic and political turmoil. To name only a few historical cases, consider Argentina's workplace takeovers of 1964, 1975 and the recent case of ERTs that we will discuss shortly; or Chile's growth in cooperatives and *coordinadoras industriales* between 1970 and 1973; Portugal's self-managed factories and farms in the early 1970s; post-colonial Algeria's brief movement of *auto-gestión* in 1962; Iran's self-management experiments around the 1979 revolution; Catalonia's self-managed industrial and agricultural sectors between 1936 and 1939; Spain's worker take-overs of failing firms in the 1970s, 1980s, and in more recent years with their Sociedades Laborales; Italy's *bienno rosso* of 1919 to 1920, where over 200,000 workers self-managed their places of work, and again in Italy's own version of worker-recuperated enterprises in the 1970s and 1980s; or the Russian Soviets of 1917 and early 1918 under the Bolsheviks, which, for a brief time, experimented with actual workers' control on shop floors. In other words, self-management is a common practice, not a historical aberration.

Historically, self-management has often been proposed as a state development policy, such as in Yugoslavia 1945 to 1985; the UK in the 1970s; Italy's Legge Marcora for workplace conversions in the 1980s and 1990s; and in Chavez's Venezuela in the first decade of the 2000s. Ideologically, self-management has also been associated with libertarian streams of certain anarchist and communist traditions, considered by them as a pillar of the future classless society (Horvat, 1983; Marshall, 1992). More reform-minded movements have also heralded it as the organization of work that most naturally reflected the collective ownership of cooperatives (Craig, 1993; Melnyk, 1985). In theoretical and historical analyses, the continued presence of competitive markets, the tensions between the political ideals of democracy in the workplace and pragmatic economic decisions, and the degree to which ruling classes react to workers' control of production have been outlined as direct challenges to self-management and to its sustainability as a viable organizational model for work (see Ness and Azzellini, 2011).

While emphasis on these different factors is important at the moment of analysis, they do not, however, completely explain why episodes of self-management have been recurrent. Historical accounts of workers taking control of and self-managing factories, hospitals, civic administration buildings or any other productive environment describe these actions as direct, democratic, unplanned and spontaneous (Bayat, 1991; Horvat, 1983; Marcuse, 1969; Seibel and Damachi, 1982; Thompson, 2009). Led by 'from-below' workplace organizing, emerging in moments of heightened struggles, and often arising independently from trade unions or organized political parties, workers have time and time again shown, through their own 'practice in struggle', an alternative way of producing and decision taking within capitalism. Though frequently this alternative has appeared as the unexpected outcome of more traditional, union-aligned labour conflicts (i.e. Italy 1919–1920, Argentina 1964, 1975), actual practices of self-management have, more often than not, developed from *the spontaneous outcome* of workers' own self-activity on shop floors. Historical cases of spontaneous, worker-led self-management include takeovers in the UK, Spain, Italy and France in the 1970s and 1980s, and more recent experiences in Latin America in the 1990s and 2000s, most exemplified in recent years by Argentina's ERT phenomenon.

Following Sheila Cohen (2011), 'the seeds and structures of potentially revolutionary episodes [of workers' struggles, including self-management] are contained in "everyday" levels of rank-and-file worker response and resistance, [or] workers' response to the "ordinary" experience of the capitalist labour process, with all its everyday aggravations' (55). While often everyday conflicts in the workplace remain hidden under the surface of 'normal' and negotiated trade union/management industrial relations, at times, as history has evidenced, workplace conflicts do explode into unintended consequences, usually in the most difficult of circumstances. At times, these conflicts transform into demands for or actual practices of workers' self-management. During these contexts of high volatility on shop floors, workplace-based organization inspired by democratic narratives and practices and driven by direct action has been noted by some to be *the* predominant form of workers' organization (Atzeni, 2010; Bayat, 1991; Beynon, 1984; Cohen, 2006, 2011; Darlington, 1994; Fantasia, 1999).

These dynamics clearly point to the close connections existing between self-management, workplace struggles and the establishment of workers' democratic organizations. In general, these dynamics suggest that the emergence of alternatives to capitalist organization of work is from within the same capitalist system. Thus, on the one hand, self-management, rather than being a utopian and impractical blueprint for organizing work, is an actual alternative to capitalist work organization. On the other hand, as a form of workers' collective action and due to the conflictual nature of the employment relationship within capitalism, self-management can be considered as a direct manifestation of the class nature of workers' struggles.

Explaining these structural or systemic factors for self-management is important. Indeed, the historical development of capitalism and of workers' struggles within it provides the possibility of thinking about a future in which new, generalized or isolated, episodes of self-management can appear.

The transformative side of self-management

Democracy, participation, equality and solidarity are the values that have emerged, often spontaneously, as the leading principles inspiring workers' self-managed production and organization. These directly contrast with authority, lack of democracy and participation, inequality, and competitiveness, which dominate the organization of work in capitalist business (Braverman, 1974; Friedman, 1977). Why do some workers struggle for and adopt a system of work and decision making so radically opposed to the traditional capitalist organizational model? And, can we argue that self-management is transformative in nature?

In part, the answer to these two questions is found in the very structure of the labour process within capitalism. The capitalist labour process is not just a simple process of producing useful objects. As we saw in Chapter 1, it is also a system of *valorization* for market exchange to take place (Marx, 1976). Objects are produced within capitalism not just because they satisfy humans' physical and social needs (i.e. use value) but also because, as commodities, they can find a willing buyer in the market (i.e. exchange value). In turn, market competition imposes on individual capitalists the need to reduce costs and full control of the whole production process in order to organize it in the most 'efficient' and, ultimately, most profitable way. Thus, a management system needs to be in place in order to *control* workers' efforts in production (Braverman, 1974). This control is assured through a vertical command-and-control structure responding to the will and profit-seeking demands of the ownership. In this structure, work in effect is divided between planning and execution, between managerial autonomy to make decisions on what is to be produced and how it is to be produced and the tasks of waged ulabourers who ensure that this production is carried out, often resulting in their de-skilling (Burawoy, 1985). Moreover, in this comparatively authoritarian system of production, income is distributed unequally by virtue of this imposed division of work.

As we shall see below with the case of Argentina's worker-recuperated enterprises, self-management within a capitalist system is a double-edged sword. All forms of workers' control still ensconced within a capitalist economy remain dependent on the market and its demands in order to create sufficient revenues to keep the firm afloat and pay salaries (McNally, 1993). But, workers' appropriation of the means of production nevertheless also brings with it radical changes to the labour process despite the continued presence of markets (Lebowitz, 2003). Such transformations, for instance, almost immediately impose collective ownership and restructure the labour process around collective decision making. The substitution of the private shareholders and bosses with the co-management of work by workers opens up spaces for innovations that turn the former organization of work upside down. Vertical management structures will tend to disappear as instruments of discipline, and coordination rather than authority becomes the *leitmotif* in organizing production. Workers' assemblies rather than CEOs and managers democratically decide the most fundamental aspects of the life of the collective.

These tendencies, and the underlying democratic principles inspiring them, are to be found in most historical accounts of workers' control (i.e. Bayat, 1991; Horvat, 1983). Moreover, workplace conversions into worker-managed spaces transform workers' originally economistic struggles into collective actions, contesting the very rights crucial to the capitalist economic system – property rights, the rights of managerial control and authority, and the dictum which equates ownership of capital with control of the firm. In successive phases of workers' control, reflecting changes in workers' consciousness as they negotiate the intricacies of organizing and consolidate their projects of self-management, practical and transformative proposals are implemented to change the organization of work, income distribution, the rules governing collective responsibility, and the internal life of the new organization. Argentina's ERTs, as we will see, show ample evidence of these transformations.

In sum, the substitution of individual ownership and self-interest with cooperative ownership and collective interests acquired by workers in their moments of struggle is key to explaining why self-management develops forms of organization, production and decision making that are intrinsically transformative of the nature of work relations within capitalism. Contesting private property means indeed contesting the system of work and social relations associated with it. It is for this reason that episodes of self-management have been almost invariably repressed by the dominant classes and have often been short-lived. However, what remains striking about episodes of self-management are the structural conditions that tend to generate, as in a chain reaction, the emergence of an alternative. As the recent case of Argentina's ERTs epitomizes, workers that spontaneously occupy their places of work are, initially, usually impelled by defensive and economic needs generated by the crises of individual capitalists or the system as a whole. That is, structural factors rather than ideals or politics seem to be the most usual creators of the conditions for workplace-based class actions. In turn, in the process of struggling and learning collectively how to self-manage their workplace, workers gradually transform into something other than employees. Rather than remaining separated workers labouring for themselves, they become self-managed associates, or *compañeros*, within a socialized labour process. Acting as a counterforce to projects of workers' control, however, competition in the market, as we will see next and in the case study that follows, imposes compromises on workers' self-management projects and on its transformative potential.

Limits and possibilities within the market

We have been arguing for the existence of a transformative/disruptive dialectical characteristic to self-management, directly connected to the class nature of workers' attempts to control production. Workers' practical engagement with self-management has also been frequently associated with the cooperative form. The cooperative movement has gained recognition within capitalism as a legitimate social movement and, together with trade unions, has historically represented effective ways of defending and enhancing workers' interests. No doubt, the democratic, egalitarian and empowering principles inspiring cooperatives have produced forms of organization different in scope and practices from the capitalist one (Craig, 1993; MacPherson, 2004; Zamagni and Zamagni, 2010; Webb and Cheney, this volume). Thus, cooperatives have represented a real and positive enhancement for workers in general. But, as business organizations and institutions operating within a market system, cooperatives have often struggled to keep their democratic values unaltered. This dual nature of cooperatives – their 'dual realities' as we term it – has for a long time been an object of analysis. In Marx's view, producers' cooperatives, in particular, by eliminating managerial control of the labour process and giving to each worker equal representation and rights in the decision-making process, represented practical examples of the unnecessary role of capital in organizing production and work. In this respect, for Marx, worker/producer cooperatives were a form through which workers' emancipation could be achieved. While with the establishment of cooperatives workers have demonstrated that they could exert control and take independent decisions about the internal life of the organization for themselves, cooperatives, however, have proven problematic when evaluating the extent of their self-determination within the context of capitalism as a system dominated by market competition. Cooperatives, according to Marx, would also then 'naturally reproduce in all cases, in their present organization, all the defects of the prevailing system, and must reproduce them' (Marx, 1981: 571). Market competition and the reproduction of capitalism as a system would impose limits on implementing the democratic and participative principles, inspiring cooperatives which would constantly be under threat of internal contradictions; small islands of socialism in a sea of capitalism, as Rosa Luxemburg famously put it.

A negative view of cooperatives for real workers' emancipation has long dominated the debate among Marxists. More recent contributions, however, recognizing the limits that even the most democratically self-managed cooperatives encounter in a capitalist market, have stressed the fundamental role that coops can play towards real social change if they are accompanied by strategies aimed at defending the most radical achievements of workers' self-organization (Jossa, 2005). Egan (1990), for instance, has underscored the importance of the existence of a broader self-organizing environment, produced within a context of working-class mobilization and a politics of radicalization, as a way of bypassing the effects of market forces. This situation has clearly favoured the emergence and consolidation of the recuperated enterprises in Argentina, as we will see in the next section. Baldacchino (1990), in contrast, has emphasized the role of the state in setting up an institutional context that would promote and protect the democratic values of self-managed cooperatives against the most degenerating effects of market competition. Current developments in Venezuela seem to be going in this direction (Larrabure et al., 2011).

In a more reformist vein, other authors, while also acknowledging the limitations imposed by competition, have focused on the positive effects that the expansion of the cooperative sector can have on the market economy, both in terms of generalizing the diffusion of cooperative values (for example, Galera, 2004; Mellor et al., 1988; Melnyk, 1985) and inspiring alternative forms of work organization (for example, Schneiberg et al., 2008; Cheney, 2002).

Quite independently from the political perspective adopted in a particular case, all critical research on cooperatives agrees in stressing the distorting effects market competition has on the everyday management of self-managed workplaces. The existence of forces in the market which workers have scarce or no control over, and that express values that are opposite the collective and democratic decision making adopted by workers, constantly impinge upon workers' independent will (i.e. their 'autonomy') in production. Research shows, for instance, how market forces, rather than in the abstract, appear to workers as impelling needs that require very pragmatic and tangible responses which confront and influence workers' control and democratic decisions about production on a daily basis. This can drive decisions towards centralization and delegation – reducing production costs and overheads, maximizing revenues in order to cover workers' salaries, reducing salaries, provisioning 'competitive' products, meeting clients' needs and so on. There is thus a tangible dimension through which market logics are constantly reasserted in self-managed workplaces, jeopardizing workers' alternatives. In this sense, while workers' subjective attitudes in promoting and defending changes and a collective consciousness of the distortive effects of the market on their organization are important counter-forces, they will still need to face material obstacles (i.e. guaranteeing production inputs, paying salaries) and overcome barriers to assert their own will and control on the organization (i.e. competitive pressures, upgrading machinery, upgrading skills, financing the firm and so on).

To put this in Marxist terms, while self-managed workers enjoy independence and autonomy in the sphere of production, freely and collectively deciding about the life of their organization, when they engage in the sphere of circulation (i.e. buying raw materials and resources, selling the outcome of their production), they will almost certainly remain exposed to system-based forces over which they have little control (i.e. prices, crises, supply and demand constraints and so on).

As we will see in the next section, and as we describe elsewhere in greater detail (Vieta, 2010, 2012a, 2012b; Atzeni and Ghigliani, 2007), the pressure of competition on the self-managed firm can be detected in different forms and at different levels of analysis. It certainly manifests itself in the form of time constraints on the democratic decision-making processes adopted by workers (Cheney et al., 2011: 239). The time needed to engage in democratic decision making, as one worker will tell us in the next section, also comes into tension with the need to produce on time and at the required quality level. Competition imposes speed, urgency and the respect of standards (fixed deadlines, fixed quality levels), flexibility (as with rapid increases in demand) and adaptability (to meet new business opportunities, to overcome unexpected production problems) that places real time limits on democratic deliberation that lead towards delegation and overall to a centralization of decisions. The same time constraints affect the possibility of changes in the labour process. Job rotation, a practice of which workers are in principle supportive, and that is practised to some extent in Argentina's worker-recuperated firms, requires time off from production to retrain workers and time for the adaptation of each worker to the new job. As a consequence of these challenges, the separation between manual/productive and intellectual/directive work might be reinforced. On a different level, labour market competition for skilled workers threatens the equal salary policies desired by workers to strengthen solidarity and cooperative values.

Notwithstanding these limitations, the example of Argentina's ERTs shows us important alternative work practices at play. Favoured by the elimination of managerial and supervisory positions and by the central role of workers in the decision-making process, the system of control at ERTs has been fundamentally changed and the labour process has been de-centralized. Cooperation and sentiments of *compañerismo* (camaraderie) and values of solidarity (rather than control and imposition from above) become the leading motives used to solve problems in a less authoritarian environment. Shared experiences of struggle against former bosses have been transformed into horizontalized workspaces with egalitarian remuneration schemes and cooperative divisions of labour.

Self-management and Argentina's worker-recuperated enterprises[1]

Background

Argentina's ERTs began to emerge in the mid- to late 1990s as more and more small and medium-sized enterprises (SMEs) began to fail or declare bankruptcy as a result of the country's sharp neo-liberal turn. As a consequence, by the first quarter of 2002, well over 20 per cent of Argentina's active, urban-based workers had entered the ranks of the structurally unemployed (Levy *et al.*, 2007). Those workers that were still employed often suffered heightened exploitation by bosses who could not keep their firms afloat. This often included not paying employees' back wages, overtime pay, holiday pay, the employer's portion of social security contributions, or severance upon dismissal. And some business owners would enter bankruptcy proceedings only to then pay off court trustees, asset strip their own firms, and open up shop somewhere else with cheaper labour. By the apogee of the neo-liberal crisis in late 2001 and early 2002 – a period highlighted by the popular revolt of 19/20 December 2001 and the announcement of Argentina's default on its national debt a few days later – the national month-to-month business bankruptcy rate had reached its highest point in the country's modern history, soaring from an average of 772 bankrupted firms per month in 1991 to over 2600 per month by December 2001 (Magnani, 2003: 37).

In this context, traditional union tactics were unable to address workers' needs, and an impotent state was on the defensive as social, economic and political crises rendered it incapable of responding to soaring unemployment, underemployment, business failure and poverty (Patroni, 2004; Vieta, 2012b). Tapping into the long-held Argentine working-class practice of occupying workplaces in times of intense conflicts between employees and employers (Munck *et al.*, 1987), and merging with the radicalization of organizations of marginalized groups throughout the country during these years of crises, some workers took matters into their own hands by occupying and reopening failing firms overwhelmingly as worker cooperatives. By late 2009, almost 9400 workers were self-managing their working lives in over 200 ERTs across Argentina's urban economy in sectors as diverse as printing and publishing, metallurgy, foodstuffs, waste management, construction, textiles, shipbuilding, tourism and health (Ruggeri, 2010: 7).

Rather than being compelled by traditional union demands or the leadership of mainstream political parties, the emergence of ERTs was at first localized and defensive tactics carried out by desperate workers willing to face violent repression by the state and returning owners in order to save their jobs, continue to feed their families and safeguard their self-dignity (Palomino, 2003; Rebón, 2004, 2007; Ruggeri, 2009). As we explore next, these shared lived experiences of crises, however, would go on to shape workers' cooperative and self-managed labour processes, which eventually transformed into more than defensive labour tactics against capital. ERTs; in short, they are testimony to workers' capacities to innovate alternatives and to cooperatively reorganize and self-manage their own working lives despite the perpetual crises and contradictions of capital.

ERTs as worker cooperatives and the 'dual realities' of self-management

As of late 2009, 95.3 per cent of ERTs were self-organized as worker cooperatives. Moreover, 63 per cent of all ERTs benefited from the temporary or permanent expropriation of the firm as 'public goods' by provincial legislatures on behalf of the cooperative, a process innovated by the lobbying efforts of ERT political umbrella organizations. These legal innovations protect these worker-run firms from property claims by previous owners or taking responsibility for the firms' previous debts (Ruggeri, 2010: 24). In most cases, almost all workers just starting an ERT have had no previous experience with cooperatives (Fajn, 2003; Rebón, 2007). Initially, these workers reopen their firms as coops for pragmatic reasons: in order to re-establish the business as a formal productive entity as quickly as possible, to do so within a legally recognized organizational form, and to legitimize the coop with financing institutions, suppliers and customers. At the same time, becoming a workers' cooperative rather than another form of entity (such as a partnership) protects the worker-members from the seizure of their personal property should the cooperative fail, offering them a form of limited liability. As such, ERT workers become cooperators, initially, as an unintended consequence of their struggles. ERT protagonists identify much more with Argentine working-class organizations than with its traditional cooperative movement. 'We come from the working-class. First we are *laburantes* (workers), then cooperators', as one worker told us. Summarizing the view of a majority of the ERT workers we interviewed concerning their take-up of the cooperative form, another worker stated that:

> We became *cooperativistas* out of obligation, not because we wanted to be *cooperativistas*. . . .
> We formed cooperatives as an alternative for the continuity of our jobs, in order for us to keep on working. From that starting point, we begin to work as a cooperative. I formed into a *cooperativista* from inside, from here, in the process of working here.

Despite these pragmatic beginnings, most ERT workers interviewed told us that they eventually do come to realize that the workers' cooperative form is indeed the most robust organizational model for restructuring their collective decision making, production and egalitarian remuneration plans. In sum, the workers' cooperative model essentially serves to give concrete procedural shape to their self-management visions and projects.

Because most ERTs must still compete within capitalist markets once they restart production, however, their workers are constantly affected by the tensions that inevitably arise between, on the one hand, their desires for democratically restructuring their work and, on the other, the production and market challenges that impose themselves palpably upon the depleted firm they have taken over. Considering the conflictual beginnings of ERTs, their technological limitations from inheriting deteriorated production infrastructure, the reduced size of their workforce, the lack of access to credit from banks, and the lack of governmental assistance in general due to a paucity of coherent state policies for assisting ERTs in Argentina, it is not surprising that most ERTs produce at between 30 per cent and 60 per cent of their potential capacity when compared to their production runs during the 'best' days of private ownership (Ruggeri *et al.*, 2005: 65–76).

Given these challenges, and as with other experiences of labour-managed firms that must operate in competitive markets, ERTs live in a tension or a 'dual reality' (Vieta, 2012b). On the one hand, out of a sheer need for survival, ERTs must attempt to maximize production and revenues as much as possible within competitive markets in order to pay salaries and keep the firm afloat. On the other hand, they must also take into account the social and solidarity objectives and values of the cooperative, which include keeping its members working and making a living and, with some ERTs, redistributing portions of revenues to community projects. This dual reality at times conflicts with the social dimensions and values of *companerismo* (camaraderie) inherent in self-management. These at times contradictory values – the coop's economic prerogatives vs. its social aims – were, in almost all interviews we have conducted with ERT workers, constantly in tension. That is, ERT workers both recognize the need for taking care of each other and taking care of the communities that surround them while also recognizing, almost in the same breath, their cooperative's need to stay competitive, upgrade their technologies, or keep growing economically. The treasurer of an ERT medical clinic in the city of Córdoba highlighted these tensions:

> As treasurer I try and take to the workers' assembly proof that we are growing. We have to eat and live and look out for each other, for sure, this is one major responsibility [we have] . . . but *this project also has to grow*. . . . We have to put some of our earnings back into the firm, right? We have to grow so people – society, our patients, the state, our competitors – won't doubt the ERTs.

Underscoring the role of market pressures in compromising the social values of cooperatives, the former president of an ERT in the highly competitive Argentine newspaper and printing sector further articulates this tension in perhaps starker terms when asked how his firm measures 'success', particularly commenting on 'how time [is] a problem in . . . egalitarian groups . . . because of the process to achieve . . . consensus or . . . agreement' (Cheney *et al.*, 2011: 239):

> I think our major success has been at the human level here . . . we have great solidarity, and with minimal conflicts. . . . We have challenges [however] at the organizational level that have to do with bettering our products, making decisions to introduce new and improved quality standards for our newspaper's layout, for example, and improving our production processes. . . . You see, we have issues, I would say, with our *times*. That is, the time it takes for us to turn around ideas into products, because we always have to consult things with the membership.

The tensions inherent in this 'dual reality', of course, are a situation not uncommon to workers' coops and labour-managed firms operating within competitive markets, where they must compete with capital-managed firms while being further tasked, unlike their private competitors, with needing to also abide by the social objectives of their cooperative (Craig, 1993; Melnyk, 1985).

Challenging a strict focus on how market pressures affect labour-managed firms, many other ERT workers, on the other hand, related to us how better working life is at their cooperative when compared to the previous firm, because of how they have 'humanized' their workplaces. How 'success' is conceived of by ERT workers thus often takes on non-economic dimensions as well. Rather than instrumentalizing work within the mainstream economic discourse of the 'transaction costs' of labour as a production input (Hansmann, 1996), ERT workers, when conceptualizing the factors that are important to their self-managed projects, will often consider the well-being of members, quality-of-life issues on and off the job, and even reject product orders if the collective feels that burdensome overtime will have to be incurred. These reconceptualizations of work are testament to how ERT workers further transform these firms beyond the economistic prerogatives of growth and profit making guiding strictly capitalist firms.

Indeed, worker coops have well-documented 'spill-over effects . . . for communities', where workers' 'potential and creativity can flourish', and where workers see improved health (Pérotin, 2012: 2). As Erdal (2000) succinctly puts it, 'people thrive in a social environment characterized by employee ownership' (par. 1; see also Erdal, 2011). One worker at an ERT print shop in the city of Buenos Aires, for example, stated it this way when asked to compare working at the ERT with working for a boss:

No, no, I like working here now much better! Things are much calmer now. There's no comparison with what this place used to be like. Before you couldn't even drink a *mate*[2] during work hours. Now we're all so much more relaxed! . . . But when we have to work, when we're on a deadline, we work hard too. . . . No, it is so much better now. Even if there wasn't any work before, the manager would insist that we grab a broom and sweep the floor, we had to always be doing something, picking up a piece of paper, whatever . . . we couldn't be seen doing nothing.

ERTs, then, are transformative organizations for their protagonists, as they proceed from being employees to self-managed workers. As another ERT worker evocatively put it:

Early on in the struggle to reclaim our work we started fighting for our salaries, for getting out of our severe debt loads that the boss had left us. Now, looking back on our struggle, I can see where the change in me started, because it begins during your struggles. First, you fight for not being left out on the street with nothing. And then, suddenly, you see that you've formed a cooperative and you start getting involved in the struggle of other *empresas recuperadas*. You don't realize it at the time but within your own self there's a change that's taking place. You realize it afterwards, when time has transpired.

Cooperativizing the workplace

The transformative nature of ERTs is also witnessed in the horizontalization or lateralization of the labour process and in the direct democracy that takes shape on shop floors. These democratic transformations, as many ERT workers told us, are not only practical ways of reorganizing production, they are also practices that serve to contrast the exploitative nature of their work in the previous firm.

Horizontalized decision-making and labour processes

Formally, ERTs are administered by a *consejo de trabajadores* (workers' council), made up of at least a president, a treasurer and a secretary elected from the membership and with a mandate of one or usually two years, and the *asamblea de trabajadores* (workers' assembly). On the whole, unlike in many cooperatives throughout the world, but like many smaller worker coops, management responsibilities are not taken up by hired managerial staff at ERTs but are, rather, divided up amongst the workers' assembly and the workers' council. The workers' council (or worker members that directly report to it) takes on the role of administering the business, engaging in duties such as signing cheques, following up accounts receivable, keeping the books up-to-date, and dealing with suppliers and customers. Also, members of the workers' council, emulating in practice (if not consciously in most ERTs) the anarcho-syndicalist and council communist model of recallable delegates, can be removed from office at any time if a majority of the workers' assembly decides to do so. All ERTs also hold compulsory meetings of the entire workers' assembly, gathering either on a regular periodic basis (usually monthly) or when major issues arise, or both. This practice far exceeds Argentine cooperative legislations' requirements of having one yearly members' meeting. The workers' assembly is involved in debating larger issues that affect all members on an ongoing basis, such as electing the workers' council; deciding on when and whom to hire as new members; when to enter new markets, seek out loans, buy new machinery; and whether or not the ERT should collaborate with certain community groups.

Communication flows on shop floors are usually informal, open and flexible. Day-to-day concerns relating to production issues are worked out on an ad hoc basis on the actual shop floor via production processes that are (re)organized around temporary work teams and consensus. These teams tend to be informally led by the expert in that product line or task on a per-project basis. Larger and more complex ERTs deploy more formalized or hierarchical production processes, while a representative from the workers' council, or even a full-time production organizer, might be responsible for allocating particular tasks to certain work teams. Often, one also witnesses informal job rotation where one *compañero* might temporarily relieve another from a work task when attending to a personal matter or when needing to learn new skills. In sum, at almost all ERTs both decision-making and production processes become profoundly more democratic than in the previous firm.

Egalitarian pay schemes linked to common struggles, solidarity and the size of the ERT

Another way one witnesses how *compañerismo* unfolds within an ERT is to look at their remuneration practices. Between 56 per cent (Ruggeri *et al.*, 2005) and 71 per cent (Fajn, 2003) of workplaces that become ERTs eventually take up egalitarian remuneration practices. Indeed, the issue of whether or not to practise pay equity is the topic of continued discussion within most ERTs. Those that do not practise complete pay equity usually, due to the pressure of needing to retain certain skilled workers, take up slightly more hierarchical forms of remuneration. Underscoring the continued importance ERT workers place on their origins in struggle, whether or not workers were present during the initial moments of occupation (that is, whether or not they are 'founders'), also at times dictates pay differentials. It is clear that the strong tendency amongst ERTs is to practise far more egalitarian forms of remuneration than when they were under the control of proprietors. Rather than specific skills or command hierarchies, one finds that collective struggle, cooperation and workers' sense of their collective labour dictate the measure of compensation.

The degree to which egalitarian remuneration practices prevail at ERTs is not necessarily common amongst traditional workers' coops. Again, empirical evidence suggests that pay equity at ERTs is linked to the high level of *compañerismo* and the strength of the social bonds created out of workers' common struggles and their collaborative labour processes. These social bonds first form during the most exploitative days of the previous capitalist firm and continue to coalesce during the moments of struggle to recuperate the firm and afterwards as the ERT consolidates (Vieta, 2010).

Specifically, egalitarian pay schemes and how directly democratic decision-making structures are implemented and practised are related to the conflict and turmoil that the workers' collective had to traverse during the turbulent last years of the previous firm and the occupation phase and *the size of the firm* (Vieta, 2010, 2012a, 2012b). For instance, ERTs that had to traverse more intensive struggles of occupation and resistance are 60 to 70 per cent more likely to practise egalitarian pay schemes and directly democratic decision making when compared to ERTs with less conflictive beginnings. And pointing to the stronger social bonds that form in smaller work teams, 64 per cent of smaller ERTs (20 workers or fewer) practise egalitarian pay schemes, compared to 47 per cent of ERTs with 20 to 50 workers that do so, and 54 per cent of ERTs with more than 50 workers that do so (Ruggeri *et al.*, 2005: 67).

Possible market distortions on ERTs' self-management practices

In addition to the positive correlations between the level of conflict and the egalitarian nature of an ERT, there also seems to be a parallel relationship between the level of market competition and the hierarchical nature of some ERTs, underscoring the point we made earlier that market competition distorts the democratic and radical potential of self-managed firms. As with the Córdoban ERT newspaper we have already mentioned, or as observed in a well-known tractor-manufacturing ERT that exports to foreign markets, ERTs that must do business in highly competitive markets are constantly pushed to continue hierarchical production and practise more marked salary differentials amongst members, in effect emulating the divisions of labour of investor-owned firms in their sector. For instance, the distribution and paper supply chain of Argentina's newspaper sector is dominated by its largest media group, Grupo Clarín, followed by many smaller regional distributors. As such, this highly centralized and competitive market has encouraged this ERT to continue to organize itself within a hierarchical production process in order to, as they related to us, control its quality, guarantee speed to market, and publish daily editions of the paper on time. Organizationally, and in contrast to the more fluid labour processes of most ERTs, each of the newspaper's production teams is headed by an appointed *encargado*, or chief, as in 'chief corre-spondent', 'editor-in-chief' and 'chief of production'. Moreover, these worker-*encargados* tend to be paid more than their fellow members in the same team. Not surprisingly, it was evident in our visits to this ERT that it tends to mostly focus on the task of producing a newspaper rather than further consolidating and horizontalizing their cooperative model. This is espe-cially exemplified in the fact that attendance at workers' assemblies is not mandatory at this ERT as it is with most other ERTs we visited in Argentina. Moreover, the members we interviewed here also tended to have the weakest personal changes in community-focused values and attitudes.

On the whole, despite the continued hierarchical labour processes of some ERTs engaged in particularly competitive sectors, these self-managed firms undoubtedly tend to privilege workers' necessities and the necessities of the communities within which they find themselves over the logics of markets, capital accumulation and the profit motive. This is especially so when compared to traditional capital-managed firms. Their widespread practices of egali-tarian remuneration, horizontalized labour processes, and community-based projects and development across the ERT phenomenon can be seen as promising experiments in forms of organizing work and production that move beyond perpetual crises and the exploitative practices intrinsic to capital–labour relations.

Argentina's ERTs in light of other experiences of workers' control

Worker takeovers of firms or even entire national economic sectors are, of course, not new from a world historical perspective, appearing at different historical junctures of socio-economic crises or political upheaval as we mapped out earlier. Latin America, in particular, provides ample evidence of workspace occupations and attempts at co- or self-management, usually centred on temporary union tactics occurring over short periods of time in the pursuit of bargaining demands, against rationalization drives or firm closures and/or carried out in support of other political ends (like in the cases of the nationalization of strategic economic sectors as in Chile during the time of Allende and in Bolivia in the 1950s). However, compared to Argentina's ERTs, they tended not to be long-term instances of workers both *controlling* and *owning* the means of production and did not tend to last as long.

The practice of self-management in the Argentine context of ERTs has not been about the revolutionary takeover of the state by the working class; nor is it about the reinforcing of an already established or aspiring socialist state under the rubric of co-managed factories or farms, as in the state-owned and worker-run factories or agricultural entities in Tito's Yugoslavia, Allende's Chile, the *ujamaa* experience in Nyerere's Tanzania, or with Chavez's government in Venezuela (Bayat, 1991; Lebowitz, 2005; Petras and Veltmeyer, 2003). Argentina's ERT phenomenon is also not about fighting for sectoral labour rights or better collective agreements via the pressure of temporary workspace takeovers, such as the experiences of earlier Argentine factory occupations, or worker takeover of plants throughout the global North in recent years (Vieta, 2012b). Nor do Argentina's ERTs emerge out of workplace buyouts, as with some Employee Share Ownership Plans (ESOPs) in the United States (Jensen, 2011).

The phenomenon of worker-recuperated enterprises as we know it today in Argentina (and, to a similar extent in Uruguay and Brazil) is, rather, in many ways a working-class response to the social crisis produced by the hegemonic neo-liberal political and economic order within a developing and heavily indebted country. The emergence of ERTs in Argentina, then, more resembles, *at first*, other situations of self-management that emerge in other conjunctures during downward economic cycles that see a large and sustained rise in unemployment and business closures during moments of economic crisis and sociopolitical turmoil. In these situations, as Birchall (2003) asserts, 'the most direct response' to the effects of economic depression, deregulation and globalizing markets has been in some cases 'to set up workers' cooperatives that took over failing firms or parts of firms that were still viable' (48). Similar surges in worker coops as solutions to the growing rate of unemployment and economic crisis occurred, for example, with the noticeable expansion in labour coops in Finland in the 1990s in the wake of the economic disruption of that country's white-collar and service sectors, caused in part by the breakup of the Soviet Union; or the exponential growth in the Industrial Common Ownership worker coop movement (ICOM) in the United Kingdom during its deep economic recessions in the late 1970s and early 1980s (Birchall, 2003; Melnyk, 1985; Oakeshott, 1990).

That the ERT phenomenon is multi-sectoral and can be found across Argentina's entire territory highlights the fact that, contrary to mainstream economic assumptions, self-management is not just possible in labour-intensive sectors but capital-intensive ones as well. That they have been long-lasting, with more and more ERTs emerging in recent years and with low comparative failure rates when compared to capitalist start-ups, also underscores that workers' self-management, in general, is not just transitory and that workers' 'human capital' and commitment to solidarity (their 'we-rationality', 'pro-social', tendencies and 'intrinsic motivators', as some economists put it) form strong foundations for sustaining firms long term. And this, despite the ups and downs of the business cycle, again counters the pessimistic view of the labour-managed firm by mainstream organizational and economic theory.

Conclusion

In short, and despite the challenges they face from having to compete in competitive markets, ERTs point to the promise embodied in all self-managed firms: less-alienated labour, less exploitation from workers controlling their own surpluses, a return to associated forms of work under collective control, an engagement with 'bottom-up' community development projects which entrenches a productive entity within the communities that surround them, and, most noticeably, in the radical acts of horizontally rethreading the labour processes and the organizational structures of formerly capitalist firms.

There is no doubt that self-managed firms that still must work within markets live in a 'dual reality'. Their workers must constantly reassess and even redesign the organization of their production to most effectively meet production requirements, customer orders and market demands, *while also* taking into account workers' internal democratic and egalitarian obligations and any external community commitments they may have. This tension shows that there are real limits to self-management within a continued capitalist system. As with Argentina's ERTs, self-managed firms, however, also point to how alternative work organizations begin to counter market competition in the very restructuring of the labour process along more democratic work flows and horizontal decision-making structures. That is, while their continued existence within competitive markets challenges their cooperative organization, it also impels its workers to find innovative solutions to continued market pressures. They begin to communicate through mostly informal channels and more autonomous and project-based work teams all along the process of production. They de-emphasize economic growth for growth's sake and decentre or even remove the pursuit of profits while redistributing surpluses equitably amongst the membership. And, more often than not, they privilege worker-members' and the firm's surrounding communities' well-being above all else. Eventually, these self-managed businesses become workplaces where workers feel – and are – infinitely more empowered than when working for a boss. They show, ultimately, how class-based actions and struggle can – and often do – radiate into emancipative instances of workers' control 'from below'.

Notes

1 The methodology used to gather the data we report on in this section of the chapter, including all interview sources, can be found in Vieta (2012b).
2 The bitter green tea sipped through a metal straw out of a gourd and consumed throughout South America's Southern Cone region.

Resources

Atzeni, M. (ed.) (2012). *Alternative Work Organizations*. London: Palgrave Macmillan.
Bayat, A. (1991). *Work, Politics and Power: An International Perspective on Workers' Control and Self-Management*. New York: Monthly Review Press.
Ness, I. and Azzellini D. (eds) (2011). *Ours to Master and to Own: Worker's Control from the Commune to the Present*. Chicago, IL: Haymarket Books.
Vieta M. (ed.) (2010). 'The New Cooperativism' – available online at http://affinitiesjournal.org/index.php/affinities/issue/view/4/showToc
Workerscontrol.net – available online at www.workerscontrol.net

References

Atzeni, M. (2010). *Workplace Conflict: Mobilization and Solidarity in Argentina*. London: Palgrave Macmillan.
Atzeni, M. and Ghigliani, P. (2007). Labour process and decision making in factories under workers' self-management: Empirical evidence from Argentina. *Work, Employment and Society, 21*(4), 653–672.
Baldacchino, G. (1990). A war of position: Ideas on strategies for workers' cooperative development. *Economic and Industrial Democracy, 11*(4), 463–482.
Bayat, A. (1991). *Work, Politics and Power: An International Perspective on Workers' Control and Self-Management*. London: Zed Books.
Beynon, H. (1984). *Working for Ford*. London: Penguin Books.

Birchall, J.R. (2003). *Rediscovering the Co-operative Advantage: Poverty Reduction through Self-help*. Geneva, Switzerland: International Labour Organization.

Braverman, H. (1974). *Labor and Monopoly Capital*. New York: Monthly Review Press.

Burawoy, M. (1985). *The Politics of Production: Factory Regimes under Capitalism and Socialism*. London: Verso.

Cheney, G. (2002). *Values at Work: Employee Participation Meets Market Pressure at Mondragón*. Ithaca, NY: Cornell University Press.

Cheney, G., Christensen, L.T., Zorn Jr., T.E. and Ganesh, S. (2011). *Organizational Communication in an Age of Globalization: Issues, Reflections, Practices*. Long Grove, IL: Waveland Press.

Cheney, G., Staub, J., Speirs-Glebe, L., Stohl, C., DeGooyer, D., Whalen, S., Garvin-Doxas, K. and Carlone, D. (1998). Democracy, participation, and communication at work: A multidisciplinary review. *Communication Yearbook: International Communication Association, 21*, 35–91.

Cohen, S. (2006). *Ramparts of Resistance: Why Workers Lost their Power and How to Get it Back*. London: Pluto Press.

Cohen, S. (2011). The red mole: Workers' councils as a means to revolutionary transformation. In I. Ness and D. Azzellini (eds) *Ours to Master and to Own: Workers' Control from the Commune to the Present* (pp. 49–65). Chicago, IL: Haymarket Books.

Craig, J.G. (1993). *The Nature of Cooperation*. Montreal: Black Rose Books.

Darlington, R. (1994). *The Dynamics of Workplace Unionism: Shop Stewards' Organisation in Three Merseyside Plants*. London: Mansell.

Dow, G.K. (2003). *Governing the Firm: Workers' Control in Theory and Practice*. Cambridge: Cambridge University Press.

Egan, D. (1990). Toward a Marxist theory of labor-managed firms: Breaking the degeneration thesis. *Review of Radical Political Economics, 22*(4), 67–86.

Erdal, D. (2000). Employee ownership is good for your health. Available online at http://cog.kent.edu/lib/erdal-health.htm (accessed 9 July 2011).

Erdal, D (2011). *Humanity Working*. New York: Bodley Head/Random House.

Fajn, G. (2003). *Fábricas y empresas recuperadas: Protesta social, autogestión, y rupturas en la subjetividad*. Buenos Aires: Centro Cultural de la Cooperación, Instituto Movilizador de Fondos Cooperativos.

Fantasia, R. (1999). *Culture of Solidarity: Consciousness, Action and Contemporary American Workers*. Berkeley, CA: University of California Press.

Friedman, A. (1977). *Industry and Labour: Class Struggle at Work and Monopoly Capitalism*. London: Macmillan Books.

Galera, G. (2004). The evolution of the co-operative form: An international perspective. In C. Borzaga and R. Spear (eds) *Trends and Challenges for Co-operatives and Social Enterprises in Developed and Transition Economies* (pp. 17–38). Trento, Italy: Edizioni31.

Hansmann, H. (1996). *The Ownership of Enterprise*. Cambridge, MA: Harvard University Press.

Horvat, B. (1983). *The Political Economy of Socialism: A Marxist View*. Armonk, NY: M.E. Sharpe Inc.

Jensen, A. (2011b). *Insolvency, Employee Rights, and Employee Buy-outs: A Strategy for Restructuring*. Unpublished PhD dissertation, University of Sydney, Sydney, Australia.

Jensen, M.C. and Meckling, W.H. (1976). Theory of the firm: Managerial behavior, agency costs and ownership structure. *Journal of Financial Economics, 3*(4), 305–360.

Jossa, B. (2005). Marx, Marxism, and the cooperative movement. *Cambridge Journal of Economics, 29*(1), 3–18.

Larrabure, M., Vieta, M. and Schugurensky, D. (2011). The 'New Cooperativism in Latin America': Worker-recuperated enterprises and socialist production units. *Studies in the Education of Adults, 43*(2), 181–196.

Lebowitz, M. (2003). *Beyond Capital: Marx's Political Economy of the Working Class*. London: Palgrave Macmillan.

Levy Yeyati, E. and Valenzuela, D. (2007). *La resurrección: Historia de la poscrisis argentina*. Buenos Aires: Editorial Sudamericana.

McNally, D. (1993). *Against the Market: Political Economy, Market Socialism, and the Marxist Critique*. London: Verso.

MacPherson, I. (2004). Remembering the big picture: The co-operative movement and contemporary communities. In C. Borzaga and R. Spear (eds) *Trends and Challenges for Co-operatives and Social Enterprises in Developed and Transition Economies* (pp. 39–48). Trento, Italy: Edizioni31.

Magnani, E. (2003). *El cambio silencioso: Empresas y fábricas recuperadas por los trabajadores en la argentina*. Buenos Aires: Promoteo Libros.

Marcuse, H. (1969). *An Essay on Liberation*. Boston, MA: Beacon Press.

Marshall, P. (1992). *Demanding the Impossible: A History of Anarchism*. London: HarperCollins.

Marx, K. (1976). *Capital, Volume I: A Critical Analysis of Capitalist Production*. Harmondsworth, UK: Penguin Books.

Mellor, M., Hannah, J. and Stirling, J. (1988). *Worker Co-operatives in Theory and Practice*. Milton Keynes: Open University Press.

Melnyk, G. (1985). *The Search for Community: From Utopia to a Cooperative Society*. Montreal: Back Rose Books.

Munck, R.M., Falcon, R. and Galitelli, B. (1987). *Argentina from Anarchism to Peronism: Workers, Unions, and Politics, 1855–1985*. London: Zed Books.

Ness, I. and Azzellini, D. (2011). *Ours to Master and to Own: Workers' Control from the Commune to the Present*. Chicago, IL: Haymarket Books.

Oakeshott, R. (1990). *The Case for Workers' Co-ops* (2nd edn). Basingstoke: Macmillan.

Palomino, H. (2003). The workers' movement in occupied enterprises: A survey. *Canadian Journal of Latin American and Caribbean Studies*, *28*(55), 71–96.

Patroni, V. (2004). Disciplining labour, producing poverty: Neoliberal structural reforms and political conflict in Argentina. *Research in Political Economy*, *21*, 91–119.

Pérotin, V. (2012). Worker cooperatives: Good, sustainable jobs in the community. Paper presented at the 'Promoting the Understanding of Cooperatives for a Better World' conference, 15–16 March, San Servolo, Venice, Italy.

Petras, J.F. and Veltmeyer, H. (2002). Autogestión de trabajadores en una perspectiva histórica. In E. Carpintero, J.F. Petras and M. Hernández (eds) *Produciendo realidad: Las empresas comunitarias: Grissinopoli, Río Turbio, Zanón, Brukman y Gral. Mosconi* (pp. 53–62). Buenos Aires: Topía Editorial/La Maza.

Rebón, J. (2004). *Desobedeciendo al desempleo: La experiencia de las empresas recuperadas*. Buenos Aires: Ediciones PICASO/La Rosa Blindada.

Rebón, J. (2007). *La empresa de la autonomía: Trabajadores recuperando la producción*. Buenos Aires: Ediciones PICASO.

Ruggeri, A. (ed.) (2009). *Las empresas recuperadas: Autogestión obrera en argentina y américa latina*. Buenos Aires: Facultad de Filosofía y Letras, Universidad de Buenos Aires.

Ruggeri, A. (ed.) (2010). *Informe del tercer relevamiento de empresas recuperadas por sus trabajadores: Las empresas recuperadas en la argentina, 2010*. Buenos Aires: Programa Facultad Abierta, Facultad de Filosofía y Letras, Universidad de Buenos Aires.

Ruggeri, A., Martinez, C. and Trinchero, H. (2005). *Las empresas recuperadas en la Argentina: Informe del segundo relevamiento del programa*. Buenos Aires: Programa Facultad Abierta, Facultad de Filosofía y Letras, Universidad de Buenos Aires, Programa de Transferencia Científico-Técnica con Empresas Recuperadas por sus Trabajadores (UBACyT de Urgencia Social F–701).

Schneiberg, M., King, M. and Smith, T. (2008). Social movements and organizational form: Cooperative alternatives to corporations in the American insurance, dairy, and grain industries. *American Sociological Review*, *73*(4), 635–667.

Seibel, H.D. and Damachi, U.G. (1982). *Self-management in Yugoslavia and the Developing World*. London: Palgrave Macmillan.

Thoburn, N. (2003). *Deleuze, Marx and Politics*. London: Routledge.

Thompson, E.P. (2009). *Customs in Common*. London: The Merlin Press.

Vieta, M. (2010). The social innovations of *autogestión* in Argentina's worker-recuperated enterprises: Cooperatively organizing productive life in hard times. *Labor Studies Journal*, *35*(3), 295–321.

Vieta, M. (2012a). From managed employees to self-managed workers: The transformations of labour at Argentina's worker-recuperated enterprises. In M. Atzeni (ed.) *Alternative Work Organisations* (pp. 129–156). Basingstoke: Palgrave Macmillan.

Vieta, M. (2012b). *Taking Destiny into their Own Hands: Autogestión and Cooperation in Argentina's Worker-recuperated Enterprises*. Unpublished doctoral dissertation, York University, Toronto, Canada.

Ward, B. (1958). The firm in Illyria: Market syndicalism. *American Economic Review*, *48*(4), 566–589.

Zamagni, S. and Zamagni, V. (2010). *Cooperative Enterprise: Facing the Challenge of Globalization*. Cheltenham: Edward Elgar Publishing.

5

Worker-owned-and-governed co-operatives and the wider co-operative movement

Challenges and opportunities within and beyond the global economic crisis

Tom Webb and George Cheney

Introduction: the rise of co-operativism and worker co-operatives today

The Great Recession that began with the burst of the housing bubble in the US in 2007 and spread to the markets of much of the world was in certain ways a tipping point: it gave legitimacy to discussions about the growing instability and long-term problems of transnational, free-market capitalism. The Great Recession also underscored another phenomenon: a large and slowly growing part of the economy, co-operatives, including worker-owned-and-governed ones, in some places out-performed the public or private investor-owned business model (Birchall and Ketilson, 2009).

We argue that there are a number of reasons embedded in the nature of the co-operative, and particularly in the worker co-operative business model, that make these firms significantly less likely to produce economic implosions like that experienced in 2007 to 2008. These reasons include comparatively less pressure to maximize profit, democratic and dynamic decision-making structures, the marriage of labor and capital with social purpose, and connections to member and community need.

What's more, experimentation with employee ownership and other types of co-operatives has become an important response to the Great Recession, even though it has had scant attention in the mainstream media, especially in North America but also in Europe (Alperowitz, 2012). A variety of types of co-operatives (consumer, housing and financial, for example) achieved modest growth during this period. But from the standpoint of economic stability, it was the performance of worker-owned co-operatives that truly demonstrated the value of the co-operative business model. In both northern Italy and in the Basque Country, Spain, the worker co-operative rich economies of the Emilia Romagna and Mondragon co-operatives, respectively, remained surprisingly stable while laying off less than 1 percent of their workers as at the same time unemployment around them soared.

Although the mainstream press has offered precious little reporting on alternative organizational forms, especially co-operatives, documentary filmmaking has recently featured principles and examples. Films such as *Collapse* (2009)*, Money and Speed: Surviving Progress* (2011), *Capitalism: A Love Story* (2009), *The Four Horsemen* (2009), *Surviving Progress* (2011), and *Meltdown* (2011) began to raise general questions about economic inequality and the structure of the global financial system. Films like *The Take* (2004), *Civilizing the Economy* (2011), *The Rochdale Pioneers* (2012), and *Shift Change* (2012) specifically considered the potential of co-operatives, and among them worker co-operatives, to respond to economic issues.

The United Nations International Year of Co-operatives, 2012, spurred co-operatives on six continents to share with each other and the world the potential for co-operative enterprises to build a better global economy focused on broader welfare and common wealth rather than the increased concentration of wealth and control. Moreover, the designated year coincided with new reports of economic inequalities in many nations and the instability and suffering created by particular financial and free-market policies (Galbraith, 2012). Logic tells us that widening income inequality has social and political consequences. It makes sense that the poorest 20 percent globally or in a country or a province or state would be likely to experience health, social and political impacts. The seminal study by Pickett and Wilkinson (2009), *Spirit Level: Why More Equal Societies Almost Always Do Better*, conclusively documents the logical or common-sense conclusion.

The United Nations International Year of Co-operatives (IYC) was the catalyst for major co-operative events around the world that brought together thousands of co-operative leaders, economists, and others. The events began with a gathering of more than 2,500 at the International Co-operative Association's (ICA's) International Congress in Mexico in November, 2011, following the launch of the IYC at the UN in New York earlier in the month. Major planning events included Imagine 2012: The International Conference on Co-operative Economics 2012 and the International Co-operative Summit, both held in Quebec City, Canada in October 2012. These assemblies were followed by the International Co-operative Alliance (ICA) Congress and the Co-operatives United and International Co-operative Expo in Manchester, UK in November 2012. This series of events led into the Co-operative Decade resolution passed by the Manchester Congress with the goal of having the IYC blossom into a co-operative decade in which co-operatives would become the fastest-growing part of the world economy.

The global economic crisis heightens the need for new ideas and creative experiments in entrepreneurship and community economic development (Birchall and Ketilson, 2009; Deller *et al.*, 2009). A number of studies have shown the important role that the co-operative economy can play in the contemporary economy and society, especially as a new center of creative energy across both the private and third sectors (Gijselinckx and Develtere, 2008; Neamtam, 2005). Moreover, co-operative business forms are increasingly playing key roles in community and regional economic development plans.

> A co-operative is an autonomous association of persons united voluntarily to meet their common economic, social, and cultural needs and aspirations through a jointly-owned and democratically-controlled enterprise. Co-operatives are based on the values of self-help, self-responsibility, democracy, equality, equity **and** solidarity. In the tradition of their founders, co-operative members believe in the ethical values of honesty, openness, social responsibility and caring for others.
>
> *(ICA, 2013)*

Contrary to continuing stereotypes of co-operatives as marginal and inflexible enterprises, we wish to stress that co-operatives may be found in many areas of commerce: service, retail, health care, skilled trades, manufacturing and engineering, technology, education, media and the arts, and agriculture. The growing number of worker co-operatives in the home health care industry (for example, in Wisconsin, Missouri, New York and Pennsylvania, in the U.S. and Nova Scotia, Quebec and Manitoba in Canada) show how the co-operative model is being applied to contemporary needs and how formal cooperation can function well even in a context where activities and members are widely dispersed in geographic terms. As discussed in Chapter 10 of this volume on networks, virtual collaboration also allows for a variety of kinds of knowledge and cultural work to be organized in terms of principles of cooperation and relying on established models of worker-owned co-operatives as well.

We believe this is, in many ways, a new phase of development and opportunity for worker/employee co-operatives and co-operatives in general. While we do not have the space here to chronicle the history of employee ownership, worker co-operatives, or co-operatives in general, we point in particular to overviews by Zeuli and Cropp (2004) and others, who have explained well the similarities and differences across examples from the past 200 years, especially the well-known cases associated with Robert Owen, William King and the Rochdale pioneers in the United Kingdom. Shaffer (1999) also offers a cross-national list of co-operatives in general, dating back to 1750 in the United States.

Furthermore, there is now a substantial amount of research to demonstrate employee ownership's viability, economic efficiency, contributions to job satisfaction, roles in job retention, and capacity for community wealth creation and revitalization. Still, bits of knowledge and experience in the financial and organizational sides of employee ownership are scattered and seldom brought together in the most usable ways (see e.g. Arando *et al.*, 2011; Reese, 2012; Sauser, 2009). At the same time, this research underscores such factors as market fit, the strength and persistence of value commitments, collective engagement in strategic planning, the presence and reproduction of capable and inspiring leadership, and the pursuit of diversified training. More broadly, the advantages of worker co-operative models include: enhanced solidarity of the workforce, the function of local economic stabilization, and community and regional social resilience (Gijselinckx, 2012; Hoover, 2011: 1). Erdal (2012) has also amassed empirical evidence to support the premise that areas with a high concentration of worker and other co-operatives may show health benefits for the population, in line with recent macro-level research on economic (in)equality and health (Pickett and Wilkinson, 2009).

While there exist other forms of employee ownership, including employee stock ownership plans (or ESOPs), democratically run LLCs and community-controlled enterprises, this chapter focuses on worker/employee-owned-and-governed co-operatives, firms where 100 percent (or very close to that, allowing for limited private non-voting shares) of the equity is held by employees and where a system of governance is built upon the principle of one person, one vote (see also Chapter 4 in this volume).

Worker co-operatives have been cast in many ways along a broad continuum, from utopian idealized organizations to unrealistic departures from conventional capitalist businesses. With the example of Mondragon co-operatives alone, we find drastically different accounts, ranging from Morrison's (1991) vision of a harmoniously balanced set of business structures in tune with their larger environment, to Kasmir's (1996) dismissive tale of co-optation. The other notable point here is, of course, that worker co-operatives themselves have evolved over time, for example, in becoming both more business savvy and more oriented toward community and environmental objectives than was typically the case as recently as the end of the twentieth century (Azkarraga *et al.*, 2013).

Still, a key question emerges in discussions of worker co-operatives, and it is expressed from multiple political and economic standpoints: are worker co-ops *serious* alternatives? Can they be financially viable over the long term? Can they have substantial economic impact? These questions are especially important to consider because many countries lack a strong worker co-operative base, even as worker co-operatives are being considered more seriously as alternative business forms. Also, we argue that worker co-operatives are particularly attuned to dealing with pressing questions such as energy use, food distribution, income inequality, and environmental stewardship (Birchall, 2004; Birchall and Ketilson, 2009).

In the remainder of this chapter, we will consider the definitions and scope of worker co-operatives, within the context of a range of organizations, the common principles underlying the worker co-operative movement and their associated practices, key organizational and institutional challenges to worker co-operative development and maintenance, and the internal and external transformative potential of worker co-operatives and the larger movement. Along the way, we will cite relevant academic, professional, and firm-specific documents. We will be highlighting the cases of the Mondragon co-operatives and the co-operatives of Northern Italy; however, we will cite numerous other cases as well.

Types and scopes of co-operatives and the focus on worker co-operatives

As already suggested, worker co-operatives themselves, and co-operatives in general, may be seen as part of a much wider array of business and organization types. Moreover, their distinctions from, and similarities to, other firms to some extent depend on national and state/provincial legal, tax, and regulatory contexts (Hoover, 2011). We do not have space to consider all of these organizational and business types in this chapter. However, it is important for us to observe and explain the diversity of co-operatives before we delve more deeply into the principles, structures, functioning, benefits and challenges of worker-owned-and-governed co-operatives in particular.

There are four key pillars of the co-operative business model that set the co-operative family of businesses apart from other business forms, and these pillars apply as well to the specific domain of worker-owned-and-governed co-operatives. Broadly speaking, the four pillars are the purpose of the business, internationally accepted frameworks of values and principles, and a founding ethic of economic fairness or justice. People often form co-operatives because they seek a fair outcome to a market situation they regard as unfair or unjust. Consumers feel they are paying unfair prices or obtaining poor quality. Citizens may find it impossible to borrow or that the rates are usurious. Farmers and fishers may encounter highly unstable cost and price structures. Workers may experience arbitrary managerial policies and the inability to share equitably in the profits of the business. For many employees or ex-employees in today's global economy, worker co-operatives offer an avenue to self-determination in the workplace or work processes, as well as a means of ensuring a fair share in the firm's profits. Worker co-operatives make shared equity the foundation of the enterprise.

Options in the formation and development of worker co-operatives are also important to recognize because they have implications in terms of structure, process, and outcomes. For example, we may find bottom-up co-operative development fostered by community of interest; charismatic leadership; employee takeovers or business spin-offs; and union co-op projects – which are now beginning to appear on the scene (Witherell, Cooper and Peck, 2012).

Top-down co-operative creation can occur with the efforts of a co-operative development organization or agency (in any sector) or through coordinated community development

(Nembhard *et al.*, n.d.). Alternatively, worker co-operatives can result from the conversion of an existing business under a number of possible circumstances: a family business may lack a successor; a business may be failing for a variety of reasons; a business owner may feel he or she would like to pass on the business to their employees. *Empresas recuperadas* (or worker-recuperated firms) have become significant features of the economy in Argentina, for example, since the banking collapse in that country in 2001 (see Atzeni and Vieta in this volume).

Generally speaking, worker co-operatives that are started with some outside resource as a catalyst have a greater chance of success, both in the short and the long term. The challenges of starting worker co-operatives were noted by Alexander Laidlaw in his 1980 speech to the ICA Congress in Moscow entitled *Co-operatives in the year 2000*. His presentation resulted in the Moscow conference passing a resolution on technical assistance for new co-operatives. As Webb (1987) noted, commenting on Alexander Laidlaw's presentation,

> His [Laidlaw's] experience told him that a strong capable co-operative development mechanism was a necessary part of any effort to develop co-operatives, be they retail, credit unions or housing co-operatives. Worker co-operatives are even more difficult than these other forms. One reason is the varied nature of their business.
>
> *(p. 139)*

The purpose of a worker co-operative is to meet the needs of its members as an outlet for their productive work while at the same time striving to meet community need and adhere to co-operative values and principles (Hoover, 2011). Increasingly, worker co-ops are widening their vision and scope to consider further contributions to the community and, in many instances, to society. This is significantly different from the investor-owned business model (whether publicly traded or not) whose purpose is to maximize the return to shareholders based on the size of their investment. The co-operative model is avowedly employee-centered while the investor-owned model is more wealth-centered for owners and beneficiaries. This is not to deny diversity of objectives and practices within any class of firms or organizations, but it is to emphasize the principles as starting points for worker-owned-and-governed businesses.

The co-operative manager has an obligation to meet member and community needs. In cases of publicly traded private enterprises, the investor-owned business manager has a fiduciary responsibility to maximize shareholder value. Even in the cases where some equity of the firm is shared with the employees (ESOPs) or the community (partially community-owned businesses), pressures can more easily be exerted to pull the firm away from the collective wishes of its members. Ultimately, worker-owned-and-governed co-operatives offer a valuable mix of individual and group incentives; however, these must be put into practice in a given case through the design of work processes as well as governance structures. For example, ESOP participants must be allowed to vote their allocated shares on major questions dealing with the future of the company but they do not necessarily vote on other matters, including the selection of board members. In practice, ESOPs vary tremendously in terms of the degree of democratic governance.

Worker-owned and other forms of co-operatives

If the purpose of the co-operative is to meet member and community needs then the question, "Who are the members?" is a vital one to understand the different types of co-operatives and their governance. In a co-operative, the residual power lies with the members. There exists a wide variety of businesses and other organizations that call themselves "co-operatives" or that can be placed under the umbrella of co-operative business. These vary greatly in terms of the types of engagement of the members and in terms of what membership actually means. Among the types to note in this discussion are:

- Worker/Employee: Those who work in the business which could be in any industry such as food, agriculture, retail sales of good or services, social services, etc. This model would include collectives although most worker co-operatives would not function as collectives.
- Consumer: Consumers of various commodities such as food, insurance, funerals, financial services including credit unions, housing, utilities such as electricity or gas, farm and garden supplies, travel services, etc. This model includes mutuals.
- Small business: Producers of common products such as dairy farmers, fishers, motel owners, hardware or other retail stores, electricians, plumbers, family grocers providing themselves with shared services such as procurement, marketing, business expertise, government relations, etc.
- Solidarity: These involve members who have an interdependent relationship (dairy workers and farmers, parents and daycare workers, social workers and clients, etc.) and form a co-operative with different classes of membership to work toward shared goals.
- Second and Third Tier: Members are co-operatives rather than individuals and there is often a variation of the one-member-one-vote practice to reflect the varying individual membership level in member co-operatives. The International Co-operative Alliance is a clear example of a third-tier co-operative whose members are for the most part second tier co-operatives.
- Community: People from a community seeking to accomplish an ad hoc project or broad community improvement join together to achieve shared goals; for example, building a community hall or developing a plan for community renewal.

There are other taxonomies or classifications of co-operatives, but the above, we suggest, will accommodate every example we have identified. There will surely be some exception that does not slide effortlessly into one of the six categories above, but for now this scheme seems robust.

A key question with any type of co-operative is whether the membership structure, if it includes different classes of benefits, permits the exploitation of non-members. As was suggested in Chapter 3, co-ops vary in this regard. For example, it would be possible to imagine a set of circumstances where consumers in pursuit of lower prices, or fishers seeking a larger share of the revenue from the sale of their fish, might be tempted to offer less than fair wages to workers or less than satisfactory working conditions. Clearly, reflection on the co-operative values and principles would cause discomfort with unfair wages or unsafe working conditions. Yet in some co-operatives, for example, credit unions, workers are prevented from sitting on the board even as consumers elected by the totality of consumer members. It would be possible to imagine circumstances in a worker-owned co-operative where decisions regarding product or service quality or safety might impact negatively on the health or safety of consumers. In other words, there are multiple ways in which "co-operativeness" can be realized even within a specific category or type of business, and we know as well that the use of the label "co-operative" in any context invites probing.

A worker co-operative is based on one worker, one vote regardless of how much a worker has invested. The start-up level of investment in a worker co-operative can vary, from a token amount to significant sums that are payroll deducted over a period. The capital for the organization generally consists of some combination of some, or all, of the following:

- worker shares
- indivisible commonly owned reserves owned by the co-operative
- debt in some form
- preferred non-voting shares.

In a worker co-operative the employee-member-owners have the full authority to decide how to distribute the surplus (profit) remaining after expenses including taxes have been paid. Distributions typically include patronage dividends to the workers (normally determined by salary, hours worked, and/or seniority), community projects, reserves, education or any other purpose the workers propose. Most worker co-operatives divide their surplus among several uses.

The ultimate authority in a co-operative lies in the membership meeting or general assembly (as it is called in the Basque Mondragon co-operatives). While there are variations, in the usual governance model the membership elects a Board of Directors to oversee the business of the co-operative between membership meetings. The Board hires a general manager who in turn hires the staff. The details of this process may vary, depending on the size of the co-operative and its history. There are also many small, and a number of significantly larger, worker-owned co-operatives where they operate as a collective without a management structure. Suma co-operative in Leeds, UK (with more than 180 workers) and Rainbow Grocery co-operative in San Francisco, USA (with over 250 workers) are examples of very successful co-operatives that operate as collectives in this sense.

Because a co-operative chooses the business model at conception, its by-laws usually reflect that identity and must either be followed or changed. Co-operatives usually choose to incorporate under co-operative legislation, unless the statutes in that jurisdiction present obstacles. Incorporating under a co-operative act inevitably requires some degree of conformance to the co-operative purpose, values and principles. In a significant number of jurisdictions, it is not permissible to have different classes of members in a co-operative, and under such legislation, solidarity co-operatives with worker members along with members who may, for example, be farmers or consumers, are not possible. Having chosen the co-operative organizational model also creates expectations about conformity to values and principles among members, workers and the public, including the media.

As both authors have found in their many visits to Mondragon, leaders in the co-operative movement there regard worker or employee cooperation as the strongest form of co-operative enterprise. They argue that a person's contribution to society through work is of more importance than a typical consumer relationship. Workers, while there are generally fewer of them involved in a business than there are consumers of the goods and services of the business, have a great deal more at risk in a co-operative than do consumers. The spiritual and organizational father of the Mondragon co-operative movement, Jose Maria Arizmendiarrieta, was a strong believer that the sense of meaning that people derive from their work is usually more prized than the meaning they derive from consumption (Arizmendiarrieta, 2000: 113–117). Moreover, the individual and collective self-determination involved in shared equity and shared decision making is a solid building block for economy and community. It is also clear that if a consumer co-operative fails, the consumers of the product or service will simply seek an alternate source (Herrasti and Lezamiz, 21 October 2011). The loss of work, of course, can have serious consequences in terms of mental and physical health and family and community ties. Clearly, the more central role a co-operative plays in a person's life, the greater the incentive to participate. A 3 percent turnout at a consumer co-operative annual meeting can often be considered "good," while a 50 percent turnout in a worker-owned co-operative would most likely be seen as a sign of the co-operative being in some difficulty.

A key distinction between different types of co-operatives is not just the structure but the level of engagement of their membership. Engagement is a broad term, but it can be used to reference a number of specific ways employee-members participate in a co-operative enterprise. If we can manage best what we measure, and if engagement is crucial, then it is of paramount importance for co-operatives, especially worker co-operatives, to be able to measure *engagement*. With that in mind, the Co-operative management Education program at Saint Mary's University in Halifax, Canada partnered with Polish scholar Ryzard Stocki and worker co-operative organizations in Canada and the USA to develop the Co-op Index, a management tool based on *a total participation approach*. The Index helps co-operatives to diagnose and develop their participatory character and align their daily operations with their co-operative values. An integral part of the Index is its linkage to the co-operative values and principles based on the belief that they can be powerful source of business strength that can drive financial and membership health (Novkovic and Brown, 2012).

Even in an age where the citizen has been refashioned as a consumer, worker co-operatives attempt to privilege "citizenship" in terms of conceiving of the firm as a polity as well as a shared enterprise with common financial investments and rewards. This can be seen well at Mondragon, where currently there are efforts to reinvigorate a sense of citizenship within the co-operatives and to link that to the larger community.

Worker-co-operative values and principles

Co-operative values and principles were adopted by the International Co-operative Association (ICA) and have been modified from time to time since their original formulation by the Rochdale Pioneers. The last set of modifications occurred in 1995, at an ICA Congress in Manchester, England. The values include equality, equity, mutual self-help, democracy and solidarity. These are reinforced by the personal values expected of co-operators of honesty, openness, social responsibility and caring for others. These in turn shape and inform the seven co-operative principles:

- Voluntary and Open Membership
- Democratic Member Control
- Member Economic Participation
- Autonomy and Independence
- Education, Training and Information
- Co-operation among Co-operatives
- Concern for Community.

It is not possible to comment on governance of worker co-operatives without commenting on the set of ten co-operative principles established by the Mondragon co-operative group. The Mondragon co-operatives grew out of the work of parish priest Don Jose Maria Arizmendiarrietta, who narrowly escaped execution for his involvement on the Republican side of the Spanish civil war. Assigned to the small town of Mondragon, he started a trade school for workers. The school taught not only skills but also a co-operative philosophy aligned with Catholic social teaching that was then influential in many parts of the world.

"Arizmendi's" perspective emphasized the dignity of work and the central role it plays in the life of the community. The co-operatives that now employ 85,000 people and represent the seventh largest private firm in Spain, grew out of this vision, deliberation and planning. From the opening of a small appliance firm in 1956, the enterprise has grown to include a wide array of industrial, technological, construction, financial, educational and consumer services.

The basic principles of the Mondragon co-operatives are ten, not seven, and they reflect the thinking of Arizmendi and his colleagues on worker co-operation. The Mondragon co-operative principles are:

1. Open Admission
2. Democratic Organization
3. Sovereignty of Labor
4. The Instrumental and Subordinate Character of Capital
5. Participatory Management
6. Payment Solidarity
7. Inter-co-operation
8. Social Transformation
9. Universality
10. Education

From the perspective of the Mondragon Co-operative Experience and co-operativism more generally, these principles are interdependent and form a complete fabric. Given this integrated set of ideas, it is not surprising that the activating pillar of co-operation is fairness or justice. The initiation may come from direct or indirect experience of lack of control or unfairness.

For those familiar with the ICA principles, the Mondragon principles numbered 1, 2, 4 and 10 above require little reflection. Although there is an interesting Basque-based experience informing them, they are essentially similar to ICA principles. The sovereignty of labor is clearly a Mondragon principle which "considers labour the principle factor for transforming nature, society and human beings themselves" (Ormaechea, 1993: 148). It stresses the primacy of labor as opposed to either capital or consumption.

The principle of payment solidarity has drawn much attention from those who have become familiar with the Mondragon co-operative model. In practice, the gap between the lowest paid job in any Mondragon co-operative and the highest paid job in the whole Mondragon Group is now 1 to 9 (it started at 1:3). Within each co-operative the gap is 1:6. This also means that the payment levels in the co-operatives are closely aligned with those workers in other firms in the area. Many Mondragon visitors are convinced before they arrive that it must be very difficult to attract good managers with such pay restrictions. As sociologist and Director of Co-operative Dissemination, Mikel Lezamiz (2011) responded to Webb and his students, "If a manager wants 20 or 30 times the amount of the lowest paid we know he or she could not manage a co-operative."

While the principle of inter-co-operation is easily understood in terms of shared benefits and losses within a system of co-operatives, its practice within the Mondragon group is the strongest Webb has witnessed in any co-operative group he has studied. Co-operatives in the Mondragon group share a solidarity fund to assist co-operatives in difficulty, they move members from one co-op to another in the face of economic downturns, they share technology, they buy from each other whenever it is reasonable, and they co-operate to develop new co-operatives.

The principle of social transformation does *not* have a parallel in the ICA principles. What the Mondragon co-operators generally understand by this is that it commits them to "a process of expansion which will contribute to economic and social reconstruction and the creation of a Basque Society which is more free, just and solidary" (Ormaechea, 1993: 175). Moreover, this principle takes the co-operativism of the firm and its members outward into a larger movement. Recently, spin-off organizations have arisen to further realize this commitment.

However, it is important to recognize that ideas about solidarity and associated practices are found in the Mondragon system at seven levels: ranging from camaraderie at work to a commitment to co-operativism. In fact, Cheney (1999, 2002) found seven such meanings and levels in his fieldwork there in the 1990s:

- workplace camaraderie
- team performance and mutual support
- wage solidarity
- inter-co-operation
- community solidarity
- Basque identity
- the Co-operative movement.

This is one example of the diverse meanings and practices that can be associated with a particular value or principle. The same is true of democratic organization, which implicates the communication, governance and managerial practices of the firm. For instance, a recent study of best practices in worker co-operatives in the US (Cheney and Hernandez, in progress) highlights transparency as a key value. In fact, a number of interviewees – representatives of worker co-ops and support organizations – stressed that without a substantial commitment to open-book policies, not only does collective decision making become weakened but also cynicism about the democratic enterprise easily results. This is one way in which democratic commitments become integrated into the daily practices of the organization.

Worker-co-operative incentives and performance

The actual performance of any business model is affected by workers' choices and by the context in which it operates. Two major elements are the structure of incentives or rewards and the processes by which people work. People determined "to do the right thing" will often move toward fairly narrow goals in an investor-owned model. People not strongly motivated to support the common good may subvert the purpose, values and principles of the co-operative business model. The more directly aligned are the values, structures, and processes, the more likely are people to be incentivized.

The actual performance of a co-operative or worker co-operative can also be impacted by the context. In 1978, delegates at the Co-op Atlantic Annual General Meeting voted for the organization to have as much retail work as possible performed by full-time employees. In the debate, they recognized that in doing so they could not vary too drastically from the full-time/part-time ratios of their retail competition without significant competitive risk. They also voted to lobby provincial governments to push up the minimum levels of full-time work and make benefits mandatory for part-time workers. The business model pushed them to meet the needs of their workers. The competitive context of investor-owned firms made fully achieving their goals very difficult and risky.

As noted in Chapter 3, goal displacement, or "mission drift", is a risk for all organizations over time, as recognized long ago by Weber (1978; see also Rothschild-Whitt, 1979; Satow, 1975). For co-operatives, and worker co-operatives in particular, we must consider the reasons why departure from a strong co-operative identity can and does occur. Among the causes are:

- weak or absent educational and training programs
- absence of strong consensus around co-operative values
- limited research into the co-operative model and its functioning
- competitive pressures from the market and predatory business practices
- the wholesale adoption of standard accounting practices
- excessive recruitment of skills and expertise from outside the co-operative
- heavy reliance on traditional management
- insufficient rewards for members and clients/customers
- use of capital with investor-owned behavior and characteristics.

The pressures listed above are not the only ones but each of them plays a role in the explanation of why co-operatives do not live up to the full promise of the "better" business model. For example, if co-operatives rely completely on standard accounting tools that were developed primarily to allow investor-owned firms to measure how efficiently they use their resources to maximize return, they will fail to account for a much wider set of efficiencies or how they use their resources to achieve non-ROI goals. Similarly, even with financial goals, co-operatives need to measure financial health as opposed to maximization of return (see Chapter 18 in this volume on social accounting). Similarly, if there are few courses in schools at all levels that provide information about the co-operative business model and little or no research in business schools, the model becomes poorly understood and unlikely to be chosen or, if chosen, operated to full potential.

Organizational and institutional challenges

Capitalization and related issues of financial structure

Co-operatives often attempt to attract capital using the same rewards and incentives and under the same public policy umbrella as investor-owned firms. Needless to say, this is a difficult strategy as investor-driven financial institutions seldom understand co-operatives nor are they excited by the idea of capital as a tool with a limited return.

The Mondragon and Italian co-operatives are in a different position with regard to capital. In Italy co-operatives are taxed at a different rate than non-co-operative firms but are required to allocate 3 percent of surplus or profit to a co-operative development fund. This has ensured a growing pool of co-operative capital, *Coopfond*, to finance co-operative business. This arrangement was part of the public policy framework for co-operatives negotiated with the government in post-fascist Italy and was the outcome of an enlightened leadership and a receptive government.

In the Basque Country the solution pursued by Arizmendi, just three years after the first industrial co-operative opened, was to take advantage of a provision under the Franco Government regulation of banks which allowed a "people's savings bank" to pay slightly higher interest rates. In a region with a faltering economy, not served by railroads and connected to the rest of the Basque Country by winding, narrow mountain roads, the slogan to attract people to the Caja Laboral Popular was "savings or suitcases." While the returns did not compare to what venture capitalists would demand, many Basques flocked to put their savings in the Caja. The Caja is governed by a board drawn from its workers and the co-operatives in the MCC network.

The new financial institution became not just a savings bank but, through its *empresarial* or development division, it began to develop co-operatives in a systematic way, combining sound business practice and a strong belief in the worker-owned co-operative business model. Business failures were very few, since the Caja not only provided capital but also the entire range of business skills needed by a developing firm. The Bank of Spain, following traditional banking theories of risk management, forced the Caja to divest itself of the development division as Spain entered the European Union in 1986.

New co-operative development is now carried on by a number of other agencies, but there have been no clear studies comparing the effectiveness of the new arrangements and the old *empresarial* division. Nevertheless, the Caja still plays a creative role in financing new co-operatives using tools like loan guarantees to attract outside capital at reduced rates. As this chapter is being written, the structure of the Caja itself is being modified toward governance by capital ownership after a merger in 2012 with a non-worker-owned credit union. The implications of this structural change have yet to be played out.

Membership, including types of relations with the co-operative

Worker co-operatives are governed by their employee-member-owners. This is a much more complex matter than commonly assumed or understood: it raises the question of what proportion of the workforce are full members and what requirements and privileges come with full membership.

Webb and his students have been able to probe these issues deeply through regular visits to the co-operatives of northern Italy, as well as to Mondragon. For example, in *Società Anonima Cooperativa Meccanici Imola* (SACMI) and a number of other large Italian worker-owned co-operatives, membership is limited to a very small percentage of those working in the co-operative. This arrangement has historical roots. At one period in SACMI's history, the co-operative faced severe financial difficulties. An appeal to the membership to increase their financial investment for the health of the co-op was responded to by a relatively small percentage of their membership. After a difficult struggle to save the co-operative, this smaller group of members reached the conclusion that membership should be limited only to those members who were truly willing to put the co-operative ahead of their own immediate financial well-being. In 2010 there were only 234 members of the total workforce of over 6000.

Still, it is important to look at the case of SACMI in a wider perspective. If one were to rate variation of co-operative performance on the seven ICA co-operative principles, while it may not score high in terms of open membership, SACMI does indeed score very high on other co-operative principles. SACMI would score very highly on co-operative education, co-operation among co-operatives, autonomy, democratic control, and certainly on concern for community. On any overall score based on adherence to co-operative values and principles, SACMI would rate as high or higher than many co-operatives who would not hesitate to affirm their "co-operative identity." For example, when asked if the 234 full members might vote to sell the co-operative and achieve considerable personal financial gain, the chairman (Oliviere, 2010) responded to Webb that the members would never sell the co-operative because "it did not belong to them" in the sense that a private enterprise belongs

75

to its shareholders. Secondly, he said, " SACMI belongs to our grandfathers, our fathers, our children and the community. It could never be for sale."

Furthermore, SACMI is not alone among Italian worker co-ops. There are a significant number of others, including some of the most successful in the city of Imola, which are similar with regard to the ratio between employees and members. One result is that, in the process of justifying the exclusion of the vast majority of workers from membership, the argument has become that this is actually a necessary policy for having healthy worker co-operatives. This simply flies in the face of ample evidence of the success of policies of open membership elsewhere in Italy and around the world. In our view, the Mondragon experience, in particular, demonstrates that much higher worker-to-member ratios are also very effective.

Nonetheless, membership density can easily be eroded. Rapid expansion of Mondragon's retail co-operative, Eroski, from its base in the Basque Country across the rest of Spain to preempt a similar initiative by the retail giant Carrefour, led to the creation of Eroski subsidiaries resulting in a dramatic decline in the percentage of workers who were members not just in Eroski but across the Mondragon group. This was on top of the impact of internationalization. Together these changes meant that the overall percentage of workers who were members dropped from close to 90 percent to about 33 percent (Freundlich, 2013). Still, there is no co-operative in the Mondragon group whose members number less than 5 percent of the workers, as is the case with SACMI and several other Italian worker co-operatives.

Size, formalization, bureaucratization, and the implications for the democratic business

Another key governance issue for co-operatives relates to the size of their membership. This question is obviously important for all organizations, given tendencies toward the excessive concentration of control and bureaucratization understood well since the writings of Michels (1962) and Weber (1978). For democratic organizations, the concern is underscored because of the desire to establish and maintain a strong system of participation in decision making, as is discussed further below. Size is an under-appreciated factor in research on worker co-operatives and alternative organizations, yet it must be confronted in practice. The long-discussed "degeneration thesis" captures well the recognition that worker co-operatives are not immune to the entropic tendencies in organizations in general, and that mechanisms must be established and revisited to ensure the long-term social as well as economic viability of the firm (Cornforth et al., 1988; Whitman, 2011).

Can the workers involved in a worker-owned co-operative with thousands of members have the level of democratic control that one would aspire to in a co-operative business? Can a consumer co-operative with tens of thousands of members achieve a reasonable level of democratic member control? In this regard, co-operatives face difficult decisions, and these precise questions have been confronted at Mondragon. In order to achieve a size that would allow them to compete with large and ever-growing investor-owned competitors with greater economies of scale, the ability to influence markets and the ability to engage in predatory pricing against smaller rivals, co-operatives feel an enormous pressure to become larger and larger. If they fail to achieve a competitive size, their survival may be jeopardized. This leads into a more refined and in-depth consideration of committee and network structures, communication processes, and mechanisms for decision making.

In his book *The Tipping Point*, Gladwell (2000) suggests that about 150 is the upper limit to the size of organizations if they are to function by fully engaging all members. Cheney's

(1999, 2002) focus on three Mondragon co-ops in the 200-member range supports the idea that increased size requires increased complexity in communication systems and underscores the need for a vital and dynamic committee structure (see also Cheney *et al.*, 2011).

The experience of Rainbow Grocery in San Francisco with 250 worker-owners and that of SUMA, a co-operative in the United Kingdom with more than 180, both of which operate without a traditional management structure, demonstrates that large collectives can indeed survive and thrive using a democratic governance model. An even more experimental and complex management alternative being explored by Union Cab, a worker-owned taxi business in Madison, Wisconsin with more than 250 members, is decision making through a steering group but without a general manager.

Menzani and Zamagni (2010) offer a solution at a broader level: the formation of co-operative networks such as those found in Emilia Romagna and in the Trento region in northern Italy. A group of 32 small and mid-sized co-operatives act together as a consortium to bid on contracts that none of them could ever carry out on their own.

Democracy, committee structure, and multi-level governance

We understand governance in worker co-operatives on at least three levels: major financial and policy decisions, decisions directly affecting members, and the ways work is organized. All three are important and, ideally, all three are interconnected. Let's consider how the three have developed and played out in the Mondragon case, including important shifts in thinking and design over time.

Mondragon utilizes a complex system of governance with a strong emphasis on committee roles, vitality, and performance. The system incorporates both elected representatives, including a president, and selected or appointed managers. Of special importance are the audit committee or watchdog council and the social council because these represent important checks on and balances to the traditional concerns of management. In Cheney's research in the 1990s (1999, 2002) and in his recent visits (2008, 2009, 2012, 2013) he found that a key measure of the success and vitality of a co-operative firm could be seen in the functioning of the social council, with its fundamental grounding in the concerns of the employee-owner's (or *socio*'s) point of view and welfare.

Interestingly, however, it wasn't until the 1990s that the industrial co-operatives of the Mondragon system recognized that while their governance structures were enlightened and effective, their work production processes were in many ways throwbacks to Taylorism (Cheney, 1999, 2002). Thus, in recent years, there has been a strong effort, especially within the FAGOR group, to modify production processes and especially the communication surrounding them in a manner that will be once more democratic, humane, and dynamic. This transformation is ongoing, involving various feedback co-ops (Ortega, in progress. Udaondo, in progress).

Reinvention of democracy (including training, engaging of subsequent generations, etc.)

Authentic, comprehensive, and vital participatory management involves not only employee participation in specific decisions or activities but also in helping to shape the very future of the participative system itself (Dachler and Wilpert, 1978). In practice, this means that deep participation aims not only at involvement in particular work processes, or even particular decisions of the firm, but also the advancement of organizational democracy. Recent studies

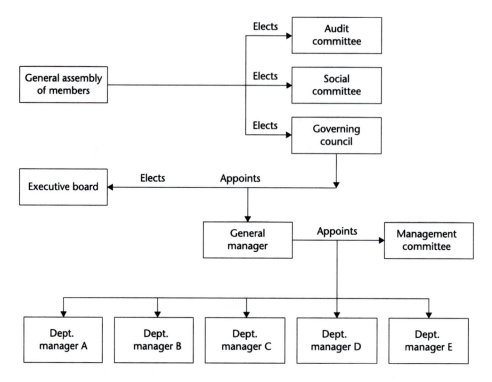

Figure 5.1 Structure of a Mondragon co-operative

by behavioral economists show that one of the most powerful sources of motivation in the workplace is workplace autonomy, which nurtures both productivity and innovation. This is a principle co-operatives in general might wish to explore. The importance of autonomy and voice is supported by the studies in *What Workers Want* (Freeman and Rogers, 1999) based on the largest surveys of employees ever conducted in the US.

There are several ways to conceive of levels and dimensions of participation, and these help to flesh out the concrete mechanisms of "engagement" discussed above. In a classic article, Bernstein (1976) identifies three dimensions of decision making in workplace participation: (1) the range of issues over which workers have control, (2) the degree of control, and (3) the organizational level at which the control is exercised. For instance, within the workplace setting, the range of issues may include employees' physical working conditions, health and safety, and work procedures. The range may or may not embrace operational issues such as hiring, training, setting wages, or issues of strategic direction, division of profits and investments. Thus employees may have complete control over their immediate work and yet have little control in other parts of the organization. These specifications help us to consider the actual meaning and workings of participation and also to explain why, in a given case, participation in one arena may not be reflected in another.

Establishing a strong sense of ownership and degree of participation is difficult enough; maintaining it over time and successive generations is even more difficult. A genuine commitment to democratic process means openness to the possibility that a new wave or generation of employees will decide to alter the system in significant ways. This is but one of the challenging, ironic, and sometimes even paradoxical aspects of democratic organizational life

(Stohl and Cheney, 2001). It also underlines the need for strong education for members to ensure that they understand the nature of co-operative business.

Networking beyond the worker-co-operative enterprise itself

Increasingly we are seeing worker co-operatives as parts of regional networks of a variety of types of co-operatives and supporting organizations within the United States. In the Bay Area of San Francisco-Oakland, co-operative enterprises are now well established and are pursuing collaborative projects. In Massachusetts, supported in part by the Economic Solidarity Network, co-operatives such as Equal Exchange have broader influence. In Madison, Wisconsin, longstanding worker co-operatives like Union Cab, and newer ones like Isthmus Engineering, are looking toward ways to leverage growth of the co-operative economy. The Evergreen co-operatives of Cleveland are to some extent modeled on Mondragon, as are the emerging union-co-op ventures in Pittsburgh and Cincinnati. In Austin, Texas, the Austin Co-operative Think Tank, with its diverse membership, together with active worker co-operative support organizations, like Cooperation Texas, are pursuing joint marketing and policy advocacy campaigns. In Denver, the Rocky Mountain Employee Ownership Center is teaming up with the Denver Foundation to develop a regional strategy. Also the Neighboring Food Co-operatives Association in New England is working closely with worker co-operatives, and agricultural groups such as the National Farmers Union on co-operative supply chains. These are but a few examples.

The Mondragon Co-operative Corporation is an umbrella organization whose constituent parts include worker co-operatives, co-operative development bodies, second-tier organizations and some solidarity co-operatives. This latter type of co-operative, solidarity co-operatives, are much more common in Italy, but one significant example in Mondragon is Eroski. In second-tier co-operatives, the controlling membership is first-tier co-operatives. An example would be Seguros Lagun Aro, the health and social security co-operative. Solidarity co-operatives are first-tier co-operatives with different classes of members. For example, in Eroski there are worker members and consumer members. The solidarity model could include dairy workers and farmers, parents and daycare workers or, as can be seen in Italy, social workers, ex-convicts, recovering drug addicts, community representatives and/or supporting co-operatives; in short, almost any combination of the key interdependent players joining together in a shared endeavor.

Solidarity co-operatives, found primarily in Europe and Quebec, are based on a different conceptual starting point from "stakeholder" co-operatives. While stakeholder co-operatives are seen as linking people with different and often conflicting interests within a single organization, solidarity co-operatives are seen as being created around the common interests of interdependent people who, while they play different roles, work in solidarity to achieve common goals. The choice of focus on interdependence or divergent interests has, at least in theory, a dramatic impact on the dynamics of the co-operatives. The dynamics are also different from co-operatives where there is only one class of membership.

Looking more broadly at the net of organizations in a community, we may find governmental community development agencies, private foundations, non-profit small-business incubators, credit unions, and other organizations involved in the support of worker co-operatives. A key question then becomes one about the autonomy of the worker co-operative. Just as we emphasize the internal structure of equal membership, so we underscore the importance of the worker co-operative's self-determination. This need becomes all the more important if the co-operative begins with outside investments as part of its capital mix when the characteristics and behavior of the capital are focused on maximum returns (Lund, 2010).

While it is possible to structure capital with characteristics and behavior consistent with co-operative business purpose, very few sources of such capital currently exist.

Engaging the market yet buffering from it in certain respects

In an era of corporate globalization, where investor-owned business has sought market control and economies of scale through massive growth, co-operatives have been forced to grow, despite a tendency to stay small and local. While co-operatives in many countries have experienced and responded to this pressure, the Mondragon co-operatives (MCC) have developed a corporate internationalization strategy. Being the largest producers in Spain of a range of products, including home appliances and car parts, they felt pressure from the early 1990s onward for them to locate plants outside the Basque Country to be able to compete with investor-owned firms (both in terms of lower wages and weaker environmental and health and safety regulations) and to respond to corporate customers who made co-located plants a term of doing business. Today, the co-ops are experimenting in green sectors as well.

This led to the establishment of subsidiaries in countries including Poland, Mexico, Brazil and China. MCC also found that they could not replicate their worker co-operative model because they felt they had to move too quickly to bring people with different languages and cultures up to speed on a complex set of arrangements they were unsure would bridge cultural divides. Their financial model with worker investments between €12,000 and €15,000 were not workable in markets like Poland's, and much less in that of China.

Internationalization or globalization has brought with it a series of challenges and problems, beginning with the fact that Mondragon's managers, for the most part, did not want to work abroad. They had created their co-operatives, among other reasons, in order that they would not have to leave the Basque County in search of work. They had little or no experience working with unions. In spite of efforts to meet and exceed safety, environmental and wage and benefits levels in the countries where they located, competitive pressure meant that pay and working conditions were below what Basque workers would have found acceptable. The issue of whether to convert plants—whether new or takeovers—abroad fully into worker co-operatives has been a point of controversy at Mondragon since the 1990s. Mondragon's global strategy did not grow organically from the co-operative model the Basque co-operatives designed for themselves. It is a survival tactic in the face of corporate globalization. While there is growing concern for widening the base of *socios*, or employee-owners, there is also concern for the co-operatives across Spain of diluting both co-operative and Basque identity through the inclusion of more and more *socios* who are distant from the Basque Country geographically, historically, and culturally.

It is interesting that while Mondragon's socios are far from unanimous, there is among them questioning of internationalization and a desire by many co-operative members to find ways to *extend* co-operative practice to subsidiaries in other countries. The debate on what to do and how to do it is persistent and energetic. In northern Italy, on the other hand, many large co-operatives like SACMI have foreign operations, but there is no mention of concern about the reality that workers outside of Italy are not able to become co-operative members.

The economic, social, and environmental possibilities for worker co-operatives

The Mondragon co-operatives do, in many ways, provide a model for financial and social resilience in times of economic crisis (Cheney, 2009). By 2012, unemployment had reached

25 percent across Spain. But in the Basque Country it hit only 12–13 percent and in the three valleys where the Mondragon co-operatives were concentrated it was less than 5 percent. This was not accidental. The Mondragon co-operatives, now a major economic engine of the Basque Country, had let go less than 1 percent of their workers and most of those were temporary or part time. During the first several years of the crisis, the worker-owners voted to accept pay cuts, reduced hours, pre-retirement options, and transfers to other co-ops, in an effort to avoid lay-offs. As of this publication, however, the co-ops face the complicated case of the effective bankruptcy of the founding industrial co-op, Fagor Electrodomésticos. This is a test not only of the cooperative system but also of the larger community, in which, as one of the founders, Alfonso Gorroñogoitia resilience and common sacrifice had diminished somewhat by consumerism.

The case of Mondragon, along with experiences of many other worker co-operatives today, bring us to consider the future potential for worker co-operatives and of co-operativism in general. Below we discuss some economic, social and environmental avenues for the future.

The development of genuinely co-operative capital

The relationship between co-operatives and capital has remained an enduring problem both in conceptual terms and in practical reality (Bajo and Roelants, 2011). In an investor-owned business, capital, in effect, hires people and all the resources of the business are at the service of capital. People may be termed simply another "resource" like raw materials, machinery and equipment. In a co-operative, the return on capital is comparatively limited, and capital is placed at the service of people.

The failure to develop a sophisticated concept of "co-operative capital" has been a major failure of co-operative thought and has been at the root of the long-standing problem co-operatives have in accumulating the capital they need to meet member needs. Investor-owned capital, as a "breed of capital," has its own set of characteristics and behavior. It seeks to maximize return. Why would one put investor-owned capital into a co-operative when the purpose of the co-operative is not to maximize return but, rather, to meet member and community need? It seems logical that investor-owned capital, inserted into a co-operative, will exercise a pervasive pressure to change the purpose of the co-operative.

It is possible to develop the concept of a co-operative breed of capital (see the chapters on community currencies and credit unions in this volume). It would have a significantly different set of behavior and characteristics than investor-owned capital. Those characteristics and behavior should include the following:

- Makes possible meeting a human need in a fair and equitable manner.
- Conducts its operations in a manner that respects the personal co-operative values: Openness; Honesty; Social responsibility; and Caring for others.
- Operates in a manner that reflects the Co-operative Principles: Open and Voluntary Membership; Democratic Member Control; Member Economic Participation; Autonomy and Independence; Education, Training and Information; Co-operation among Co-operatives; and Concern for Community.
- Returns equity upon request unless it puts the co-operative in financial jeopardy.
- Pays a limited return or fair return; members do not expect a windfall at the expense of others.
- Allows the creation of a pool of capital that is owned collectively by the members and is the indivisible common property of the membership.

But is such a concept of capital realistic as a large-scale alternative? Would it be possible for co-operative-minded persons around the world to accumulate pools of capital with these characteristics and behaviors? We believe that it is. As the authors of an essay on co-operative capital note, "It is safe to estimate that together co-operative financial institutions have assets well in excess of $2.5 trillion USD" (Robb *et al.*, 2010: 8). If 10 percent of that capital were reserved for use in developing or growing co-operatives there would be $100 billion in available co-operative capital.

There are approximately 1 billion members of co-operatives around the world. It is not unreasonable to expect that they are at least as interested in socially responsible investing (SRI) as the general population.

- According to Swedish bank Stockholm's Enskilda Bank (SEB, 2013), "SRI is experiencing strong growth in the developed world. SRI is a booming market in both Europe and the US. The SRI market, in Europe today, represents as much as 15–20 percent of total assets under management."
- As of 2007 about one out of every nine dollars under professional management in the United States is involved in socially responsible investing – 11 percent of the USD 25.1 trillion in total assets under management tracked in Nelson Information's Directory of Investment Managers.

(http://sustainableperspectives.sebgroup.com/Academy/ KnowledgeBank/SRI/)

If 1 billion members of co-operatives and credit unions around the world were to invest an average of $1,000 each in co-operative capital they would generate $1 trillion (see also the Global Alliance for Banking on Values, www.gabv.org). This is a conservative estimate of the potential, given that many members in the wealthier countries of Europe, Asia and the Americas each have hundreds of thousands of dollars of savings. The challenge for co-operatives, especially financial co-operatives, is to create viable vehicles to accumulate co-operative capital and, perhaps more daunting, to face off with generally uninformed and too often hostile regulators to allow this to happen.

The revival of participation

The Mondragon co-operatives, in part because of their size and longevity, represent a giant laboratory for the study of not only workplace democracy but also the ways in which participation inside the firm – and set of firms – relates to social capital and political participation generally. While Cheney (1999, 2002) found in the 1990s that education in the philosophy and practices of cooperativism had taken a back seat to technical training, he has been pleased to find on recent visits (2008, 2009, 2012, 2013) that there are a number of projects to re-introduce, update and institutionalize co-operative training. Many of these are designed and implemented by the LANKI Co-operative Institute of Mondragon University and the management education center, Otalora.

Furthermore, with the partnership of LANKI, parts of the FAGOR industrial group of the Mondragon co-operatives are experimenting with new forms of participation internally and, at the same time, connecting those to community engagement and solidarity. These experiments are in part based on surveys and focus groups conducted in the Mondragon group from 2005 and 2008, as well as on more recent interviews and surveys with the *socios* of FAGOR Arrasate, a dynamic and innovative industrial co-op (Ortega, in progress).

Carefully and systematically taking the pulse of *socios* at Mondragon has revealed issues in the areas of the routinization of participation, the loss of a sense of co-operative identity, and barriers to communication. Both new training programs and the experiments with *consejillos*, or informal discussion groups, is aimed at addressing all three of these problems, while also fostering greater awareness of responsibilities to the larger community. Watching these programs develop will be important not just for assessing Mondragon's future but also for applying relevant lessons to a variety of other worker co-operatives and democratic enterprises throughout the world (Basterretxea and Albizu, 2010).

Broader community and environmental commitment

While co-operative principles provide room for environmental responsibility and many co-operators plausibly argue that in general co-operatives are more environmentally responsible, there are no systematic research studies that document superior co-operative performance. It remains a reasonable hypothesis. A growing number of co-operative activists have begun to push either for an addition to the ICA principle 7, Concern for community, or a new separate, eighth, principle. As presenter and participant comments at the Imagine 2012 conference stressed, co-operatives need urgently to think about how to play a leadership role in economic action to avoid environmental catastrophe. The Imagine 2012 Declaration suggested adopting a position along the following lines: "Co-operatives recognize that the human species is an integral part of an interconnected and interdependent universe and that respecting nature and life in all its expressions is not separable from respect for the dignity and value of each person."

This position is consistent with an emerging environmental consciousness in and around the Mondragon co-operatives. The investigators in the LANKI Institute for Co-operative Studies at the University of Mondragon, both as observers and as part of the Mondragon experience itself, have come to recognize the imperative that the co-operatives elevate environmental concern amongst their principles and practices. Moreover, the researchers maintain that Mondragon ought to be a leader in orienting the entire co-operative movement in this direction for the future. In fact, the same scholar-practitioners insist that without an authentic embrace of an "ecological economy," co-operatives and other parts of the broader solidarity economy cannot offer a model for replication in the twenty-first century (Azkarraga, 2007; Azkarraga, 2009; Azkarraga and Altuna, 2012; Azkarraga, Cheney and Uriarte, 2013).

Conclusion: the promise of workers and worker co-operatives

In his classic work, *A Preface to Economic Democracy* (1985), Robert Dahl persuasively makes the case that "if democracy is justified in governing the state then it is also justified in governing economic enterprises" (111). If, as Dahl argues, the rationale for political democracy applies as robustly to economic enterprises as to the institutions of the state, then reflection on this issue leads to questioning whether a democratic state can function smoothly in the long run with an undemocratic economy. It would also be logical to conclude that an economy increasingly operating in a democratic fashion would nurture the spirit and practice of political democracy.

This would be logically consistent with the following conclusions. Enterprises which engage their workers through democratic ownership, structure and process can make a greater contribution to a free democratic society than enterprises whose ownership, structure, and process are based on wealth. Enterprises controlled and governed chiefly by wealth would tend to influence public policy in a manner which protects the holders of wealth. It would also lead to the conclusion that, within the co-operative family of enterprises, including consumer and small-business co-operatives, a compelling case can be made for the democratic involvement of workers in the governance of the organization. This would be logical and consistent with co-operative values and principles, which include democracy and related values such as education, openness, honesty, equity, equality, solidarity, etc.

Taken together these considerations make a powerful case not just for worker-owned co-operatives but for broader solidarity co-operatives where key participants who are interdependent (for example, farmers and dairy workers, parents and daycare workers, farmers and consumers, consumers and retail workers) can recognize the legitimacy of each other's needs. In solidarity co-operatives, workers would always be recognized as key participants.

The claim is not that a significant shift to economic democratic democracy would solve the entire range of problems facing democracy and humanity. Once again, we would point to Dahl.

> A system of self-governing enterprises would not, of course, eliminate conflicting interests, goals, perspectives, and ideologies among citizens. But it would tend to reduce the conflict of interests, give all citizens a more nearly equal stake in maintaining political equality and democratic institutions in the governance of the state and facilitate the development of a stronger consensus on standards of fairness.
>
> *(1985: 110)*

If we think about the need for business firms to operate in a manner that does not have them externalizing costs such as worker health and safety, community erosion or environmental damage, the co-operative business model, with its focus on meeting member and community needs as opposed to maximizing returns to shareholders, is in principle a better model. If our focus is on meeting human need, whether for goods or services, or an opportunity to express human talent, the co-operative business model again seems superior. If the focus is on delivering a smaller gap between the highest and lowest paid or stability in challenging times, the track record of co-operatives from 2007 to now presents evidence of a better perform-ance than the investor-owned model. Co-operatives, especially when worker-owned-and-governed, offer a powerful response to today's, and tomorrow's, economic, social and environmental needs.

Resources

http://co-operative-curriculum.wikispaces.com/
www.geo.coop/node/15
www.ica.coop
www.mondragon-corporation.com
www.oeockent.org
www.usworker.coop
www.uwcc.wisc.edu
http://www.MMCCu.coop

References

Abrams, J. (2005, 2008). *Companies we Keep: Employee Ownership and the Business of Community and Place.* White River Junction, VT: Chelsea Green.

Adams, F.T., and Hansen, G.B. (1992). *Putting Democracy to Work* (rev. edn). San Francisco: Berrett-Koehler.

Alperowitz, G.A. (2005). *America beyond Capitalism*. Takoma Park, MD, and Boston, MA: Democracy Collaborative Press and Dollars and Sense Magazine.

Alperowitz, G.A. (2012). *What Then Must We Do?* Burlington, VT: Chelsea Green Publishing.

Arando, S., Gago, M., Jones C.D. and Kato. T. (2011). Efficiency and job satisfaction in employee-owned enterprises: An econometric case study of Mondragon. (IZA Discussion Paper No. 5711). Available online at http://cep.lse.ac.uk/conference_papers/26_05_2011/kato.pdf

Arando, S., Pena, I. and Verheul I. (2008). Market entry of firms with different legal forms: An empirical test of the influence of institutional factors, *International Entrepreneurship and Management Journal, 1*, 77–95.

Arizmendiarrieta, Don Jose Maria (2000). *Reflections*, a translation of Pensamientos, Otalora, Mondragon Co-operative Corporacion.

Azkarraga, J. (2007). *Mondragon ante la globalización: la cultura cooperativa vasca ante el cambio de época*, Cuadernos de LANKI, n° 2, Mondragon Unibertsitatea, Eskoriatza, Basque Country, Spain.

Azkarraga, J. (2009). El cooperativismo como conciencia crítica, *Nexe. Quaderns d'autogestió i economía cooperativa,* n° 25.

Azkarraga, J. and Altuna, L. (2012). Cooperativismo, economía solidaria y paradigma ecológico. Una aproximación conceptual, *Ecología Política*, n° 44, Icaria.

Azkarraga, J., Cheney, G. and Udaondo, A. (2012). Workers' participation in a globalized market: Reflections on and from Mondragon. In M. Atzeni (ed.) *Alternative Work Organizations* (76–102). London: Palgrave Macmillan.

Azkarraga, J., Cheney, G. and Uriarte, L. (2013, March). Worker cooperativism, the solidarity economy, and the ecological economy: Strengthening the interconnections and exploring further possibilities. Eskoriatza, Basque Country, Spain.

Ayuso, S., Ricart, J.E. and Rodriguez, A.M. (2006). Using stakeholder dialogue as a source for new ideas: A dynamic capability underlying sustainable innovation (Working Paper No. 633). Available online at www.iese.edu/research/pdfs/DI-0633-E.pdf

Bagchi, A. (2007). Varieties of employee ownership: Some unintended consequences of corporate law and labor law, *University of Pennsylvania Journal of Business and Employment Law, 10*, 305.

Bajo, C.S. and Roelants, B. (2011). *Capital and the Debt Trap: Learning from Co-operatives in the Global Crisis*. London: Palgrave Macmillan.

Bakan, I., Yuliani S. and Pinnington, A. (2004). The influence of financial participation and participation in decision-making on employee job attitudes, *International Journal of Human Resource Management, 15*(3), 587–616.

Basterretxea, I. and Albizu, E. (2010). Management training as a source of perceived competitive advantage: The Mondragon Co-operative Group case, *Economic and Industrial Democracy, 32*, 1–24.

Bernstein, P. (1976). Necessary elements for effective worker participation in decision making, *Journal of Economic Issues*, 10(2): 490–522.

Birchall, J. (2004). Co-operatives and the millennium development goals. Available online at www.ilo.org/public/english/support/lib/resource/subject/coop/birchallbook_2004.pdf (accessed 20 January 2012).

Birchall, J. and Ketilson, H.L. (2009). Resilience of the co-operative business model in times of crisis. International Labour Office, Sustainable Enterprise Programme, Geneva. Available online at www.ilo.org/wcmsp5/groups/public/---ed_emp/---emp_ent/documents/publication/wcms_108416.pdf

Cheney, G. (1999, 2002). *Values at Work: Employee Participation Meets Market Pressure at Mondragon*. Ithaca, NY, and London: Cornell University Press.

Cheney, G. (2009). *Arizmendi topaketak: The Importance of Co-operative Values During Times of Economic Crisis*. Mondragon, Basque Country, Spain: Gizabidea.

Cheney, G., Christensen, L.T., Zorn Jr, T.E. and Ganesh, S. (2011). *Organizational Communication in an Age of Globalization: Issues, Reflections, Practices* (2nd edn). Prospect Heights, IL: Waveland Press.

Cheney, G. and Hernandez, A. (In progress). *Best Practices in Worker Cooperatives*. Working papers, Kent State University, Ohio, USA.

Cheney, G. and Hernandez, A. (2011, May). Worker co-operative values and ownership culture. Available online at http://co-operative-curriculum.wikispaces.com/

Cheney, G., Lair, D.J., Ritz, D. and Kendall, B.E. (2010). *Just a Job? Communicaton, Ethics, and Professional Life*. New York: Oxford University Press.

Corcoram, H. and Wilson, D. (2010). The worker co-operative movements In Italy, Mondragon and France: Context, success factors and lessons. Available online at www.canadianworker.coop/sites/canadianworker.coop/files/CWCF_Research_Paper_International_16-6-2010_fnl[1].pdf

Cornforth, C., Thomas, A., Lewis, J. and Spear, R. (1988). *Developing Successful Worker Co-operatives*. London: Sage.

Curl, J. (2009). *For All the People*. Oakland, CA: PM Press.

Dachler, H.P. and Wilpert, B. (1978). Conceptual dimensions and boundaries of participation in organizations: A critical evaluation, *Administrative Science Quarterly*, *23*, 1–39.

Dahl, R.A. (1985). *A Preface to Economic Democracy*. Berkeley: University of California Press.

Deller, S., Hoyt, A., Hueth, B. and Stukel-Sundaram R. (2009). Research on the economic impact of co-operatives. Available online at http://reic.uwcc.wisc.edu/

Erdal, D. (2012). Employee ownership is good for your health, *Journal of Co-operative Thought and Practice*, *1*, 4–7.

Forester, J. (2006). Making participation work when interests conflict: Moving from facilitating dialogue and moderating debate to mediating negotiations, *Journal of the American Planning Association*, *72*, 447–455.

Freeman, R.B. and Rogers, J. (1999). *What Workers Want* (updated edn). Ithaca, NY, and London: Cornell University Press.

Freundlich, F. (2013, January–March). Personal communications with the authors.

Galbraith, J. (2012). *Inequality and Instability: A Study of the World Economy Just Before the Great Crisis*. New York: Oxford University Press.

Gijselinckx, C. (2012). Co-operative answers to societal challenges: 9 Insights from 2 × 9 cases. In M-J. Brassard and E. Molina (eds), *Texts Selected from the International Call for Proposals* (403–417). Quebec, Canada: International Summit of Co-operatives.

Gijselinckx, C. and Develtere (2008). The co-operative trilemma: Co-operatives between market, state and civil society. Working papers on social and co-operative entrepreneurship, WP-SCE 08-01. Leuven, Belgium: University of Leuven.

Giszpenc, N. (2003, April). Human resources and company performances. Available online at www.ownershipassociates.com/hr_performance.shtm.

Gladwell, M. (2000). *The Tipping Point*. New York: Little Brown and Company.

Greenwood, D. and Gonzalez, J.L. (1992). *Culturas de FAGOR*. San Sebastian, Basque Country, Spain: Editorial Txertoa.

Herrasti, J. and Lezamiz, M. (2011, 21 October). Interview with J.T. Webb, Mondragon, The Basque Country, Spain.

Hoover, M. (2011, April). Worker co-operative curriculum. Available online at http://co-operative-curriculum.wikispaces.com/file/view/WorkerCoops-Hoover.pdf

International Co-operative Alliance (1986). *ICA Policy for Co-operative Development, Studies and Reports*. London: ICA.

International Co-operative Alliance (2013). Co-operative identity, values and principles. Available online at http://ica.coop/en/what-co-op/co-operative-identity-values-principles (retrieved 8 March 2013).

Iuviene, N., Stitely, A. and Hoyte, L. (2010). *Sustainable Economic Democracy: Worker Co-operatives for the 21st Century*. Available online at http://web.mit.edu/colab/pdf/papers/Sustainable_Economic_Democracy.pdf

Kasmir, S. (1996). *The Myth of Mondragon*. Albany: State University of New York Press.

Kruse, D.L., Freeman, R.B. and Blasi, J.R. (eds) (2010). *Shared Capitalism at Work*. Chicago, IL: University of Chicago Press.

Kruse, D., Freeman, R., Blasi, J., Buchele, R. and Scharf, A. (2003). Motivating employee owners in ESOP firms: Human resource policies and company performance (Working Paper No. 10177). Available online at www.nber.org/papers/w10177

Laidlaw, A.F. (1982). Co-operatives in the Year 2000 (address). Ottawa: Co-operative Union of Canada.

Lawless, G. and, Reynolds, A. (2004). Worker co-operatives: Case studies, key criteria. University of Wisconsin Center of Co-operatives (UWCC Staff Paper No. 3). Available online at www.uwcc.wisc.edu/pdf/Staffpercent20Papers/staff03.pdf

Lindenfeld, F. (2003). Commentary on "The Organization of Work as a Factor in Social Well-Being," *Contemporary Justice Review*, *6*(2), 127–131.

Logue, J. and Yates, J. (2005). *Productivity in Co-operatives and Worker-owned Enterprises: Ownership and Participation Make a Difference!* Geneva: International Labour Organization.

Lund, M. (2010). Solidarity as a business model. Available online at www.oeockent.org/home/publications-a-research

MacLeod, G. (1997). *From Mondragon to America: Experiments in Community Economic Development.* Sydney, NS, Canada: University College of Cape Breton Press.

Majee, W. and Hoyt, A. (2011). Co-operatives and community development: A perspective on the use of co-operatives in development, *Journal of Community Practice, 19*(1), 48–61.

Mathews, R. (1999). *Jobs of Our Own.* Sydney: Pluto Press.

McDonnell, D., Macknight C.E. and Donnelly, H. (2012). *Democratic Enterprise: Ethical Business for the 21st Century.* Available online at http://cets.coop/moodle/course/view.php?id=2

Menzani, T. and Zamagni, V. (2010). Co-operative networks in the Italian economy, *Enterprise and Society, 11*(1), 98–127.

Merrett, C.D. and Walzer, N. (2007). *Bibliography of Co-operatives and Co-operative Development.* Springfield: Illinois Institute for Rural Affairs.

Michels, R. (1962). *Political Parties: A Sociological Study of the Oligarchical Tendencies of Modern Democracy.* New York: Collier Books.

Morrisson, R. (1991). *We Build the Road as we Travel.* Gabriola Island, Canada: New Society Publishers.

Neamtam, N. (2005, July–August). The social economy: Finding a way between the market and the state, *Policy Options,* 70–76.

Nembhard, J.G., Johnson, M., Johnson, J., Krimerman, L. and Ifateyo, A.N. (n.d.). Worker-co-operative development models: A brief overview. Available online at http://www.geo.coop/node/627

Northcountry Co-operative Foundation. (2004). Using Worker Co-ops to Enhance Economic Well-being of Rural Residents: A Report for The United States Department of Agriculture. USDA-RCDG.

Novkovic, S. and Brown, L. (eds) (2012). *Atlantic Canada's Social Economy: Communities, Economies, and Solidarity.* CBU Press: 161–177.

Oliviere, D. (2010, 14 October). Interview with J.T. Webb, Imola, Italy.

Ormaechea, J.M. (1993). *The Mondragon Co-operative Experience.* Mondragon, Basque Country, Spain: Mondragon Co-operative Corporation.

Ortega. (In progress). New participative systems in FAGOR Arrasate: Design, implementation and assessment. Dissertation, Mondragon Unibertsitatea, Basque Country, Spain.

Paranque, B., Bouchon, C., Plasse, A. and Benoit, M. (2011). Co-operatives and governance: Forward-looking or stuck in the past? *Annals of Public and Co-operative Economics, 83*(3), 21.

Pateman, C. (1970). *Participation and Democratic Theory.* Cambridge, UK: Cambridge University Press.

Pickett, K. and Wilkinson, R. (2009). *Spirit Level: Why More Equal Societies Almost Always do Better.* London: Allen Lane.

Ramirez, R. (2001). Understanding the approaches for accommodating multiple stakeholders' interests. *International Journal Agricultural Resources, Governance and Ecology, 1,* 264–285.

Reese, A. (2012). Identity, participation and firm longevity: An analysis of worker co-operatives through the lens of Argentina's recovered firm movement. In M-J. Brassard and E. Molina (eds). *Texts Selected from the International Call for Proposals* (389–402). Quebec, Canada: International Summit of Co-operatives.

Restakis, J. (2010). *Humanizing the Economy: Co-operatives in the Age of Capital.* Gabriola Island, BC, Canada: New Society Publishers.

Robb, J.A., Smith, H.J. and Webb, J.T. (2012). Co-operative capital: What it is and why our world needs it, *Journal of Co-operative Thought and Practice, 1,* 7–38.

Rothschild, J. and Whitt, J.A. (1986). *The Co-operative Workplace.* Cambridge, UK: Cambridge University Press.

Rothschild-Whitt, J. (1979). The collectivist organization: An alternative to rational-bureacratic models, *American Sociological Review, 44,* 509–527.

Sarasua, J. (2008). Mondragon in a new century: Brief reflection on the course of the co-operative experience. In A.L. Gabilondo (ed.) *Experiencia Cooperativa de Mondragon.* Eskoriatza, Gipuzkoa, Basque Country, Spain: Lanki Institute, Mondragon University.

Satow, R.L. (1975). Value-rational authority and professional organizations: Weber's missing type, *Administrative Science Quarterly, 20,* 526–531.

Sauser Jr, I.W. (2009). Sustaining employee owned companies: Seven recommendations, *Journal of Business Ethics 84*, 151–164.

Shaffer, J. (1999). *Historical Dictionary of the Co-operative Movement*. London: Scarecrow Press.

Stockholms Enskilda Bank (SEB). Available online at http://sustainableperspectives.sebgroup.com/Academy/KnowledgeBank/SRI/

Stohl, C. and Cheney, G. (2001). Participatory processes/paradoxical practices: Communication and the dilemmas of organizational democracy, *Management Communication Quarterly, 14*, 349–407.

Tchami, G. (2006). Handbook on co-operatives for use of workers' organizations. Available online at www.ilo.org/wcmsp5/groups/public/#caed_emp/#caemp_ent/documents/publication/wcms_094046.pdf

Udaondo, A. (in progress). Assessing the impact of cooperative education: A multi-method analysis. Dissertation. Mondragon Unibertsitatea, Basque Country, Spain.

United States Department of Agriculture. (1998). The impact of new generation co-operatives on their communities. Available online at www.rurdev.usda.gov/rbs/pub/rr177.pdf

Webb, J.T. (1987). *Worker's Co-operatives: A People Centered Approach to Regional Development, Research Report No. 5*. Moncton, NS, CA: Canadian Institute for Research on Regional Development.

Weber, M. (1978). *Economy and Society*, 2 vols. Berkeley: University of California Press.

Whitman, J. (2011). The worker co-operative life cycle. Available online at http://co-operative-curriculum.wikispaces.com/file/view/WorkerCoops-Whitman.pdf

Whyte, W.F. and Whyte, K.K. (1991). *Making Mondragon* (2nd edn, rev). Ithaca, and London: Cornell University Press.

Williams, C.R. (2007). *The Co-operative Movement: Globalization from Below*. Burlington, VT: Ashgate Publishing.

Witherell, R., Cooper, C. and Peck, M. (2012). Trade unions and co-operatives: Challenges and perspectives. Working paper. Pittsburgh: United Steelworkers Union.

Zamagni, S. (2012, 17 October). Seminar in Master of Management: Co-operatives and Credit Unions program, University of Bologna, Italy.

Zamagni, S. and Zamagni, V. (2010). *Co-operative Enterprise: Facing the Challenge of Globalization*. Glasgow, UK: Edward Elgar Publishing.

Zeuli, K. and Cropp, R. (2004). Co-operatives: Principles and practices in the 21st century. Available online at www.uwcc.wisc.edu/info/uwcc_pubs/primer.html

6

Communes and intentional communities

Donald E. Pitzer (with Donald E. Janzen,
Docey Lewis and Rachel Wright-Summerton)

Introduction

As social laboratories, communes and intentional communities have proven, virtually any organizational structure is viable if the participants agree to its requirements – from the most authoritarian and hierarchical, to the most democratic and egalitarian. Those who voluntarily accept the disciplines of communal living do so for the survival, solidarity and security it offers. Members of communal organizations enjoy a high level of fellowship, from work to worship. They also exercise a freedom to pursue the utopian visions, beliefs and lifestyles prescribed by their founding leaders and movements, only bounded by the laws and mores of their locales. Economic union is the distinctive alternative characteristic of communal organization, a union that may range from community of goods to cooperative sharing.

Intentional communities, like all organizations, must maintain an economic base, producing income at least equal to expenses. Yet they are noted for placing a higher value on the well-being of their members than on profit-making and consumerism. This does not detract, however, from their commitment to produce high-quality products and provide trustworthy services. Their internal organizational structures and managerial practices have distinct advantages, including a willing workforce committed to a common economic and ideological purpose. Many achieve full employment of able-bodied members and full participation in a decision-making process of open communication. Their financial success, if that is what they want to achieve, stems from their ability to be inwardly cooperative and outwardly competitive. Some communities have been satisfied simply to sustain their lifestyles, while others have sought a significant place in the local, national and international marketplace. Most importantly, the organizational alternative of communes and intentional communities presents an example that could lead to a more peaceful, humanitarian and sustainable future.

This chapter starts by introducing communal organization in terms of its ability to provide for survival, solidarity and security. The following section – intentional communities in action – presents three case studies of contemporary communities to analyze their internal composition and workings. Drawn from two communities in the United States and one in Senegal, these case studies focus on distinctive organizational factors related to leadership, labor, and large markets that have contributed to their communal and financial success. The concluding section suggests that developmental communalism and transformative utopianism are two processes central to the long-term survival of communities.

Communal organization for survival

Cooperation is key to human survival (Nowak, 2012). Cooperative organization has been essential from kinship and tribal groups to nation states. In fact, all life forms have cooperated to survive since stromatolite bacteria formed colonies for protection from ultraviolet sunlight more than three billion years ago. Both living and fossilized stromatolites are still found today (Sagan and Druyan, 1992). Only since the Industrial Revolution and the rise of global capitalism has competition supposedly supplanted cooperation in human consciousness and made cooperative communities seem like alternatives to the norm.

Communal living is a method of social organization that has been available to all peoples, governments and movements from time immemorial. Since communal organization offers security, solidarity and survival it is often employed, voluntarily or involuntarily, at an early stage, during emergencies, and for experimentation and social reform (Pitzer, 1989, 1997, 2009). Hunters, gatherers, and agricultural and nomadic peoples used numerous cooperative arrangements to endure, and sometimes thrive, over long periods of time. The communistic Soviet Union and Maoist China forced millions into collective farms and the people's commune. The democratic United States set up garden cities and communal homesteads which thousands joined voluntarily during the Great Depression (Conkin, 1959). Religious, social and economic reform movements, which are the focus of this chapter, have also employed communal living from ancient times. Modern reformers have often turned to communitarianism, a term coined in 1840, as a voluntary, immediate and nonviolent method of social change, an alternative to individualism, gradual reform through legislation, and the bloodshed of revolution (Bestor, 1950).

Communal organization for solidarity

Solidarity is fundamental to the definition, purpose and function of communes and communal societies; those formed since the 1950s are generally called "intentional communities." All might be defined as small, voluntary social units, partly insulated from the general society in which their members intentionally bond together around an ideology, an economic union and a lifestyle, and attempt to implement their ideal systems – social, economic, governmental, religious, philosophical, ecological and sustainable – often in hopes that their utopian vision will be realized worldwide by divine aid or human effort (Pitzer, 2009; Miller, 2010; Questenberry, 1995). Historically, the predominant internal economic union of communitarians was purely communistic (Nordhoff, 1875). Therefore, most have been referred to as communes or communal societies. In the East, community of goods can be traced to Hindu ashrams as early as 1500 BCE and Buddhist monasteries after about 500 BCE. In the West, the communal tradition dates to the Essene community at Qumran on the Dead Sea in the second century before Christ and the first-century Christian congregation in Jerusalem (Acts 2, 4, 5). Holding all property in common continues among Roman Catholic religious orders following the founding of communal (cenobitic) monasticism by Saint Benedict in sixth-century Italy (McCrank, 1997). The Protestant Reformation produced the pietistic, communal Hutterite movement, and 40,000 followers still share all in 470 patriarchally led *bruderhofs* in the United States and Canada (Evans, 2010; Hostetler, 1974;

Huntington, 1997; Rubin, 1993). By the nineteenth century, religious sects in America, from the Shakers and Harmonists to the Inspirationists and Zoarites, were noted for the social solidarity and financial prowess of their charismatically led, communistic organizations.

Nevertheless, in the more than 1,500 communal groups established in North America before 1965 and the many thousands since, diversity increasingly came to characterize their internal communal structure while always preserving the essential element of solidarity (Fogarty, 1990; Pitzer, 1997; Miller, 1999). Less complete economic sharing and more cooperative arrangements, or less charismatic and patriarchal leadership and more democratic and egalitarian governance became evident (*Communities; Communities Directory;* Miller, 1999; Pitzer, 1997). Escape and experimentation lured hundreds of thousands of counterculture and millennialistic youth worldwide into hippie communes, Jesus communities and ashrams in the 1960s and 1970s (Miller, 1999). Economic and environmental concerns induced tens of thousands more to seek the benefits of communal cohousing, ecovillages and retirement centers by the 1980s and 1990s. These groups have gone by many names according to their financial and legal, often purposefully tax-exempt, organizational structures. We find their solidarity expressed as cooperatives, collectives, corporations, associations, partnerships, trusts, and a host of sub-categories (Butcher *et al.*, 1995; Kozeny, 2010).

Ever since the Industrial Revolution, the business world has been especially fascinated with the success of the economic organization and management produced by the solidarity of the most prominent communes and intentional communities. These exclusive enclaves have never comprised more than a small minority of the population, yet the results of their unity of purpose have exercised an influence far beyond their numbers (Pitzer, 2013). In his *The 60s Communes*, Timothy Miller observed that "Tens of thousands of communes with hundreds of thousands of members constituted a large social phenomenon – or a small one, when one considers that those who even dabbled in communitarianism constituted a minor fraction of one percent of the American population" (Miller, 1999: 237–238). The outside society continues its insatiable interest in alternative communal solidarity, leadership, beliefs and practices. Many realize that communal societies are social microcosms, voluntary laboratories that, like all businesses, must maintain loyalty and financial solvency to continue. Internally, they must satisfy the interests and needs of their own members (the investors); and, externally, they must compete profitably in the market economy. Long-time kibbutz member and communal historian, Yaacov Oved, concludes in his *Globalization of Communes: 1950–2010* that "the communes, kibbutzim, and cooperative communities were and still are small islands exposed to external forces," that "even though they are a minority their contribution has always been unique," and that "there is increasing interest in the endeavors of the various types of communes and cooperative communities as social laboratories to establish a life of cooperation and solidarity" (Oved, 2013: 302).

Organizationally and economically, many groups have proven the long-term viability of communal solidarity, especially when built on religious belief. For centuries, abbot- and abbess-led Roman Catholic monastic orders established the now nearly universal reputation of successful communal groups organized upon honest dealing, quality products and reliable services. Monastic enterprises from farming and brewing to schools and hospitals became their financial lifeblood (McCrank, 1997). By the early nineteenth century, twenty Shaker settlements loyal to immigrant English messiah, Ann Lee, spread across the United States. They supplied the best early evidence that communal groups could grow very large in membership and profitability, organized around equally empowered eldresses and elders on an agricultural and handicraft economic base. Shaker garden seeds, medicinal herbs, furniture and flat brooms (which they invented) sold in a wide market (Brewer, 1986). The

Harmony Society, united around German prophet George Rapp, became the first communal group to make an economic breakthrough in America with significance for international trade. By the 1820s, with shrewd business leadership and hundreds of religiously committed, hardworking and skilled laborers, the Harmonists proved that manufacturing could be made a community's basic source of income, providing enough self-sufficiency to free it from most foreign imports (Arndt, 1972). This unwelcome news reached the ears of intimidated European mercantilistic monopolists just as the Harmonists and Robert Owen established a second town, New Harmony, on the Indiana frontier, from which it sent its products to twenty-two states and nine foreign countries. The broader implications were all too clear. The former British colonies were poised to supply most of their own industrial needs while protecting domestic-made goods by tariffs in what became known as "the American System" which the communal Harmonists fully supported. If this were not enough, the Harmony Society went on in a third town, Economy, Pennsylvania, to help lead communitarians and the Western world into the age of heavy industry and finance capitalism by their successful investments in railroads, oil wells, pipelines and automobiles (Pitzer, 2011).

In the twentieth century, examples of communally united success abound. The Zionist movement inspired more than 250 Jewish kibbutzim that helped bring about statehood for Israel in 1948 (Near, 1992, 1997; Bartelt, 1997). Often in desert conditions, and sometimes under physical attacks, Kibbutz settlers have stood shoulder to shoulder using democratic decision-making processes, agriculture, light industry, outside employment and government assistance to survive to the present. In America, the Christian prophetess Mary Purnell's City of David defied the Great Depression. Reorganized from the Israelite House of David in Benton Harbor, Michigan in 1930 under the direction of Mary and her successors, it has persisted to the present on income from traveling baseball teams, a tourist resort, a vegetarian restaurant serving kosher food, and agricultural industries (Mary's City of David website). The Farm at Summertown, Tennessee was founded in 1971 by college professor and guru, Stephen Gaskin, and became the largest hippie commune to spring from the youth movement. Gaskin and able managers led the community to prosper mostly on outside employment in construction work and soy bean production until that market became glutted in the 1980s. This forced a healthy economic diversification that brought The Farm to create its Ecovillage Training Center and other revenue-producing enterprises (The Farm website). The Damanhur Community in the Valchiusella valley of northern Italy has grown to 1,000 members with their own convenience currency while operating eighty businesses, an international university, and centers worldwide (Damanhur website). The Habitat for Humanity International initiative in humanitarian capital investment sprang from communal roots. It has built more than 400,000 affordable homes for deserving families in eighty countries with volunteer labor and donated building material and appliances (Monterey Herald website). Habitat grew from providing homes for members with interest-free loans and "sweat equity" labor at the interracial Koinonia Farm in Americus, Georgia. Now, volunteers include former President Jimmy Carter and his wife Rosalynn, and corporations large and small choose to donate as social entrepreneurs.

Collective organization for security

The question remains, "What do communes and intentional communities teach us about alternative organization?" Collective organization offers built-in advantages for security. Communal groups with astute, business-savvy, even charismatic leadership often meet with success on many fronts. Laird Schaub, long-time communitarian, consensus decision-making consultant, and executive secretary of the Fellowship for Intentional Community, concludes, "I've come to the belief that there are definite skills involved in management and some people are flat better at it than others. People are no more interchangeable parts when it comes to decision making than they are in the auto shop or the classroom" (Schaub, 2011: 54). Effective leaders, from monastic abbots to the charismatic Mormon prophet Joseph Smith, make decisions quickly and see them carried out efficiently by a willing workforce committed to a common religious or secular vision in which workers' futures are heavily invested. In her *Commitment and Community: Communes and Utopias in Sociological Perspective*, Rosabeth Moss Kanter identified continuance, cohesion and control as increasingly more effective commitment mechanisms employed in the most economically successful and long-lived historic American communal groups up to 1865 (Kanter, 1972). Members feel a strong sense of cooperative ownership and a pride of workmanship. They are laboring for their brothers and sisters, their family and friends, and often the utopian goals of a movement. Shakers built their religious perfectionism into their furniture as their motto became "hands to work, hearts to God." Where the diversity of jobs permits, intentional communities often encourage members to enjoy changing their work assignments. Internal production of the most successful communal groups is characterized by excellent quality control and a flexible, developmental approach to the variety of products and services offered.

Policy decision making and management options cover the gamut from authoritarian and council forms to democratic and consensus methods. In recent decades, most intentional communities have preferred electoral processes. Consensus decision making may produce greater compatibility and cooperation but requires time-consuming meetings and may deny groups some of the harmony and innovative progress of creative diversity (*Communities*, 2012; Pitzer, 2011). Tax-exempt status may be achieved and is a definite advantage. Unemployment and poverty, which plague capitalism, are rarely problems in intentional communities, especially in groups that concentrate on agriculture and animal husbandry. Economy of scale can be a significant benefit for people sharing lodging, food and transportation costs. Downturns in the general economy make the financial and social security of communal organization especially attractive (Cothron, 2009; Hall, 2009; Roth, 2009; Valles, 2009).

Regardless of how distinctive and isolated the most successful communal societies may be internally, they have had to reach out to distribute their goods and services externally. Many have engaged vigorously with the larger market economy. Some interact only to procure commodities and to generate income. Others also wish to impact upon the world with their utopian ideologies. The Amish live in more than 450 highly cooperative communities in North America, though they have never adopted community of goods. They pride themselves on their religious separation from the world whose people they still call "the English." Yet these Christian sectarians have proven to be among the world's most successful entrepreneurs. Recent surveys reveal that as many as 95 percent of new Amish businesses are still operating after five years, a startling rate compared to only 50 percent of traditional start-ups (Wesner, 2010; Williams, 2010). Perhaps the unique Amish combination of cooperative, family-oriented organization along with private, capitalistic initiatives by individuals or groups of members is the secret to their success. At the other extreme, The Twin Oaks community, founded in 1967, has successfully sought both economic and ideological engagement with the wider world. Welcoming visitors, giving tours, circulating publications and holding conferences have aided its promotion of ecology, egalitarianism, peace and feminism. Indexing books, selling its tofu, making hammocks and chairs (for years for Pier One Imports), and growing organic seeds for the Southern Exposure Seed Company have provided a solid financial base (*Communities Directory*, 2010; The Twin Oaks website).

Intentional communities in action

The following case studies suggest three factors that have made alternative communal organizations successful – leadership, labor force and large markets. In the first study, anthropologist Donald Janzen uses his knowledge from personal interviews and organizing the group's archival sources to explain the major role played by communal charismatic leadership in the organization and financial achievements of the Shiloh Family in New York and Arkansas.

The Shiloh Family: alternative organization for faith and pioneering organic foods

The Shiloh Family, a small Christian communal group, had a modest beginning on several hundred acres of farmland near Sherman, New York, purchased by the Reverend E. Crosby Monroe in 1942. Ordained a minister of the Apostolic Church of England, he conducted Bible study sessions that attracted a number of followers. Concepts developed at these sessions led to the founding of the Shiloh Bible School shortly after World War II (Monroe, 1952). Monroe was a charismatic speaker, yet he never intended to start a communal group and withdraw from mainstream society. It appears that it was just the opposite. He was a teacher, and his goal was to help those in need and impart the message of Christian love and fellowship that others could carry into the world. However, the atmosphere of his school was so appealing that instead of leaving after their training, many wanted to remain and live together communally as directed in the book of Acts (2:44–45) (Clough, n.d.: 7). This led to the formation of an intentional community in which the residents referred to themselves as the "Shiloh Family."

Shiloh's signature industry started modestly when one member's offer to bake bread earned him the role of community baker. Working from a kitchen oven that baked seven loaves at a time, what became Shiloh's Sun Rise Acres Bakery was launched. Shiloh members delivered not only baked goods but also dairy products, meats and organic vegetables from their large garden to customers around Sherman.

E. Crosby Monroe, perhaps influenced by the prophet Isaiah (55:2), urged the community to eat and produce healthy foods: "Wherefore do ye spend money for that which is not bread? Hearken diligently unto me, and eat that which is good, and let your soul rejoice" (Clough, n.d.: 5). Monroe believed that pesticides and processed foods should be avoided. Consequently, the community adopted a twelve-point dietary code and began using wholegrain flours and natural sweeteners and oils while avoiding pesticides (Dietary Code, n.d.). Today "organic" is a common word in the consumer's twenty-first century vocabulary. In fact, according to the Organic Trade Association, in 2010 the organic food industry was the fastest growing segment of all food sales (News Release, 2011). Fifty years ago, the emergence and growth of organic foods in the US was fostered by this pioneering enterprise called Shiloh.

In 1963, several members attended the Natural Foods Associates convention in Binghamton, New York (History of Shiloh, n.d.: 1). They learned that the nation was beginning to demand organically grown foods. With two trucks, one refrigerated, the Shiloh organization began solving the problem of how to link the producers of organic foods with customers. To insure their high standards, foods brought in from sources outside the community were tested in the Shiloh laboratory so they could be certified as organic. By 1967, the two Shiloh trucks were logging 9,000 miles a month shipping such products as fish from the North Atlantic, honey from Israel, maple syrup from Vermont, potatoes from Ohio, cheese from Wisconsin, and pinto beans from Colorado (Story of Shiloh, 1967). For better location and climate, in 1969 Shiloh relocated to Sulphur Springs, Arkansas (Clough, n.d.). This gave them ample space to expand the size of the bakery and more efficiently move Shiloh Farm products around the country, products eventually delivered to over 1,200 stores in forty-four states (Condition, n.d.).

In the beginning, there was no need for a structured business plan. While some people worked at a particular job more frequently than others, there was no established hierarchy of managers and workers. Some tasks were organized around a division of labor based on sex, while both men and women participated in others. Men were involved in farm work, butchering of animals and delivering products. Men *and* women worked in the community's garden and prepared eggs for sale.

As Shiloh's business changed from retail sales to the wholesale distribution of organic food products, with $4 million in annual sales, there was a corresponding change in their business structure. Shiloh Farms, Inc. was established with a highly efficient tiered organizational plan. This included the standard Board of Directors and an array of managers who oversaw everything: manufacturing, purchasing, distribution, sales and accounting. In addition, personnel were in charge of segments of the company such as pricing, printing, bagging and office supplies (Shiloh Organizational Chart). The division of labor became less patriarchal, women serving on the Board and positions of importance. The bakery became the main business within the community, with women and men working together on the production line. Jobs were rotated periodically in the bakery so that individuals became familiar with the entire process, now known as multitasking.

As the demand for products grew, the membership could no longer meet the labor demands, so people from outside the community were hired. For cooperative communities that choose to separate themselves from mainstream society, hiring outside labor can involve risks since it brings the members in contact with people who have a lifestyle they are trying to avoid. Since it was always Shiloh's intention to participate in mainstream society, the introduction of people from outside the community into its workforce presented no problems. However, Shiloh created a highly structured way of hiring outsiders. A potential employee was given a thirty-two-page booklet titled "Shiloh Farms: Your Company and You." The Table of Contents of this booklet covered twenty-two items ranging from anti-nepotism and overtime policies to timekeeping, pay schedule, transfers and promotions, fringe benefits, safety, accident procedures, first aid kits, and termination. The last page was an "Agreement" that employees must sign, indicating they had read the book and would abide by all the requirements ("Shiloh Farms").

While Shiloh's business model mirrored that of many corporations in mainstream society, there were significant differences. The profit motive was still important, but as a Christian communal society this was not their main goal. Shiloh formalized the interconnection of their economic, belief and social systems into what they called their "Trinity of Relationships." This was symbolized by a triangle with the angles labeled Worship, Work and Family. Shiloh thus adopted what can be called Communal Capitalism, a fusing of their corporate model with their religious and social philosophies. As a communal society, Shiloh took care of the main requirements of their members, such as food and lodging. To care for unexpected expenses, such as travel to the funeral of a family member, Shiloh established a "Needs Committee" to cover these costs.

While employees from outside the community received a wage, each Shiloh member was given a monthly stipend. The amount was the same for everyone, a board member, production manager, or a person working on the line in the bakery. Historically, Shiloh's equalization of the value of work is reminiscent of the labor note system used in Robert Owen's socialistic New Harmony, Indiana in the 1820s and in the labor exchange and time store experiments of Josiah Warren at Equity and Utopia, Ohio and Modern Times, New York between 1833 and 1863 (Bestor, 1950: 185; Lockwood, 1905: 295–303; Pitzer, 2011).

Currently, these compensation plans bear similarity to many workers' managed enterprises (see Atzeni and Vieta, this volume), as well as to the international TimeBanks movement begun in 1995 and now headquartered in Washington, D.C. which "promotes equality and builds caring community economies through inclusive exchange of time and talent" (timebanks.org/about; see North, this volume). Shiloh's egalitarian compensation is a radical departure from that of the corporations of mainstream society where the differences in pay are extreme.

At the turn of the twenty-first century, James Janisch, by then the spiritual head of the community, decided that Shiloh's business enterprise had grown to the point that it overshadowed the community's original spiritual goals. Their Trinity of Relationships was no longer in balance and the corporate aspect was dwarfing Worship and Family. Once again, the members followed the wisdom of their respected leader. In a bold move, they withdrew as a major player in the organic food business while retaining the name Shiloh Farms. Today, Garden Spot Distributors sells organic foods bearing the Shiloh Farms label from coast to coast.

The Shiloh Family story shows that communal capitalism is an alternative to mainstream, global capitalism and a tiered system of compensation. A group of people, never numbering over 200, were not only able to launch a successful, nation-wide business, but they were able to do it within an atmosphere of fellowship and family love.

★ ★ ★

Even a capable, charismatic leader needs a united and committed labor force. As noted in E. Crosby Monroe's Shiloh Family, this natural advantage of voluntary communal organization is also prominently featured in the second case study about Daniel Wright's patriarchal Padanaram Settlement in Martin County, Indiana. Daniel so closely equated labor to the survival of his community that he incorporated a biblical directive into Padanaram's spiritual and philosophical foundation: "If a man will not work, he shall not eat" (II Thessalonians 3:10 NIV). He expected his workers to be self-motivated, reminding them that "from everyone who has been given much, much will be demanded" (Luke 12:48). Yet, Daniel wisely fostered an atmosphere of partnership and high morale under his patriarchal leadership.

Rachel Wright-Summerton describes Padanaram through the eyes of a resident and its archivist whose parents founded the community in 1966. United around the utopian vision of "Kingdomism," Padanaram has found financial security by operating the largest sawmill in Indiana, diversifying its products, and doing business in several countries.

Padanaram Settlement: alternative organization for "Kingdomism"

Padanaram was founded by a non-demoninational minister, Daniel Wright, after being inspired by a spiritual experience – in 1966 after being led to a valley where he said God told him "Here men will take off their shoes; this is holy ground" (Wright, 2007: 62). That September, twelve individuals ("the dirty dozen") pooled their resources to purchase 86 acres on that ground in the rolling hills of southern Indiana near Bedford. This was the new "nation within a nation," the pattern for Kingdomism: a vision of small, self-sufficient communities that would spread around the globe. "It is dedicated to equal education, philosophical analysis, social idealism, economic independence, and religious non-denominationalism" (Padanaram, 1998). Padanaram built a foundation for success on several basic principles: Leadership

("Wisdom is the leader; truth is the guide"), Ownership ("Hold all things in common"), Familyism ("Care for your neighbor"), Partnership ("He that won't work, shall not eat"), and Adaptation, Growth and Expansion – "Change is inevitable" (Wright, 2007: 592–602).

The immediate aim was survival. The only housing available was a dilapidated farmhouse where sleeping bags lined the walls for the first few months. Logs were dragged from the woods with a mule, and a three-storey log-cabin-style building was slowly erected. The plan was for a building that would "last a hundred years." Farming seemed like a viable option, but heavy rains soon dampened the spirits as well as the pocketbook. The alternative possibility was a market for pulp wood in nearby Bedford. This temporary effort provided funds for food and the bare necessities.

The first lodge was finished by 1968. Families had a room or two while single people had a bunk around the fireplace. As for many "voluntary simplifiers" (see McDonald, this volume), it was a primitive lifestyle – a wooden cook stove, simple meals, water from a spring, outhouses, and a guitar or two. This was the 1960s, and many young people traveled through the region and became joiners.

The dire need for housing and a dairy barn triggered the idea of a small sawmill, just for the villagers' needs. A Corley mill was purchased for $6,000. A couple of the men knew tree species and a little about sawmilling. Daily, on-the-job training produced a sawyer, grader and lumber stackers. It was hard work – long hours during the week (sometimes a double shift) and carpentry on weekends. It was communal work, communal dining and communal living.

"These things affected me right where I lived. Philosophies of 'how to' didn't help. It's what I lived, what I experienced, and sometimes it was raw! It was the nitty-gritty of communal life, the daily ups and downs. It is called 'working together' " (Wright-Summerton, 1996: 22). One of the favorite songs over Saturday night beer was, "If you can't take it buddy, hit the road. This ain't no place for the meek or weak-hearted. If you can't take it buddy, hit the road."

Word of mouth brought farmers who placed orders for lumber, and a business was born. Income for the first year was $4,000. The three-mile dirt pathway became a thoroughfare for transporting lumber. Within a few months, the Internal Revenue Service knocked at the door. They found fault with the idea of a "partnership." However, a partnership it remained. The land, the money and the profits belonged to the people. Padanaram was not founded as a religious organization, so taxes had to be paid and a bookkeeper was needed to keep detailed records of the business transactions.

The main income from 1968 to 2000 continued to be from renewable forest products – sawmilling, selective timber buying, veneer sales and land improvement. Profits were visible in purchased farms, material for the schoolchildren, home-canned foods, and special suppers celebrating the growth of the community. Camaraderie, commitment and high spirits characterized the workplace. The workers owned the means of production and the distribution of the goods. The village business was outwardly competitive but inwardly cooperative. The geographical spot called Padanaram (the acreage) and the business were two separate entities. The land was held in a trust governed by seven elders while the businesses remained partnerships. The land would be held in perpetuity regardless of the membership; it could not be divided or sold.

The community flourished with schools, gardens, a bakery, and numerous arts and crafts, including blacksmithing and leatherwork. Soon 30, 50, 80-plus people resided in the community. Several log lodges, barns and outbuildings dotted the landscape. By 1972, the first school was operating; six students walked down the road to a black and white trailer which had a library in the refrigerator, fish in the bathtub, and bearded men cut out from Sunday school literature.

By 1976, the small agricultural setting with limited access to the roads no longer sufficed. For the first time, the villagers traveled to Bloomington to work in what had become the largest mill in Indiana and surrounding states. In 1996, this community-owned mill grossed $7 million. But in the late 1990s, changes in the economy and a fluctuating timber market forced a restructuring of the community and its businesses. The common purse of "one sawmill" was replaced by a "storehouse fund." This fund paid property taxes and maintained the community's roads and buildings. It was equally contributed to by all members, male and female. Retired persons donated if they wished. Payments of electricity, gas, food, and other personal expenditures were individual responsibilities as one mill could no longer provide for the group.

This led to the expansion of smaller businesses within the logging industry, as well as other businesses (painting and wallpapering, landscaping, window washing) and outside jobs (teaching, marketing, etc.). Diversity gave strength to the seasonal wood business – while one business was dormant, the other businesses offered employment. It was "success" together – sharing good times and bad. In 2002, the lumber business expanded into international trade, exporting veneer logs and lumber to Spain, India, Hong Kong, Italy, China and Vietnam (Wright Timber website). Longtime business associates were going overseas; there were expanded markets for hardwoods from the Midwest. Business practices with these associates entailed trust and friendship and long-term business relationships (not just quick profits). It was a win-win for both parties. Young people with forestry degrees had the expertise to eliminate the middle men and make the business even more profitable.

Currently, the lumber business extends into four states: Indiana (logging, mulch and organic soils), Kentucky (logging operation), Missouri (two portable sawmills), and a new expansion into Pennsylvania. A second community in Arizona (started in the 1980s) has an organic date company and plans for a solar panel plant. Numerous smaller businesses (10–15) continue to multiply in the areas of home improvement, landscaping, construction, gardening/herbal products and food operations. Many of the younger generation are furthering their careers in business, health care, law, teaching and media/computer technology which will, in turn, lead to the creation of new businesses and employment for the community.

The 2011 population of "the valley" is 150 men, women and children who reside in the beautiful, park-like environment. Gardens, lakes, streams, hiking paths and country living provide a peaceful atmosphere. Attention to the land remains of primary importance. There are 2,000 acres of land, plus numerous farms and business property: 1,000 acres of classified or sustainable forest; 500 acres of regular forest – managed for wildlife habitat, recreation, hunting and fishing; 200 acres in farm ($20,000 a year helps pay taxes); and three lakes.

In 1999, a resolution presented in the Indiana General Assembly honored the late Daniel Wright and his Padanaram Settlement. Praising their prosperity, ideal of building a better world, and teaching job skills to the homeless, it concluded that "Daniel Wright and his community have proved that people of all kinds can live together harmoniously" (House Resolution, 1999: 2).

★ ★ ★

In Rachel Wright-Summerton's words, a communally organized business must be "inwardly cooperative" but "outwardly competitive." Even though the Shiloh Family was insulated by its religious beliefs and Padanaram was isolated by its backwoods location, both found it profitable to connect with the wider world for economic well-being. The third case study illustrates this need to operate in a larger market in a much more urgent context. From her own on-site experience, Docey Lewis describes how native Senegalese people living in a communally oriented Muslim kinship group, and employed by Ndem's Maam Samba company, are developing organizational, marketing and other skills with assistance from a new type of international social entrepreneur, micro-philanthrocapitalists. An investment consortium of such entrepreneurs, including Lewis, is on the cutting edge of philanthropic enterprise, basing its projects on the indigenous structure of communities in the Third World and using revenues from consortium members' for-profit businesses to support humanitarian not-for-profit activities. Docey calls this new, community-based frontier of philanthropy "micro-philanthrocapitalism" – an outgrowth of philanthropic/altruistic capitalism and social enterprise (Kikkoman Advertisement, 2011; Kirkpatrick, 2011; Coster, 2011). She is pioneering this method in Ndem, Senegal and elsewhere in the spirit of her ancestor Robert Owen. He became famous for social reforms that improved the health, education and environment of workers, initially in his cotton mill town of New Lanark, Scotland (Donnachie, 1993; Pitzer, 2011).

Micro-philanthrocapitalism: alternative organization in the kinship community of Ndem, Senegal

The survival of communes and semi-communal kinship groups, especially ones geographically or socially isolated, depends on their economic base. Their communally organized businesses face unusual pressures for reaching into larger, external markets. In good times, such businesses can afford the often slower process of communal decision making and the nurturing of inefficient production units and weaker producers, but hard times can drive a community toward accepting more hierarchical leadership and better defined work regulations. Hard times can also bring out the best and the worst in individuals fighting for their personal and family survival within the context of commitment to their community. Just such a challenge recently faced the Maam Samba clothing and home décor business of the village of Ndem, Senegal (Maam Samba).

Ndem is situated in the arid landscape of the Baol region, 75 miles west of the capital of Dakar. Over a hundred years ago, the area was the birthplace of the founder of the Baye Fall Islamic group, a sect that descends from the Mourides which is one of the largest Islamic Brotherhoods in Senegal. They view work as a form of prayer. Many worshipers choose to live near their spiritual leader in a village-within-a-village known as a *dara*. In the Ndem *dara*, housing, food and livelihood are enjoyed by the members and their families who eat together, work together, pray together, and make decisions together. Their spiritual leader, Babacar Mbow, a Sorbonne-educated sociologist with a dynamic French wife and ambitiously holistic plans for his village, has transformed a difficult environment into a thriving community. In 1985, the Ndem Villageois d'Artisanat was organized under a General Assembly and grew to include 189 men and 176 women from the *dara* as well as from 13 surrounding villages. They established schools, craft workshops, bio-fuel manufacturing, a health clinic, a community well, drip irrigation organic gardens, microfinance programs and a health insurance scheme. At its peak in the early 2000s, the village regularly exported containers of crafts to European fair trade importers.

Just as Maam Samba was gearing up for expansion, the global economic downturn of 2008 hit them full force. Several large clients defaulted on payments. Orders were canceled. The government instituted power cutting which, in turn, badly affected the generators that powered the village well. The slow-down of business affected the entire social structure of the village. During the good times, both managers and workers had become complacent. Many of the artisans were on a fixed salary, and whether they came to work regularly or produced a reasonable quantity of quality saleable crafts became less important over time. The international market for crafts became more competitive, and tastes changed. The first wave of artisans were becoming too old to work, and a new pool of workers, who were not necessarily from the *dara* and who did not fully share the values of the original founders, changed the overall environment. The perfect storm arrived in the summer of 2010 when Maam Samba was repeatedly unable to meet its payroll, there were few orders, and the craft center was, for all practical purposes, bankrupt. In spite of the still strong guidance of its spiritual leader, artisans who once cooperated for mutual benefit were not equipped for such negative change and, consequently, turned on one another and on the organization they had created. Ndem had to rethink the organizational structure that once worked and adapt to changing times.

Under those circumstances, a consortium – including 3Form, Docey Lewis Designs, Aid to Artisans and Vital Edge Aid – was created. With a philosophy of giving back to the communities it worked with and committed to a form of micro-philanthrocapitalism, it began providing grants and low interest loans for specific interventions like building spinning wheels and looms. For their part, the artisans volunteered their time to learn new skills like textile design. The interventions were developed in partnership with the community and with other NGOs who are also active in the areas of food security and access to health, education and technology. Swiss, French and Italian NGOs participated in developing interventions for solar technology, a marketing center, Internet capacity and raw materials supply. 3Form focused on developing the products with the most potential – those using organic cotton – where the community could control the full supply chain, from field to retail store. The farmers and artisans of Ndem now plant their own cotton, gin, card, spin, dye, weave, knit and sew products they supply to their retail store two hours away in the seaside tourist village of Saly. The organic cotton products are paid for in full when they are delivered to the store, and the artisans who produce them are paid for their labor regardless of whether their fellow artisans in other media have been able to make sales.

The store received a loan to upgrade its display, replace its inventory and improve its bookkeeping. A merchandiser acts as a bridge between the village and the store to supply accurate information about what sells and to make sure high quality is maintained. The management of the artisan center has been shifted from a committee to a temporary CEO who will be replaced by a trained CEO with the skills to run a complex business. Artisans have been hired according to their skills and productivity and are paid fairly for each piece they produce that passes quality inspection. No one is hired if there are no orders to fulfill. The focus has shifted from export market with low profit margins to the local niche markets of tourists, hotels, restaurants and the burgeoning middle class. If orders slow down, artisans shift to agricultural activities in their community-owned, drip-irrigated organic garden. The lesson learned is that in a community that produces many kinds of products, each section needs to be treated as its own profit center, and there needs to be the flexibility to shift labor to the most profitable work. Business requires both financial and leadership discipline. While it may be possible to institute committee-style management in the future, new skills will need to be learned in order to enable those running Maam Samba to make timely and tough decisions. Once Ndem put its economic engine back on track, the shared vision of stewardship of the environment, the importance of appropriate economic activity, belief in education, and the need for a holistic approach to community development is once again clear.

Conclusion

Two theories help clarify the processes at work in communes and intentional communities and the movements that found them. Developmental communalism suggests that the most vital movements and their model communities seize opportunities, adjust to changing circumstances, and adopt new procedures, methods and structures (Pitzer, 1989, 1997, 2009). This includes flexibility in communities' and movements' policy making, management and product marketing, as seen in the case studies. The developmental process is a chief element in their long-term survival and their contributions to their own adherents and the general society. In some cases, this development takes the movement away from the communal method of organization altogether. From the first Christians, the Moravians and Mormons to the socialistic Owenites, the developmental process paved the way for vast expansion in numbers and more effective general acceptance of basic beliefs and reforms. Ndem illustrates how the developmental process and the need to survive led a community away from some of its communal assumptions. Groups which are too slow to develop creatively often see their communities and movements wither or die. The Harmonists and Shakers have suffered this fate. The theory of transformative utopianism concentrates on developmental communalism in its ultimate stage, one in which movements that create communes and intentional communities sometimes witness the integration of their progressive ideals and innovations into the broader culture and foster wider senses of change (Lockyer, 2009; Pitzer, 2013).

The Shiloh Family, Padanaram Settlement and Ndem's kinship community are graphic examples of the distinctive communal alternative organization and orientation involving leadership, labor force and large markets. The value systems of these groups, and of all economically successful communal societies, place them in a unique position of both tension and compatibility with the profit-making mindset of traditional capitalistic enterprise. Shiloh is a prime example where the delicate balance between communal spiritual values and economic success got out of kilter, and they responded by downsizing the business. Notably, each of the case studies focuses on a religiously based community, underscoring the fact that most of the longest-lasting communes have been founded on religious or spiritual movements. Ideologies that promise eternal rewards have obviously called forth the strongest, most enduring, communal commitment (Kanter, 1972). Yet, this is not meant to ignore the reality that many cooperative communities established by non-sectarian and secular movements have also thrived (Fogarty, 1990; Hine, 1953; LeWarne, 1975; Miller, 1999; Pitzer, 1997, *Communities*, 2012).

Today, intentional communities are teaching vital lessons. The question of whether civilization can survive in an age of global capitalism under the threats of nuclear weapons, perpetual warfare, climate change and the exhaustion of fossil fuels remains at the top of the human agenda. Optimistic communitarians see a bright, communally oriented future of nonviolent, humanitarian, agriculturally based but market-engaged sustainable lifestyles in which conflicts are resolved peaceably and people are freed from poverty and unemployment. Attitudes and reforms put forward by the two waves of communal usage in the second half of the twentieth century are having noticeable effects in the early twenty-first century. The people who lived in counterculture, Jesus and other types of communes in the 1960s and 1970s are now seeing their practical utopianism manifest broadly in healthier eating habits, socialized health care, gender equality, multiculturalism, interfaith dialogue and peace initiatives (Pitzer, 2013). Communes are not just about the organization of economic production, but also of reproduction and of the relationships between work and life, and as such can potentially call into question gender relations and contribute to greater equality (see Dale, this volume).

The most valuable contemporary contribution of experimental communal models to the world at large may come in the arena of sustainability from the ecologically oriented wave of communities that began in the 1980s and 1990s (see the chapters by Cato, and Ganesh and Zoller, this volume). Thousands of ecovillages around the world are pioneering workable solutions. The secret to this alternative organization is not only cooperative economic structures but also a system of permanent organic agriculture ("permaculture"), vegetarian diets, green technology, and natural building materials and techniques (*Communities*, 2008, 2009, 2010). As fossil fuels shrink toward the vanishing point, the world is reluctantly adopting the environmentally conscious methods of recycling and harnessing the solar, wind and thermal renewable energy sources long advocated and exhibited by communes and intentional communities (*Communities*, 2008, 2009, 2010, 2012; Pitzer, 2013). If they can make these ideas increasingly attractive to society in general, they will have produced one of the most fundamental communal products of all alternative organizations – sustainability (Lockyer, 2010; Toray Advertisement, 2011: S26; Trainer, 2010).

Resources

Christian, D. (2003) *Creating a Life Together: Practical Tools to Grow Ecovillages and Intentional Communities*. Gabriola Island, BC: New Society Publishers.
This book is a fine introduction to the workings of ecovillages and other forms of communal living.

Cohousing Association of the United States. www.cohousing.org/
This website gives access to a vast amount of information on cohousing.

Communal Studies: Journal of the Communal Studies Association. http://www.ic.org.csa
This periodical contains the latest scholarly description and analysis of communes and intentional communities, past and present.

Communities: Life in Cooperative Culture
This quarterly publication of the Fellowship for Intentional Community carries articles about all matters related to communal living, mostly by communitarians.

Kanter, R. (1972) *Commitment and Community: Communes and Utopias in Sociological Perspective*. Cambridge, MA: Harvard University Press.
This study identifies commitment mechanisms that have produced longevity in communal organizations.

References

Arndt, K. (1972) *George Rapp's Harmony Society: 1785–1847*. Rutherford, NJ: Fairleigh Dickinson University Press.
Bartelt, P. (1997) 'American Jewish Agricultural Colonies', in D. Pitzer (ed.) *America's Communal Utopias*. Chapel Hill, NC: University of North Carolina Press, 352–374.
Bestor, A. (1950, 2012 reprint with new introduction by Donald Pitzer) *Backwoods Utopias: The Sectarian Origins and Owenite Phase of Communitarian Socialism in America*. Eugene, OR: Wipf and Stock, vii–viii, 1–19, 185.
Brewer, P. (1986) *Shaker Communities, Shaker Lives*. Hanover, NH: University Press of New England.
Butcher, A., Bates, A. and Christian, D. (1995) 'Legal Options for Intentional Communities', *Communities Directory: A Guide to Cooperative Living*. Langley, Washington, D.C.: Fellowship for Community (1995 edition): 141–149.
Clough, W. (n.d.) Unpublished interview by Frank Barhydt for 'Let's Live', 5, 7. Shiloh Family Collection, Rice Library, University of Southern Indiana, Evansville, Indiana.

Communities: Life in Cooperative Culture, 2008, 139(3); 2009, 143(3), 144(4); 2010, 146(2), 147(3); 2012, 155(3), 156(4). Available online at www.communities.ic.org

Communities Directory, 1990, 1995, 2000, 2005, 2007, 2010. Rutledge, MI: The Fellowship for Intentional Community.

'The Condition that is Shiloh' (n.d.), 3. Unpublished Shiloh document, Shiloh Family Collection, Rice Library, University of Southern Indiana, Evansville, Indiana.

Conkin, P.K. (1959) *Tomorrow a New World: The New Deal Community Program*. Ithaca, NY: Cornell University Press.

Coster, H. (2011, 19 December) 'Can Venture Capital Save the World?', *Forbes*, 188(11): 66–75.

Cothron, B. (2009) 'Food Security in Community', *Communities: Life in Cooperative Culture*, 144(4): 54–56, 79.

Damanhur Community website: www.damanhur.org (accessed 1 December 2011).

Dietary Code of Church of Shiloh (n.d.) Unpublished document, Shiloh Family Collection, Rice Library, University of Southern Indiana, Evansville, Indiana.

Donnachie, I. and Hewitt, G. (1993) *Historic New Lanark: The Dale and Owen Industrial Community since 1785*. Edinburgh: University of Edinburgh Press.

Evans, S. (2010) 'Alberta Hutterite Colonies: An Exploration of Past, Present, and Future Settlement Patterns', *Communal Societies: Journal of the Communal Studies Association*, 30(2): 27–63.

Fogarty, R. (1990) *All Things New: American Communes and Utopian Movements, 1860–1914*. Chicago, IL: University of Chicago Press.

Hall, R. (2009) 'Establishing Community in Hard Times: A Swedish Case', *Communities: Life in Cooperative Culture*, 144(4): 42–45.

Hine, R. (1953, 1966, 1983) *California's Utopian Colonies*. Berkeley: University of California Press.

'The History of Shiloh', 1. Unpublished Shiloh document, Shiloh Family Collection, Rice Library, University of Southern Indiana, Evansville, Indiana.

Hostetler, J. (1974) *Hutterite Society*. Baltimore, MD: Johns Hopkins University Press.

House Resolution HR 15539/DI, Indiana House of Representatives (1999), 2.

Huntington, G. (1997) 'Living in the Ark: Four Centuries of Hutterite Faith and Community', in D. Pitzer (ed.), *America's Communal Utopias*. Chapel Hill, NC: University of North Carolina Press, 319–351.

Kanter, R. (1972) *Commitment and Community: Communes and Utopias in Sociological Perspective*. Cambridge, MA: Harvard University Press.

Kikkoman Advertisement (25 July 2011) 'Perfectly Seasoned', *Fortune*, S25.

Kirkpatrick, D. (26 September 2011) 'Social Power and the Coming Corporate Revolution', *Forbes*, 188(5): 72–81.

Kozeny, G. (2010) 'Flavors of Community', *Communities Directory*. Langley, Washington, D.C.: Fellowship for Intentional Community, 1995 edition, 16–17.

LeWarne, C. (1975) *Utopias On Puget Sound 1885–1915*. Seattle: University of Washington Press.

Lockwood, G. (1905) *The New Harmony Movement*. New York: D. Appleton and Company.

Lockyer, J. (2009) 'From Developmental Communalism to Transformative Utopianism: An Imagined Conversation with Donald Pitzer', *Communal Societies: Journal of the Communal Studies Association*, 29(1): 1–14.

Lockyer, J. (2010) 'Intentional Communities and Sustainability', *Communal Societies: Journal of the Communal Studies Association*, 30(1): 18–30.

Maam Samba website: http://timbuktuchronicles/maamsamba (accessed 26 March 2012).

Mary's City of David website: www.maryscityofdavid.org

McCrank, L. (1997) 'Religious Orders and Monastic Communalism in America', in D. Pitzer (ed.) *America's Communal Utopias*. Chapel Hill, NC: University of North Carolina Press, 204–252.

Miller, T. (1999) *The 60s Communes: Hippies and Beyond*. Syracuse, NY: Syracuse University Press.

Miller, T. (2010) 'A Matter of Definition: Just What is an Intentional Community?', *Communal Societies: Journal of the Communal Studies Association*, 30(1): 1–15.

Monroe, E. (1952) 'The Shiloh Aim', 1. Unpublished document, Shiloh Family Collection, Special Collections Department, Rice Library, University of Southern Indiana, Evansille, Indiana.

Monterey Herald website: http://www.monteryherald.com/living/ci_19535746 (accessed 13 December 2011).

Near, H. (1992, 1997) *The Kibbutz Movement: A History*, 2 Vols. Oxford: Littman.

News Release of the Organic Trade Association (2011, 21 April) Brattleboro, Vermont. Shiloh Family Collection, Rice Library, University of Southern Indiana, Evansville, Indiana.

Nordhoff, C. (1875, 1965 reprint) *The Communistic Societies of the United States*. New York: Schocken Books.

Nowak, M. (2012, July) 'Why We Help', *Scientific American*, 307(1): 34–39.

Oved, Y. (2013) *Globalization of Communes: 1950–2010*. Piscataway, NJ: Transaction Publishers.

Padanaram Settlement Blue Booklet (1998) Williams, Indiana: Padanaram Press, 1. Padanaram Collection, Rice Library, University of Southern Indiana, Evansville, Indiana.

Pitzer, D. (1989) 'Developmental Communalism: An Alternative Approach to Communal Studies', in D. Hardy and L. Davidson (eds) *Utopian Thought and Communal Experience*. Middlesex: Middlesex Polytechnic, 68–76.

Pitzer, D. (1997) *America's Communal Utopias*. Chapel Hill: University of North Carolina Press.

Pitzer, D. (2009) 'Response to Lockyer's "From Developmental Communalism to Transformative Utopianism" ', *Communal Societies: Journal of the Communal Studies Association*, 15–21.

Pitzer, D. (2011, April) 'How the Harmonists Suffered Disharmony: Schism in Communal Utopias', *American Communal Societies Quarterly*, 5(2): 55–75.

Pitzer, D. (2013) 'Developmental Communalism into the Twenty-first Century', in E. Ben-Rafael, Y. Oved and M. Topel (eds) *The Communal Idea in the Twenty-first Century*. Leiden, Netherlands: Brill Academic Publishers, 33–52.

Pitzer, D. and Jones, D. (2011) *New Harmony Then & Now*. Bloomington: Indiana University Press.

Questenberry, D. (1995) 'Who We Are: An Exploration of What "Intentional Community" Means', *Communities Directory*, 33–38.

Roth, C. (2009) 'Community in Hard Times', *Communities: Life in Cooperative Culture*, 144(4):15.

Rubin, J. (1993) 'The Abuse of Charismatic Authority within the Bruderhof', address given at The Elizabethtown Anabaptist Conference, Elizabethtown, Pennsylvania, June 1993. Available online at www.perefound.org/jhr_arch.html (accessed 26 March 2012).

Ryder World (1979) 'Organic Foods go to Market in Ryder Trucks (Naturally)', *Ryder World*, (4):16.

Sagan, C. and Druyan, A. (1992) *Shadows of Forgotten Ancestors*. New York: Random House.

Schaub, L. (2011) 'Managing Management', *Communities: Life in Cooperative Culture*, 152(4):54–55.

Shiloh Family Collection, Special Collections Department, Rice Library, University of Southern Indiana, Evansville, Indiana.

'Shiloh Farms: Your Company and You.' Shiloh Family Collection, Special Collections Department, Rice Library, University of Southern Indiana, Evansville, Indiana.

Shiloh Organizational Chart (n.d.). Shiloh Family Collection, Special Collections Department, Rice Library, University of Southern Indiana, Evansville, Indiana.

The Farm website: www.thefarm.org (accessed 10 April 2011).

'The Story of Shiloh', New York: 1942–1967 (1967), 23. Shiloh 25th Anniversary publication.

Time Banks website: www.timebanks.org/about (accessed 29 August 2012).

Toray Advertisement (2011, 25 July) 'Sustainable Growth', *Fortune*, S26.

Trainer, T. (2010) *The Transition to a Sustainable and Just World*. Australia: Envirobook Publishing.

Twin Oaks website: http://twinoaks.org (accessed 23 August 2012).

Valles, J. (2009) 'Hard Times, Good Life, Community', *Communities: Life in Cooperative Culture*, 144(4): 20–23.

Wesner, E. (2010) *Success Made Simple: An Inside Look at Why Amish Businesses Thrive*. San Francisco, CA: Jossey-Bass.

Williams, G. (2010, 4 May) 'Why Amish Businesses Don't Fail'. Available online at www.money.cnn.com/2010/05/04smallbusiness/amish (accessed 30 December 2011).

Wright, D. (2007) *My Word Shall Guide Thee*. Bloomington, IN: AuthorHouse.

Wright-Summerton (1996) 'Padanaram: The Valley of the Gods', in W. Metcalf (ed.) *Shared Visions, Shared Lives*. Findhorn, Scotland: Findhorn Press, 22.

Wright Timber website: www.wright-timber.com/veneer/importsales,php (accessed 15 October 2011).

7

Non-commodified labour

Colin C. Williams

A popular and recurring assumption across academia and beyond is that commodification is steadily stretching its tentacles wider and deeper into everyday life and that its continuing encroachment is inevitable, inescapable and irreversible. In other words, goods and services are viewed as increasingly being produced for monetized exchange for the purpose of financial gain, while non-commodified labour practices, which do not involve monetized exchange and/or are not driven by the profit-motive, disappear as commodified labour colonizes every nook and cranny of daily life. Since the turn of the millennium, however, a small but growing tributary of post-structural, post-development, post-colonial and critical scholarship has started to question this depiction of commodification by drawing attention to the persistence of non-commodified labour practices in contemporary economies. The aim of this chapter is to review this emergent stream of literature and to provide an analytical lens for both evaluating critically the reach of commodification as well as displaying the continuing existence of non-commodified labour practices in contemporary societies. The intention in so doing is to open up the future to alternative forms of organizing and organization.

Introduction

The story of commodification is that over the long run of history, the capitalist mode of production has slowly but surely become ever more dominant, co-opting, replacing and colonizing all other forms of production. In this view, non-commodified forms of production are residues or leftovers from some earlier mode of production that, although persisting in a few marginal enclaves of the global economy, are steadily disappearing from view as commodification has become extensive, totalizing and hegemonic. This is the dominant narrative whether one reads the history of economic development of particular nations, portrayed in the stories of industrialization and the growth of market economies, or whether one reads the history of global development, with its tales about how capitalism has become an all-conquering force and the failure of all alternatives (e.g. socialism, communism). The resultant, widely held belief is that the ongoing permeation of capitalism into everyday life is a progressive and inevitable process. Indeed, today, this is seldom questioned. The aim of this chapter, however, is to do so. By displaying the widespread existence in the here and now of a plurality of non-commodified labour practices, I will critically evaluate the dominant narrative of capitalist hegemony and in doing so, begin to open up the future to alternatives beyond the hegemony of a totalizing capitalist mode of production.

To do this, the first part of this chapter shines a spotlight on the widespread belief that a process of commodification is occurring, and this is followed by a discussion of how this has begun to be contested by a small but growing body of literature that draws attention to the persistence of non-commodified labour practices in everyday life. An analytical lens will then be outlined that highlights the continuing existence of a multiplicity of non-commodified labour practices in the contemporary world. The second section will use this analytical lens to evaluate the ongoing existence of non-commodified labour by providing case studies of: the range of labour practices employed to undertake the task of cooking; the labour practices used by one person over the course of a day; the diverse labour practices employed in a voluntary sports organization; and the multifarious repertoire of labour practices used by the population of an English locality. These will begin to unravel the shallow reach of commodification and its highly uneven penetration as well as how, contrary to those depicting an increasingly commodified world, the use of a multiplicity of non-commodified labour practices in daily life remains the norm.

Before doing so, it is worthwhile rehearsing why it is important to question the hegemony of commodification. It might be assumed that my reason for questioning whether or not we live in a commodified world is because I have some 'problem' with commodification and dream of some alternative non-commodified world. This, however, is inaccurate. Rather, my concern is that it is those who believe that we live in an increasingly commodified world, and that the further encroachment of commodification is inevitable, who are failing to recognize the lived practices of work organization in the present and the range of possible futures for work. In this chapter, therefore, I want to provide a wake-up call. There is not only one, single, future for work: namely, a commodified world in which people take a formal job to earn money, and then use that money to purchase goods and services produced and distributed by profit-motivated commercial organizations. Instead, there are many ways to produce, distribute and consume goods and services, both in the here and now as well as in the future. This is not some chapter by a 'dreamer' wishing for the advent of some alternative to a commodified world. Rather, it is the opposite. It is a call to stop believing the dreams of those who want a capitalist world and who erroneously portray economies in the present as near enough entirely commodified in order to promulgate the notion that there is only one possible feasible future. With this in mind, let us begin.

Beyond commodified labour

A widespread belief across the social sciences and well beyond is that the encroachment of commodification into every aspect of daily life is inevitable and irreversible (Carruthers and Babb, 2000; Comelieau, 2002; Castree *et al.*, 2004; De Soto, 2001; Fulcher, 2004; Gudeman, 2001; Gough, 2000; Harvey, 2000; Kovel, 2002; Shutt, 2010; Rifkin, 2000; Ruskola, 2005; Slater and Tonkiss, 2001; Watts, 1999). On the one hand, this is argued by those of a neo-liberal persuasion who celebrate the advent of commodification, such as De Soto (2001: 1), who rejoices that "capitalism stands alone as the only feasible way rationally to organize a modern economy". On the other hand, it is also argued by those opposed to the continuing incursion of commodification due to its negative impacts, but who nevertheless believe that its ongoing encroachment is irreversible. As Fulcher (2004: 127) asserts, "the search for an alternative to capitalism is fruitless in a world where capitalism has become utterly dominant". Similarly, Castree *et al.* (2004: 16–17) contend "that this is a predominantly capitalist world seems to us indisputable . . . this system of production arguably now has few, if any, serious economic rivals". Consequently, a widespread and recurrent assumption is that only one future is possible and probable, and it is one where all labour becomes commodified in the sense that all goods and services are produced for monetized exchange for the purpose of profit.

Since the turn of the millennium, however, this has begun to be contested. An assorted and loose grouping of post-capitalist, post-development, post-colonial, post-structuralist and critical scholars have started to question the extent to which there has been a commodification of labour and in doing so, have opened up the future to alternative economic possibilities both in relation to the majority, Third World (e.g. Escobar, 2001; Esteva 1985; Whitson 2007) and East Central Europe (Round *et al.*, 2008a, b; Smith, 2007, 2010; Smith and Stenning, 2006; Williams, 2011a; Williams *et al.*, 2011) as well as with regard to western so-called "market" economies (e.g. Chakrabarty, 2000; Gibson-Graham, 1996, 2006, 2008; Fuller *et al.*, 2010; Leyshon *et al.*, 2003; St Martin, 2005; Williams, 2004, 2005, 2011b). As Samers (2005: 876) puts it, their intention has been to "relinquish a vision of a largely unimaginable socialism as capitalism's opposite, and instead, recover and revalorize a multitude of non-capitalist practices and spaces that disrupt the assumption of a hegemonic capitalism". By de-centring the notion that there has been a commodification of labour by re-evaluating the persistence of a multitude of non-commodified labour practices, the intention has been to open up the future to alternatives beyond a commodified world (Bourdieu, 2003; Chowdhury, 2007; Gibson-Graham 2006, 2008; Williams, 2003, 2004, 2005).

One way in which this can be pursued is by adopting a dichotomous depiction of a sphere of commodified labour and a separate sphere of non-commodified labour and then displaying the persistence of non-commodified labour in the contemporary world. The problem with pursuing this approach, however, is that commodified labour is not a separate and discrete sealed chamber that is distinct from non-commodified labour in terms of its values, economic relations and motives. Although commodified labour, for example, is sometimes depicted as composed of rational economic actors pursuing for-profit motives, while the separate realm of non-commodified labour is represented as involving social actors embedded in more intimate reciprocal relations, commodified labour in lived practice often possesses elements of emotion and sociability, and non-commodified labour elements of rational economic action and even, sometimes, the profit motive (Gibson-Graham, 2006; Williams and Zelizer, 2005; Zelizer, 2011). For example, private sector organizations are increasingly claiming to be motivated by social responsibility and sustainability, while non-commodified labour working in public and third sector organizations are increasingly being driven by the motive of surplus or profit because of the withdrawal of state funding.

The outcome is that the spheres of commodified and non-commodified labour are not wholly separate and discrete. Instead, the boundaries between them are, in practice, fuzzy and blurred. Although there are, of course, pure forms of commodified labour (which produce and deliver goods and services in the commercial economy for monetized exchange purely for the purpose of financial gain) and pure forms of non-commodified labour (where there is no monetized exchange and/or the profit motive is entirely absent), there are many 'hybrid' varieties in between these two ends of the spectrum.

Therefore, in order to move beyond the dichotomous depiction of commodified and non-commodified labour as separate and discrete, an analytical framework is required that unravels the multitude of labour practices in the contemporary world. One such analytical framework is the "total social organization of labour" approach developed by Glucksmann (2005: 28) who reads "the economy as a 'multiplex' combination of modes, rather than as a dualism between market and non-market forms". Until now, those using this more multi-layered understanding of the diverse repertoire of labour practices in the contemporary world to transcend the conventional commodified/non-commodified dichotomy have done so by locating labour practices along a spectrum from commodified to non-commodified practices, and have cross-cut this analysis against whether a practice is monetized or non-monetized (Glucksmann, 1995, 2005; Taylor, 2004).

A 'multiple labour practices' approach

Here, a slightly revised and extended view of the total social organization of labour is used to understand the multiple labour practices in contemporary societies. As Figure 7.1 displays, there is, first, a spectrum ranging from wholly commodified to wholly non-commodified labour practices at each end, with many hybrid varieties in between, but secondly, and cross-cutting this, a further spectrum (rather than dichotomy) from wholly non-monetized, through gift exchange and in-kind practices, to wholly monetized labour practices. Overlapping circles with hatched lines are deliberately used in order to display the borderless continuum, rather than strict separation, between labour practices, each overlapping and merging into one another. The outcome is a vivid representation of the seamless fluidity of a diverse repertoire of labour practices which are not discrete but entwined together (Williams, 2010, 2011a, b; Williams *et al.*, 2011).

These ten overlapping labour practices each possess within them different varieties of labour and merge at their borders with a range of other practices. First, "formal paid labour in the private sector", defined as paid work in the private sector which is registered by the state for tax, social security and labour law purposes, has conventionally been seen as the pure form of "commodified labour" and separate from all other (and "othered") non-commodified labour practices, including "formal paid labour in the public and third sectors", as is so clearly expressed in discourses surrounding the private/public sector dualism. However, given that private sector organizations are increasingly claiming to pursue a triple bottom line, while public and third sector organizations are also pursuing profit (albeit in order to reinvest so as to achieve wider social and environmental objectives), these two zones are far from separate and are, in practice, merging into each other.

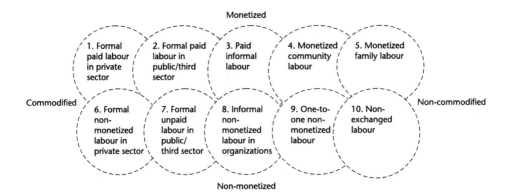

Figure 7.1 A typology of the diverse repertoire of labour practices in contemporary societies

This supposedly pure form of commodified labour, which is far from pure once the varieties which pursue social and sustainable practices are taken into consideration, also overlaps and merges with other labour practices, not least "paid informal labour" and "formal non-monetized labour". Paid informal labour here refers to paid labour unregistered by or hidden from the state for tax, social security and labour law purposes (Williams, 2009). Multifarious varieties exist, ranging from wholly paid informal labour where none of the payment is declared for tax, social, security and labour law purposes, through formal self-employment where people do not declare a portion of their earnings, to under-declared formal employment where formal employees receive an additional undeclared wage from their formal employer alongside their formal declared wage (Williams, 2009). Although it has been conventionally assumed that a job or labour contract is either formal or informal, under-declared formal employment clearly shows how labour can be simultaneously both formal and informal, further blurring the divide between commodified forms of labour (formal paid labour in the private sector) and non-commodified labour practices.

Formal paid labour in the private sector not only overlaps with paid informal labour but also "formal non-monetized labour", both in the private sector as well as in the public and third sectors. In the private and public sectors, such formal non-monetized labour takes many forms, including unpaid internships, unpaid periods of work experience or limited-period unpaid trials. Sometimes, however, it also occurs when businesses fail to pay their formal employees for protracted periods (Shevchenko, 2009). It is in third sector organizations, nevertheless, that formal non-monetized labour is perhaps most extensive; here it is commonly termed "formal volunteering" and refers to "giving help through groups, clubs or organiza-tions to benefit other people or the environment" (Low et al., 2008: 11). In some instances, this can transmute into "informal non-monetized labour in organisations", when help is again provided through groups to benefit other people or the environment, but the required formalities required by the law have not all been fulfilled, such as when a children's football coach volunteers but without having undertaken the required police checks.

Labour provided on an own-account one-to-one basis, meanwhile, can either be provided in exchange for money, gifts, on an in-kind basis and/or a non-monetary basis. "One-to-one non-monetized labour" refers to unpaid labour provided on an individual level to members of households other than one's own, such as kin living outside one's household, friends, neighbours and acquaintances. This ranges from individualized, one-way giving (often termed "informal volunteering") to two-way reciprocity. When reciprocity is involved, such unpaid endeavour often blurs into "monetized community labour", or what might be termed paid favours, since the reciprocity may take the form of either in-kind labour or gifts in lieu of payment, or monetary exchanges. Indeed, whether such labour is situated as monetized community labour or paid informal labour depends on the economic relations, values and motives involved. Paid informal labour is more commodified, since financial gain is more prominent and more distant social relations are involved, while mone-tized community labour is less commodified, since redistributive and relationship-building purposes are more prominent and it is conducted for and by closer social relations, with many combinations and overlaps in between. Peter North, in Chapter 12, moreover, provides a fascinating review of an organizational form, namely community currencies, which is seeking to harness monetized community labour in a manner that not only encourages new social relations of exchange that transcend the profit motive but also provides greater opportunities for such non-commodified exchanges to take place so as to provide an alternative to mainstream commodified exchange.

Turning to the kinds of labour furthest from commodified labour, there is, firstly, "non-exchanged labour" which refers to unpaid work conducted by household members for themselves or for other members of their household, and is further discussed by Karen Dale in Chapter 8 on family and household reproduction. Sometimes, nevertheless, there is a blurring between this and "monetized family labour", where family members are reimbursed for tasks conducted for and by other household members using money, gifts or in-kind reciprocal labour. There is a blurring not least because what is often seen as non-exchanged labour (e.g. housework) is rarely conducted in couple-households on a purely non-exchanged basis, with no expectation of reciprocity, since couples often reciprocate labour (e.g. "you do the cooking and I will do the washing up"). Moreover, with the rise in divorce rates and remarriage, and ongoing disassembly and reassembly of families, what constitutes family and non-family is by no means always clear-cut, and therefore differentiating family work (non-exchanged labour) from one-to-one non-monetized labour in the wider community is sometimes difficult, since current acquaintances, friends and even neighbours in areas with low geographical mobility might well be past or future family.

Evaluating multiple labour practices in everyday life

Given this analytical lens which captures the diversity, fluidity and overlaps between the multitude of labour practices in societies, I will now turn to showing how this analytical framework can be used to evaluate the labour practices used in daily life. To do this, four case studies are employed: the multifarious labour practices that can be used to undertake the task of cooking; the types of labour practices used by one person over the course of a day; the multifarious labour practices used by a voluntary sports organization; and the repertoire of labour practices used by the inhabitants of an English locality.

Case study 1: the task of cooking

Tasks cannot be assigned to a particular labour practice (e.g. cooking is undertaken as non-exchanged labour and web design as formal paid labour in the private sector). Instead, any task or activity can be conducted using any of the ten labour practices identified above. To demonstrate this, the task of cooking is here considered. Taking each of the ten labour practices in turn, examples can easily be found of how this labour practice can be used to undertake the activity of cooking:

- Formal paid labour in the private sector – paid formal employment as a chef in a restaurant;
- Formal paid labour in the public/third sector – paid formal employment as a cook in the canteen of a town hall;
- Paid informal labour – working as a cook in a "burger van" at an event for which one is paid "cash-in-hand";
- Monetized community labour – preparing sandwiches for a community event for which one is given some money as a "thank you" for doing the favour;
- Monetized family labour – paying your children "pocket-money"/"bribes" to cook the Saturday evening meal;
- Formal non-monetized labour in the private sector – doing an unpaid internship with a chef in a restaurant to gain work experience;

- Formal unpaid labour in the public/third sector – working as a formal volunteer in a homeless shelter cooking their meals;
- Informal non-monetized labour in an organization – preparing and selling on an unpaid volunteer basis food at a church event when it does not have a licence to sell food;
- One-to-one non-monetized labour – cooking for friends for a dinner party;
- Non-exchanged labour – cooking on an unpaid basis for oneself or other members of the household.

Of course, not all of these labour practices are used to the same extent in daily life to undertake the task of cooking. Non-exchanged labour probably remains by far the most commonly used labour practice to do this task. However, it is perhaps increasingly the case, as exemplified by ready-prepared meals bought in supermarkets, that non-exchanged labour is increasingly being used only for the final stage of cooking and that formal paid labour in the private sector is being increasingly used for earlier stages in the production process, such as the production of the ready-prepared meal for reheating.

This case study of cooking also displays the strong relationship between gender and the labour practices used to undertake tasks. Cooking when undertaken as paid formal labour in the private sector is strongly associated with men, but with women when undertaken as paid formal labour in the public and third sectors. When undertaken using some labour practices, moreover, it attains a higher social status (e.g. being a chef employed in the private sector in paid formal employment) than when it is conducted using other labour practices, reflecting not only how the labour practices associated with men are privileged over those associated with women, but also the privileging of commodified labour over other labour practices.

It is also the case that if one examines any food product in terms of how it moves through the "commodity" chain from its production to consumption, many labour practices might be used during its journey. Take, for example, an apple. The tree might have been planted many years ago by somebody on a paid informal or "cash-in-hand" basis when they planted an apple orchard on a former grassland field. The apple might then be picked either by unpaid family labour if it is a family-owned orchard, or by "cash-in-hand" labourers organized by a gang-master, before being sold by the formal apple-farming business to a formal retailer who uses formal labour to bring it from the farm to the retail superstore. Once in the retail superstore, it is worth remembering that the "consumer" employs unpaid self-provisioning to pick the apple from the shelf, put it in their trolley, process it at a self-checkout counter and then transport it in their self-driven car from the supermarket to their home where they unpack it and store it until use. They then again use unpaid self-provisioning to prepare it for consumption, whether that is peeling it or making some product such as an apple pie with it before eventually consuming it. Multifarious labour practices, in consequence, are involved in the so-called "global commodity chain" of the production, distribution and consumption of the food products involved in cooking.

Case study 2: a day in the life of a person

It is not just tasks such as cooking that can be conducted using each and every labour practice. Just as tasks cannot be assigned to a specific labour practice, neither can individuals (e.g. individual A engages in formal paid labour in the private sector and individual B in paid informal labour). Instead, in daily life, individuals engage in a repertoire of diverse labour practices. Table 7.1 divides a normal day into 30-minute segments and provides an example of the diverse labour practices a person may undertake.

Table 7.1 Example of an individual's daily repertoire of labour practices

Time	Activity	Labour practice
07.30	Brush teeth, shower and make breakfast at home	Non-exchanged labour
08.00	Drive to work. Pick up colleague on way (who gives petrol money on fortnightly basis)	Monetized community exchange
08.30	Do web design work in office	Formal paid labour in private sector
09.00	↓	↓
09.30		
10.00		
10.30		
11.00		
11.30		
12.00		
12.30		
13.00	Do some clothes shopping for children in lunch hour	Non-exchanged labour
13.30	Do web design work in office	Formal paid labour in private sector
14.00	↓	↓
14.30		
15.00		
15.30		
16.00		
16.30		
17.00		
17.30	Leave work and drop off work colleague	Monetized community exchange
18.00	Pick up medicine from chemist for elderly neighbour and drop it off	One-to-one non-monetized labour
18.30	Cook dinner for family	Non-exchanged labour
19.00	Take child to football training	Non-exchanged labour
19.30	Do food shopping	Non-exchanged labour
20.00	Give some of the children a lift home	Informal non-monetized labour in organization
20.30	Help child with homework	Non-exchanged labour
21.00	Work on a website design for a friend	Paid informal labour
21.30	↓	↓
22.00	Wash up and tidy up house	Non-exchanged labour
22.30		

This displays not only the diverse repertoire of labour practices used by an individual on a daily basis, but also how some labour practices are more commonly used, and for longer time periods, than others. It is not just individuals who cannot be assigned to a specific labour practice. Neither can organizations.

Case study 3: labour practices in a voluntary sports organization

Just as individuals engage in a diverse repertoire of labour practices, so too do organizations. To see this, consider the example of a voluntary sports organization, such as a children's football club run by volunteers and which is registered as a charity. At first glance, one might believe that there is only one form of labour involved in such an organization, namely formal unpaid labour in the third sector, or what is often termed "formal volunteering" and refers to "giving help through groups, clubs or organizations to benefit other people or the environment" (Low *et al.*, 2008: 11).

In lived practice, however, a much wider array of labour practices is prevalent in such an organization. Here, just a few examples are provided. First, the use of "informal non-monetized labour in organizations" is widespread, which is when help is provided through groups to benefit other people or the environment but the formalities required by the law have not all been fulfilled. In a children's football team, this form of labour is one of the dominant forms of labour used, since although the football coach may have had the required police checks undertaken, this is often not the case for those who give children other than their own a lift to the football matches and take responsibility for caring for them. Similarly, the first-aider will often not have had the required police checks so, again, is engaged in informal non-monetized labour in the organization.

The persistence and survival of this organization, moreover, is premised on unpaid self-provisioning. Indeed, without the football kits being washed, the lifts given to children to football matches by their parents, and so forth, the organization would be unable to undertake its core activity. Neither would it survive without one-to-one non-monetized labour such as other parents giving lifts to children to matches and to training sessions. Some parents, moreover, engage in monetized family labour, paying children for goals scored and giving them their pocket-money for washing and preparing their own football kit. There is also a good deal of paid informal labour or cash-in-hand work in such organizations. Each week, teams hold a raffle during the football match, the proceeds of which do not go "on the books" of the club but rather are used to acquire goods and services (e.g. new footballs, training equipment, end-of-season awards to players).

This organization that superficially appears to be a voluntary organization engaged in not-for-profit activities, moreover, often engages in for-profit activities, which uses the surpluses generated to fund the continuation of the organization. Each year, for example, a summer football camp may be held during the school summer holidays to provide a facility during the day for local children, and the profits will be used to fund the continuation and development of the wider organization, such as paying for training facilities in the winter months. They may also hold "social evenings" for profit-making purposes such as discos.

An organization, therefore, might be classified as a third sector or a private sector organization, but this does not mean that all of the labour practices involved in that organization are of one variety. Any organization uses a multiplicity of labour practices in order to survive and grow. This is similarly the case at a locality level. To start to understand the different participation rates in various labour practices in various localities, as well as how some are more commonly used than others, the fourth case study reports the labour practices used by the inhabitants of an English locality.

Case study 4: labour practices in a North Nottinghamshire locality

How widely and deeply has commodified labour actually spread its tentacles in everyday life in different populations? Are there other labour practices beyond those conducted for profit-motivated monetized exchange in the private sector that persist in everyday life and, if so, what types? And does the prevalence of these other labour practices vary across populations? To answer these questions, a survey was conducted in late 2002 in the English local government area of Bassetlaw in North Nottinghamshire (Williams and Nadin, 2010). Some 120 face-to-face interviews were conducted across the most affluent ward, the middle-ranking ward and the most deprived ward, as classified by the Index of Multiple Deprivation (Department of Communities and Local Government, 2000).

To evaluate the depth of penetration of commodification across the different types of wards, Table 7.2 documents the participation rates of the inhabitants in each labour practice. This shows that only one-fifth (20 per cent) of participants in the deprived community and just half (50 per cent) in the more affluent community had participated in paid formal employment in the private sector over the 12 months prior to interview. Compared with participation in non-exchanged labour (which all respondents conducted over the prior 12 months) and one-to-one non-monetized labour (which three-quarters of respondents in the deprived community and over one-half in the affluent community undertook over the previous year), participation in commodified labour is thus confined to comparatively small pockets of the population.

It is not only engagement in formal paid labour in the private sector that displays variations across these populations; so does participation in other labour practices. Participation rates in all ten labour practices (with the exception of one-to-one non-monetized community labour and informal non-monetized labour in organizations) are higher in the affluent than the deprived ward. In consequence, the inhabitants of the relatively affluent ward can be read as a "work-busy" community more likely to participate in nearly all ten labour practices. The inhabitants of the relatively deprived community, meanwhile, can be seen as "work deprived" in that they are less likely to engage in not only commodified labour but most other labour practices, with the exception of unpaid one-to-one community labour and informal unpaid labour in organizations.

It is not just participation rates that reveal the persistence of a diverse repertoire of labour practices in everyday life. This study also analysed the labour practices households last used to undertake 42 common domestic tasks covering house maintenance, home improvement, housework, making and repairing goods, car maintenance, gardening and caring activities.

Table 7.2 Participation rates in various labour practices: by type of community

% of respondents who in last year participated in:	Deprived area	Middle-ranking area	Affluent area	All three areas
Monetized practices				
Formal paid labour in private sector	20	36	50	35
Formal paid labour in public and third sector	20	25	25	23
Paid informal labour	4	8	10	7
Monetized community labour	10	21	30	20
Monetized family labour	3	4	6	4
Non-monetized practices				
Formal unpaid labour in private sector	0	1	2	1
Formal unpaid labour in public and third sector	15	24	35	25
Informal non-monetized labour in organizations	2	0	0	1
One-to-one non-monetized community labour	72	60	53	62
Non-exchanged labour	100	100	100	100

Williams and Nadin (2010, Table 1)

Table 7.3 Labour practices used to conduct 42 domestic tasks: by type of neighbourhood

% of tasks last conducted using:	Deprived district	Middle-ranking district	Affluent district	All areas
Monetized practices	18	26	29	24
Formal paid labour in private sector	12	18	19	16
Formal paid labour in public and third sector	2	1	1	1
Paid informal labour	3	3	4	4
Monetized community labour	1	3	4	2
Monetized family labour	<1	<1	1	1
Non-monetized practices	82	74	71	76
Formal unpaid labour in private sector	<1	<1	<1	<1
Formal unpaid labour in public and third sector	<1	<1	<1	<1
Informal non-monetized labour in organizations	<1	<1	<1	<1
One-to-one non-monetized community labour	4	2	2	3
Non-exchanged labour	78	71	70	73

Williams and Nadin (2010, Table 3)

As Table 7.3 reveals, just 16 per cent of the 42 common domestic tasks were last conducted using the formal paid labour of private sector organizations. Despite the widespread assumption of a commoditization of domestic services, this survey reveals that even if some groups are outsourcing their domestic workload and/or specific tasks to the commodified realm, the overall penetration of commodified labour into the domestic sphere is relatively shallow in this part of the UK. Indeed, only a small proportion (24 per cent) of tasks were even monetized. The vast majority of activities (76 per cent) were carried out on a non-monetized basis, with some 73 per cent undertaken by household members on an unpaid basis using non-exchanged labour.

There are also significant variations across populations in the repertoire of labour practices employed. Residents living in the affluent ward were more likely to use monetized labour in general, and formal paid labour more particularly, than households in the middle-ranking or deprived communities. In the deprived community, meanwhile, there was a heavier reliance on non-monetized labour practices in general and non-exchanged labour and unpaid one-to-one labour more specifically. In sum, this study reveals the shallow and uneven permeation of commodified labour and the continuing persistence of a multitude of labour practices in daily life in all the populations surveyed.

Conclusions

To move beyond the popular and recurring assumption across academia and beyond that commodification is steadily disembedding social relations, and that its continuing encroachment is inevitable, inescapable and irreversible, this chapter has started to chart the diverse repertoire of labour practices in contemporary societies. To do this, it has first produced an analytical lens for understanding the "multiple labour practices" used in daily life. This transcends the commodified/non-commodified labour dichotomy by viewing multiple labour practices existing along a continuum from wholly commodified labour to wholly non-commodified labour, cross-cut with a further spectrum from non-monetized, through gift exchange and in-kind reciprocal labour, to monetized labour practices. This has resulted in ten loose types of labour practice being identified, representing a borderless continuum, rather than separate practices.

This analytical lens has been then applied to understanding the multiple labour practices used in daily life through four case studies. First, this revealed that tasks cannot be assigned to different labour practices (e.g. it cannot be claimed that cleaning is undertaken as non-exchanged labour and web design as formal paid labour in the private sector). Instead, and taking the example of cooking, it has revealed that any task or activity can be conducted using any of the ten labour practices identified. Just as tasks cannot be assigned to specific labour practices, the second case study revealed that neither can individuals. Instead, in daily life, individuals engage in a repertoire of different labour practices. It is similarly the case with organizations. Just as individuals engage in a diverse range of labour practices, so too do organizations. Contrary to what might be assumed, a voluntary sports organization does not only use unpaid formal volunteering. Instead, a diverse repertoire of labour practices is employed to ensure its continuing persistence and development. To begin to understand the extent and nature of the different labour practices in contemporary societies, a fourth and final case study then analysed their usage in an affluent, middle-ranking and deprived neighbourhood of an English locality. This revealed the limited penetration of the commodified realm. Not only is participation in private sector formal employment found to be confined to small pockets of the population, ranging from 20 per cent of the adult population in the deprived neighbourhood to 50 per cent in the affluent neighbourhood, but formal employment is also rarely used to complete domestic tasks. Indeed, only 16 per cent of the 42 common domestic tasks surveyed were last conducted using formal paid labour employed in the private sector, although this is greater in the affluent than deprived neighbourhood (19 per cent compared with 12 per cent).

Indeed, to see how a diverse array of labour practices persists in contemporary economies, a fairly simple exercise can be undertaken. For example, choose any task (e.g. doing the laundry, tidying a garden, cleaning a computer's hard drive, writing, cutting hair, shopping for food, driving a car). Then consider whether this task can be conducted using each of the ten labour practices identified above. For each task, one might then consider what is the most popular labour practice used to undertake it in the contemporary world and whether there has been a shift over time in the labour practices most commonly used to do this task. The outcome will be very informative about whether in practice there has been a deeper encroachment of commodified labour into our daily life.

Another way of seeing the relatively shallow permeation of commodification in daily life is for readers to break down what they did yesterday into 30-minute segments, to write down the tasks undertaken from when they opened their eyes until when they went to sleep, and classify these according to the ten labour practices discussed in this chapter. This may not only reveal that your daily life has not been entirely commodified, but also highlight the barriers to a hegemonic capitalism where all tasks are conducted in the commodified realm. Indeed, it is worth reflecting on whether all the tasks conducted yesterday could have been undertaken using purely commodified labour (paid formal labour in the private sector). What problems would have been confronted if you had tried to do so? The answers provide a telling insight into the feasibility of a world in which the commodified realm is the only form of labour used and whether it will ever be possible to live in an economy other than one characterized by multifarious labour practices.

In conclusion, the outcome of this chapter has been to begin to outline the limited reach of commodified labour and the persistence of a range of labour practices that are in differing ways, and to varying degrees, non-commodified. This persistence of a repertoire of labour practices in the present opens up the future to alternative ways of organizing and organization beyond capitalist hegemony. If this chapter therefore stimulates further questioning of whether a commodified world is inevitable, and an opening up of the future to alternative possibilities such as those described in this book, then it will have achieved its objective.

Resources

Ertman, M.M. and Williams, J.C. (eds) (2005) *Re-thinking Commodification*. New York: New York University Press.
This edited volume contains case studies of the debates concerning whether to commodify or not and reflects on whether this is an appropriate question to ask. It transcends the idea of whether commodification is good or bad by exploring the quality of the social relationships involved in each form of work in different contexts, including slavery, organ transplants and sex work.

Gibson-Graham, J.K. (1996) *The End of Capitalism (As We Knew It)?: A Feminist Critique of Political Economy*. Oxford: Blackwell.
This volume provides a critical exploration of the breadth and depth of the penetration of capitalism so as to demonstrate the feasibility of alternative futures beyond capitalist hegemony.

Rifkin, J. (1996) *The End of Work: The Decline of the Global Labor Force and the Dawn of a Post-market Era*. New York: G.P. Putnam.
This populist book contains many case studies of how the Western world is moving into a post-capitalist era in which non-capitalist practices are emerging to replace capitalism.

Williams, C.C. (2005) *A Commodified World? Mapping the Limits of Capitalism*. London: Zed Books.
This book seeks to document the extent to which non-commodified practices persist across the world and reveals the geographical and social variations in the hegemony of capitalism. www.WeAreEverywhere. org – this website reports the multifarious activities of groups aligned with the "anti-globalisation"/"anti-capitalist" movement.

References

Bourdieu, P. (2003) *Firing Back: Against the Tyranny of the Market 2*. London: Verso.
Carruthers, B.G. and Babb, S.L. (2000) *Economy/Society: Markets, Meanings and Social Structure*. Thousand Oaks, CA: Pine Forge Press.
Castree, N., Coe, N.M., Ware, K. and Samers, M. (2004) *Spaces of Work: Global Capitalism and the Geographies of Labour*. London: Sage.
Chakrabarty, D. (2000) *Provincializing Europe: Postcolonial Thought and Historical Difference*. Princeton, NJ: Princeton University Press.
Chowdury, S.A. (2007) *Everyday Economic Practices: The 'Hidden Transcripts' of Egyptian Voices*. London: Routledge.
Comelieau, C. (2002) *The Impasse of Modernity*. London: Zed Books.
De Soto, H. (2001) *The Mystery of Capital: Why Capitalism Triumphs in the West and Fails Everywhere Else*. London: Black Swan.
Department of Communities and Local Government (2000) *Index of Multiple Deprivation*. London: Department of Communities and Local Government.
Escobar, A. (2001) 'Culture sits in places: Reflections of globalism and subaltern strategies of localization', *Political Geography*, 20(2): 139–174.
Esteva, G. (1985) 'Beware of participation and development: Metaphor, myth, threat', *Development: Seeds of Change*, 3: 77–79.
Fulcher, J. (2004) *Capitalism: A Very Short Introduction*. Oxford: Oxford University Press.
Fuller, D., Jonas, A.E.G. and Lee, R. (eds) (2010) *Interrogating Alterity: Alternative Economic Practices and Political Spaces*. Aldershot: Ashgate.

Gibson-Graham, J.K. (1996) *The End of Capitalism (As We Knew It)?: A Feminist Critique of Political Economy.* Oxford: Blackwell.

Gibson-Graham, J.K. (2006) *A Post-Capitalist Politics.* Minneapolis: University of Minnesota Press.

Gibson-Graham, J.K. (2008) 'Diverse economies: Performative practices for "other worlds" ', *Progress in Human Geography,* 32(5): 613–632.

Glucksmann, M. (1995) 'Why work? Gender and the total social organisation of labour', *Gender, Work and Organisation,* 2(2): 63–75.

Glucksmann, M. (2005) 'Shifting boundaries and interconnections: Extending the "total social organisation of labour" ', *The Sociological Review,* 53(2): 19–36.

Gough, I. (2000) *Global Capital, Human Needs and Social Policies.* Basingstoke: Palgrave.

Gudeman, S. (2001) *The Anthropology of Economy.* Oxford: Blackwell.

Harvey, D. (2000) *Spaces of Hope.* Edinburgh: Edinburgh University Press.

ILO (2002) *Decent Work and the Informal Economy.* Geneva: International Labour Organization.

Kovel, J. (2002) *The Enemy of Nature: The End of Capitalism or the End of the World?* London: Zed Books.

Leyshon, A., Lee, R. and Williams, C.C. (eds) (2003) *Alternative Economic Spaces.* London: Sage.

Low, N., Butt, S., Ellis Paine, A. and Davis Smith, J. (2008) *Helping Out: A National Survey of Volunteering and Charitable Giving.* London: Office of the Third Sector.

Rifkin, J. (2000) *The Age of Access.* Harmondsworth: Penguin.

Round, J., Williams, C.C. and Rodgers, P. (2008a) 'Everyday tactics and spaces of power: The role of informal economies in Ukraine', *Social and Cultural Geography,* 9(1): 171–185.

Round, J., Williams, C.C. and Rodgers, P. (2008b) 'Corruption in the post-Soviet workplace: The experiences of recent graduates in contemporary Ukraine', *Work, Employment & Society,* 22(1): 149–166.

Ruskola, T. (2005) 'Home Economics: What is the difference between a family and a corporation?', in M. Ertman and J.C. Williams (eds) *Rethinking Commodification: Cases and Readings in Law and Culture.* New York: New York University Press, 324–341.

Samers, M. (2005) 'The myopia of "diverse economies", or a critique of the "informal economy"', *Antipode,* 37(5): 875–886.

Scott, A.J. (2001) 'Capitalism, cities and the production of symbolic forms', *Transactions of the Institute of British Geographers,* NS 26(1): 11–23.

Shevchenko, O. (2009) *Crisis and the Everyday in Postsocialist Moscow.* Indianapolis: Indiana University Press.

Shutt, H. (2010) *Beyond the Profits System: Possibilities for a Post-capitalist Era.* London: Zed Books.

Slater, D. and Tonkiss, F. (2001) *Market Society: Markets and Modern Social Theory.* Cambridge: Polity.

Smith, A. (2007) 'Articulating neoliberalism: Diverse economies and everyday life in "postsocialist" cities', in H. Leitner, J. Peck and E.S. Sheppard (eds) *Contesting Neo-liberalism: Urban Frontiers.* London: Guildford Press, 204–222.

Smith, A. (2010) 'Informal work in the diverse economies of "post-socialist" Europe', in E. Marcelli, C.C. Williams and P. Joassart (eds) *Informal Work in Developed Nations.* London: Routledge, 47–65.

Smith, A. and Stenning, A. (2006) 'Beyond household economies: Articulations and spaces of economic practice in postsocialism', *Progress in Human Geography,* 30(1): 1–14.

St Martin, K. (2005) 'Mapping economic diversity in the First World', *Environment and Planning A,* 37: 959–979.

Taylor, R.F. (2004) 'Extending conceptual boundaries: Work, voluntary work and employment', *Work, Employment & Society,* 18(1): 29–49.

Watts, M. (1999) 'Commodities', in P. Cloke, P. Crang and M. Goodwin (eds) *Introducing Human Geographies.* London: Arnold, 305–315.

Whitson, R. (2007) 'Hidden struggles: Spaces of power and resistance in informal work in urban Argentina', *Environment and Planning A,* 39: 2916–2934.

Williams, C.C. (2002) 'A critical evaluation of the commodification thesis', *The Sociological Review,* 50(4): 525–542.

Williams, C.C. (2003) 'Evaluating the penetration of the commodity economy', *Futures,* 35: 857–868.

Williams, C.C. (2004) 'The myth of marketization: An evaluation of the persistence of non-market activities in advanced economies', *International Sociology,* 19(4): 437–449.

Williams, C.C. (2005) *A Commodified World? Mapping the Limits of Capitalism.* London: Zed Books.

Williams, C.C. (2009) 'Formal and informal employment in Europe: Beyond dualistic representations', *European Urban and Regional Studies,* 16(2): 147–159.

Williams, C.C. (2010) 'Beyond the market/non-market divide: A total social organisation of labour approach', *International Journal of Social Economics*, 37(6): 402–414.

Williams, C.C. (2011a) 'Geographical variations in the nature of community engagement: A total social organisation of labour approach', *Community Development Journal*, 46(2): 213–228.

Williams, C.C. (2011b) 'Socio-spatial variations in community self-help: A total social organisation of labour perspective', *Social Policy and Society*, 10(3): 365–378.

Williams, C.C. and Nadin, S. (2010) 'Rethinking the commercialisation of everyday life: A "whole economy" perspective', *Foresight*, 12(6): 55–68.

Williams, C.C., Nadin, S., Rodgers, P., Round, J. and Windebank, J. (2011) 'Beyond the formal/informal labour dualism: Mapping the social organization of labour in Moscow', *Sociological Research On-Line*, 16(1). Available online at www.socresonline.org.uk/16/1/13html

Williams, J.C. and Zelizer, V.A. (2005) 'To commodify or not to commodify: That is not the question', in M. Ertman and J.C. Williams (eds) *Rethinking Commodification: Cases and Readings in Law and Culture*. New York: New York University Press.

Zelizer, V. (2005) *The Purchase of Intimacy*. Princeton, NJ: Princeton University Press.

Zelizer, V. (2011) *Economic Lives: How Culture Shapes the Economy*. Princeton, NJ: Princeton University Press.

8

Family and household reproduction

Karen Dale

Home is a name, a word, it is a strong one; stronger than magician ever spoke, or spirit ever answered to, in the strongest conjuration

Charles Dickens

There is nothing like staying at home for real comfort

Jane Austen

Going home must be like going to render an account

Joseph Conrad

Where is 'home'? What is 'home'?

'Home is where the heart is', as the saying goes. It might evoke images of love, a comfortable fireside, leisure . . . or maybe family conflict, poverty or domestic violence. Whatever emotions it stirs up, you are probably asking just how relevant is the home in the context of this book, what does it have to do with alternative organization? Why bother thinking about or changing the home at all?

You are not alone! In writing about the home I have come up against lack of interest and even hostility from many academics – after all, they (we!) often come 'to work' to avoid those domestic issues. The political significance of the home lies exactly in this indifference and its taken-for-granted everydayness – we don't question it, challenge it or change it; indeed, by and large, we don't even recognize its importance in the reproduction of dominant power relations in society.

In this chapter I argue that unless we address the relations of the home, we will not be able to find alternative ways of living and organizing. I explore how the home is far from a non-organized backstage, and argue that the way the home is managed contributes to the reproduction of class and gender relations, and of capitalism itself as the dominant 'mode of organizing' in contemporary society. Just as management within work organizations is not neutral, but advances the interests of certain groups and values, so too 'household management' is political as well as personal.

Recognizing the significance of the everyday domestic world is the starting point to being able to develop alternative ways of living. To this end, the chapter looks first at how reproductive and household work have been devalued, and how the household has been ideologically separated from the 'spheres' of paid employment and 'public' life and with what consequences. I then challenge this separation, arguing that organization and management pervade the household, although this is rarely recognized. I look at the historical development of household management techniques, which has been ignored in most management history. I also argue that the household, far from being external to politics and the economy, is central to the flexible adaptation and reproduction of capitalist relations. Finally, I look at some alternatives, turning historically to the 'material feminists' of the nineteenth century and their plans for kitchenless houses and the socialization of housework, and then looking at contemporary co-housing projects as a way of challenging and changing our assumptions about how we organize our home lives.

The politics of reproduction and the construction of 'separate spheres'

Production – the process of producing goods and services, and the economic arrangements, technologies and labour that are involved in this – is placed centre stage in much analysis of alternative forms of organizing, especially in alternatives to capitalism where the relations of production are seen as a principal source of exploitation and power inequalities. This is reflected in the number of chapters in this book which take this as their starting point. In this chapter, however, I want to draw attention to the equally significant need for alternatives to current forms of reproductive labour and, further, to argue that productive and reproductive labour are intertwined so intimately that any form of alternative which is going to produce meaningful change has to involve both.

As we will see, 'reproduction' has a number of meanings, although it is mainly associated with childbirth and childcare. Because of this, it is frequently dismissed as 'biological', 'natural' and assumed not to be 'socially' or 'culturally' organized (as production is seen to be) and thus not open to political change. Even feminist thought and action have been dominated by a focus on changing women's status and rights in employment and law. Feminism has mainly seen domestic and reproductive labour as a barrier to equality from which women should be liberated, rather than considering the need for wholesale transformation of the reproductive 'sphere' and its relationship with economic structures and cultural norms.

One writer who has challenged this and drawn attention to the 'politics of reproduction' is Mary O'Brien (1981). Her analysis of how reproductive labour has been devalued in practice and theory has a bearing on alternative forms of organizing in two ways: in its relations to production and to property. First, O'Brien addresses the ways in which reproduction has been dismissed as 'natural'. This means that women's role in reproduction is devalued, and only labour associated with men and the 'public' world is recognized as meaningful or creative. She argues that throughout history, in male-dominated views of the world, 'children evidently arrive without any theoretically important assistance from their mothers, so that the mediative nature of labour and the formation of female reproductive consciousness remain unanalysed. In fact, of course, children are the product of labour' (1981: 31).

Second, O'Brien locates the characteristics of property relations within this gendered separation around reproduction: 'the family has amongst its functions the care for biological and emotional life via the activities of women, on the one hand; on the other hand, it protects the family's material wealth via the proprietorial activities of men' (1981: 32). This latter is sustained through laws of inheritance and property ownership which protect patriarchy.

Within societies where property and power are passed down the generations from father to son, there is a greater need for men to secure and establish their *continuous* part in reproduction. Women are clearly *biologically* involved in reproduction from start to finish, through pregnancy and birth, but this has to be established for men through the *social* structure of the family. O'Brien (1981: 60) describes this as the 'privatization' of women and children within a clear family structure, which separates women from productive labour that is socially and economically valued, and from access to property relations. In Marilyn French's classic feminist novel *The Women's Room* (1977), the central character describes her privatized situation as a woman: 'She felt bought and paid for, and it was all of a piece; the house, the furniture, she, all were his, it said so on some piece of paper' (1977: 168). The nineteenth and early twentieth centuries saw the overt struggle of women in many western societies against these limitations on property ownership. However, economic disadvantage and cultural norms still leave women highly disadvantaged in access to property despite being legally 'equal'.

Meanwhile, the association of women with reproductive labour, and the privatization of this within the home, has led to an uneven division of labour between the genders and between productive and reproductive labour. Since reproductive and domestic labour is excluded from economic relations, it becomes hidden. 'Work' comes to be conflated with 'paid employment', and the home associated with leisure and rest from employment. The labour which goes into the household is forgotten and devalued, both in status and in real economic terms. Feminists have been active in trying to raise awareness of the political significance of domestic work. Reproduction is not simply 'natural', but is economically crucial. The workforce that is necessary for private and state wealth is reproduced within the family. This is both through producing the children who become the next generation of employees and through the daily production of food, shelter and other aspects of care which enable workers to continue to expend their energies within the formal economy. Feminists in the 1970s called for the recognition of this hidden labour in the same economic terms as other labour with demands for 'wages for housework'. A feminist song expresses this point:

> I'm not your little woman,
> your sweetheart or your dear,
> I'm a wage slave without wages,
> I'm a maintenance engineer
>   (in Hayden, 2002: 121).

Ultimately this demand failed. Moreover, the family, and women's unpaid labour within it, continues to be the 'fall-back' position whenever there are societal failures or state withdrawal of welfare support for children, the elderly, disabled and ill (see Williams' chapter in this volume).

Society has tended to grant more status to men who are able to support their family without their wives' employment, although this has differed over time and between classes. However, economic reality means that the majority of women do participate in the labour market. Yet their participation is often stigmatized as different from that of men, due to part-time work and periods of time spent out of employment in full-time household labour or even for a minimum period for maternity leave. Meanwhile, women still carry an unequal weight of reproductive and domestic labour in addition to their paid work. This has become known as the 'dual burden' or 'second shift', and is illustrated in Table 8.1.

Table 8.1 Paid and unpaid work amongst couples with a child under 5, 1999, UK

| Family type | Dual-earner | | | Dual-earner | | | Single (male) earner | | |
| | Woman full time | | | Woman part time | | | Woman housewife | | |
	Man	Woman	Couple	Man	Woman	Couple	Man	Woman	Couple
Paid work hours per week	34.3	24.5	58.8	34.3	18.9	53.2	34.3	2.8	37.1
Unpaid work hours per week	21.7	51.8	73.5	21.7	49.1	70.8	21.7	49.5	71.2
Total hours worked per week	56	76.3	132.3	56	68	124	56	52.3	108.3

Derived from OECD Employment Outlook 2001, after data supplied by K. Fisher, Essex University (Gray, 2003: 30)

OR

| Family type | Dual-earner | | | Dual-earner | | | Single (male) earner | | |
| | Woman full time | | | Woman part time | | | Woman housewife | | |
	Man	Woman	Couple	Man	Woman	Couple	Man	Woman	Couple
Paid work hours per week	34.3	24.5	58.8	34.3	18.9	53.2	34.3	2.8	37.1
Unpaid work hours per week	21.7	51.8	73.5	21.7	49.1	70.8	21.7	49.5	71.2
Total hours worked per week	56	76.3	132.3	56	68	124	56	52.3	108.3

Derived from OECD Employment Outlook 2001, after data supplied by K. Fisher, Essex University (Gray, 2003: 30)

Not only do women do more housework than men and not get paid for it, their unequal burden in housework affects the wages they receive in employment. Hersch and Stratton (2002), using data from the National Survey of Families and Households in the USA, conclude that housework has a negative effect on women's wages, whatever their marital status. Where women participate in the labour market they continue to be marked by their unequal relationship to reproductive labour. Phillips and Taylor's classic work on the sex stereotyping of skills argues that 'Skill definitions are saturated with sexual bias. . . . Women workers carry into the workplace their status as subordinate individuals, and this status comes to define the value of the work they do' (1980: 79). Where paid jobs use the skills usually associated with reproductive labour, such as cleaning, sewing, caring and cooking, they are generally some of the lowest paid and lowest status within the economy. This devaluing of skills associated with women's role in the domestic sphere is given a global slant when linked with corporations seeking new sources of cheap and replaceable labour. Sharpston gives an example from Morocco where 'in six weeks, girls (who may not be literate) are taught the assembly under magnification of memory planes for computers – this is virtually darning with copper wire, and sewing is a traditional Moroccan skill' (1976: 334).

Thus there is a global dimension to the politics of reproduction. Within western countries, reproduction has historically been kept *outside* formal economic relations. Yet on a global scale we can see that even where reproductive labour is brought into the economy as waged labour this does not have simple benefits for the position of women. For example, half of the world's 120 million legal and illegal migrants are women, and this is predominantly made up of millions of poor women who leave their families to fill the 'care deficit' of westernized countries, in personal services such as cleaners and nannies (Ehrenreich and Hochschild, 2003).

Rowena Bautista's account is typical:

> [She] left a village in the Philippines to work as a domestic in Washington DC – one of about 800,000 legal household workers (plus armies of illegal workers). In her basement room she has photos of four children, two of her own whom she has left behind and two of her American charges to whom she has to some extent transferred her love and care. She left her own children in the care of their grandmother five years ago when the youngest, Clinton, was only three: she could find no work to provide for them. The children's grandmother is herself so hard-pressed that she works as a teacher from 7am to 9pm each day, so Rowena has hired a local woman to cook, clean and care for the family in her long absence. (In her turn, that woman leaves her own child in the care of a very elderly grandmother). Rowena hasn't managed to get home to the Philippines for the last two Christmases, but the family relies on the money she sends. Rowena calls the American child she tends 'my baby'. She says: 'I give Noa what I can't give my own children'. Last time she saw her own son, he turned away from her, asking resentfully: 'Why did you come back?'
>
> *(Toynbee, 2003)*

One way in which this 'politics of reproduction' is reinforced is through the ideology of 'separate spheres' between 'home' and 'work' or between the 'private' and 'public' aspects of social life. Alexis de Tocqueville reported in his *Democracy in America* (1840: 101) on the position of women, saying that 'the inexorable opinion of the public carefully circumscribes [her] within the narrow circle of domestic interests and duties and forbids her to step beyond it.' Despite significant changes in women's employment and roles in society, the ideology of 'separate spheres' remains powerful.

The idea of 'separate spheres' is influential because it expresses a cultural assumption and preference. Even though everyday life does not easily conform to it, it still has material effects because it expresses a view that this is how social life should and could be. Despite it being a metaphor, much effort goes on in society to maintain these supposed boundaries. The metaphor of a 'sphere' has a constraining and limiting sense to it, as de Tocqueville noted, yet this applies to women and not men, who easily straddle both public and private domains.

The separation of spheres can be traced to the Industrial Revolution, when men's and women's occupations and roles became more distinct. Fredrich Engels examined it in his book *The Origin of the Family, Private Property and the State* (1884). He links the effect this public – private split had in changes in the control of space: 'With . . . the single monogamous family . . . household management lost its public character. . . . It became a *private service*' (1972: 137).

Thus the other side of the 'dual burden' of housework/employment for the employed woman is the 'problem with no name' for the full-time housewife, as described by Betty Friedan in her influential *The Feminine Mystique* (1963). She articulated the experience felt by many isolated housewives:

The problem lay buried, unspoken, for many years in the minds of American women. It was a strange stirring, a sense of dissatisfaction, a yearning that women suffered in the middle of the 20th century in the United States. Each suburban wife struggled with it alone. As she made the beds, shopped for groceries . . . she was afraid to ask even of herself the silent question – 'Is this all?'

(1963: 15)

As Friedan describes it, the problem is not just economic and social, but also spatial. The aspirational home in the USA, and many other westernized societies, is the single-family home. These have been predominantly developed in suburban residential enclaves: they make concrete the ideals of private life, away from the urban problems of the city. But, at the same time, they isolate the housewife away from public facilities and traditional community. Inside, the architecture is 'filled with gender stereotypes, since houses provide settings for women and girls to be effective social status type achievers, desirable sex objects, and skillful domestic servants, and for men and boys to be executive breadwinners, successful home handymen, and adept car mechanics' (Hayden, 2002: 33–34). In this way, the ideology of the separate spheres is built in material form. We only have to think of the mythology of the masculine space of the garden shed, frequently drawn upon in popular culture, or the abiding feminization of the kitchen and bedroom within the social imaginary.

Calculating selves and calculable spaces: how household management reproduces social structures

The power of the 'separate spheres' ideology means that today the home and management or organization are seen as two distinct and separate arenas of social life. However, as I have argued above, this is a failure of historical understanding, and might even be said to be a form of institutionalized discrimination, stemming from the development of the separation of paid employment from the home which has occurred post-Industrial Revolution. The home came to be seen as a privatized, purely domestic, sphere of family life and associated with a devalued, gendered division of labour. However, when we take a broader historical perspective, we can see that the household has been central to the development of many management and accounting techniques which are today assumed to be purely related to the development of industrial organization and professional management. And when we look to today, we can also see that organization and management pervade the supposed 'private' home and, as they do so, they facilitate the reproduction of relations of class and gender, and the continuation of capitalist structures.

The modern word 'economics' comes from the Ancient Greek words *oikos* meaning dwelling and *nomos* meaning laws or management. This refers to the careful administration of the home and its goods in order to provide for the whole household. In this context, the household was broader than the modern idea of family, and was concerned with both managing property and material possessions, and with the organization of all the people involved in the household. 'Management' is typically seen as deriving etymologically from the Italian *maneggiare*, horse-handling, linked to the Latin *manus* for hand. However, it also has roots in the household economy, which are often forgotten, from the French *mesnagement*, later *ménager*, related to estate management and housekeeping.

In fact, if we look at the household in England in medieval times, we can see the beginnings of coherent managerial and accounting techniques. At this time, the household was the unit of state taxation and economic policy: a key site of economic and social relations which facilitated the development of mercantile capitalism. During the fourteenth century, within the propertied classes of gentry and merchants, there was a widespread use of the household account book, many of which survive to this day and provide an insight into these practices. These households employed accounts clerks to keep records and take responsibility for the control of the household resources. The practices and the ideology of household management are transmitted through a number of 'how to' texts. These books, such as *Walter of Henley's Husbandry* (1276, 1971), present household management as a way of preventing misfortune and of gaining control over the world. In order to do this, all the lands and products of the household have to be made measurable and comparable.

Accounting is a way of achieving this, through making individuals, objects and organizations more visible, and therefore governable:

> Far from being neutral devices for mirroring the social world, the calculative technologies of accountancy are complex machines for representing and intervening in social and economic life. Along with allied expertises, the creation of calculating selves and calculable spaces enables a normalization of individual lives that is cast in financial terms. The visibility conferred on the calculating self who occupies a specific locale within a loosely assembled network of calculable spaces is intrinsically linked to norms of financial performance. Ways of organizing and ways of calculating have developed hand in hand.
>
> *(Miller, 1992: 78–79)*

And the relations of the household and reproduction are at the centre of these, not in some 'separate sphere'.

From this brief snapshot we can see the household was important in the development of managerial and accounting techniques, and also an unacknowledged feature of the development of mercantile capitalism as a forerunner of industrial capitalism. However, this is not simply an obscured and forgotten aspect of dusty history. The home continued after the Industrial Revolution to be a significant site for the reproduction of capitalist relations, and it does so to this day. I would argue that this is important because it allows for a degree of flexibility in the way in which capitalism can adapt to changing social and cultural conditions. This means that any forms of alternative organizing cannot afford to ignore the home, because it is already part of wider economic and political relations.

The house, then, has long been a central part of economic and social structures, where market, management and organization permeate what appear to be private and privatized everyday lives, but this is generally forgotten because of the pervasive influence of the image of the home as haven, and as a 'separate sphere'. The places that we live in and through have a very powerful effect on us, as we construct our day-to-day habits through their routes and routines. Yet we tend to take our homes for granted, commonly seeing them as an expression of freedom of choice, of taste, of personal history and an expression of lifestyle and identity. Thus, the spaces of the home and its organization tie us into particular ways of living in the world, although these are implicit and embodied.

From the time of the Industrial Revolution, 'home' was spatially separated from the workplace. But rather than being the antithesis of public life, the home remained an integral part of it, requiring just as careful management as did commercial ventures:

> the house and its mistress in fact served as a significant adjunct to a man's business endeavors. Whereas husbands earned the money, wives had the important task of administering the funds to acquire or maintain social and political status. Running the

middle-class household, which by definition included at least one servant, was an exercise in class management.

(Langland, 1992: 291)

with the increase of wealth from the
reasingly dependent on the manipula-
e was not sufficient for social status; a
equired, which marked out who was
mid-1900s an increase in manuals on
most famous of which is *Mrs Beeton's*
vas the centre of the reproduction of
this ideological and material labour,
ngements of everyday life in the right
y in control of this domestic stage; as
!006: 1). Despite this, the dominant
vity and dependence, rather than as

twentieth century, we can again see
nd social relations. With a growing
oods, companies required workers to
he engine of capitalism. The home
the 1920s, manufacturers turned to
r large-scale hotels and restaurants.
t fitted with an ideology of 'labour-
m' exacerbated by the effects of war-
servants into jobs in the growing
e in female participation in employ-

lian Gilbreth, were central to these
deologues of the antifeminist, pro-
derick applied F.W. Taylor's ideas of
hold Engineering (1920), and popular-
old consumption in her *Selling Mrs*

for corporations and both sat on the
planning committee for President Hoover's 'Conference on Home Building and Home
Ownership' (1931), which developed the political strategy that if all families were encouraged
to have their own home, this would produce thrift and civil harmony and as a result, a docile
populace. Those who have a vested interest through ownership (even mortgaged!) are much
less likely to challenge or damage those economic and social structures which seem to promise
them this desired lifestyle. Even further, as fuel to the capitalist machine, greater consumption
could be achieved by each nuclear family in its own individual home. A private, owner-
occupied dwelling became the ideal to which people should aspire.

All aspects of house construction, furnishings and decoration became a prime vehicle for
corporate involvement and profit. The suburban house could be mass produced by industrial
methods, cheap for builders to construct and to reap large profits from the desires of the
population to gain the status of 'homeowners' and the convenience of modern dwellings.
Houses were deliberately designed to maximize consumption. During the 1930s, a competition for 'The House for Modern Living' was sponsored by *Architectural Forum* and General

Electric. It celebrated the nuclear family and demonstrated the centrality of electricity to their lives: the winner incorporated 32 electrical appliances from GE in its design (Hayden, 2002: 148–149).

In the UK, too, the design of new estate houses in the 1930s and the spatial organization of the estate itself had an effect on the organization of the household, reinforcing the separation of domestic and work spheres, and the differentiation between the labour of husband and wife. For example, the designer of houses in Salford, UK argued that kitchens should face south, since 'the housewife spends nine hours in the scullery for one she spends in the living room' (Glucksmann, 2000: 142). Glucksmann comments that

> with the enhanced status of the housewife [as a symbol of the success and status of the working husband], the physical layout and equipment of houses assumed a new importance: they had to be modern, efficient and hygienic, facilitating the wife's duties as scientific household manager.
>
> *(2000: 142)*

Yet in Glucksmann's (2000) portrayal of the lives of women in the textile industry in Lancashire, we gain a glimpse of a possible alternative: communal domestic labour. The women's accounts show how they continued to use the municipal wash-house for laundry, ironing and bathing, often three times a week, until it was closed down:

> You used to book about 6 o'clock. You'd go home and get your washing the night before all ready in bundles, didn't we, your woollens, your whites, your coloureds. . . . And you watched my washing while I'd go and have a bath and we used to watch their washing while they went to have a bath.
>
> *(2000: 59–60)*

However, privatized housekeeping and facilities were, with the influence of corporate power, imposed as the norm. In Salford, there was a struggle over the provision of communal facilities. Feminist Labour Councillor, Harriet Mitchell, tried to pressure for municipal wash-houses on the new estates, but her critics derided her by claiming: 'Mrs Mitchell would go as far as to omit wash boilers and ovens too – from all future corporation estates, so that communal arrangements for cooking as well as washing may become a matter of course' (Glucksmann, 2000: 142). As we shall see in looking at the work of the material feminists, far from being an extreme way of thinking this might have provided many opportunities for alternative organization of gender and class, but unfortunately she was swimming against the tide of popular desire and corporate marketing for the most up-to-date technological conveniences which could be shown off in the setting of one's own home.

This pattern of privatized domestic consumption continues in the modern phenomenon of interior design and renovation projects. The processes involved in the creation of a 'beautiful home' influence a huge market. For example, in a Mintel study on the market for kitchen furniture (2007), 37 per cent of 25,000 people agreed that they were always looking for new ideas to improve their home. A homeowner, quoted in a UK home interest magazine, comments that they 'enjoy de-cluttering and starting again, so we were really keen to find our next home, and my next decorating project' (*25 Beautiful Homes*, November 2007: 93). As Lefebvre says, 'change is programmed: obsolescence is planned. Production anticipates reproduction; production produces change in such a way as to superimpose the impression of speed onto that of monotony' (1987: 10). In this way capitalist reproduction of the market is integrated right into the heart of private life, becoming part of the identity project of the 'ideal home' (Dale, 2010).

The idea of the home as an expression of identity is closely bound up with notions of good management and sound investment. Far from a haven in a heartless world, home life is often based on consumer culture, and characterized by a notion of managerialism rooted in economic exchange – the concept of a 'return on capital' for money, time or energy expended on the home, as one homeowner explains: 'This particular area of South London offers great value for money because there's no tube station, and it has transformed itself in the last 5 years into a fantastic upmarket village' (Dale, 2010: 171). The home is also seen as something that is subject to good management skills of the sort used within employment: ' "The best tip I have for a project like this is to plan well, install up-to-date equipment and make your contractors aware of those small but vital details," says William. "We have, and now our household runs like clockwork" ' (ibid.: 168). The home also becomes part of a wider career and life project, as a trainee accountant voices: 'It's all about ladders, I mean, not just work but getting married and having kids, or houses and cars and things like that. You're always trying to make yourself get one stage further on. You have to have something to aim for, don't you?' (Gray, 1994: 496).

Having recognized that the home is imbued with the organized logic of the market, consumption, managerialism, status relations and gender stereotypes, it is time to look at possible alternative forms of domestic organization that might provide ways of challenging and changing these so as to achieve more sustainable and egalitarian ways of living.

Alternative forms of organizing the household

A PhD student once recounted to me how his brother, having found himself temporarily without accommodation, had managed to construct himself a place to sleep in the office he worked in! In some ways, this challenges the typical direction whereby the economic rationale of employment comes to dominate other spaces and times 'outside' paid work (e.g. Massey, 1995; Taylor and Spicer, 2004). However, as a strategy for changing relations between production and reproduction, moving the domestic into the space of employment has limited potential in transforming either – although moving the domestic into public spaces, as Occupy have recently done to protest about the economy, can have an important political effect. Thus alternatives to these forms of social organization tend to be focused on the 'home'. In what follows I describe the ways that nineteenth-century 'material feminists' (Hayden, 1982) reshaped domestic arrangements and compare this with contemporary 'co-housing' initiatives. In different ways, these examples open up possibilities and challenges involved in attempting to live differently.

The 'material feminists': socializing domestic work

During the second half of the nineteenth century a now largely forgotten feminist tradition challenged industrial capitalism with its 'physical separation of household space from public space, and the economic separation of the domestic economy from the political economy' (Hayden, 1982: 1). Hayden has described them as 'material feminists' because 'they dared to define a "grand domestic revolution" in women's material conditions' (ibid.). Their work can still be seen as crucial to alternative organizing today.

The material feminists proposed payment for household labour, along with a complete transformation of the social and spatial design of not only homes but also neighbourhoods and cities. As Hayden comments:

Their insistence that all household labor and child care become social labor was a demand for homelike, nurturing neighbourhoods. By that emphasis, they linked all other aspects of feminist agitation into one continuous economic and spatial struggle undertaken at every scale from the home to the nation. Because their theoretical position represented the logical extension of many ideas about women's autonomy, material feminists exercised influence far beyond their numerical strength.

(1982: 5)

Indeed, they influenced socialist and feminist thinking across the US and Europe.

From about 1860 to 1917, there were a large number of diverse experiments to socialize housework. Melusina Fay Pierce, in a series of articles in the *Atlantic Monthly*, 1868–1869, was one of the first to make an economic critique of domestic labour and to call for 'co-operative housekeeping'. She called for women to group together to perform domestic work collectively, charging their husbands for their labour. This led to her proposals for forms of neighbourhood planning and house design that would facilitate this through communal facilities and 'kitchenless houses'. Although she had little success herself in putting these schemes into practice, her ideas were highly influential on later feminists.

In the 1880s and 1890s, there was an increase in collective and co-operative services. 'Apartment hotels' were built with collective kitchens, laundries and other facilities, but these were primarily for wealthy owners (for example, Haight House in New York and Hotel Kempton in Boston in the 1870s). This did not sit well with more democratic visions, and 'public kitchens' were established. These aimed to provide food for poorer workers, to help against malnutrition, provide more economic use of fuel and other resources, and support women workers who had no time to prepare food (Hayden, 1982: 155). 'Social settlements' were perhaps the most successful of the co-operative housekeeping projects. These were innovative residential communities, which aimed to bring together public kitchens with childcare facilities and co-operative housing. In the US, by 1913 there were 413 settlements in 32 states. One of the best-known projects is Jane Addams' Hull House, created in an immigrant area of Chicago in 1889. As well as food, childcare and housing, it provided evening classes, trade union organizing, social clubs, a public bathhouse and a consumers' co-operative for buying coal (Hayden, 1982: 164). Walter Lippmann, in *A Preface to Politics* (1913), said of Hull House:

A few hundred lives can be changed, and for the rest it is a guide to the imagination. Like all utopias, it cannot succeed, but it may point the way to success. If Hull House is unable to civilize Chicago, it at least shows Chicago and America what a civilization might be like.

(www.spartacus.schoolnet.co.uk/USAhullhouse.htm)

In an unhappy twist, financial problems caused the Hull House Association in Chicago to close after 120 years on the very day that I was writing this. It had continued to operate as a social services agency, providing childcare, job training and housing assistance, even though the original Hull House building, reprieved from demolition when part of the University of Chicago was built in the late 1960s, continues to exist as a museum.

Some of the difficulties in these nineteenth-century experiments with co-operative living forms were the continued divisions between classes, education and ethnicity. Some of these were even reinforced by the middle-class, white women who organized these experiments, and who did not question, or even saw as natural, the use of lower class women to carry out the labouring in their communal kitchens. This is an earlier echo of the contemporary global trade in low-paid care work, and Hayden's comment is relevant to all alternative forms of organizing: 'women can never gain their own liberation from stereotypes of gender at the expense of other women of a lower economic class or another race whom they exploit by paying them low wages to do sex-stereotyped work' (1982: 299).

Nevertheless, these experiments give us an important insight into how assumptions about individualized and privatized domestic arrangements might be challenged. They provide a glimpse of other ideals and alternative possibilities, where nurturing and collective work are socially significant and valued, and where these are put into practice in material and spatial form.

Co-housing: challenging individualized and privatized domestic relations

These experimental alternatives have continued from the times of the material feminists to the present, even though often hidden from mainstream history. A contemporary alternative to the privatized household, which is growing in significance across many countries, is 'co-housing'. This is a form of intentional community: a community set up to achieve a common purpose (see Pitzer, this volume), a term that covers a range of forms including housing co-operatives, alternative communities, communes, permaculture communities and residential land trusts. Co-housing combines private homes with shared facilities, and is organized and managed by its residents through participatory and non-hierarchical decision-making processes. They share a range of activities communally like cooking, dining, child-care, gardening and governance. Like the material feminists, they have common kitchens, dining rooms, laundry and nurseries, as well as facilities such as communal offices, Internet access, guest rooms and recreational amenities. These communities do not usually combine shared employment or a community economy (www.cohousing.org/six_characteristics). Residents often go outside the community to their paid employment, and co-housing usually excludes community businesses, although some do host businesses which are run by individuals or sub-groups within the community.

Two forms of co-housing projects which are growing in popularity are 'eco-villages' (see Cato, this volume) and senior co-housing projects. Eco-villages aim to be small, sustainable communities set up as a lived response against corporate globalization. Senegal is the first country to officially adopt the idea of the eco-village as an alternative development model (Jackson, 2004). Senior co-housing projects provide alternatives to living in an institution or being isolated in private homes in traditional urban arrangements. Co-housing is also seen as a better way of collectively raising children, giving women an alternative to the isolation of sole childcare responsibility or daycare institutions.

Co-housing is often seen as originating in Denmark in the 1970s, with the Tynggarden project. This consisted of six courtyards with about 15 families in each. Each family gave up 10 per cent of its interior space to create a shared neighbourhood centre, which contained mailboxes, laundry equipment, community kitchen, space for residents' activities and childcare. But its roots are earlier and more diverse, as Pitzer's chapter in this volume on communes and intentional communities shows.

One of the longest running co-housing communities in the UK is the Postlip Community in the Cotswolds, based within a shared manor house since 1968. A more recent example of a 'brownfield', inner city eco-village is the Beddington Zero Emissions Development, or BedZED, in south London, UK. The project was initiated by the Peabody Trust, a large housing association, along with an environmental organization called BioRegional. There are 82 living units with passive solar design, super-insulation and triple-glazed windows, eliminating the need for central heating, as well as water-saving appliances and rain collection. Energy needs are provided by an on-site power plant using waste timber. Figures show enormous energy savings relative to the average UK figures – 56 per cent on water consumption and 55–65 per cent on electricity bills. A 'green transport plan' with the support of the local community promotes walking, cycling, and a car pool with electric vehicles charged by on-site photovoltaic cells, and good public transport links. In addition, residents have a link to a local organic farmer, while many grow their own food and compost their waste (Jackson, 2004). This is in stark contrast to the impetus for ever greater consumption which as we have seen is designed into conventional private family housing.

Close to where I live is Lancaster Co-housing (http://lancastercohousing.org.uk/), which provides an example of a greenfield project, based in the village of Halton in Lancashire, UK, on the banks of the River Lune. It is currently at the stage of building houses and communal facilities, having been created in 2005. It aims to be a fully integrated, intergenerational community, with a range of private homes from one-bed flats to three-bed houses, all built to high environmental standards using the Passivhaus ultra-low energy system, with south-facing aspect, high levels of insulation and heat recovery systems. It includes a community hydroelectric scheme developed in collaboration with the local village and is thought to be the first 'district heating system' in the UK to combine biomass and solar thermal energy sources. This means that instead of each house having its own boiler, there is a single, highly efficient boiler powered by woodchip (biomass). This is supplemented by solar thermal collectors on south-facing roofs, which provide domestic hot water. The site contains an old mill building, to be refurbished as work space for members. This links to a desire to reduce car use, with the majority of members undertaking not to own a car and the pedestrianization of the whole community.

One of the most important features of the Lancaster co-housing project is a common house, with living, dining and cooking areas for the use of all residents. It includes guest accommodation, a playroom and laundry room. The aim is that the communal areas come to feel like an extension of private homes, although it is recognized that this is not necessarily easy, as people have very different expectations as to how spaces will be used ('A Community Built On Ecological Values' at http://lancastercohousing.org.uk/Documents/Residents%20 Handbook). Although people have freedom as to what they can do in their private homes, this sort of living creates greater awareness of how privatized actions might affect the whole community, such as using energy-inefficient appliances or chemicals which might affect local wildlife.

The co-housing movement recognizes the need for time and commitment to community processes: not always easy given the time-poverty and the expectation of long working hours within contemporary culture. Lancaster Co-housing, for example, is set up as a company limited by guarantee as a non-profit-making body, with rights and responsibilities of members and a management committee. The community is looking to develop a method of consensual decision making (see e.g. www.seedsforchange.org.uk/fresources). A draft proposal suggests that members over the age of 14 are involved in shared maintenance tasks. Everyone is expected to give eight hours a month to communal activities. This includes activities such as cooking and cleaning for the planned communal meals; annual 'workdays' for cleaning the common house and gardening; and the necessary meetings to organize collective living. There has been some debate as to whether these duties can be substituted by money – which is an interesting discussion because it brings in marketized relations through economic exchange rather than the desired alternative communal social relationship, and takes us back to the discussion about the relationship between socially valued paid employment and devalued unpaid household labour. Nevertheless, co-housing has a huge potential to challenge the norms that have developed around privatized domestic arrangements, and how these are integrated with capitalist structures. As an alternative, it is a step towards collective, participatory, sustainable living.

Conclusions and challenges

In this chapter I have sought to recover the political understanding of the household and reproductive labour. Reproductive and household labour continue to be socially and economically devalued, yet they are just as central to capitalism as the 'public' sphere of production and economics. Indeed, the household has developed in such a way as to be thoroughly imbued with, and incorporated into, capitalism. 'The home' has such an emotional hold on our imaginations that we often find we 'invest' our energies, resources *and identities* into it. In the process, we contribute to the greater individualization and rationalization of social life, re-creating divisions of class, gender and opportunity within our most intimate spaces. In constructing private places that we see as reflecting our identity and taste, we end up consuming ever more in the desire to 'keep up with the Joneses', bolstering corporate profits and damaging the environment. The ideology of the sanctity of the home also contributes to the failure to deal with problems such as poverty, domestic violence and mental illness, where they are literally hidden behind closed doors and become privatized rather than social issues.

This is an area of our lives which we take particularly for granted, and believe to be private and unique to ourselves and our families. By analysing how far the domestic is permeated by social and economic organization, I hope to point towards the need to find alternative ways to organize the household. The alternatives shown by the material feminists and co-housing communities provide some ideas as to how we might do this. They show how we need to rethink our attitudes to our 'home' lives, and the challenges that are involved in community living. They also show us that communitarian *ideology* is not enough, that we have to *materially* change our spaces and places. They pose challenging questions which we need to ask ourselves: Can we let go of our conventional dreams of 'home'? Are we willing to develop different social identities, not based on self-expression through consumption and display? Are we willing to open ourselves, our time and energies to a wider community, not just the nuclear family? Can we let go of the suburban dream and live in mixed communities, where we can care and be cared for, but with the challenges of differences and the labour involved in communication and community building?

These are critical political challenges, for '[t]o advance a theory of everyday life is to elevate lived experience to the status of a critical concept – not merely in order to describe lived experience, but in order to change it' (Kaplan and Ross, 1987: 1). Personal matters are political matters, and the organization of the home reflects political assumptions.

Resources

Co-housing Association of the United States: www.cohousing.org/six_characteristics
The UK Co-housing Network: www.cohousing.org.uk/
Fellowship of Intentional Communities website: www.ic.org/
Hayden, D. (2002) *Redesigning the American Dream*. New York: W.W. Norton and Company.

Jackson, R. (2004) 'The Ecovillage Movement', *Permaculture Magazine*, no. 40, summer: http://files. uniteddiversity.com/Ecovillages_and_Low_Impact_Development/JTRJ_EV-Movement2004.pdf

References

Beeton, I. (2006, 1861) *Mrs Beeton's Household Management*. Ware, Herefordshire: Wordsworth Editions.

Dale, K. (2010) 'Ideal Homes? Managing the Domestic Dream', in P. Hancock and M. Tyler (eds) *The Management of Everyday Life*. Basingstoke: Palgrave Macmillan.

Ehrenreich, B. and Hochschild, A.R. (2003) *Global Woman: Nannies, Maids and Sex Workers in the New Economy*. London: Granta Books.

Engels, F. (1972, 1884) *The Origin of the Family, Private Property and the State*. New York: International Publishers.

French, M. (1977) *The Women's Room*. London: Abacus.

Friedan, B. (1963) *The Feminine Mystique*. New York: W.W. Norton.

Glucksmann, M. (1990) *Women Assemble: Women Workers and the New Industries in Inter-War Britain*. London: Routledge.

Glucksmann, M. (2000) *Cottons and Casuals: The Gendered Organization of Labour in Time and Space*. Durham: sociologypress.

Gray, A. (2003) *Towards A Conceptual Framework for Studying Time and Social Capital*. Families and Social Capital ESRC Research Group. London: South Bank University

Grey, C. (1994) 'Career as a project of the self and labour process discipline', *Sociology* 28.2: 479–497.

Hayden, D. (1982) *The Grand Domestic Revolution*. Cambridge, MA: MIT Press.

Hayden, D. (2002) *Redesigning the American Dream*, New York: W.W. Norton and Company.

Hersch, J. and Stratton, L. (2002) 'Housework and Wages', *Journal of Human Resources*, 37, 1, 217–229.

Jackson, R. (2004) 'The Ecovillage Movement', *Permaculture Magazine*, 40. Available online at http://files. uniteddiversity.com/Ecovillages_and_Low_Impact_Development/JTRJ_EV-Movement2004.pdf

Kaplan, A. and Ross, K. (1987) Introduction, *Yale French Studies*, 73, 1–4.

Langland, E. (1992) 'Nobody's Angels: Domestic Ideology and Middle-class Women in the Victorian Novel', *PMLA*, 107, 2, 290–304.

Lefebvre, H. (1987) 'The Everyday and Everydayness', *Yale French Studies*, 73, 7–11, transl. C. Levich, 'Quotidien et Quotidiennete', from *Encyclopaedia Universalis*.

Lippmann, W. (1913) *A Preface to Politics*. New York: Henry Holt.

Massey, D. (1995) 'Masculinity, Dualisms and High Technology', *Transactions of the Institute of British Geographers*, 20, 4, 487–499.

Miller, P. (1992), 'Accounting and Objectivity: The Invention of Calculating Selves and Calculable Spaces', *Annals of Scholarship*, 9, 1–2, 61–86.

Mintel International Group (2007, August) *Kitchen Furniture – UK*. London: Mintel International Group.

O'Brien, M. (1981) *The Politics of Reproduction*. London: Routledge and Kegan Paul.

Phillips, A. and Taylor, B. (1980) 'Sex and Skill', *Feminist Review*, 6, 1, 79–88.

Sharpsten, M. (1976) 'International Subcontracting', *World Development*, 4, 4.

Taylor, S. and Spicer, A. (2004) 'You Can Checkout Anytime but You Can Never Leave', *Human Relations*, 57, 1, 75–94.

Tocqueville, A. de (1840) *Democracy in America*. London: Saunders and Otley.

Toynbee, P. (2003) 'Mothers for Sale', *Guardian*, 19 July. Available online at http://www.guardian. co.uk/books/2003/jul/19/highereducation.shopping

Walter of Henley (1971, 1276) in D. Oschinsky (ed.), *Walter of Henley and Other Treatises on Estate Management and Accounting*. Oxford: Clarendon Press.

9

Immigrants and immigration

Josiah Heyman, Nicholas Fischer and James Loucky

Introduction

Migration is today, as in the past, a major domain of the social, cultural and political struggle for justice, in which alternative organizations play a central role. The principal regulator of migration is the nation-state, such as the United States Department of Homeland Security, or entities like FRONTEX, a multi-state European agency. Because immigrant[1] advocates often criticize state policies, it is important to emphasize that states often permit or even create or encourage migration, including family reunification, permanent and temporary labor migration, and asylum. Not all state policies are oppressive, but some are. The private sector, and more broadly the world capitalist economy, likewise helps "organize" migration, even encouraging undocumented migration, as we will discuss below. But we can hardly term their activities alternatives to dominant power.[2] Immigrant organizations are also affected by home nation-states, religious organizations, labor organizations and large philanthropic funders, so that it would be naïve to envision "alternative" as being pure, clear and separate.

Alternative organizations in this arena are best defined by their values and the emergent trajectory they embody: (1) valuing human dignity, well-being, and agency for immigrants in the face of state regulation and repression; (2) championing the particular needs of refugees from violence and persecution; and (3) transcending the dehumanizing treatment of immigrants as controlled units of labor in managed migration programs. (For extended discussions of values in immigration debates, see Heyman, 1998a; Ho and Loucky, 2012.)

Alternative immigration organizations confront the crucial opportunities and challenges of the contemporary era. On the one hand, dynamic patterns of movement, social change and cultural mixing offer new goals, values, participants and coalitions, including ones that cut across conventional boundaries of nation-states and race/ethnicity. On the other hand, uncertainties and divisions of nationality, legal status, resources and fluidity challenge immigration organizations. We identify, in particular, divisions between action at the local and national (obviously, not the same) versus cross-national ("transnational") scales, which threaten to reproduce the barriers that immigration promises to overcome. To conceptualize the opportunities and challenges we see in alternative immigration organizing, we present a three-part conceptualization of possible futures: (1) bounded nationalism; (2) cosmopolitanism from above; and (3) cosmopolitanism from below.

Bounded nationalism refers to ideologies of clear, bounded national communities, and laws and practices related to that. Although this is the main basis for stigmas and punitive policies toward immigrants, especially unauthorized ones, it nevertheless affects most immigrant organizations, both in terms of their own identifications with sending countries, and also ways in which their social and political action is channeled toward existing national frames. Cosmopolitanism, in general, is knowledge of, and fellow feeling with, people outside of narrow locales (including, in the modern world, nation-states). Cosmopolitanism from above involves bonds of social practice and values that cut across conventional national boundaries, which expresses the interests of various forms of capital in the international economy, with inputs (including immigrants) and outputs crossing conventional boundaries. It promotes migration but also subordinates migrants, as seen in labor relations. Cosmopolitanism from below expresses the ways that migrants and other non-elites forge new bonds of recognition, solidarity and justice in law, rights and respect across conventional borders.[3] This latter is a fragmented and partial development, with many limitations, but also represents the lasting contribution of alternative immigration organizations to broader understandings of alternative organization.

We begin the chapter by delineating the many dimensions of variation among alternative immigration organizations. Not only does this summarize the main patterns of organizations and approaches, but it offers brief illustrations of diverse entities that help the reader envision the subject matter. We then probe a specific issue, the entanglement of alternative organizations in state legal and administrative structures, which both provide arenas and vocabularies of contestation, but also partial collaboration with dominant power systems. This is exemplified by an extended case study of three immigrant advocacy organizations in France, dealing with immigrant detention and deportation, and the ways in which they use law to struggle for immigrants, but also are caught up in the practices of detention and the boundaries of existing law.

We move next to consider labor. We identify this as a central domain of social justice, specifically because it enables us to begin to distinguish globalization from above – in the ways that large employer interests and state managers guide and exploit migrant workers – from globalization from below – in the ways that workers and communities organize for dignity and a fair share of the social surplus. This provides an opportunity to deepen our concept of globalization from below by examining a real-world case study centered on the global electronics and information industry and immigrant workers. We then conclude by deepening this notion of cosmopolitanism from below as a new path toward the future, an emerging set of values and practices, especially in counterpoint to elite-dominated globalization.

Diverse characteristics of alternative immigration organizations

In what follows, we delineate important features of immigrant organizations, with illustrative examples. To make our presentation efficient, we rely on static types. That facilitates communicating key ideas, but does not fully capture the complexity, hybridity and "processuality" of living organizations. Alternative immigrant organizations tend to cluster around key human values, as described in the introduction. However, even value-orientations are a source of complexity, as some organizations are radical and others reformist, some are focused on advocating only for one immigrant nationality or home region and others are universalist,[4] and so on. Organizations vary considerably in their geographical and social bases, their membership, and the background of their staff or key activists, including whether the core of the organization tends to be immigrants themselves or host society sympathizers. Organizations vary considerably according to their key activities. Among many possible variations, a major distinction is between organizations that mainly provide services or mutual aid and those that mainly advocate and publicly represent.

The variability of kind of activity is often connected to variability of location and scale of action. While organizations often have local bases in areas of immigrant settlement, the importance of national policies tends to create a different spatiality, focused on capital cities and national activities. This is ironic, given the values of alternative organizations, but the transnational dimension of immigration is often hardest to realize, though instances do exist. Often related to kind of activity and sometimes to membership, alternative immigration organizations vary according to their resources, ideological, material and committed personnel. This is partly internal, but it also involves their connections to non-immigrant organizations, including philanthropic funders, labor unions, religious organizations, and so forth, which of course bring various values and commitments with them. A closely related dimension is fields of organizations, which includes counterparts of alternative organizations (e.g., employers, government agencies) as well as coalitions of pro-immigrant organizations.

Many organizations emerge from the immigrant community itself. Others are launched by non-immigrant activists, unions, religious entities, and so forth. This distinction is not neat: organizers sent from outside entities may themselves be immigrants while grass roots immigrant participation may go well beyond an initial, parochial impetus. Among the organizations that emerge from immigrant communities themselves, a common and important phenomenon (see Portes *et al.*, 2011) is immigrant hometown/region associations in the new society, and relatedly local mutual aid, protection and advocacy societies. Local or small entities sometimes merge into federations or other large associations, perhaps national or ethnic alliances, that can have substantial impact.

An important example is the *Frente Indigena de Organizaciones Binacionales* (Indigenous Front of Binational Organizations, FIOB), an alliance of indigenous associations in the United States and Mexico, mainly California, Baja California and Oaxaca (http://fiob.org/; see Fox and Rivera-Salgado 2004). Besides a variety of cultural and language efforts, FIOB has clear political goals, notably the interrelated rights to migrate (broadly, issues entering and inside the United States) and the right to not migrate (broadly, cultural and economic issues in Mexico). In the north, those rights are intricately connected to immigration reform, while the right to stay home hinges on local opportunities that can make migration a matter of choice rather than a forced outcome of poverty. The latter domain addresses equitable price structures for corn, protections from genetic contamination and organic cultivation, as well as programs for reforestation and marketing of artisan and woven products.

Another grassroots pattern of immigrant self-organization is media in the language and/or the cultural orientation of immigrant groups. Spanish-language radio in the United States, for example, helped spark the 2006 immigration rights marches. As the examples of ethnic media and hometown associations suggest, some immigrant-community-rooted organizations are created by or centered on petit bourgeois (small business, labor contractor, etc.) leadership (Griffith, 2012). Likewise, they may be disproportionately male. Of course, exceptions can be found (e.g., working-class women concerned with schools, as documented by Zlolniski (2006)). Such bases mean that immigrant organizations may simultaneously be alternative to the dominant, anti-immigrant or assimilationist order, and yet embody social

Table 9.1 Typological characteristics of immigration organizations

Typological theme	Illustrative organization	Notable characteristics, if any
Immigrant-based organizations	*Frente Indigena de Organizaciones Binacionales*	Indigenous peoples in Mexico (especially Oaxaca) and the United States; transnational
Immigrant-based organizations	Multiple cases summarized	Survey reported in Portes *et al.* (2011); transnational connections and activities in country of origin
Tactics: mass demonstrations	US immigration marches of 2006–2007	
Tactics: rights education and other incremental approaches	Border Network for Human Rights	
Tactics: cultural and artistic expression	Culture Strike	Grassroots, multi-ethnic immigrant organization
Non-immigrant groups organizing immigrants (labor)	Service Employees International Union, Justice for Janitors	Discussed in labor section
Non-immigrant groups organizing immigrants (religious, social movement)	People Acting in Community Together (linked to Catholic Church)	Discussed in labor section
Service providers and advocates (legal representation)	*Ligue des droits de l'homme; Groupe d'Information et de Soutien aux Immigrés*	Discussed in legal strategies section
Service providers and advocates (social services, legal representation)	*Comité inter-mouvements pour l'aide aux déplacés et aux évacués*	Discussed in legal strategies section
Funders	Ford Foundation Close to Home Initiative	Identified and supported human rights groups working inside United States
Coalitions	Border Network for Human Rights; National Immigration Forum	Collaboration between a community-based entity, oriented toward a specific region (US–Mexico border), and an expert advocate-based entity, oriented toward national center
Coalitions	Multiple cases of transnational Maya interactions	Overview in Loucky and LeBaron (2012)
Radicalism	No Borders Network	United Kingdom; rejects borders
Reformism	National Network for Immigrant and Refugee Rights	United States; advocacy for change in US national immigration policy and practice

inequality and power within immigrant communities. Finally, because these organizations begin by emerging from the immigrant community, they often have other agendas (such as hometown associations raising money for sending community health services) before they are drawn into immigrant rights struggles in the new setting.

Immigrants, and the groups that serve them, have many values, goals, needs and interests. While important, rights for unauthorized migrants are but one part of a diverse scene (e.g., to FIOB, indigenous cultural expression is as important as border and migration policy). As a result, alternative immigrant organizations vary widely in their tactics and means of expression, a topic that still awaits comprehensive review. Perhaps the most visible and dramatic mode of action is mass marches, such as those in the United States in 2006 and 2007 (Voss and Bloemeraad, 2011). Much quieter, but perhaps more enduring, is week-by-week, year-by-year training in organization, issues and rights when dealing with government officers, employers, landlords and the public (e.g. Heyman, 2010). Tactics and forms of expression must be suited to specific audiences, agendas and moments in the struggle. For example, in an era in which outsiders are stigmatized in dominant, wealthy societies, seen either as dangerous threats or as backward helots, in need of assimilation, some individuals and alternative immigrant organizations have made considerable progress through artistic expression and public performances (e.g., Culture Strike, http://wordstrike.net/).

Immigrant community-based entities can be contrasted with non-immigrant, activist or expert (e.g., lawyer) staffed organizations. Such entities may serve the needs of communities, at least as sympathizers perceive them, but may not help to develop capacity and autonomy among community members. As immigrants make up increasingly large segments of the working classes of prosperous societies, especially in economically dynamic urban and rural regions, movements for social justice have slowly recognized the need for including immigrants. Notable among the outside organizations that have moved toward engaging immigrants are religious organizations (Hondagenu-Sotelo, 2008)[5] and labor unions. A relevant case study, identifying the possibilities and limitations of non-immigrant organizing of immigrants, is presented later in this chapter, in the section on labor.

An important class of alternative organizations provides specific services and material goods for immigrants, by contrast with organizations that press for social and policy change. As the extended French example later in this chapter narrates, organizations provide legal defense, affirmative legal support (e.g., applications for asylum), and advocacy for improved conditions of detention, removal and release. They also provide housing and shelter, food, health services, non-migration legal representation (e.g., labor rights), language courses and other education, job training, childcare and other assistance for children, support and protection for women, support and protection for LGBT persons, support and protection for the disabled, and so forth. The immigrant condition is often accompanied by other needs and disadvantages, so the role of such service providers is obvious – indeed, need often overwhelms the resources available. Such organizations are often relatively large, in both budgets and paid personnel, but also limited by the specialization that also provides these resources: the daily, compelling call for services can constrain the political capacity and imagination of such organizations. However, practical service provision sometimes does evolve into something more, in providing social and physical spaces for immigrant self-organization and campaigns for justice beyond the immediate and practical.

The agendas of organized funders – large capitalist philanthropies, religious organizations, political parties, labor unions, and so forth – inevitably affect "alternative" immigrant organizations (the word alternative in quotation marks precisely indicates the blurring of that label). Large, personal donors sometimes do also, through fund-raising events, donation campaigns, and boards of directors. Of course, some organizations avoid or simply have not tapped large external funders, but that significantly limits their organizational capacities, in particular because of few or no paid staff, as well as reduced funding of transportation, offices, communications, printing, and so forth. There is no question that funders attempt to shape the organizational forms and political and social goals of immigrant-based or immigrant-serving groups (an example being the Ford Foundation's initiative to identify human rights groups working inside the United States, which ultimately lead to funding the growth and policy engagement expansion of the Border Network for Human Rights, described below; see www. fordfoundation.org/pdfs/library/close_to_home.pdf). At the same time, alternative organizations also sell initiatives and approaches to funders. The Border Network was already deeply grounded in the immigrant community and committed to border enforcement policy change; Ford simply reinforced and amplified this development. Likewise, alternative organizations often maintain a gap or autonomy between real operations and the vision presented to outsiders – not a fraud, but a pattern of managed, partial communication.

The conclusion, then, is that the relation between funders and organizations does involve unequal power, but is not purely one-sided, with agency on both sides. Likewise, funders, organizations and communities may share similar goals, modes of action, discourses, and so forth, so that one cannot say that the relationship must be one of distortion and domination. The agendas of major funders of alternative migration organizations have not been well documented and much is yet to be discovered about main funder themes in recent history, such as human rights, community organization, public policy impact, immigrant integration, and so forth. It seems reasonable to say that funders do not, conspiratorially, bring immigrant organizations into being, but that they are a strong force shaping them once they emerge, consolidate and grow.

Alternative immigration organizations vary considerably according to their wider affiliations: ethno-national, religious, political philosophies and parties, and so forth. Using an important survey of Colombian, Dominican and Mexican immigrant organizations on the US east coast, Portes et al. (2011) characterize some important patterns of organizational form in a particular set of immigrant entities. These are specifically ones formed by immigrants with connections back to their home country, although organizations may also have activities in the new society (they focused on "transnationalism," which is involvement in various ways across borders). They found that, in all cases, people who had been in the United States longer actually participated more in immigrant organizations; that is, transnational bonds persisted over time, at least for the immigrant generation.

However, there were significant differences otherwise between nationalities, which are of interest not just for those specific populations, but because they indicate some important factors shaping immigrant organizations. Mexicans, for example, were poorer, younger, and more likely to be undocumented, though also more closely affiliated with sending country governments (especially province and locality). This resulted in less well-funded, smaller organizations with more emphasis on assistance to hometowns, including indigenous and rural ones. Dominicans and Colombians tended to have larger organizations, based on their older, more prosperous and educated, and legal immigrant community bases. The survey of Portes et al. emphasizes the separate national character of each set of immigrant organizations.

The network character of migration, in which people use kinship and geographic origin connections to decide when, how and where to move, how to obtain housing and work, and how to form social affiliations, means that immigrant association initially tends to be parochial. However, the existential and political issues faced by immigrants are often widely shared. To address such issues, there is power in coalitions and numbers. For example, a single, local immigrant organization may only have a modest political presence, but a cross-geographic coalition can impact many politicians at a national scale. The most difficult but also most important line to cross is that of different national origins, to go from being (say) Mexicans to being advocates for all immigrants, thereby changing the political agenda.

Unifying across diversity is thus an important challenge for immigrant organizations and coalitions. Yet building coalitions is difficult, because of varied bases, styles, resources, leaderships, locations, languages, ideas and goals. Studies of immigrant organization coalition processes and outcomes are thus needed (e.g., Heyman, 2011). For example, an important category of alternative immigration organizations focuses on educating and lobbying key politicians and administrators, and are often located in national capitals. Such expert organizations have knowledge of and connections into core policy processes, but to some extent lack knowledge of on-the-ground issues and goals, and likewise need the legitimacy of immigration-community-based entities themselves. One of us (Heyman) has participated in coalition relations between the Border Network for Human Rights (BNHR, www.bnhr.org; also see Heyman, 2010), an El Paso, Texas and southern New Mexico-based immigrant organization with about 4,000 working-class, mostly Mexican-origin members and a small professional (mostly immigrant) staff, and the National Immigration Forum, a Washington, D.C.-based professional public policy organization (www.immigrationforum.org/) without a specific national-origin affiliation. In general, they have cooperated excellently, with positive outcomes in the policy process. BNHR has provided a clear policy vision about the concerns of border communities, under conditions of intensive immigration and drug enforcement, while the Forum has opened doors of political access in the national Congress and Executive Branch. BNHR policy language has been included in comprehensive immigration reform legislation since 2007, albeit so far unsuccessfully. At the same time, there are hints of underlying tension over the Forum's sensitivity to pragmatic political concerns (i.e., concessions to intensified border enforcement) counterposed to BNHR's stronger stance for reform, rooted in community concerns emerging from their policy-setting General Assembly. In general, however, this periphery – core coalition has been impressively effective, because of balanced strengths and mutual respect.

The coalition just described operates within a *nation-state frame*. But alternative immigration coalitions frequently challenge such boundaries, either consciously or (perhaps more often) simply because of shared values and activities that cut across borders. A special issue of *Practicing Anthropology* (LeBaron and Loucky, 2012; Loucky and LeBaron, 2012) addresses partnerships between organizations in North America and Mesoamerica, especially the Maya. The indigenous peoples of Mesoamerica have particularly strong self-identity and cultural resources for creating and maintaining transnational bonds. These bonds are useful in creating projects in origin communities, involving remittances (resources returned home from new settlement communities) of both funding and knowledge, and providing solidarity in new arrival areas. At the same time, such bonds are buffeted by complex interpretations and delicate interpersonal relations not only within sending and immigrant communities, but also with engaged non-immigrants. Immigrants face several forces of risk and erosion, including arrest and deportation and loss of indigenous identities, cultural content and languages by youth who grow up in the new society (such youth, however, also have new capacities, such as command of modern communications technology). Transnational coalition formation thus is always fragile, a process of communication and exchange that requires participation and reinforcement to survive the gaps of distance and localism and re-nationalization.

Alternative immigration organizations differ according to their approach toward the existing political and administrative process, and more generally their attitudes toward international borders. This may be expressed as the difference between radicalism (in the sense of going to the root of issues) and reformism (in terms of bringing about incremental improvement in the world as we face it), allowing for the reality of greater subtlety and complexity of issues. Migration brings up fundamental questions of bounded territorial spaces, profound economic inequality in those spaces, and asylum from violence and persecution. At the same time, there are innumerable compelling needs for amelioration, such as non-abusive policing, humane detention, and reduction of death and injury in unauthorized border crossing. Such amelioration accepts (perhaps not in the long run, but as an immediate fact) the existing territorial state legal and political system. Radicals and reformists tend to differ in goals, tactics and rhetorics. Perhaps the most important division is between those organizations that operate more or less within the existing nation-state frame and those that articulate a vision of a borderless, universal world. For example, the British NoBorders Network (http://noborders. org.uk/), which calls for universal freedom of movement, tends toward direct protest action aimed at broad changes in public values, whereas the US National Network for Immigrant and Refugee Rights (http://www.nnirr.org/~nnirrorg/drupal/) focuses on specific US laws, policies and administrative actions, though their stance remains quite militant within that frame, using protest events and issuing critical reports. The Border Network for Human Rights, cited above, exemplifies an even more reformist approach to existing politics and policies, proposing very specific modifications to existing laws and administrative practices. Each orientation has value, when understood properly; the radical vision has the potential to change the long-term frame for political choice toward a more global sense of shared humanity, while the reformists respond to compelling instances of immediate human suffering.

Yet at the same time, this dichotomy – admittedly simplistic – poses key dilemmas of being "alternative." The challenge is that alternatives often mean humanizing existing practices and ideas of power, addressing the suffering individual even as the collective pattern becomes more and more tightly controlled (Fassin, 2012). Clearly, this is a peril for reformist, ameliorative agendas, but the recent radical rhetoric of humanity, human rights, and so forth seems also to point in this direction (as opposed to a radical, communist agenda of mass, class-based redistribution in the world system, say). Migration, as a form of mobile and flexible labor supply, unquestionably serves the agenda of unbound and often exploitative capitalism (Heyman, 1998b; Krissman, 2005). Even as alternative migration politics and organizations resist some agendas – such as racism and the bounded, territorial state—they may adhere to other power orders. But then, as we saw in Chapter 3, no forms of organizing are ever above suspicion. The next two sections address these ironies and entanglements of the "alternative" project, starting first with an extended case study from France that exemplifies how immigrant advocacy becomes bound up with the web of law and administration.

Legal strategies and ambiguities: a case study of human rights advocacy for deportable immigrants in France

This section, based on fieldwork and analysis by Fischer, focuses on the involvement of human rights organizations in France in the controversial issue of detention and forced removal of deportable immigrants, and the ways in which this involvement has resulted in the "legalization" of advocacy. The resource of law enables activists to successfully challenge civil servants in court, but it can also lead to cooperation between these two sets of actors. The shared "framework of contention" provided by law illustrates a broad issue: the ambiguous relationship between critical actors and state administrations.

As in most European countries, France relied extensively on an immigrant workforce to sustain its reconstruction and the economic boom that followed World War II (Noiriel, 1988). The 1974 end to the guest worker program began a shift toward legal and technical means of immigration restriction, including forced removal for undocumented foreigners and police identity checks and arrests. Today, "undesirable" foreigners may be locked up in one of the 25 immigration detention centers (*centres de rétention administrative*) – institutions that have developed from scattered and small-scale locales designed for a maximum confinement of six days to a network of large, specialized facilities able to hold up to 140 migrants for up to 45 days (Fischer, 2012). The country's integration in the Schengen area resulted in lighter controls of most EU citizens residing in France but an increased pressure on "third country nationals" who could not claim similar rights (Bigo and Guild, 2005).

In parallel, special rights for immigrants, including for those facing deportation and confinement, have emerged since the early 1980s. This involves a shift away from enforcement by street-level bureaucrats who enjoyed high levels of discretionary power, and whose only legal references consisted of barely compulsory and mostly unpublished government regulations (Spire, 2005). In the late 1970s and early 1980s a general legal frame slowly appeared, as local decisions were referred to binding national laws adopted through parliamentary debate and subject to judicial review. Meanwhile, external actors – local and national courts, and human rights advocates – began intervening in immigration enforcement. These developments were complementary, as most of the advances in immigrants' rights were triggered by legal actions taken by advocates and case lawyers, thus prompting judges to produce case law and declare certain practices as illegal (Israël, 2003; Sarat and Scheingold, 2006).

Immigration control thus presents a contradictory scenario. On the one hand are highly repressive detentions and deportations, and on the other legal provisions which have not stopped these activities, but rather have added to them guarantees for the immigrants and limits to arbitrary decisions from state officials. The opportunities opened by the "legalization" of immigration control were rapidly seized by many Human Rights organizations. As Sarat and Scheingold express it, "speaking law to the state" means using the very substance of the state in order to modify its regulation (Sarat and Scheingold, 1998). This kind of intervention – whether through negotiation or litigation – has important consequences for organizations' positions and collective identities: they become critical co-producers of public policies, with contrasts depending on the political options of each group and on the social and professional background of its members.

The first two organizations we describe use the law to influence the production of immigration policies and, in certain cases, their local enforcement. The *Ligue des droits de l'homme* (the Human Rights' League, or LDH) is mostly composed of professional lawyers experienced in filing motions in favor of deportable immigrants/deportees who claim rights to legally stay in France (Agrikoliansky, 2002). Similarly, most of Gisti's (the *Groupe d'Information et de Soutien aux Immigrés*) members are administrative or legal experts, among whom many are professional barristers (61 of 210 in total). Gisti played a major role in the emergence of a protective legal status for foreigners through cases its lawyers won in court – some decisions of the supreme courts known as the *arrêts Gisti* ("Gisti judgments") are now part of the core administrative law taught in law schools (Agrikoliansky, 2002; Israël, 2003).

Both the Gisti and the LDH primarily use the law through litigation at a national level, challenging general laws and decrees before the French supreme courts or defending symbolic individual cases in order to obtain decisions of principle. Their main form of cooperation with local state agencies occurred during periods of undocumented immigrant "legalization" (in all senses of the word), running street-level legal clinics that received immigrants' claims for residence permits, preparing applications before sending them to local immigration officers (for a US equivalent see Hagan, 1994). Both organizations refused, however, to be associated with openly repressive policies. The Gisti, for instance, remains hostile to the very principle of immigrant deportations and detention, as well as to all forms of repressive border control (in the terms introduced above, it is more radical and less reformist).

A contrasting option was chosen by the *Comité inter-mouvements pour l'aide aux déplacés et aux évacués* (Joint Committee for the Relief of the Displaced and the Evacuated, Cimade) when they made an agreement in 1984 with the Ministry of Social Affairs to become part of detention center staff. A Christian Protestant group, Cimade was not originally created as a legal action-oriented organization, but rather for the defense of internally displaced and confined populations in the context of World War II. After the war, the organization focused on the defense of immigrants, but its members only adopted legal forms of action in the 1980s, after "cause lawyering" became a common means of political contention (Drahy, 2004).

Cimade's history influenced its choices regarding immigration control. The organization's creation around camps made its members particularly concerned with the return to immigrant administrative detention in the 1980s. Since its beginnings, the organization's leaders also maintained a logic of "close relationship" with state administrations. While taking an active part in campaigns and rallies against restrictive immigration policies, they kept contacts and negotiation with state officials, an approach that clearly separated Cimade from other French human rights organizations.

In 1984, Cimade and the Ministry of Social Affairs signed an agreement enabling the organization to perform a double task inside detention centers: first, providing individual social relief for the deportees; second, making a general review of conditions of detention leading to a confidential annual report sent to ministry officials. Fellow advocates reacted toward Cimade with disapproval, if not outward denunciation of what was sometimes called "collaboration" with an overtly violent and repressive policy. Cimade officials justified their decision by reviving the historical tradition of the group – to help the detained from the inside of confinement devices, and to "bear witness" (a religiously significant notion) to what happened to them. Central to their arguments was the idea that detention centers that were actually legalized and judicially monitored could not be reduced to the intolerable internment camps of the past, and they also pointed to the intention of Cimade members to keep their critical autonomy and publicly denounce the situation inside detention centers.

The passage of time changed the mission of Cimade members, and significantly reorganized an advocacy network around it. As detention centers became perennial, specialized institutions, the organization's members themselves became professionals and specialists, above all, of legal issues concerning the deportation process, first renamed "legal information" in 1991 and then officially "legal counsel" in 2001 – when most Cimade members had already been running de facto legal clinics for years within the centers. The recruitment of the organization's "detention teams" evolved in consequence: while Cimade traditionally drew on the voluntary involvement of spiritually motivated Protestant activists, the typical profile of immigration detention workers now involved a strong legal formation – up to the master's degree and sometimes above – combined with a clear involvement in the political Left.

This evolution changed both the internal organization of Cimade, and its position within the field of immigrant rights advocacy. Internally, Cimade's professionalized "detention workers" went from volunteers to wage-earning employees, while interorganizationally, Cimade's official but critical involvement in the enforcement of immigration detention became a key resource for all advocates concerned with deportations: the annual public reports on the state of detention centers provided convincing first-hand material on the evolution of French immigration policies. This long-term critical activity guaranteed sustained public attention to detention centers, both from other human rights advocates and from specialized journalists. In the day-to-day defense of arrested immigrants, the organization's members became expert insiders that other advocates could turn to when following individual cases. They progressively gained the legitimacy to reassess and negotiate the enforcement of forced removals before courts or through direct, regular contacts with police officials and their superiors.

The choice of a "cooperative" legal strategy is interesting organizationally, as it confirms the contemporary blurring of the traditional boundaries between "the state" and "civil society." Thus, we conclude by emphasizing the insurmountable ambiguity of legal strategies (Sarat and Scheingold, 1998). The legal knowledge of Cimade professionals gave them sufficient expertise to win cases in the courtroom and enabled them to be accepted as interlocutors by local and national state officials, while sometimes publicly criticizing the very same officials' actions. However, laws and regulations are shaped at a different political level, and after decades of restrictive policies, legal tactics provide increasingly narrow opportunities for challenging state repression. When Fischer conducted his fieldwork in detention, this situation was acknowledged by Cimade lawyers who repeatedly had to tell detained immigrants that nothing could be done, within the frame of the increasingly restrictive law, to help them. Inside the organization, this led to an ongoing debate over the definition of the "limit" – the point beyond which the organization's commitment would cease to be helpful, and be reduced to a mere collaboration with police repression.[6]

While "legalization" has its own specific logic, the lessons of this case study apply across diverse alternative organizations. Because the values of such organizations present alternatives to the status quo, and because they are critics of standard immigration policies and practices, does not mean that they romantically stand apart from the processes of the existing system. Their commitments include the state, their own memberships, wider immigrant communities, and various discourses and ideological contexts. Their action can create alternative spaces but, in doing so, can also enter wider governing processes.

Immigrant advocacy, labor and transnationalism

It is not only legal and administrative systems that envelop alternative immigrant organizations; this is also the case for the capitalist economy at local, national and global scales. Hence, labor and economic development are crucial aspects of immigrant organizing. While the labor concerns of immigrants and supporters are widely shared, the challenges are considerable. Global economic interests have vast financial and political resources for driving policy regimes that favor cheap and predictable labor, and consequent wealth flows to the global North. Workers, on the other hand, are generally in positions that provide little security or leverage. For their part, developing countries often depend on remittances to try to meet huge debt payments, pay for social services, and dampen potential discord over poverty and joblessness. Increasingly, the benefits that both corporations and countries gain from displaced labor are leading to a growing interest in shared regulatory systems for both supplying and controlling it.

Contract labor has a lengthy history, including "guest worker" or "temporary worker" programs in the US and those referred to as "managed migration" in much of Europe (an informative resource is Griffith, 2006). These arrangements have helped fuel the economic growth in these countries until recently. With sudden global retrenchment since 2008, however, plans for managing the flow of migration have grown. Contract labor systems are particularly closed and difficult for alternative organizations to penetrate, but they do generate worker concerns and voices. In Canada, for example, Justicia for Migrant Workers combines on-the-ground publicity and organizing (www.justicia4migrantworkers.org/) while Industrial Accident Victim's Group of Ontario (www.iavgo.org/legal_ressources.html) provides expert support in the area of occupational health (see McLaughlin, 2007).

Underlying the expansion of a global pool of available labor is *vulnerability*. As awareness has risen about the disempowerment inherent in the conflation of corporate profitability with immigration policies, so also has arisen a range of challenges. The North American Free Trade Agreement (NAFTA) is emblematic of the economic "reforms," including privatization and the end of subsidies, that are mandated by international trade agreements and global institutions like the World Trade Organization (WTO), yet have massive implications for displacement of people and communities. Insufficient or bottlenecked visas, sustained by anti-immigrant politics, results in policies of intensified border entry enforcement, interior immigration status and employment enforcement, detention, and deportation, such as the French case described above; this likewise heightens vulnerability and exploitability (DeGenova, 2002; Heyman, 1998b).

Given this scenario of vulnerability, it is easy to assume that immigrant workers, especially undocumented ones, are too afraid to engage in labor organizing. Yet workplaces generate both discontent and solidarity in highly varied ways. Undocumented workers specifically (Delgado, 1993; Zlolniski, 2006) and immigrant workers more generally (Milkman, 2000, 2006) have responded to campaigns by larger scale unions and have organized among themselves. In many countries, unions that at first formed substantially among children of immigrants had, by the mid- to late twentieth century, become either fearful of or simply oblivious to immigrants. However, as workforces again are filling with new immigrants, and as the capitalist war against organized working people gains momentum, unions have generally become more pro-immigrant and have created new, effective immigrant-based organizing strategies (Milkman, 2006).

Christian Zlolniski (2006) provides a particularly rich ethnography of Mexican working-class immigrant organizing, both inside and outside the workplace. Janitors, working for a small firm contracted to a large transnational electronic corporation, linked their previously unorganized discontent to a unionization campaign brought by national labor organizers (the Service Employees International Union's Justice for Janitors Campaign). Their own concerns were with the contractor – interestingly, owned by an immigrant from another, more relatively privileged national origin group – but the national union was able to leverage public pressure against the main corporation. However, the workers were later "disorganized" (their employment and unionization fractured) through flexible capitalism, the rearrangement of subcontracts and state coercion – raids on undocumented workers by the immigration service.

In parallel, the working-class community held an unorganized variety of needs, concerns and aspirations outside the workplace. The city of San Jose, California approached the community, via externally organized community meetings, with a top-down set of quality-of-life and crime-reduction initiatives; even though these activities spoke to community concerns and were generally appreciated (with some reservations), they were broadly resented as being imposed, reflecting lack of trust and connection, and disempowering rather than engaging with their organizational potentials. A highly disciplined community public advocacy organization (People Acting in Community Together), with Catholic affiliations, obtained more involvement from the community by teaching people systematic forms of organizing and advocacy to act on their own behalf, rather than just doing things *for* the community. Despite initial successes in educational services, the rigid training and action frameworks of that organization eventually alienated or exhausted key immigrant community activists. The demands of survival on the bottom of the rung in the host society resulted in people dropping out or fracturing, in an erosive process somewhat similar to the unionization experience. Finally, as Zlolniski points out, there were spontaneous community movements, with weaker form and less persistence, generally made up of interpersonal networks around energetic individuals, "often remaining invisible to government officials and outsiders alike" (43) that accomplished significant self-chosen goals, such as obtaining bilingual Spanish – English education in the local school. Clearly, immigrants are limited by the broad patterns of inequality and power, but they do display agency within constraints in terms of goal-setting and desire for self-determination in organizing.

Big capital is mobile on continental and global scales. Ironically, immigrant mobility resembles that of and is connected to capital mobility. Most people, even today, are not so globally mobile, and nationalist politics hence tends to mix together the mobility of capital and migrants. Immigration debates thus tend to be nationalized, and do not attend to the differences of mobility of the powerful and the powerless. The political and legal architecture of the territorial nation-state, including immigrant admission and enforcement of restrictions, as well as community and workplace conditions, tends to focus inside the bounded nation. This even affects many alternative immigration organizations.

Yet when we consider the lives of immigrants, and we attend to global labor – capital relations, we realize that alternative organizing needs to cross conventional borders (Evans, 2010). This "transnational" tendency, breaking with the conventional national frame, is on the cutting edge of immigrant organizing in a number of domains, including both labor (Gordon, 2007) and cultural and political rights (see the FIOB case study, above). Transnational communities are creating new ways of looking at citizenship and residence that correspond more closely to the reality of migration. While not directly transnational, the union organizing described by Zlolniski was successful (at least temporarily) precisely because of the sensitivity of a major information technology corporation to global public criticism. Transnational organizing is difficult (see Staudt and Coronado, 2002), but seems essential in the contemporary world.

Conclusion: what does being "alternative" mean in a world of power over immigration?

The struggle over immigration has profound implications for the kind of global future we will have and value. But alternative immigration organizations, or any others apart from separatist intentional communities (see Pitzer's chapter in this volume), cannot magically separate themselves from wider contexts. The starting point of alternative immigration organizations is often repressive acts or policies or wider patterns of discrimination in the dominant society. But from that starting point, alternative organizations fashion positive forms of sociality, culture and politics, grounded in a vision of human worth beyond narrow nation-state membership. This evolution from challenge to creative response is found in a number of chapters in this volume, an excellent example being the worker-controlled enterprises discussed in the chapter by Atzeni and Vieta. The organizational values and forms thus created are indeed "alternatives" to an inhumane status quo, but they often exist within and adapt to those social and economic fields. As the case study from France demonstrated, alternative immigration organizations cannot simply make contemporary legal regulation vanish, and might even in some ways reinforce it, even as such rules are rendered more "humane." Likewise, immigration is deeply bound up in the widespread and intensive mobility of factors of production within contemporary capitalism. The movement of immigrant workers is part and parcel with the movement of investment capital and global commodities.

So what difference does it make to be "alternative"? A useful entry point is to consider the emerging trend of managed migration, discussed above. It appears to satisfy the needs of employers and of managerialist state elites (Heyman, 2008). Yet it is restrictive, controlling, and fundamentally treats migrants as units of production, not as people. In important ways, it reproduces on a global scale the South African design of apartheid, segregating a lower order of laborers, allowing them in for work but not for full societal membership (Sharma, 2006). This is cosmopolitan design from above, the making of a mobile world on behalf of the prosperous and powerful. The alternative is cosmopolitanism from below, the development of a world of strong rights claims and robust worker organizations on a transnational scale.

In this emerging scenario, and others like it, which cosmopolitanism we advocate matters for elites and working-class migrants. A need to belong, to family as well as to group or community, is a powerful force in human behavior. Identity and affiliation in today's world had been associated with nationality; this is now challenged from above by big capital and mobile elites, and from below by immigrants and their allies. Citizenship is an ever more complex issue in a world where transnational migrant communities span borders, and exist in more than one place simultaneously. Residents of transnational communities do not see themselves simply as victims of an unfair system, but as actors capable of reproducing culture, of providing economic support to families in their towns of origin, and of seeking social justice in the country to which they have migrated.

A sensible immigration policy would recognize and value the communities of migrants, and see their support as desirable. It would reinforce indigenous culture and language, rather than treating them as a threat. At the same time, it would seek to integrate immigrants into the broader community around them and give them a voice in it, rather than promoting social exclusion, isolation and segregation. It would dedicate as much as possible the value produced by the mobility of factors of production – contemporary economic globalization – toward increased *human capabilities* rather than private accumulation (see also Ferrell's chapter on scrounging in this book). From effective organization comes meaningful redistribution, and a more generous understanding of the relationship between alternative organizing and space. Above all, it would protect the rights of immigrants as a part of protecting the rights of all working people.

Notes

1 In this chapter, we use the terms immigration and immigrants, because that is a conventional usage for most readers. In reality, the broader term migrants refers to all those persons moving between political and social settings, the larger group, while immigrants refers narrowly to those who settle in the new society for some substantial period of time.
2 Unauthorized immigrants and small-scale smugglers, David Spener (2009) argues, engage in a vigorous struggle against the nation-state acting as an enforcer of global spatial separation and inequality ("global apartheid"). In this regard they are "alternative" to the dominant order, and Spener argues against a purely negative stereotype of smugglers. Small-scale smugglers are not, however, distinct organizations, while organized, large-scale smugglers tend to be more exploitative of immigrants.
3 We draw on two related ideas: "globalization from below," a concept proposed by Mathews *et al.*, (2012) for small-scale economic activities that span borders, and philosopher Seyla Benhabib's (2006) concept of "another cosmopolitanism," the evolution of rights and norms above and beyond bounded nation-states, especially around migration and asylum.
4 Hence, not all alternative immigrant organizations are cosmopolitan in their explicit membership and values, even though they stand as cosmopolitan alternatives to the closed, territorial nation-state.

5 Hondagneu (2008) and, before her, Cunningham (1995) have described an important religious theme of militant civil disobedience against borders, such as smuggling refugees and sheltering them in the host society ("sanctuary"), humanitarian assistance to migrants at risk of dying in the crossing process (e.g., No More Deaths, http://www.nomoredeaths.org/), and symbolic protests of religious and humanitarian universalism against state boundaries, walls, fences, and so forth.

6 For the sake of space, some developments after 2008 have been skipped here.

Resources

American Friends Service Committee (USA): https://afsc.org/project/immigrants-rights
Migrant Rights International (worldwide): www.migrantwatch.org/index.html
Migration Policy Institute (worldwide): www.migrationpolicy.org/
National Immigration Forum (USA): www.immigrationforum.org/
National Network for Immigrant and Refugee Rights (USA): www.nnirr.org/drupal/

References

Agrikoliansky, É. 2002. *La Ligue française des droits de l'homme et du citoyen depuis 1945 sociologie d'un engagement civique*. Paris, Budapest and Torino: l'Harmattan.

Benhabib, S. 2006. *Another Cosmopolitanism*. Oxford and New York: Oxford University Press.

Bigo, D. and Guild, E. 2005. *Controlling Frontiers: Free Movement into and within Europe*. Aldershot, UK: Ashgate.

Cunningham, H. 1995. *God and Caesar at the Rio Grande: Sanctuary and the Politics of Religion*. Minneapolis: University of Minnesota Press.

DeGenova, N. 2002. Migrant 'Illegality' and Deportability. *Annual Review of Anthropology* 31: 419–447.

Delgado, H.L. 1993. *New Immigrants, Old Unions: Organizing Undocumented Workers in Los Angeles*. Philadelphia, PA: Temple University Press.

Drahy, J. 2004. *Le droit contre l'État? droit et défense associative des étrangers, l'exemple de la CIMADE*. Paris, Budapest and Torino: l'Harmattan.

Evans, P. 2010. Is it Labor's Turn to Globalize? Twenty-first Century Opportunities and Strategic Responses. *Global Labour Journal* 1(3): 352–379. Available online at http://digitalcommons.mcmaster.ca/globallabour/vol1/iss3/3 (accessed 10 April 2012).

Fassin, D. 2012. *Humanitarian Reason: A Moral History of the Present Times*. Berkeley: University of California Press.

Fischer, N. 2012. *Le territoire de l'expulsion: La rétention administrative des étrangers dans l'Etat de droit*. Lyon: Presses de l'ENS Lyon.

Fox, J. and Rivera-Salgado, G. (eds). 2004. *Indigenous Mexican Migrants in the United States*. La Jolla, CA: Center for US-Mexican Studies and Center for Comparative Immigration Studies, University of California, San Diego.

Gordon, J. 2007. Transnational Labor Citizenship. *Southern California Law Review* 80: 503–587.

Griffith, D.C. 2006. *American Guestworkers: Jamaicans and Mexicans in the U.S. Labor Market*. University Park, PA: Pennsylvania State University Press.

Griffith, D.C. 2012. Immigrant Heterogeneity and Class Consciousness in New Rural US Destinations, in E.P. Durrenberger (ed.), *The Anthropological Study of Class and Consciousness*, pp. 201–222. Boulder, CO: University Press of Colorado.

Hagan, J.M. 1994. *Deciding to be Legal: A Maya Community in Houston*. Philadelphia, PA: Temple University Press.

Heyman, J.M. 1998a. *Finding a Moral Heart for U.S. Immigration Policy*. Arlington, VA: American Anthropological Association.

Heyman, J.M. 1998b. State Effects on Labor Exploitation: The INS and Undocumented Immigrants at the Mexico–United States Border. *Critique of Anthropology* 18: 157–180.

Heyman, J.M. 2008. Constructing a Virtual Wall: Race and Citizenship in US–Mexico Border Policing. *Journal of the Southwest* 50: 305–333.

Heyman, J.M. 2010. The Border Network for Human Rights: Building an Immigrant Movement in the Besieged Borderlands. Available online at www.race-talk.org/?p=4210 (accessed 10 April 2012).

Heyman, J.M. 2011. An Academic in an Activist Coalition: Recognizing and Bridging Role Conflicts, *Annals of Anthropological Practice* 35(2): 136–153.

Ho, C.G.T. and Loucky, J. 2012. *Humane Migration: Establishing Legitimacy and Rights for Displaced People.* Sterling, VA: Stylus.

Hondagneu-Sotelo, P. 2008. *God's Heart has No Borders: How Religious Activists are Working for Immigrant Rights.* Berkeley: University of California Press.

Israël, L. 2003. Faire émerger le droit des étrangers en le contestant, ou l'histoire paradoxale des premières années du GISTI. *Politix* 16 (62): 115–143.

Krissman, F. 2005. Sin Coyote Ni Patrón: Why the "Migrant Network" Fails to Explain International Migration. *International Migration Review* 39: 4–44.

LeBaron, A. and Loucky, J. (eds). 2012. Mesoamerican/North American Partnerships for Community Wellbeing. *Practicing Anthropology* 34(1): 2–3.

Loucky, J. and LeBaron, A. 2012. Introduction: Mesoamerican/North American Partnerships for Community Wellbeing. *Practicing Anthropology* 34(1): 2–3.

Mathews, G., Ribeiro, G.L. and Vega, C.A. 2012. *Globalization from Below: The World's Other Economy.* New York: Routledge.

McLaughlin, J. 2007. Falling through the Cracks: Seasonal Foreign Farm Workers' Health and Compensation across Borders. *The IAVGO Reporting Service* (The Industrial Accident Victims Group of Ontario) 21(1). Available online at www.injuredworkersonline.org/Documents/ONIWGconfMcLaughlin.pdf (accessed 10 April 2012).

Milkman, R. 2000. *Organizing Immigrants: The Challenge for Unions in Contemporary California.* Ithaca, NY: ILR Press.

Milkman, R. 2006. *L.A. Story: Immigrant Workers and the Future of the U.S. Labor Movement.* New York: Russell Sage Foundation.

Noiriel, G. 1988. *Le Creuset français: histoire de l'immigration, XIXe-XXe siècles.* Paris: Éd. du Seuil.

Portes, A., Escobar, C. and Radford, A.W. 2011. Immigrant Transnational Organizations and Development: A Comparative Study, in J. Shefner and M.P. Fernández-Kelly (eds), *Globalization and Beyond: New Examinations of Global Power and its Alternatives.* University Park, PA: Pennsylvania State University Press.

Sarat, A. and Scheingold, S.A. 1998. *Cause Lawyering: Political Commitments and Professional Responsibilities.* New York: Oxford University Press.

Sarat, A. and Scheingold, S.A. 2006. *Cause Lawyers and Social Movements.* Stanford, CA: Stanford Law and Politics.

Sharma, N.R. 2006. *Home Economics: Nationalism and the Making of "Migrant Workers" in Canada.* Toronto: University of Toronto Press.

Spener, D. 2009. *Clandestine Crossings: Migrants and Coyotes on the Texas–Mexico Border.* Ithaca, NY: Cornell University Press.

Spire, A. 2005. *Étrangers à la carte l'administration de l'immigration en France, 1945–1975.* Paris: Grasset.

Staudt, K.A. and Coronado, I. 2002. *Fronteras No Más: Toward Social Justice at the US–Mexico Border.* New York: Palgrave Macmillan.

Voss, K. and Bloemraad, I. (eds). 2011. *Rallying for Immigrant Rights: The Fight for Inclusion in 21st Century America.* Berkeley: University of California Press.

Zlolniski, C. 2003. Labor Control and Resistance of Mexican Immigrant Janitors in Silicon Valley. *Human Organization* 62: 39–49.

Zlolniski, C. 2006. *Janitors, Street Vendors, and Activists: The Lives of Mexican Immigrants in Silicon Valley.* Berkeley: University of California Press.

10

Toward a politics of anonymity

Algorithmic actors in the constitution of collective agency and the implications for global economic justice movements

Ned Rossiter and Soenke Zehle

Introduction

Social media has transformed itself into a set of interlocking operating systems, designed not simply to facilitate established forms of communicative usage and political organization but to serve as platforms for a new generation of commercial services. As users shift their online activity to social media sites, they accelerate the decline of a destination web whose open protocols are being replaced by closed environments modeled on the walled-garden architectures of online stores. Organized around user-as-product paradigms that encourage information sharing to build massive databases, the political economy of this transformation of user agency has already been analyzed as biolinguistic capitalism, or the social production of value. Complementing these analyses of an expropriation of leisure time, the effective enmeshment of communicative and economic practice, and the integration of users into stream-based paradigms of information sharing, we argue that alternative modes of organization must engage the production of standards and protocols that shape the codes and infrastructures of expression within which organization subsists. At stake is not simply the role of real-time media in processes of organization, but a politics of anonymity that acknowledges the central role of algorithmic actors in the constitution of collective agency. By "algorithmic actors" we mean the grammar, rules or parameters of code which can shape the organization of people and things (Galloway, 2006; Fuller and Goffey, 2012). Just like organizing, code has political effects.

The widespread adoption by users of social network media has increasingly rendered the border between life and labor indistinct in ways not fully imagined before the networked society. The human soul has been put to work, formatting its informatic expression in clouds without freedom (see Berardi, 2009a). Some of the most radical political events witnessed over the past few years – the Arab Spring, the European Austerity Protests and the Occupy movements – have been notable in their choice of commercial social media services such as Facebook and Twitter to facilitate techniques of organization (Maeckelbergh, this volume). How these political mobilizations sustain themselves over time remains an open question, but one that nevertheless requires concepts and models of organization to take into account the politics of code. Beyond a political economy of user-as-product approaches, we contend that it is the figure of anonymity that most effectively identifies the stakes of a new protocol politics. The question of anonymity is at the heart of an emergent politics of information governance, addressing the role of protocols, policies and practices in systems of networking.

To facilitate such a shift in perspective, this chapter offers a brief overview of the decline of the destination web following the migration of users to closed commercial media platforms. We go on to examine the emergence of communication networks based on open hardware protocols and the repoliticization of the design of infrastructures of expression beyond a politics of information rights. This brings us to our core interest in the way anonymity shapes political organization at both technological and social levels. Across finance capitalism, hacker cultures and political movements, algorithmic anonymity has become the architecture of organization coincident with networked forms of communication. As such, it warrants critical inspection and analysis hitherto overlooked by organization studies. In short, organization studies must take seriously how algorithmic actors shape the ways in which individual and collective agency is constituted and mobilized.

After the destination web

Never simply about the utopia of friends happily connected in a global village, the communicative work of social media users is well and truly intregrated with operations specific to 'biolinguistic capitalism' (Berardi, 2009b; Marazzi, 2008).[1] Algorithmic tracking of how you communicate generates profiles so comprehensive that they have become a major commercial asset, and it does not come as a surprise that an entire industry of data dealers has emerged. The analysis of online social networks has focused much of its attention on the "user-as-product" approach adopted by commercial social media platforms: software encourages users to generate their own social data, which in turn allows for the construction of dynamic user profiles whose commercial value lies in their unprecedented scope and scale as "big data" to be endlessly modeled and recombined.

An entire cottage industry has developed based on the monetization of these data flows, from mortgage lending to debt service monitoring. And as the shift from contextual and behavioral advertising to deep packet inspection illustrates, such analyses are no longer simply content-based: as advertisers partner with Internet Service Providers (ISPs) to better reach their target audiences, they effectively become part of the networked infrastructure.

> Deep Packet Inspection (DPI) is a computer network packet filtering technique that involves the inspection of the contents of packets as they are transmitted across the network. DPI is sometimes referred to as 'complete packet inspection'. Owing to the volume of traffic on most networks, DPI is usually automated and performed by software based on criteria set by the network operator. Deep Packet Inspection can be used to determine the contents of all unencrypted data transferred over a network. Since most Internet traffic is unencrypted, DPI enables Internet Service Providers to intercept virtually all of their customers' Internet activity, including web surfing data, email, and peer-to-peer downloads.
>
> *(http://epic.org/privacy/dpi)*

Analyses are based on a logic of aggregation: as the automated adjustment of prices or credit lines depends on what people in your networks do, "weblining" follows the "redlining" of an earlier era, when people were denied mortgages based on where they live. Some of these actors are brand names well known on college campuses yet rarely the focus of analytical attention. Take LexisNexis – the same company that offers online access to research literature also provides the tools to monitor whether you have paid your student loan (Accurint for Collections) or come in conflict with the law (Accurint for Law Enforcement).[2]

Following her analysis of this data industry, Lori Andrews (2012) has proposed a "Social Network Constitution" to protect constitutional rights to privacy in the "Facebook Nation."[3] Yet Evgeny Morozov (2012) has sharply criticized Andrews' transfer of social contract theory to describe the relationship between social media corporations and their customers; he also wonders why she does not at all engage the new social movements that have emerged in response to these threats to privacy. He doesn't miss a social constitution as much as the political capacity to resist the violation of such rights: "the mere right to privacy – even if enshrined in a constitution – is not going to be enough. Someone also needs to make a powerful argument about the dangers of sacrificing that right" (Morozov, 2012). And as long as consumers don't weigh the cost of being denied a loan against the benefit of a discount after showing their coupon-apps to the teenager at the cashier, this won't change.

Rather than assuming that users will eventually recognize the cost of sharing within commercial "user-as-product" infrastructures, we believe that organizing starts by exploring the affect of sharing beyond a critique of corporate ownership of networking platforms.[4] Because users love to share (Tamir and Mitchell, 2012). Any reflection on organization, be it in terms of a traditional dynamic of institutionalization or the "instituent practices" (Raunig, 2009) of social movements, needs to take this into account. And if life and labor mesh in our communicative practice, the lack of popularity of independent social media services would suggest the need for new figures of organizational thought – of what it means to build and sustain collective agency in the world of real-time networks, or any other technology (see also Chapter 21 on appropriate technologies).[5]

Meshworks of freedom

Information technology plays an increasingly important role in the way we create, communicate and collaborate. As this happens, our autonomy is increasingly affected by the degree and scope of our control over these technologies. Over the past thirty years, the free software movement has worked to protect this autonomy. However, the last decade has witnessed a rise in the role of computing as a service, a massive increase in the use of web applications, the migration of personal computing tasks to data centers and the creation of new classes of service-based applications. Through this process, some of the thinking, licenses, tools and strategies of the free and open-source software movements are being adapted to address the challenges posed by these network services.

As Yochai Benkler (2008) has noted, "[t]he critical policy questions of the networked environment revolve around the battles between the decentralization of technology and the push of policy to moderate that decentralization by limiting the distribution of authority to act" (52). A few years ago, Alexander Galloway (2004) predicted that "[i]t is very likely if not inevitable that the core Internet protocols, today largely safe from commercial and state power, will be replaced by some type of proprietary system."[6] The rise of cloud-based computing has raised the question of non-proprietary standards anew. Grasping the scope of this technological transformation, Nicholas Carr (2008) has compared it to the development of electricity as a utility and prompted the suggestion that if the cloud is best understood as a utility it should be regulated like one.[7]

As computing comes to be seen and experienced increasingly in terms of a networked service, new concerns arise regarding the autonomy of users now positioned on new grids largely controlled by a few corporations. Lawyer and free software activist, Eben Moglen, likens such grids of control to an "architecture of the catastrophe":

> So "cloud" means servers have gained freedom, freedom to move, freedom to dance, freedom to combine and separate and re-aggregate and do all kinds of tricks. Servers have gained freedom. Clients have gained nothing.
>
> *(Moglen, 2010a)*

Because "we lost the ability to use either legal regulation or anything about the physical architecture of the network," contends Moglen, "what we need to do is to make free software matter to the problem that we have which is unfree services delivered in unfree ways really beginning to deteriorate the structure of human freedom." Free software advocate, Richard Stallman (2010), understands the cloud primarily in terms of a "Software-as-a-Service" (SaaS) business model. Yet an exodus from the cloud is a complex matter, cautions Benjamin Malo Hill (2010): all network services tend to "involve some SaaS features and some non-SaaS features". To leverage the "dematerialization of the network" and return it to "peerage," Moglen (2010b) has already encouraged software developers to create "Freedom Boxes" – small servers (encrypted web proxies) that will "turn the net into an infrastructure for federated services," extending software freedom beyond the local installation of free operating systems and applications. Such a practice takes organization into the realm of distributed networks of open hardware.

From the collaborative process of decentralized software development in peer-to-peer networks to the role of free licenses as radical manifestos on the information form, the social and technological protocols that govern the dynamic of free software have often been considered a key net.cultural dynamic. To understand the web is to understand, first of all, free software. But the "Freedom Box" advocated by Moglen and others connects software to another trend, free hardware, and more broadly the question of how we relate to the material infrastructures that enable and sustain our communicative practices. In one attempt to "take back the network," Commotion Wireless proposes a different infrastructure: the automated connection of communication devices owned by users in a "device-as-infrastructure" distributed communications platform.[8] Inspired in part by the experience of the Arab Spring, where governments used their control of ISPs to disrupt network communications, such decentralized "meshworks" grow more stable as new users are added to the network (Dibbel, 2012).

Yet the development toward technological decentralization Moglen foresees is unlikely to occur. For "venture communist" Dmytri Kleiner (2012b), "the question we need to address is not so much how we can invent a distributed social platform, but how and why we started from a fully distributed social platform and replaced it with centralized social media monopolies." As long as communication platforms exist to return a profit, they will be designed as apparatuses of capture and control. For Kleiner (2012a), "[c]ommercialization has made online rights irrelevant." We are more circumspect about such claims when considered in a longer trajectory of communication media within social situations. Privately owned presses, newspapers, radio and television stations have not, for example, made information or privacy-related rights irrelevant. That said, the transfer of a politics of rights to the world of online networks is more complex than perhaps frequently assumed. Nuanced and far-reaching examples of information rights can be seen in debates on data-sharing agreements, Stop Only Piracy Act (SOPA), Preventing Real Online Threats to Economic Creativity and Theft of Intellectual Property Act (PROTECT IP Act, PIPA), Anti-Counterfeiting Trade Agreement (ACTA), network neutrality and Internet governance. To paraphrase Jacques Rancière

(2004): who is the subject of online rights, how is this subject constituted as a rights-bearing subject and what is the role of organization in constituting collective actors capable of claiming such rights?[9]

Algorithmic actors

In their analysis of key contemporary political events – the Arab Spring, European Austerity Protests, Occupy encampments – observers have rarely failed to assert the centrality, if not indispensability, of social media to the organizational dynamic in question. Such assertions range from techno-utopian enthusiasm to affirmations of a desire for offline life. Either way, the power of code makes it tempting to see technology as a determining force. Despite frequently voiced concerns about issues of privacy for users of social media, there is little inclination by participants involved in political movements to adopt platforms based on free or open-source software to facilitate the work of organization. Facebook, it seems, reigns supreme even among radicals. Even within projects explicitly geared toward a critique of commercial social media platforms, there is only modest enthusiasm for Facebook alternatives.[10] Organizing takes place within and not outside of corporate spheres of communication. The question of software alternatives within social media networks involved in political organization arises not simply in response to the rise of social media monopolies. In a world that sees labor and life as inseparable from informational technologies and their modes of organization and economy, it is the very constitution of political subjectivity that is at stake, not only the political economy of online networking (see also LaFrance and Nathan, 2012).

On a macro scale, the algorithmic operations of finance capitalism – as registered in the trade of financial instruments such as derivatives, for example – are one of many instances of the invisible status of *algorithmic anonymity* that precipitated what is broadly referred to as the global financial crisis (see Martin, 2007; LiPuma and Lee, 2004). The relative autonomy and invisibility of algorithmic actors has accorded them a central role in the analysis of contemporary crises and the social dynamics of mobilization that have emerged in response – from governmental attempts to regulate high-frequency trading to the politicization of financial secrecy pursued by the Occupy and Tax Justice movements. On a micro scale, such responses to algorithmic anonymity manifest as resistance to the enmeshment of mobile communications in broader architectures of surveillance.[11] Despite the impact of these socio-technological developments, reflective of broader developments toward the incorporation of algorithmic assemblages across the terrain of culture, economy and politics, and therefore much discussed across the fields of communication and media studies, organization studies have (aside from the occasional use of free and open-source software to support radical portals) not prioritized investigations of the relation between computational systems of organization and the production of political agency or subjectivity.[12] This is surprising, as the question of technology and agency is of direct relevance to the development of alternative forms of organization, including issues of centralization – decentralization, governance and transparency, and local to global connection (see also Chapters 15 on localism, 16 on transition towns, 19 on the commons, and 23 on governance). Technology does not, of course, serve as a neutral backdrop to the content of politics and the work of organization, but structures modes of relation as well as possible outcomes. The sophistication of contemporary architectures of code suggests that it will not suffice to maintain a general awareness of technological trends. As emerging analytical frameworks such as software studies assert, code is content and must find its way into theories of organization.

A politics of anonymity

These emergent algorithmic assemblages from finance capital to political insurrection are not without social articulations, but our theories of individual and collective agency may not be capable of comprehending them. Adopting a framework of (online) rights, for example, appears to facilitate the self-empowerment of users, but it also fails to foreground the extent to which algorithmic actors upset analytical assumptions. Rather than framing analytical approaches in terms of openness, participation and transparency, we therefore suggest that a term that is itself only reluctantly acknowledged by democracy-theoretical perspectives becomes the point of departure: anonymity.[13] Political thought, as far as we understand it, necessarily structures more broadly reflections on organization as institution and process. Yet instead of assuming that political thought revolves around the question of identity and representation, we contend that it is the desire for anonymity itself – shared by actors across micro and macro scales – that has become, once again, a terrain of contestation.

Aiming to contribute to the field of organization studies as well as to the analysis of the dynamics of self-organization, we argue that anonymity is an exemplary figure that corresponds with alternative modes of organization and political projects. To explore data-mining, electronic surveillance, derivatives software, supply-chain management programs, risk management calculators, GIS mapping applications, military modeling or simulation software is to, above all, challenge the anonymization of the algorithmic actors engaged in these dynamics of machinic self-organization.[14] With the proliferation of architectures of code that create constellations of algorithmic actors ("ubiquitous computing"), anonymity shapes political organization at both technological and social levels. Broadly speaking, we understand anonymity as an affect capable of sustaining new modes of relation and collaborative constitution as well as an operating principle at the infrastructural core of algorithmic cultures and its institutions.[15] Anonymity allows us to bring together seemingly disparate, disconnected actors into a singular plane of analysis in order to discuss questions of information governance and modalities of organization.

The emphasis on the conceptual figure of anonymity not only brings into view a wide array of algorithmic apparatuses; it also acknowledges the power anonymity continues to hold over the political imagination: "Hacker Ethos," "WikiLeaks" and, above all, "Anonymous/4Chan." Not coherent as a social movement, but nonetheless clearly identifiable as a social-political desire and technical hack expressed in the form of playful acts of "civil disobedience," Anonymous came to prominence in 2008 with a series of viral media pranks against the Church of Scientology. But it wasn't until late 2010 and early 2011, with the formation of AnonOps, that Anonymous shifted focus from mischief-making to political campaigns. As media anthropologist, Gabriella Coleman, notes of Anonymous operations during the Arab Spring, "Anonymous attacked government websites but soon began acting more like a human rights advocacy group, enabling citizens to circumvent censors and evade electronic surveillance and sending care packages with advice and security tools" (Coleman, 2012a; see also Coleman, 2012b). The preferred mode of organization for AnonOps includes the use of IRCs (Internet relay chats), imageboards and online forums with social networking media such as Twitter, YouTube and Facebook serving to connect planned actions with broader publics.

Anonymous offers a collective critique of political economy, a critique mediated by a combination of online communication platforms and tactical stagings of public action. The grammar of attack takes the form of botnets that take down government and corporate websites instigating a DDoS (distributed-denial-of-service), hacking email and mobile phone accounts. Such techniques of computational sabotage attracted widespread media reporting during the campaign in 2010 against financial institutions preventing the transfer of funds by donors to WikiLeaks. In a sense, Anonymous refuses the mantra of openness common across much of the open-source software and cultures movement. But a more apt target of attack here would be social media, in which openness is synonymous with the expropriation of privacy as users become the commercial product of social connectivity machines.[16] Facebook and other networks have little patience with users who desire forms of social connection but would rather not have private details of their life data-mined and sold to third parties.[17] While the lack of transparency does not prevent Anonymous from standing up for actions and entities that champion openness and transparency – the WikiLeaks campaign being most obvious here – the constitution of Anonymous as a political actor remains a puzzle to analyses predicated on idioms of identity and representation favored by democratic theory. Yet what interests us here, more than the question of whether or not Anonymous exemplifies the "multitude" of post-representational political theory is the practical possibility that such a "movement that needs no name" offers a perspective that seeks to assess the role of anonymity as a central principle of communicative practice. "The search for a name for the movement is just the start. By finding it, we open up a space in which profound questions about social transformation can be asked" (Kahn-Harris, 2010). This is true only if we include the full range of actors involved – including algorithmic actors. So we understand "finding the name" as a practice of cultural translation rather than an attempt to integrate these movements in a politics of representation (see Buden, 2006). This question strikes to the heart of the question of agency which remains a pressing practical, as well as a theoretical concern, not only for the move to collective action but also because of discourses of inevitability that characterize neo-liberalism, growth and consumption.

New rules of algorithmic engagement

The (re)emergence of anonymity – as political desire, as principle of socio-technological organization – signals a major transformation in the relationship between public and private. To focus exclusively on the political economy of an expropriation (or subsumption) of leisure time that makes "user as product" approaches to social media possible obscures the extent to which the "decline of the destination web" has given rise to stream-based paradigms of information sharing that radically transform user agency.[18] Organizing must, for example, enter the terrain of "big data," without being side-tracked by the "false confidence" that data analysis and a new generation of real-time media metrics tools inspire (Fader, 2012).

So-called big data is "data that exceeds the processing capacity of conventional database systems" (Dumbill, 2012). As Edd Dumbill notes, "[t]oday's commodity hardware, cloud architectures and open source software bring big data processing into the reach of the less well-resourced." Such low thresholds of entry allow new investigative approaches and, we would suggest, alternative modes of organization, as political campaigns, advertising or cultural production (including journalism) increasingly rely on the vast amounts of data generated by real-time communicative practices. Data analysis of communicative practices complements existing methodologies of organization and cultural analysis based on "surface data" (quantitative methods) and "deep data" (humanities methodologies such as "hermeneutics, participant observation, thick description, semiotics, and close reading") (Manovich, 2012: 462). Making the case for new alliances with new data science disciplines like social computing, "[w]e want humanists to be able to use data analysis and visualization software in their daily work, so they can combine quantitative and qualitative approaches in all their work" (Manovich, 2012). What is perhaps needed even more than data analysis (and hence the capacity to engage new actors in data-driven information governance regimes) is a machinic theory of social value predicated on the role of data as the new ground or source of valorization.

As new algorithmic assemblages generate data based on our real-time communicative practice, organizing is confronted with a new resource that is both social and technological. Such a focus quickly returns us from software studies to the terrain of organizing as we know it. As the Occupy movements have demonstrated, the politics of data are developed from within a horizon of financialization, and it should not be forgotten that the campaigns around student debt occur on the terrain of "big data" as well.[19] The same holds for international campaigns around tax justice that have shifted the focus from "capital outflows" (and the implication that neo-liberal tax policies might stem such outflows) to the "secretive jurisdictions" that organize the "illicit inflow" of international capital to Europe and the US, weakening the capacity to tax (and hence self-determine local affairs) elsewhere.[20] To effectively address such concerns, the need to develop a conceptual idiom capable of comprehending the scope of a "politics of anonymity" becomes all the more apparent. From anonymous grassroots activists in support of independent media to hackers able to control industrial infrastructures, from the anonymity of high-frequency trading that complicates the analyses of financial crises to the anonymity of users who prefer to cooperate in their exodus from the world of corporate communications infrastructures. These dynamic, loosely coupled and mission-oriented "extra-organizational" networks deserve attention from scholars as well as activists.

But above all, we must develop our conceptual devices on the algorithmic terrain that both structures and sustains our communicative practices. In its search for new forms of alliance, grassroots creativity must match and mobilize the artificial intelligence that drives cultural data analytics. Data analysis involves "techniques of artificial intelligence like natural-language processing, pattern recognition and machine learning" (Lohr, 2012; see also Loukides, 2010). Given the sobering analyses of the financial crisis of 2008, we are not fully convinced that "the requirements of mobile financial services development coincide with prerequisites for a thriving data common" (WEF, 2012). But we agree that data is a new asset class, and that perhaps we must open up the horizon of our media ecologies to include the "data exhaust" generated by our daily practices.[21] And if it is true that "We need to have a much more material, much more mundane, much more immanent, much more realistic, much more embodied definition of the material world if we wish to compose a common world" (Latour, 2010: 484; see also Deseriis and Dean, 2012), then algorithms must be included as we continue to create visions of such a common world, of such a commons.

Notes

1 In our usage of "biolinguistic capitalism" we refer to the work of Marazzi (2008) as well as Berardi (2009b), who have focused on the becoming-linguistic of labor and the centrality of linguistic conventions in their analysis of contemporary capitalism.

2 http://accurint.com. Others, however, you have never heard of: major actors in "predictive analytics" include Acxiom, FICO or Splunk.

3 See www.socialnetworkconstitution.com

4 We mean "affect of sharing" very deliberately here. As many working in affect theory have shown, the term *affect* is not reducible to terms such as sentiment or emotion, but rather encompasses a range

of sensations and senses coincident, in our argument, with distributed modes of communication. See Massumi (2002); see also Gregg and Seigworth (2010).

5 Key alternatives include http://crabgrass.riseuplabs.org, http://diasporaproject.org and http://identi.ca/

6 See also DeNardis (2011).

7 Of course, such a suggestion puts aside the fact that in many countries, utilities have been privatized as part of the neo-liberal agenda.

8 https://code.commotionwireless.net. See also http://fabfi.fablab.af

9 Rancière: "The strength of those rights lies in the back-and-forth movement between the first inscription of the right and the dissensual stage on which it is put to test" (2004: 305).

10 See Unlike Us: Understanding Social Media Monopolies and their Alternatives, a critical Internet studies project organized by the Institute of Network Cultures, Amsterdam. http://networkcultures. org/wpmu/unlikeus

11 See, for example, US Patent No. 8,254,902, "Apparatus and methods for enforcement of policies upon a wireless device," granted to Apple Inc. in 2012. The patent allows Apple the remote disabling of mobile phone cameras in Apple devices.

12 One of our favorite online journals for critical organization studies – *ephemera: theory & politics in organization* – is frequently addressing the topic of alternative organization. Though even here, the preoccupation is not with alternative figures of organization, such as the rise of anonymity as a disruptive critical persona. Instead, contributing writers to *ephemera* are more often engaged with how Foucault's writings on power and subjectivity alongside the Italian autonomist theories of biopolitics and immaterial labor can be incorporated within the field of organization studies. We don't see this as a shortcoming or oversight within organization studies so much as an indication of where the field is at in terms of its disciplinary horizon of thought. http://www. ephemeraweb.org

13 For a brilliant PhD dissertation that undertakes a much-needed critique of the politics of openness and the depoliticization of collaboration, see Tkacz (2012).

14 We use the term "machine" to refer to socio-technological assemblages of human and non-human actors. See Raunig (2010). On assemblage as an analytical term that acknowledges the way such machines cut across macro/micro distinctions, see DeLanda (2006). Assemblage can (but does not always) convey a critical awareness of conflict and power relations; see also note 16.

15 Here, we invoke the term *institution* in a twofold way: (1) as a machinic arrangement of *instituent* practices; and (2) as a *dispositif* of power. We deploy the term *dispositif* on various occasions as a way of signaling the more nuanced, comprehensive and political inflection of what in English is rendered as "apparatus." Associated with the work of Foucault, *dispositif* has been summarized by Giorgio Agamben (2009) as follows: "a) It is a heterogeneous set that includes virtually anything linguistic and nonlinguistic, under the same heading: discourses, institutions, buildings, laws, police measures, philosophical propositions, and so on. The apparatus itself is the network that is established between these elements. b) The apparatus always has a concrete strategic function and is always located in a power relation. c) As such, it appears at the intersection of power relations and relations of knowledge" (3). Proponents of Bruno Latour, actor-network theory and a politically eviscerated invocation of Deleuze and Guattari prefer to adopt the term and concept of "assemblage" in order to speak of material complexities. Our preference is to retain the sense of power, strategy, knowledge and technical arrangements assumed of *dispositifs*.

16 Beyond sidestepping the issue of the free labor powering user-generated content (note that such references to "generation" conveniently obscure the question of labor and the role of social media in its ongoing transformation), the emphasis on "participation" in analyses of "liberation technology" fails to draw attention to its own paradoxes – that participation has ceased to be a practice exclusively associated with the political (as in Hannah Arendt's political philosophy) and is now a practice that produces economic value. See Zehle and Rossiter (2009). See also Mejias (2012).

17 See http://datadealer.net for a game-based analysis of the political economy of social networks.

18 For an analysis of the "decline of the destination web" see Berry (2011).

19 www.occupystudentdebtcampaign.org; www.edu-factory.org/wp/campaign-against-debt. On financialization, see Crouch (2011); on debt as a cultural and economic practice, see Graeber (2011); and on alternatives devised by the Occupy Student Debt campaign to the debt-financing of education, see Ross (2012).

20 See www.taxjustice.net, www.financialsecrecyindex.com, and Shaxson (2012).
21 On data created as a by-product of other transactions, see WEF (2012: 11ff.).

Resources

Fibreculture Journal: http://fibreculturejournal.org
Organized Networks – Mobile Research Labs, Beijing: http://orgnets.net
TechCrunch: http://techcrunch.com
Transit Labour: Circuits, Regions, Borders: http://transitlabour.asia
xm:lab: www.xmlab.org

References

Agamben, G. (2009, 2006). *What is an Apparatus?* (D. Kishik and S. Pedatella, trans.). Stanford, CA: Stanford University Press.

Andrews, L. (2012). *I Know Who You Are and I Saw What You Did: Social Networks and the Death of Privacy.* New York: Free Press.

Benkler, Y. (2008). The University in the Networked Economy and Society: Challenges and Opportunities. In R.N. Katz (ed.), *The Tower and the Cloud: Higher Education in the Age of Cloud Computing*, Louisville (pp. 51–61). Col.: Educause. Available online at www.educause.edu/thetowerandthecloud

Berardi, F.B. (2009a). *The Soul at Work: From Alienation to Autonomy* (F. Cadel and G. Mecchia, trans.). Los Angeles, CA: Semiotext(e).

Berardi, F.B. (2009b). *Precarious Rhapsody: Semiocapitalism and the Pathologies of the Post-Alpha Generation.* London: Minor Compositions.

Berry, D.M. (2011). *The Philosophy of Software: Code and Mediation in the Digital Age.* London: Palgrave Macmillan.

Buden, B. (2006) Cultural Translation: Why it is Important and Where to Start with It. *Transversal*, 06. Available online at http://eipcp.net/transversal/0606/buden/en

Carr, N. (2008) *The Big Switch: Rewiring the World, from Edison to Google: Our New Digital Destiny.* New York: Norton.

Coleman, G. (2012a, January 13). Our Weirdness is Free. *Triple Canopy.* Available online at http://canopycanopycanopy.com/15/our_weirdness_is_free

Coleman, G.E. (2012b). *Coding Freedom: The Ethics and Aesthetics of Hacking.* Princeton, NJ: Princeton University Press.

Crouch, C. (2011). *The Strange Non-Death of Neo-Liberalism.* London: Polity Press.

DeLanda, M. (2006). *A New Philosophy of Society: Assemblage Theory and Social Complexity.* New York: Continuum.

DeNardis, L. (ed.). (2011). *Opening Standards: The Global Politics of Interoperability.* Cambridge, MA: MIT Press.

Deseriis, M. and Dean, J. (2012, March 1). A Movement Without Demands? *Possible Futures.* Available online at www.possible-futures.org/2012/01/03/a-movement-without-demands

Dibbel, J. (2012). The Shadow Web: Future of Media Control and Information Activism. *Scientific American*, 3, 61–65.

Dumbill, E. (2012, January 19). What is Big Data? An Introduction to the Big Data Landscape. *O'Reilly Radar.* Available online at http://radar.oreilly.com/2012/01/what-is-big-data.html

Fader, P. (2012, May 3). Is there Money in Big Data? *MIT Technology Review.* Available online at www.technologyreview.com/business/40320

FCIC. (2011, January). Conclusions of the Financial Crisis Inquiry Commission. In *The Financial Crisis Inquiry Report: Final Report of the National Commission on the Causes of the Financial and Economic Crisis in the United States.* Available online at http://fcic-static.law.stanford.edu/cdn_media/fcic-reports/fcic_final_report_conclusions.pdf

Fuller, M. and Goffey, A. (2012). *Evil Media.* Cambridge, MA: MIT Press.

Galloway, A. (2004). *Protocol: How Control Exists after Decentralization.* Cambridge, MA: MIT Press.

Galloway, A.R. (2006). *Gaming: Essays on Algorithmic Culture.* Minneapolis: University of Minnesota Press.

Graeber, D. (2011). *Debt: The First 5,000 Years*. London: Melville House Publishing.

Gregg, M. and and Seigworth, G.J. (eds). (2010). *The Affect Theory Reader*. Durham, NC: Duke University Press.

Hill, B.M. (2010). Richard Stallman on SaaS. Available online at http://autonomo.us/2010/03/richard-stallman-on-saas

Kahn-Harris, K. (2010, June 22). Naming the Movement. *openDemocracy*. Available online at http://www.opendemocracy.net/keith-kahn-harris/naming-movement

Kleiner, D. (2012a, May 15). Commercialization makes your online rights irrelevant, more thoughts from my talk with @ioerror at #rp12. Posting to liberationtech mailing list. Available online at liberationtech@lists.stanford.edu

Kleiner, D. (2012b, June 8). Privacy, Moglen, @ioerror, #rp12. Available online at www.dmytri.info/privacy-moglen-ioerror-rp12

LaFrance, D. and Nathan, L. (2012, February). Revolutionaries Will Not Be Friended: "Owning" Activism through Social Networking. iConference 2012, Toronto, Canada.

Latour, B. (2010). An Attempt at a "Compositionist Manifesto". *New Literary History*, 41, 471–490. Available online at http://blogs.sciences-po.fr/speap/files/2011/08/manifesto_speap.pdf

LiPuma, E. and Lee, B. (2004). *Financial Derivatives and the Globalization of Risk*. Durham, NC: Duke University Press.

Lohr, S. (2012, November 2). The Age of Big Data. *New York Times*. Available online at www.nytimes.com/2012/02/12/sunday-review/big-datas-impact-in-the-world.html

Loukides, M. (2010, June 6). What is Data Science? *O'Reilly Radar*. Available online at http://radar.oreilly.com/2010/06/what-is-data-science.html

Manovich, L. (2012). Trending: The Promises and the Challenges of Big Social Data. In M.K. Gold (ed.), *Debates in the Digital Humanities* (pp. 460–475), Minneapolis: University of Minnesota Press. Available online at http://lab.softwarestudies.com/2011/04/new-article-by-lev-manovich-trending.html

Marazzi, C. (2008). *Capital and Language: From the New Economy to the War Economy* (G. Conti, trans.). Los Angeles, CA: Semiotext(e).

Martin, R. (2007). *An Empire of Indifference: American War and the Financial Logic of Risk Management*. Durham, NC: Duke University Press.

Massumi, B. (2002). *Parables for the Virtual: Movement, Affect. Sensation*, Durham, NC: Duke University Press.

Mejias, U.A. (2012). Liberation Technology and the Arab Spring: From Utopia to Atopia and Beyond. *Fibreculture Journal*, 20. Available online at http://twenty.fibreculturejournal.org/

Moglen, E. (2010a). Freedom In the Cloud: Software Freedom, Privacy, and Security for Web 2.0. Available online at www.softwarefreedom.org/events/2010/isoc-ny/FreedomInTheCloud-transcript.html

Moglen, E. (2010b). How We Can Be the Silver Lining of the Cloud. DebConf10. Available online at http://penta.debconf.org/dc10_schedule/events/641.en.html; see also http://freedomboxfoundation.org

Morozov, E. (2012, January 27). The Dangers of Sharing. *New York Times*. Available online at www.nytimes.com/2012/01/29/books/review/i-know-who-you-are-and-i-saw-what-you-did-social-networks-and-the-death-of-privacy-by-lori-andrews-book-review.html

Rancière, J. (2004). Who is the Subject of the Rights of Man. *South Atlantic Quarterly*, 103(2/3), 297–310.

Raunig, G. (2009). Instituent Practices: Fleeing, Instituting, Transforming. In G. Raunig and G. Ray (eds), *Art and Contemporary Critical Practice: Reinventing Institutional Critique* (pp. 3–11). London: MayFly Books.

Raunig, G. (2010). *A Thousand Machines: A Concise Philosophy of the Machine as Social Movement* (A. Derieg, trans.). New York: Semiotext(e).

Ross, A. (2012). Democracy and Debt. In C. Beltrán, A.J. Bauer, R. Jaleel and A. Ross (eds), *Is this What Democracy Looks Like?* New York: Social Text/Periscope. Available online at http://what-democracy-looks-like.com/democracy-and-debt/

Shaxson, N. (2012). *Treasure Islands: Uncovering the Damage of Offshore Banking and Tax Havens*. London: Palgrave MacMillan.

Stallman, R.S. (2010). What Does That Server Really Serve? Available online at www.gnu.org/philosophy/who-does-that-server-really-serve.html

Tamir, D.I. and Mitchell, J.P. (2012, June 7). Disclosing Information about the Self is Intrinsically Rewarding. *PNAS Early Edition*, 1–6. Available online at http://wjh.harvard.edu/~dtamir/Tamir-PNAS-2012.pdf

Tkacz, N. (2012). *Wikipedia and the Politics of Openness* (Doctoral dissertation, University of Melbourne, Melbourne).

WEF (2012). Big Data, Big Impact: New Possibilities for International Development. Davos: World Economic Forum. Available online at www.weforum.org/reports/big-data-big-impact-new-possibilities-international-development

Zehle, S. and Rossiter, N. (2009). Organizing Networks: Notes on Collaborative Constitution, Translation and the Work of Organization. *Cultural Politics*, 5(2), 237–264.

Section 3
Exchange and consumption

The main objective of this section of the book is to reflect upon the sort of relations that are implicated in exchange and consumption. In particular, the chapters presented here redefine exchange in terms of social and environmental relations rather than purely economic ones.

As we noted in Chapter 1, neo-liberalism envisages the market as a place populated by free, rational, calculating individuals who exchange so as to maximize their own interests. Thus consumers will supposedly seek to obtain maximum value at minimum price from any exchange, irrespective of any damaging effect this may have on others or the environment, as long as they don't have to bear the cost themselves. Yet the consumers we encounter in the chapters that follow seem a long way from these self-maximizing individuals; they are moved by solidarity and responsibility (see Chapter 3) rather than just self-interest. So we see consumers who care about the impacts of their consumption – for example, on producers or the environment – and are prepared to take responsibility for what, if the free market had its way, would remain 'externalities'. We also see the possibility of exchange becoming an act of solidarity where concerns for the fair sharing of resources take precedence over self-interest maximization. The types of consumption and exchange presented in the chapters below also have important implications for the way in which we understand the 'good life'. This becomes articulated less in terms of the accumulation of material goods, and more in terms of the quality of the relationships we have with each other and our environment. Ultimately, reading through these chapters, the image of the calculating and greedy consumer, so central to capitalism and its need for endless growth, starts disintegrating. Instead, acts of exchange, consumption (and non-consumption) emerge as complex webs of social, ethical and economic relations.

In Chapter 11, Laura Raynolds and Jennifer Keahey discuss some of the challenges that Fair Trade faces in creating more egalitarian networks of exchange between producers in the global South and consumers in the global North. Fair Trade seeks to transform the market from within; it relies on the market to promote justice, but tries to address its failures by accounting for social and environmental costs. However, the recent expansion of Fair Trade has created certain tensions between market dynamics and commitment to social justice, tensions which Raynolds and Keahey explore through their analysis of Fair Trade Roiboos tea in South Africa.

If Raynolds and Keahey look at ways to instil social justice in global trade, several other chapters in this section explore how exchange can be re-localized. Complementary currencies are one way of doing so and, in Chapter 12, Peter North reviews the various ways in which local currencies are organized (e.g. how they value goods or services, their convertibility and geographical scale) to meet objectives ranging from radical attempts to develop alternative economic relations, to more moderate agendas related to boosting local economic development. He suggests that if complementary currencies are to be instrumental in creating more sustainable economies, they will need to take diverse forms and operate at different levels in order to reconcile ethical commitments to the local area with the sort of geographical scale that would attract businesses.

In Chapter 13, Alf Rehn argues that the continuous presence of gift exchange in contemporary economies (for example, in free open-source software, or blood and organ donations) suggests the possibility of more ethical alternatives to the calculating rationality of market exchange. However, he warns against idealized images of gifting, reminding us that while gift relations imbue economic exchange with personal relations, these relations can be coercive or competitive. In addition, while gift exchanges can create and distribute significant economic value, they are limited to certain domains, times or spaces. Thus while gift relations in contemporary society are significant enough to challenge the supposed supremacy of market exchange, the possibility of a gift economy remains more elusive.

In Chapter 14, Seonaidh McDonald introduces us to voluntary simplifiers. Here the key issue is not so much to exchange or consume differently as to exchange and consume less. Voluntary simplicity involves deliberately reducing income and consumption in order to enjoy a better quality of life, defined in terms of having more time. Thus, implicitly if not explicitly, voluntary simplicity stands as a strong criticism of capitalism and its reliance on endless growth and consumption. Maybe the most significant contribution of voluntary simplicity is its redefinition of the 'good life' from material to immaterial goods (time, relationships). This is a theme that is taken up by the following two chapters.

In Chapter 15, Molly Scott Cato argues that capitalism's need for endless growth is incompatible with the earth's natural limits. She proposes the idea of the bioregional economy as a framework for designing localized, self-reliant economies that are not only more sustainable but also put questions of the fair distribution of resources at the forefront. By calling into question the pursuit of endless growth, the bioregional economy also invites us to re-examine the way we think about ourselves: in terms of relationships rather than consumption. Throughout her discussion, Cato provides various examples of the ways in which bioregional economies could allocate resources equitably, and through participatory processes.

In their discussion of eco-localism and the transition movement in Chapter 16, Shiv Ganesh and Heather Zoller pick up on the issue of grass-roots participation and its potential tension with environmental imperatives. The transition movement provides a framework for moving from a high-energy to a low-energy economy that can be more resilient to the shocks associated with climate change and peak oil. In doing so, it confronts two potential tensions – the first between the need to achieve environmental outcomes while maintaining a democratic process, and the second between the localized economy it proposes and large-scale systemic change. Ganesh and Zoller suggest that the way the transition movement articulates the concept of resilience – as a collective process for designing more fulfilling, post-carbon, liveable futures – goes a long way to addressing these tensions.

11

Fair Trade

Social justice and production alternatives

Laura T. Raynolds and Jennifer Keahey

Introduction

Fair Trade represents an important form of alternative organizing that seeks to promote social justice by creating more egalitarian commodity networks designed to link marginalized producers with progressive consumers. Fair Trade works to alleviate poverty and empower producers in the global South by providing better prices, stable market links and development resources. In the global North, Fair Trade provides consumers with opportunities to purchase more socially and environmentally responsible products. Over the past 20 years, Fair Trade has come to represent a critical alternative to the destructive relations characteristic of conventional globalization, particularly in the agro-food system (Raynolds et al., 2007).

As a form of alternative organization, Fair Trade joins an array of non-capitalist social economy arrangements that integrate social justice concerns with alternative economic practices (Raynolds, 2012). The Fair Trade movement works to re-embed production in social relations (Raynolds, 2000), seeking to transform the market from within (Keahey et al., 2011; Raynolds, 2002). Fair Trade represents an example of the social economy experiments that Wright (2010: 17) suggests "could potentially constitute a component of a process of transcending capitalism." For Fair Trade fuels a challenge to each of the three core capitalist principles which the editors outline in their introductory chapter: (1) private appropriation of the means of production and the division between capital and labor, (2) profit motive, and (3) free market reliance. First, Fair Trade's smallholder producers challenge the separation between capital and labor by democratically organizing into cooperatives that collectively own the means of production. Second, Fair Trade exchange relations challenge the profit imperative by redefining quality in terms of social well-being and environmental sustainability, shifting profit shares to producers in the form of guaranteed minimum pricing and social premium funds. Third, Fair Trade harnesses free market forces, in particular the neoliberal thirst for value addition, in the pursuit of global trade regulation. However, despite Fair Trade's considerable promise in supporting alternative organizational forms, as this chapter explores, the initiative's rapid expansion raises a number of challenges to its core, social justice principles.

This chapter analyzes Fair Trade's contributions and challenges in developing alternative production and marketing networks. We focus particularly on movement and market dynamics as they relate to Africa, since this region is currently experiencing the most rapid growth in the production of Fair Trade certified commodities. Our analysis highlights the dynamic tensions driving fair market divergence and convergence at transnational and regional levels. We ground our discussion with a case study of the South African Rooibos tea sector, where Fair Traders are striving to increase farm ownership and capacity among "emerging" farmers of color who historically have been denied access to agricultural land and markets. While Fair Trade offers opportunities for combating acute agriculture inequalities, production growth is increasingly being dominated by large hired-labor estates. We argue that while Fair Trade's production and marketing networks are not immune from mainstream market pressures, there are dynamic openings for emerging farmers and their organizations to refashion Fair Trade in South Africa and to shape alternative market networks at regional and international levels.

Fair Trade's alternative marketing networks

A brief history

Fair Trade grew out of a set of post-World War II initiatives that were led by church and development groups who wished to assist impoverished producers by providing preferential markets for their products. These groups established alternative trade organizations (ATOs) to import handicrafts at favorable prices and sell them in dedicated craft shops. Third World solidarity and cooperative movements in the 1960s and 1970s expanded ATO efforts across Europe and North America, and into new commodities (Raynolds and Long, 2007).

In the late 1980s, a new strand of Fair Trade was established with the introduction of product certification and labeling. Fair Trade groups created alternative networks for certified products to introduce food items into mainstream supermarkets where the majority of people do their shopping. This move acknowledged the continued centrality of agro-export production for poor people in the global South and the rise of specialty markets in the global North for products differentiated based on their social or ecological attributes. In creating the first certified Fair Trade networks, international solidarity groups collaborated with Mexican coffee cooperatives to secure markets for small-scale coffee farmers threatened by world price declines (Renard, 2005). Transnational alliances between solidarity and development groups, Fair Trade organizations, and producer associations have fueled the creation of alternative marketing networks in a growing range of products.

Fair Traders work to alleviate poverty and empower producers and farm workers in the global South by providing them with better prices, stable market links and development resources. In the global North – as well as in nascent Southern markets such as South Africa – Fair Trade certification provides consumers with opportunities to purchase more socially and environmentally responsible products, and over the past 20 years the movement has come to represent a critical alternative to the destructive relations characteristic of conventional globalization, particularly in the agro-food system (Raynolds et al., 2007).

Decades of growth have transformed the movement from a model of charitable intentions to one of commercial success (Keahey et al., 2011). Although Fair Trade products represent a minor share of the world market, annual certified sales are valued at nearly US$5 billion and continue to rise, despite the current economic downturn (FLO, 2010a). Fair Trade producer organizations in 60 countries across Latin America, Africa and Asia export 20 certified products to alternative markets across Europe, North America and the Pacific. Less often recognized is the movement's potential for combating acute racial and gender inequalities. Fair Trade maintains specific gender standards to promote female leadership and enables under-represented producers to enter into alternative commodity networks, where they may access technical training and strengthen their participation in multilateral trade networks (Raynolds and Keahey, 2009). In response to these opportunities, grass-roots practitioners have worked to bring less advantaged farmers into the Fair Trade system as a development strategy, but, despite the promise of Fair Trade in supporting alternative production organizations, its recent expansion raises a number of challenges to the movement's core, social justice principles.

Alternative market dynamics

Fair Trade joins a growing array of market-based initiatives that promote social and environmental concerns through the sale of alternative and often certified commodities. In this sense, Fair Trade is related to environmental certifications found largely in food and forest products, and ethical certifications found largely in apparel and footwear (Vogel, 2010). Yet Fair Trade distinguishes itself from other certification efforts in its breadth in incorporating both environmental and social concerns and its depth in reshaping trade and production conditions (Raynolds, 2000). Operating at the intersection of market critique and re-regulation, Fair Trade challenges dominant "unfair" trade practices and promotes alternative "fair" market norms (Raynolds, 2012). Fair Trade's ATO and certification strands have worked together to forge a common understanding of the movement's foundational principles and alternative organizing model.

> Fair Trade is a trading partnership, based on dialogue, transparency and respect, that seeks greater equity in international trade. It contributes to sustainable development by offering better trading conditions to, and securing the rights of, marginalized producers and workers – especially in the South. Fair Trade organisations (backed by consumers) are engaged actively in supporting producers, awareness raising and in campaigning for changes in the rules and practice of conventional international trade.
>
> *(FINE, 2003)*

As this statement suggests, Fair Trade operates both "in and against the market," working through market channels to create alternative commodity networks for items produced under more favorable social and ecological conditions, and simultaneously working against the conventional market forces that create and uphold global inequalities (Raynolds, 2000, 2002).

In working against the market, Fair Trade is positioned within the Alternative Globalization/Trade Justice movement. Fair Trade has clear institutional and ideological ties with anti-sweatshop and social movement union initiatives in manufacturing and agro-ecology, food sovereignty and land reform initiatives in agriculture. These diverse global civil society efforts coalesce around critiques of corporate globalization and efforts to advance an alternative globalization agenda, based on core human rights and sustainability precepts (Vogel, 2010). Social movement groups have aligned with non-governmental organizations (NGOs) and socially responsible enterprises in pursuing these alternative initiatives in local, national and transnational arenas. In Fair Trade, NGOs have played a key role in pressuring corporations to improve their practices, and in working with innovative entrepreneurs to create non-corporate alternatives. What accounts for Fair Trade's popularity is its ability to combine visionary goals with the pragmatic construction of alternative trade networks (Raynolds, 2002).

Working within the market, Fair Trade groups promote alternative values, practices and institutions to "shorten the distance" between producers and consumers (Raynolds, 2000). These alternative networks hinge on personal relations of trust and on information exchanges which humanize economic transactions. Fair Trade questions the legitimacy of industrial and market conventions that value commodities based solely on efficiency and price considerations, and it promotes a revaluation of goods based on civic and relational values. Rather than being abstracted from their roots, Fair Trade seeks to re-link commodities to the people and places from which they originate (Raynolds, 2002).

Fair Trade certification organization

Fairtrade International (FLO) has coordinated the rapid growth in certified commodity networks. This umbrella organization links 18 national labeling initiatives in Northern markets (such as the UK Fairtrade Foundation) with 942 producer groups organized into three regional producer networks (including the African Fairtrade Network). FLO's certification system is based on a set of core requirements for producers and buyers (FLO, 2010a). Affiliated producers must be organized into democratic groups of small growers or workers who uphold high social and environmental standards. Fair Trade buyers must in turn pay FLO guaranteed prices, provide a social premium, and offer producer credit and stable contracts.

Fair Trade's rapid growth over recent decades has fueled a process of bureaucratic growth in the FLO certification system. FLO originally acted as both standard-setting body and certifier. Certification was in the early years informal and free to producer groups, but has become formalized with auditing costs billed to producers. To decrease conflicts of interest, FLO-Cert was spun off as an independent certifier. FLO-Cert is charged with overseeing compliance and auditing producers (via onsite interviews and document reviews) and buyers (through a review of purchase records). In FLO's bureaucratic development, Fair Trade standards have become increasingly specific, involving now an extensive list of producer entry and progress requirements. FLO has moved to transform Fair Trade's alternative norms into a business management plan as Mutersbaugh (2002) suggests, although its standards continue to diverge from commercial norms in stipulating non-quantifiable expectations like "democratic" representation. Even though FLO has increasingly adopted mainstream auditing practices, its normative standards appear to make Fair Trade relations less susceptible to market rule than, for example, organic certification where standards are increasingly interpreted as a set of input restrictions (Raynolds, 2004).

FLO was founded and originally controlled by Northern market members, but over the has become more a multi-stakeholder organization. While FLO's Board of Directors once comprised only labeling initiative representatives, this group now holds only five of 14 seats. There are in addition two seats reserved for certified trader representatives and three for independent civil society experts. The most important change has come in producer representation, with four Board seats reserved for representatives from FLO certified producer organizations (at least one from each of the African, Asian and Latin American producer networks). Fifty producer representatives participate in the annual FLO General Assembly which decides on membership issues, approves the budget and ratifies new Board members. Although producer representation in FLO governance has increased substantially over the years, analysis of key decisions, such as the establishment of minimum prices, reflects continued North/South inequalities. For example, coffee producer representatives were recently able to secure a significant price floor increase, but not without significant struggle against the conventional market forces that continuously challenge Fair Trade's alternative model (Bacon, 2010; Reinecke, 2010).

Fair Trade market growth

The global Fair Trade market is booming. FLO certified sales were valued at US$4.7 billion in 2009, with growth averaging 46 percent per year (FLO, 2010a). Markets for non-certified Fair Trade items, comprised largely of handicrafts, have been growing more slowly, adding US$363 million to global sales (Krier, 2008). Certified commodities have made major inroads across Europe and North America and represent one of the most rapidly growing segments in the agro-food industry. As noted in Table 11.1, Europe has the largest Fair Trade certified market, led by the United Kingdom with annual purchases of US$1.25 billion. FLO's certified commodities are readily available in government offices, universities, supermarkets, restaurants and specialty outlets across Europe. UK consumers spend an average of US $16 per year on labeled Fair Trade items (Krier, 2008). Although North American Fair Trade markets are less well developed than those in Europe, the United States has emerged as the second largest national market, with certified sales worth US$1.19 billion per year. The availability of Fair Trade certified products is more limited in the United States, where per capita spending averages only US$3 annually (Krier, 2008). Some of the most rapid sales growth is now being experienced in newer Fair Trade markets in the Pacific Rim.

Table 11.2 outlines sales figures for Fair Trade's key certified commodities. Coffee remains Fair Trade's signature commodity, with roughly 74,000 metric tons sold each year. Cocoa and tea represent Fair Trade's other top commodities. Of these key commodities, tea has seen the

Table 11.1 Fair Trade certified sales in major markets (US$ 1,000)*

Countries by Region	2005	2007	2009
Europe	812,546	1,802,174	2,495,076
UK	344,588	965,666	1,250,409
France	135,819	287,931	400,970
Switzerland	166,568	216,771	251,053
Germany	88,263	194,285	372,724
Austria	31,869	72,394	100,332
Netherlands	45,439	65,127	119,588
North America	471,693	1,111,140	1,467,887
USA	428,370	1,002,000	1,186,431
Canada	43,323	109,140	281,456
Pacific Rim	7,345	23,309	55,764
Australia/NZ	3,112	14,808	40,041
Japan	4,233	8,501	15,723
Total**	1,409,762	3,264,589	4,729,800

Compiled by the authors using data from FLO (2006, 2008, 2010a)

Notes: *Euros are converted to dollars using the US Federal Reserve average annual exchange rate (2005: US$1.24 = 1 Euro; 2006 US$1.26 = 1 Euro; 2007: US$1.37 = 1 Euro; 2008: US$1.47 = 1 Euro; 2009: US$1.39 = 1 Euro).
** Total includes countries not listed on the chart.

Table 11.2 Sales volumes of top Fair Trade certified commodities (metric tons)

Commodity	2005	2007	2009
Coffee	33,992	62,209	73,781
Tea	2,614	5,421	11,524
Cocoa	5,657	7,306	13,898
Sugar	3,163	15,074	89,628
Bananas	103,877	233,791	311,465
Other fresh fruit/juices	13,145	24,919	65,673
Total*	168,076	354,611	575,620

Compiled by the authors using data from FLO (2006, 2008, 2010a)

Notes: * Includes other labeled commodities measured by weight (e.g., rice and honey), but not those measured by item or volume (e.g., flowers, cotton, sports balls, wine and beer).

most rapid recent growth, with yearly sales rising to reach almost 12,000 metric tons in 2009. Fair Trade certification was initiated in the mid-1990s in traditional tea and expanded in the mid-2000s to include Rooibos (or Red Bush), camomile, hibiscus, mint and other herbal teas.[1] UK consumers drink roughly 70 percent of the world's Fair Trade certified tea. Despite not being a traditional tea drinking country, the United States currently has the world's second largest certified tea market. Here, the most rapidly rising sales are for herbal teas like Rooibos which are caffeine free and claim a broad range of health benefits (Raynolds and Ngcwangu, 2009).

Fair Trade's alternative production networks

Fair Trade production growth

Fair Trade production has seen dramatic expansion across the global South. Northern demand has generated lucrative markets for an increasing volume and variety of certified food exports, and producers' interest in these new markets has been fueled by neo-liberal policies, which have undercut domestic prices and reoriented agro-exports toward specialty markets. Producers around the world have sought to differentiate their products according to social or ecological attributes in order to secure more stable and higher-priced sales. Development NGOs and allied groups have worked to bolster the opportunities for less advantaged farmers and workers to tap the income-generating and community development benefits of participating in Fair Trade's alternative market system (Bacon, 2005; Raynolds, 2004).

The number of FLO-affiliated producer enterprises rose from 433 to 942 between 2004 and 2009 (FLO, 2005; 2010a). There are now 1.5 million farmers and workers across Latin America, Africa and Asia producing Fair Trade certified commodities. As noted in Table 11.3, Latin America, the traditional home of Fair Trade production, has the largest number of FLO certified groups. There are 536 FLO certified enterprises in Latin America and the Caribbean, the vast majority of which are small, farmer cooperatives. Latin America continues to supply most of the world's Fair Trade certified coffee, bananas and sugar as well as much of its cocoa (FLO, 2010b).

Africa has seen the largest increase in Fair Trade production in recent years and is the world's second most important supplier. The number of FLO affiliates in Africa rose from 78 in 2004 to 259 in 2009 (FLO, 2005, 2010a). Fair Trade certified commodities are produced

Table 11.3 Fair Trade certified producer groups by region

Region	Number of producer countries	Number of FLO certified enterprises	Share of certified enterprises that are coops
Latin America and the Caribbean	20	536	84%
Africa	28	259	51%
Asia	12	147	72%

Compiled by authors using data from FLO (2010b)

in 28 African countries, most importantly in South Africa, Ghana, Uganda, Tanzania and Kenya. The continent is the largest source of Fair Trade certified traditional and herbal tea as well as cocoa and is a secondary, but critical, supplier of certified coffee and bananas. Africa is also the world's major supplier of newly FLO labeled items like flowers and wine. The number of certified producer groups in Africa has risen across a number of commodity areas, with certified enterprises in the tea sector increasing from 17 in 2005 to 48 in 2009.

Alternative production dynamics

Fair Trade raises the potential for empowering small farmers in Africa and transforming trade practices historically framed by colonialism (Raynolds and Keahey, 2009). However, FLO's rapid expansion into new commodities and territories has involved a shift in the organizational foundations of production. While smallholder cooperatives still comprise the backbone of production, hired-labor estates represent an important and growing share of production. This is particularly true in Africa where, as noted in Table 11.3, roughly half of the enterprises certified by FLO are large enterprises that rely on hired labor. In coffee, cocoa and sugar, FLO certification excludes plantation enterprises. In tea and bananas, FLO certifies both large and small enterprises and plantations have come to outnumber and out-produce farmer cooperatives.

The most direct Fair Trade benefits for smallholders come from the higher guaranteed prices and the financial and development support provided for producer cooperatives. For larger enterprises, FLO rules help ensure that International Labor Organization and national labor standards are upheld and that workers are collectively represented. Both Fair Trade producer arrangements benefit from the social premium paid by buyers for certified products. Producer and worker associations are responsible for determining the allocation of premium funds, which are invested largely in education, health and housing projects (FLO, 2010b). The most important benefits of Fair Trade engagement for both producers and workers appear to come from the multifaceted informal and formal support mechanisms provided for organizational capacity building (Raynolds, 2012).

Fair Trade certified tea, like its conventional counterpart, is primarily produced and processed by large enterprises (Raynolds and Ngcwangu, 2009). Tea certification was initiated with progressive plantations which operated their own tea factories. The extension of Fair Trade certification to herbal teas and the efforts of dedicated ATO buyers have reinforced the position of small farmer cooperatives. Cooperatives still make up less than half of the 89 enterprises exporting Fair Trade certified tea (FLO, 2010b). Despite their more limited numbers, smallholder cooperatives are a critical avenue for integrating less advantaged producers into alternative networks: there are roughly 126,000 tea farmers who are members of Fair Trade certified cooperatives, 27 percent of whom are women (FLO, 2010b).

Table 11.4 African Fair Trade certified traditional and herbal tea producer organizations

Countries	Producer organizations	Types of tea produced
Kenya	20	Camomile; traditional tea
South Africa	7	Rooibos; traditional tea
Tanzania	6	Camomile; mint; traditional tea
Malawi	5	Camomile; traditional tea
Uganda	4	Camomile; traditional tea
Egypt	2	Camomile; hibiscus; mint
Burkina Faso	2	Hibiscus
Rwanda	1	Camomile
Senegal	1	Traditional tea
Total	48	

Compiled by the authors using data from FLO-CERT (2011b)

Table 11.4 outlines the characteristics of Fair Trade certified producers of traditional and herbal teas in Africa. FLO entrance into tea and herbal tea has stimulated the growth of African Fair Trade certified groups producing camomile, hibiscus, mint and traditional tea. Out of the continent's 48 Fair Trade tea enterprises, 20 are located in Kenya. The predominance of Kenyan producers in certified networks reflects this country's historically central role in the traditional tea trade (Dolan, 2007), as well as its more recent entry into camomile exports. South Africa, Tanzania, Malawi and Uganda have the next largest number of FLO certified tea enterprises, with four to seven producer organizations in each country. All of these countries, except South Africa, are historically important producers of traditional tea which have moved in recent years into certified markets for both traditional tea and newly established herbal varieties. Although South Africa historically has played only a minor role in the traditional tea trade, the recent boom in Fair Trade production in this country has encouraged producers to enter certified markets for Rooibos tea, a uniquely South African product (Raynolds and Ngcwangu, 2009).

South African production dynamics

South African Fair Trade is dominated by hired-labor production, and movement growth is primarily occurring in the wine and temperate fruit sectors where large, white-owned estates hire predominantly colored[2] and black workers. As noted in Table 11.5, the number of Fair

Table 11.5 Fair Trade certified producer organizations in South Africa

	2005	2011
Fresh fruit	22	58
Wine	22	17
Tea	5	7
Fruit juice	2	4
Dried fruit	1	1
Total	52	87

Compiled by the authors using data from FLO-CERT (2005; 2011b)

Trade certified producer organizations in South Africa has increased substantially in recent years in tea and other commodity areas, but the most rapid growth is currently occurring within the fresh fruit sector which has been collaborating with European supermarkets to launch Fair Trade citrus. Although Table 11.5 suggests that the number of enterprises in the wine sector has declined, this is due to the amalgamation of 11 growers under a multi-estate certificate. In real terms, there has been a growth of six certified producer groups.

In South Africa, Fair Trade offers important opportunities for combating numerous agricultural inequalities (Bek et al., 2007; Kruger and du Toit, 2007). Nearly all national Fair Trade production is concentrated within the hired-labor sector because FLO has prioritized hired-labor involvement to secure farm worker rights. Commercial agriculture in the colonial and Apartheid eras was controlled by the white minority, limiting the participation of black and colored farmers. To counter this legacy, the post-Apartheid government instituted a series of Black Economic Empowerment (BEE) policies that promote non-white ownership, management, procurement and capacity building. In the early 2000s, FLO revised South African hired-labor standards to incorporate BEE requirements which required workers of color to acquire a 25 percent share of certified enterprises, enter management, and gain access to capacity-building programs (AgriBEE, 2005).[3] In recent years, the government has sought to expand benefits by developing a Broad-Based Black Economic Empowerment (BBBEE) system that engages scorecards to track labor relations (Department of Trade and Industry, 2009; du Toit et al., 2008). Ongoing Fair Trade/BBBEE alignment has been lauded as the means to reducing exploitation, but while there are sterling enterprises, broader results remain inconclusive (du Toit et al., 2008, Ferrer and Lyne, 2008, Kruger and du Toit, 2007).

Emerging smallholders also have experienced historical exclusion from market access and agricultural production, but BBBEE standards do not apply to this group because they do not operate as farm laborers on white-dominated commercial farms. Smallholder needs necessarily differ from those of farm laborers, but emerging producers of color require similar access to support mechanisms, including managerial and production training. In theory, Fair Trade's smallholder cooperatives could become involved in BBBEE, and would likely score quite highly in the scorecard system as such cooperatives are entirely owned and managed by underrepresented groups. However, cooperatives would reap few, if any, benefits from pursuing BBBEE compliance. There are some moves to brand the concept of BEE tea outside of the Fair Trade system, but few smallholders are involved in South African Fair Trade, and potential linkages have yet to be adequately explored.

The case of Rooibos tea

Rooibos is a member of the Cape *fynbos* floral kingdom, which among the world's six floral kingdoms is the smallest and wholly contained within South Africa (Wilson, 2005; Binns *et al.*, 2007). Production of this legume has traditionally been limited to the Greater Cederberg Biodiversity Corridor (GCBC). Whereas commercial production extends from the wetter western slope into the valleys along the Atlantic coast, emerging Rooibos production occurs on the northeastern slope, in and around the mountains of Wupperthal and in the southern Bokkeveld plains to the north, and these two areas comprise the core of emerging farmer production. Colored Cederberg communities traditionally have gathered wild Rooibos, and helped develop early cultivated varieties. More recently, these communities have sought to enter Rooibos markets by expanding cultivation, and the industry has recognized the high quality of their tea.

Within the smallholder sector, European ATOs pursuing a solidarity agenda have established direct market ties with emerging Rooibos producers. Enterprising smallholders first organized into democratic farmer associations to capture organic certification and began selling tea through ATOs in 2002. The two emerging Rooibos groups organizationally restructured into formal cooperatives in 2005 to secure certification, becoming the first smallholders in South Africa to enter the FLO system. In accordance with Fair Trade guidelines these cooperatives were democratically organized, with a governing board elected by member vote, and the means of production jointly owned by its membership base. Prior to certification, the two entities had begun plans to add product value by instituting a joint Fair Trade packaging effort which was launched at the same time as certification. The cooperatives developed an organizational model in which each would own one-third shares, with the third portion going to a South African packager who instituted company operations (Raynolds and Ngcwangu, 2010).

Despite this promising start, cooperative efforts outpaced Fair Trade standards development. Emerging producers initially believed Fair Trade would limit Rooibos to smallholder production, but the placement of this product on FLO's tea registry enabled the entry of hired-labor enterprises and Fair Trade markets were flooded with newly certified Rooibos. Market prices plummeted due to a broader industry glut. The packaging firm collapsed and participating groups splintered into different factions. One cooperative was able to survive these difficulties. But the largest organization experienced extended conflict as it was unable to pay its members; this cooperative was decertified in 2009 and subsequently liquidated. In the area, a smaller cooperative has formed to regain certification, but the broader community is struggling to rebuild Rooibos ties.

In many ways, emerging Rooibos farmers faced a perfect storm as they entered Fair Trade markets. First, members became certified at a time when standards were not fully developed. Second, emerging Rooibos farmers produce in extremely low volume due to land shortages. Third, South African Fair Traders have prioritized hired-labor production as a means of redressing Apartheid-era farm worker abuses, and emerging producer support has been nascent. Fourth, hired-labor firms were similarly obtaining Rooibos certification and the industry as a whole was entering into a commodity glut that lowered pricing. As a consequence, hired-labor firms now dominate both conventional and Fair Trade Rooibos markets.

Progressive industry actors have sought to assist emerging farmers through these difficulties by supporting their market access. However, most emerging producers reside on marginal land where scant rainfall and regional conservation protocols limit farming potential (Binns et al., 2007; Nel et al., 2007). Some own land but most do not, and because rented parcels are insufficient, farmers must locate other income, with many turning to tourism. As they seek to expand into broader product markets, emerging farmers recognize the need for multiple certifications; yet multiple audits are prohibitively expensive. Inadequate telecommunications and road infrastructure further limit emerging farmer potential (Sandra Kruger and Associates, 2010).

Rooibos estates are equipped with better infrastructure and operate on larger tracts of land in the more productive western slope. These privileges enable hired-labor estates to more efficiently meet market demands. Emerging Rooibos farmers compete with approximately 300 large commercial producers (de Lange, 2004). Total national production now averages about 12,000 tons per year, half of which is destined for export.[4] Despite this rapid growth, Rooibos distribution remains highly concentrated, with one firm controlling 90 percent of domestic sales and 70 percent of exports (Binns et al., 2007). Table 11.6 delineates South Africa's Fair Trade certified Rooibos producers and traders.

FLO did not introduce minimum pricing requirements until 2008 when it set minimum per kilo prices for Rooibos small producer organizations at US$3.93 (30 South African

Table 11.6 South African Fair Trade certified Rooibos producers and traders

Small farmer groups	Hired-labor estates	Traders
Driefontein	Bergendal Boerdery	Cape Natural Tea Products
Heiveld	Erfdeel Farming Trust	Carmien Tea
Wupperthal Original	Mouton Citrus	Coetzee & Coetzee
	Weidouw Estate	I & M Smith
		Khoisan Tea
		Rooibos Ltd

Compiled by the authors using data from FLO-CERT (2011b)

Rand/ZAR), with a US$0.66 social premium (5 ZAR). Hired-labor estates receive the same amount, albeit with a lower floor price and higher premium to better serve FLO's farm laborer constituents (FLO, 2007; Raynolds and Ngcwangu, 2010). It is unclear whether this minimum pricing is sufficient. Rising agricultural input and living costs mean that absolute prices are similar to those in the 1980s, and Rooibos pricing is highly volatile due to this product's susceptibility to drought. Climate change is of relevance to tea producers because of this crop's susceptibility to drought cycles and desertification (Fairtrade Africa, 2011). Emerging Rooibos groups likewise live in fragile production areas, and operate within a commodity sector that is marked by cyclical gluts and droughts. While Fair Trade price guarantees buffer producers from market volatility, certification is by no means a panacea.

FLO membership offers access to technical support, but delivery has been problematic. Given their relative lack of infrastructure and managerial experience, it is more difficult for emerging groups to access FLO pre-assessment requirements; yet producer organizations must initiate the process and modify internal operations to suit external interests. In the case of Rooibos, lack of technical capacity engendered the decertification of a major cooperative, and the resulting conflict threatened community well-being. To succeed within the Fair Trade system, less advantaged producers must rapidly obtain technical expertise, often with minimum support. Without effective training, Fair Trade may fall short of its promise, leaving impoverished producers buffeted by an external system of which they have negligible knowledge and over which they have little influence.

Finally, some emerging farmer groups want more flexibility than FLO's current producer standards offer. Those with greater levels of technical expertise wish to use certification as a pathway to commercialization but feel that FLO's bifurcated, producer designation system (the smallholder vs. hired-labor distinction) hinders their growth potential. Whereas smallholders must organize into cooperatives to access Fair Trade benefits, hired-labor firms retain independence, and some emerging farmers believe the differing organizational requirements for Fair Trade's hired-labor and smallholder producers reinforce racial separations by locking farmers of color into more marginal modes of production, while white-dominated firms reap a greater portion of Fair Trade's benefits.

South Africa's responses to Fair Trade's organizational challenges

As South African Fair Traders are managing both production and domestic Fair Trade markets, they are uniquely aware of Fair Trade's multifaceted concerns and have been collaborating to foster improvements. In regard to producer designation tensions, FLO-based practitioners can assist emerging producers who wish to enter under hired-labor standards, and the South African Fair Traders are expanding technical assistance mechanisms to further assist smallholders. South African efforts likewise offer insights into the potential for broader movement alignment. Viewing differing movement approaches as an opportunity to expand impact, regional Fair Trade groups are implementing strategies to harmonize services, advocacy and growth. In 2010, FLO-aligned Fair Trade South Africa voted to provide Board space to ATO entities engaged in handicrafts and tourism. Indeed, South Africa may be the first nation to offer both consumers and producers an integrated Fair Trade network.

In South Africa, certain industries are progressive, and Fair Traders may more effectively collaborate within these domains. The South African Rooibos Council has led efforts to secure right of origin for Rooibos to maintain its status as a Cederberg-biodiversity commodity and has advanced a Right Rooibos sustainability initiative that may institute an industry-wide label designed to surpass global standards. The advent of stringent industry-based labels would enable producers to capture multiple certifications in a single auditing stream, and Fair Traders may work with industry networks to streamline regulatory potential. In response to timber-market complexities, FLO has developed a Fair Trade Associations system to align differing production groups within an umbrella framework that allows for producer-designation flexibility (FLO, 2011b). By embedding such a Fair Trade approach within specific industries, diverse Fair Trade producer groups would be able to collaborate on shared issues such as producer representation, production challenges and market access.

Finally, South African Fair Trade engagement offers particular insight in regard to Fair Trade's race-based power dimensions. As this nation has been struggling to emerge from decades of Apartheid-era inequalities, South African fair traders have explicitly integrated BBBEE precepts into hired-labor standards. While their efforts may be imperfect, South African steps may inform a more global examination of the systemic racial inequalities operating within Fair Trade's networks, thereby illuminating prospects for improved social justice.

Fair Trade critiques

Traditionally, ATOs have sought to construct Fair Trade relations by promoting direct producer–consumer interactions (Raynolds, 2002; Keahey *et al.*, 2011). However, as the movement has grown, organizational protocols have become increasingly bureaucratized and Fair Trade's trust-based relationships are being replaced with formalized rules that drive market transactions within certified networks. Producer groups have, over recent years, increased their role in FLO governance, but the certification system remains largely controlled by market country groups and priorities. These factors make it more difficult to maintain a relational orientation to trade (Gendron *et al.*, 2009) and broader movement goals may be threatened by mainstream actors who are more interested in ensuring product traceability than in realizing social justice in trade (Raynolds, 2009).

These considerations point to a core Fair Trade tension. By striving to reform markets from within, the movement essentially puts itself at permanent risk of mainstream cooptation (Raynolds, 2002, and see the final chapter in this volume). The question is whether or not Fair Trade is serving to transform global trade relations, or if it is merely reinforcing structural trade inequalities. Social justice outcomes are mixed and hotly contested. Some argue that Fair Trade replicates colonial trading relations via its organizational model of Southern production for Northern consumption. Indeed, FLO has rejected the notion of certifying producer groups located in the global North. However, some Northern production groups are developing ATO relationships and Fair Traders have been active in terms of building

South-South trade networks, with South Africa launching domestic Fair Trade sales in 2009, and Brazil, India and Kenya initiating domestic standards as well (FLO, 2011a).

Another common critique of Fair Trade is that by attempting to add value to social dimensions, the movement ultimately fetishizes producers, thereby deepening their level of exploitation (Fridell, 2007; Hudson and Hudson, 2003). Depending on one's perspective, Fair Trade efforts may serve to commodify peoples and cultures or bridge peoples and cultures by connecting consumers with those who produce goods. Although the commodification critique has some merit, it focuses on the economic mechanisms of Fair Trade labeling and concedes the market to corporate actors, downplaying the engagement of diverse social groups, including producers and consumers, in shaping market arrangements. Globalization is rapidly reshaping human societies and, despite its challenges, Fair Trade offers a critical counterpoint to free trade. The movement diminishes the distance between production and consumption by promoting more equitable and trust-based trade relationships, enhancing intercultural awareness (Raynolds, 2002). Fair Trade efforts thereby complement the more localized forms of alternative organization discussed elsewhere in this volume.

Finally, as our case study demonstrates, Fair Trade engagement requires a great deal of organizational management as well as multilateral network coordination. Given the negative impact that hired labor expansion may be having on smallholder involvement, Fair Traders should revisit core organizational ethics. Hired labor involvement is an important avenue for securing farm worker rights, but without meaningful smallholder engagement the Fair Trade system may inadvertently force less advantaged producers into marginalized roles. As Fair Traders seek to engender empowerment within global trade networks that have long been marked by systemic abuses of power, movement actors should consider how marketing networks may better respond to production difficulties that derive from deeply entrenched inequalities – for example, by instituting peace and reconciliation mechanisms to resolve organizational disputes.

Conclusions

Fair Trade refers to a critique of the historical inequalities inherent in international trade and to a belief that trade can be made more socially just. This chapter has focused on outlining the parameters of the recent challenges raised against neo-liberal globalization and the types of alternative material and ideological networks created by Fair Trade. Fair Trade represents an important form of alternative organizing that promotes social justice by creating more egalitarian commodity networks. The true significance of Fair Trade lies not in its impressive markets, but in the extent to which this movement challenges core capitalist principles (Raynolds, 2012).

Conventional markets are guided by the profit motive which drives prices below the full ecological and social costs of production, encouraging the degradation of environmental and human resources, particularly in the global South. The Fair Trade movement makes visible the ecological and social relations embedded within a commodity and asks that consumers shoulder the true costs of production. The movement shortens the distance between producers and consumers through dense information as well as resource flows. By demystifying global trade and creating more equitable relations of exchange, Fair Trade goes further than other social or ecological certification initiatives in challenging conventional market practices (Raynolds, 2000; 2002).

This chapter has examined Fair Trade's contributions and challenges in developing alternative production and marketing networks, with particular emphasis on African dynamics, since this region is currently experiencing the most rapid growth in certified production. Though the potential benefits of Fair Trade for producers and workers in the global South are substantial, increased geographic spread, product diversification and organizational variation threaten those benefits. The spread of Fair Trade production across dozens of countries requires adjusting this model to local circumstances, but regional groups can learn from the efforts of one another.

Our case study of the South African Rooibos tea sector demonstrates how historical inequalities and current movement priorities shape the dynamics of alternative organizations working to produce for Fair Trade markets. As we demonstrate, emerging Rooibos producer groups have been central to Fair Trade's smallholder growth in South Africa, yet remain underrepresented. Fair Trade has aligned its hired-labor standards with BBBEE policies to address farm worker inequalities, but neither Fair Trade nor the South African government has effectively addressed the empowerment needs of emerging farmers. This producer group is innovatively struggling to gain access to land and markets (Everingham and Jannecke, 2006), but while emerging Rooibos farmers have engaged with Fair Trade, membership benefits remain elusive.

Fair Trade offers numerous opportunities for combating acute inequalities, but the movement must develop protocols to transcend mainstream market pressures and more effectively address interrelated production and market tensions. Support agencies may begin to address such concerns by developing peace and reconciliation mechanisms that may be enacted when there is organizational conflict. Punishing the producers via decertification is a facile excuse for non-action, particularly when higher-level decision making disproportionately affects those at the base. Indeed, Fair Trade benefits outcomes are lost if producer members do not have the appropriate resources to put knowledge into practice. Ultimately no one group is entirely to blame, but neither is any group blameless. As the movement continues to grow, the question of producer participation is increasingly salient. If the Fair Trade movement is to continue to challenge core capitalist principles, and thereby maintain its position as an alternative trade leader, Fair Traders must align organizational efforts and commit to extending more meaningful levels of participation to its least advantaged communities.

Notes

1 Although these herbal varieties are generally called tea, they do not derive from the tea plant.
2 In South Africa, the term "colored" denotes mixed race and/or indigenous individuals.
3 FLO incorporated BEE standards into its hired-labor sector in response to concerns that existing FLO standards, designed for poorer countries, could be met by most firms in relatively well-off South Africa, thus driving other countries out of Fair Trade markets and ignoring glaring South African inequalities (Kruger and du Toit, 2007; Kruger and Hamman, 2004).
4 Total Rooibos production has doubled over recent years and the share exported has risen from 30 to 50 percent (Wilson, 2005).

Resources

For information on Fairtrade International, please visit: www.fairtrade.net
For information on the World Fair Trade Organization, please visit: www.wfto.com
For information on Fair Trade USA, please visit: www.fairtradeusa.org
For information on The Center for Fair and Alternative Trade, please visit: http://cfat.colostate.edu/
For information on becoming a Fair Trade College or University, please visit: www.fairtradeuniversities.org
For information on becoming a Fair Trade Town, please visit: www.fairtradetowns.org

The following books and articles will provide further insight into Fair Trade issues:

Fridell, G. 2007. *Fair Trade Coffee: The Prospects and Pitfalls of Market-Driven Social Justice*. Toronto: University of Toronto Press.

Keahey, J.A., Littrell, M.A. and Murray, D.L. 2011. Business with a Mission: The Ongoing Role of Ten Thousand Villages within the Fair Trade Movement. In Weaver, A. E. (ed.) *A Table of Sharing: Mennonite Central Committee and the Expanding Networks of Mennonite Identity*. Telford, PA: Cascadia Publishing House.

Linton, A. 2012. *Fair Trade from the Ground Up: New Markets for Social Justice*. Seattle, WA: University of Washington Press.

Raynolds, L.T. 2012. Fair Trade: Social Regulation in Global Food Markets. *Journal of Rural Studies*, 28: 276–287.

Raynolds, L.T., Murray, D.L. and Wilkinson, J. (eds). 2007. *Fair Trade: The Challenges of Transforming Globalization*. London: Routledge.

References

AgriBEE. 2005. Broad Based Black Economic Empowerment: Draft Transformation Charter for Agriculture. AgriBEE.

Bacon, C. 2005. Confronting the Coffee Crisis: Can Fair Trade, Organic, and Specialty Coffees Reduce Small-scale Farmer Vulnerability in Northern Nicaragua? *World Development*, 33: 497–511.

Bacon, C. 2010. Who Decides What is Fair in Fair Trade? The Agri-environmental Governance of Standards, Access, and Price. *Journal of Peasant Studies*, 37: 111–147.

Bek, D., McEwan, C. and Bek, K. 2007. Ethical Trading and Socioeconomic Transformation: Critical Reflections on the South African Wine Industry. *Environment and Planning*, 39: 201–319.

Binns, T., Bek, D., Nel, E. and Ellison, B. 2007. Sidestepping the Mainstream: Fairtrade Rooibos Tea Production in Wupperthal, South Africa. In Maye, D., Holloway, L. and Kneafsey, M. (eds) *Alternative Food Geographies: Representation and Practice*. Amsterdam: Elsevier Ltd.

de Lange, A. 2004. The Evaluation of Empowerment Policies, Strategies and Performance within the Agricultural Sector. Final NDA Report.

Department of Trade and Industry. 2009. Codes of Good Practice on Broad Based Black Economic Empowerment. Government Gazette.

Dolan, C. 2007. A gift that keeps on giving: Fair trade in Kenyan tea fields. Workshop on Democracy and Transparency in Certified and Ethical Commodity Networks, University of Kentucky, Lexington.

du Toit, A., Kruger, S. and Ponte, S. 2008. Deracializing Exploitation? 'Black Economic Empowerment' in the South African Wine Industry. *Journal of Agrarian Change*, 8: 6–32.

Everingham, M. and Jannecke, C. 2006. Land Restitution and Democratic Citizenship in South Africa. *Journal of Southern African Studies*, 32: 545–562.

Fairtrade Africa. 2011. *A Fair Climate Deal for Fairtrade Producers*. Nairobi: Fairtrade Africa. Available online at www.fairtradeafrica.net/news/press-releases/ (accessed 7 November 2011).

Federal Reserve System. 2011. *Foreign Exchange Rates*. Washington, D.C.: Federal Reserve System. Available online at www.federalreserve.gov/releases/G5A/Current/ (accessed 9 November 2011).

Ferrer, S.R.D. and Lyne, M.C. 2008. Product Labelling of Wine and Fruit to Promote Black Economic Empowerment in South Africa: A Case Study of the Thandi Empowerment Label. *Actahort (ISHS)*, 794: 127–132.

FINE. 2003. What is FINE? Available online at www.rafiusa.org/programs/Bangkok%20 proceedings/12What%20is%20FINE.pdfFLO 2005. Annual Report 2004/5 – Delivering Opportunities. FLO, Bonn.

FLO. 2006. Annual Report 2005/6 – Building Trust. FLO, Bonn.

FLO. 2007. FLO International Announces Fairtrade Minimum Prices for Rooibos Tea. Bonn. Available online at www.fairtrade.net/single_view1.html?andL=titleandcHash=463691687dandscale=0a ndtx_ttnews[tt_news]=35 (accessed 12 November 2011).

FLO. 2008. An Inspiration for Change: Annual Report 2007. Bonn: Fairtrade Labelling Organizations International.

FLO. 2010a. Annual Report 2009/2010: Fair Trade Leading the Way. FLO, Bonn.

FLO. 2010b. The Benefits of Fairtrade, 2nd edition: A Monitoring and Evaluation Report of Fairtrade Certified Producer Organizations for 2008. FLO, Bonn.

FLO. 2011a. Challenge and Opportunity: Annual Review 2010–11. Fairtrade International, Bonn.

FLO. 2011b. *Fairtrade Standards for Timber for Forest Enterprises: Sourcing from Small-scale/Community-based Producers*. Bonn: Fairtrade Labelling Organizations International.

FLO-CERT. 2005. Fairtrade Certification. Prepared by Frank Brinkschneider. Unpublished PowerPoint Presentation.

FLO-CERT. 2011. Operators. Bonn. Available online at www.flo-cert.net/flo-cert/113.html (accessed 12 October 2011).

Fridell, G. 2007. Fair-Trade Coffee and Commodity Fetishism: The Limits of Market-Driven Social Justice. *Historical Materialism*, 15: 79–104.

Gendron, C., Bisaillon, V. and Rance, A. 2009. The Institutionalization of Fair Trade: More Than a Degraded Form of Social Action. *Journal of Business Ethics*, 86: 63–79.

Hudson, I. and Hudson, M. 2003. Removing the Veil? Commodity Fetishism, Fair Trade, and the Environment. *Organization and Environment*, 16: 413–430.

Keahey, J.A., Littrell, M.A. and Murray, D.L. 2011. Business with a Mission: The Ongoing Role of Ten Thousand Villages within the Fair Trade Movement. In Weaver, A.E. (ed.) *A Table of Sharing: Mennonite Central Committee and the Expanding Networks of Mennonite Identity*. Telford, PA: Cascadia Publishing House.

Krier, J. 2008. Fair Trade 2007: New Facts and Figures from an Ongoing Success Story. Dutch Association of Worldshops, Culemborg, Netherlands.

Kruger, S. and du Toit, A. 2007. Reconstructing Fairness: Fair Trade Conventions and Worker Empowerment in South African Horticulture. In Raynolds, L.T., Murray, D.L. and Wilkinson, J. (eds) *Fair Trade: The Challenges of Transforming Globalization*. London: Routledge.

Kruger, S. and Hamman, J. 2004. *Guidelines for FLO's Empowerment Strategy in South Africa*. Unpublished consultation paper, Programme for Land and Agrarian Studies (PLAAS) University of the Western Cape, South Africa.

Malgas, R. and Oettle, N. 2007. *The Sustainable Harvest of Wild Rooibos*. Cape Town: Environmental Monitoring Group Trust.

Matten, D. and Moon, J. 2008. "Implicit" and "Explicit" CSR: A Conceptual Framework for a Comparative Understanding of Corporate Social Responsibility. *Academy of Management Review*, 33: 404–424.

Murray, D.L. and Raynolds, L.T. 2007. Globalization and its Antinomies: Negotiating a Fair Trade Movement. In: Raynolds, L.T. *et al. Fair Trade: The Challenges of Transforming Globalization*. New York: Routledge.

Mutersbaugh, T. 2002. The Number is the Beast: A Political Economy of Organic Coffee Certification and Producer Unionism. *Environment and Planning A*, 7: 1165–1184.

Nel, E., Binns, T. and Bek, D. 2007. "Alternative Foods" and Community-based Development: Rooibos Tea Production in South Africa's West Coast Mountains. *Applied Geography*, 27: 112–129.

Rainforest Alliance. 2011. *Our Work*. Available online at www.rainforest-alliance.org/work (accessed 9 July 2011).

Raynolds, L.T. 2000. Re-embedding Global Agriculture: The International Organic and Fair Trade Movements. *Agriculture and Human Values*, 17: 297–309.

Raynolds, L.T. 2002. Consumer/Producer Links in Fair Trade Coffee Networks. *Sociologia Ruralis*, 42: 404–424.

Raynolds, L.T. 2004. The Globalization of Organic Agro-food Networks. *World Development*, 32 (5): 725–743.

Raynolds, L.T. 2009. Mainstreaming Fair Trade Coffee: From Partnership to Traceability. *World Development*, 37: 1083–1093.

Raynolds, L.T. 2012. Fair Trade: Social Regulation in Global Food Markets. *Journal of Rural Studies*, 28: 276–287.

Raynolds, L.T. and Keahey, J.A. 2009. Fair Trade, Gender, and the Environment in Africa. In Gallagher, K. (ed.) *The Elgar Handbook on Trade and Environment*. Cheltenham: Edward Elgar.

Raynolds, L.T. and Long, M.A. 2007. Fair/Alternative Trade: Historical and Empirical Dimensions. In Raynolds, L.T. *et al.* (eds) *Fair Trade: The Challenges of Transforming Globalization*. London and New York: Routledge.

Raynolds, L.T. and Ngcwangu, S.U. 2010. Fair Trade Rooibos Tea: Connecting South African Producers and American Consumer Markets. *Geoforum*, 41: 74–83.

Raynolds, L.T., Murray, D. and Wilkinson, J. (eds). 2007. *Fair Trade: The Challenges of Transforming Globalization*. London and New York: Routledge.

Reinecke, J. 2010. Beyond a Subjective Theory of Value and Towards a "Fair Price": An Organizational Perspective on Fairtrade Minimum Price Setting. *Organization*, 17(5): 563–581.

Renard, M-C. 2005. Quality Certification, Regulation and Power in Fair Trade. *Journal of Rural Studies*, 21: 419–431.

Sandra Kruger and Associates. 2010. *Rooibos Socio-Economic Study*. Cape Town: Ministry of Agriculture, Nature, and Food Quality.

UTZ Certified. 2011. *What Is UTZ Certified*. Available online at www.utzcertified.org/aboututzcertified (accessed 9 July 2011).

Vogel, D. 2010. The Private Regulation of Global Corporate Conduct. *Business and Society*, 49: 68–87.

Wilson, N.L.W. 2005. Cape Natural Tea Products and the US Market: Rooibos Rebels Ready to Raid. *Review of Agricultural Economics*, 27: 139–148.

Woolworths Holdings Limited. 2010. *Our News: Producing Woolworths Rooibos Tea Invigorates a Previously Disadvantaged Community*. Available online at www.woolworthsholdings.co.za/media/news/news_display.asp?Id2=380 (accessed 1 October 2011).

Wright, E.O. 2010. The Social Economy – A Niche in Capitalism or a Pathway Beyond? Preliminary Notes Towards an Analysis. Paper prepared for the meeting of the Analytical Marxism Group, Oxford, June 2010.

12

Complementary currencies

Peter North

Introduction

'There are now hundreds of projects underway that are utilising new kinds of money . . . My forecast is that 90–95% of these projects will not survive; but the remaining 5% will succeed in permanently changing our economies, our societies, our civilization, and our world'.

(Lietaer, 2001: 27)

Recent years have seen a mushrooming of complementary currencies such as Local Exchange Trading Schemes (LETS), electronic and paper-based currencies denominated in time (Ithaca Hours, Time Banks), and local script circulating in small towns (BerkShares, Lewes Pounds). The economic crisis of 2001 that devastated Argentina's economy led to mass use of community and NGO created scrip, as cashpoints jammed up in an attempt to limit the effects of a bank run on the Argentine Peso (North, 2007), a phenomenon emerging in equally devastated Greece as the Eurozone crisis continues to hit (Donadio, 2011). Concerns about the continuing credit crunch, and about more long-term crises in the form of climate change and resource crises, have led to the emergence of a new social movement in the form of Transition Initiatives that look to relocalize economies to build in (or we should say, rebuild) resilience to shocks and to cut down on the emissions and fossil fuel consumption associated with globalization (North, 2010a, b; Hopkins, 2011; Ganesh and Zoller, this volume). Local money, that circulates only in a small town and its hinterland, has been a key tool for localization (North, 2010a) as, it is argued, the existence of an alternative form of money that is not accepted outside of a smaller local economy will act as a method of 'structuring' spending away from globally circulating goods and services, towards local ones (North, 2005).

This chapter examines the usefulness of complementary currencies as alternative organizational forms and tools for social change. I argue that the use of complementary currencies is underdeveloped. Lietaer (2001) is right in arguing that 95 per cent of what is being pioneered today will not achieve the potential its supporters expect; but also that long-term, complementary currencies will have a greater role to play at greater economic and geographic scales than they do today. If not, a future, capitalist and hyperglobalized world will be a poorer, depleted, climate-ravaged place. This chapter explores the strengths and weaknesses of the pioneer complementary currencies by analysing the range of designs and organizational features of differing models, which have a different ethos, objectives, and work at different scales. The chapter concludes by arguing that new initiatives at a more regional, than local, scale, being pioneered mainly in Germany, are more likely to realize the full potential of alternative organizational forms of money that might make a difference to the climate, resource and economic problems humanity faces. What we do not know, and, perhaps cannot yet know, is whether alternative organizational forms of money can have the power to change economic activity in the same way that the emergence of banking and of the joint stock and limited liability companies did (Ferguson, 2008). Where local or regional currencies are strong, does this act as a reflection of the form of the local economy, or does a local or regional currency help bring about the sort of convivial, sustainable, locally owned and controlled economy that proponents hope to see?

A typology of organizational features

This part of the chapter is built around a discussion of the strengths and weaknesses of a range of organizational features pertinent to different complementary currency models, which make them more or less effective as social change vehicles. These organizational features include:

1. methods of valuation
2. currency design and physical form
3. convertibility
4. managing the currency supply
5. commitment-building mechanisms and the translation of any group ethos into management practices
6. the geographical extent of space an alternative currency system covers.

Valuation

Time-based currencies

Local Exchange Trading Schemes (in the UK), Talente (in Germany and Hungary), and Grains of Salt (France) are community-based local trading networks that first emerged in the 1990s, using a local currency based on a number of units per hour, sometimes with a locally significant name; such as 'Tales' in Canterbury, 'Brights' in Brighton or 'Bobbins' in Manchester (Williams, 1996a, 1996b; North, 2006). To establish a LETS scheme, a directory of services provided by network members is put together and trading takes place using local currency, and preferably without the use of any national currency. Accounts are kept, usually on a computer, and start with an opening balance of zero. In LETS, no money actually exists in the form of coins or notes. Users write a cheque in the local money to pay for goods and services, which they back with a 'commitment' to earn, at a later date, sufficient local money to return their account to zero. In LETS, currency does not have to be earned before it is spent, so some members go into 'debt' while others simultaneously earn. The person commissioning the work has their account debited, and the person doing the work is credited the same amount; so the totality of credits paid in and out of all accounts balances out at zero. All members' balances and turnovers are publicly available, and members are expected to take their accounts back to zero before they leave the network, to prevent default by a member before they have provided reciprocal services. These latter facets are designed to facilitate trust. Some LETS networks now have over 20 years' trading experience (North, 2010c).

Time Banks connect people who need and offer services, match their requirements and skills, and facilitate the service with time-based credits (Cahn, 2000; Seyfang, 2003). Credits are valued at a straight hour-for-hour swap and consequently avoid national currency alignment. No directory or cheque book is issued; rather, members phone through to a central administrative point which finds someone to meet their needs and records accumulated credits. Finally, there is no obligation for people to give and receive services in equal measure, although all are encouraged to do both. Rather, the philosophy is that members contribute to and receive from the Time Bank as a collective. If a member needs more than he or she can give back, that is not a problem.

The other North American time-based currencies are watermarked, often exceptionally high-quality, scrip notes which circulate in Ithaca (New York), Salmon Arm (British Columbia) and up to 40 other cities in North America. The Ithaca Hour project has been spectacularly successful, particularly in involving significant numbers of local businesses (Glover, 1995; Maurer, 2003, 2005), something LETS schemes or Time Money in the UK have conspicuously failed to do (North, 1998). Ithaca's success inspired Argentina's Red Global de Trueque (North, 2007). Over a million scrip notes (denominated in *creditos*) circulated amongst a loose network of self-identified prosumers meeting at markets.

National currency equivalents

Scrip-based, complementary currencies linked explicitly to national currencies, including 'Deli Dollars', 'BerkShares' and 'Berkshire Farm Preserve Notes', are local scrip notes aligned to the Dollar and redeemable in a number of small towns in Massachussetts (Solomon, 1996). In turn, BerkShares inspired the UK transition currencies currently in Totnes, Lewes and Brixton, London (North, 2010b). The world's most successful complementary currency, the Swiss *Wirschaftsring* (Business Ring), involves over 70,000 small and medium businesses and with a turnover in 1995 of 2521 million *Wir* units, equivalent to Swiss Francs (Douthwaite, 1996: 100). After making a cash deposit, participants receive a credit card with an interest-free credit of 5 per cent of their deposit, and they can then trade these *Wir* units, equivalent to Swiss Francs in value, with other participants. WIR, the only survivor of the 1930s Freework movement, inspired the German regional currencies that emerged in the early twenty-first century. Having a local currency at parity with the national currency has many advantages but, as we see below, it can be contested.

The social construction and contestation of valuation

Until the recent rise of the transition currencies, the majority of complementary currencies have tended to stress their dissimilarity with national currency values, taking an hourly rate, a rate that floats against national currency, or a rate as disconnected from national currency rates as possible. For example, many UK LETS schemes argued that a LETS unit is 'like' a pound, and that a recommended hourly rate should be charged that reflects a 'fair' rate in the conventional economy. Others argue for a rate that specifically does *not* align with sterling: for example, the Bright Exchange's (Brighton, UK) rate of 12 units to the hour was felt to be specifically non-decimal and therefore discouraged valuations aligned to sterling. Belfast used the pint.[1] Ideal LETS, in Bristol, set a rate of 20 Ideals an hour, reflecting a desire by many of its well-paid members for rates that reflected their expected sterling hourly rates.

The arguments for and against various rates are as follows. Time-based money mainly appeals to those who want to value work in ways unconnected to the capitalist nexus whereby, for example, a lawyer is paid more than a cleaner. It echoes Robert Owen's – and Marx's – argument that the basis of all wealth is labour, and it puts the need for problems to be solved before the need for money to be in existence (North, 1999). A strict, hourly rate appeals to those for whom equality and equity in trading relations is of major importance. The downside is that valuing labour time in hours is easy (enough), but what if I work harder, or more efficiently than you, and do more with my hour than you do? What if an hour of a lawyer's time is actually 20 years' experience and training concentrated into an hour? The absence of any national currency referent led to confusion in pricing goods in time-based money (how many hours for a fridge?). Having a time-based currency basically restricts your currency to those with supportive political views, who want to trade roughly equivalent services. It generally excludes conventional businesses.

The practical issues involved in trading goods and involving the small numbers of businesses that join LETS schemes consequently suggested a move away from strict equality, but values allied directly to national currency were seen by the more political members attracted to LETS in its early days as replicating the inequalities of the conventional economy (North, 2006).

In practice, LETS members have developed a range of diverse moral values for the currency. These valuations included:

- Exactly a pound, with hourly rates calculated by directly translating members' expectations of their worth at mainstream prices.
- Like a pound, with the hourly rate referent happily accepted.
- A gesture: One LETS unit would be paid, irrespective of the time taken to provide a service.
- Distrusted: Others distrusted complementary currencies which they saw as commodification of co-operation that would have happened irrespective of the existence of the currency. They used the network to share, without using the currency.
- Variable valuation: All or some of the above, depending on the quality of the relationship between traders, how much or little a trader wished to or enjoyed providing a service, or the relative level of accounts.

The problem with this early diversity was that these currencies failed to act as either an effective measure of value or an accepted means of exchange (North, 2006). Problems arose when traders with essentially different value systems had to interrelate and felt that their differing value systems led to unequal outcomes. For example, cleaners could feel that an accepted rate of 10 LETS an hour compared favourably with the going rates in the pre-minimum wage UK, while a homoeopath could feel that her hourly rate should include recompense for her hours of training. As Viviana Zelizer (1997) shows, we value money differently. This differential meant that LETS money failed to act as a store of value if a trader who charged above the odds could then buy more labour per hour than someone earning a lower rate. On the other hand, others felt that as they had access to unlimited currency, the fact that one person charged more than another seemed irrelevant as all that is traded is points: unlimited currency did not need to function as a store of value. In a third scenario, market mechanisms worked and the trader charging above the odds began to store up un-spendable credits and lowered their prices. The problem was that strong bonds of trust were not developed in the absence of a universally accepted currency valuation, either imposed on the network by a strong organizational structure running the network, through rules, regulations and/or penalties, or through the construction of a shared and accepted ethos.

Consequently, a range of accepted community 'norms' arose to make sense of, and to bring some order to, the diversity. In LETS, this was for a LETS unit to be 'like' a pound, and a recommended hourly rate. Time Banks insisted that everyone's time was equivalent to everyone else's, with one time credit for one hour's work. Ithaca Hours settled on an hourly rate of 10 Hours, within an Hour equivalent to a US$, for an hour's work: thus enacting a community-based living wage from below. This facilitated easy pricing, while avoiding the enforced equality associated with hour-based systems. However, the confusion associated with these social struggles over valuation put many people off LETS and, in particular, acted as a disincentive to business participation. Many of the paper-based currencies that followed avoided this by explicitly relating their currency to national currencies, while allowing those who used the currency to decide for themselves how much to pay for what in different circumstances. Many LETS advocates felt this was a step backwards, an unacceptable political compromise.

Physical form and design

The physical manifestation of the currency can communicate the ethos and politics of the currency. It varies from the virtual to beautifully designed paper currency notes that compare favourably with any produced by nation states. Believing that money is 'just information', and should not be valuable in its own right, Michael Linton's original 1984 LetSystem design did not give the currency any physical form: users recorded transactions on an answer-phone, before being logged onto the computer database. While this had the advantage of being simple and easy to set up, a design flaw was that a virtual currency is so far removed from common understandings about money that new members found the concept difficult to grasp (North, 1996). Money, especially in the 1990s before the widespread use of electronic cash, was a physical 'thing', like a bank note, many felt. The lack of corporeality of LETS meant it was often not taken seriously. If money is merely a number on a computer printout, people often displayed an over-casual attitude both to the value of the currency and to the need to return accounts to zero (Aldridge and Patterson, 2002). Banknotes and credit cards use design specifically to bestow grandeur and communicate the solemnity and timeless value of currency: they have 'moneyness' (Cohen, 1998).[2]

While fiat currencies, disconnected from any relation to a tangible value base such as gold, are intellectually tenable (Dodd, 1994; Ingham, 2004), a currency with no alternative method of demonstrating its credibility will have problems in gaining usage and respect beyond those who accept these claims made about money in advance as part of a wider programme of social reform, or as part of a challenge to power relations associated with money (North, 1999). Those who have more conventional understandings of money, who see it as in some way 'hard', limited, and connected to something tangible in the real world, will be less attracted to alternative organizational forms of money that diverge too strongly from uncontested or unconsidered attitudes about money. Third, an answer-phone or computer-based system is clumsy. Users must remember to phone each transaction through, and they may forget to make the call, or get identity numbers wrong. Someone needs to process the transactions: a problem for businesses with a large number of small transactions. When large numbers of people use an alternative currency (as they did in the Argentine crash), bookkeeping is impractical: the accountant will be quickly overwhelmed. Finally, a telephone-based system is inappropriate for the poorest communities. While North America at the time had free local calls, in the UK the cost of phoning in the 1990s acted as a deterrent to poorer members (North, 1996). Those without access to a phone were excluded completely.[3]

From the early 1990s, UK LETS schemes began to address these problems by using home-designed cheques as the most popular physical manifestation of the currency. This had the advantage of being familiar, providing easy corporeality, and being relatively easy to produce and process. Problems included the unfamiliarity of cheques for poorer members excluded from access to conventional banking services, and the often poor quality of many cheque designs, which again reduced confidence in the reliability and exchangeability of the currency. Cheques were still unwieldy for small transactions, and larger schemes found the processing of large numbers of transactions, big or small, onerous. High street businesses began to see cheque usage decline as electronic point-of-sale technologies became more widespread, although many tradespeople continue to use cheques regularly. Finally, a big problem, specific to the US, was that any organization offering a computer-based currency scheme was subject to the same regulations as business-to-business barter: the organizers were responsible for notifying members' details to the Internal Revenue Service for tax purposes. This was a major structural barrier, which led to the innovation of moving to a paper currency.

The issuance of scrip notes, like Ithaca Hours, does not come up against the volume problem as no central records are kept. If well designed and watermarked (as recent scrip notes often are), the notes bestow credibility and confidence in the currency. Notes are quicker and easier to take in and out of tills and wallets, speeding up transactions immeasurably – of crucial importance to businesses. Everyone is used to paper money, so the concept resonated with accepted views of what money should do. Well-designed alternative money seems 'serious', although on the other side of the coin poorly designed notes can seem too much like 'monopoly money' and lead to a lack of respect for the currencies, with the result that businesses might not be attracted to them. A second objection to a paper currency is that, unlike personal credit money, services must be provided in the first place which again can exclude the poorest who might feel they have few skills and resources that others might need. The Argentine Red Global de Trueque overcame this problem by issuing 30 to 50 notes in advance, but issued unbacked currency to the extent that this eventually had major inflationary effects which resulted in the catastrophic loss of faith in the currency. Some German regional currencies have experimented with more limited and controlled advance issuance for socially excluded currency users.

Managing the circulation of the currency

The supply of any new currency, and how it circulates, must be managed in some way. There are two approaches. With 'personal credit' money, like LETS and Time Money, currency issue is governed by the users of the currency themselves with the simple act of commissioning work and paying for it to be done with local credits, backing it with their labour in the future: their personal 'promise to pay the bearer on demand'. Here a second set of design features relates to the management of individual accounts. To what extent are there credit or debit limits? Are members expected to earn as much as they spend, periodically returning their account to a zero balance as in LETS; or should needs be met irrespective of the existence or otherwise of credits to pay for received services? Can an account with a growing debit be tolerated? Should balances be made public, proactively or otherwise? What account information should be made available and how important is it that account statements are accurate?

The LETS design pays close attention to accurate account management. Members are expected to periodically balance their accounts. Some LETS schemes impose credit or debit limits, and can actively enforce them either through the proactive publication of balances or through oversight by the management group. Green Dollar schemes in New Zealand are particularly proactive in this regard, and have gone as far as taking members to small claims courts to enforce the payment of debts they don't feel are being repaid (North, 2002). LETS schemes often go out of their way to regularly provide account statements, and pay considerable attention to their accuracy. These account management systems are, it is argued, necessary to maintain the integrity of the currency and confidence in it. Public access to account balances is necessary to ensure that all traders are contributing to the scheme, and that a member who takes more from others than they contribute will find that opportunities to trade reduce when the depth of the imbalance is known. In reality, the extent that individual members do check up on the credit balances of others and regulate their trading relations to ensure equitable contributions is questionable, especially in the absence of regularly published balances. The publication of individual balances can cut against cultural conceptions of privacy. In New Zealand, Green Dollar committees involved themselves in the management of individual accounts in ways that a UK audience might find intrusive, yet felt that the open publication of accounts would invade members' privacy. The design of accounts must balance close attention to cultural conceptions of what should or should not be made public with the need for feedback mechanisms.

With Time Money, the emphasis is on meeting needs and on people making whatever contribution they feel they can, irrespective of whether the volumes of services given and received are in balance in any individual case. Account statements are often not provided, to avoid putting those in a situation where they have more needs than things they can put back feeling beholden, or holding back from accessing services. Time Money is thereby better at meeting the needs of those who have to take more than they can ever give back, and who might feel unwilling to go into 'debt' with LETS. The concept of 'debt' does not exist in the same way, as participants are seen to collectively give to and take from 'the bank', rather than manage an individual account. The ethos of Time Banks is of 'co-production'; of people meeting their needs collectively, of providing as well as receiving help (Cahn, 2000). These are conceptions more closely allied to social service provision than to trade, and consequently are less resonant with businesses.

With scrip such as 'Hours', the Red Global de Trueque, the transition currencies and German Regional Currencies, a central issuing authority decides how much scrip to issue. If too many notes are issued, as we saw in Argentina, they may (perhaps catastrophically) lose value in an inflationary cycle as too many notes are chasing too few trading opportunities. If too few are issued, needs may still be unmet for lack of currency to pay for them, recreating the pathologies of the conventional currency. How many notes to issue is a delicate decision, and it is unclear who has the right, or knowledge, to make a decision that affects the fundamental integrity of the system. Some of the more radically minded currencies decide collectively at open meetings how much currency should be issued. Regiogeld and BerkShares, which do involve significant numbers of businesses, are formally organized by NGOs, with the support and participation of local banks. In the UK, some of the transition currencies have suffered from a perception that they are not professionally organized and managed. Levels of organization enabling individuals to exchange childcare and gardening are obviously different in both importance and extent when compared with what is necessary to facilitate business-to-business exchange, together with the tax and (potentially) regulatory liabilities associated with the latter.

Convertibility

To maintain the distinctiveness of the complementary currency system, few LETS schemes actively facilitated the transfer of complementary currencies into national currency. Time Banks prohibited it and refused to make any connection between an hour and national currencies. The result is that traders with popular services could often be left with a store of un-spendable credits. While participants in Time Banks saw themselves as exchanging favours, and had a relaxed view about their account balance, in LETS an inability to spend what could be seen as hard-earned cash could, in time, become problematic. This was a particular problem for those able to earn large amounts of a local currency, especially businesses, and acted as a disincentive to their continued participation. They would stop taking on new work until they had spent their balances, or drop out, writing off their balance. If enough people did this, the network would fail. Sometimes, for example, in Ithaca the organizer of the currency spent a considerable amount of time working with businesses to help them find new ways to recirculate the currency. In time, it became clear that this was a previously underemphasized managerial requirement for an alternative currency network. A bank does not need to help account holders to spend conventional money; there is, in the form of advertising, a considerable infrastructure that does this.

Two more organizational solutions were also utilized to facilitate the circulation of the currency. In Germany, Bavaria's Chiemgauer regional currency is experimenting with demurrage, whereby a currency depreciates, or 'rusts', over time unless a stamp or voucher is periodically purchased which revalidates it so it can be spent again. Inspired by Rudolf Steiner's views on money, Chiemgauer currency notes are withdrawn from circulation in time, so they cannot be hoarded over long periods. The advantage of demurrage is that a huge pressure is put onto holders of currency to move it on before the validation date. The problem is that demurrage can exacerbate the unattractiveness of complementary currencies to those providers of in-demand services who are willing to spend their accumulated credits, but lack opportunities to do so. A balance losing value over time is likely to ensure that providers of such services quickly cease accepting currency, and disproportionately penalizes those who have provided the most services. Interestingly, though, recent evidence from Germany suggests that, in an environment where there are many opportunities to trade, demurrage can incentivize recirculation to avoid having to revalidate the notes.

The second solution to this problem is to have a local paper currency that is fully backed by national currency, which those who struggle to spend can easily exchange back into national currency. This is the solution taken by BerkShares, and by the transition currencies. It solves the problem of what to do with unspent balances, but can, in turn, create three new problems. First, these currencies can only be obtained in exchange for national currency, which is banked, so as to be available for those who later want to change it back. Why would anyone change universal money into a more limited form of money, unless they had a political or affective commitment to their local economy? Secondly, those without national currency are still excluded from participation in the network: it is not new, 'poor people's money'. Third, what is the point of having a currency that does not circulate widely through the local economy, but is just banked straight away? The structuring elements of a local currency are missing: why should a business try to spend the local currency with those with whom they do business if they can just bank it? One problem is solved, three new ones emerge.

BerkShares and the transition currencies consequently incentivize new users by offering a favourable exchange rate between local and national currencies. For example, nine dollars bought you ten BerkShares, giving you a 10 per cent boost to your spending power. They disincentivize banking, rather than recirculating, the currency, as if the business then exchanged them back into US dollars they would only get nine dollars back for their ten BerkShares. Businesses that could spend their local currency were not penalized, and many businesses could afford to offer a 10 per cent discount: this is normal business practice. Many businesses reported that the local currency featured prominently in the media, and provided good publicity for the town: the price was worth paying. But businesses that were popular with many users, but who could not spend high volumes of a local currency, struggled with what they began to describe as a '10 per cent' hit. The E.F. Schumacher Society responded to this by reducing the discount to 5 per cent, a practice replicated by the transition currencies. This seems more sustainable.

Commitment-building mechanisms

A debate that goes back to the beginning of the modern wave of complementary currencies centres on the question: is this a tool for anyone to use, for whatever they want to, or a community, a social movement arguing for a different form of money that will help to build a sustainable, convivial, low-carbon world? Is it protest, economic development, or a mix of the two? This has implications for ways of organizing the currency network. Those who see the local currency as a tool for building communities and strengthening local economies are more likely to be interested in a complementary currency that is organized by a democratically accountable management group that is fairly small, and operates within a geographically tight area or homogeneous community. They are likely to favour those design elements that build community and commitment, such as directories and newsletters with a strong 'alternative' or 'community' feel, trading days, and a brokerage service which actively puts members in touch with each other on the Time Bank model. They will enjoy and appreciate strong boundaries: a feeling that the community that uses the currency is distinct or special, and 'doing things in a different way'. Time Banks are especially strong in providing the organizational structure necessary to make sure that vulnerable members are looked after, their needs are met, and that they are protected by a duty of care.

In contrast, those who prefer to use a complementary currency as a ladder into mainstream employment, or as a way to strengthen local economies, may prefer a larger, more diverse, anonymous community, and feel stifled by commitment-building mechanisms that those with a stronger commitment to community may appreciate. Here, how prospective members find out about the opportunities to use a complementary currency, and what it means to use the currency matters. Which groups in society do those organizing the currency target to get them to participate, and why do they target some groups and not others? How does the management group go about developing the range of services available within the currency, if at all?

LETS groups rarely actively identified target markets or systematically attempted to explain the benefits of complementary currencies to potential new users. Promotional materials were, and still are, often poorly produced, if at all. Many LETS groups did little more than rely on their directory to convey the flavour of resources accessible. Others simply relied on word of mouth. Often this could be deliberate. Community-based complementary currency networks relied on significant levels of trust in the absence of methods of enforcing payment, and the personal or home-based nature of many services meant that many users sought assurances that they would feel 'comfortable' with their fellow traders. Time Banks managed who would and who would not be allowed into the network, often insisting on Criminal Records checks. Many more radical members of LETS specifically set out to be part of a hidden network of tranquillity and fair exchange, and actively sought to create a border against a wider world 'gone mad', actively opposing any active promotional strategy. These processes all build a shared identity, but beyond obvious problems with equal opportunities also restrict the size of the network, keep the benefits to a small group, and can cut off new blood, skills and energy. But if borders were sufficiently porous to let new members in, and commitment-building mechanisms (opportunities to meet, communication methods, rules and regulations, punishments for defection, or processes of constructing a group feeling and identity) were strong enough to keep group identity, then a diverse and resilient trading network can emerge that can last over time. Rosabeth Moss Kanter's (1972) study of US nineteenth- and twentieth-century intentional communities identified both borders and commitment-building mechanisms as crucial to the longevity of such groups: this remains the case for alternative currency networks (see also Pitzer, this volume).

Yet the problem more radical complementary currency schemes like LETS came up against in attempting to move from a small, radical network and grow into something more robust was that promotional approaches that pictured complementary currencies as mainstream tools that businesses could use did not inspire activists to do the legwork necessary to recruit new membership beyond those who join on the basis of a political standpoint. It was only when NGOs, such as the US E.F. Schumacher Society, Argentina's Programma de Autosuficiencia Regional or the UK's New Economics Foundation, put organizational resources behind business-focused currency networks, and the need to relocalize economies to avoid dangerous climate change was identified as a new rationale for local currencies, that networks involving local businesses to any extent were built. Unless they found ways to formalize their organizational form into something more sustainable, community-based action alone struggled to provide the levels of support local businesses needed to find ways to spend a local currency. In Germany and in the Berkshires, a promising solution has been a partnership between the community-based activists centred on a Steiner school (Germany) or the NGO (US) who first created the currency, and the ethical and regional banks that helped provide the infrastructure and legitimation that made them work.

Conclusion: horses for courses?

A final issue is to think about what the vision is: a small-scale, community or neighbourhood exchange scheme, or a larger economic development tool, perhaps working at a regional level. In Europe or the US, might more robust regional currencies circulate alongside the Euro and dollar, in time perhaps becoming a real alternative to the dollar or Euro in times of crisis? Many LETS schemes and Time Banks have evolved over time into sustainable, long-lasting exchange networks that meet the needs of their members. But to address issues of climate change, financial crisis and resource constraint, something else is needed. We need a diverse ecosystem of complementary currencies that are more finely attuned to the needs of those using them, from the Euro down to the Bobbin. One size does not fit all.

Diversity and targeting are necessary as, for example, businesses run by people who do not have a pre-existing ecological or egalitarian political perspective are not likely to be attracted to a small, local, hour-based currency. Similarly, a currency aligned directly to pound, dollar or Euro is frequently seen as an unwelcome commodification of sharing by those attracted to Time Money. The list goes on. Businesses have shown themselves to be attracted to a tightly managed, hard currency – yet few join LETS schemes (and are not targeted by Time Banks). A community of anarchists is likely to reject any form of currency governance beyond consensus-based grass-roots management. Business may see this as unaccountable and flaky, instead requiring formal, accountable forms of organization, rules and regulations, and the confidence that those running the currency know what they are doing, and that they can get their money back if necessary. Those looking to build communities or help needy groups will want to get together as a community to work out how to collectively meet their needs. Business will want to use the currency as and when they feel it necessary, without being expected to participate in group identity-building exercises.

As well as a diversity of organizational forms, we need a diversity of spatial scales. Just as social and economic life has spatiality, so do complementary currencies. Indeed, as local currencies, they have a specific geographical component that currently limits their usage. Currencies have a moral geography (Lee, 1996), raising a number of questions: How widely should they circulate? What is an 'optimum currency area' (Mundell, 1961) in terms of economic efficiency, and to what extent does an optimal area map onto, or clash with, socially constructed conceptions of what is a locality? How far 'away' is 'too far'? When do 'we' end and 'they' begin? LETS members, and to a lesser extent Time Bank users, wish to locate economic relations at a specific geographical scale – the very local or, at the largest extent, a city or sub-region. They feel that it is a problem if wealth leaves this particular scale to move to a place where it may secure a higher return. A community or ecological currency will need to be limited to a local neighbourhood, whereas one facilitating significant business involvement will need to be at least at a city-wide level, if not regional, to encompass the full range of supply linkages necessary to make complementary currencies spendable in the absence of existing localized economies. German Regiogeld operate at a regional level, while BerkShares circulate in the western part of a US state: these seem to be scales that mix an ethical attachment to the 'local' at a scale that enough businesses join to make circulations possible. Generally, the UK transition currencies, at a town level, have struggled to generate much recirculation. Their borders are too tight. But conversely, regional currencies are likely to operate at too big a scale for LETS and Time Bank members, but might work for credit unions (see Cutcher and Mason, this volume).

If complementary currencies are to become serious tools for building the sorts of resilient, localized, convivial economies activists want, participants will need access to the economic resources controlled by business. To fully promote sustainable development, inter-business trading at the regional level needs to be developed. In the future, the vision is for robust localization organizations to emerge that control their own regional currency and, crucially, are able to issue it in the form of loans to develop the sort of local production that activists want to see. Evidence from Germany's Chiemgauer regional currency suggests that where there are many locally owned *mittelstand* (or small and medium-sized) businesses in a local economy, then a local currency can circulate between them in an area that does, subjectively, feel 'local'. What we don't know is the extent that a regional currency is a strong enough organizational innovation to create a locally owned economy where one does not exist. This is an issue for the future of alternative currency development, and will be critical for the 5 per cent of current schemes that Bernard Lietaer believes will change our future.

Notes

1   'I'll buy you a pint if you . . .'.
2   This is perhaps less of an issue in an era of credit cards, supermarket points, and mobile phone-based and contactless payment systems. Many people now rarely use cash.
3   Although note the recent success of the African M-PESA SMS-based money transfer system in poor communities with affordable mobile phone services.

Resources

For a practical guide to community currencies see:
North, P. (2010) *Local Money: How to Make it Happen in Your Community*. Totnes: Transition Books.

Alternative currency websites

Bernard Lietaer's website on alternative currencies: www.lietaer.com
Tom Greco's websites: www.reinventingmoney.com and http://beyondmoney.net
These two websites are by interesting, local currency advocates and are full of useful information.

The Bibliography of Community Currency Research: www.cc-literature.org
The online Complementary Currency Resource Center: www.complementarycurrency.org
These two websites attempt to pull together written research on alternative currencies.

The International Journal of Community Currency Research, an online, open-access, academic but accessible journal of recent research on alternative currencies: www.uea.ac.uk/env/ijccr

Regional and local currency resources

LETSLink – UK: www.letslinkuk.net
Système d'Échange Locaux (SEL) – France: www.selidaire.org (in French)
Tauschringe – Germany: www.tauschring.de (in German)
Chiemgauer – Germany: www.chiemgauer.info/ (in German)
Ithaca Hours – USA: www.ithacahours.org

Also see Paul Glover's website: www.ithacahours.com
This includes links to a wide range of hour-based currencies in the USA at www.ithacahours.com/otherhours.html

BerkShares: www.berkshares.org
Run by the E.F. Schumacher Society, this is a good place to find out more about some of the practicalities of BerkShares, and get up to date with latest developments. It has some good links to YouTube films about BerkShares that give you more of a flavour of how it works.

References

Aldridge, T. and Patterson, A. (2002). "LETS get real: constraints on the development of Local Exchange Trading Schemes." *Area* 34(4): 370–381.
Cahn, E. (2000). *No More Throw Away People*. London: Harper Collins.
Cohen, B. (1998). *The Geography of Money*. Ithaca, NY: Cornell University Press.
Dodd, N. (1994). *The Sociology of Money*. New York: Continuum.
Donadio, R. (2011). "Battered by economic crisis, Greeks turn to Barter Networks." *New York Times*, New York.
Douthwaite, R. (1996). *Short Circuit: Strengthening Local Economies for Security in an Uncertain World*. Totnes, Devon: Green Books.
Ferguson, N. (2008). *The Ascent of Money: A Financial History of the World*. London: Penguin Books.
Glover, P. (1995). Ithaca Hours. In S. Meeker Lowry, *Invested in the Common Good*. New York: New Society Publishers, 72–80.
Hopkins, R. (2011). *The Transition Companion*. Totnes: Green Books.
Ingham, G. (2004). *The Nature of Money*. Cambridge: Polity.
Kanter, R. (1972). *Commitment and Community: Communes and Utopia in Sociological Perspective*. Cambridge, MA: Harvard University Press.
Lee, R. (1996). "Moral Money? LETS and the social construction of local economic geographies in Southeast England." *Environment and Planning A* 28(8): 1377–1394.
Lietaer, B. (2001). *The Future of Money*. London: Random House.
Maurer, B. (2003). "Uncanny exchange: the posibilities and failures of 'making change' with alternative money forms." *Environment and Planning D: Society and Space* 21(3): 317–340.
Maurer, B. (2005). *Mutual Life, Limited: Islamic Banking, Alternative Currencies, Lateral Reason*. Princeton, NJ: University of Princeton Press.
Mundell, R. (1961). "A theory of optimum currency areas." *American Economic Review* 51(4): 657–665.

North, P. (1996). "LETS: a tool for empowerment in the inner city?" *Local Economy* 11(3): 284–293.

North, P. (1998). "LETS, Hours and the Swiss business link: local currencies and business development programmes." *Local Economy* 13(2): 114–132.

North, P. (1999). "Explorations in Heterotopia: LETS and the micropolitics of money and livelihood." *Environment and Planning D: Society and Space* 17(1): 69–86.

North, P. (2002). "LETS in a cold climate: Green Dollars, self help and neo-liberal welfare reform in New Zealand." *Policy and Politics* 30(4): 483–500.

North, P. (2005). "Scaling alternative economic practices? Some lessons from alternative currencies." *Transactions of the Institute of British Geographers* 30(2): 221–233.

North, P. (2006). *Alternative Currencies as a Challenge to Globalisation?: A Case Study of Manchester's Local Money Networks.* Aldershot: Ashgate.

North, P. (2007). *Money and Liberation: The Micropolitics of Alternative Currency Movements.* Minneapolis: University of Minnesota Press.

North, P. (2010a). "Eco-Localisation as a progressive response to peak oil and climate change – a sympathetic critique." *Geoforum* 41(4): 585–594.

North, P. (2010b). *Local Money.* Dartington: Green Books.

North, P. (2010c). The longevity of alternative economic practices: lessons from alternative currency networks. In D. Fuller, A. Jonas and R. Lee *Interrogating Alterity: Alternative Spaces of Economy, Society and Politics.* London: Ashgate, 31–46.

Seyfang, G. (2003). "Growing cohesive communities one favour at a time: social exclusion, active citizenship and time banks." *International Journal of Urban and Regional Research* 27(3): 699–706.

Solomon, L. (1996). *Rethinking Our Centralised Money System: The Case for a System of Local Currencies.* London: Praeger.

Williams, C.C. (1996a). "Informal sector responses to unemployment: an evaluation of the potential of LETS." *Work, Employment and Society* 10(2): 341–360.

Williams, C.C. (1996b). "Local exchange trading systems: a new source of work and employment?" *Environment and Planning A* 28(8): 1395–1415.

Zelizer, V. (1997). *The Social Meaning of Money.* Princeton, NJ: Princeton University Press.

13

Gifts, gifting and gift economies

On challenging capitalism with blood, plunder and necklaces

Alf Rehn

Introduction

This chapter discusses the gift, one of the most romanticized and misunderstood economic phenomena in history, and the alternative forms of organization it can create. It will also address the manner in which this can be understood as a challenge to simplified notions about capitalism and the market economy, but rather than arguing for gift economies as a simple substitute for market economies, I will herein discuss the fact that the gift can be understood as being a permanent question to the notion of a triumphant market economy. I will, in this chapter, try to highlight the fact that even in the most craven and simplistic idea of market exchange there remains a social component that cannot be reduced to mere calculative rationality, and do so by way of examining the (not so) simple act of exchanging gifts and through this establishing relations.

A key challenge to writing about gifts, and one that needs to be addressed at the start of any serious engagement with the same, is that they evoke strong emotional responses. The gift, as should be well known, in addition to the obvious work done in anthropology (e.g. Boas 1897, Malinowski 1922, Sahlins 1972, Orenstein 1980, Godelier 1999, Benthall 2001, Sigaud 2002, Sykes 2005) has been utilized by a plethora of scholars, including people in fields such as feminist theory (Strathern 1990, Tyler and Taylor 1998, Cameron and Gibson-Graham 2003), sociology (Camerer 1988, Carrier 1991, Berking 1999), economics (Akerlof 1984, Offer 1997, Kolm and Ythier 2006, Falk 2007, Eisenstein 2011), philosophy (Hyde 1979, Schrift 1997, Teubner 2001), organization studies (Rehn 2004, Jensen 2008, Dunne and Spoelstra 2010), marketing and consumer research (Belk 1979, Marcoux 2009) and information science (Raymond 1999). This has often built on the desire to present an assumedly ethical alternative to more craven forms of human interaction and exchange – something that, unsurprisingly, is high up on the contemporary agenda (see Graeber 2012). The idealized gift – selfless and inherently good – is simply too lovely a sentiment not to create strong socio-moral feelings in a commentator's mind. The gift seems like such a perfect Other to the cold, hard reality of market exchange that it can quite easily be cast as a fundamentally good thing, an iconic representation of a pure and ethical alternative to the market. This is further strengthened by the fact that the literature on the gift tends to have a strong intellectual impact on people, to the point where this too becomes idealized. More specifically, individuals are often highly moved by Marcel Mauss's seminal essay on the gift (Mauss, 1925, 1954), hereafter simply *The Gift*, to the point where they start believing themselves to be among the few people to 'really get it'. I have personal experience of how several individuals, upon learning that I worked with notions on gift economies and had published on the matter, enthusiastically suggested that I read a little book they happened to know of – namely *The Gift* – as it might be of interest to me. As I pointed out, this is akin to suggesting to a theologian that they might find a little-known tract called *The Bible* interesting. At least one of the above individuals acted surprised that I'd already heard of it. Such is the power of the gift, as a concept, that we easily make it our own: our personal alternative, presented as a gift to the community around us.

At the same time, the gift is far from a simple thing, and has been highly resistant to oversimplified theorizing. It has been boosted by Benedict (1934) and derided by Derrida (1992), treated as a trusted go-to concept for economic anthropologists and as an anything-goes concept by more pundits than I care to mention, and yet it retains a degree of both mystique and explanatory power. Rather than being one specific thing, the gift might best be seen as a dynamic, the capacity for human exchange to retain a both/and, a back and forth of social relations. This, in the end, rather than any romanticized notion of an economy completely freed from calculative rationalities, might be the true power of the concept – its capacity to challenge the market economy by way of continuously reintroducing the social into economic exchange.

The gift and The Gift

Why the gift? Simply put, the notion of gift exchange as an alternative to other forms of economic organization – most notably that of market exchange – arose from anthropological evidence that it was possible to structure complex exchange systems without invoking notions such as price, or at least without having such as the predominant form of exchange. By inquiring into how cultures had developed complex forms of economic organization without giving precedence to market mechanisms, early anthropologists such as Marcel Mauss, Franz Boas and Ruth Benedict tried to show that rather than being 'primitive', non-Western cultures had systems quite as complex as their Western counterparts, but that these often followed different logics. This wasn't necessarily a political project, but rather an attempt to develop the field of anthropology towards a more mature incarnation – one without preconceived notions of what 'correct' forms of economic organization might look like.

While one could point to a number of predecessors and earlier influences, most histories of the study of gift economies start by referring to the aforementioned two-part essay of the French anthropologist Marcel Mauss, published in 1925 in *L'Année Sociologique* as *Essai sur le don. Forme et raison de l'échange dans les sociétés archaïques*. The essay was later republished as a book, first in French in 1950, but is perhaps best known under the name it got when translated into English in 1954 – *The Gift* (Mauss 1925, 1954). The book is fairly short, and at heart a meditation on the 'forms and functions of exchange in archaic societies'. As a seminal piece of work in anthropology in general, and economic anthropology in particular, it has generated an immense amount of commentary, and stands as the foundational work on gift economies.

As a result, two of the key cases in Mauss's work have become something akin to archetypal forms through which gift exchange is discussed. On one hand we have the *Kula ring*, a cycle of ongoing gift exchange where the ritual movement of specific gifts – the necklaces known as *soulava* that travel 'clockwise' and armbands known as *mwali* that are gifted 'counter-clockwise' – and the weaving together of a dispersed community constituted the key economic organization of a group of islands in the Massim archipelago of Papua New Guinea. Here, the ritual donation of the symbolically valuable Kula objects constituted the main reason to engage in any kind of exchange, and served as the framework for social organization more broadly. This, however, did not mean that market exchange was alien to the participants of the Kula exchanges. On the contrary, the gifting of Kula objects was normally accompanied by another process, namely the *gimwali*, in which commodity objects were exchanged in barter. For the people participating in these exchanges, the difference between the two was, however, sacrosanct. Kula could never be conducted like *gimwali*, as the two forms of exchange – where the former was seen as far more important – had to be treated as separate.

The Kula might thus be seen as an ordering framework for both economy and social behavior in the communities engaged in the same. The gifting that took place in the Kula exchanges was ritual and social, something that had to be conducted according to strict rules of reciprocity and keeping the cycle alive. Sooner or later the *soulava* or *mwali* needed to be given forward, prompting the holder of these objects to set out on a journey. That these journeys also created an opportunity to barter, trade and gossip was a beneficial by-product of the Kula ring, but it was the gift exchange that was the necessary form of economic organizing. In other words, gift exchange, and the economy that evolved around this, was the main form of economy for those communities that engaged in the same – effectively disproving the assumption that trade and barter were necessarily the primary forms of economic engagement for a society. Nor was this just an isolated case, for while the economy around the Kula exchange is quite limited in size, it doesn't represent a unique form. Similar exchanges have been found in other parts of Papua New Guinea (e.g. the Sepik Coast exchange), as well as among the Maori (e.g. the custom of Koha).

Despite this, the Kula ring was not to be the most famous of Mauss's examples. This accolade goes to the practice of *potlatch*, particularly among the Kwakwaka'wakw of the First Nations (sometimes, and in Mauss, incorrectly referred to as the 'Kwakiutl indians'). The *potlatch*, a term that comes to us from the Chinook trading jargon word 'patshatl', which in turn was derived from the Nuu-chah-nulth word *paƛiƛ*, was a gift-giving economy practiced on the Pacific Northwest Coast of North America among at least the Kwakwaka'wakw, the Nuu-chah-nulth, the Tlingit, the Haida and the Nuxalk cultures. As the social structure that existed around the *potlatch* (and, for that matter, the Kula, and definitively that of the Koha) is far more intricate than can be captured in a single chapter, let alone in part of one, I am here forced to present only a very truncated explication of the same (cf. Codere 1950).

A central part of the social system of the *potlatch* is the eponymous gift-giving festival. Here, a chief or comparable leader invites one or more other chiefs to a feast at which gifts are ceremoniously given to the guests. This gifting is also accompanied by a number of ceremonial aspects such as dances and songs, many of which celebrate the chief giving the *potlatch* – although it should be noted that there are variations between the cultures how *potlatches* are given. The aspect that interested Mauss, and which has become the most discussed and commented-upon feature of the *potlatch* (to the point that it is at times seen as synonymous with the same), is that the gifting, rather than being a limited and symbolic thing, in fact represented a central aspect of economic exchange in the cultures engaging in *potlatch* festivals. The gifts given often represented considerable material wealth, and the *potlatch* stood as the main process for the redistribution of wealth among, for example, the Kwakwaka'wakw.

However, this should not be understood as the ritual wrappings of a sharing and caring economy, nor as pure altruism. The *potlatch* was rather, in the memorable phrasing of Helen

Codere (1950), 'fighting with property'. A chief giving a *potlatch* was engaged in a ritualized game of honor, one in which the giving of, for example, pelts, valuable metals or fish oil was a way to exhibit dominance. One might even say that those receiving gifts were 'subjected' to a *potlatch*, and even shamed in the same. The giving of a *potlatch* was a way to show off the wealth you and your family or tribe had amassed, and the, at times, casual manner in which a great deal of wealth might be redistributed during the festivals needs to be understood as a way of showing (feigned) indifference to wealth. To give was to show oneself to be honorable, and the more one gave the greater the honor. Being the guest at a *potlatch* also came at a price. A leader of a community that had been the recipient in a *potlatch* was now bound by the obligation to give a *potlatch* in turn, preferably a greater *potlatch*, although this too differed among cultures.

Over time, this led (in some cultures) to ever-greater *potlatches*, and also to situations where wealth was not only given away, but also ceremoniously destroyed. In some, exceedingly rare and possibly exaggerated cases, this even led to the greatest possible forms of sacrifice – that of human beings. To be part of the gift economy of the *potlatch* was to accept being part of a hierarchy, and to potentially become part of a kind of competitive generosity. This manner in which *potlatches* could engender quite extreme positions of squandering and waste also inspired the economic works of Georges Bataille (1933, 1997, 1949, 1988; see also Rehn and Lindahl 2011), who in the *potlatch* found an example of expenditure so radical he started talking of an 'accursed share', mankind's drive towards wastefulness and ecstatic expenditure.

The Kula and the *potlatch* are thus both gift economies, but they are far from identical. Where the Kula emphasizes the continuous circulation of (mostly) the same objects – the most valuable Kula objects are those with a long history – the *potlatch* emphasized the show of honor that came with the giving of gifts. In both cases, however, the key logic was one of *reciprocity*, that the giving of a gift establishes a relation between the giver and the receiver that needs to be addressed. In the case of the Kula this meant that the ceremonial objects need to be given forward, whereas in the case of the *potlatch* this meant that every festival of gifting required a reply in the form of a (grander) festival of gifting. Continuously present in the work of Mauss, and thus in most of the work on gift economies, was thus also a third concept, one at times forgotten but which has also given rise to fierce debate. This is the notion of the 'spirit of the gift', at times referred to by the Maori word *hau*. Mauss's insight was that the gift was neither merely something that existed in a circle of exchange, nor a mere token in a battle of shame and honor, but rather something imbued with a very specific kind of relational spirit. For the people engaged in a gift economy, the gift contained part of the giver's spirit – a force that imbued it with the power to demand reciprocity. But this force also meant that the giving of a gift meant you invested yourself in the giving – the gift always carried part of the giver or, if you prefer a less individualized interpretation, the gift-relation. Gifts were thus inalienable in a way that commodities could never be.

Gift exchange and gift economies

The notion of inalienability also led Mauss to the conclusion that no gift was ever completely 'free', as all gift-giving contained a tacit assumption of reciprocity, making the gift exchange a 'total prestation' that bound the participants of the exchange rather than freeing them. Where a market exchange is a very temporary relationship, where both parties are free after payment has been agreed upon and handed over, the gift creates ties that bind. This famously led Derrida (1992) to argue that there is an *aporia* surrounding the gift, and that no gift in a gift exchange represents a genuine gift – as the assumption of reciprocity annuls the gift as gift. In his reading, the only true gift, then, would be one where an anonymous giver is not even aware that she is giving a gift, and the recipient isn't able to acknowledge receipt thereof, making a genuine gift an impossibility. Laidlaw (2000) has argued that free gifting does exist in some charitable contexts, for example, where the giver may give for religious or charitable reasons and thus expect no reciprocity, and the receiver may be unable (again, for example, for religious reasons) to acknowledge the gift as something meaningful.

Herein lies an important distinction, one curiously often ignored in the debate on gifts. We need to distinguish between the notions of the gift-as-is (i.e. the gift as a symbolic entity), gifting, gift exchanges and gift economies. Mauss's interest, and the interest of a number of anthropologists after him, was the gift exchange and its capacity to develop into a gift economy. Derrida's interest rested on the possibility of the gift as a phenomenon and an entity. Discussions of charity, such as the critique presented by Testart (1998), focus more specifically on gifting behaviors, i.e. the giving of gifts that do not require set behaviors of reciprocity and which do not tend to create gift economies. This separation may seem somewhat nerdy, but is in fact central if we are to consider how the gift can create alternative economic forms.

A *gift economy*, as I define it here, is a form of economic organization that exists over a longer period of time and in which gift exchanges function as the central framework of economic activity. In a gift economy, there exists an ongoing giving and receiving of gifts that is socially meaningful and socially structured, normally in such a way that a symmetry of exchange is achieved over time – i.e. some form of reciprocity organizes the distribution of wealth in the society over time.

Gift exchange is the term for the manner in which gifts are given and acknowledged, by parties that may or may not be hierarchical equals. Such exchanges can be so structured as to give rise to more limited or more general gift economies, but need not be so. Gift exchange is, however, structured by all parties being aware of the structure within which this takes place, and an adherence to some shared rules regarding proper decorum when engaging in gift exchange – for instance, knowing one is supposed to show gratitude, if not full reciprocity, when presented with a Christmas gift.

Gifting, again, is the general form in which a gift is presented from one agent to another. This *can* occur within a gift exchange or a gift economy, but does not need to do so. For instance, giving coins to a beggar does not, in most cultures, contain an assumption of some specific form of decorum – the assumption is often that the two parties will never meet again. Similarly, religious offerings may well be given in a stylized manner by the giver but met with religiously prescribed indifference by the recipient (see Laidlaw 2000).

Thus, when talking about the gift we are potentially talking about at least three structures or figurations within which this can exist, from the general structure of gifting to the highly specific form of the gift economy. A problem in the discussion regarding the gift in the economy has thus been that the differences inherent in these levels or figurations haven't always been acknowledged, something which has also affected the manner in which the gift has been seen as an economic alternative.

The gift as economic alternative

Is gift exchange or gift economy, then, an alternative to more well-known forms of economic organization, more specifically capitalist market exchange? It is, although it should be noted that the 'being alternative' here can be interpreted in several ways (see also Chapter 3). The existence of the archaic gift economies documented in the anthropological literature is obviously in itself proof that there are cases where calculative economic rationality is not the key framework for economic exchange – although this conclusion used to be hotly debated between representatives of the substantivist and the formalist positions in economic anthropology (see Plattner 1989, cf. Graeber 2012). This, in itself, can serve as an important reminder that while notions of utility maximization may well be the defining characteristic of almost all large-scale economic systems, this does not mean that alternatives are nonexistent (see also Chapter 2). Through this, the anthropological work on gift exchange can be read as a falsification of reductionist, neoclassical economic models. Further, by pointing to the continuing existence of more limited forms of gift exchange in contemporary society – during, for instance, Christmas (see Lemmergaard and Muhr 2011, Hancock and Rehn 2011, cf. Waldfogel 1993) – one can show that even within the dominant notion of a triumphant market economy there remain pockets of alternative logics and through this a potential for resistance (Gibson-Graham 1996, Yang 2000, Williams, this volume).

This, however does not address the larger issue of whether ideas of gift economies carry the potential to become large-scale alternatives to contemporary economic systems. Some have looked at the work by Mauss, and the works that have sprung up in its wake, and seen the promise of a new kind of economy, often a morally superior kind of economy. As the 'archaic' societies Mauss and his fellow anthropologists studied seem far removed from the excesses and the ethical dilemmas inherent in contemporary capitalist society, the gift economy has at times served as an icon for an economic Other to the market economy. Notions such as 'pay it forward' and 'freeconomy' (see www.justfortheloveofit.org/) have often co-opted the anthropological notion of the gift economy, and the theorization of the same has been invoked in alternative economic organizational forms – including but not limited to trials with local currencies and in the organizing of autonomous communes such as Freetown Christiania (see www.christiania.org/ and the chapters by Pitzer and North, this volume).

It is however important to note the difference between the socio-ethical interpretations of gift economies and their actual functioning. One of the challenges in studying gift economies has been that examples tend to come in two forms – the archaic, pure forms or more modern, diluted examples which have more in common with gift exchange than fully fledged gift economies. In the former, we normally have small communities structuring their economic exchanges around rituals, in contexts where close social ties and strong reciprocity support the prolonged existence of ongoing gift exchanges, i.e. an economy unto itself. In the latter, there has been a tendency to conflate barter-systems, pooling-systems (e.g. give-away shops and the like) and gift exchanges under umbrella terms such as 'social economies' (cf. Bowen 1977, Fontan and Shragge 2000), so that, at times, the gift economy is presented as more prominent in a new form of economic organization than its actual contribution might allow. As Guerin (1970) has pointed out, a functioning modern gift economy would represent a kind of anarchist utopia, one where neither state nor market would interfere with individuals giving (and receiving) according to need and capacity.

A key limitation in a move towards such forms, utopian or not, is the social structure necessary to support this alternative kind of organization. For instance, if we assume a cyclical model – one reminiscent of the Kula – we need to be able to ensure both that the cycle of gifting continues and that the 'free rider' problem (i.e. the issue of how many participants only take part of the system as recipients and whether the system can sustain such a level) is controlled. This may require introducing controlling and sanctioning processes, which in the original forms often came from existing structures of kinship and social pressure. Similarly, if we assume a more competitive notion of gift exchange – one reminiscent of the *potlatch* – we need to have a shared notion of achievement for there to be incentives for giving in order to achieve status.

Claims such as the ones above will no doubt anger at least some proponents of gift economies as alternatives to the market, as they do not allow for an economy of pure altruism, i.e. systems where people share and give out of the goodness of their hearts without being coerced by social pressures or rewarded by status (see Vaughan 2007). The anthropological problem here is that from what we know of gift economies, 'big-man' economies (see Sahlins 1963) and the like do not function in a purely altruistic fashion, but are conditioned by the social structure from which they've emerged. In other words, the anthropological evidence for purely altruistic gift economies is scant, disallowing some historical evidence of anarchic or religious communities that have operated in such a manner (see Haude 2000, cf. Dana 2007). This said, some suggestions and some evidence regarding altruistic gift economies can be found when looking at some of the modern forms of gift exchange, which is why this is what I will turn to next.

Blood and plunder: on modern gift exchanges

For an insight into how gift exchanges – and, potentially, gift economies – might function *within* the contemporary market economy, I will here refer the reader to some of the most widely used examples of gift exchange in contemporary capitalist society, examples somewhat removed from the works of self-sufficiency and communal organization discussed elsewhere in this volume. These examples have all, in their own way, served to further the argument that some form of gift economy might be possible in our modern, 'advanced' societies, and, in some cases, even that such societies might be more capable of supporting it.

Even though one could list a number of examples, I will here limit myself to the following two. My cases here will be:

- Internet gift exchanges, i.e. FOSS, warez and Wikipedia
- Blood and organ donorship

A great deal of the literature on the gift has, as indicated above, focused on the gifting of material objects. Although some of these seem to have very limited material value, or use value, they are still the tokens through which the spirit or the *hau* (by any other name) of the gift is transferred. In many ways, gift theory has been biased towards the manner in which something that could be seen as a commodity can also escape this fate by becoming part of another kind of economy. A necklace could be either/or – a commodity or a gift object imbued with history and great symbolic value – depending on the system in which it was placed.

The limitation inherent in this has always been that the material value of the object still remained, even if it existed in a gift economy – something which in 1884 led to a ban on *potlatches* in Canada, as the European colonists viewed the practice as wasteful. Throughout history, one has had the possibility of *either* selling/consuming an object one has acquired *or* giving it away. Doing both was, for a very long time, impossible. And then came the Internet.

Although it is impossible to give a full picture of the manner in which ICT affected our view on production, distribution and (the potential for) gifting in the confines of a chapter, it is important to note that this may well represent one of the most thorough re-evaluations of these concepts in history (see Rossiter and Zehle, this volume). For the purposes of this chapter, we can simply state that the development, first, of digital goods, and then the protocols for the distribution of the same, removed many of the barriers that made large-scale gift exchange difficult or impossible, making gift exchanges created and supported by ICT a qualitatively different form of the same.

We should differentiate between those Internet gift exchanges that build upon original knowledge work and those that build on the sharing of digital goods. The former would include things such as the FOSS movement (Free and Open-Source Software) and the creation of Wikipedia, whereas the latter would include file-sharing and software piracy (AKA the culture around 'warez'). Unsurprisingly, much of the positive media attention has focused on the former.

FOSS builds on several of the key elements identified in classic gift economies (see Raymond 1999, Rehn 2004, Bergquist and Ljungberg 2008). Participants in the communities around FOSS emphasize the importance of contributions to the greater community, and that these are supposed to be done without any direct compensation. At the same time, there is no assumption of pure altruism. Those who are seen to have contributed the most (i.e. given the greatest gifts) rise in the hierarchy and are afforded more respect than those who haven't. Some also rise to the level of gatekeepers and, for instance, decide which 'gifts' should be included in the greater project – for example, which parts of code should be included in a new build of Linux. The gift economy of FOSS is thus more akin to an honor economy, one where those who have given away the most are seen as the most important actors in the community – or outside of it, as participants in the FOSS community have been able to translate success in the same into lucrative consulting contracts.

If we compare this to the community I've referred to as the warez community (Rehn 2001, 2004), i.e. the community that has grown up around the competitive practice of distributing pirated commercial software for free across the Internet (and the similar communities that exist in related fields such as pirating movies, music, books and the like), the aspect of producing the gift is lessened, but the same does not go for the honor aspect. In cultures of online piracy, the greatest honor goes to those who are seen as contributing the most to the community, i.e. those who have given away the most.

In other words, warez and FOSS are reminiscent of the kinds of gift economies where honor is a key element, and where gifting is less a case of pure altruism and more a case of one-upmanship. Regardless of the ethical elements inherent in this, such competitive gift exchange has in both cases been able to create a semi-permanent, powerful form of economic organizing that has shown itself capable of creating (in the case of FOSS) and/or distributing (in the case of warez) a great deal of economic value. Both cases thus represent the kind of example that can serve to falsify simplistic views of the contemporary economy, but at the same time neither necessarily shows us forms of economic engagement that in themselves can supplant the market economy.

A very different case can be found in a form of gift economy that exists in most countries and which supports a critical infrastructure of contemporary health – the donation of blood and organs. As Titmuss (1970) has shown, treating blood as something that was voluntarily donated rather than as a commodity increased the blood supply, proving that the market was not always the most efficient way to organize exchanges.

Some, such as Boas (2011), have, in this area, deployed the term 'restricted altruism' to separate between donations as social goods and donations made as personal gifts. Arguably, blood donorship would in such a scheme fall outside of a gift economy and belong to a more general field, a field without the assumptions of direct reciprocity that normally define the former, even though one might assume that there remains the possibility of a more vicarious or general reciprocity (e.g. a blood donor later being a blood recipient, or a blood donor having a close relative being a blood recipient at a later date). At the same time, we can in the donorship of blood and organs see how gifts can represent efficiencies that the market economy cannot easily replicate.

When dealing with things such as blood, the basic economic value of the same cannot necessarily affect donors in a manner which would optimize supply. Rather than seeing their 'property' as having a set economic value, donors will be more easily moved to give by viewing their acts through the lens of gift exchange, regardless of whether reciprocity or not plays a part. Thus, the gifting relationship may exist outside of the spirit of the gift, and create a different kind of gift economy, at least in a restricted fashion.

Blat and other 'economies of favors'

In both the Internet gift economies and the case of donorship, a key element is the final 'product'. For the community-building Wikipedia, this stood as the symbol of their endeavors, much as the zero-day release (i.e. a piece of software that is 'gifted' to the community on the same day as it is commercially released, if not earlier) is an icon for those engaged in warez. In the donorship of blood and organs this obviously becomes even more material, and directly (literally) visceral. Still, much of the work of Internet gift economies is knowledge work, and the end-results are immaterial. This is, of course, in line with the general trend of post-industrialism, where knowledge-work becomes ever more important.

Some have, with this as a starting point, noted that one of the larger gift economies in contemporary societies is science and academia. Even though most academics are salaried and work in the public sector, a great deal of their work has similarities with gift exchange. Academics write articles, chapters and books without expectation of direct payment for their scholarly output (even though they may be compensated for this in the long run through career advancement, for example), and also serve as reviewers and editors with little or no pay. In doing so, academics serve the greater community with the gift of an increased body of knowledge, often far beyond any stated requirement for output and, somewhat surprisingly, often for the benefit of commercial publishers (Harvie et al. 2012).

In this, a great deal of the work could be referred to as 'favors'. An academic agreeing to being an external advisor or a reviewer rarely does it for any direct compensation (none such are forthcoming in the latter case, and only trifling amounts in the former), but does so as such favors are built into the system and participation is a requirement for the system to work. Being a reviewer or convening a workshop is thus, in a manner of speaking, a gift given to the community of academics with the assumption that others will partake in the same way – a kind of more generalized reciprocity.

Something similar can be seen in what we might call communal economies. Working communes normally contain at least some elements of a gift economy, particularly when it comes to the gift of time (Butcher 1999). Many smaller and more permanent communities, however, operate more with principles of sharing and controlled inputs (cf. Kinkade 1994, Janzen 1996), even to the point where it might be more correct to talk of a social economy with alternate currencies rather than a gift economy as such. Still, this hasn't stopped more large-scale and temporary communes exhibiting behaviors that might be described as time-limited gift economies. Of particular interest here are large religious gatherings, such as those organized by mega-churches in the US, or other community-led festivals. In the former, gifting in the form of potluck dinners (a word derived from *potlatch*) is seen as a natural part of organizing such an event, and participants are assumed to give freely of their time in order to make such events possible.

A radical example of this is the Burning Man festival (Chen 2009). This event, held yearly from the last Monday in August to the first Monday in September, is founded on the notion of self-reliance, inclusion and gifting, stating explicitly that:

> Burning Man is devoted to acts of gift giving. The value of a gift is unconditional. Gifting does not contemplate a return or an exchange for something of equal value.
>
> *(From the stated principles of Burning Man)*

Although the festival isn't completely cash-free – tickets are still sold, as is coffee, fuel and some sanitation services – most of the economic activity of the festival is structured by gift exchange, which is why it can be said to represent a limited (and delimited) form of gift economy. Although many have, in the working of the festival, seen something akin to a potential alternative to the market economy, one needs to acknowledge that such festivals tend to represent very temporary organizations. Their existence depends on the accumulation of value in market economies, and their capacity to act as an alternative is thus somewhat adulterated.

For a very different form of gift economy we could look to the phenomenon of *blat* which existed as an 'economy of favors' (Ledeneva 1998) in the Soviet Union (Rehn and Taalas 2004). Here, the stifling structure of a state-run economy had created an almost permanent state of lack, one where even getting hold of basic necessities could be a chore. As a result, the Soviet economy – which forbade market exchange – gave rise to a shadow economy of favors, one which most Soviet citizens had to take part in. Simplifying somewhat, a Soviet citizen utilized the resources and access to the resources that s/he had, and leveraged the favors that s/he could offer in order to be able to access other parts of the economy.

A baker with access to bread might thus gift the occasional loaf of bread to a pharmacist, who might in return enable a worker at a radio factory to get hold of some medicine, who might in turn help the baker out with a radio. Direct exchanges (medicine for bread or radios for medicine) were rare, partly as this would have meant one committed a more grievous crime, but the circle of favors was very much an integral part of Soviet society. In other words, gifting became a second economy, one which emerged as the primary economy proved itself unable to support society in a functional manner.

The *blat* combined elements of honor economies – the more one could give, the higher in the *blat* hierarchy one could rise – and the circular notions of reciprocity found in other gift economies. More importantly, the *blat* was something close to a total system, one that most members of the community/society engaged with at least in some degree. Where the gift economy of academia exists as a sub-system of the greater (market) economy, and one where only a fraction of society are engaged, and where festivals such as the Burning Man are temporary exceptions to the market economy, the *blat* was a permanent and generally used system.

Economies of favors can thus represent an alternative form of economy, but not only the market economy. In our quest to figure out exactly what the gift is an alternative to, we thus need to be sensitive to the contexts in which it emerges, and the peculiar efficiencies brought on by the same. The gift can be an alternative, but gift exchanges can function in a myriad of ways – some of which may well be co-opted by the system it tries to be an alternative to.

Co-opting the gift

As many in the various movements criticizing contemporary capitalism and searching for alternatives for it were lauding the notion of gift economies, often using the FOSS movement as an example (Berry 2008), a subtle shift occurred in the very market economy these movements criticized. At play here was the fact that the same technological developments that had made many forms of gifting both a great deal easier, and in many cases very cheap, also represented an opportunity for economic agents such as corporations and entrepreneurs.

Gift-giving has of course always played a part in market capitalism. Free samples have in all likelihood been a part of marketing for as long as the market has existed, and as Pink (2012: 11–12) notes in his discussion of the Fuller Brush salesmen:

> [O]ffering a free vegetable scrubber known as a Handy Brush as a gift, they tried to get what quickly became known as 'a foot in the door. [. . .] In 1937 alone, door-to-door Fuller dealers gave away some 12.5 million Handy Brushes.'

Such promotional gifting has come in many forms, including the classic capitalist paradox of 'free gift with purchase' and the bundling of products in order to give the impression of the consumer receiving gifts in addition to his/her purchase, all of which utilized the logic of reciprocity inherent in gift-giving – albeit for purposes very far removed from that of real gift-exchange. But while this kind of gifting has a long history, this was for a very long time limited by the basic logic of the material commodity, i.e. that an agent within a capitalist logic cannot give away things for very long without amassing hard-to-cover losses.

However, the same logic that enabled the FOSS and software piracy movements to establish gift economies of their own enabled companies to experiment with new forms of old market gifting. As indicated above, free software has always played a part in the coding community and in the adoption and widespread use of computers. Such 'freeware' was often the product of coders wishing to share their work or market their skills. As the use of personal computers and the access to networks/the Internet spread, some companies saw potential in this model and started experimenting with the notion of 'shareware' or 'trialware'. A watershed moment in this, thanks to the popularity of the titles, was the decision of iD Software to release the first episode (ten missions/levels) of *Wolfenstein 3D* (1992) as a free-to-download demo, in order to entice gamers to buy the full version. As this was quite successful, the company used the same method to sell their follow-up game of 1993, *Doom*. This became a runaway success, and established the model of giving away a limited version of a game or a program in order to sell customers on the extended or more advanced version.

Today, this business model is known as 'freemium', and represents something of a default assumption in much of the software industry. The notion has also given rise to a business bestseller with Chris Anderson's (2010) *Free: How Today's Smartest Businesses Profit by Giving Something for Nothing*, which argued that such models could be adapted to almost any business, and that such strategies represented the future of the market economy. Giving things away, argues Anderson, is necessary in a market culture in which consumers have become accustomed to receiving things for free and getting to try-before-you-buy. In other words, Anderson argues that the market economy has evolved to a point where the giving away of products and services would represent 'business as usual', and thus, in extension, that a kind of gift or attention economy would be on its way to becoming integrated into the market economy.

And this is not merely the question of companies enticing their customers with gifts, with the assumption that the spirit of the gift would get many of the said customers to reciprocate by way of purchases. At the same time as Anderson and others have proselytized for freemium as a business model, many other corporations have embraced notions such as crowdsourcing and open innovation, often looking to the aforementioned Wikipedia as an iconic example.

As ICT has made it possible to collect input and various kinds of contributions from customers, consumers and the general public in a manner never before practically possible, the notion of being able to have the public solve your business problems – be this by helping in picking out your product portfolio, writing advertising copy or contributing with ideas for innovations – has been close to irresistible to companies and engendered a business literature all of its own (see Chesbrough 2005, Howe 2009, Gansky 2010, Tapscott and Williams 2010a, Tapscott and Williams 2010b).

In such 'open' forms of engagement between the public and the corporation, a problem or a question is posed to the former, with the assumption that members of the public will devote their time and intellect to providing solutions or ideas, often with little more incentive than the chance to win a small reward or merely being recognized as the progenitor of an idea. If successful, this represents a tremendous business opportunity for a corporation, as it can benefit from the 'wisdom of crowds' (Surowiecki 2005) without paying more than a pittance. The participants may well see themselves as participating in a form of honor-based gift economy, one where the act of giving your input and insight to the community is a key form of identity formation. For the companies enabling the same, the logic may well be quite different, as the goading of participants into this kind of competition may well result in attracting far more commercially usable input than would be possible by utilizing solely market-based mechanisms.

In other words, where many are looking to the gift as an alternative to capitalist appropriation, the corporate world are looking to the same as a new engine for the very same appropriation. For the corporate world, the gift truly represents a gift that keeps on giving.

The promise of the gift?

What, then, can we say about the promise of the gift economy as a contemporary alternative to the market economy? As I've hopefully managed to show, this is not an easy question to answer. It is easy to the point of triviality to show that gifts exist, that they affect societies and that they create exchanges of value that are important enough to falsify simplistic notions of the supremacy of market exchange. At the same time, finding 'complete' gift economies is not necessarily easy.

FOSS and warez represent fields in which great economic values are created and distributed in a manner that cannot be explained by the simple hypothesis of market exchange. However, they are technologically limited and function mainly within the field of digital goods.

Blood donorship shows that people are moved by more than economic incentives, and that organizing things merely through market exchange and trusting in the 'natural egotism' of individuals isn't necessarily efficient. Similarly, the processes of academia prove that even very well-educated people are more easily moved by the demands placed on them by their community than by monetary incentives. This chapter, written at a time when its author could have made much more filthy lucre by writing columns or other commercial texts, but chose not to do so out of a sense of duty to the editors and the community, stands as proof of this.

Communities such as those created around temporary organizations such as Burning Man, or more permanent ones such as the *blat*, show that even more large-scale sharing and gifting still exists in contemporary societies, but the generality of these and the context within which they emerge aren't necessarily given.

All in all, the gift *shows* us an alternative, but this does not mean that it *is* an alternative. It may be, but it may also be perverted, or limited, or co-opted, or might only emerge in very special conditions. For us to truly make it an alternative, we need to look closely at the conditions that make it possible – those technical, social and cultural states of exception that can make or break our current way of viewing the potential of the economic.

Resources

The obvious starting point for an engagement with the gift as an economy and as a creator of organizations is the book that started it all:

Mauss, M. (1925/1954). *The Gift: Forms and Functions of Exchange in Archaic Societies*. London: Cohen & West.

Another book that has been seen as quite influential in bringing the logic of the gift to a general public is:

Hyde, L. (1983). *The Gift: Imagination and the Erotic Life of Property*. New York: Vintage Books.

A nice introduction to the *economy* of gifts and gifting and their relation to market economies can be found in:

Offer, A. (1997). "Between the Gift and the Market: The Economy of Regard", *Economic History Review*, 50(3): 450–476.

For one of the more influential modern texts on the potential of gift economies in the digital sphere, see:

Raymond, E.S. (2001). *The Cathedral and the Bazaar – Musings on Linux and Open Source by an Accidental Revolutionary* (revised edition). Sebastopol: O'Reilly Media.

However, for a critique, see http://thebaffler.com/past/the_meme_hustler and Stallman, R. (2002). *Free Software, Free Society*. Boston, MA: GNU Press.

The gift economy of the Burning Man has been showcased in a documentary, http://giftingitthemovie.com/ and in Chen's ethnography:

Chen, K. (2009). *Enabling Creative Chaos: The Organization Behind the Burning Man Event*. Chicago, IL: University of Chicago Press.

For a radical call to action for a (specific kind of) feminist gift economy, see www.gift-economy.com/

For a call to a general altruism, including a move towards gift economies, see www.altruists.org/

References

Akerlof, George A. (1984). "Gift Exchange and Efficiency-Wage Theory: Four Views", *The American Economic Review*, 74(2): 79–83.

Anderson, C. (2010). *Free: How Today's Smartest Businesses Profit by Giving Something for Nothing*. New York: Hyperion.

Bataille, G. (1933/1997). "The Notion of Expenditure", in *The Bataille Reader* (ed. F. Botting and S. Wilson, trans. A. Stoeckl *et al.*). Oxford: Blackwell.

Bataille, G. (1949/1988). *The Accursed Share*, Vol I. New York: Zone Books.

Belk, R. (1979). "Gift Giving Behavior", in J. Sheth (ed.) *Research in Marketing*, pp. 95–126. Greenwich, CT: JAI Press.

Bell, D. (1991). "Modes of Exchange: Gift and Commodity", *The Journal of Socio-Economics*, 20(2): 155–167.

Benedict, R. (1934). *Patterns of Culture*. New York: Houghton Mifflin.

Benthall, J. (2001). "Time to Look 'The Gift' in the Mouth", *Anthropology Today*, 17(4): 1–2.

Bergquist, M. and Ljungberg, J. (2008). "The Power of Gifts: Organizing Social Relationships in Open Source Communities", *Information Systems Journal*, 11(4): 305–320.

Berking, H. (1999). *The Sociology of Giving*. London: Sage.

Berry, D. (2008). *Copy, Rip, Burn: The Politics of Copyleft and Open Source*. London: Pluto Press.

Boas, F. (1897). *The Social Organization and Secret Societies of the Kwakiutl Indians*. Canadian Institute for Historical Microreproduction.

Boas, H. (2011). "Where Do Human Organs Come From? Trends of Generalized and Restricted Altruism in Organ Donations", *Social Science and Medicine*, 73(9): 1378–1385.

Bowen, H.R. (1977). *Toward Social Economy*. Southern Illinois University Press.

Butcher, A.A. (1999). *Time-Based Economics: A Community-Building Dynamic*. Denver, CO: Author.

Camerer, C. (1988). "Gifts as Economic Signals and Social Symbols", *The American Journal of Sociology*, 94: 180–214.

Cameron, J., and Gibson-Graham, J.K. (2003). "Feminising the Economy: Metaphors, Strategies, Politics", *Gender, Place and Culture: A Journal of Feminist Geography*, 10(2): 145–157.

Carrier, J. (1991). "Gifts, Commodities, and Social Relations: A Maussian View of Exchange", *Sociological Forum*, 6(1): 119–136.

Chen, K. (2009). *Enabling Creative Chaos: The Organization Behind the Burning Man Event*. Chicago, IL: University of Chicago Press.

Chesbrough, H. (2005). *Open Innovation: The New Imperative for Creating And Profiting from Technology*. Cambridge, MA: Harvard Business School Press.

Codere, H. (1950). *Fighting with Property: A Study of Kwakiutl Potlatching and Warfare, 1792–1930*. New York: American Ethnological Society.

Dana, L.P. (2007). "A Humility-Based Enterprising Community: The Amish People in Lancaster County", *Journal of Enterprising Communities: People and Places in the Global Economy*, 1(2): 142–154.

Derrida, J. (1992). *Given Time: I. Counterfeit Money*. Chicago, IL: University of Chicago Press.

Dunne, S. and Spoelstra, S. (2010). "The Gift of Leadership", *Philosophy Today*, 54(1): 66–77.

Eisenstein, C. (2011). *Sacred Economics: Money, Gift, and Society in the Age of Transition*. Berkeley, CA: Evolver Editions.

Falk, A. (2007). "Gift Exchange in the Field", *Econometrica*, 75(5): 1501–1511.

Fontan, J.M. and Shragge, E. (2000). *Social Economy: International Debates and Perspectives*. Montreal: Black Rose Books.

Gansky, L. (2010). *The Mesh: Why the Future of Business Is Sharing*. New York: Portfolio.

Gibson-Graham, J.K. (1996). *The End of Capitalism (As We Knew It): A Feminist Critique of Political Economy*. London: Blackwell.

Godelier, M. (1999). *The Enigma of the Gift*. Chicago, IL: University of Chicago Press.

Graeber, D. (2012). *Debt: The First 5,000 Years*. New York: Melville House.

Guerin, D. (1970). *Anarchism*. New York: Monthly Review Press.

Hancock, P. and Rehn, A. (2011). "Organizing Christmas", *Organization*, 18(6): 737–745.

Harvie, D., Lightfoot, G., Lilley, S. and Weir, K. (2012). "What Are We to do with Feral Publishers?", *Organization*, 19(6): 905–914.

Haude, S. (2000). *In the Shadow of Savage Wolves: Anabaptist Münster and the German Reformation During the 1530s*. Leiden: Brill.

Howe, J. (2009). *Crowdsourcing: Why the Power of the Crowd is Driving the Future of Business*. New York: Crown Business.

Hyde, L. (1979). *The Gift: Imagination and the Erotic Life of Property*. New York: Vintage Books.

Janzen, D. (1996). *Fire, Salt, and Peace: Intentional Christian Communities Alive in North America*. Evanston, IL: Shalom Mission Communities.

Jensen, T.E. (2008). "Experimenting with Commodities and Gifts: The Case of an Office Hotel", *Organization*, 15(2): 187–209.

Kinkade, K. (1994). *Is it Utopia Yet?: An Insider's View of Twin Oaks Community in its 26th Year*. Louisa, VA: Twin Oaks Publishing.

Kolm, S.C. and Ythier, J.M. (eds). (2006). *Handbook of the Economics of Giving, Altruism and Reciprocity: Foundations*. New York: North-Holland.

Laidlaw, J. (2000). "A Free Gift Makes No Friends", *Journal of the Royal Anthropological Institute*, 6: 617–634.

Ledeneva, A. (1998). *Russia's Economy of Favours: Blat, Networking and Informal Exchange*. Cambridge: Cambridge University Press.

Lemmergaard, J. and Muhr, S. (2011). "Regarding Gifts: On Christmas Gift Exchange and Asymmetrical Business Relations", *Organization*, 18(6): 763–777.

Malinowski, B. (1922). *Argonauts of the Western Pacific: An Account of Native Enterprise and Adventure in the Archipelagoes of Melanesian New Guinea*. London: George Routledge & Sons.

Marcoux, J-S. (2009). "Escaping the Gift Economy", *Journal of Consumer Research*, 36(4): 671–685.

Mauss, M. (1925, 1954). *The Gift: Forms and Functions of Exchange in Archaic Societies*. London: Cohen & West.

Offer, A. (1997). "Between the Gift and the Market: The Economy of Regard", *Economic History Review*, 50(3): 450–476.

Orenstein, H. (1980). "Assymetrical Reciprocity: A Contribution to the Theory of Political Legitimacy", *Current Anthropology*, 21(1): 69–91.

Pink, D. (2012). *To Sell is Human: The Surprising Truth About Moving Others*. New York: Riverhead.

Plattner, S. (1989). *Economic Anthropology*. Stanford, CA: Stanford University Press.

Raymond, E. (1999). "The Cathedral and the Bazaar", *Knowledge, Technology and Policy*, 12(3): 23–49.

Rehn, A. (2001). *Electronic Potlatch – A Study on New Technologies and Primitive Economic Behaviors*. Stockholm: Royal Institute of Technology.

Rehn, A. (2004). "The Politics of Contraband – the Honor Economies of the Warez Scene", *Journal of Socio-Economics*, 33: 359–374.

Rehn, A. and Lindahl, M. (2011). "Georges Bataille", in Jensen, T. and Wilson, T. (eds), *On the Shoulders of Giants*. Lund: Studentlitteratur.

Rehn, A. and Taalas, S. (2004). " 'Znakomstva I Svyazi' (Acquaintances and Connections) – Blat, the Soviet Union, and Mundane Entrepreneurship", *Entrepreneurship and Regional Development*, 16(3): 235–250.

Sahlins, M. (1963). "Poor Man, Rich Man, Big Man, Chief; Political Types in Melanesia and Polynesia", *Comparative Studies in Society and History*, 5(3): 285–303.

Sahlins, M. (1972). *Stone Age Economics*. Hawthorne, NY: Aldine de Gruyter.

Schrift, A. (1997). *The Logic of the Gift: Toward an Ethic of Generosity*. London: Routledge.

Sigaud, L. (2002). "The Vicissitudes of the Gift", *Social Anthropology*, 10(3): 335–358.

Strathern, M. (1990). *The Gender of the Gift: Problems With Women and Problems With Society in Melanesia*. Berkeley: University of California Press.

Surowiecki, J. (2005). *The Wisdom of Crowds: Why the Many Are Smarter Than the Few and How Collective Wisdom Shapes Business, Economies, Societies and Nations*. New York: Knopf Doubleday.

Sykes, K. (2005). *Arguing With Anthropology: An Introduction to Critical Theories of the Gift*. London: Routledge.

Tapscott, D. and Williams, A.D. (2010a). *Macrowikinomics: Rebooting Business and the World*. New York: Portfolio.

Tapscott, D. and Williams, A.D. (2010b). *Wikinomics: How Mass Collaboration Changes Everything*. New York: Portfolio.

Testart, A. (1998). "Uncertainties of the 'Obligation To Reciprocate': A Critique of Mauss", in *Marcel Mauss: A Centenary Tribute*. New York: Berghahn Books.

Teubner, G. (2001). "Economics of Gift: Positivity of Justice The Mutual Paranoia of Jacques Derrida and Niklas Luhmann", *Theory, Culture and Society*, 18(1): 29–47.

Titmuss, R. (1970). *The Gift Relationship: From Human Blood to Social Policy*. London: Allen & Unwin.

Tyler, M. and Taylor, S. (1998). "The Exchange of Aesthetics: Women's Work and 'The Gift' ", *Gender, Work and Organization*, 5(3): 165–171.

Vaughan, G. (ed.). (2007). *Women and the Gift Economy: A Radically Different Worldview is Possible*. Toronto: Inanna Publications and Education.

Waldfogel, J. (1993). "The Deadweight Loss of Christmas", *The American Economic Review*, 83(5): 1328–1336.

Yang, M. (2000). "Putting Global Capitalism in Its Place: Economic Hybridity, Bataille and Ritual Expenditure", *Current Anthropology*, 41(4): 477–509.

14

Voluntary simplicity

Seonaidh McDonald

Voluntary simplicity: what it is, and what it is not

Etzioni describes voluntary simplifiers (VS) as people who choose, "out of free will – rather than by being coerced by poverty, government austerity programs, or being imprisoned – to limit expenditures on consumer goods and services, and to cultivate non-materialistic sources of satisfaction and meaning" (1998: 620). Although there are many different definitions of voluntary simplicity (Johnston and Burton, 2003), this definition is useful because it includes the three major elements that set this movement apart from others: free will; limiting consumerism; and alternative sources of satisfaction. In the three sections that follow, I will discuss each of these elements in turn.

Non-voluntary simplicity

The first element of Etzioni's definition is free will. Voluntary simplifiers are changing their lifestyles of their own volition. This is an important point because there are lots of people, especially during the recent economic downturn, who have simplified their lifestyles in some way out of necessity. They may stop buying certain goods or services that they do not deem necessary or wait longer to make luxury purchases, but because their motivation is to save money, or to live on an income that has been reduced through wage cuts, unemployment or redundancy, they would not be considered voluntary simplifiers. If someone takes public transport simply because they cannot afford a car, rather than to reduce the environmental impact of their lifestyle, and would change to driving a car if their income allowed, then their simplification is non-voluntary. Mitchell (1983), for example, makes a distinction between the Needs-Driven poor and the Inner-Directed voluntary simplifiers. In other words, voluntary simplifiers are individuals who have access to resources such as wealth, education, and unique skills that *could* be traded for high income, but who have elected not to do so (Craig-Lees and Hill, 2002). For a more extended discussion of simplicity and poverty see Segal (1999: 20–22).

Limiting consumerism

The second component of a voluntary simplicity lifestyle is that there is a focus on reducing (or changing) personal or household (or even community) consumption (Cherrier and Murray, 2002). Here there is an overlap with much that is written about "green consumers" who are driven by environmental values (Moisander and Pesonen, 2002) to reduce the amount of impact their lives have on natural resources through, for example, waste reduction or water and energy conservation. There is also resonance with the tenets of the "ethical consumer" who seeks to shop in such a way as to promote social justice and equity (Shaw and Newholm, 2002; Raynolds and Keahey, this volume). However, like the notion of sustainable consumption, voluntary simplicity will contain all of these elements. And while most voluntary simplifiers would, due to their reduced consumption patterns, be considered to be "green", not all green consumers would necessarily be considered voluntary simplifiers, as the examination of the final element of voluntary simplicity will demonstrate.

Alternative sources of satisfaction

Although frugality is a central tenet of this movement, voluntary simplicity does not just mean having less of everything (Shama, 1996). While voluntary simplifiers aim to have less of some (material) things, they also aim to have more of others (non-material). A common trade-off made is the reduction of monetary income through giving up, cutting down or changing paid employment in order to have more time to spend on family, creative endeavours or self-development. Thus the motivation behind a simplified lifestyle can be focused on either part of this equation: some people are driven to simplify through a rejection of consumerism, or Western notions of career; for others the drive is to increase the time they have with their families (Craig-Lees and Hill, 2002) or the meaningfulness of the work they do.

This trade-off points to an overlap between voluntary simplifiers and downshifters. Downshifters are characterized as individuals who give up the pursuit of income in order to increase the amounts of unstructured time available to them (Hamilton and Mail, 2003). Often this means working part-time, changing careers or giving up urban lifestyles in order to raise families, to have more leisure time or to take up more rewarding work. The end result of downshifting does look similar to a voluntary simplicity approach, but the decision to downshift is often focused solely on personal interests, such as reducing work-related stress or illness whereas simplicity addresses these but also encompasses broader concerns for the environment or society (Shaw and Newholm, 2002). Taylor-Gooby (1998: 647) notes that "downshifting indicates a movement of social values away from ostentation, but it is not clear that downshifters will abandon income disparities or ecologically damaging consumption practices".

Another aspect of voluntary simplicity not shared by other movements is the explicit link with spiritual aspects of life. Elgin (1981) describes voluntary simplicity as an "examined life" and for many people their expressions of simplicity are linked to specific religious or spiritual philosophies. This spiritual element of voluntary simplicity is almost always absent in the discussion of downshifting, offering a further distinction between these movements. Over the past few decades however there has been a tendency for voluntary simplicity discourses to rely more on more general expressions of spiritualism such as self-development or harmony with nature than on the teachings of specific religious or spiritual movements (Zavestoski, 2002). Rudmin and Kilbourne (1996: 190) have termed this the "secularization of simplicity". Contemporary voluntary simplicity might therefore be argued to represent a philosophy in its own right, rather than something that is practised as part of an organized religion.

Table 14.1 Distinguishing voluntary simplicity from other social groups

Social group	Deliberately reduced consumption	Deliberately reduced income	Spiritual element
Voluntary simplifiers	✓	✓	✓
Low income	✓	✗	✗
Downshifters	✓	✓	✗
Green consumers	✓	✗	✗
Ethical consumers	✗	✗	sometimes

In summary, then, voluntary simplicity has kinship with a number of other social movements, such as downshifters and green consumers, but it can be distinguished by the presence of three elements: voluntary simplifiers have deliberately reduced their consumption; they have deliberately reduced their income in order to gain more quality of life; and they are guided by a spiritual "examination" of their lives and their selves which may or may not be linked to an organized religion.

Table 14.1 summarizes the differences between voluntary simplifiers and other groups within society who may embrace certain elements of the voluntary simplicity life. I close this section by offering the classic and enduring (Johnston and Burton, 2003) definition of voluntary simplicity, as coined by Elgin and Mitchell in their early writing about this movement more than 30 years ago (see Figure 14.1).

Elgin and Mitchell (1976, 1977a, 1977b) identify five key, interdependent values of voluntary simplifiers:

- **Material simplicity** which implies consuming less (but not necessarily cheaper) products and services. Included in this is the favouring of items which are resource-efficient, durable, not mass produced and have a smaller ecological impact.
- **Human scale** denotes a commitment to working and living in environments which are smaller, decentralized, and less complex. The aim is to reduce the anonymous nature of much industrialized work experience which decouples the contribution made by individuals from the end results.
- **Self-determination** involves a reduced reliance on large corporations and institutions such as supermarkets and finance companies. This is portrayed as an increase in personal control. Self-determination also includes notions of self-sufficiency such as home food production, mending and doing without. It also means looking to your own values to guide you rather than being driven by the media or the expectations of others.
- **Ecological awareness** is an important aspect of VS which centres on resource conservation, reduction of waste and pollution and the protection of nature. It also extends to the promotion of social responsibility, equality, diversity and caring for others implying increased community involvement.
- **Personal growth** denotes a concern for self-realization through the development of practical, creative or intellectual abilities.

Figure 14.1 Elgin and Mitchell's classic definition of voluntary simplicity

Voluntary simplicity in the academic literature

Voluntary simplicity is not new. Ascetic lifestyles that have their basis in Chinese and Greek philosophies of the ancient world are still revered by many of the world's major religions today (Rudmin and Kilbourne, 1996; Zavestoski, 2002). The American movement is underpinned by the writing of the philosopher Henry Thoreau (1854, 1937), who wrote *Walden; or, Life in the Woods* as a powerful expression of a life of "plain living and high thinking" (Rudmin and Kilbourne, 1996: 194) which inspired many and has become synonymous with voluntary simplicity. However, the writer who has introduced these ideals to the wider public is Duane Elgin (1981) whose straightforward text is the cornerstone of most contemporary voluntary simplicity.

The academic literature on voluntary simplicity is centred on the social psychology literature and, to a lesser extent, the marketing literature. Following Elgin and Mitchell's early work (1976, 1977a, 1977b) several commentators produced conceptual, or even speculative (Craig-Lees and Hill, 2002) pieces on the theme of voluntary simplicity. What these pieces lacked in evidence they made up for in enthusiasm, often extolling the virtues of voluntary simplicity in "rosy-eyed" (Maniates, 2002: 206) tones.

A second group of researchers took up the challenge of designing quantitative instruments which would distinguish voluntary simplifiers (VS) from non-voluntary simplifiers (NVS)[1] and measure their attitudes and behaviours (Shama, 1981, 1988; Leonard-Barton, 1981; Shama and Wisenblit, 1984; Iwata, 1997; Iwata, 1999, 2001; Huneke, 2005). This work is often in the "market segmentation" tradition which aims to find out the demographic or psychographic profile of simplifiers and it parallels the search for the "green consumer" in the marketing literature, both in its approach and in its ultimate failure to identify simplifiers consistently (McDonald *et al.*, 2012). A number of issues have been raised with this body of work, including the size and nature of the samples used (McDonald *et al.*, 2006), the use of self-reports as a way of collecting data about behaviours (Rudmin and Kilbourne, 1996) and the bias of the research instruments towards environmental issues (Craig-Lees and Hill, 2002), which, as was argued above, only constitutes a proportion of the range of voluntary simplicity.

The third tranche of work in this area has begun to look at voluntary simplifiers using qualitative research approaches. The aim here is to understand the simplifiers and the motivations that underpin their life choices (Moisander and Pesonen, 2002; Zavestoski, 2002). Craig-Lees and Hill (2002) have found that although VS and NVS groups may own the same items, they do so for different reasons, and ultimately attribute different meanings to them. This insight offers an interesting dimension to the research problem and suggests that it will not be possible to "define" VS groups in terms of their consumption behaviours alone. Another facet of simplicity that is challenging for researchers is that it exists in so many forms and with so many different emphases. In line with the myriad of definitions of voluntary simplicity (Johnston and Burton, 2003), Shaw and Newholm's work (2002) has uncovered several distinct ways of being a voluntary simplifier. This is a common theme in the literature where commentators have distinguished between groups of simplifiers, either in terms of different "degrees" of voluntary simplicity (Etzioni, 1998) or different "kinds" of voluntary simplicity in terms of their lived experience (Shaw and Newholm, 2002) or their motivations (Zavestoski, 2002). Taken together, the need to examine the meanings given to possessions, the diversity of motivations that drive these lifestyles and the difficulty of defining simplicity either as a concept, or as a lived experience, mean that this body of work does not perhaps offer the answers that marketers might seek, but it certainly underlines the need for qualitative approaches to studying voluntary simplicity.

Some writers predicted a huge growth in the numbers of people simplifying their lifestyles by the end of the twentieth century (Elgin and Mitchell, 1976; Shama, 1985). While this has not come to pass, the voluntary simplicity (sometimes called simple living) movement gained some momentum in both the US (Zavestoski, 2002) and in Western Europe (Etzioni, 1998) at the close of the millennium. Voluntary simplicity has not provided the challenge to mainstream capitalism that many of its proponents might have liked, but it survives as a lived reality for a modest proportion of the population today.

Organizational practices[2]

As suggested above, it is difficult to make generalizations about the organizational practices of voluntary simplifiers because they are diverse and dispersed individuals, many of whom may not even think of themselves as belonging to a movement or a group. Nevertheless, although it is not easy to make generalizations about their practices, it is possible to discern a degree of underlying similarity in their conceptualizations of, and approaches to, their practices. At the root of voluntary simplicity is an implicit rejection of many of the assumptions that underpin capitalism. For example, capitalism privileges notions of growth, efficiency and scale. Elgin and Mitchell's tenets of voluntary simplicity, as set out above, are often read as a practical way forward for a better way of living, but they can equally be understood as an extensive and political critique of the ideas underpinning capitalist social and commercial structures. Thus most voluntary simplifiers share a common disquiet about dominant social assumptions about ways of living and how these ultimately shape people's lives. Some voluntary simplifiers are explicit in their rejection of the tenets of capitalism, while for others the questioning of social norms remains implicit, embedded in their practices and lived out through their choices about how they spend their time and money. Although voluntary simplifiers all share a commitment to question and rethink these assumptions at an individual (or, more accurately, household) level in terms of their own practices, some also address these issues at a societal level, in terms of community practices, or in political spheres.

Since the organizing practices of voluntary simplifiers stem from this underlying (implicit or explicit) belief that dominant social norms are privileging the wrong things, it is helpful to consider some of the interrelated ideas that are presented in opposition to these norms in order to support a discussion of how these lead to alternative ways of doing things. In the discussion that follows, attention will be given to *Mindfulness*, the value of *Time* (as opposed to money), and how these influence the practical choices that voluntary simplifiers make. This is followed by a short commentary on the *Environmental Impact* of voluntary simplicity lifestyles.

Mindfulness

Elgin (1981) talks about an "examined life". This idea runs through the narratives of many voluntary simplifiers. Some people use the tenets of a specific religion as a starting point to examine their lives. Thus, for example, Buddhism and different forms of Christianity (especially Quakerism) have been associated with voluntary simplicity. However, there are also many secular interpretations of voluntary simplicity. What these views share is a commitment to thinking through life choices, starting from the point of view of a specific set of values, whether they are associated with a specific religion, a broader sense of spirituality or a position of environmental concern. In this way, voluntary simplifiers tend to begin their journeys by questioning social norms and establishing their own internal compass in terms of what they are going to privilege and then working these values through into the practical realms of their lives by asking themselves what those values would look like once they were operationalized in everyday life.

So rather than looking at current levels of household waste and devising a domestic system to sort recyclables and divert more material away from landfill, a voluntary simplifier is more likely to ask themselves how and why they are producing so much waste in the first place and think about how they could live differently in order to produce less waste. As an example, this contemplation might lead to an observation that packaging waste was a symptom of shopping at supermarkets, an implicit decision for many people, which in turn is due to a lack of time to undertake weekly food shopping, which is driven by working long hours. Thus the voluntary simplifier may ultimately tackle their waste concern by starting to work less, giving them more time to shop in a different way which generates less packaging and reduces their household waste. The outcomes might look very similar (less waste) but the process is characterized by a deeper level of examination of the interrelated nature of issues, and is more likely to take a holistic approach and/or include (or consider) a rejection of what is regarded as "normal" to others.

Time

At the basis of our society is the notion that money and time are inextricably linked: the value of something is how much time you have to work to pay for it. One of the most common strategies among voluntary simplifiers is to rearrange their lives in a way that does not maximize the money that they have, but seeks to maximize the amount of time they have instead. One of the most significant impacts of deciding that time is more important than money is in terms of the choices that voluntary simplifiers make about work. For example, rather than taking a job with an employer that would pay a premium for their specialist Masters degree, they might choose a lower paid position which they perceived as more fulfilling, or less stressful. Some of them emphasize changing the amount of work that they do (by going part time or limiting their hours of work for salaried positions) while others are more concerned with changing the kind of work they do (for example, changing career to do work that they find more meaningful). This shift in emphasis from money earned to time spent can often mean that income is reduced or restricted and so voluntary simplifiers' practices often adjust accordingly.

In the marketing literature, a distinction is made between *consuming differently* and *consuming less* (Peattie, 2010). So people who tackle the sustainability agendas by buying environmentally friendlier versions of the products they use (such as recycled paper), and adopting technological approaches to reducing the environmental impact of their lifestyles (such as switching to use a car with high fuel efficiency and low CO_2 emissions for their daily commute to work), are characterized as consuming differently. The group who *consume differently* may reduce their carbon footprint, but they do not change the way they live. The group who *consume less* would be more likely to car share or take the bus and, over time, they may change jobs or move house in order to avoid having to commute in the first place. There is a parallel here to be drawn between these groups of green consumers and the decisions that are made by voluntary simplifiers. Partly because they are inclined to reflect upon their practices, and partly because of their reduced income, voluntary simplifiers are less likely to be drawn to high-cost, technology-mediated solutions. Instead they are attracted by simpler solutions. So a voluntary simplifier seeking to reduce their electricity use would be more likely to choose an extra jersey rather than solar panels. As they have deliberately made a trade-off between time and money in favour of more time, they are also able to employ time-rich measures, such as growing their own vegetables, rather than simply switching their buying behaviour by buying organic instead of non-organic vegetables as part of their weekly supermarket shop, for example. Some voluntary simplifiers come to see Local Exchange Trading Schemes (LETS) and other systems of local currency as a way to address the relationship between time and money in a different way and these are examined in more detail in North's chapter in this volume.

Environmental impact

Although a number of the practices cited so far would be recognized by those engaged in environmental protection, it is worth reiterating here that not all voluntary simplifiers are driven by values associated with sustainability. Although many of their practices do reduce their environmental impact, that is not necessarily the purpose of the behaviour change for all voluntary simplifiers. Many are driven by spiritual values or are committed to redressing their work–life balance in order to spend time with family or pursue their own spiritual or artistic development. In other words, an extra jersey does not always denote an eco-warrior: it could equally signify a simplifier who does not wish to sacrifice family time or a day of painting in order to earn the money to sustain a higher heating bill. Nevertheless, while a reduction in environmental impact (in the widest sense) is not always the primary driver of voluntary simplification, it is nearly always the result.

One of the issues quickly exposed to be self-perpetuating and self-defeating by the joined-up thinking of the voluntary simplifier is built-in obsolescence. Thus products that are designed to become out of date, fuelling the need for repeat purchases before a product is worn out, such as technology-based products and fashion clothing, become understood differently by the voluntary simplifier. Once people begin to weigh their lives in terms of time rather than money, it becomes hard to see replacing a television set which is not broken, at X cost which will take Y hours to earn, as anything other than a non-essential drain on your most precious resource: time. The voluntary simplifier therefore seeks out different relationships with material goods. Once they begin to operate on the basis of need and function rather than brand or innovation, voluntary simplifiers often start to purchase on the basis of how long-lasting or hard-wearing an item is. Many also purchase items such as furniture or clothing second-hand. They also seek out other solutions for ownership, such as sharing, for larger items which are used infrequently. So simplifiers may informally share the cost of a purchase of garden tools or a car trailer with like-minded friends or neighbours on the understanding that they may use them whenever they need. Or they may enter into sharing arrangements more formally, by purchasing an item as a community. These practices all reduce the environmental impact of voluntary simplifier lifestyles, whether that is the primary intention or not.

Becoming a voluntary simplifier

Voluntary simplifiers often refer to their process of simplification as a journey. Many begin their journeys in isolation. Their changes in practices come from the mindfulness described above which is often brought on by a sense of growing dissatisfaction: with the way they are living their lives, with the pace and demands of modern life and/or with the effects their life-style is having on their health, the welfare of others or on the planet. In many cases, they do not know that they are simplifiers until they have reached the limits of their own ingenuity in terms of solving practical problems, or feel the need for support from like-minded individuals and begin to reach out to others. The help and support that they seek has traditionally been in the form of handbooks and self-help guides. Over the past decade, some of these resources have been translated to websites (see the resources section for suggestions of handbooks and websites). This relationship between the "wise" and the "new" voluntary simplifier, conducted through reading and contemplation, is characteristic of how many voluntary simplifiers learn or deepen their practices. Many cite inspirational texts (including Thoreau's *Walden*) which they return to again and again in their thinking about how best to remodel their lives in line with their simplicity values.

Voluntary simplifiers are change-oriented. The changes they are working towards are quite radical in that they challenge many of the norms of mainstream consumer society, and yet the typical simplifier tends to move incrementally towards their goals (or, more precisely, away from the lifestyle that has caused their dissatisfaction) making small changes to their way of life over a period of many years, gradually simplifying their lifestyle. Sometimes their simplification goes unnoticed by friends and family until they reach a point where they need to make a major lifestyle change in order to progress, such as changing career, downsizing or relocating their house or giving up a car.

All voluntary simplifiers are engaged in personal change, but a minority are also involved with campaigning for change on a local or national stage, some in terms of changing laws, others in changing norms, for example, through the Transition Towns movement discussed in Chapter 16. Some offer help to others seeking support for their own changes, through writing new books or online resources.

In summary: the complexity of a simple life

The mindfulness that characterizes voluntary simplifiers, and their rejection of money as a way to measure life in favour of time, presents a significant challenge to many of the assumptions about how modern lives could (or should) be lived. Voluntary simplicity is undoubtedly a conceptual journey from acceptance of the norms that surround us to an examined, change-focused life driven by self-determined values. In particular, this shift in thinking about time and money reveals the interrelatedness of decisions about work, housing, food and mobility, and how each of these systems is locked into each other. For many people it is simply not possible to reduce the amount of time that they spend at work, or change their career without that having an impact on where and how they live. Making a change in how you travel has a knock-on effect on where and how you shop and socialize, but it can also mean deciding between changing jobs and moving house. Unpicking these relationships and trying to tackle these basic issues is much more difficult than *consuming differently*. For each voluntary simplifier, the outcome will be a deeply personal solution, crafted over time in dialogue with their own values and priorities.

Notes

1 Note that the term NVS refers to everyone who is not a voluntary simplifier and not the non-voluntary simplifiers (those who simplify out of necessity) discussed above.
2 The descriptions of voluntary simplifiers in the sections that follow are drawn from data gathered as part of an ESRC project (award RES-388-25-0001). For more information about how these data were gathered, please see McDonald *et al.* (2012).

Resources

For a full discussion of the history and development of voluntary simplicity, see:
Rudmin, F.W. and Kilbourne, W.E. (1996). The meaning and morality of voluntary simplicity: History and hypothesis on deliberately denied materialism. In R.W. Belk, N. Dholakia and A. Venkatesh

(eds) *Consumption and Marketing: Macrodimensions* (pp. 166–215). Cincinnati, OH: South-Western College Publishing.

Shi, D.E. (1986). *In Search of the Simple Life*. Salt Lake City, UT: Peregrine Smith Books.

For an overview of the treatment of voluntary simplifiers in the academic literature, see:

McDonald, S., Oates, C.J., Young, C.W. and Hwang, K. (2006). Towards sustainable consumption: Researching voluntary simplifiers. *Psychology and Marketing*, 23(6): 515–534.

For an analysis of the many voluntary simplicity handbooks, see:

Zavestoski, S. (2002). The social–psychological bases of anticonsumption attitudes. *Psychology and Marketing*, 19(2): 149–165.

There are a whole host of handbooks and self-help manuals dedicated to voluntary simplicity, but the original and most quoted is by Duane Elgin:

Elgin, D. (1981). *Voluntary Simplicity: Toward a Way of Life that is Outwardly Simple, Inwardly Rich*. New York: William Morrow.

Cecile Andrews is one of the best-known proponents of voluntary simplicity in the US. She has written several handbooks on the process and value of simplifying. She offers individual consultations and runs workshops for groups interested in working towards a simpler lifestyle:
www.cecileandrews.com/

To follow individuals who have simplified their lifestyles and see how they have tackled specific issues, see:
www.choosingvoluntarysimplicity.com/
http://adventuresinvoluntarysimplicity.blogspot.com/

References

Cherrier, H. and Murray, J. (2002). Drifting away from excessive consumption: A new social movement based on identity construction. *Advances in Consumer Research*, 29: 245–247.

Craig-Lees, M. and Hill, C. (2002). Understanding voluntary simplifiers. *Psychology and Marketing*, 19(2): 187–210.

Elgin, D. (1981). *Voluntary Simplicity: Toward a Way of Life that is Outwardly Simple, Inwardly Rich*. New York: William Morrow.

Elgin, D. and Mitchell, A. (1976). Voluntary simplicity. Business Intelligence Program, SRI International. Reprinted in Elgin, D. and Mitchell, A. (1977). Voluntary simplicity (3). *The Co-Evolution Quarterly*, 3(summer): 4–19.

Elgin, D. and Mitchell, A. (1977a). Voluntary simplicity: Lifestyle of the future? *The Futurist*, 11(4): 200–261.

Elgin, D. and Mitchell, A. (1977b). Voluntary simplicity. *The Co-Evolution Quarterly*, 3(summer): 4–19.

Etzioni, A. (1998). Voluntary simplicity: Characterization, select psychological implications, and societal consequences. *Journal of Economic Psychology*, 19(5): 619–643.

Hamilton, C. and Mail, E. (2003). *Downshifting in Australia: A Sea-change in the Pursuit of Happiness*. Discussion Paper Number 50, The Australia Institute.

Huneke, M.E. (2005). The face of the un-consumer: An empirical examination of the practice of voluntary simplicity in the United States. *Psychology and Marketing*, 22(7): 527–550.

Iwata, O. (1997). Attitudinal and behavioural correlates of voluntary simplicity lifestyles. *Social Behaviour and Personality*, 25(3): 233–240.

Iwata, O. (1999). Perceptual and behavioural correlates of voluntary simplicity. *Social Behaviour and Personality*, 27(4): 379–386.

Iwata, O. (2001). Attitudinal determinants of environmentally responsible behaviour. *Social Behaviour and Personality*, 29(2): 183–190.

Johnston, T.C. and Burton J.B. (2003). Voluntary simplicity: Definitions and dimensions. *Academy of Marketing Studies Journal*, 7(1): 19–36.

Leonard-Barton, D. (1981). Voluntary simplicity lifestyles and energy conservation. *Journal of Consumer Research*, 8: 243–252.

Maniates, M. (2002). In search of consumptive resistance: The voluntary simplicity movement. In T. Princen, M. Maniates and K. Conca (eds) *Confronting Consumption* (pp. 199–235). Cambridge, MA: MIT Press.

McDonald, S., Oates, C.J., Young, C.W. and Hwang, K. (2006). Towards sustainable consumption: Researching voluntary simplifiers. *Psychology and Marketing*, 23(6): 515–534.

McDonald, S., Oates, C.J., Alevizou, P.J., Young, C.W. and Hwang, K. (2012). Individual Strategies for Sustainable Consumption. Special issue of *Journal of Marketing Management* on Re-Visiting Contemporary Issues in Green/Ethical Marketing, 28(3–4): 445–468.

Mitchell, A. (1983). *The Nine American Lifestyles*. New York: Warner Books.

Moisander, J. and Pesonen, S. (2002). Narratives of sustainable ways of living: Constructing the self and the other as a green consumer. *Management Decision*, 40 (4): 329–342.

Peattie, K. (2010). Green consumption: Behavior and norms. *The Annual Review of Environment and Resources*, 35: 8.1–8.34.

Rudmin, F.W. and Kilbourne, W.E. (1996). The meaning and morality of voluntary simplicity: History and hypothesis on deliberately denied materialism. In R.W. Belk, N. Dholakia and A. Venkatesh (eds) *Consumption and Marketing: Macrodimensions* (pp. 166–215). Cincinnati, OH: South-Western College Publishing.

Segal, J.M. (1999). *Graceful Simplicity: Toward a Philosophy and Politics of Simple Living*. New York: Henry Holt and Company.

Shama, A. (1981). Coping with stagflation: Voluntary simplicity. *Journal of Marketing*, 45(3): 120–134.

Shama, A. (1985). The voluntary simplicity consumer. *The Journal of Consumer Marketing*, 2(4): 57–63.

Shama, A. (1988). The voluntary simplicity consumer: A comparative study. *Psychological Reports*, 63(3): 859–869.

Shama, A. (1996). A comment on "The meaning and morality of voluntary simplicity: History and hypothesis on deliberately denied materialism". In R.W. Belk, N. Dholakia and A. Venkatesh (eds) *Consumption and Marketing: Macrodimensions* (pp. 216–224). Cincinnati, OH: South-Western College Publishing.

Shama, A. and Wisenblit, J. (1984). Values of voluntary simplicity: Lifestyle and motivation. *Psychological Reports*, 55(1): 231–240.

Shaw, D. and Newholm, T. (2002). Voluntary simplicity and the ethics of consumption. *Psychology and Marketing*, 19(2): 167–185.

Taylor-Gooby, P. (1998). Comments on Amitai Etzioni: Voluntary simplicity: Characterization, select psychological implications, and societal consequences. *Journal of Economic Psychology*, 19(5): 645–650.

Thoreau, H.D. (1937). Walden. In H.S. Canby (ed.) *The Works of Thoreau* (pp. 243–465). Cambridge, MA: Riverside Press.

Zavestoski, S. (2002). The social–psychological bases of anticonsumption attitudes. *Psychology and Marketing*, 19(2): 149–165.

15

The bioregional economy

Reclaiming our local land

Molly Scott Cato

Summary

This chapter addresses the question of how an alternative economic organization might be conceptualized and developed in response to the need to end economic growth. It begins by offering evidence that economic growth, the shibboleth of capitalist economies, cannot be compatible with sustainability, and that finding ways of divorcing growth from energy and resources, known as 'decoupling', cannot be practically achieved. With this in mind, I argue that the globalized economy is wasteful of energy and needs to be replaced by a system of self-reliant local economies. I then propose the 'bioregion' as an alternative geographical area by which these local economies could be defined. A bioregion is an area defined by geographical rather than political boundaries; in a bioregional economy each bioregion would seek self-reliance in the provisioning of food, shelter, fuel, clothing and so on, and would also seek to absorb or reuse all its waste products. In a world organized in this way, and which respected the planetary boundary, questions of how resources are shared would become more important. In a bioregional economy, resources are considered to be held in common and shared according to participatory processes. I argue that an economy based within a bioregion could help us replace our present consumer identities, based around the purchase of material possessions, with identities based on closer relationships with each other and with the natural world. I conclude by offering examples of communities that are already on the path of transition to developing sustainable local economies, and throughout the chapter I present case studies of alternative organizations from my home community of Stroud.

Global market or bioregional economy?

When Nicholas Stern identified climate change as 'the greatest market failure of all time' (2007) he was both identifying the need for a total redesign of our system of production and distribution – what green economists prefer to call provisioning in recognition of the fact that we may meet our own needs directly rather than through market exchange – and demonstrating the limitations of the thinking of mainstream economics. Climate change, and the ecological crisis more broadly, requires us to radically rethink our economic systems to live

Table 15.1 The rapid process of globalization in figures

	China	Germany	India	Kenya	UK
Imports (as a percentage of GDP)					
1980	11	25	9	36	25
1990	16	25	9	31	26
2000	21	33	14	32	30
2008	28	40*	30	39	29*
FDI, net inflows (current $ USm)					
1980	570.0	342.4	79.2	79.0	10122.8
1990	3487.0	3003.9	236.7	57.1	33503.7
2000	38399.3	210085.4	3584.2	110.9	122156.8
2007	138413.2	51543.3	22950	727.7	197766.2
Mobile phones (per 100 people)					
1980	0	0	0	0	0
1990	0	0	0	0	2
2000	7	59	0	0	74
2008	48	131	30	42	123
Energy use (kg of oil equivalent per capita)					
1980	610	4597	304	486	3575
1990	760	4477	377	479	3708
2000	876	4174	453	481	3971
2006	1433	4231	510	491	3814

Data from the World Bank's World Development Indicators database
* data are for 2006.

within planetary limits, to recognize that the market system itself is a failure and to envision something better, more just and more secure. The bioregional economy is a proposal for how we might do this.

The bioregional economy is proposed as an alternative to the globalized economy that dominates current systems of provisioning. I do not have space here to make a full critique of these systems (for such a critique see Chapter 12 of my 2011 book, and Chapter 1 of this volume), but Table 15.1 begins to illustrate what is meant by 'globalization'. While it is often discussed in terms of an increase in trade, we can see from the table that what has increased most rapidly over the past 30 years are flows of investment capital and communications, both supported by vast increases in energy use. It has been estimated that at the turn of the millennium, around 97 per cent of the money that flowed through the global economy was speculative finance, which had no connection with real goods and services.

While money has flowed more rapidly this has not led to an equalization of levels of wealth, in fact quite the reverse. There is a great deal of data from authorities such as the IMF and the World Bank to underpin this case:

> Over the past two decades, income inequality has risen in most regions and countries. At the same time, per capita incomes have risen across virtually all regions for even the poorest segments of population, indicating that the poor are better off in an absolute sense during this phase of globalization, although incomes for the relatively well off have

increased at a faster pace. Consumption data from groups of developing countries reveal the striking inequality that exists between the richest and the poorest in populations across different regions.

(IMF, 2008)

Similarly, Stiglitz (2000) has pointed out that certain countries, particularly those that have large internal markets and control their currencies, have been able to benefit much more from globalization.

It is to replace this system of energy and money flows, leading to an increase in CO_2 emissions and growing levels of inequality, that a more local system of self-reliant economies is proposed under the heading of 'the bioregional economy'. I should make it clear, at the outset, that many of the proposals made here run counter to existing legal and institutional structures. In the following section I argue for a devolution of more powers to lower tiers of government, or community, and, if I had space, I would also raise the issue of landownership, which I think is crucial to any sustainable economic future (see Wightman, 2011). Similarly, a bioregional economy could not flourish within the existing regime of world trade, presided over by the WTO and dominated by multinational corporations which demand an end to 'protectionism'. But some changes are already possible without institutional and legal change, as illustrated by the case studies presented throughout the chapter.

The following section provides a short argument about the need for our economic system to recognize planetary limits, something which is impossible within an economy organized according to capitalist principles. I then introduce the idea of the bioregion and discuss how an economy organized along bioregional lines might work. Following that, I address the link between sustainability and equity and explore the implications of this connection for a system of allocation. After that, I consider some of the wider benefits and critiques of bioregional economies, and conclude with a challenge to reclaim our economies and re-imagine them along bioregional lines.

Limits to growth

The bioregional economy is one way of theorizing self-reliant local economies to replace the globalized economy of today. One of the critiques of globalization is that it has eroded individual differences between places and local cultures, so that we have clone towns within countries and uniformity between nations. For Uruguayan economist Eduardo Galeano, this is a hidden form of violence:

> The invisible violence of the market: diversity is the energy of profitability, and uniformity rules. Mass production on a gigantic scale imposes its obligatory patterns of consumption everywhere. More devastating than any single-party dictatorship is the tyranny of enforced uniformity. It imposes on the entire world a way of life that reproduces human beings as if they were photocopies of the consummate consumer.
>
> *(Galeano, 1998: 252)*

Aside from questions of cultural deprivation and inequity, at a fundamental level any economy we would propose must fit within a very important limit: that of the planet itself.

In 1977 Herman Daly, a US economist who previously worked for the World Bank, published a book called *Steady State Economics*. In it he challenged the growth logic of the economic system that predominated then, and has become more powerful since. The force of his argument is hard to deny: the planet is limited and so an economy whose central design feature is growth is bound to run into difficulties when it reaches the planetary boundary. Richard Douthwaite (1992) suggested that the economy is also failing in its own terms: it is undermining rather than enhancing human well-being. This need to limit growth has been a central tenet of green economists for the past 40 years.

Once climate change became widely accepted as a scientifically validated reality, the defenders of the growth-based economy had to find a response to the call for 'limits to growth'. They did this, first, by focusing attention solely on climate change and away from the myriad other ecological crises that threaten our future, and, second, by arguing that we could have 'green growth' by finding ways of generating economic activity that are not dependent on fossil fuels, sometimes referred to as 'decoupling' (see Weizsäcker et al., 2009). In 2009, Tim Jackson, working as the Economics Commissioner for the UK's Sustainable Development Commission, provided convincing evidence that such a decoupling is not feasible within the necessary timeframe.

His data show that if we assume the same lifestyle for all the people in the world, and an increase of the world population to 11 billion by 2050, we would have to increase the carbon efficiency of our productive systems some 128-fold in order to keep our economy within sustainable limits. Jackson argues that it is not conceivable that technological developments can take place so rapidly as to ensure this rate of energy efficiency gain, and therefore we have to make structural changes to the way our economy functions and to reconsider what we mean by a good life.

Jackson (2009) also makes clear the link between an economy that is in balance with the natural world and equity. If you cannot keep expanding the quantity of material production, you have to think more carefully about how you allocate what has been produced. This essential link between sustainability and equity is often overlooked, but it is clear from the history of globalization and the growth economy that an increase in production has been used to sideline questions of equity. Phrases like 'a rising tide lifts all boats' are used to mean that, while some become wealthy faster than others, in a dynamic and growing economy all will gain over time. It is clear that the market system is very effective in creating innovation and growth, but it undermines rather than improves equity (Stiglitz, 2000). So what other proposals are there for organizing the economy in a way that pays greater attention to the fair allocation of goods and services?

How local is the local economy?

Green economists have long suggested that a sustainable economy needs to be organized around a system of interactive and self-reliant local economies, rather than as a single globalized system made up of competitive economies within nation-state boundaries (Douthwaite, 1996; Hines, 2000). Less clear, however, has been their answer to the question of how such a local economy might be defined, how its boundaries might be established, and to what extent it would be self-sufficient. The proposal of a bioregional economy begins to provide answers to these questions.

The world we live in today is divided into political units known as nation-states. This is a relatively recent situation, with most nation-states coming into existence around 150 years ago and many, particularly in the non-European world, having a history of less than a century (Anderson, 1991). Historically there have been many different forms of social, economic and political organization and the one we have today is a result of growing population and increasing conflict over land and other resources, which the nation-state system was developed to mediate. Its rise also paralleled the rise in the exploitation of fossil fuels, which facilitated the production and transport of consumption goods and gradually undermined our reliance on local soil for the provisioning of our needs (Heinberg, 2005).

As a result of the process of globalization (of the development of a single global market to replace individual national economic systems) and of the use of market rules to overrule national legislation (especially through the World Trade Organisation), the system of nation-states is breaking down (Ohmae, 1996). The global financial system recognizes little distinction between sovereign nations and corporations when it is choosing who to lend money to and many corporations have a larger turnover than the world's smaller economies.

This growing power of corporations within a globalized economy has removed economic power from local areas and politicians. The bioregional economy proposal is an attempt to regain power for people within areas that they can feel responsible for. It also locates people clearly within their local land and landscape. Bioregionalists argue that part of the reason that the environment is being destroyed is that people do not feel they have a stake in it (McGinnis, 1999).

Bioregions are natural geographical units, defined by topographical and hydrological features, as well as by species that thrive in the particular climates and ecosystems that these natural features favour. According to Kirkpatrick Sale:

> It is any part of the earth's surface whose rough boundaries are determined by natural characteristics rather than human dictates, distinguishable from other areas by particular attributes or flora, fauna, water, climate, soils, and landform, and by the human settlements and cultures those attributes have given rise to.
>
> *(1991: 55)*

Amongst proponents of bioregionalism, globalization is seen as a system that divorces people from their locality; bioregionalism helps them to relearn their place in space, a process that is inherent in restructuring our relationship with our planet (Drenthen, 2009).

The concept of the bioregion is useful in rethinking an economic system that is localized rather than globalized. The aim of bioregional economic planners would be to make the bioregion as self-reliant as possible; to make it responsible for its own waste; and to maximize the amount of consumption that was based on local production. This has significant implications in terms of production, since it would imply a policy focused on meeting needs as much as possible from within the boundary of the bioregion. This implies a far greater emphasis on seasonal foods, vernacular architecture and local textile crops. At present in the UK we might live in a house built out of bricks, heated by imported oil, and wear clothes made of Egyptian cotton. In a bioregional economy we would be more likely to live in wooden homes, heated by wood or other local biofuels, and wear clothes made from our domestic textile crops: hemp, flax and wool.

The bioregional economy proposal is powerful because it imposes direct accountability for our resource use. This is most clear for the case of carbon emissions, when at present we are exporting these to China and elsewhere, as demonstrated in Figure 15.1. The figure illustrates the direct, indirect and transport-related emissions arising from various aspects of our consumption. The indirect emissions are much higher for consumption goods than direct emissions, because they are emitted in China rather than in the UK. They are not usually counted when we report our emissions, which means that the most effective way for companies to reduce their 'carbon footprint' is to move their productive facilities overseas. However, in a bioregional system carbon emissions would have to be measured on a

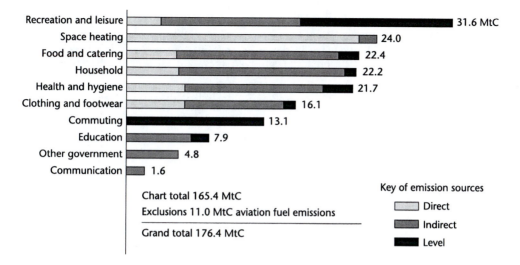

Figure 15.1 The carbon emissions in all that we consume (Carbon Trust, 2006)

consumption basis; this would have the indirect benefit of relocalizing production and revitalizing a local economy.

Once the fuzzy boundaries of the bioregion are established we can begin to map its resources. It is useful to begin with a consumption audit identifying the most important needs – for water, energy and food – as a first step towards providing for these from the resources of the bioregion. Beginning to see local resources in this way can be empowering – indicating how abundant nature is – and can also lead to the establishment of projects and businesses, such as community orchards, woodland co-operatives or community-owned renewable energy plants.

Stroud Woodland Co-operative in England is an example of an enterprise built on local resources that could be reproduced in any community with access to a small amount of woodland. It is related to Stroud Community Agriculture, which we will meet later in the chapter, in that the woodland is located on land belonging to the same adult education college. The co-operative began as a small group of friends who heated their homes using wood-burning stoves and needed a supply of fuel. They came to an arrangement with the landowner that they would manage the woodland in exchange for use of the fuel produced during the felling and trimming of trees. They engaged a woodland expert to teach them the necessary skills during the first season, and now take care of the woodland and share the wood. This provides directly for the heating needs of some ten local families from a small area of woodland. Additional benefits are a closer relationship to the land for the families, as well as a better maintained woodland.

So how can we begin to move our own local economies towards a bioregionally embedded one? The first step is to consider what the boundaries of our local economy might be. The Australian government has divided their national territory into 86 bioregions which are used for the purposes of environmental planning. Countries vary in terms of the variety of their climatic and watershed characteristics, but the bioregion should be large enough to include a variety of essential resources while still maintaining a community with a shared and ecologically rooted identity. In the Pacific North-West, where bioregional thinking is well established, the bioregions are defined according to watersheds. Some bioregions appear to have survived the bureaucratization of local planning, and traces of bioregional thinking can be found in the local areas that people identify with – say, the Cotswolds in my area or the Quercy of South-West France – although these are no longer reflected in local political systems.

Another crucial aspect of rebuilding local production is developing skills. The global economy has encouraged our helplessness so that even simple tasks such as cooking our own meals can be outsourced to the market, enabling the generation of profit. Meanwhile traditions of thrift based around skills such as making and mending clothes have been lost, again requiring us to buy more products in the marketplace. In the UK, the Transition Towns movement has initiated a process called The Great Reskilling, where skills ranging from self-building sustainable homes to preserving surplus crops for winter consumption are shared within local communities (see Ganesh and Zoller in this volume). Perhaps the most fundamental and widespread area of activity is in food growing on allotments and in gardens. English law includes a provision that local councils must provide land for food growing if there is sufficient demand from local people, and this offers support to the transition towards self-provisioning.

Reclaiming control of resources

The first step in keeping our economies within energy and resource limits is to have a sense of how much energy each of us can use within a set time-period without threatening the climate system. A guide for determining this energy limit is provided by the Contraction and Convergence model.[1] It begins with a scientific assessment of the carrying capacity of the planet in terms of CO_2 and then divides this by the size of the human population. In very general terms, this gives us a sense of our fossil energy quota for the year. In this way a bioregional economy would set a global limit to each person's fossil energy use, no matter which bioregion the source of energy originated from. So, while bioregions can claim control of their own resources, they are still operating within global limits on issues of global concern.

Although many of the consequences of climate change are unpredictable there is one clear trend that will have a major impact on economic organization. As a consequence of the exhaustion of oil supplies and the reduction in fossil fuel use to combat climate change, energy prices will rise. This will lead to an increase in the price of most goods, since energy is used in their manufacture. It will also mean that goods made closer to home will become relatively cheaper, since the cost of transport will also rise. So there may be a natural movement in the direction of local production – as the higher labour costs in Western economies are offset by the greater cost of transporting goods – and most of the things we buy and sell today, whether cars or bread, are likely to be considerably more expensive than they are now.

In a market system, goods are allocated on the basis of ability to pay and priced in terms of money. However, in a world of rapidly rising prices this will lead to a much lower standard of living for those on lower incomes, and may mean that some of those who have the greatest need, say, an old person needing their home heated, are going to be deprived. As for money prices, these may not be the best way to ensure that the limited energy that is available is used to produce the most socially important goods and services.

The market system encourages us to think as individual, self-interested consumers; when we are shopping we are motivated to put our own interests first. According to the proponents of the free market, the self-interested decisions of millions of people will ensure the optimal outcome for all (see Chapter 1, this volume). The problem is that this theory is not working well in terms of finding solutions to the ecological crisis. The self-interested decisions of people in North America to fly abroad are guaranteeing that the inhabitants of Vanuatu will lose their island; the self-interested decisions of bond traders in the City of London are ensuring that pensioners in Scunthorpe will not receive adequate social care. We need to find a way to make decisions, as a society, that are in the best interests of society as a whole.

In a bioregional economy, resources will be taken to belong in common to the people of that bioregion. This is in stark contrast to the pseudo-colonial system of the early twenty-first century, where national governments grant concessions to corporations to exploit their resources, often with very little value accruing to local people. This is as true of the rights to seek shale oil through fracking in South Wales as it is of the extraction of petroleum in the Niger Delta or the Chinese prospecting for rare earths in Africa. When it would be inefficient to extract resources on a very small scale, we might wish to enable established companies to do that on behalf of the community, but companies granted concessions would be required to pay a realistic price that reflects the benefit they acquire from the community. Although this seems improbable within an Anglo-American worldview, there are examples where everybody receives a share of the wealth that the country or region's resources generate, as in the cases of the Alaska Permanent Fund and the Norwegian Oil Fund.[2]

This idea of ownership in common may seem utopian and unrealistic – though see the chapter by De Angelis and Harvie in this volume – but in fact systems of land distribution are being changed by government land reform policies in many countries across the world.[3] Similarly, the ownership of new resources such as minerals is vested in national political authorities, who choose to allocate licences via a market system. A simple, legal change could ensure that the value of these resources passed to local communities rather than to private individuals (Wightman, 2011).

Once we decide that the only acceptable moral position is that the natural resources of a region belong to its citizens, and take on board the point made earlier about the boundaries set for the sustainable economy reinforcing the importance of equality, we need to propose an alternative system of allocation to that of the competitive market: a market within social and ecological boundaries. Such a system does not yet exist, although there are some examples that give us a clue about how we might establish something along these lines. One is the participatory budgeting process of Porto Alegre in Brazil. Since 1989, spending on public services in Porto Alegre has been decided by a participatory budgeting process. A process of decentralized and democratic decision-making in the city's neighbourhoods identifies spending priorities for the $200 million annual budget for infrastructure and services. The process is not fully participatory – about 50,000 of the city's 1.5 million inhabitants take part – but is distinct from the systems of representative democracy that decide budgeting in cities of a similar size the world over.[4]

In order to establish a fair system for the allocation of our bioregional resources we need a process that enables social priorities to enter into market allocations. We might propose three possible pre-conditions for such a process:

- A system for making decisions that is more responsive to the wishes of citizens than representative democracy.
- A way of encouraging citizens to behave in the general good of society rather than in their personal self-interest.

- A clear idea of our energy budget, and measures to enable or enforce people to live within it.

Once we have established the energy limit for our bioregion following the Contraction and Convergence model, we could set up a system of Citizens' Juries to decide how that energy budget could be spent.[5] Asking individuals to become part of these juries would require them to act as citizens rather than consumers, to rise above their self-interest and make decisions in the interests of the society they are part of. They would have to take responsibility for the consequence of their decisions; for example, travelling by plane might mean that the energy needed to undertake a heart operation was not available. This is one way in which a bioregional approach to economics requires that people take responsibility for their behaviour, in a way that is impossible in the global marketplace.

For example, food is one of the most essential products that we need for happy and healthy lives; for this reason, it has been the greatest focus of activity for those who are seeking to relocalize our sources of supply. The English city of Bristol has a food plan entitled 'Who Feeds Bristol?' and is an excellent example of how local authorities can approach this question which, while not explicitly within their remit, is of vital importance to their citizens. The plan was drawn up by Joy Carey with support from the City Council and the National Health Service. It covers a range of areas from local, food-related and catering businesses to the nature of the distribution networks, food waste, local production and community food growing. The plan's focus is on resilience (see Ganesh and Zoller in this volume) so, as well as data on all these areas, it includes ideas on how we might assess the resilience of a local food supply, and policies for enhancing resilience in Bristol. The report makes it clear that to have anything like self-reliance in food, we would need significant changes in how and where people live and work (www.bristol.gov.uk/page/food-bristol).

It is important to stress that we are not talking about the abolition of markets and the creation of some form of central planning; the Citizens' Juries would not decide how many bicycles should be made in Vladivostok or the size of the turnip harvest in the Ukraine. Their role would be to inform governments about which goods and services were valued most highly. This information would then be used to adapt the taxation system to one in which incentives were created for people to consume in a way that made sure the energy used achieved the maximum in terms of social well-being; for example, by imposing higher sales taxes on the least-valued, high-energy products, and exempting from taxation goods that are locally grown or made from locally sourced materials.

It is quite possible for communities to begin a process of establishing Citizens' Juries now; even though their decisions might not carry political weight, they could influence local governments in terms of their carbon management strategies, or their plans for building resilient local communities. Encouraging a wider range of people to consider a low-energy future is a useful exercise in itself, since it involves sharing knowledge about the size of reductions required, as well as helping people share their hopes and anxieties about the process of transition.

It is constitutive of the bioregional proposal that control over the three strategic resources of a green economy – land, energy and water – passes to the bioregion. These could be designated as belonging to the community of the bioregion, and some redistribution through a process of participatory decision-making could be expected in most bioregions. If a decision is made that some common resources should be managed or administered by private bodies then this is likely to be via a non-profit arrangement (as in the Glas Cymru model: see Bruijn and Dicke, 2006), or in return for a tax to give the value received to the community at large (as is argued in the case of a Land Value Tax: see Wilcox, 2010). Once this reallocation is achieved, the bioregional authority could be empowered to maximize provisioning of the community, being responsive to local priorities about the competing uses of land for the production of food, fuel or material crops and the consequent attainable lifestyles. Such decisions could be enforced through planning guidance, backed up by land tax systems with variable rates to provide incentives to dedicate land to meet socially agreed priorities. At the community level, communities would be encouraged and trained to engage in participatory planning, as discussed by Ganesh and Zoller in this volume, and practised widely in Venezuela (see Azzellini, 2010).

We also need to consider the implications of the proposal of a bioregional economy for spatial organizing. The present pattern of habitation has resulted from industrialization and the availability of cheap supplies of fossil fuels. Within such a framework it does not matter that people live far from their basic resources, since transport is cheap. However, now that we need to take into account the advent of peak oil and the need to reduce carbon emissions (Kemp and Wexler, 2010), the energy intensity of provisioning patterns takes on a much greater significance. In this context, urban living begins to appear as an outmoded, if not obsolete, solution. Girardet (2006) calculated that London currently has a footprint equivalent to 80 per cent of the entire UK landmass. A transition to a lower-energy inhabitation of the world's productive land is likely to result in high rates of migration that to some degree reverse the pattern of migration that occurred in response to industrialization.

The bioregional economy seems feasible in the context of a semi-rural community like that of Stroud, where I live, but how practical would it be in the case of the world's largest cities, which at present rely on drawing resources in from many miles away? Since the growth of cities was fuelled by fossil energy it seems inevitable that, at least in their current form, they will be superseded as fossil fuels become depleted. As we saw, the City of Bristol is considering its own ability to provide food for itself and its relationship with the productive hinterland which traditionally fed the City. The Transition Towns (see Ganesh and Zoller, this volume) focus on the energy efficiency and conviviality of the market town, while Kirkpatrick Sale (1991) evokes the memory of the Italian city-states of the Renaissance. Both of these patterns of spatial organizing share similar features: urban settlements of limited size drawing on rich rural hinterlands. In this context, Girardet (2011) proposes moving towards 'regenerative cities'. Building on the work of nineteenth-century German economic geographer, Johann Heinrich von Thünen, he describes the original urban settlements as 'agropolis', with the city surrounded by fertile land that provided its resources. From this we have moved to what Girardet characterizes as 'petropolis', an urban settlement that relies on fossil fuels to bring in its resources and remove its wastes. His regenerative city would be an 'ecopolis', returning to the model of an urban settlement linked to its hinterland but made of energy-intensive structures and powered by renewable sources of energy.

For example, Stroud Community Agriculture is a model for local food production and distribution that balances the needs of the farmers and those who want to eat their food. The co-operative was established in 2001 when a group of local people decided to find a shared solution to their need for organic, locally produced food. They rented some land and employed a farm to tend it for them. The co-operative now rents around 50 acres on two sites and employs two full-time and three part-time farmers. Together they produce enough seasonal vegetables to supply 200 families every week of the year. While day-to-day decisions are taken by the farm team, strategic decisions are taken by a core group elected from the members. They also organize seasonal events to mark the turning of the year. As well as paying a membership fee and a monthly charge for their vegetables, members are expected to participate in the work of the farm, although this is not compulsory (see www.stroudcom-munityagriculture.org).

Wider benefits and critique of bioregional economics

The *Prosperity Without Growth* report from the UK's Sustainable Development Commission (Jackson, 2009) called for us to re-examine what it means to lead a good human life and to learn how to 'flourish within limits'. At present many people derive their sense of identify largely from their consumption, through their attachment to brands or the exotic locations they fly to during their holidays (Bauman, 1998). The attachment to travel can be seen positively as a commitment to living as a global citizen, but more negatively it can be seen as an attempt to escape from our local place and our everyday lives which have become dissatisfying, unpalatable even. Polanyi (1944) discusses this divorce from our society and our environment as a response to the market economy and the alienating consequences of both labour and land becoming commodities to be bought and sold.

The bioregional economy would be one in which we were much more closely embedded in our local place and lived in stronger and more convivial communities. To some this offers a strengthened identity and sense of spiritual connection; while to others it can seem limited and stifling. The process of re-embedding is not a passive or intellectual one that can be engaged in while lying in bed or sitting at a computer: it requires physical interaction with the local environment. In my own community this is supported by a group called Walking the Land, which organizes encounters with nature – supported walks with activities to encourage active engagement with features of the local landscape – as well as the production and display of works of art inspired by the surrounding countryside. (For more details on Walking the Land see Cato and Myers, 2010.)

As has already been said, in a bioregional economy we would be defined much more strongly by our relationships and less by our consumption habits. We might extend this to consider our needs in a different way. If our first motivation is to keep production local we might try to adapt our needs so that they can be met from local production as often as possible. For example, in the globalized economy we might discover a craving for a pineapple and drive to the supermarket to buy one, even if it is November. In a bioregional economy we might try to adjust this 'need' for a pineapple into a desire for fresh fruit, and cycle to the local community orchard to pick an apple or pear.

A local product, one that thrives in the environmental conditions of the bioregion, could start to define that area and also its people. In Britain, different regions have traditionally been identified with specific types of production. This is easy to see in the case of food products, such as apples in Herefordshire, where one of the country's leading cider producers, Bulmers, is still based. In the case of craft, the Somerset levels, where the watery environment is ideal for the production of willow for basket-making, became renowned for the production of wicker goods, which were exported widely. This is an example that the bioregional economy could follow: the local environment favouring the production of certain crops, which then define the focus of local production and lead to the concentration and evolution of particular skills. We can see the beginnings of such regional specialization in the Transition Towns movement, with Totnes designating itself as the country's first nut town, and Stroud following by becoming an apple town.

A key critique that can be levelled at the idea of a bioregional economy is that, if we define our provisioning units according to areas of similarity in terms of climate and species, then this will mean that we have a great uniformity of production and little variety. It is certainly true – and inevitable, I think – that we will have less variety and more seasonality than we have today. This will have decided benefits, since the excitement over the arrival of strawberries in summer or tangerines at Christmas will replace the easy satiety of today's consumer. However, the bioregional economy does not imply the ending of all trade.

A local currency can both encourage more local production and, once a greater range of variety is available, facilitate its exchange (see North, this volume). In the European context, the most successful local currency is the German *Chiemgauer*, which is now used in 600 shops, has 1800 consumer members and 200 charitable associations which are supported by donations when the currency is exchanged for Euros. Nearly half a million *Chiemgauers* are in circulation, generating a transaction volume value of more than €4m.

The question of exchange between bioregional economies must begin with a visit to the work of nineteenth-century economist David Ricardo. It was his theory of comparative advantage that set the scene for the rapid expansion of international trade and the model of export-led growth that we live with today. This Theory of Comparative Advantage suggested that even if a country was less efficient in the production of all goods than potential trading partners, it would still benefit by specializing in whatever it produced most efficiently, compared to its other productions, and trading for all other goods.

The Theory of Comparative Advantage is an argument about specialization, but sidelines all discussion about how the goods are traded and whether the trading relationships are based on equal power relationships (see a more detailed critique in Cato, 2006: ch. 4). In addition, it ignores the lengthy supply chains that typify the global economy and are both energy intensive and vulnerable to the unpredictable weather events that it is predicted climate change will cause. By contrast a bioregional approach to economics proposes the idea of trade subsidiarity. By analogy with political subsidiarity, this principle states that we should begin to meet our needs locally, and only look further afield when the product we need is not available locally.

Deeper political and cultural criticisms of the bioregional proposal can also be raised. A world of low-energy use, where people are more deeply embedded in their local places, could threaten the cosmopolitan world we have grown used to. Some of the original theorists of bioregionalism suggested a kind of uniformity of culture which could be associated with an unacceptable form of political exclusion, as in Sale's suggestion that 'Outside or asystemic agents are normally detected and rejected, so that total population is stable, and within the system population levels of the species are maintained in a dynamic equilibrium' (1991: 73). He was writing here of ecosystem dynamics, but such comments could easily be misrepresented by proponents of exclusionary political philosophies, which is why maintaining a commitment to cultural diversity and social openness is of critical importance (see Ganesh and Zoller, this volume).

In a similar way, some critiques of the early environmentalist movement traced its roots to Nazi Germany (Bramwell, 1989). Evanoff has expressed concern that 'the emphasis bioregionalists place on localism might be construed as promoting insularity, ethnocentrism, and racism' and concludes that 'such worries are legitimate and point to the need for bioregionalism to develop a wider perspective that transcends a purely local focus and promotes greater cross-cultural understanding and cooperation' (2007: 152). Part of the point of the proposal of a bioregional economy is to offer twenty-first-century citizens, who have grown used to establishing their identity through a large number of novel material goods, a strong alternative source of identify in their local land (here bioregionalism has similarities with proposals for 'voluntary simplicity' as outlined by McDonald in this volume).

While some have interpreted the bioregional proposal in terms of its potential political exclusion, others have suggested the possibility of a kind of 'bioregional cosmopolitanism'

(Tomashow, 1999), and as Heater reminds us, in the original Greek sense, 'A person thus described [as a cosmopolitan] was . . . someone conscious of being part of the whole universe, the whole of life, the whole of nature, of which all human beings, let alone just the community of the person's political state, were but tiny portions' (Heater, 1999: 137). Meredith (2005) also suggests the possibility of a bioregional communitarianism, which fits neatly with the appeal for a shared approach to resource ownership and a participatory approach to the sharing of local resources outlined earlier.

Transition economics and self-provisioning

Imagining entirely different systems for social and economic organization is difficult because we tend to take the system we live with as some sort of general norm. Assuming that the market economy is the normal system of economic organization could not be further from the truth (see Williams, this volume). In reality, capitalism represents an aberration from systems of provisioning based around norms of reciprocity and mutualism. It has existed for little more than two centuries, and for only the past 30 years or so has been the daily reality for a minority of the world's citizens.

In his book *The Great Transformation*, Polanyi (1944) documents the move from these self-provisioning, socially guided economies towards the market economy, where money was the supreme power and people were forced to compete against one another. He clearly establishes that the market economy is not typical of historical patterns of economic and social organization: 'previously to our time no economy has ever existed that, even in principle, was controlled by markets . . . though the institution of the market was fairly common since the later Stone Age, its role was no more than incidental to economic life' (45).

Despite its novelty, the market form of economic organization has rapidly come to dominate, but this domination has been bought at a series of economic and social costs, as we have lost our traditional habits of reciprocity and exploited our environment. The bioregional economy is proposed as a way of responding to these social and environmental costs. We can already see evidence of the shoots of a new economy based on just relationships between people, the species they share the planet with, and the planet itself.

To attempt to compare the advantages of the bioregional economy against the charms of the high-energy, 24/7, globalized shopping mall we live in today is rather to miss the point. The starting point of this proposal is not that such a life would be preferable in all respects, but rather that it would be sustainable and equitable. We need to find a way to live within energy and resource limits: the bioregional economy is a proposal for enabling us to do this while creating the best possible human life. Other proposals are possible, of course, in fact to be welcomed in the spirit of diversity and freedom, but only those which respect environmental limits are tenable.

The globalized economy seems powerful and succeeds especially in convincing us of its invincibility and our powerlessness. The reality could not be more different. The lengthy supply chains and energy intensity of the global marketplace mean that it cannot survive the transition to a sustainable economy. More urgently, it relies on a system of ports, almost all of which are located at sea level, while the most rapid consequence of global warming is the melting of polar ice and rises in sea levels. This threatens the ports on which we now rely for our most basic resources. By contrast, a bioregional approach to provisioning can put us back in touch with our local environment, offer us local and secure ways of meeting our needs, and would need us to relearn skills and rebuild our economy through the creation of real, productive jobs and close economic relationships.

While the global economy continues to provide for our needs, carrying out a bioregional mapping exercise or auditing our energy resources can seem artificial, almost like a game. But the need for us to make the transition to locally based economies could arise more rapidly than we anticipate and, unless we learn the necessary skills soon, we could be left dangerously vulnerable.

Notes

1 Contraction and Convergence is a model for sharing the ability of the atmosphere to absorb CO_2 emissions on a global, per capita basis. It begins by establishing a limit on emissions based on the best available science; this total is then divided between all the world's population and allocated to national governments on behalf of their citizens. Find out more at: www.gci.org.uk/contconv/cc.html

2 The Alaska Permanent Fund shares a proportion of the value of Alaska's oil wealth with citizens of the state (www.apfc.org); in Norway, pensions are funded from money taken from the value of the country's oil wealth, formerly called the Government Petroleum Fund and now called the Government Pension Fund Global (www.nbim.no/en/About-us/Government-Pension-Fund-Global/).

3 Significant reallocations of land are taking place in the Philippines, South Africa (Wily, 2000), Bolivia (Sikor and Müller, 2009) and Brazil (Castañeda, 2006).

4 Source: Albert (2003); and the article published online here: www.zmag.org/znet/viewArticle/7269

5 For an example of how such Citizens' Juries might work in a more limited environmental context see Ward, 1999.

Resources

The issues discussed here are considered at considerably more length in my book *The Bioregional Economy: Land, Liberty and the Pursuit of Happiness* (2012, Earthscan). I explore the sorts of policies that would support a transition to a provisioning economy based on bioregions in my earlier book *Green Economics* (2009, Earthscan). I also have a website where I have uploaded a range of information and other resources: www.greeneconomist.org

A bioregional economy entails a completely different attitude to land, one informed by the indigenous perspective. As an introduction to this approach to land, and as an initial point of contact with the lifeworld of an indigenous people, I would recommend Bruce Chatwin's book *The Songlines* (1987, London: Cape). For further detail on issues of land rights and the campaign for land reform readers are recommended to read *The Land* magazine: www.thelandmagazine.org.uk/

Conaty, P. and Mayo, E. (2012), 'Renewable energy co-operatives', *Journal of Co-operative Studies*, 44, shares practical insights into successful energy co-operatives, while Westmill Windfarm is an inspiring example of community renewables in action: www.westmill.coop/westmill_home.asp. *The Resilience Imperative* by Pat Conaty and Mike Lewis gives further details on participatory economic solutions (2012, Gabriola Island, BC: New Society Publishers).

If you are inspired to start a local currency the best book is North, P. (2010), *Local Money: How to Make it Happen in Your Community* (Totnes: Green Books). The most successful local currency in an industrialized economy is the *Chiemgauer*: www.chiemgauer.info/

References

Anderson, B. (1991), *Imagined Communities: Reflections on the Origin and Spread of Nationalism*. London: Verso.

Azzellini, D. (2010), *Partizipation, Arbeiterkontrolle und die Commune: Bewegungen und soziale Transformation am Beispiel Venezuela*. Hamburg: VSA Verlag.

Bauman, Z. (1998), *Work, Consumerism and the New Poor*. Buckingham: Open University.

Bramwell, A. (1989), *Ecology in the Twentieth Century*. New Haven, CT: Yale University Press.

Bruijn, H. de and Dicke, W. (2006), 'Strategies for Safeguarding Public Values in Liberalized Utility Sectors', *Public Administration*, 84/3: 717–735.

Carbon Trust (2006), *The Emissions in All That We Consume*. London: Carbon Trust.

Castañeda, J.G. (2006), 'Latin America's Left Turn', *Foreign Affairs*, 85/3.

Cato, M.S. (2006), *Market Schmarket: Building the Post-Capitalist Economy*. Gretton: New Clarion Press.

Cato, M.S. (2011), *Environment and Economy*. London: Routledge.

Cato, M.S. and Myers, J. (2010), 'Education as Re-embedding: Stroud Communiversity, Walking the Land and the Enduring Spell of the Sensuous', *Sustainability*, 3/1: 51–68.

Daly, H. (1977, 1992), *Steady State Economics*. London: Earthscan.

Douthwaite, R. (1992), *The Growth Illusion: How Economic Growth Has Enriched the Few, Impoverished the Many and Endangered the Planet*. Totnes: Green Books.

Drenthen, M. (2009), 'Ecological Restoration and Place Attachment: Emplacing Non-Places?', *Environmental Values*, 18/2: 285–312.

Evanoff, R. (2007), 'Bioregional and Cross-Cultural Dialogue on a Land Ethic', *Ethics, Place and Environment*, 10/2: 141–156.

Friedman, T. (2005), *The World is Flat: A Brief History of the Twenty-First Century*. New York: Farrar, Straus and Giroux.

Galeano, E. (1998), *Upside Down: A Primer for the Looking Glass World*. New York: Picador.

Girardet, H. (2006), *Creating Sustainable Cities*, Schumacher Briefing no. 6. Totnes: Green Books.

Girardet, H. (2011), *Creating Regenerative Cities*. Berlin: Heinrich Böll Foundation.

Heater, D. (1999), *World Citizenship: Cosmopolitan Thinking and Its Opponents*. London: Continuum.

Heinberg, R. (2005), *The Party's Over: Oil, War and the Fate of Industrial Societies*. West Hoathly: Clairview Books.

Hines, C. (2000), *Localisation: A Global Manifesto*. London: Earthscan.

IMF (2008), 'Globalization: A Brief Overview', available online at www.imf.org/external/np/exr/ib/2008/053008.htm

Jackson, T. (2009), *Prosperity Without Growth: The Transition to a Sustainable Economy*. London: SDC.

Kemp, M. and Wexler, J. (2010), *Zero Carbon Britain 2030: A New Energy Strategy*, the second report of the Zero Carbon Britain project, pp. 50–52. Machynlleth: Centre for Alternative Technology.

Khor, M. (2001), *Changing the Rules: An Action Agenda for the South*. Penang: Third World Network.

McGinnis, M.V. (ed.), (1999), *Bioregionalism*. London: Routledge.

Meredith, D. (2005), 'The Bioregion as a Communitarian Micro-region (and its Limitations)', *Ethics, Place and Environment*, 8/1: 83–94.

Ohmae, K. (1996), *The End of the Nation State: The Rise of Regional Economies*. New York: Harper Collins.

Polanyi, K. (1944, 2011), *The Great Transformation: The Political and Economic Origins of our Time*. Boston, MA: Beacon Press.

Sale, K. (1991, 2000), *Dwellers in the Land: The Bioregional Vision*. Athens, GA: University of Georgia Press.

Sikor, T. and Müller, D. (2009), 'The Limits of State-led Land Reform: An Introduction', *World Development*, 37/8: 1307–1316.

Stephens, P.H.G. (2001), 'Blood, Not Soil: Anna Bramwell and the Myth of "Hitler's Green Party" ', *Organization and Environment*, 14/2: 173–187.

Stern, N. (2007), *The Economics of Climate Change*, The Stern Review. Cambridge and New York: Cambridge University Press.

Stiglitz, J. (2000), *Globalisation and its Discontents*. Harmondsworth: Penguin.

Thomashow, M. (1999) 'Toward a Cosmopolitan Bioregionalism', in M.V. McGinnis (ed.) *Bioregionalism*, pp. 121–132. London: Routledge.

Ward, H. (1999), 'Citizens' Juries and Valuing the Environment: A Proposal', *Environmental Politics*, 8/2: 75–96.

Weizsäcker, E. von, Hargroves, K., Smith, M., Desha, C. and Stasinopoulos, P. (2009), *Factor 5: Transforming the Global Economy Through 80% Increase in Resource Productivity*. London: Earthscan.

Wightman, A. (2011), *The Poor Had No Lawyers: Who Owns Scotland (And How They Got It)*. Edinburgh: Birlinn.

Wilcox, C. (2010), *Taxing Natural Rents:* Special Issue of *Tax Justice Network* newsletter, 6/1. London: Tax Justice Network.

Wily, L. (2000), 'Land Tenure Reform and the Balance of Power in Eastern and Southern Africa', *ODI Natural Resource Perspectives*, 58, June.

16

Organizing transition

Principles and tensions in eco-localism

Shiv Ganesh and Heather Zoller

Over the last fifty years, studies of alternative organization have evidenced an interesting tension in what counts as alternative forms of organizing. On one hand, what is constituted as "alternative" is historically and politically responsive to extant dominant forms of organizing. At the same time, regardless of the specific kind of dominating force that shapes alternative spaces, be it capitalism, patriarchy or colonialism, studies of alternative organizing/organizations have been concerned with enduring and transcendent issues of democracy. Chief among them are principles of collective participation, dialogue and community (Cheney *et al.*, 1997, and Chapter 3 in this volume).

This tension between responsive and transcendent aspects of alternative organizing informs our discussion and assessment of the transition initiatives movement, a popular eco-local movement that began in Ireland in 2005. Eco-localism has attracted much academic attention and critique in recent years. As conceptualized by Curtis (2003), it is a model of place-based economics that rejects large-scale, place-less rational economic models upon which the current global economic order is built. Instead, it propounds a mode of organizing that advocates "place-rooted local contexts" (p. 86) where economic decisions are made by communities who understand the vital role played by local eco-systems. As a form of eco-localism, the transition movement advocates principles and templates for community organizing to deal with the twin crises of peak oil and climate change by building resilience to manage potential shocks and reducing or eliminating carbon dependence.

In this chapter, we investigate the potential of the transition movement to transform communities through bottom-up, democratic organizing and resist dominant discourses and relations of power that support neo-liberal conceptions of economic growth and deny the environmental consequences of late capitalism. Although several critiques of the transition movement focus on what authors cast as the inherent limitations of eco-localism as a form of meaningful resistance to capitalism, often from an explicitly socialist point of view (e.g. Albo, 2009), our point of departure is relatively pragmatic. It is well established that all social movements struggle with issues of democracy, power and scale (Tarrow, 2005), and like other movements and practices discussed in this volume such as alternative food reclamation (in Chapter 20 of this volume), non-commodified labour practice (in Chapter 7) and alter-globalization (in Chapter 23), the transition movement faces similar issues. In order to prevent critical attention to this social movement from lapsing into disengagement, our approach in this chapter is deliberately affirmative and our assessment is aimed at understanding the potential of the movement as well as identifying issues and challenges it may face. Accordingly, we discuss how the transition initiatives movement attempts to be simultaneously responsive to current global environmental and economic crises, while also engaging substantively and deeply with issues and dilemmas of democracy.

After briefly describing the transition movement, we examine how it has constituted resilience as a key responsive principle. We argue that the movement's conceptualization of resilience challenges increasingly popular individualistic and neo-liberal articulations of the term, with significant implications for sustainability organizing. Following this, we discuss some enduring democratic principles of alternative organizing that are also evident in the transition movement. We highlight some pragmatic responses to common organizing tensions that may allow transition towns to balance imperatives for participation and material outcomes, which in turn may enable the movement to scale up over time. In doing so, we draw from the organizing framework proposed in the *Transition Handbook* and other publications that act as guides for local action, as well as examples from different parts of the world. In concluding, we identify key challenges for the movement in resisting dominant economic and political power relations to achieve sustainable economic and civic models and democratic principles.

Transition towns and the transition movement

The transition movement, like all eco-local initiatives, is shaped against what it identifies as two monumental and intertwined crises generated by capitalism: anthropogenic global warming or climate change, and the related problem of peak oil. Evidence of human-induced changes in the atmosphere was established in the 1970s, and its impact on the planet's climate has been measured and modelled with increasing certitude since that time (Hansen, 2009). Concurrently, analysts have established that the world has approached, or is close to approaching the moment of "peak oil", a term first coined by Shell petroleum engineer Marion Hubbert in 1956 to describe the moment when the rate of extraction of petroleum would finally be overtaken by the rate of consumption (Deffeyes, 2004). Scholars, scientists and engineers have theorized the economic and environmental consequences when the energy returned on energy invested (EROI) reaches equivalency or a net loss (King and Hall, 2011).

Starting with the supposition that macro-level policy initiatives are too slow, ineffectual, compromised and partial to deal with these crises (Ganesh and Dann, 2011), a slew of initiatives worldwide have emerged to act on these issues by mobilizing communities and transforming local civic and economic organizing. These eco-local movements (Curtis, 2003) privilege place-based organizing as a means of resisting larger capitalist economics that are predicated on universal and continual growth, without regard to the consequences of such growth in specific locales or even on the planet as a whole (Meadows *et al.*, 2004). Thus, eco-local movements encourage communities to make economic decisions based on their under-standing of the vital role played by local eco-systems. Eco-local initiatives tend to be diverse and creative, including ventures such as community agriculture, local exchange economies, urban gardens and time banks (see Chapters 12 and 15 in this volume).

Eco-localism is obviously not without its sceptics. Many critiques of eco-localism tend to reflect larger socialist critiques of anarchism by arguing that the retreat into localism implies a rejection of large-scale society, which is unrealistic and abandons the larger struggle against corporate globalization and capitalism in general (Marshall, 2008). Albo (2009), for example, argues that eco-localism is rooted in an impractical rejection of universal or large-scale change, modernization and centralization. Likewise, Sharzer's (2012) critique of localism argues that it supports neo-liberal economics by promoting micro-markets, is restricted to the professional and creative classes, and endorses an incremental approach to change that will transform capitalism. Although both of these critiques offer important assessments about the difficulty involved in scaling up social movements and local practices, they also conflate all forms of localism with small-scale and market-based initiatives. The transition movement, for instance, cannot be easily equated with forms of "green capitalism" or "buy local" movements.

We maintain, along with several other chapters in this volume (see Chapter 15, for example), that the idea of developing place-based economic systems is not incommensurate with large-scale, systemic change. Indeed, we believe, along with Homer-Dixon (2006), that renewed attention to locality is a crucial, powerful and pragmatic *starting point* for any meaningful intervention into the ecological devastation wrought by capitalism, precisely because capitalism is amnesiatic about location. Any critical assessment of eco-local initiatives therefore needs to carefully examine to what extent it self-consciously grapples with questions of systemic change: in Rao's (2010) conception, the extent to which it is cosmopolitan.

The transition initiatives (or sometimes simply "transition") movement indexes the popularity of eco-localism. Started in Kinsale, Ireland in 2005 by permaculturist Rob Hopkins, it now has more than 500 chapters worldwide (Transition Towns, 2010). It is a particularly good instance of an eco-local movement due to its emphasis on the need to "transit" out of a high-energy, densely connected industrial economy towards local, loosely connected low-energy economies that can more robustly manage shocks associated with climate chaos. As the Transition Network website says:

> Transition Initiatives, community by community, are actively and cooperatively creating happier, fairer and stronger communities, places that work for the people living in them and are far better suited to dealing with the shocks that'll accompany our economic and energy challenges and a climate in chaos.

Thus, the movement is premised on the idea that viable, sustainable and creative solutions to the intertwined problems of peak oil and climate change can be found by creating new and alternative forms of locality. This idea is closely linked with permaculture, which involves ecological design for sustainable agriculture and ecosystems, creating synergies that achieve maximum sustainable yield through each element of farming and landscaping (Mars, 2005).

The transition movement was originally known as the "Transition Towns" movement but the reference to "towns" has been increasingly dropped in the last four years, as various initiatives spring up in various parts of large metropolises. By all accounts, the term "Transition Town", itself an evocative discursive referent to a shifting yet small sense of place, was coined by Rob Hopkins and his students as part of an attempt to lobby the Kinsale council to adopt low-energy and sustainable food practices. As Hopkins took these ideas to Totnes, England, they evolved into the development of a detailed template for action called an Energy Descent Action Plan (EDAP), which is often described in terms of the popular slogan "the big step down", An EDAP involves creating "a clear vision of how a lower energy future could be, and then identifying a clear timetable for achieving it" (Hopkins, 2005, p. ii). According to the Kinsale report:

The late renowned ecologist Howard Odum coined the term "energy descent" for the transition from a high fossil fuel use economy to a more frugal one, also coining the term "a prosperous way down" to show that, if planned, this could be an opportunity for great inventiveness and abundance.

(Hopkins, 2005, p. 4)

The Transition website (www.transitionnetwork.org) also cautions that EDAPs should be considered a provisional and emergent part of the movement rather than a proven template. The model emphasizes the process through which communities develop the EDAP more than the outcomes (Heinbert and Lerch, 2012), encouraging communities to focus on their assets and identify their strengths rather than approach sustainability in deficit terms. As a way to capture that process and guide other communities, a *Transition Handbook*, authored by Hopkins and based on his work in Totnes, describes twelve major steps or dimensions involved in the process of developing and implementing the EDAP (see Table 16.1), which we discuss in the second half of this chapter.

Hopkins' template was quickly adopted in various parts of England before rapidly becoming global, moving on to Canada, Australia, Aotearoa New Zealand, and then to the United States, Brazil, Portugal, France, Japan, Hungary, Spain and elsewhere. The movement has been facilitated by technology, and all countries that have Transition initiatives have regional websites that are affiliated with www.transitioninitiatives.net, in much the same way that the Independent Media Centre, or Indymedia, grew in the late 1990s and early 2000s (Pickard, 2006). As mentioned earlier, the name of the movement itself began to be shortened to Transition initiatives in 2008–2009 in order to describe villages and entire cities that were adopting the model. To be called a formal initiative, communities have to have a small amount of training and communication with the original group in Totnes, as well as have progressed through several stages of the twelve-step process. Additionally, there are many hundreds of informal initiatives all over the world that have adopted one or the other aspects of the Transition initiative.

While these initiatives are often in tension with government priorities and mainstream discourses on sustainability and development (Ganesh, 2007), they are influencing community and environmental health and well-being, and can have surprising effects during emergencies and disasters (Folke *et al.*, 2010). In the following sections, we identify ways in which the transition movement challenges dominant, neo-liberal conceptions of the economy and democracy. The first is by casting resilience in collective and potentially transformative terms, and the second by promoting participative methods.

Transition and resilience

Understanding how the transition movement has appropriated and defined resilience as a core organizing term not only helps clarify how the movement is responsive to contemporary environmental, political and economic issues, but also how it crafts a cosmopolitan notion of localism. Indeed, resilience is such a central organizing concept in the transition movement that it is an explicit identity term: the very title of the founding document by Hopkins (2008) is titled *The Transition Handbook: From oil dependency to local resilience*. The *Handbook* says:

> The concept of resilience is central to this book. In ecology, the term resilience refers to an ecosystem's ability to roll with external shocks and attempted enforced changes. Walker *et al.* define it thus: "Resilience is the capacity of a system to absorb disturbance

and reorganise while undergoing change, so as to still retain essentially the same function, structure, identity and feedbacks."

(Hopkins, 2008, p. 6)

The *Handbook* goes on to characterize three major features of resilience: diversity, modularity and tightness of feedbacks. Diversity in the context of community resilience refers to the ability of a community to generate diverse forms of multiplicity, such as multiple sources of energy, multiple forms of land use, and multiple sources of livelihood. Modularity, following from this, implies that the collapse of one portion of the community does not result in the automatic collapse of the rest of the community. Finally, tightness of feedbacks refers to how quickly and responsively portions of a community can respond to crises in other parts of it.

The *Handbook* also makes an effort to distinguish between resilience and sustainability, arguing that specific sustainability initiatives do not necessarily contribute to community resilience. A recycling programme, for example, might help with the more sustainable production of plastics, but it does nothing to decrease the community's reliance on plastics itself. On the other hand, measures that reduce animal and food transportation not only reduce global energy consumption, they also help with local community resilience because they increase modularity by reducing a community's dependence on global industrial agriculture for its protein sources. Likewise, creating an alternative currency helps enhance diversity by creating new, personal economic relationships and encouraging local enterprise.

The transition movement's conceptual appropriation of resilience, then, is distinct from how it is used in academic studies grounded in social psychology or organizational studies, as well as in programmatic applications informed by these disciplines. For example, the US army recently renamed its "Battlemind" programme as "resilience training". The programme attempts to train soldiers to be immune from the psychologically devastating effects of combat, which include, of course, violence and death. Interestingly enough, the programme is advised by Martin Seligman, a key figure in the positive psychology movement (Ehrenreich, 2010) that has dominated how the concept has been appropriated both in social psychology as well as organizational studies.

Although psychology and organizational studies treat resilience in very complex terms and at multiple levels, they continue to rely on Rutter's (1987) conception of psychosocial resilience as the "degree to which people can protect themselves against the psychological risks associated with adversity" (p. 316), which results in resilience being understood relatively narrowly as a form of coping and as a social adaptation to risk at the individual level. Doing so, however, does not enable us to focus on actions and practices that change the source of the risk itself. For instance, Sutcliffe and Vogus (2003) developed the notion of organizational resilience within the framework of positive organizational scholarship, but, like others, consider resilience in terms of exposure and positive adaptation to a threat or risk rather than a process of systemic renewal that can change the risk itself.

There may be several reasons for the paradoxical bias towards adaptation in studies of resilience influenced by positive organizational studies. For one, positive psychology and positive organizing rarely address contexts of power, particularly in terms of accounting for what might be considered "positive" experiences and behaviours, as well as the role of power and critique in changing and shifting systemic risks and threats themselves. The focus on adaptation might also stem from the tendency to depict threats and risks as negative, fixed and immutable, and therefore outside the purview of such analysis. And finally, the tendency to understand resilience in individual rather than community terms may also lead to a focus on adaptation.

However, the political and historical circumstances that motivate the transition movement have resulted in a significantly different and cosmopolitan definition of resilience, which focuses not only on local adaptation, but also on systemic renewal. It draws from more ecological notions of resilience, as demonstrated by its association with the Resilience Alliance, a collaborative consortium of scientists who explore the dynamics of social-ecological systems, The Alliance offers a threefold definition of resilience, stating that it refers to:

> i) the amount of change the system can undergo and still retain the same controls on function and structure, or still be in the same state within the same domain of attraction; ii) the degree to which the system is capable of self-organization; iii) the ability to build and increase the capacity for learning and adaptation.
>
> *(Resilience Alliance, 2012)*

This definition positions resilience as distinct from stability, and as part of a cyclical self-organizing system that involves systemic renewal as well as adaptation (Berkes *et al.*, 2003).

The transition movement's conceptualization of resilience is thus significant because it calls attention to larger relationships of power that are created and sustained through dominant neo-liberal economic discourses predicated on growth and energy consumption. Developing resilience entails formulating a steady-state economy focused on establishing economic security in an equitable way within the capacity of the ecosystem (Rees, 2010). In this way, the concept represents a form of resistance to prevailing discourses of austerity and disaster capitalism that defines financial resources in terms of scarcity and ecological resources as plentiful (Klein, 2011). The transition movement instead inverts this discourse by reframing finance as potentially plentiful and scarcity as ecological. Human capital as the capacity for creativity is treated as unbounded, whereas environmental capital is treated as finite. This, of course, has implications for how localism itself is conceptualized. As Rees (2012) argues, economic planning should occur at a manageable scale, which leaves the question of scale to the practical experience of organizers on the ground. Rees' approach also implies the need for cooperation among different economic planning regions, and does not conceptualize localism and regionalism in terms of discrete and sequestered units.

In addition to challenging taken-for-granted neo-liberal economic models, this conceptualization of resilience pragmatically challenges popular opinion that casts environmental conscientiousness as nay-saying. Asking citizens accustomed to the consumption patterns of late capitalism to radically rethink their assumptions about growth (Heinberg and Lerch, 2010) and extensively modify their lifestyle is likely to be dismissed out of defensiveness and fear. Denial is particularly easy when proponents of the status quo promise technological fixes so that environmental concerns can be ignored. The transition movement thus uses "positive" discourse as a means to go beyond this problem. The movement has been helpful in that it places optimistic attention onto what the future might actually look like. As the *Handbook* says, "It is one thing to campaign against climate change and quite another to paint a compelling and engaging vision of a post-carbon world in such a way as to enthuse others to embark on a journey towards it" (Hopkins, 2008, p. 67). Building resilience is not framed in terms of sacrifice and loss, but is about creating liveable futures that focus on developing human happiness through meaningful relationships, a sense of purpose and environmental harmony rather than the accumulation of material goods.

For instance, in the US, transition town advocates seek to redefine prosperity by measuring well-being rather than wealth (the GDP), drawing from the idea of the "Genuine Progress Indicator" (GPI) used in places like Maryland. Building community resilience, as one organizer put it, involves using an appreciative inquiry approach, or a "cooperative search for solutions, to go where people want the community to go. That more than anything else is effective because it demonstrates that we can do things" (personal communication, May 2010). Functional demonstrations of this vision are important given that the level of optimism expressed by the movement can itself be a shortcoming. Indeed, one of the organizers we spoke with said, "our biggest challenge is people thinking we are silly" (personal communication, May 2010).

In sum, it is significant that transition groups frame resilience at the system level rather than the individual level. Groups assume that environmental realities must be faced and addressed, but their framing treats extant relations of economic and social power as something that can be changed through grass-roots action rather than something to which we must adapt locally. The movement builds a narrative in which doing with less (material goods) produces greater levels of equality, happiness and community than many citizens experience today (Fodor, 1999). And although adaptation continues to be positioned as an important aspect of resilience, it is contextualized in terms of a broader need for sweeping social and ecological transformation and renewal.

Envisioning democracy: organizing principles in the transition movement

The systemic and eco-centric notion of resilience adopted in the transition movement therefore carries significant potential as a means of consolidating and responding to economic and environmental crises wrought by capitalism. The heavy emphasis on process means that much of this potential depends upon how the transition movement engages with the enduring concerns of alternative organizing efforts for democratic ideals. Significantly, movement advocates construct these democratic principles with a strong blend of pragmatism, perhaps because it frames the need for resilience as being strong, urgent and immediate. Thus, democratic ideals are often discussed in highly practical terms, and there are three terms in particular that are common in the movement and merit attention: *inclusivity, Open Space decision making* and *open-endedness*. However, each of these terms is held in pragmatic and often productive tension with the need to achieve practical outcomes. Inclusivity is understood with reference to the need for local power brokers to get involved, Open Space decision making is encouraged alongside the need to engage in education and awareness about ecological crises, and open-endedness is held alongside the need for a pragmatic vision about outcomes. We take up each tension in turn.

Inclusivity and the need to get local power brokers involved

Historically, participation has been an enduring concern for alternative organizing, and it remains a central principle of contemporary democratic and grass-roots organizations. Bottom-up, grass-roots change results from involving community members and giving them voice in the organizing process and in substantive decisions, reflecting the tenets of participative democracy. The transition model encourages this in a number of ways, understanding participation in terms of the need for inclusivity. In "How to Start a Transition Initiative", the *Handbook* insists that citizens do not need funding or expertise to initiate the process. "Funding is a very poor substitute for enthusiasm and community involvement, both of which will take you through the first phases of your transition. Funders can also demand a measure of control, and may steer the Initiative in directions that run counter to community interests and to your original vision" (Hopkins, 2008, p. 146). The model encourages the use of Open

Space technology (which we describe later) to co-create goals and principles and to "involve everybody in the transformation" (p. 149). As sub-groups form, members should continually question, "Who isn't here who should be here?" (p. 159). "Go-Rounds" give sub-groups five to ten uninterrupted minutes at meetings to share what has been happening with their groups and check in on how they are feeling. Hopkins suggests that members should be trained in such meeting facilitation and collaboration techniques to promote widespread participation.

Of course, an inclusive, bottom-up project has to start somewhere, often with visionaries or leaders who initiate the process and encourage participation (Zoller, 2000). In Kinsale, Hopkins and his permaculture students initiated the project by identifying and inviting participants from relevant community sectors. The group might hold an event about food and invite speakers to address that topic, followed by an open meeting on the subject. For some, this leadership role calls into question the democratic or dialogic nature of the process (Bohm, 1996). Pragmatically, though, we may be able to separate the context of initiating the process from the conversations and models that ensue. A good example of this comes from the *Handbook*, which recommends that organizers "set up a steering group and design its demise from the outset" (p. 148). This can be seen as a type of planned organizational obsolescence, an occurrence that in most sectors is difficult to imagine (Cheney, 2002).

Participative tensions also arise because at the same time as the model focuses on inclusivity and a bottom-up approach, it also recognizes the need to involve local officials and power brokers in order to build credibility, promote scale and create policy change. Hopkins described a "community think tank" intended to initiate organizing in Kinsale "in order to hear the community's ideas about how energy descent would affect the community and what might be done about it. We sent personal invitations to the movers and shakers in the town" (Hopkins, 2008, p. 123). Enrolling powerful participants can also be seen as a transgression against a grass-roots approach. Pragmatically though, *The Transition Handbook* stresses that Lesson One from the Kinsale process is "Avoid 'them' and 'us' ". Treating local officials as a source of the problem and as separate from citizens does not translate into effective action. Involving policy makers and others, like influential decision makers, does require vigilance in managing power imbalances. "The power of the Transition process is its potential to create a truly community-led process which interfaces with local politics, but on its own terms. The role we identify for Local Authorities in this process is to support, not to drive it" (p. 144).

This pragmatic tension has resulted in some projects being more visibly led by community members, and others being obviously and visibly folded into larger policy goals. For example, the Mayor of London's office collaborated and funded several transition-related groups to create a "Capital Clean-up" campaign, in time for the 2012 London Olympics. Here, the pragmatic goals of the City of London were arguably much more about tourism and promotion than about ecological sensitivity; yet, the other groups that participated in the exercise, including the transition-related group Thames 21 (thames21.org.uk), were much more connected and supported by local communities, and were able to realize important goals related to wildlife and water conservation as a result.

Other transition-related efforts are entirely locally initiated, without much initial input from local, state or national government, but with support coming from them in later stages. For example, the Waitati Energy Project began in Otago, New Zealand with the impetus of local activists, who used the aftermath of a major 2006 flood that compromised their power networks, as an opportunity for a range of community members to get involved in creating and promoting alternative energy sources in Waitati and Blueskin Bay. The local residents have been successful by many indicators: they have engaged with national government to develop small wind turbines and micro-hydro projects to create local off-the-grid energy networks, as well as create a successful household energy efficiency programme. In both cases, it is clear that projects flourished because they were inclusive; but in one case, the initiative was driven by policy needs and in the other, by local exigencies.

The question of who participates and the degree of diversity and broad representation of involved communities remains a significant, and sometimes vexing, issue; indeed, it predicts the ability of a transition initiative to embed itself in an existing matrix of community organizing around environmental issues. In one small town in the northwestern United States, for example, the first author's participant observation over a period of three months showed that one reason that the local transition initiative had failed to reach the point of "the great unleashing" was because the core group of organizers were not seen as credible by other key actors. These included not only the local university or members of the city council, but also the local food bank, members of a permaculture collective, and even a local Occupy group.

Awareness raising and Open Space decision making

Collaboration is often conceived in dialogic terms as an equitable and open interchange that does not privilege particular viewpoints (Isaacs, 1993). This ideal can lead to tension with organizations that need to engage in advocacy by raising awareness and building public support for the issues they seek to address. This need for persuasion may exist in tension with the need for dialogic interaction. The transition model provides a pragmatic blueprint for managing this tension. For instance, Hopkins cautions that organizers should not assume community members understand basic environmental concepts let alone more complicated, abstract and specific issues of peak oil and climate change, so they must "prepare the ground" (Hopkins, 2008, p. 149) by educating audiences through film showing (for example, *Peak Oil: Imposed by Nature* or *The Power of Community*) and speaking events. These events should build a groundswell of enthusiasm and energy for participation, which is critical for successful initiatives. Reflecting their pragmatic approach, Hopkins suggests that this education process also serves the function of building the social networks needed for a transition initiative as audience members get to know one another. "Education" as it is framed here involves persuading people that we need to respond to environmental crises and that the transition model is an effective way to do so.

This persuasion is not "one-way" communication in the sense that public events should encourage dialogue among audience members. Education can be understood in Paulo Freire's terms as a set of moves that culminates in dialogue (Burbules, 1993). In practice, it may be more appropriate to view persuasion and education as intertwined with dialogue, as ideas that result from group discussion must be promoted throughout the community in order to cultivate participation. Interestingly, the persuasive needs for awareness, education and inspiration are part of a stages of change model that derive from studies of addiction – indeed, the very idea of a "twelve-step model" for change is discursively related to recovery from alcoholism. Here, addiction models are used metaphorically to explicitly understand energy use in terms of addictions and dependencies. Consequently, public meetings and discussions have to allow time for people to be weaned from their energy dependencies. Still, persuasive efforts do stand in tension with the idea of collaborative and open decision making.

The *Handbook* describes Open Space technology as involving a group of people who come together "to explore a particular topic or issue, with no agenda, no timetable, no obvious co-ordinator and no minute-takers" (p. 162) that creates opportunity for expression, networking and the development of visions (as well as typed notes). The movement imports this highly open-ended deliberative procedure from Owen's (1997) discussion of the subject.

As a process, open-ended procedures do not specify agendas or desired outcomes: they begin purely with a topic for discussion. Discussion formats are always in circular formation, begin with people describing their passions, and inviting participation from others for sub-group breakout discussion. In this manner, the group goes where its participants want it to go, and as sessions and sub-sessions evolve, the larger group begins to convene less regularly. The longer the session, the greater the need to record deliberation. The transition model adopts this need to record deliberation by creating a Wiki website where drafts of Energy Descent Plans can be shared and edited collaboratively. The town of Hertfordshire ran an online Wiki successfully for four years to discuss, debate and understand notions of energy descent and visions of the future until 2010, when its participants decided that its purpose for successful visioning, deliberation and support for surrounding transition groups had been fulfilled. They then moved to a formal website and a Facebook page to facilitate continued interaction.

A significant challenge that emerges for transition groups is to manage tensions that might arise from these very collaborative efforts, and ways in which this is done can impact the enthusiasm behind specific efforts. An organizer for a transition initiative in Aotearoa, New Zealand reported to us some recent dynamics in their local group where participants were split on whether they should create a new level of organization that they were trying to define as a "resilience network". Some people felt that it was critical to create such a trans-local group because it would help different communities learn from each other, create a more consolidated front to lobby the regional council, and help build better awareness about systemic aspects of resilience. Others felt that it would dilute energy behind efforts to grow and manage more local ventures such as the local time bank, and that they would not accomplish anything "real" with the network. In the absence of a consensus, one influential organizer stepped in and made a decision on behalf of the group to get involved in the network. This, understandably, violated the expectation of several members that they make decisions consensually and collaboratively, and created a fair amount of bitterness.

Visioning and open-endedness

The tension between education and Open Space decision making as the key means through which communities make decisions and deliberate together is echoed in another tension about the goals of the movement between focused visioning versus the need for open-endedness. This reflects a common dilemma in community-based organizing between allowing new ideas to emerge through the process and creating a concrete vision and mission of where the organizing will go that creates enthusiasm (Medved et al., 2001). For instance, in a Healthy Communities initiative, facilitators and community members clashed over whether unstructured dialogue was the key to creating change or an impediment to action (Zoller, 2000). Missions help groups coordinate their action and cohere a common identity, but they can also limit groups' potential. On one hand, Open Space decision making, in its very title, encourages an open-ended vision. The four key principles of Open Space, according to Owens (1997), are:

- whoever comes are the right people
- whatever happens is the only thing that could have
- whenever it starts is the right time
- when it's over, it's over.

(Owen, 1997, p. 95)

Table 16.1 Twelve key ingredients to the transition model

1. Set up a steering group and design its demise/transformation from the start
2. Start raising awareness
3. Lay the foundations with existing groups and activists
4. Organize a great unleashing
5. Form theme (or special interest) groups
6. Use Open Space decision-making techniques
7. Develop visible manifestations of the project in the community
8. Facilitate the great reskilling or the desire to change habits
9. Build a bridge to local government
10. Honour the elders
11. Let it go where it wants to go
12. Create an Energy Descent Action Plan.

Adapted from www.transitionnetwork.org

On the other hand, the principle of open-endedness is balanced by the need to remain focused on the core goals of the movement, to enhance resilience and to empower communities to deal with ecological crises. Some important features of the transition movement help balance this tension in a pragmatic way.

For example, take the "twelve key ingredients of transition" identified in the *Handbook*. These include setting up a core group of dedicated activists, raising community awareness about peak oil and climate change, a "great unleashing" or setting up a memorable milestone or a project that resonates with the community, a subsequent division of labour and the creation of specialized sub-groups, initiating Open Space democratic decision-making techniques, engaging with local government, and culminating in the creation of a specific EDAP. The directiveness of these twelve steps is offset by the caution:

> They don't take you from A–Z, rather from A–C, which is as far as we've got with this model so far. These steps don't necessarily follow each other logically in the order they are set out here, every Transition initiative weaves a different way through the Steps, as you will see.
>
> *(Hopkins, 2008, p. 148)*

The *Handbook* recommends that readers view the steps not as prescriptions but as pieces of a puzzle they may wish to use. The particular form a transition project takes depends on the community itself. For instance, Bloomington, Indiana in the US developed an energy descent plan in a somewhat top-down form through a task force coordinated by the city council. Further, as is evident from the title of Table 16.1, discussion in recent years has reframed the "steps" to "key ingredients" in an attempt to reduce the apparent linearity and overt prescriptiveness of the process.

The tension between the paradoxical goals of visioning and open-endedness echoes extant discussions in studies of community dialogue of tensions between talk and action (Zoller, 2000). Here, open-ended processes run the risk of being seen as "all talk" with a significant tension between the need to allow emergent decisions to guide the group rather than adopt action for its own sake, and the need to see concrete results in order to maintain enthusiasm and participation. To ameliorate this issue, the movement suggests demonstrating concrete manifestations of the movement early on. Drawing from other grass-roots initiatives, Hopkins suggests that "your project needs, from an early stage, to begin to create practical manifestations in the town, high visibility signals that it means business" (p. 163). Such initiatives could include activities from tree plantings to an experiment in alternative currency. Stressing the pragmatic theme, the *Handbook* recommends uncontroversial events that will result in positive press, part of the "great unleashing" that is discussed in detail in the "twelve key ingredients". The challenge for the movement is to ensure that such actions do not substitute for more transformative changes, and to discuss whether particular activities themselves count as "talk" or "action". This is evident from an example discussed in the previous section, where participants in a transition group were torn about whether or not to join a resilience network, because they could not agree whether it counted as just "talk" or as a meaningful systemic intervention.

Discussion

As we explained at the outset, it is tremendously difficult to catalogue the success of any social movement because such efforts depend upon what counts as a successful outcome of movement organizing. Rather than interpret movement success purely in material terms or with regard to the achievement of the formal goals of the movement, Tilly (2006) suggests that we understand successful movement mobilizing in terms of WUNC – Worthiness, Unity, Numbers and Committedness. From that perspective, the transition movement has been consequential in communicating the importance of acting locally on both peak oil and climate change to many hundreds of communities all over the world. Participants have managed the enactment of dialogic and democratic forms of communication, the number of transition initiatives has grown at an unprecedented rate, and it is clear from studies (Ganesh and Dann, 2011; Ganesh, 2012) as well as media coverage that participants are committed to the success of the movement. The broader potential of the transition movement stems from its reframing of resilience in systemic terms that paint a picture of energy descent and climate change as an opportunity for a happier and more fulfilling future, rather than merely the abrupt end of the consumption party. Collective resilience becomes a powerful means of changing social norms of radical individualism as well as received views about the necessity of growth as an economic model.

Some of the movement's success may also result from the pragmatic approach we describe above that balances concerns about facilitating the growth of emergent solutions through bottom-up participation with the need for some of the basic tools of political organizing: building enthusiasm, involving existing power brokers and moving towards concrete action. Obviously, these tensions are significant and, as our discussion demonstrates, they can be managed poorly or well. Initiatives must remain focused on avoiding losing that sense of balance if the movement is to continue to thrive in terms of WUNC.

Given the enormity of unfolding environmental crises, it is also crucial to understand the success of transition initiatives in material terms. Because these are still early days for the movement, its influence cannot be fully understood. At a minimum, individual transition efforts can provide working models as effects of climate change and peak oil become more visible to power brokers and the general public. Nonetheless, in moving forward the movement needs to address several challenges. In closing, we identify three.

First, it is arguable whether all communities are equally fertile grounds for transition. Indeed, communities that are particularly vulnerable to ecological devastation are often those that are characterized by hierarchies of exploitation, ranging from powerful global, corporate or state actors to local elites (Shiva, 1989). Persuasive and participative communication practices to encourage change in impoverished and marginalized communities, particularly in the third world, are often stymied by powerful national and transnational interests. The template offered by the transition movement needs to take such material and power issues into account if it is to build a truly global community resilience, which might stretch to its limit the ability of the movement to balance democratic organizing with the pragmatic need for outcomes.

A second challenge that transition initiatives face is the question of local ownership: whether communities truly own the process and outcome of transition efforts, or whether they are incorporated into the service of larger, extraneous or even non-related policy objectives. The City of London's use of transition groups to improve its image before the 2012 Olympics is a case in point. While critics such as Albo (2009) focus on capitalism itself as the prime obstacle to any effective eco-localization effort, we believe that local ownership of transition efforts is an important first step in materially shifting the scale of change enabled by transition.

Finally, the actual process of transition involves a fundamental shift in economic livelihoods, social practices and political relationships. While we have described how three major tensions in the transition movement are often balanced against each other, it is also the case that the scale of change that the movement is asking for may make such balance supremely difficult to maintain in the long run. In practical terms, the effort the movement requires may be difficult to sustain in the face of the change needed. Further, the optimism of the principles espoused in the movement may themselves make the movement easy for critics to dismiss. It is precisely for these reasons that we need to continue examining potential obstacles facing the movement, not only in terms of the material scale of the challenges involved, but also in terms of how these initiatives enact their own prefigurative politics (see Chapter 23 in this volume) and addresses questions of power in terms of participation and decision making at the local level. Perhaps, with such self-examination, the movement itself will continue to be resilient in the face of its many challenges.

Resources

Heinberg, R. and Lerch, D. (eds). (2010). *The Post Carbon Reader*. Healdsberg, CA: Watershed Media.
Hopkins, R. (2008). *The Transition Handbook: From oil dependency to local resilience*. Foxhole, Dartington, UK: Green Books.
Resilience Alliance website: www.resalliance.org
Transition Network website: www.transitionnetwork.org/

References

Albo, G. (2009). The limits of eco-localism: Scale, strategy, socialism. *Socialist Register*, 43, 1–27.
Berkes, F., Colding, J. and Folke, C. (eds). (2003). *Navigating Social-Ecological Systems: Building resilience for complexity and change*. Cambridge, UK: Cambridge University Press.
Bohm, D. (1996). *On Dialogue*. New York: Routledge.
Burbules, N.C. (1993). *Dialogue in Teaching*. New York: Teacher's College Press.
Cheney, G. (2002). *Values at Work: Employee participation meets market pressure at Mondragon*. Ithaca, NY: Cornell University Press.
Cheney, G., Straub, J., Speirs-Glebe, L., Stohl, C., DeGooyer, D., Whalen, S., Garvin-Doxas, K. and Carlone, D. (1997). Democracy, participation, and communication at work: A multidisciplinary review. In M. Roloff (ed.) *Communication Yearbook 21*. Thousand Oaks, CA: Sage, 35–91.
Curtis, F. (2003). Eco-localism and sustainability, *Ecological Economics*, 46, 83–102.
Deffeyes, K. (2004). *Hubbert's Peak: The impending world oil shortage*. Princeton, NJ: Princeton University Press.
Ehrenreich, B. (2010). *Bright Sided*. New York: Macmillan.

Fodor, E. (1999). *Better Not Bigger: How to take control of urban growth and improve your community.* Gabriola Island, BC, Canada: New Society Publishers.

Folke, C., Carpenter, S.R., Walker, B., Scheffer, M., Chapin, T. and Rockström, J., (2010). Resilience thinking: Integrating resilience, adaptability and transformability. *Ecology and Society*, 15(4), 20.

Freire, P. (1973). *Education for Critical Consciousness.* New York: Seabury Press.

Ganesh, S. (2007). Sustainable development discourse and the global economy: Promoting responsibility, containing change. In S. May, G. Cheney and J. Roper (eds) *The Debate over Corporate Social Responsibility.* New York: Oxford University Press, 379–390.

Ganesh, S. (2012). Reconfiguring resilience for organizational communication studies: Eco-localisation and the transition towns movement. Organizational Communication Division, National Communication Association Annual Convention. Orlando, FL, November.

Ganesh, S. and Dann, C. (2011). Eco-localisation: Strategies for resistance, resilience and renewal. *Organization, Identity and Locality (OIL) VII: Local Theory.* Massey University, 10–11 February, 46–49.

Hancock, T. (1993). The evolution, impact and significance of the Healthy Cities/Healthy Communities Movement. *Journal of Public Health Policy* (spring), 5–17.

Hansen, J. (2009). *Storms of my Grandchildren: The truth about the coming climate catastrophe and our last chance to save humanity.* London: Bloomsbury.

Heinberg, R. and Lerch, D. (eds). (2010). *The Post Carbon Reader.* Healdsburg, CA: Watershed Media.

Homer-Dixon, T. (2006). *The Upside of Down: Catastrophe, creativity and the renewal of civilization.* Toronto, CA: Alfred A Knopf.

Hopkins, R. (ed.). (2005). *Kinsale 2021, An Energy Action Descent Plan Version 1.* Kinsale: Kinsale Further Education College.

Hopkins, R. (2008). *The Transition Handbook: From oil dependency to local resilience.* Foxhole, Dartington, UK: Green Books.

Isaacs, W.N. (1993). Taking flight: Dialogue, collective thinking, and organizational learning. *Organizational Dynamics*, 22(2), 24–39. DOI: 10.1016/0090-2616(93)90051-2

King, C.W. and Hall, C.A.S. (2011). Relating financial and energy return on investment. *Sustainability*, 3(10), 1810–1832.

Klein, N. (2011, 6 October). Occupy Wall Street: The Most Important Thing in the World Now. The Nation.

Koschmann, M. and Laster, N.M. (2011). Communicative tensions of community organizing: The case of a local neighborhood association. *Western Journal of Communication*, 75(1), 28–51.

Lassen, I., Horsbøl, A., Bonnen, K. and Pedersen, A.G.J. (2011). Climate change discourses and citizen participation: A case study of the discursive construction of citizenship in two public events. *Environmental Communication: A Journal of Nature and Culture*, 5(4), 411–427. DOI: 10.1080/17524032.2011.610809

LeGreco, M. and Leonard, D. (2011). Building sustainable community-based food programs: Cautionary tales from "The Garden". *Environmental Communication: A Journal of Nature and Culture*, 5(3), 356–362.

Mars, R. (2005). *The Basics of Permaculture Design.* White River Junction, VT: Chelsea Green Publishing.

Marshall, P. (2008). *Demanding the Impossible: A history of anarchism.* Oakland, CA: PM Press.

Meadows, D., Randers, J. and Meadows, D. (2004). *Limits to Growth: The 30-year update.* Oxford: Earthscan.

Medved, C. (2003). Tensions in community health improvement initiatives: Communication and collaboration in a managed care environment. *Journal of Applied Communication Research*, 29, 137–152.

Medved, C.E., Morrison, K., Dearing, J.W., Larson, R.S., Cline, G. and Brummans, B. (2001). Paradox in community health improvement initiatives: Communication and collaboration in a managed care environment. *Journal of Applied Communication Research*, 29, 137–152.

Minkler, M. (ed.). (1997). *Community Organizing and Community Building for Health.* New Brunswick, NJ: Rutgers University Press.

Owen, H. (1997). *Open Space Technology: A user's guide*, Second edition. San Francisco, CA: Berrett-Koehler Publishers.

Pickard, V. (2006). Assessing the radical democracy of Indymedia: Discursive, technical and institutional constructions. *Critical Studies in Media Communication*, 28(1), 19–38.

Rao, R. (2010). Disciplining cosmopolitanism. *Transnational Legal Studies*, 1(3), 393–420.

Rees, W. (2010). Thinking "resilience". In R. Heinberg and D. Lerch (eds) *The Post Carbon Reader*. Healdsberg, CA: Watershed Media, 25–42.

Resilience Alliance. (2012). Resilience. Available online at www.resalliance.org (accessed 21 February 2012).

Rutter, M. (1987). Psychosocial resilience and protective mechanisms. *American Journal of Orthopsychiatry*, 57(3), 316–331.

Sharzer, G. (2012). *No Local: Why small scale alternatives won't change the world*. Blue Ridge Summit, PA: Zero Books.

Shiva, V. (1989). *Staying Alive*. New Delhi: Kali for Women.

Sutcliffe, K.M. and Vogus, T. (2003). Organizing for resilience. In K.S. Cameron, J.E. Dutton and R.E. Quinn (eds) *Positive Organizational Scholarship: Foundations of a new discipline*. San Francisco, CA: Barrett-Koehler, 94–110.

Tarrow, S. (2005). *The New Transnational Activism*. Cambridge: Cambridge University Press.

Tilly, C. (2006). WUNC. In J.T. Schnapp and M. Tiews (eds) *Crowds*. Stanford, CA: Stanford University Press, 289–306.

Transition Towns. (2010). "Official" initiatives. Available online at http://transitiontowns.org/TransitionNetwork/TransitionCommunities (accessed 3 November 2010).

Zoller, H.M. (2000). "A place you haven't visited before": Creating the conditions for community dialogue. *Southern Communication Journal*, 65(2 and 3), 191–207.

Section 4

Resources

In this final section, we turn our attention to the resources that are mobilized in alternative organizing. This will involve considering the bits and pieces that get assembled in constructing modes of organizing that hold true to the three principles outlined in Chapter 3: autonomy, solidarity and responsibility. These resources may look very similar to those used in capitalist organizations: money, knowledge, natural resources, social networks, technologies in a broad sense. But the ways they are constituted and deployed may be very different. Here it is useful to go back to the relationships between means and ends discussed in Chapter 3.

All the contributions in this section show that questions of means and ends cannot be separated; the resources we use to build alternatives must be consistent with the alternative values we want to promote. So, for example, if we want to build more equal and democratic modes of organizing, it won't do to leave control over essential resources (be it money, knowledge or technology) in the hands of powerful banks, corporations or experts; rather, we need to reclaim some collective ownership of these resources. Similarly, it would seem contradictory to promote autonomy or equality through hierarchical decision-making processes. In all the chapters below, organizational resources are revealed as being more than mere ends; they also embody, or prefigure, alternative values.

While banks may be considered the epitome of the greed and competitive drive that led to the global financial crisis in 2008, Leanne Cutcher and Peter Mason (Chapter 17) show that they can be organized on the principle of mutuality rather than competition. Credit unions and saving clubs are cooperative financial organizations that are owned and managed by communities; they are not only a means of providing affordable financial services to those often excluded by conventional banks, but also serve the broader social objective of members' empowerment. There are many ways of thinking about banking and finance, and we discussed microcredit in Chapter 3, but this chapter opens the possibility of local responsibilities shaping financial priorities.

In Chapter 18, Kelum Jayasinghe and Dennis Thomas argue that accounting practices are not neutral techniques but embody particular interests. What we decide to measure, to account for, reflects values about what we think is important (profit, social or environmental goods). So we can expect alternative organizations to account differently from capitalist ones. Alternative organizations do use accounting, for example, to access resources, build legitimacy, or gain cultural and political acceptance from members, but rely on a 'spectrum of calculative practices' that respond to different organizational objectives and contexts. Showing that we can 'account' differently also shows that we can organize differently, and that 'the bottom line' is only ever a line that we make up.

In Chapter 19, Massimo de Angelis and David Harvie argue that commons are not just a resource, or a means, but also embody alternative values and practices. Commons are 'social systems in which resources are shared by a community of users/producers, who also define the modes of use and production, distribution and circulation of these resources through democratic and horizontal forms of governance'. As such, commons provide an essential space for organizing ourselves independently of capital, but can also all too easily be co-opted by capitalism. The commons thus emerge as a terrain of struggle between 'antagonistic value practices', but then we should never fall into the trap of believing that any one space or form of organization provides the final answer.

To a large extent, the chapters that follow all speak of this struggle, and of communal modes of governance through which people develop and share resources independently of markets and hierarchies. Jeff Ferrell, in Chapter 20, offers a fascinating twist on the relationships between means and ends by showing that the goods we are continuously compelled to purchase in consumer capitalism all too quickly lose their exchange or symbolic value and get discarded as waste. But this waste becomes a resource for alternative, or oppositional, forms of social and economic organizing based on scrounging, a mode or organizing that has its own arrangements, norms and values.

In Chapter 21, Joshua Pearce discusses Open Source Appropriate Technology (OSAT) as a knowledge commons that opposes the private appropriation of knowledge through Intellectual Property law. OSAT is open access, often simple and small-scale, participatory technology that is designed to match the needs and purposes of users, rather than to maximize profit. Technology, Pearce argues, reflects social values. If technology is society made durable, as Bruno Latour suggests, then we need to be clear what sort of society is embedded into the technologies we use.

For The Trapese Collective (Chapter 22), popular education is also a way of creating a knowledge commons; it is 'education by the people for the people'. For example, the way education is practised in contemporary social movements challenges the instrumental orientation of traditional schooling and is an attempt to reclaim education as a collective, non-hierarchical process through which we can change our lives, and 'practice freedom'. Popular education is thus not just a toolkit or a method, but a laboratory for practising greater justice and equality.

In the final commissioned chapter, Marianne Maeckelbergh explores how decision-making practices in the alterglobalization movement address the democratic gap in supposedly representative forms of democracy. She argues that reclaiming the political power to determine the decisions affecting our lives requires particular forms of governance based on consensus, horizontality and diversity. These three principles are prefigurative in the sense that they ensure that the ways in which decisions are made now reflect the alternative world participants want to build. This emphasis on prefiguration offers a fitting end to this collection, for all the alternatives discussed in the book represent attempts to enact future organizational possibilities in the here and now.

We conclude with a chapter by the editors which tries to bring together the strands in these twenty chapters, as well as realistically appraising the challenges and limitations faced by anyone who is concerned to imagine a world organized differently.

17

Credit unions

Leanne Cutcher and Peter Mason

Introduction

This chapter provides an overview of credit unions as alternative organizations in the financial services sector. Credit unions are financial co-operatives whose members combine their deposits to create a local loan pool. This model of savings and loans is underpinned by the notion of mutuality wherein members benefit from shared norms of reciprocity. The chapter highlights the ongoing and consistent commitment to the ideals of co-operation that has underpinned credit union development across time and in different economic and geographical contexts. With a focus on the southern hemisphere we identify the challenges faced by credit unions in developed and developing economies, including regulatory constraints or limitations, shifting discourses and pressure to conform to market-based norms and organizational practices. At the same time we show how credit unions are best placed to offer a viable alternative to low-income financial consumers who might otherwise find themselves financially excluded from the market. Overall, we argue that credit unions are a long-standing form of alternative organization that continues to attest to the benefits of co-operation over competition (see the section in Chapter 3 on microfinance for an instructive comparison).

The series of events that began with the collapse of the sub-prime mortgage market in the US and continue to ricochet around the globe have led some to question the practices and ethics of large global banks. It seems an apt time to remind ourselves that there are alternative ways of organizing and managing financial services and that these alternatives have been with us since the nineteenth century. Since the mid-1800s credit unions have offered a different form of savings and loans, one that is based on principles of mutuality not competition. This commitment to providing low-cost financial service products and affordable credit products continues today with credit unions offering an important alternative to the broader fringe lending market that includes pawnbrokers and payday lenders. A report by the Australian Consumer Action Law Centre found that borrowers who have accessed credit through pawnbrokers or payday lenders expressed a sense of shame or humiliation at having to resort to such high-cost, short-term loans (Gillam, 2010). Credit unions can play an important role in offering an alternative that not only provides affordable loans but also educates financial services consumers in financial literacy.

Credit unions are able to offer this kind of alternative because they are not-for-profit financial co-operatives that provide savings, loans and other financial services to their members. As
co-operatives (see Chapter 5, this volume), credit unions are member-owned and controlled
organizations. Credit union membership is based on a common bond, a linkage shared by
savers and borrowers who work for the same employer, are involved in a social group, or reside
in a particular geographical area (Jones, 2001). Credit unions pool their members' savings
deposits and shares to finance their own loan portfolios rather than rely on outside capital.
Members benefit from the fact that any surpluses are returned to the members in the form of
higher returns on savings, lower rates on loans, member education and improved services.
This aligns with the co-operative principle of "member economic participation" where
surpluses are used for the development of the co-operative and benefit of the members.

Central to what is often called the "credit union difference" is the concept of mutuality.
Mutualism has been described as a sort of communitarianism or collectivism, in which individuals are tied to others through a variety of economic and social links (Parker et al., 2007).
A mutual organization then is owned by the people that do business with it. As Cato reminds
us in this volume, social and economic forms of organization based on notions of reciprocity
and mutualism long pre-date the market-based economy that is so often presented as the
norm. In the case of credit unions, members are both customers and owners of the organization. On joining the credit union, each member is asked to purchase a share for a nominal
amount and this entitles them to an equal say in the running of the credit union. The member
has the right to vote at Annual General Meetings and when electing the Board of Directors.
Members can also stand for positions on the Board. Each member has one vote, regardless of
the volume of business they have with the credit union.

Credit unions are also committed to the co-operative principle of member education and
training and focus on improving the financial literacy of their members and the communities
in which they operate. The provision of financial services and increasing rates of financial
literacy are both key to overcoming financial exclusion. Financial exclusion is a lack of access
to the financial system or the lack of participation in savings and loans activities. Individuals
experience financial exclusion not because they do not have money, but because they don't
have access to low-cost, fair and safe financial products from mainstream suppliers. Those most
likely to be affected by financial exclusion are people living in remote regions, those with low
incomes, and people with low rates of financial literacy. Financial exclusion is largely a result
of who you are and where you live (Leyshon et al., 1998). Jones makes the important point that
financial exclusion is a result of poverty, but also leads people into greater poverty and over-
indebtedness. He argues that it is credit unions that are best placed within the financial services
industry to make an impact within financially excluded communities (2007: 2144).

In this chapter, we explore why this is the case, as well as outlining some of the challenges
credit unions face in not only meeting the needs of the financially excluded but also in maintaining a commitment to the co-operative principle of mutuality. We discuss these issues first
in relation to credit unions in developed economies, with a particular focus on Australia, and
then, in relation to credit unions in developing economies, focusing on the South Pacific and
South East Asia. Before doing that we provide a brief overview of the history and philosophical traditions of the worldwide credit union movement.

Credit unions: antecedents and principles

The concept of credit unions originated in 1850 in Delitzsch, Germany. A liberal Prussian
parliamentarian, Hermann Schulze-Delitzsch, responded to the hardship experienced by

urban labourers and trades-people during a severe winter of 1846 by establishing a number of co-operatives, including a credit co-operative society (Crapp and Skully, 1985: 11). Founded on notions of self-help and open membership, Schulze-Delitzsch's co-operatives were the precursor to the European people's banks (Lewis, 1996: xxi). Friedrich Raiffeisen, a German burgomaster, adapted Schulze-Delitzsch's ideas to the needs of his rural constituents and in 1854 established an independent farmer-based credit association, called the Heddesdorf Society (Lewis, 1996: xx). Raiffeisen developed the notion of "limitless liability, achievable through a bond of association, whereby a person's trusted standing in the community and the knowledge co-operators had of each other acted as security in seeking loans from a community pool of funds" (Lewis, 1996: xxi). By the end of the 1880s societies founded on Schulze-Delitzsch and Raiffeisen principles had spread throughout Europe. Across the seas, in Canada, Alphonse Desjardins, a parliamentary reporter inspired by the Papal Encyclical *Rerum Novarum* (1891), developed his own philosophy for credit unions (Lewis, 1996: xxi). The first Canadian credit union was opened in 1901 at Levis, near Quebec, and by 1914 there were 150 co-operative banks in Canada. Credit unions developed on Desjardins' model were founded in Massachusetts in the United States around the same time. By 1921 there were 1,999 credit unions in various parts of the United States (Lewis, 1996: xxii).

The legacy for credit unions of this rich cross-cultural history is an emphasis on co-operation around a set of unifying principles and common identity. Today these are reflected in the principles set down by the World Council (WOCCU) under which 51,013 credit unions across 100 countries operate (World Council, 2011: www.woccu.org). These principles include open and voluntary membership to all within the group accepted by the credit union, democratic control, non-discrimination, service to members, equitable distribution of surpluses, financial stability, ongoing education to promote thrift and wise use of credit, co-operation among co-operatives, and social responsibility (WOCCU, 2011). Credit union principles align very closely to the seven co-operative principles outlined by the International Co-operative Alliance; voluntary and open membership, democratic member control, member economic participation, autonomy and independence, education, training and information, co-operation among co-operatives and concern for community (see Webb and Cheney, this volume).

Credit unions in developed economies

Even though credit unions in developed economies may be at different stages of maturity, they share some similar challenges. The first challenge is the increasing competition they face in deregulated financial service markets. In seeking to compete with other financial service providers, credit unions have adopted many of the practices of for-profit banks. As Jayasinghe and Thomas observe in Chapter 18, there has been pressure on credit unions in the UK to borrow and adapt mainstream accounting models from the commercial sector rather than develop their own systems. Australian credit unions face the same pressure to conform to the dominant market logics; for example, they are often criticized for their high cost-to-income ratios. A 2010 report by Pottinger, a financial and strategic advisory consulting firm, found that the largest credit unions had cost-to-income ratios of 73 per cent compared with the four largest retail banks that had average cost-to-income ratios of 46 per cent. Reporting of Pottinger's analysis frames the credit unions with high ratios as inefficient and doomed to fail (Drummond and Searle, 2011). Such criticism assumes that all organizations should be focused on driving down costs and fails to understand that credit unions' relatively high cost structures are because they are co-operative organizations that are not focused on delivering the highest possible returns to shareholders. Instead their focus is on providing high-quality member service through branch networks, in many cases in places that the large, for-profit retail banks have abandoned because they found them too costly to service.

Shifts in the practice of credit unions in developing economies have also been accompanied by discursive shifts in the meaning attached to notions of mutuality (Cutcher, 2008; Cutcher and Kerr, 2006). Analysis of discourse used by credit unions in both Ireland and Australia (Cutcher, 2008; Mangan, 2009) has identified a shift away from a discourse of mutuality to a "discourse of enterprise" with its emphasis on "market forces" and "entrepreneurial principles" (cf. du Gay, 1996; du Gay and Salaman, 1992). This has led in some cases to credit unions emulating the strategies of the large retail banks by introducing customer segmentation and sales strategies. As a result the credit union member is constructed as a "profit-source" rather than a fellow co-operator.

A second challenge relates to garnering and maintaining government support and recognition of the distinctive role they can play. Research across the UK (Jones, 2007), Ireland (Mangan, 2009) and Australia (Cutcher, 2008) highlights how legislation can play a key role in either supporting or stymieing the development of credit unions. In the UK (French et al., 2008; Midgeley, 2005) and Australia (Connelly and Hajaj, 2002) large retail banks and mainstream providers have continued to withdraw from providing services to low-income individuals and communities, leading to increasing rates of financial exclusion. If developed economies are going to rely on credit unions to ensure the financial inclusion of all members of society then government needs to support this role, for example, through the provision of tax exemptions.

A third challenge is balancing growth with an ongoing commitment to the philosophy of mutuality and co-operation. In some respects credit unions can also become victims of their own success because as they grow and increase the diversity of their membership base it becomes increasingly difficult to maintain a "bond of association" and as a result the concept of mutuality loses much of its meaning. The member relationship with the credit union moves closer and closer to that of a traditional customer relationship and members lose sight of the fact that they are owners of their credit union.

The remainder of this section sets out the specific challenges for the Australian credit union movement as a way of offering insights into the pressures faced by credit unions in developed economies.

Australian credit unions

Perhaps in keeping with a particularly pragmatic Australian identity, the motivation of the early credit union pioneers in Australia is retold by business historians (see Lewis, 1996; Crapp and Skully, 1985) as simply a way to make personal credit available to ordinary working people. During World War II the personal credit market was dominated by loan sharks and hire-purchase finance companies, who often charged interest rates in excess of 80 per cent. In a bid to regulate this burgeoning market the NSW government enacted the 1941 NSW Small Loans Facilities Act. Lewis (1996) argues that this legislation provided the impetus for development of credit unions in Australia. In line with credit unions in Britain, Ireland and Eastern Europe (Jones, 2001), Australian credit unions were developed out of the North American model. Yates, who some consider to be the founder of the Australian credit union movement, had been stationed in Canada during World War II and he transplanted ideas from the Canadian movement back to Australia (Lewis, 1996). The early Australian credit unions relied on the zeal of the pioneers, the work of thousands of volunteers, and the co-operation and donations of employers and church groups in order to stimulate the formation of new credit unions (Cutcher, 2008).

In Australia, up until the 1980s, credit unions were subject to their own legislative requirements and were afforded tax incentives. Not being subject to the same strict reporting requirements as the large mainstream banks and benefiting from reduced taxes helped sustain a wide range of credit unions who serviced discrete memberships. However, a range of structural changes – most notably, demutualization of consumer and producer co-operatives, privatization of the public sector, and, deregulation of the financial services sector – made it increasing difficult for smaller credit unions to survive. The result was a raft of amalgamations which saw credit union numbers fall from 549 in 1983 (Lewis, 1996: 4) to 90 in 2013 (Australian Prudential and Regulatory Authority, 2011). While credit unions are an important part of the Australian financial landscape, with over 4 million Australians belonging to a credit union (ABACUS, 2011), as they have amalgamated they have also struggled to maintain a commitment to the key credit union principles. Large credit unions with diverse membership bases have adopted similar strategies to the large retail banks and are a long way removed from the kinds of organizations envisaged by the pioneers of the credit union movement. Since 2011, some of the largest credit unions have changed their name to Mutual Banks.

This is in part a response to the structural shifts that have occurred in the Australian retail banking market as a result of the Global Financial Crisis (GFC). As Johnston (2009) reports, the big four banks – Westpac, Australia and New Zealand Bank, National Australia Bank, and the Commonwealth Bank of Australia – have used their position to acquire weaker rivals and take over banking business from smaller banks, non-bank lenders and mortgage brokers. Australia, which already had the most consolidated banking market in the world, has become even more consolidated. For example, in 2009 the big four banks were writing more than 90 per cent of the nation's new mortgages, compared with approximately 60 per cent before the GFC (Johnston, 2009). The incumbent Labor government has sought to increase competition in the sector by promoting the idea of the "mutual" sector, credit unions and mutual building societies, as a fifth force of banking (Fell, 2011). This aligns with reforms in other sectors both in Australia and the UK where not-for-profit, co-operative organizations are seen as key to pluralism of supply and increased competition (Kelly, 2007).

The peak body representing credit unions and other financial mutuals in Australia, COBA, has embraced the Labor government's competition discourse and in July 2009 adopted a Mutual Banking Code of Practice (a copy of the code can be downloaded at customerownedbanking.asn.au). While it is a code of practice for mutuals, there is no discussion of the meaning of mutuality in the document nor mention of the philosophy of co-operation that is said to underpin the work of mutuals. The 10 principles outlined in the code could read as generic statements offered by any financial services institution, with the exception of Principle 7 which states: "We will recognize members' rights as owners." However, this translates into a right to information only. The shift to call themselves "Mutual Banks" represents a significant shift in credit union discourse and practice. This is most notable in the way that "members" are now referred to as "customers": that is, from owners of a financial institution to that of service recipients. The professionalization and marketization of credit unions has seen the shift from locally owned and focused institutions into corporatized financial institutions that bear little resemblance to their forebears and members relate as customers not owners of the credit union.

There are, of course, credit unions still operating in Australia whose operations closely align with the principles of credit unions set down by the World Council. They are able to maintain a strong commitment to the principles of mutuality and co-operation in the main because they service particular communities (for example, Traditional Credit Union serving Indigenous people in the Northern Territory) and low-income individuals (such as the Fitzroy and Carlton Community Credit Co-operative[1], which we will explore below). In many respects these organizations are attempts to return economic power to local areas, as outlined by several of the chapters in this volume. These organizations serve particular communities and are focused on creating a sense of mutuality not only amongst members but also between the organization and the community. One way this manifests itself is the strong focus these credit unions place on educating members in financial literacy.

An emphasis on financial prudence and literacy underpins Traditional Credit Union's (TCU) work in the Northern Territory. TCU is Australia's only Indigenous-owned deposit-taking institution. With a head office in Darwin, the capital of the Northern Territory of Australia, it provides banking services in local languages delivered by Indigenous staff in 11 remote Aboriginal communities across the top end. They reinvest any surpluses they generate back into the provision of financial literacy training in remote Indigenous communities and into the training and development of their Indigenous staff. Their approach to employing Indigenous people, delivering financial literacy programmes and crafting locally responsive banking services has seen them win a number of national awards.

TCU was established as a Yolngu-initiated response to the ongoing market failure and associated withdrawal of financial services by major banks from remote communities in the Northern Territory. Without the services that TCU provides people living in these communities would have to travel thousands of kilometres to access banking services. The wide geographical spread of the branches and the very long distances between these places makes providing services to these communities very expensive. For example, the cost of chartering a plane from Darwin to travel to the branch at Ramingining in North West Arnhem land is $2,000.

In offering financial services and financial literacy training in the local languages of the communities, TCU ensures that Aboriginal and Torres Strait Islander people have the ability to participate fully in Australia's financial system. This is important because being financially illiterate and not having access to banking facilities perpetuates the cycle of disadvantage for many Indigenous Australians. TCU also provides local Indigenous people with the opportunity to improve their numeracy and literacy skills. TCU's management consider the role they play as a training provider as important as their role as a financial services provider. In 2011 they won the Northern Territory Employer of the Year award and Deb Say, TCU's Head Trainer, won the Trainer of the Year award. While Sam Wees, the Branch Manager at Warruwi, in the Arufura Sea, won the Aboriginal and Torres Strait Islander Trainee of the Year award (www.tcu.com.au).

Fitzroy and Carlton Community Credit Co-operative's commitment to social justice principles manifests itself in the provision of low-cost and flexible financial services to ensure the financial inclusion of economically and socially disadvantaged people living within a discrete geographical location. The credit union has strong links to social justice groups working in the area, most notably the Brotherhood of St Laurence. Based in inner city Melbourne, it is an example of an independent community-managed credit union that provides what it calls "appropriate and supportive" financial services to people on low incomes. There is an emphasis on teaching thrift – a word that seems to have almost disappeared from financial services parlance. FCCC is located in the heart of Brunswick Street which is home to both a vibrant arts scene and large public housing estates. FCCC's "bond of association" is with this community, a large proportion of whose main source of income is government benefit or allowance and people on very low household incomes. In 2010 FCCC had 9,640 members and deposits close to $11 million.

People on low incomes face difficulties in gaining access to low-cost, fair and safe financial products from mainstream suppliers. In some instances this leaves them at the mercy of non-mainstream credit providers, such as pawnbrokers, "payday lenders" and loan sharks, thereby increasing the cost of borrowing money and their exposure to risk. FCCC offers small loans at affordable rates to people who would not qualify for credit at another financial institution. Most of these loans are for household goods, schools costs, car repairs, debt consolidation, and for emergencies like family sickness and death. The focus is not on making profits but on providing services aimed at encouraging saving and avoiding problematic debt among those on low and fixed incomes. Much of the work of FCCC is undertaken by a team of volunteers. Many of the volunteers have used their experience at the Co-operative to move into paid work with other organizations. FCCC recognizes that this training is a key part of their work in the community (www.fccc.com.au).

Credit unions, such as the two above, with their direct and hands-on approach to financial service delivery, remind us that ensuring equitable access to finance is more complex than simply boosting financial literacy, "which may be a worthwhile objective but does not in its own right secure positive economic outcomes for individuals and households" (Erturk et al., 2007: 555). Investing their surpluses back into staff training and development is important not only because it means the credit unions are meeting any prudential and compliance require-ments, but also because research shows that financially excluded people want financial prod-ucts and services to be delivered by professional providers with well-trained staff (Collard et al., 2003) and that they are prepared to pay a reasonable upfront monthly fee for a trans-parent and fair current account (Jones, 2007). These communities do not want to be further stigmatized by having their financial services provided by anything less than an efficient and well-run financial services organization. So the challenge credit unions face is to offer programmes that target poorer consumers while at the same time appealing to middle- to high-income consumers. This is important because cross-subsidization of services by more affluent consumers is central to credit unions' viability and because as Jones (2007: 2143) writes "the poor person's bank appeals least to the poor themselves".

In Australia at the same time that governments have pushed for standard regulation of the financial services sector they continue to look to the credit union sector to meet the needs of low-income earners and those living in remote and regional communities who have to a large extent been abandoned by the large retail banks. While research shows that credit unions are best placed to combat financial exclusion, it is disingenuous at best for governments to place this expectation on credit unions while at the same time taxing and regulating them as if they were just another bank and making it very difficult for them to remain viable or to compete with the large for-profit Australian banking industry.

Credit unions in emerging economies

Credit unions in emerging economies face a different set of challenges to their counterparts in more developed economies. In the main these challenges relate to lack of prudential and regula-tory frameworks and the difficulties and costs of service delivery caused by geographical remoteness (Oceanic Confederation of Credit Union Leagues, 2011). The diverse structures of the credit unions within a context of limited financial literacy of volunteers, staff and manage-ment highlight both the need for regulation but also the challenges in developing and imple-menting sound organizational structures that offer members somewhere safe to save and lend. These challenges are exacerbated by the way in which regulators in developing economies struggle to understand the credit union's philosophical commitment to the twin goals of providing financial services and developing communities (Levi and Davis, 2008). Further, the credit union model of institutional development does not always produce organizational outcomes that are predictable and measurable, and therefore it is sometimes difficult for regulators to appreciate the inherent value of the community capacity building that occurs (Simmons and Birchall, 2008). As a result existing legislation and oversight arrangements for credit unions have proven inadequate in many cases, and a number of serious problems have occurred that undermine the stability or even the very existence of individual credit unions (Riechel, 2001).

Despite these challenges credit unions continue to play an important role in the sustainability and growth of many developing economies. There is an emerging credit union movement across the South East Asia and South Pacific Regions, operating both formally and informally in rural and remote areas. These credit unions offer poor communities a safe place to save and provide them with a means of budgeting. At the individual level, the ability to save reduces the need for short-term, high-interest loans. While at the community level, the amassed savings of members form a low-cost loan pool for all members to access. These loans assist credit union members in establishing micro-businesses and the extra income circulates around the communities.

In the next two sections of this chapter we focus on the work of credit unions in the South Pacific and South East Asian regions and show how these credit unions balance organizational and operational requirements with their cultural and social obligations. As many of the chapters in this volume attest, this generally results in alternative organizations being organized around notions of "trust, tradition and reciprocity" and with management practices based on a "mix of written and oral" systems.

South Pacific Region credit unions

In the past, credit unions in the South Pacific Region have struggled to develop an environment that opens up space for community participation and at the same time incorporates the administrative and regulatory requirements of a financial institution (Woolcock, 1998). More recently, credit unions in the South Pacific have sought to meet this challenge through the use of what Jayasinghe and Thomas (in this volume) call "interpretive reporting practices" which are influenced more by narratives and social values rather than numerical data and financial values. For example, in the Pacific Melanesian Wantok[2] social system, social ties and obligations of reciprocity and hierarchy are inherent within everyday relationships and are aligned with the credit union concept of mutuality. In this context, loan applications are viewed through the filter of social obligation and not through the prism of a loan criteria document.

The development of less formal credit unions, called Savings Clubs, in the Solomon Islands is another example of the way in which using a mix of written and oral accounting systems leverages off close family and village bonds. As a result the development of savings clubs has enabled communities that were financially excluded from mainstream financial providers to now have places to safely save and borrow. There are nearly 300 savings clubs throughout the Solomon Islands, many in extremely remote areas. These savings clubs share a number of common features: first, they are initiated by the local community; second, they build on existing forms of trust, shared social norms and forms of cultural reciprocity; and, third, they offer simple savings and loan products. The loan products are usually designed to meet emergency needs and traditional obligations such as weddings and funeral ceremonies (Asian Development Bank, 2001: 97). The savings clubs have also provided a conduit to the formal and monetized economy. Prior to the introduction of the saving clubs, inhabitants of some of the more remote villages simply bartered their goods to secure their daily requirements. The use of money in their everyday lives was seen as of little benefit, until they needed to access medical care outside of the village or wanted to be able to send their children to higher education in the capital Honiara. In addition to offering a place for safe, communal saving, the savings clubs also offer villagers a safety net by providing a range of health, education and other material benefits that would assist the village in ways that are agreed upon by the community as a whole.

The road to the village of Lengalau, on Guadalcanal, in the Solomon Islands, is a narrow dirt track which becomes almost impassable in the rainy season. The village families, with five to nine children, live in houses made from leaf fronds and timber. The villagers share a single water supply and have no toilets in their houses. Until the Lenga Savings Club was established (Drummond and Noel, 2010), the villagers had no access to local commercial banking facilities as the population is too remote, too small and far too poor to attract the attention of commercial banks. While the community has traditionally titled land it does not belong to any one person and therefore is of no use as collateral for any commercial banking purposes. Further, the villagers of Lengalau cannot join a commercial bank because customers are required to provide evidence of identification, and many of them do not have a birth certificate, passport or driving licence.

In this context, community leader, Roslyn Tapolia, established the Lenga Savings Club. Roslyn works in the capital of the Solomon Islands, Honiara; however, local, cultural tradition means she is obligated to help her family and those within her local village. The Savings Club is her way of giving back to her family and the local villagers of Lengalau. A savings club is an informal group of people who come together to save and receive loans. A year after Lenga Savings Club was established, its 133 members – both adults and children – have combined savings equivalent to about US$6,700. The Lenga Savings Club provides villagers with small loans to enable them to convert their houses into more permanent structures and install toilets. They have also been able to save for their children's education, providing local children with the opportunity to study in Honiara, a three-hour drive away. This financial empowerment has enabled the community to develop stronger links to the formal economy and to access services and goods that they were previously denied.

The club hopes to introduce a loans facility as soon as the community has developed sufficient capacity to manage and service this type of financial product. Roslyn Tapolia assists other community members in keeping meticulous financial records. This not only meets an organizational need but builds the capacity and financial literacy of members of the Lengalau community which helps them in many other aspects of their lives. The accuracy and transparency of the accounting system provides members with assurances and builds trust which encourages them to maintain the habit of saving.

In Fiji, a country that has a larger formally educated population than that of many other Pacific nations, the success of the credit union movement has been in the way in which it has been able to offer ongoing member education as well as having members play an active role in their governance structures (Elder, 2010). In this way, the credit unions in Fiji are further investing in the country's human capital by helping members and staff develop the skills required for effective participation in institutional decision making. Indeed, as Fiji's several military coups attest, many Pacific nations have weak governance structures at the level of the state, and the credit unions offer one way for people living in these countries to participate and gain first-hand experience of democratic decision-making processes. The credit unions present a local example of organizational responsiveness, accountability and transparency that can be used as a model for good governance on a broader scale (see Evans et al., 2006).

South East Asian credit unions

Throughout South East Asia, there is plenty of evidence of credit unions combating financial exclusion and increasing the participation of citizens. The development of these credit unions follows some similar patterns. Initially credit unions are staffed by volunteers that may get a small amount of funds to cover their transport costs. As the organization matures, paid staff and management are employed. Initially at the commencement of operations the board or committee meets several times a week to oversee the operation with subcommittees formed to approve loans and membership applications. The boards and committees are elected by the membership and should be good savers themselves. The organization will have a set of by-laws (constitution) that govern the procedures and operation of the organization. During the early stages of the organization's development a board or committee member would usually oversee the volunteer staff until such time as the organization has matured and they are able to pay for the services of a manager. The credit unions would also have regular member meetings, usually on a monthly basis, to provide a forum for member education, promote membership, make special announcements and consult the members regarding the operations of the credit union. Members of these organizations often use the credit union membership and meetings as a forum to engage in wider community issues (Mason, 2012).

There are many different ways that members are able to interact and engage with each other that not only provide a platform for mutual aid but also help in the creation and maintenance of shared norms and values that strengthen their communities. For example, the Women's Co-operative in Sri Lanka has over 85,000 members and seeks to improve the lives of very poor communities. The credit union is their core focus; however, they undertake a number of other mutual aid activities such as health committees which operate clinics for their members (see Webb and Cheney, this volume). The Women's Co-operative also has a disaster committee which they mobilized to assist the victims of the 2004 tsunami and they offer educational scholarships to members' children who are academically gifted.

The Akphiwat Credit Union in Battambang Province, Cambodia is a typical example of how communities can collectively organize to address local issues. For example, farmers have pooled resources to work with each other at harvest time and have now come together to jointly purchase irrigation pumps and farm machinery with the aid of the credit union. This village savings bank is based in a village called Kompong Chhlong in the province of Battambang and has 1,300 members. A member of the Akphiwat Community Village Savings Bank shares its story:[3]

> The leaders and our members have tried to work hard to achieve the vision and mission of our savings bank. Our savings bank is stable because we have a formal building [many savings banks operate from people's homes] and our members trust each other. Our savings bank has been developing and growing from year to year. We have seen the growth as we have saved more money in the savings bank and it has become more developed and stable. The leaders have led us very well and they have given us new skills and knowledge to run our savings bank. The leaders are very good at communication, good at preparing letters and lists, have a good relationship with the community and have high education and knowledge which help us run our savings bank.

The bank member explained that the savings bank usually has a meeting once a month where members debate and agree upon the savings bank's principles and regulations:

> For our savings bank, we have a specific meeting time, every month on the 24th. When we have any new information or problems, the leaders always call us to join a meeting

and try to find solution together. When we have had discussion and find the solution we disseminate it to our members immediately in the meeting.

The bank is open for all people to join, there is no discrimination and membership is voluntary. Most members are poor rice farmers from the local area. The member explained why he joined the savings bank:

> I wanted to borrow some money and the leaders explained to me about the benefit of saving that is why I have decided to be member. After we had a vote to choose the volunteers and staff, I was chosen to be a volunteer. My volunteer activities can help my village know how to save money and because of this they will have a good future.

He went on to explain how:

> members have borrowed money from those microfinance institutions and sometimes they were late to repay money so they had to borrow from other microfinance institutions to pay back the money to the others. Some people lost their land to these microfinance institutions. Some members previously got into a lot of financial trouble with microfinance institutions as they didn't understand how to use money and how to save for the future.

The savings bank has helped people understand how saving is important to individuals and their families.

This type of co-operation would have been unimaginable only 10 to 15 years ago. Indeed, it is in Cambodia where the role of trust building by credit unions is most apparent. Cambodia is a country that was ripped apart during the Pol Pot regime and is only now beginning to rebuild (Hughes, 2009). Trust in Cambodia was decimated during that time: trust in both the financial system as well as between neighbours (Gardère, 2010). Social capital generated from the act of institutional building has acted as glue (Bjornskov and Svendsen, 2003) that has seen many fractured communities heal and build trust. The trust generated by the organization of a credit union does not belong to the individual or even to the credit union but resides in the relations between the actors (Field, 2006). These relations are underpinned by a philosophical commitment to co-operation. Relations of trust are underpinned by a shared network of financial arrangements and vice versa. In Cambodia credit unions have offered communities a way to relearn the value of mutual self-aid albeit within a context that continues to recognize the need to acknowledge political elites with the Village Chief or Commune Governor invariably being given a seat on the credit union as a way of "paying respects" to those in power and at the same time giving the organization an "informal" licence to operate within the community.

Credit unions in a range of emerging economies share some general common features, most notably location within, and access to, strong hierarchical social structures. Lazega (2000: 195) argues that "social relations among members are the key to the process of mutual adjustment, i.e. the way in which a formally egalitarian organization obtains this quasi-voluntary compliance with its rules and agreements". The way in which credit unions can benefit from leveraging off these social structures and family bonds varies. Strong family ties within a South East Asian context enable institutions to lower transaction costs because of the trust inherent within the relationship. However, in the South Pacific region, close family ties sometimes allow for opportunist behaviour to occur at the local level in the form of nepotism and corruption, and the credit union has to guard against and manage this. This compliance must be negotiated within a localized cultural and social framework, particularly in respect of hierarchical and family bonds.

Concluding thoughts

At this point in history when many financial institutions are failing it would seem time to give greater consideration to Kropotkin's notion that "co-operation is a more basic principle than competition" (cited in Parker *et al.*, 2007: 187). Following the crisis of 2008, governments in developed economies have looked to mutuals to provide a range of essential services. For example, in the UK the Prime Minister, David Cameron, has promoted mutuals as part of his "Big Society" agenda (Fell, 2011), whereas in Australia, the Gillard Labor government has been championing smaller, not-for-profit financial mutuals, including credit unions, as a fifth competitive force in retail banking. There is no doubt that credit unions, and other mutual banking institutions, have played a key role in providing access to affordable financial services throughout Australia's history. The philosophy of co-operation which drives their operating model has meant that they are, in many cases, best placed to meet the needs of consumers who might otherwise find themselves excluded from accessing financial products and services from the market.

However, there is a risk that promoting credit unions through a discourse of competition puts the mutual philosophy of co-operation under threat. These forms of co-operation are the reason why credit unions are best placed to make an impact for financially excluded groups within developed economies (Jones, 2007). Primarily, it rests on the way in which mutuality and co-operation at the local level encourages savings. If the aim of governments in developing economies is to ensure the ready availability of fair and reasonably priced financial services then it may do better to look to the forms and norms of "co-operation" rather than competition. Credit unions have a long history of equitable and fair service provision in financial services through co-operation. We suggest that rather than look to the not-for-profit sector as a source of competition the key lesson to be learnt from credit unions is the benefit of co-operation.

Communities across the Pacific and South East Asia have learnt the benefit of co-operation by saving together and pooling their resources under the auspices of a credit union. They have learnt that participating in savings can, as Jones (2007: 2147) argues, "change the way [they] feel about themselves and enables them to be more open" to not only participating in financial services but in broader, democratic participation. This is because for credit unions in developing countries it is communal, not institutional, trust that is critical to their success. While credit unions are not the only institutions and mechanisms of rebuilding trust in communities, the nature of their structure underpinned by notions of co-operation does mean that they have played an important role in ensuring not only financial but also social inclusion in villages across South East Asia and the South Pacific.

It is the case that credit unions in both developed and developing economies are effective primarily because they are locally initiated, owned and managed. However, it must also be acknowledged that they sit within a broader global financial system and need their local structures to be supported by effective regulatory frameworks at the national and global level. In developing economies, credit unions operate in an under-regulated environment and are forced to rely on the capacity of the local community to either create or build on existing forms of trust and reciprocity in order to remain viable. A supportive and strong regulatory environment is needed because, as Amin (2007) argues, regeneration cannot be a localist affair or a matter of local responsibility alone but needs to be part of a wider political economy. Credit unions have proven that they are a model that works in creating sustainable and financially included communities but they deserve and need the support of facilitating regulation for credit union members in developing economies to fully participate as global citizens.

Notes

1 As this book went to press Fitzroy and Carlton Credit Co-operative was acquired by Bank MECU. Bank MECU is the first of the mutual banks to be formed under the new mutual code of practice. Fitzroy and Carlton Credit Co-operative is the 55th credit union acquired by Bank MECU and its acquisition is evidence of the increasing consolidation of the sector as small credit unions find it increasingly difficult to comply with the regulatory and reporting requirements imposed on them and to compete with the larger for-profit and mutual banks.
2 Wantok meaning *one talk* or speaker of the same language.
3 Source: Interview with Peter Mason, CEO of the Credit Union Foundation of Australia.

Resources

The World Council is the peak body for credit unions around the world. It is their mission to be the world's leading advocate, platform, development agency and good governance model for credit unions. On their website you will find a good number of publications and resources, including case studies, information about women and leadership programmes, and member services: www.woccu.org

The Credit Union Foundation of Australia has been working with communities for over 40 years. Their programmes focus on providing disadvantaged communities with access to financial services in the South East Asia and Pacific region. You can read more about these programmes, including some of the case studies discussed in this chapter, at www.cufa.com.au

Abacus – Australian Mutuals is the industry body for the Australian mutual financial services sector, a strong alliance of mutual building societies, credit unions, mutual banks and friendly societies. You can find out more about their strategies to increase market share at http://abacus.org.au/home

The report on the effects of payday lending by Zac Gillam and the Australian Consumer Law Centre can be downloaded from the Consumer Action website at www.consumeraction.org.au/publications/policy-reports.php. This report details qualitative research with consumers who have used payday lending services.

References

Amin, A. (2007), 'Local Community on Trial', *Economy and Society*, 34(4): 612–633.
Asian Development Bank (2001), 'Financial Sector Development in the Pacific Developing Member Countries', *Regional Report* (Vol 1; Manila), 1–197.
Australian Prudential and Regulatory Authority (2011), 'Quarterly Performance Statistics for Credit Unions and Building Societies', available online at www.apra.gov.au/
Bjornskov, C. and Svendsen, G.T. (2003), 'Measuring Social Capital: Is there a single underlying explanation?' in *Aarhus School of Business Department of Economics, Denmark Working Paper*, 03–05.
Collard, S., Kemson, E. and Dominy, N. (2003), *Promoting Financial Inclusion: An Assessment of Initiatives Using a Community Select Committee Approach*, Bristol: The Polity Press.
Connolly, C. and Hajaj, K. (2002), *Small Business Banking Issues Paper*, Financial Services Consumer Policy Centre, University of New South Wales, Sydney, April, 1–40.
Crapp, H. and Skully, M. (1985), *Credit Unions for Australians*, Sydney: Allen & Unwin.
Credit Union Foundation Australia (2010), 'Sri Lanka – Women's Cooperative Project Monitoring Report', in *International Development Working Group Sydney: Credit Union Foundation Australia*, 1–15.
The Customer Owned Banking Association, available online at customerownedbanking.asn.au
Cutcher, L. (2008), 'Strong Bonds: Maintaining a commitment to mutuality in a deregulated environment – the case of Australian credit unions', *Journal of Co-operative Studies*, 41(1): 22–30.
Cutcher, L. and Kerr, M. (2006), 'The Shifting Meaning of Mutuality and Co-operativeness in the Credit Union Movement from 1959 to 1989', *Labour History*, 91: 31–46.
Drummond, C. and Noel, H. (2010), 'Savings in the Solomons', *Connexus Magazine*, 33 (summer): 48.
Drummond, M. and Searle, J. (2011, 24 January), 'Mutual Inadequacies', in *Australian Financial Review*.
Du Gay, P. (1996), *Consumption and Identity at Work*, London: Sage.

Du Gay, P. and Salaman, G. (1992), 'The Culture of the Customer', *Journal of Management Studies*, 29(5): 615–633.

Elder, F. (2010), 'Fiji Country Report – Credit Unions', Suva: Oceanic Confederation of Credit Union Leagues.

Erturk, I., Froud, J., Johal, S., Leaver, A. and Williams, K. (2007), 'The Democratization of Finance? Promises, outcomes and conditions', *Review of International Political Economy*, 14(4): 553–575.

Evans, A.C., Grell, S. and Klaehn, J. (2006), 'A Technical Guide to Increasing Citizen Participation: How credit unions strengthen democracy', available online at http://www.woccu.org/publications/techguides

Fell, E. (2011), 'A Third Way on Services', *Australian Financial Review*, 19 January.

Field, J. (2006), *Social Capital*, New York: Routledge

Fiji Ministry of Education National Heritage Culture and Arts (2008), 'Education For All: Mid-decade Assessment Report', in Government of Fiji (ed.), Suva: United Nations Education Scientific and Cultural Organization.

French, S., Leyshon, A. and Signoretta, P. (2008), ' "All Gone Now": The Material, Discursive and Political Erasure of Bank and Building Society Branches in Britain', *Antipode*, 40(1), January: 79–101.

Gardère, J-D. (2010), *Money and Sovereignty: An Exploration of the Economic, Political and Monetary History of Cambodia*, Phnom Penh: National Bank of Cambodia, 369–429.

Gillam, Z. (2010), 'Pay Day Loans: Helping Hand or Quicksand?', report of the Australian Consumer Law Centre, 1–294.

Hughes, C. (2009), *Dependent Communities: Aid and Politics in Cambodia and East Timor*, New York: Southeast Asia Program Publications.

Johnston, E. (2009), 'Banks Given Too Much Power, Says Keating', *Business Day, The Sydney Morning Herald*, 23 September, p. 7.

Jones, P.A. (2001), *The Growth of Credit Unions and Credit Co-operatives – is the Past Still Presented?* in E.C. Mayo (ed.), *Banking and Social Cohesion, Alternative Responses to Global Market*, Oxford: Jon Carpenter Publishing.

Jones, P.A. (2007), 'From Tackling Poverty to Achieving Financial Inclusion – The Changing Role of British Credit Union in Low Income Communities', *The Journal of Social Economics*, 37: 2141–2154.

Kelly, J. (2007), 'Reforming Public Services in the UK: Bringing in the Third Sector', *Public Administration*, 85(4): 1003–1022.

Lazega, E. (2000), 'Rule Enforcement Among Peers: A lateral control regime', *Organization Studies*, 21(1): 193–214.

Levi, Y. and Davi, P. (2008), 'Cooperatives as the "Enfants Terribles" of Economics: Some implications for the social economy', *Journal of Socio-Economics*, 37: 2178–2188.

Lewis, G. (1996), *People Before Profit: The Credit Union Movement in Australia*, Sydney: Wakefield Press.

Leyshon, A., Thrift, N. and Pratt, J. (1998), 'Reading Financial Services: Texts, consumers, and financial literacy', *Environment and Planning D: Society and Space*, 16: 29–55.

Mangan, A. (2009), 'We're Not Banks: Exploring self-discipline, subjectivity and co-operative work', *Human Relations*, 62(1): 93–117.

Mason, P. (2012), 'Social Capital Adequacy of the Australian Mutual Sector', World Council of Credit Unions Conference 2012, 18 July, Gdansk, Poland.

Midgley, J. (2005), 'Financial Inclusion, Universal Banking and Post Offices in Britain', *Area*, 37(3), September: 277–285.

Oceanic Confederation of Credit Union Leagues (2011), 'Operational and Statistical Report 2010/2011 on Fiji', in Oceanic Confederation of Credit Union Leagues, available online at www.occul.org

Parker, M., Fournier, V. and Reedy, P. (2007), *The Dictionary of Alternatives: Utopianism and Organization*, London: Zed Books.

Riechel, K. (2001), 'Financial Sector Regulation and Supervision: The case of small Pacific Island countries', *International Monetary Fund*, PDP/01/6: 1–17.

Simmons, R. and Birchall, J. (2008), 'The Role of Co-operatives in Poverty Reduction: Network perspectives', *Journal of Socio-Economics*, 37: 2131–2140.

Woolcock, M. (1998), 'Social Capital and Economic Development: Toward a theoretical synthesis and policy framework', *Theory and Society*, 27(2): 151–208.

World Council of Credit Unions (2011), available online at www.woccu.org

18

Alternative and social accounting

Kelum Jayasinghe and Dennis Thomas

This chapter presents an analysis of the socially driven accounting practices used by alternative organizations. Using two short case studies it attempts to discuss three main issues:

1. the form of accounting systems and calculations that exist in alternative organizations
2. the role that accounting calculations play in alternative organizations
3. the impact such calculative practices make on the socio-economic performances of alternative organizations.

The chapter reveals the "spectrum of calculative logics", ranging from rational to cultural and political disclosure, used by alternative organizations to achieve their diverse organizational and strategic objectives. In contrast to Anglo-American accounting systems used in capitalist business enterprises, accounting in alternative organizations relies on a mix of written and oral practices and involves several alternative forms: "blended value" accounting, ethno-accounting and reward-token systems. These accounting systems and calculations do not merely account for financial and economic performances, but are also open to cultural and political interpretations. They operate as "rhetorical strategies" and formulas and symbolically provide "substantively rational" structures and justifications for the stakeholders of alternative organizations, with regard to their socio-economic performances. The chapter concludes by raising further questions concerning the role of accounting in alternative organizations, and argues for more comprehensive social accounting research.

Introduction

This chapter focuses on socially driven accounting practices in alternative organizations, such as credit unions, cooperatives, local trading systems, social firms, charities and community businesses (see chapters in this volume), that are characterized by mixed organizational values (economic, social and political) and substantively rational economic calculations. In contrast to capitalist business organizations that are driven by the rational calculative logic to maximize profit for shareholders and owners, alternative organizations (either in profit or non-profit form) apply business like strategies and culturally and politically motivated logic to achieve their organizational objectives – primarily about improving human and environmental well-being at a community level.

These alternative organizations arrange their internal structures and micro-form financing by using social forms of accounts that specifically value and measure social costs, benefits and wealth. Their accounting systems are driven largely by social expectations and are "substantively rational" in that they are informed by cultural and political values. These systems attempt to facilitate the organizations' socio-economic performances and also communicate the social effects of their economic actions. As such, the socially driven accounting systems make these organizations economically visible, measurable, accountable and amendable to their members and other key stakeholders in society (Miller, 2001).

In this context, the chapter specifically examines three main issues:

1. the forms of accounting systems and calculations that exist in alternative organizations
2. the role that accounting calculations play in alternative organizations
3. the impact such calculative practices make on the socio-economic performances of alternative organizations.

In addition, the chapter identifies the spectrum of "calculative logics" and socially driven accounting systems used by alternative organizations in different cultural and political economic contexts. It uses two selected cases – the Colchester Credit Union Ltd (in UK) and the Kalametiya Fish Production System (in Sri Lanka) – to contextualize the form, role and impact of alternative organizational accounting practices.

The chapter is organized as follows: the first section explains the specific role of accounting in organizations and society and discusses accounting as a calculative practice. This is followed by an examination of how socially driven accounting systems are used in alternative organizations, with particular attention to two selected cases. The final sections present a discussion and concluding remarks.

The role and impact of accounting in organizations and society

Marx (1974a, 1974b) and Weber (1947, 1978, 1992) both highlighted the relationship between accounting or bookkeeping and capitalism. According to Marx (1974a, 1974b), it is important for a capitalist to keep a set of books to calculate transformations of the forms of capital from commodities into money, and from money into commodities. For Weber (1978), the spirit of capitalism is a process of rationalization, with accounting being an essential element in this process. The calculative practices of bookkeeping and both budgeting and capital accounting have helped capitalist enterprises organize their economic activities so as to rationally pursue profits (Weber 1978).

In modern capitalist enterprises, accounting is generally perceived as a "business technology" with the purpose of providing a reliable and accurate record of the transactions of an organization. It performs the task of providing financially oriented information to permit informed judgements and decisions by internal users, namely managers (management accounting), and also by interested external users, such as investors, tax agencies and banks (financial accounting). However, the use of accounting is not limited to rational/economic decision making and control; it can also be used symbolically to provide rational structures and significance to budgeting, planning and evaluation processes in organizations (Boland and Pondy, 1983; Hopwood, 1983). Accounting systems and language, in the form of numbers, categories (e.g. profits, cost) and records (e.g. profit and loss statement), thus give meaning and visibility to people's experience of organizational problem solving and development (Jayasinghe and Wickramasinghe, 2011).

As both a calculative instrument used for decision-making purposes and a symbolic device for giving meaning to experience (Boland and Pondy, 1983), accounting is basically used for two purposes in organizations:

1. to make sense of transactions, e.g. in planning and decision making
2. to establish the legitimacy of transactions, e.g. hiring and firing employees (Carruthers and Espeland, 1991).

When used in this second way, accounting becomes a "rhetorical strategy" whose purpose is not primarily to inform, but to convince the interested parties (Mueller *et al.*, 2004). Accounting rhetoric is characterized by the use of "accounting logic" (Broadbent, 1998: 272), which emphasizes "hard" information (numbers representing incremental profits, costs, etc.) and creates visibilities in the form of factuality, objectivity and neutrality (Carruthers and Espeland, 1991).

In sociological terms, accounting is viewed as a broader calculative practice, which creates the "visibility" and "measurability" of modern economy and society (Weber, 1978; Miller, 2001). It operates as a dominant force of modern economic life, separating businesses from households, as suggested by Dale in this volume, and enabling the formation of capitalist enterprises. So, accounting and organizations are fundamentally interrelated and interdependent, and the links between them are mutually constitutive. Moreover, the economic calculations in the language of accounting (e.g. numbers, encryptions, records) assist people to organize their operations, standardize their future ambitions, and discount their economic futures for rational decision making (Miller, 2001; Jayasinghe, 2006, 2009). Ultimately, calculative practices tend to recreate the capacities of people and organizations, by rationalizing and influencing their actions (Hopper and Powell, 1985; Miller and Napier, 1993; Hopwood and Miller, 1994; Miller, 2001; Vollmer, 2003; Jayasinghe and Wickramasinghe, 2007).

As we saw in Chapter 3, Weber (1978) distinguished between two major forms of calculative rationalities: "formal" and "substantive". By "formal rationality", of which accounting is a part, Weber referred to the type of decision making which is subject to calculation and value-neutral judgements, and where problems are solved by the application of some technical criteria. This form of rationality has the capacity for controlling activity through calculations. In contrast, "substantive rationality" is an evaluative concept that emphasizes the degree to which decision making is subject to values and an appeal to ethical norms. Substantive rationality is concerned with the substance of the values, ends and needs of specific social groups. That said, economic actions are substantively rational if they are consistent with the values, ends and needs of specific social actors, groups or institutions (Clegg, 1989). In practice, formal rationality tends to conflict with the substantive values of different social groups (Colignon and Covaleski, 1991).

For example, in organizations and communities operating in remote villages in less developed countries (LDCs), the rational "institutional conditions" necessary for the "calculative rationalities" found in modern capitalist organizations and society do not prevail, but are intertwined with more traditional, non-capitalist arrangements (Colignon and Covaleski, 1991; Jayasinghe, 2009). In these contexts, cultural and political values such as reciprocity, trust or patronage often reshape rational imperatives (Taylor, 1979; Jayasinghe and Wikramasinghe, 2007; Jayasinghe, 2009; Cutcher and Mason, this volume). In the specific case examined later in this chapter, local fish merchants have control over the relatively powerless fish workers, and both parties are involved in political and strategic battles over assets, liabilities and profits; accounting practices in this context reflect power relations and conflicting interests (Slater, 2002; Jayasinghe, 2009).

As suggested by Hopwood (1989), accounting calculations have come to be regarded as an "interesting endeavour". As he argues, "[r]ather than being seen as merely residing in the technical domain, serving the role of neutral facilitator of effective decision-making, accounting is slowly starting to be related to the pursuit of quite particular economic, social and political interests" (p. 141). In other words, accounting as a calculative practice is "socially constructed" and "socially constructing"; it is both firmly situated in a particular social, cultural and political context, and reproductive of that context (Tinker and Lowe, 1984; Tinker, 1985). Thus, as an intellectual and pragmatic tool in social domination, accounting calculations are exposed as an ideology; a way of rationalizing or explaining the appropriation of the production of one social class by members of another (Tinker, 1985). For example, during the recent financial crisis, US accounting standards such as fair value accounting have contributed to the failure of the US banking and finance system. Overall, the complicity of accounting in matters such as off-balance sheet financing, manipulation of fair value measurements and misuse of financial instrument accounting systems by bank and finance companies have been reported as a major cause for the global financial crisis (Sikka, 2009). Given this background, the next section introduces the form, role and impact of accounting calculative practices in alternative organizations and, for the purpose of contextualization, two distinct cases are used, one from the global North and one from the global South.

Accounting in alternative organizations

In contrast to modern capitalist enterprises, the accounting practices used in alternative organizations present a spectrum of different characteristics. Despite the presence of high levels of literacy in the form of reading and writing (as in developed economies) and external institutional influence (e.g. NGOs in less developed countries) in terms of training and development, participants in alternative organizations still do not, to a large extent, use fully developed modern accounting systems. Instead, they tend to rely on some historically established shared meanings and substantively rational calculative practices, or use accounting systems "tailor-made" for their organizational purpose. For example, the Local Exchange Trading Systems (LETS) (UK) use traditional barter practices in their trading system, and adopt a token system which is based on reciprocity and trust as their form of accounting (see North, this volume).

There are many unsolved issues regarding how and what to measure and report in the alternative organizations' accounts, as there are no standardized, universally accepted, calculative mechanisms for their social value creation, nor any comparative unit of measurement. The activities of alternative organizations range from macro-level interventions that fill "institutional voids" in societies to micro-level technological solutions for local market failures (Cornforth, 2003). In the context of developed countries such as the UK, most alternative organizations are registered legally either as charities, unincorporated voluntary organizations or community interest companies (CICs). These are commonly identified as social enterprises or networks attempting to enhance or reconfigure existing institutional arrangements to address the inadequate provision or unequal distribution of social and environmental goods. Examples of such organizations in the UK are voluntary and community organizations, community businesses, cooperatives, credit unions, development trusts, fair trade companies and work integration enterprises.

Because of the complexity and diversity of their activities, most alternative organizations struggle to establish a balance between their input factors, such as grants, volunteers, market income, social capital, etc., and their mission objectives, e.g. creating social impacts. Unlike modern capitalist enterprises, these alternative organizations operate across all areas of society and, as a consequence, are associated with a wide diversity of resource inputs, e.g. donations, grants, membership fees, volunteer time, government subsidies, commercial income. In addition, many alternative organizations find it difficult to recruit people with the required skills and competencies in accounting and financial management onto their managerial committees and governance boards. They also struggle between different models of committee and board operations (governance), e.g. community representatives versus expert board members. In particular, this is a problem for grass-roots-driven credit unions, where the organization tends to be informal, with volunteers carrying out operational duties and representing community welfare interest at the board level while the expert directors in areas such as finance tend to encourage ways to establish formal control and ethos.

As suggested by Nicholls (2009, 2010), alternative organizations, such as social enterprises, adopt unique "blended value accounting" systems which involve a range of accounting and disclosure logics used to access resources, and report on organizational missions and strategic objectives to key stakeholders. For instance, their accounting and reporting systems may adopt numerical data such as "financial figures – costs, benefits" to satisfy their regulatory needs (financial values), together with social impact reporting (narrative reporting) such as "community development initiatives" to build and maintain organizational legitimacy and social accountability with other key stakeholders (social values). Furthermore, alternative organizations follow functional reporting practices such as "financial reports and quantitative data" for the purpose of their own performance improvement checks (managerial values). They also undertake so-called "reliable monitoring" of social grant outcomes to facilitate their external resource acquisition effort aimed, for example, at the government (political values). Overall, accounting still plays a key role in the management of alternative organizations, but it is not just a "business technology" as it tends to be perceived in modern capitalist enterprises, but a technology that creates "blended values" to the multiple stakeholders (Nicholls, 2009).

The accounting systems employed in some alternative organizations, such as LETS (see North, this volume) and some other grass-roots organizations such as the Funeral Society and Women's Saving Society in Sri Lanka (Chandrasekara, 2009), take totally different forms to that of capitalist business enterprises. For example, many LETS schemes employ a "reward-token system" and do not use a conventional system of accounts. The system helps to measure and value people's time in the services exchanged. To empower the marginalized, LETS often counts people's time as equal. Rather than following traditional cost plus or target cost pricing approaches, LETS uses three unique approaches to price (value) their member services (Aldridge et al., 2001). One approach involves the use of uniform standard rates for all kinds of work, a second approach uses "caps" and "floors" to control the variance of the rates charged for work, while a third favours a liberal and laissez-faire strategy that devolves responsibility for the pricing of work to the parties involved in the exchange.

Accounting again operates differently in grass-roots-level organizations in rural societies in the global South. In such organizations trust and reciprocity, rather than rationality and generally accepted capital accounting principles (GAAP), constitute the main principles underpinning the accounting calculations (see also Cutcher and Mason, this volume). They adopt historically and culturally established "ethno accounting systems" (Chandrasekara, 2009), where members' savings or funeral allocations are organized in an "oral accounting system" rather than through conventional records or bookkeeping, In the case of the Funeral Society and Women's Savings Society in Sri Lanka, the treasurer (as a trusted member) calculates the total savings and reports orally to the members at informal and formal meetings. The other members trust the figures (numbers) and narratives (how the money was spent) presented by the "caretaker" of the funeral fund. Such socially driven rules, economic calculations and conventions are well supported by the historically established hierarchical structures; and we'll see another example of this with the role of patronage in the local Fish Trading System at Kalametiya in one of our case studies.

The above discussion reflects the complexity and diversity of accounting systems used in alternative organizations. These systems (i.e. blended value accounting systems, reward-token systems and ethno-accounting systems) contrast with generally accepted capitalist accounting systems in that they adopt a spectrum of calculative practices, ranging from written to oral, based on their diverse organizational objectives and contextual needs. These "substantively rational" accounting calculative practices are suited to the values, ends and needs of specific social groups and their institutional environments. Therefore, the information produced by these tailor-made accounting systems is not restricted to measuring financial and economic performances, but is also used by members to make various cultural and political interpretations and justifications.

The following two case studies selected from the UK (Colchester Credit Union Ltd) and rural Sri Lanka (Fish Production System at Kalametiya) are intended to further illustrate the diverse formats, roles and impacts of socially driven accounting systems in alternative organizations. Together, these case studies highlight a range of responses to the challenges of record keeping and information reporting; they also set out a larger landscape of socially driven accounting practices that will be analysed in the subsequent discussion section.

Accounting in Colchester Credit Union Ltd (Essex, UK)

Colchester Credit Union Ltd was formed in 2002 as a savings and loans cooperative targeting people over the age of 18 years who live, work or study in the Colchester Borough or District of Tendring. In addition, there is a Young Savers Club for young people under 18 years, which educates schoolchildren with regard to local savings methods and good money management, with collection points at a number of schools in the Colchester Borough area.

Regenerating the bond of association among community members (common bond), the Colchester Credit Union Ltd organizes safe and easily accessible savings and expands opportunities for the local community to obtain short-term credit facilities (small-scale loans) on fair terms and at reasonable rates. The membership is allowed to have individual savings up to a maximum of £5,000, with the frequency of payments agreed according to the saver's individual circumstances. In order to qualify for loans, the members must have a minimum short period of saving at the credit union, although small-scale emergency loans can be obtained outside this policy according to individual circumstances and needs.

The accounting system at the Colchester Credit Union is based on a specific credit union software called "Curtains Too The SQL", which has been developed by Kesho Systems, a company specializing in the development of credit union software. The software is loosely based on a two-tier structure. The first tier is the domain of the system administrator who sets the basic standards around which the system operates. This can involve setting the rate of interest, the credit period, and general terms and conditions for membership borrowing. The second tier involves the data entry operator, who is responsible for issues such as opening accounts for new members, updating the accounts as and when members pay in/borrow money, credit control, etc. Other than transaction posting on a daily basis, the system also facilitates things such as the preparation of fixed asset schedules, bank reconciliation, quarterly returns and, most importantly, the production of financial statements.

The Colchester Credit Union Ltd has a diversity of resource inputs, including donations from membership, grants from Colchester Borough Council, membership fees, volunteer time and government subsidies. The Credit Union recruits volunteers with the required skills and competencies to manage their accounting system, enter computer data and undertake everyday management activities. The voluntary staff carries out all operational duties, and the organization's board members do not receive any remuneration for their work.

Every year, the Colchester Credit Union Ltd has to file a set of financial statements to the Financial Service Authority (FSA), to fulfil the regulatory requirements. These include financial information in terms of an abbreviated balance sheet and full financial disclosure, such as that regarding incomes and expenditures. Because of these formal obligations, the credit union is compelled to adopt "Generally Accepted Accounting Principles" (GAAP) as required in the Community Interest Companies (CICs) in the UK. The union presents the main financial and social mission information from their annual accounts to their membership at the Annual General Meeting (AGM) in order to communicate their managerial efficiency and establish organizational legitimacy. As such, the credit union's main annual accounts (numerical sections) are carefully structured to reflect both their financial and social impact performances. In addition, they prepare monthly cash flow statements and bank reconciliation statements for their internal financial management purpose. In summary, the Colchester Credit Union Ltd's accounting system targets multiple objectives and creates "blended values". Its financial management and reporting reflects managerial values, social values related to its obligations towards the local community, and political values related to the establishment of organizational legitimacy (Nicholls, 2009).

Accounting in a local fish production system (Kalametiya, Hambanthota District, Sri Lanka)

In a Sri Lankan local fish production and trading system based in the village of Kalametyia, a distinct mode of accounting calculations exists, involving more than numerical computations of costs, profits, losses and returns. As powerful fish merchants dominate the local fish production and trading system, there is considerable disparity of ownership patterns between the local fish merchants and fish workers. This has implications for production relationships in the village economy with respective costs such as capital expenses, labour and materials calculated differently. The hegemonic influence of capitalist fish merchants determines the values of goods, services and labour in terms beyond the parameters of free markets. Furthermore, the seasonality of fish production distorts the accounting period and leads to seasonal accounting systems.

On the basis of tradition, the calculation of profit is inextricably linked with a historically reproduced and culturally accepted norm rather than an economic rationale. The labour process in the fish production system is governed by politics and traditions, rather than economic efficiency. Thus, patronage labour dominates fish production and trading, and provides the basis for informal credit systems, with the resultant calculative practices "rational" only in cultural and political terms. These practices are "readable" and accepted by everybody engaged in the village fish market production and trading system. But these generally accepted practices of recording are embedded in trust relations and oral calculations, rather than in the formal bookkeeping conventions prevalent in modern market systems. The budgeting and financial practices are localized in households under the responsibility of the women who spend the money for various domestic activities.

A key feature of Kalametyia's fish production and trading system is a practical awareness among the villagers of the fish-catch sharing arrangement. The fish landing by a single boat is shared between the boat owner (exclusively male) and his partner(s) who are fish workers, adopting a historically agreed 50–50 formula. Thus, the boat owner is entitled to a 50 per cent share from the daily fish-catch, as he uses his capital for the fishing trip (e.g. production inputs such as craft and oil, and depreciation or damage to craft and fishing nets), while the remaining 50 per cent is allocated to (usually) two fish workers who work on the fishing trip. However, if the owner goes on the trip with one fish worker, then he is entitled to another half of the remaining 50 per cent, so that a single fish worker receives only a quarter of the total fish-catch. As a trip with a multi-day craft, usually involving 28 days of deep sea fishing, requires at least four fish workers, each fish worker receives only one-eighth of the total fish-catch, with 50 per cent of the total fish-catch going to the owner fish merchant, for his capital investment (see Jayasinghe, 2009; Jayasinghe and Thomas, 2009).

As another example, the small-scale fishermen employ "oral records" and "trust" when they pay back loans obtained from the fish merchants to cover their expenses for fish production (e.g. engine oil, baits and boat-hiring cost). In fact, they hand over their fish-catch as a repayment, without relying on any recorded accounting information regarding total debt values. Because of this practice of making loans that are repaid through fish sales at pre-arranged (below-market) prices, the powerful fish merchants trap fishermen into lifelong indebtedness. In the same fashion, the fish merchants carry out an oral cash-flow analysis on fishermen's overall ability to repay before granting the informal loans (normally based on average, daily fish-catch).

This accounting system appears to be an equally applicable common rule for everybody in the fishing village. The practice is historically rooted and culturally bounded, so that everybody must adhere to it. This traditional rule for the calculation of profit and loan payment rates shapes the entire political economy of the village, even though the fish production and finance systems do not necessarily preclude mainstream rationality or formal record-keeping systems.

In comparison with rational accounting systems in modern capitalist enterprises, the accounting employed in local fish production systems primarily manifests itself through the prevalence of oral performances such as the fishing-catch sharing ritual, and is usually accompanied by and grounded in face-to-face social events (see Goody and Watt, 1968). Overall, the Kalametiya fish production and trading system represents a typical example of "ethno-accounting" systems (Chandrasekara, 2009). Thus, while fishermen and fish traders both use basic principles of accounting in terms of profit sharing, pricing and cost calculations, their judgements and interpretations are largely determined by the historically established local cultural and political logics, such as the fish-catch sharing system. Rather than formal rationality, substantively rational logics such as patronage relations dominate their transactions.

In direct contrast to the above, a formally recorded accounting system exists at the local Kalametiya Fishermen's Cooperative Society (KFCS) and its allied Idiwara/Fisheries Bank, both of which have been established from the membership of the local fisher community (mainly fish labourers and small-scale fish merchants) and are managed by office bearers who are elected annually. The KFCS is the main institution that maintains relations with international and national NGOs, as well as with the state institutions (particularly local government), while the Idiwara Bank manages, and is accountable for, the state and NGO allocated funding. The KFCS is mainly responsible for the benefits and welfare of the local community, through its involvement in the distribution of fish production resources and the dissemination of knowledge via training and development programmes in collaboration with the NGOs. For example, fishing boats donated by an international NGO were distributed to the village of Kalametiya by KFCS. Additionally, vulnerable fishermen use cooperative society meetings as a forum for discussing issues such as fishing problems, credit and welfare matters (such as houses, community halls, pre-schools), as well as loans and repayment, and aspects of coastal conservation.

Certain types of accounting reporting are also used to create financial and social accountability at KFCS. Thus, both the Idiwara Bank and KFCS are supposed to prepare accounting reports, progress reports and accounting information on the project expenses (and any return payments made by participants) to the state bureaucracy (e.g. Coast Conservation Department), and provide final reports directly to international donors. This information is expected to be openly available for public scrutiny at open forums, such as AGMs at Idiwara Bank and KFCS. Additionally, as an internal control system, all the Idiwara Bank's transactions are expected to get prior approval from the KFCS.

Overall, the KFCS also adopts a "blended value accounting" system (Nicholls, 2009), using a formally recorded accounting system (similar to Colchester Credit Union Ltd) to achieve the society's various strategic objectives such as financial management, legitimacy and sustainability, and create blended values in financial, social and political terms.

Socially driven accounting and the spectrum of calculative logics in alternative organizations

The previous section has revealed the various forms, roles and impacts of accounting practices in alternative organizations. These alternative organizations are shown to adopt different models of accounting systems and social and economic performance reporting based on the contexts of their operation and their strategic organizational objectives. While it is true that alternative organizations adopt some basic principles from the standard/conventional accounting practices (e.g. GAAP), their unique organizational characteristics (e.g. formal vs. informal, oral vs. written modes of communication, cash vs. reward-token basis) make it difficult for their accounting practices to cohere into formally rational reports of performance.

In this context, accounting in alternative organizations represents innovative and unique practices and disclosure logics based around a set of substantive rationalities to address their own social or environmental objectives (Weber, 1978; Jayasinghe, 2009; Jayasinghe and Thomas, 2009; Nicholl, 2009, 2010). In addition, these alternative models of social accounting practices blur traditional boundaries between business and social spheres, and between the formal and the informal.

Building on the above discussion, the range of socially driven accounting practices (either written or oral) in alternative organizations, i.e. blended value accounting, reward-token accounting and ethno-accounting, can be conceptualized as a "spectrum of calculative logics" (see Table 18.1).

These "calculative logics" represent many different cultural and political economic parameters shared by organizational members to access resources and achieve the strategic objectives and contextual needs of key stakeholders. They do not merely account for financial and economic performances, but also act as cultural and political logics that provide substantively rational justifications for the stakeholders of alternative organizations with regard to the organization's socio-economic performance. These socially driven accounting systems do not represent a prescriptive set of logics for rational accounting calculations and reporting, but

Table 18.1 Socially driven accounting systems and spectrum of calculative logics

	Blended value accounting system	Ethno accounting system	Reward-token system
Form	Use formal and written accounting and reporting systems (GAAP). Adopt rational disclosure logics set by the regulators.	Use oral and written accounting systems and adopt historically, as well as culturally and politically, motivated (substantive rational) calculative logics. Mode of "recording" is embedded in trust relations.	Use a reward-token system for recording. Adopt culturally and politically motivated calculative logic, i.e. count people's time as equal. Doesn't use the conventional system of accounts
Role	Maintain a strategic balance between their input factors, such as grants, volunteers, market income, social capital, etc. and the mission objectives, e.g. creating social impacts. Operate as a "rhetorical strategy".	Facilitate local resource allocations and economic exchanges. Operate as a "rhetorical strategy".	Offer an alternative to capitalist accounting system. Facilitate local trade and exchange systems. Help to measure and value people's time in the exchange. Operate as a "rhetorical strategy".
Impact	Enhance operational performance (better financial management and social impact). Build and maintain organizational legitimacy and help obtain more resources. Create blended values, such as financial, social and political, for multiple stake holders. Symbolically provide rational structures and significance to budgeting, planning and evaluation processes.	Maintain local traditions, historical rules and norms, while reproducing political and economic relations. Symbolically provide substantively rational structures and significance to budgeting, planning and evaluation processes.	Empower marginalized people in the community. Re-create a stronger bond among local communities through reciprocal relations. Symbolically provide substantively rational structures and significance to budgeting, planning and evaluation processes.

Adapted from Boland and Pondy (1983); Hopwood (1983); Nicholls (2009); Chandrasekara (2009): LETSLINK UK (2012)

rather create a calculative basis for substantively rational political and economic behaviour (Weber, 1978).

These substantively rational social accounting calculations promote and capture multiple values for multiple stakeholders, and enable different combinations of accounting logics to be established over time. For instance, the ethno–accounting system prevalent in Kalametiya fish production and trading connects many different social groups such as fish merchants, small-scale fishermen, fish workers, small-scale fish traders, etc. and establish "culturally motivated logics" such as patronage relations as the rational ("right practice") to determine fish market prices and the fish-catch sharing ratio. Following a different logic, the accounting system in Colchester Credit Union Ltd uses blended values (Nicholls, 2009), such as financial and social, to record and report its financial data.

Overall, this "spectrum of calculative logics" in alternative organizations presents distinct sets of practices that can be combined to capture the complexity and diversity of organizational arrangements and impacts.

Depending on the context of an organization's operations, its accounting practices will be subject to the politically motivated interests of its users. This could involve manipulative accounting, responses to financial crises, or political issues affecting budgeting and resource allocation. In general, the economically or culturally and politically motivated "calculative logics" operate as "rhetorical strategies" and are used symbolically to provide rational or substantively rational structures and significance to budgeting, planning and evaluation processes in both mainstream and alternative organizations (Boland and Pondy, 1983; Hopwood, 1983). In particular, as the case analyses in this chapter reveal, decision making in alternative organizations tends to be dominated largely by cultural and political logics rather than rational imperatives. For instance, the main purpose of the LETS reward-token system is to facilitate local economic exchanges (calculative logic) and promote reciprocal relations within the local communities (cultural logic). By using a token system, LETS also provide an alternative to mainstream currency and attempt to create alternative solutions to members' financial issues (political logic) (see North, this volume, for more details).

Concluding remarks

This chapter has presented an analysis of socially driven accounting practices in alternative organizations and, more specifically, of the organizational construction and consumption of accounting calculative practices. It has revealed the ways alternative organizations use accounting to assure their continued existence, access resources, build organizational legitimacy, and gain cultural and political acceptance from the membership. It has proposed a way of conceptualizing socially driven accounting, its form, role and impact, in terms of blended value accounting, ethno-accounting and reward-token accounting.

The chapter has also shown that alternative organizations use both rational as well as substantively rational calculative logics (e.g. political and cultural logics) to calculate and measure their economic and social performances. The accounting practices in most of these organizations draw upon substantively rational and culturally and politically shaped lay conceptions.

Such practices do not constitute generally agreed rational calculative mechanisms (Weber, 1978) and, as a consequence, the interpretive context of a given stakeholder's perspective on the organization's cultural and political performances can directly affect the mode of calculations. This resonates with the findings of Jacobs and Kemp (2002) according to which social capital factors such as patronage, reciprocity and trust dominate the accounting calculations within local production and trading systems and organizations, while mainstream rational accounting techniques and principles are mainly absent from decision making.

The findings also confirm the "socially constructed" and "socially constructing" nature of accounting calculations in organizations (Hopwood, 1983; Tinker and Lowe, 1984; Tinker, 1985). The social accounting practices within alternative organizations have implications not only for the operations of individuals and organizations, but also for society as a whole. For instance, the ethno-accounting system applied in the Kalametiya fish production and trading system becomes an influential mode of management in both organizational and social arrangements. It is used as a powerful tool in social domination and as a way of rationalizing or explaining the appropriation of the daily fish-catch of small-scale fishermen by powerful fish merchants.

Overall, the chapter has attempted to map the landscape of socially driven accounting practices in alternative organizations. However, this has only been a partial inquiry, limited most notably to two short case studies that clearly require further empirical exploration. It would clearly be valuable to use a range of theoretical approaches to further understand social accounting practices, perhaps in terms of their broader organizational functions and institutional settings (e.g. Jayasinghe and Wickramasinghe, 2007; Jayasinghe and Thomas, 2009). Despite these limitations, the empirical analysis drawn from the two cases provides interesting reflections on how alternative organizations use accounting in diverse organizational contexts, and opens the possibility that accounting might be done differently.

Resources

Hopwood, A.G, and Miller, P. (1994) *Accounting as Social and Institutional Practice,* Cambridge: Cambridge University Press.
This book presents a socio-historical analysis of accounting in practice in multiple arenas. It provides an understanding of the conditions and consequences of accounting as a calculative technology.

Jayasinghe, K. and Thomas, D. (2009) Preservation of indigenous accounting systems in a subaltern community. *Accounting, Auditing and Accountability Journal,* 22(3), pp. 351–378.
Based on a case study, this paper reveals how indigenous ethno-accounting practices are mobilized in the daily life of subaltern communities. Its findings reflect the role of social accounting as the common language of the inhabitants in their everyday life.

LETSLINK UK (2012): www.letslinkuk.net/
This website provides detailed accounts of the LETS activities and explains how the reward-token system operates as an alternative currency in local exchanges.

Nicholls, A. (2009) We do good things, don't we?: "Blended Value Accounting" in social entrepreneurship. *Accounting, Organizations and Society,* 34, pp. 755–769.
This paper focuses on the emergent reporting practices used by social entrepreneurs to achieve their institutional and strategic objectives. Based on the findings from five in-depth case studies, it develops a new theoretical construct termed "blended value accounting" by the author.

Weber, M. (1978, 1956) *Economy and Society,* Berkeley, CA: University of California Press.
This book provides a comprehensive analysis and comparison of social structures and orders in history. It reveals how the protestant ethos in Western society has contributed to rational economic development.

References

Aldridge, T.J., Tooke, J., Lee, R., Leyshon, A., Thrift, N. and Williams C.C. (2001) Recasting work: The example of Local Exchange Trading Schemes. *Work, Employment & Society,* 15(3), pp. 565–579.
Boland, R.J. Jr. and Pondy, L.R. (1983) Accounting in organizations: A union of natural and rational perspectives. *Accounting, Organizations and Society,* 8(2/3), pp. 223–234.
Broadbent, J. (1998) The gendered nature of "accounting logic": Pointers to an accounting that encompasses multiple values. *Critical Perspectives on Accounting,* 9(3), pp. 267–297.
Carruthers, B.G. and Espeland, W.N. (1991) Accounting and rationality: Double-entry book keeping and the rhetoric of economic rationality. *The American Journal of Sociology,* 97(1), pp. 31–69.
Chandrasekara, I. (2009) Why is finance critical? A dialogue with a women's community in Sri Lanka. *Ephemera: Theory and Politics in Organization,* 9(4), pp. 300–317.
Clegg, S.R. (1989) *Frameworks of Power,* London: Sage.

Colignon, R. and Covaleski, M. (1991) A Weberian framework in the study of accounting. *Accounting, Organizations and Society*, 16(2), pp. 141–157.

Cornforth, C. (ed.) (2003) *The Governance of Public and Non-profit Organizations: What Do Boards Do?*, London: Routledge.

Goody, J. and Watt, I. (1968) The consequences of literacy. In J. Goody (ed.), *Literacy in Traditional Societies* (pp. 27–68), New York: Cambridge University Press.

Hopper, T. and Powell, A. (1985) Making sense of research into the organizational and social aspects of management accounting: A review of its underlying assumptions. *Journal of Management Studies*, 22(5), pp. 429–465.

Hopwood, A.G. (1983) On trying to study accounting in the contexts in which it operates. *Accounting, Organizations and Society*, 8(2–3), pp. 287–305.

Hopwood, A.G. (1989) Organizational contingencies and accounting configurations. In B. Friedman and L. Ostman (eds), *Accounting Development – some perspectives – in Honour of Sven-Eric Johansson* (pp. 23–44), Stockholm: Economic Research Insitute.

Hopwood, A.G, and Miller, P. (1994) *Accounting as Social and Institutional Practice*, Cambridge: Cambridge University Press.

Jacobs, K. and Kemp, J. (2002) Exploring accounting presence and absence: Case studies from Bangladesh. *Accounting, Auditing & Accountability Journal*, 15(2), pp. 143–161.

Jayasinghe, K. (2006) Micro-entrepreneurship in a rural community of Sri Lanka: A phenomenological study of emotionality, power and calculative practice. Unpublished PhD thesis. Bradford: University of Bradford.

Jayasinghe, K. (2009) Calculative practices of the rural: Emotionality, power and micro-entrepreneurship development. PhD monograph. Germany: VDM Publishers.

Jayasinghe, K. and Thomas, D. (2009) Preservation of indigenous accounting systems in a subaltern community. *Accounting, Auditing and Accountability Journal*, 22(3), pp. 351–378.

Jayasinghe, K. and Wickramasinghe D. (2007) Calculative practices in a total institution. *Qualitative Research in Accounting and Management*, 4(3), pp. 183–202.

Jayasinghe, K. and Wickramasinghe, D. (2011) Power over empowerment: Encountering development accounting in a Sri Lankan fishing village. *Critical Perspectives on Accounting*, 22(4), pp. 396–414.

Marx, K. (1974a, 1887) *Capital* Volume I, London: Lawrence & Wishart.

Marx, K. (1974b, 1893) *Capital* Volume II, London: Lawrence & Wishart.

Miller, P. (2001) Governing by numbers: Why calculative practices matter. *Social Research*, 68(2), pp. 379–396.

Miller, P. and Napier, C. (1993) Genealogies of calculation. *Accounting, Organizations and Society*, 18, pp. 631–647.

Mueller, F., Sillince, J., Harvey, C. and Howorth, C. (2004) Discourses, rhetorical strategies and arguments: Conversations in an NHS Trust Hospital Board. *Organization Studies*, 5(1), pp. 75–93.

Nicholls, A. (2009) We do good things, don't we?: "Blended Value Accounting" in social entrepreneurship. *Accounting, Organizations and Society*, 34, pp. 755–769.

Nicholls, A. (2010) The legitimacy of social entrepreneurship: Reflexive isomorphism in a pre-paradigmatic field. *Entrepreneurship Theory and Practice*, 34(4): pp. 611–633.

Sikka, P. (2009) Financial crisis and the silence of the auditors. *Accounting, Organizations and Society*, 34(6–7), pp. 868–873.

Slater, D. (2002) From calculation to alienation: Disentangling economic abstractions. *Economy and Society*, 31(2), pp. 234–249.

Taylor, J.G. (1979) *From Modernization to Modes of Production: A Critique of the Sociologies of Development and Underdevelopment*, London: Macmillan.

Tinker, T. (1985) *Paper Prophets: A Social Critique of Accounting*, New York: Praeger.

Tinker, T. and Lowe, E.A. (1984) One dimensional management science: Towards a technocratic consciousness. *Interfaces*, March–April.

Vollmer, H. (2003) Book keeping, accounting, calculative practice: The sociological suspense of calculation. *Critical Perspectives on Accounting*, 14(3), pp. 353–381.

Weber, M. (1947) *The Theory of Social and Economic Organization*, New York: Free Press.

Weber, M. (1978, 1956) *Economy and Society*, Berkeley, CA: University of California Press.

Weber, M. (1992, 1930) *The Protestant Ethic and the Spirit of Capitalism*, London: Routledge.

19

The commons

Massimo De Angelis and David Harvie

Hang the man and flog the woman
Who stole the goose from off the common
But let the greater criminal loose
Who stole the common from the goose.

Popular rhyme, originating in the seventeenth century

The leaves, the roots, the trunk, the orchard, and the ecosystem? It is our Western conceit to focus on the apple.

David Bollier

We live in the midst of a social and economic crisis, one of the worst in capitalism's history; at the same time the environmental crisis, according to the predictions of the vast majority of scientists, is approaching catastrophe. Neither states nor markets seem able to offer solutions. On the contrary, many believe that they are the main sources of these crises. It is in this context that talks of – and social movements for – commons have become not only increasingly commonplace, but also increasingly relevant. In general terms, the commons are social systems in which resources are shared by a community of users/producers, who also define the modes of use and production, distribution and circulation of these resources through democratic and horizontal forms of governance. Such commons are not utopias, if nothing else because they exist and are produced vis-à-vis a social force – capital – that often demands their *co-optation*, if not *enclosure*. In this chapter we will examine various conceptualizations of commons, tracing a brief history of commons thinking in the process, before concluding that commons are essential to both capital and anti-capitalist social movements – and will therefore be a key focus of social antagonism over the next century.

Introduction

Talk of commons has become commonplace. Interest in the category reached a new plateau in 2009 with the award of the Nobel Memorial Prize in Economic Sciences to political economist Elinor Ostrom, for her 'analysis of economic governance, especially the commons'.

But commons (and common goods) have not always been so mainstream. Indeed, until a few years ago, the category was all but forgotten and seemed an intellectual and political back-water. So-called primitive accumulation, the process by which commons are enclosed, was understood to be a one-off process; moreover, a process that was completed several centuries ago. For example, in England 'enclosures' is a term which is usually assumed to refer to some-thing that happened in the sixteenth century. Thus commons could only be of historical interest.

In this chapter, we begin by challenging this understanding of enclosures as a one-off, historical event. We instead suggest that primitive accumulation is better interpreted as a continuous process, an interpretation that opens up the possibility that commons may still exist. We then review arguments in favour of enclosing – that is, destroying – commons, focusing on Garret Hardin's influential 1968 'tragedy of the commons' argument. In the next two sections, we critically assess two recent intellectual traditions that not only refute Hardin's thesis, but expand our understanding of the way in which commons may be sustained and extended: first, that of Ostrom and the International Association for the Study of Commons, whose primary focus is (material) resource systems; and, second, that of the peer-to-peer network, which is more focused on software and other forms of information commons.

In the final part of the chapter we return to the relationship between commons and capital. We suggest that capital might need a commons 'fix' in order to resolve its crisis (and avoid ecological and social catastrophe), but that commons also constitute the basis for anti-capitalist modes of social organization. We thus suggest that commons are the terrain of a clash between capital and commonism.

'Letters of blood and fire': enclosures, the flipside of commons

Our discussion begins with the flipside of commons, with the process that results in their destruction: enclosures or primitive accumulation. (Throughout the chapter we use the terms 'enclosures' and 'primitive accumulation' interchangeably.) According to the traditional Marxist interpretation, Marx's concept of primitive accumulation indicates the historical process that gave birth to the preconditions of a capitalist mode of production. These precon-ditions refer mainly to: first, the creation of a section of the population with no other means of livelihood but their labour-power – their capacity to work – which must be sold on an emerging labour market in exchange for wages; and, second, the accumulation of capital that may be used for emerging industries.

In part 8 of the first volume of *Capital*, which remains essential reading, Karl Marx provides rich historical detail of this process as it occurred in England (where it has 'the classic form') and Scotland over the course of the sixteenth, seventeenth and eighteenth centuries. He describes the frequently violent way in which peasants, serfs, bondsmen and other 'commoners' were forcibly expelled from the unowned land that had sustained them – from Henry VIII's Dissolution of the Monasteries, to the Highland 'Clearances', to Parliamentary Acts of Enclosure. He describes the 'bloody legislation against the expropriated', the extensive series of laws against 'vagabondage', with vicious penalties for those that broke them, by which those newly created proletarians were further 'encouraged' to become wage-labourers. And he describes the 'genesis' of both the capitalist farmer and of the industrial capitalist, who were the beneficiaries of this process of expropriation: they gained either from 'augmented' stocks of land and livestock or from a plentiful supply of 'free' labourers – or both. Contrasting his account of the origins of the capitalist mode of production to that of Adam Smith and 'Political Economy', Marx summarizes:

> As a matter of fact, the methods of primitive accumulation are anything but idyllic. . . .
> [T]he history of [nascent wage-workers'] expropriation, is written in the annals of
> mankind in letters of blood and fire.
>
> *(Marx 1976: 874–875)*

In this conception, the adjective 'primitive' corresponds to a clear-cut temporal dimension that separates the past understood as *feudalism* from the present understood as *capitalism*. However, by focusing on a definition of capital as social relation, rather than as capital as 'stock' as in Adam Smith, Marx's definition of primitive accumulation leads to another possible interpretation.[1] For primitive accumulation to be a precondition of accumulation, it must be a precondition to *the exercise of capital's power*. But the exercise of capital's power is nothing else but human production – or humans' creative and purposive activity – carried out through the relation of separation that characterizes capital. With his discourse on 'primitive accumulation', Marx is thus able to point out the presupposition of this capital-relation: 'a complete separation between the workers and the ownership of the conditions for the realisation of their labour'. From this it follows that 'so-called primitive accumulation. . . is nothing else than the historical process of divorcing the producer from the means of production' (Marx 1976: 874–875).

There is, however, a problem in the way that the traditional Marxist literature has dealt with the issue of enclosures. Primitive accumulation is marginalized from theory by making it not just a question of genealogy, but of genealogy within a *linear* model of development. The narrative goes something like this: before capitalism there are enclosures or 'primitive accumulation'. These processes of expropriation are preconditions of capitalism because they create and develop markets for commodities such as labour-power and land. But once the job is done, we can stop talking about enclosures (or primitive accumulation) and must talk instead about 'capital logic'. 'Primitive accumulation' and 'capital logic' are thus distinctly separated, both theoretically and temporally (or spatially) – and social practices occurring right in front of scholars' noses are ignored as having nothing to do with real and ongoing enclosures, since in their framework these have *already occurred* at some time in the past. (For more on this argument see De Angelis 2007, especially pp. 133–149.)

The account which suggests enclosure has already happened is problematic, both theoretically and politically. Theoretically, because if we understand capital not as a totalized *system*, but rather as a *social force* with totalizing drives coexisting with other drives which limit it, then we can argue that enclosures are not a one-off occurrence but instead a continuous characteristic of 'capital logic'. In fact, primitive accumulation plays a central role in the world we live in; we can understand it as a *value practice* clashing with other value practices.[2] As noted in Chapter 1 of this volume, one drive is capital's, to make and remake the world through commodification and enclosures; another drive is that of 'commoners' or 'humanity' to make and remake the world through counter-enclosures and commons. 'Class struggle' was how Marx described the clashing of these social forces and their correspondent value practices; Karl Polanyi (2001) theorized the resulting social development in terms of a 'double movement of society'.

The traditional framework is problematic politically because the confinement of enclosures to a question of genealogy *within* a linear model of capitalist development paralyses Marxian-inspired contributions on the question of 'alternatives'. (Here we understand 'paralysis' to mean a state of powerlessness, an incapacity to act.) Indeed, in the linear model of historical development inherited and practised by classical Marxism, the alternative to capita*lism* can only be another 'ism'. Thus ongoing struggles within global justice and solidarity movements are not appreciated for what they are: budding alternatives to capital. Marxian-inspired thinking frequently cannot connect the intellectual and political endeavours to shape alternatives in the here and now because its framework is *for* another 'ism' projected into an unqualified future, and generally defined by a model of power that needs a political elite to tell 'the masses' why power cannot be exercised from the ground up, starting from the now.

We owe much of this understanding of primitive accumulation to the political and theoretical work of the Midnight Notes Collective, who recovered the twin concepts of enclosures and commons as still-relevant political-economic categories in their 1990 document *The New Enclosures*. Midnight Notes coined the term 'new enclosures' to understand processes at work both in Africa and Latin America, in the wake of the international debt crisis of the 1980s, as the International Monetary Fund and the World Bank imposed so-called Structural Adjustment Programmes (SAPs); also, in cities such as New York and Zurich, there were fierce struggles around urban space and gentrification. SAPs involved privatization, liberalization of markets, removal of subsidies and price controls of food staples and other essentials such as cooking oil and . . . land enclosures. Silvia Federici described what was at stake:

> [T]o this day at least 60% of the African population lives by subsistence farming, done mostly by women. Even when urbanized, many Africans expect to draw some support from the village, as the place where one may get food when on strike or unemployed, where one thinks of returning in old age, where, if one has nothing to live on, one may get some unused land to cultivate from a local chief or a plate of soup from neighbours and kin.
>
> *(Federici 1990: 11)*

Reflecting on this 'discovery', three decades on, another member of the Midnight Notes Collective writes:

> It took a while after my arrival [in Nigeria] for me to recover and begin to ask, where is the class struggle here? The answer that eventually came was a surprise to me: *the commons still existed in Nigeria* and made it possible for many who are outside of the waged labor market to have collective access to land and for many waged workers with ties to the village common land to subsist when on strike.
>
> *(Caffentzis 2010: 28; emphasis added)*[3]

'The tragedy of the commons': in defence of enclosure

Primitive accumulation has not only its critics, but also its defenders and proponents. Commenting on the same processes described in *The New Enclosures*, for example, *The Economist* insisted that Africa's land 'must be enclosed, and traditional rights of use, access and grazing extinguished', because everywhere 'it is private ownership of land that has made capital work' (cited by Federici 1990: 11). Here *The Economist* is echoing the assessment of two influential economic historians on the 'old' English enclosures: 'Nevertheless, enclosure was necessary because not all open-field villages showed much progress or efficiency and because even where there was progress there were limits' (Chambers and Mingay 1966: 52).

For the past 500 years (that is, from the very first acts of enclosure in sixteenth-century England), a lively argument about primitive accumulation – with great political import, of course – has raged, from pulpits and university lecterns, and on the pages of tracts, pamphlets, books and scholarly journals. Rather than attempting to review this now-sprawling debate, we instead focus on one key contribution, by ecologist Garret Hardin. In his seminal article, 'The tragedy of the commons', published in the prestigious journal *Science*, Hardin (1968) describes a group of herders sharing common grazing land, to which each has open and free access. Hardin argues that since each herder wants to maximize the fodder for his or her cattle, or the number of animals feeding, this will inevitably lead to a problem of resource depletion.

According to Hardin, the 'rational herdsman' will keep increasing the size of his herd, because he receives all the benefits from grazing an additional animal, while the costs of over-grazing are shared by all. Of course, 'each and every rational herdsman sharing a commons' will make the same decision.

> Therein is the tragedy. Each man is locked into a system that compels him to increase his herd without limit – in a world that is limited. Ruin is the destination toward which all men rush, each pursuing his own best interest in a society that believes in the freedom of the commons. Freedom in a commons brings ruin to all.
>
> *(1968: 1244)*

Hardin's analysis is relevant to the problem of pollution and climate change. Indeed he states that the

> rational man finds that his share of the cost of the wastes he discharges into the commons is less than the cost of purifying his wastes before releasing them. Since this is true for everyone, we are locked into a system of 'fouling our own nest,' so long as we behave only as independent, rational, free-enterprisers.
>
> *(ibid.)*

This approach to commons has some clear policy and political-economic implications. To avoid the tragedy, Hardin advocates replacing commons rights with private property rights (where possible) or direct state management (where not). In other words, Hardin advocates enclosure.

Hardin's *Science* paper has been cited tens of thousands of times and remains enormously influential. But the analysis is partial. Hardin analyses commons; yet entirely absent from this analysis is any consideration of community or common*ers*, of common*ing*. To be more precise, Hardin's commons are populated by a collection of selfish, maximizing individuals. In other words, the problem with Hardin's model concerns the fact that its players are cast in a rationality and measuring process that is uniquely the type of subject portrayed by capital: *Homo economicus* – neo-liberal economic man. We can uncover the 'apologetics' and 'vulgarity' of this argument only by reclaiming different types of measures for ourselves.

From tragedy to comedy: the scholarly rehabilitation of the commons

An important moment in the intellectual rehabilitation of the commons was the establishment, in 1989, of the International Association for the Study of Common Property, which in 2006 became the International Association for the Study of the Commons (IASC). A key figure in this current of thinking was political scientist Elinor Ostrom, who, over a number of important contributions, spanning several decades until her death in 2012, has explored the institutional arrangements that govern 'common property'. The work of Ostrom – and her IASC colleagues and coworkers – thus provides a convincing refutation of Hardin.

		Subtractability of use	
		High 'rivalrous' good	Low 'non-rivalrous' good
Difficulty of excluding potential beneficiaries	High	Common-pool resources (common goods): groundwater basins, lakes, irrigation systems, fisheries, forests, etc.	Public goods: peace and security of a community, national defence, knowledge, fire protection, weather forecasts, etc.
	Low	Private goods: food, clothing, automobiles, etc.	Toll goods (club goods): theatres, private clubs, daycare centres, cable television

Figure 19.1 Commons as a type of good (adapted from Ostrom (2010: fig. 1))

Ostrom (1990) had no difficulty in pointing out that the model set up by Hardin was not one of a *commons*, but a case of *open access*. For Ostrom, commons are

> where the members of a clearly demarked group have a legal right to exclude non-members of that group from using a resource. Open access regimes (*res nullius*) – including the classic cases of the open seas and the atmosphere – have long been considered in legal doctrine as involving no limits on who is authorized to use a resource.
>
> *(Ostrom 2000: 335–336)*

If Hardin's pasture was a commons, the community (or communities) that utilized it would have set up rules of access and governance to ensure its sustainability. Through this communal governance of the shared resource, with correspondent systems of monitoring and enforcement, the 'tragedy' of resource depletion is avoided. Ostrom thus begins the journey of conceptualization of commons as social systems.

The starting point for Ostrom's analysis of commons is the 2×2 matrix by which she classifies different types of good (see Figure 19.1). Her focus tends to be on the top-left cell: goods that are *rivalrous* (my consumption of the good detracts from yours), but for which it is hard for me to prevent you from consuming the good. That is, she focuses on the commons as analysed by Hardin. But what makes such resources *commons* is that set of rules preventing the tragedy Hardin thought inevitable. Analysing several empirical studies, Ostrom goes on to distil eight such rules or 'design principles' necessary for sustainable commons:

1. *User boundaries* and *resource boundaries*: legitimate users must be clearly separated from non-users; the common pool resource must be clearly separated (or distinguished) from its wider environment.
2. *Congruence with local conditions*: the rules that govern the commons must be appropriate to the local social and environmental conditions.
3. *Collective-choice arrangements*: individuals affected by the resource regime must be able to participate in making and modifying its rules.
4. *Monitoring of users* and *monitoring of the resource*: users of the resource monitor other users' appropriation of the resource and the condition of the resource.

5. *Graduated sanctions*: there are sanctions for violations of the rules, which start very low but become more severe for repeat violators.
6. *Conflict resolution mechanisms*: arenas exist for the rapid and low-cost resolution of conflicts amongst users.
7. *Minimal recognition of rights*: local users' rights to make their own rules are recognized by the government.
8. *Nested enterprises*: when a common-pool resource is connected to a larger social-ecological system, there are multiple and nested layers of governance (Ostrom 2010: 422).

In this tradition, commons are defined as common pool *resources* (CPRs), and resources are understood, although with some limitations, in terms of *systems* that are operationally closed.

> The term 'common-pool resource' refers to a natural or man made resource system that is sufficiently large as to make it costly (but not impossible) to exclude potential benefi-ciaries from obtaining benefits from its use . . . . Examples of resource systems include fishing grounds, groundwater basis, grazing areas, irrigation canals, bridges, parking garages, mainframe computers, and streams, lakes, oceans, and other bodies of water.
>
> *(Ostrom 1990: 30)*

The following three 'classical' examples of 'sustainable' traditional commons, in which community decisions set the boundary of what is 'sustainable', demonstrate the limitations of Hardin's analysis.

> Every spring, as the snow melts and the edelweiss blooms, Swiss farmers coax their dairy cows out of the valleys and up into Alpine meadows to graze. In each village, the farmers decide collectively how many cows each farmer can send to the mountain commons. That decision is based on the number of cows the farmer can overwinter, which is, in turn, based on the farmer's valley pasturage and barn space. Overwintering capacity has little connection, if any, to the meadow's grazing capacity but somehow the system works. And it has worked year after year, with no evidence of overgrazing, for at least 500 years. . . .
>
> In the Lofoten Islands in the far north of Norway, a portion of the cod fishery is set aside for sail-powered boats. Factory trawler ships are prohibited entirely. These Norwegians know perfectly well that modern techniques would bring them greater yields. But they're not sure modern techniques will ensure them fish for their lifetime and that of their children and grandchildren. Despite repeated attempts by the govern-ment to emphasize revenues, the fishermen's primary goal is not maximum yield or profit; it's a secure fishery. The result is a relatively 'inefficient' management regime, but one with a track record: 100 years of successful management . . . and some 500 years of cod export to the Mediterranean. Similar stories can be told for long-standing small-scale, inshore fisheries around the world. . . .
>
> On Marajo Island, a large chunk of land in the mouth of the Amazon River, ranchers graze beef cattle on native grasses, getting respectable but not great yields of meat. Nearby, on the mainland, ranchers use modern methods of feeding to produce superior quantities of beef. The land and water in the mainland ranches are degrading, though, making uncertain whether their practices can continue. Meanwhile, the Marajo ranchers are expected to continue their relatively low-yield practices for a long time to come. After all, they've been doing it for some 400 years.
>
> *(Princen 2005: 23)*

An important theoretical distinction is that between the *resource system* and the *flow of resource units* that the system produces, and which are appropriated by individuals. We can understand the resource system as a stock variable, while the number of resource units it yields is a flow variable. As we would expect, there is a maximum flow of resource units above which a resource system is unsustainable. According to Ostrom and her IASC colleagues, it is the resource system which can be a commons (say a forest, a river, sea waters along the coast and so on), not the resource units (woods, water and fish) that are individually appropriated by the members of the community. Within this framework, resource units, such as the fish removed from a fishery (which fall into the bottom-left cell of Figure 19.1), are not part of the commons, since they 'are not subject to joint use or appropriation' (Ostrom 1990: 31).

This understanding of commons is summed up by one of Ostrom's IASC colleagues:

> The word 'commons' refers to resources for which people do not have to pay for to exercise their user and access rights within a confine of a set of institutions or rules to protect the resources from overuse by people who do not respect the resources' fragility or limits.
>
> *(Jumbe 2006: 5)*

The Ostrom/IASC definition certainly captures some crucial aspects of commons. The realm of the shared is understood as being a realm beyond the money nexus and therefore a realm in which social connectivity is not mediated by commodity relations, but by institutional forms of participatory governance that sustain the shared resource system by regulating individual appropriation.

But there are, in fact, also many examples of common property *regimes* which have not been based on common-pool resources, where the fish are cooked in a communal pot; here resource units are pooled together by a community of users, who then establish the governance rule of the common pool.

> [M]oney income, personal belongings, literary texts, and even children have been communalized. Thus the 15th century Taborites' first act of forming their community was to dump all their personal belongings in large open chests and begin their communal relations on an even footing.
>
> *(Federici 2004: 54)*

> On the basis of the history of common property regimes it is difficult to decide what types of goods are 'conducive' to private property and what kinds of goods are 'conducive' to common property.
>
> *(Caffentzis 2004: 22)*

So what the IASC definition fails to capture is that both resources might be claimed as commons, such as city-centre public spaces (as in the Occupy movement of 2011) and also 'rivalrous' goods ('resource units') that communities might collectively decide to treat as commons by pooling them into a 'common pot'. We will return to these questions in the final section, where we discuss common*ing*.

From peer to peer: the creation of the 'information commons'

Ostrom and the IASC have traditionally focused on physical resources. More recently, however, there has been a growing trend to also consider as commons immaterial 'public goods', such as knowledge and information. For example, the starting point for the scholars and activists of the Foundation for P2P [peer-to-peer] Alternatives is information: software, scientific databases, the electro-magnetic spectrum, the arts and so on. Such 'things' have no physical limits that must be managed to ensure 'sustainability'; they are 'non-rivalrous' goods, in the sense that your use of the good does not limit mine or anyone else's, and fall into the right-hand cells of Figure 19.1. In fact, when limits in the use of these resources are present, they are entirely socially constructed, embedded in processes of enclosures promoted by state policies on 'copyright' and 'intellectual property'.

More recently the P2P Foundation has extended its understanding of commons from cyberspace into other realms. This gives rise to long lists of commons types and several possible taxonomies of commons. A key classification relates to a commons' material quality. Thus Michael Bauwens, the P2P Foundation's founder, distinguishes three categories: 'inherited commons', such as earth, water and forests; 'immaterial commons', essentially information and 'culture'; and 'material commons', which are human-created resources, such as 'common stock, common machinery' (Betz 2011).

There is much to inspire in the peer-to-peer commoners' extensive understanding of commons and there is no doubt that they are giving shape to their own autonomous and non-commodified social space (see Rossiter and Zehle, this volume). There is much we can learn from these practices; and we should also remember that the evolution of social networks has allowed the acceleration of waves of social movements – witness the North African revolutions of 2011 (see Mason 2012: 127–152; and Maeckelbergh, this volume). According to Bauwens, this is a

> form of human network-based organisation which rests upon the free participation of equipotent partners, engaged in the production of common resources, without recourse to monetary compensation as a key motivating factor, and not organised according to hierarchical methods of command and control.
>
> *(2005: 1)*

Although there have been attempts to theorize and expand P2P production into 'material' domains, in their purest form such commons are underpinned by Internet-based coordination. Examples include the online, free encyclopedia, Wikipedia, and the thousands of applications of FLOSS – Free/Libre/Open Source Software. In all these cases, resources are shared and there exists no central place of decision-making; instead decisions emerge from the free cooperation and free association of producers, all of whom participate freely in the creation of the (mainly digital) 'output'.

But we must sound a note of caution too. Any expansion of digital commons must also problematize these commons' relationship to sustenance commons (and their potential enclosure). At present, the peer-to-peer commoning that goes on in cyberspace (i.e. in the realm of immaterial commons) does not resonate with the experience of commoners who depend on material resources for their reproduction. For it is these material resources – water and fossil fuels, as well as rare minerals and ores – that are enclosed and privatized so as to produce the IT infrastructure upon which the digital commons depend.

Richard Pithouse, an activist and researcher involved in the community struggles of the poor in Durban, South Africa, puts it in this way:

> My first concern about all the P2P stuff . . . is . . . the fact that it depends on both other modes of labour and extraction (like digging coltan in the Eastern Congo)[4] and other

modes of enforced and very material (guns, fences, guards, borders, etc.) social division within and between societies.

(Pithouse 2010)

Any distinction between immaterial and material therefore becomes meaningful only from the perspective of relatively *isolated* spheres of practice. In the P2P Foundation approach, the various spheres – and, indeed, the various types of commons within these spheres – are *operationally closed*: that is, the social practices in each sphere occur *as if* there were no relation between the different spheres. In short, despite the global information and technology industry accounting for roughly 2 per cent of global CO_2 emissions (on a par with aviation), with every Google search causing an estimated 5–10 g of CO_2 to be emitted (boiling a kettle results in 15 g of emissions) (Leake and Wissner-Gross n.d.), this is *not* a problem for the peer-to-peer commoner at the moment in which 'exploitation' or 'climate change' are typed into a search engine.

From the perspective of another world – which is possible if we accept the alter-globalist slogan – and the constitution of new social relations, then this isolation of operationally closed systems must be overcome if commons are to form the basis of any transformative politics.

Capital's commons 'fix' versus commoning

We started this chapter by discussing the enclosure of commons as part of a process of capitalist 'development' and (primitive) accumulation. In this final section we return to an explicit discussion of capital. We explore both the possibility of a new 'accommodation' between capital and the commons, and that of moving beyond capital through practices of commoning.

The award of the Nobel prize to Elinor Ostrom was undoubtedly a significant moment in the history of the conceptualization of the commons. (It was also a significant moment in the history of the economics Nobel, for Ostrom was the first woman and the first non-economist to receive it.) Her award may well reflect the fact that there are some forces pushing a paradigm shift in economics. Possibly this award is as significant as Hayek's in 1974, which anticipated the shift from Keynesian to neo-liberal orthodoxy. This should be an occasion for celebration – but also for concern. Celebration, because Nobel-prize recognition puts commons discourse firmly within the mainstream, in turn making more visible emancipatory politics grounded in commons. Concern, because any paradigm shift signalled by the Nobel may not be an epistemic shift *away* from capitalism, but rather a paradigm shift *within* the strategies of management of capitalist social relations.

With the ongoing crisis that started in 2007/8, capitalism has clearly reached an impasse. If accomplished purely on capital's terms, overcoming this impasse will produce a social and ecological apocalypse at worst, and an intensification of social conflict at best. Capital's difficulty lies in the fact that if the system is to survive it must continue to push for strategies of growth. Growth is necessary not only because of capital's essential need for accumulation, but also as a way to reconcile a profit-maximizing mode of *production* with hierarchical modes of *distribution*. If 'all boats are lifted by a rising tide' there will be less pressure to address the inequality that is contested by struggles for social justice. But today, all the strategies and 'fixes' available to capital to pursue growth in the world system will only intensify the crises of social and ecological reproduction, amplifying and widening the range of resistance even if there is no programmatic focus to this resistance.[5]

A possible way out is a shift in the mode of governance of social relations, or at least a fine-tuning of neo-liberal governance such that it can contain the costs associated with the crisis of social reproduction – these costs include public expenditures necessary to police and control rebellions generated by this crisis. Such a 'fine-tuning' might involve commons, or at least specific, domesticated versions of them. Capital needs a *commons fix* (De Angelis 2012). Since neo-liberalism is not about to give up its management of the world, it will likely have to draw on the commons to help manage the devastation. And if the commons are not there, capital will have to promote them somehow – a strategy George Caffentzis (2005) has described as neo-liberalism's 'plan B'.

But the relation between commons and capital is necessarily ambiguous, since their co-dependence and co-evolution makes it difficult to point out which of the two systems uses the other. We can illustrate this by looking at the paradigmatic function that the 'village commons' has vis-à-vis capital. In a classic study, the anthropologist Claude Meillassoux argued that the work of reproduction and subsistence performed, mostly by women, in the village commons in South Africa allowed male labourers to migrate and be available for various types of waged work. The village commons work reduced the cost of reproduction of these male workers, since the capitalists who hired them did not have to pay for the cost of their upbringing, or contribute to any social security in case of illness, unemployment or old age retirement (1981: 110–111). Meillassoux also recognized the ambiguity of the capital–commons relationship. If the subsistence-producing commons is too 'unproductive', capital loses important aspects of the 'free gift' of labour-power; but if the commons is too 'productive', fewer workers would migrate out of the village commons and would, more generally, have more power to push up wages (Caffentzis 2004).

We can see many other examples of this relationship between commons and capital. (Capital's increasing dependence on commons has not curbed its enthusiasm for continued enclosure, however, as in the case of international land grabs (Bollier 2011). Indeed, primitive accumulation and commons co-optation seem to be the two complementary coordinates of a new capitalist strategy.) We can see it in the World Bank's approach to development in the global South where, for years, it has emphasized the importance of some aspects of commons management, such as pooled resources, community participation and 'trust' as the basis of 'social capital'. We can also see it in Britain, where, since 2010, the Conservative-Liberal-Democrat coalition government is attempting to impose massive public-spending cuts while simultaneously promoting a vision of a 'Big Society' that claims to support community empowerment to address social upheavals. Implicitly rejecting his Conservative predecessor, Margaret Thatcher's, neo-liberal claim that society 'does not exist', David Cameron appears to want to harness society's social power. He claims that governments urgently need to 'open up public services to new providers like charities, social enterprises and private companies so we get more innovation, diversity and responsiveness to public need' and to 'create communities with oomph' (*The Economist* 2010).

Such an approach requires recognizing that resources are not simply financial, and that wealth doesn't just take the form of commodities. Rather, resources and wealth lie dormant in fragmented and atomized communities and must be activated through some form of what Peter Linebaugh (2008) has called *commoning*. Of course, where capital uses the commons as a fix for its crisis, commoning is harnessed by capital and, in turn, the possibilities for expanding commons are constrained. The goal here is not to provide alternatives to capital, but to make a particular node of capital – a region or a city perhaps, a 'sustainable community' – more competitive, while somehow addressing the problems of social reproduction at the same time.

But commons could create a social basis for alternative ways of organizing social production, independent from capital and its prerogatives. Indeed, it is difficult today to conceive of emancipation from capital – and achieving new solutions to the demands of *buen vivir* (good living), social and ecological justice – without at the same time organizing, on the terrain of commons, the non-commodified systems of social production. The depth of today's many crises, directly threatening various aspects of social reproduction (food, social care, health, education), and the failures of markets and states to address these crises – indeed, their co-responsibility in producing them – make the development of commons a necessity.

Since the 1970s, demands for greater democracy have grown ever louder. They have now – in the face of social, economic and ecological crises – reached a crescendo and are reverberating across the planet. We can understand these demands for democracy as grass-roots demands to control the means of social reproduction. But democratic freedoms imply personal investments and *responsibilities*, and negotiating these responsibilities and corresponding social relations and modes of production through the praxis of *commoning* is what constitutes commons. In other words, claiming ownership of the conditions needed for life and its reproduction in itself creates a commons.

We can thus see an important limitation of the Ostrom and IASC tradition, in spite of all its strengths. The institutional forms it conceptualizes as governing the commons serve only the purpose of putting fetters on social action ('a set of institutions or rules to protect the resources from overuse'). These forms are not understood as *also* promoting social practices that put constraints on, and push back, practices based on commodity production and capital accumulation. Struggle is conceptualized only as competition among appropriators; that is, a struggle within the commons, not also as a struggle *of* the commons vis-à-vis an outside social force – capital. But as the continuous character of primitive accumulation demonstrates, the real 'drama of the commons' (Dietz *et al.* 2002) is one in which commons (and commoners) exist within a web of *antagonistic* social relationships, in which – to repeat a point we made above – value practices clash with other value practices.

Thus, if we look carefully, we can see many examples of this type of commoning which are also antagonistic to capital – practices that some may see opening 'cracks' in capitalism (Holloway 2010) and others as expanding the material bases and powers of social forces alternative to capital (De Angelis 2007). In recent years, we have witnessed the development of the Occupy movement in the United States, and mass occupations of squares and plazas in Egypt, Spain and elsewhere. Argentina's financial crisis of 2001 sparked a rebellion which led, in turn, to myriad alternative social practices, including occupations, in which workers took over factories abandoned by the boss (see Atzeni and Vieta, this volume). Such struggles are distinguished by two features. First, their concern with the materialities of social reproduction: what will we eat and who will cook it? What happens if somebody gets sick? Where will we sleep? Where will we shit? And who will clean up? This attention to social reproduction is an organic part of the struggle. Second, in all these cases – and so many others – the social relations amongst participants are horizontal, not vertical, and governance of the common resources is characterized by a democratic participation that includes all in the decision-making process through various forms of consensus.

Conclusion

The 'ambiguity' between commons-within-and-for-capital and commoning-beyond-capital is in fact a razor edge that both capital and social movements must attempt to negotiate. This 'ambiguity' at the heart of the relation between commons and capital means that questions of social powers are pivotal. Moreover, the social contingencies of this struggle between capital and commoners mean that questions of whether a commons can be co-opted or not cannot be addressed *ideologically*. The question of co-optation is instead a matter of strategic power.

Hence, there a double impasse, for both capital and anti-capitalist social movements. Capital needs the commons in order to deal with the crisis. Social movements need to confront not only capital's enclosures of commons, but also its attempts to co-opt commons – and instead to create new, non-capitalist worlds on the basis of commons. Commons are thus a crucial terrain of antagonistic struggle, not only as a *resource* that may or may not be depleted by the actions of competing individuals, but as the site upon which alternative value practices clash. In spite of capital's strategies to deploy a commons fix to its problems, commons may well be part of a different historical trajectory. Capital may help conjure up social powers that will destroy it: in fact, the spectre of *commonism* may already be haunting the planet.

Notes

1 Adam Smith understood capital as the stock of buildings, machinery, raw materials and so on necessary for production (the 'means of production', in Marxist terms). Karl Marx did not reject this
   definition, but he deepened it, such that capital *also* means the social relation whereby one class of
   people (capitalists) owns capital or the means of production, while another class of people (the
   proletariat or working class) owns nothing but its ability to work; to survive, members of the
   working class must therefore labour for capitalists.
2 On value practices see De Angelis (2007), Graeber (2005) and McMurtry (1998); Graeber (2011:
   89–126) discusses the three coexisting, yet alternative, 'moral principles on which economic relations can be founded . . . communism, hierarchy, and exchange'.
3 More recently – and working in a different current of Marxism to Midnight Notes – geographer
   David Harvey also 'rediscovered' and popularized the category of enclosure or primitive accumulation. Harvey, however, prefers to describe the process as 'accumulation by dispossession' (Harvey
   2003).
4 Coltan is a relatively rare ore, whose derivatives are used in the manufacture of mobile phones,
   computers and other similar devices.
5 David Harvey (2007) uses the term 'fix' to discuss different capitalist strategies to deal with crises.

Resources

The Commoner – 'a web journal for other values', with many articles on primitive accumulation,
   commons and commoning: www.commoner.org.uk/
The Foundation for P2P Alternatives: http://p2pfoundation.net/
The International Association for the Study of the Commons: www.iasc-commons.org/
Linebaugh, Peter (2008) *The Magna Carta Manifesto: Liberties and Commons for All*, Berkeley, Los Angeles
   and London: University of California Press.

References

Bauwens, Michel (2005) 'P2P and Human Evolution: Peer to peer as the premise of a new mode of
   civilization', available online at www.networkcultures.org/weblog/archives/P2P_essay.pdf
   (accessed 4 February 2012).
Betz, Anna (2011, 8 August) 'The School spreads its wings: Graceful inaugural flight sets a successful
   precedence', posted to School of Commoning, available online at www.schoolofcommoning.com/
   content/school-spreads-its-wings-graceful-inaugural-flight-sets-successful-precedence (accessed 4
   February 2012).
Bollier, David (2011, 23 April) 'Now underway, an outrageous international land grab', available online
   at www.bollier.org/now-underway-outrageous-international-land-grab (accessed 8 February
   2012).
Caffentzis, George (2004) 'A tale of two conferences: Globalization, neoliberalism and the
   question of the commons', A talk prepared for the Alter-Globalization Conference, 9 August, San

Miguel de Allende, Mexico. Available online at www.commoner.org.uk/?p=96 (accessed 4 February 2012).

Caffentzis, George (2005) 'Dr. Sachs, Live8 and neoliberalism's "Plan B"', in David Harvie, Keir Milburn, Ben Trott and David Watts (eds) *Shut Them Down! The G8, Gleneagles 2005 and the Movement of Movements*, Leeds: Dissent! and Brooklyn, NY: Autonomedia: pp. 51–60.

Caffentzis, George (2010) 'Two themes of Midnight Notes: Work/refusal of work and enclosure/commons', in Craig Hughes (ed.) *Toward the Last Jubilee: Midnight Notes at Thirty Years*, Brooklyn, NY: Autonomedia and Washington, DC: Perry Editions: pp. 24–30.

Chambers, J.D. and G.E. Mingay (1966) *The Agricultural Revolution 1750–1880*, London: Batsford.

De Angelis, Massimo (2007) *The Beginning of History: Value Struggles and Global Capital*, London: Pluto Press.

De Angelis, Massimo (2012) 'Crises, capital and cooptation: Does capital need a commons fix?', in David Bollier and Silke Helfrich (eds) *The Wealth of the Commons: A World Beyond Market and State*, Amerst, MA: Levellers Press.

Dietz, Thomas, Nives Dol#aksak, Elinor Ostrom and Paul C. Stern (2002) 'The drama of the commons', in National Research Council, *The Drama of the Commons*, Committee on the Human Dimensions of Global Change, Elinor Ostrom, Thomas Dietz, Nives Dolšak, Paul Stern, Susan Stonich, and Elke Weber (eds), Washington, DC: National Academy Press.

Economist, The (2010, 12 August) 'Let's hear those ideas', available online at www.economist.com/node/16789766 (accessed 4 February 2012).

Federici, Silvia (1990) 'The debt crisis, Africa and the new enclosures', in Midnight Notes Collective (eds) *The New Enclosures* (Midnight Notes 10): pp. 10–17. Available online at www.midnightnotes.org/newenclos.html and reprinted in Midnight Notes Collective (eds) *Midnight Oil: Work, Energy, War 1973–1992*, Brooklyn, NY: Autonomedia, 1992.

Federici, Silvia (2004) *Caliban and the Witch: Women, the Body and Primitive Accumulation*, Brooklyn, NY: Autonomedia.

Graeber, David (2005) 'Value as the importance of action', *The Commoner*, 10. Available online at www.commoner.org.uk.

Graeber, David (2011) *Debt: The First 5,000 Years*, Brooklyn, NY: Melville House.

Hardin, Garrett (1968) 'The tragedy of the commons', *Science*, 162: 1243–1248.

Harvey, David (2003) *The New Imperialism*, Oxford: Oxford University Press.

Harvey, David (2007) *Limits to Capital*, 2nd edition, London: Verso.

Holloway, John (2010) *Crack Capitalism*, London: Pluto Press.

Jumbe, Charles (2006) 'Short commentary on "The Name Change; or What Happened to the 'P'?", authored by Charlotte Hess and Ruth Meinzen-Dick', *The Commons Digest*, 2. Available online at http://hdl.handle.net/10535/2672 (accessed 26 December 2011).

Leake, Jonathon and Alex Wissner-Gross (n.d.) 'How you can help reduce the footprint of the web', available online at www.sustainablefootprint.org/en/cms/gebruikerscherm.asp?itemId=420; (accessed 4 February 2012).

Linebaugh, Peter (2008) *The Magna Carta Manifesto: Liberties and Commons for All*, Berkeley, Los Angeles and London: University of California Press.

McMurtry, John (1998) *Unequal Freedoms: The Global Market as an Ethical System*, Toronto and Westport, CT: Garamond & Kumarian Press.

Marx, Karl (1976) *Capital: A Critique of Political Economy*, Penguin: Harmondsworth.

Mason, Paul (2012) *Why It's Kicking Off Everywhere: The New Global Revolutions*, London: Verso.

Meillassoux, Claude (1981) *Maidens, Meal and Money: Capitalism and the Domestic Community*, Cambridge: Cambridge University Press.

Ostrom, Elinor (1990) *Governing the Commons: The Evolution of Institutions for Collective Action*, Cambridge: Cambridge University Press.

Ostrom, Elinor (2000) 'Private and common property rights', in Boudewijn Bouckaert and Gerrit De Geest (eds) *Encyclopedia of Law and Economics*, Volume I: *The History and Methodology of Law and Economics*, Cheltenham: Edward Elgar: 332–379. Available online at http://encyclo.findlaw.com/2000book.pdf

Ostrom, Elinor (2010) 'Beyond markets and states: Polycentric governance of complex economic systems', in Karl Grandin (ed.) *The Nobel Prizes 2009*, Stockholm: The Nobel Foundation: 408–444. Available online at www.nobelprize.org/nobel_prizes/economics/laureates/2009/ostrom-lecture.html

Pithouse, Richard (2010) Private correspondence with De Angelis.

Polanyi, Karl (2001) *The Great Transformation: The Political and Economic Origins of Our Time*, Boston, MA: Beacon Press.

Princen, Thomas (2005) *The Logic of Sufficiency*, Cambridge, MA: MIT Press.

20

Scrounging and reclaiming

Jeff Ferrell

Introduction

Around the world, from the wealthiest of cities to the poorest of villages, people engage in the daily process of scrounging and reclaiming discarded food, clothing, electronics, plastics and metal. Often this work is organized and undertaken by those on the margins of contemporary society – the very poor, the urban homeless, rural peasants or members of lower social castes – and often such work is located in society's spatial margins as well – down back alleys or atop isolated landfills. Because of this, widespread scrounging and reclaiming are often easily enough ignored, or imagined to be an issue only for those consigned to it. But in a real sense we, too, are complicit in the process of scrounging. We are privileged enough to have the means of purchasing and consuming the goods offered by contemporary capitalist economies, and these consumerist economies, and the waste that they (and we) inevitably produce, form the primary material basis for global scrounging and reclamation. In this sense it could be said that contemporary scrounging and reclaiming are organized by the dynamics of global consumer capitalism, and by our own everyday patterns of consumption, waste and disposal. Yet, marginal as they may be, those who scrounge the material discards of contemporary society are not simply passive recipients of this waste. Instead, they regularly organize themselves into small-scale communities; they invent mechanisms by which to store, repurpose and redistribute the waste they salvage; and they develop shared structures by which to turn this reclaimed waste into dynamic forms of mutual aid and social change. In this way, contemporary scroungers not only organize themselves and their lives around waste reclamation, they reorganize the waste itself and begin to shape alternative forms of social and economic life.

Scrounging, trash picking and other forms of informal reclamation are pervasive in the United States, Europe and worldwide; while shaped by distinctly contemporary dynamics, these practices also continue a long human history of gleaning, poaching, and otherwise living from the loose ends and leftovers of conventional society. Some of this work today goes forward individually; much of it occurs within the shared spaces of informal communities, illicit subcultures and social movements. Certainly, among the millions who scrounge and reclaim discarded goods worldwide, wide variation exists in cultural practices and day-to-day conventions; as regards organizational arrangements, though, a number of common themes run through many of the collective experiences of scrounging. To begin with, the globalization of capitalism, and the ongoing financial and ecological crises that have accompanied it, increasingly shape the experiences of scrounging and trash picking. Whether homeless persons picking through the consumer waste that accumulates within large European and American cities, or peasants sorting through electronic and computer discards shipped from such cities to villages in southern China or west Africa, the contemporary practice of scrounging and informal reclamation often rests on the distinct dynamics of global capitalism. In mining the discards of global capitalism, though, scroungers regularly invoke a second, contradictory dynamic: a more or less conscious resistance to this global system of consumption and waste, such that they seek to convert its waste into the raw material for alternative forms of organization, economic survival and political engagement. This counter-dynamic is in turn often informed by ideologies of self-reliance and local sustainability. In the United States and Europe, especially, it is further animated by distinctly anarchist and anti-capitalist orientations toward direct action, decentralization and 'dis-organization'. When these orientations are deployed within the spatial and temporal environments of scrounging and trash reclamation – back streets, background spaces, and unnoticed aftermaths of mass production and retail consumption – it is little wonder that informal scrounging often incorporates yet another distinctive feature: relative economic and social invisibility.

Given this invisibility, perhaps a brief orientation to the range of contemporary scrounging and reclamation is in order. As already noted, electronic waste and other consumer trash from the United States and Europe is regularly shipped to Asia and Africa, where communities of scavengers engage in the dangerous work of reclaiming metals and other materials. In India's major cities, a complex 'urban informal economy' revolves around the scavenging and recycling of scrap materials, ranging from Pepsi cups to jerry cans (Gill, 2010). In Buenos Aires, Argentina, the economic crisis of the past two decades has spawned tens of thousands of *cartoneros*, who make a meager living from salvaging cardboard and other consumer waste materials (Ferrell, 2006: 15, 170). Outside Rio de Janeiro, Brazil, Jardim Gramacho – one of the world's largest and busiest landfills – hosts a community of *catadores*, trash pickers who first squatted the landfill during the economic crisis of the 1970s and 1980s and continue to mine it today (Walker *et al.*, 2010). Generations of scroungers – *guajeros* – have likewise scavenged the mountainous, methane-spewing landfill outside Guatemala City, Guatemala, with some second-generation scavengers even born and raised at the landfill itself (Iwerks, 2006). Today, the contemporary trash pickers of Jardim Gramacho, Guatemala City and elsewhere face an additional challenge, as ironic as it is revealing: with the ongoing and increasing disposal of consumer waste, these landfills are now leaking into surrounding areas and exhausting even their own cavernous capacity for waste. Because of this, many face closure, and, with it, the dispersal and relocation of their trash-picking populations.

Various forms of trash picking are also widespread in first world countries like the United States, where trash picking is colloquially referenced under the umbrella term of 'dumpster diving'. On a daily basis, homeless individuals and support groups scrounge trash piles and trash containers for discarded clothing, shoes, backpacks and food; many of them also dumpster dive for aluminum cans, to be sold for small amounts of cash at urban recycling centers (Botha, 2004; Pritchett, 2009). Others, impoverished but not homeless, drive old trucks or ride rebuilt bicycles around urban and rural areas, searching for sellable copper, brass, and other metals that have been discarded during building construction, or that can be extracted from trashed appliances and machinery. Among the working poor, parents dig through trash piles and trash containers, looking for home repair materials or school clothes for their children.

With the ongoing economic crisis in southern Europe, Spain and other countries are also seeing increasing numbers of residents – the homeless, the unemployed, old age pensioners – digging through trash bins in search of discarded but still edible food (Daley, 2012).

It is worth emphasizing again that these various worldwide communities of scroungers are not identical, and cannot be reduced to a single social status; the communities and the experiences of those within them vary along fault lines of cultural tradition, urbanization, shelter, age and gender. Yet as different as the life of a New York City food scrounger is from that of a Jardim Gramacho *catador*, it is also worth emphasizing again a clear commonality. Both lives, and both practices of scrounging, exist in response to the distinct patterns of contemporary consumer capitalism, and so are, in many ways, organized by them.

Consumer capitalism, consumer culture and consumer waste

Contemporary global capitalism can be understood as an essentially *cultural* enterprise which generates and legitimates a particular ideology (Ferrell, 2007). By way of global advertising and media industries, this form of capitalism manufactures physical products but also manufactures the meanings and desires that are to be associated with these products. The advertising industry is in this sense designed primarily to create the sorts of ongoing needs and desires that will sell each new round of advertised products. The consumer insatiability and elastic markets produced by this process are expanded further still by the planned obsolescence of contemporary consumer goods. Significantly, this obsolescence is accomplished not only by building in technical limitations, but by a 'planned obsolescence of desirability' (Packard, 1960: 71) whereby rapid fashion cycles and endless product 'improvements' inevitably push existing products out of style. Within this world, 'conspicuous consumption' – consumption for the sake of acquiring, maintaining or displaying status – moves from the 'leisure class' amongst whom Veblen (1953) first observed it and out into the wider social order. Whether food, clothes or cars, consumer items come to be purchased and displayed for the status that they carry and communicate – and so, once this status evaporates, so does their social and cultural worth.

In this way, contemporary global capitalism promotes both consumption and, more importantly, a pervasive *culture* of consumption – a global consumerist lifestyle structured around advertised desire, artificial need, ephemeral fashion and conspicuously acquired status. Unsurprisingly, this consumer culture spawns personal insecurity, sexual anxiety, eating disorders, financial indebtedness, and a host of other social harms (see Chapter 1 in this volume). As regards contemporary scrounging and reclamation, it produces a more direct consequence: pervasive, profligate consumer waste. In the same way that the endless manufacture of artificial needs and desires promotes the over-consumption of newly advertised goods, it promotes the discarding of existing goods now reconstructed, by default, as outdated or out of style. Likewise planned obsolescence, in both its technological and stylistic forms, predictably produces a throw-away culture of dissatisfaction and disposal. As Veblen first suggested, an item purchased for the status it can confer – for its sheen of newness and desirability – becomes culturally worthless, and so disposable, when that sheen is worn away by the next round of status-rich products. This sort of waste is not an unfortunate by-product of consumer culture; it is inherent in it (Moore, 2009). Conspicuous consumption promotes the wasteful over-consumption of manufactured items beyond basic human need, and then ensures these items' disposal, sooner rather than later, as social and cultural waste.

Across the globe, in developed and developing societies, the material consequences of this consumerist culture are increasingly calamitous, with the disposal of waste presenting intractable problems and resulting in engorged landfills, sprawling illegal dump sites, and the consequent fouling of land and water. The disposal and distribution of consumer waste reinforce other social problems as well, producing particularly virulent forms of environmental racism and ecological injustice (Pellow, 2004; South, 2010). For scroungers and trash pickers, the *content* of this pervasive consumer waste is of additional importance. Within a consumer culture that values the latest innovations, and that associates newness with status, 'trash' is conventionally conceptualized in terms of decay, dysfunction and filth – in no small part because such a conceptualization serves, once again, to push the consumer back towards the new and the immediately marketable. But as my ongoing research has shown, and as trash pickers regularly confirm, a large proportion of everyday consumer waste is neither decayed nor dysfunctional. Instead, it is made up of reusable packaging, edible food, usable toys, like-new clothing, functional appliances – even many items that retain their wrappers or price tags, having never been worn or used (Ferrell, 2006; http://empireofscrounge. blogspot.com/). This phenomenon is less surprising than it might at first seem. For large-scale retailers, mass commodification means that overstocked shelves can often be cleared most efficiently by simply discarding stock that is out of date or out of season. For consumers, panicked by the pace of modern life and eager to move on to the next round of consumption, last year's impulse purchase or this year's closet overstuffed with last year's fashions, can likewise easily enough end up in the trash bin or the curbside trash pile.

This, then, is the material basis of much contemporary scrounging and reclamation. The pervasive waste of consumer culture ensures a steady stream of scroungeable items – and the conspicuous consumption and engineered obsolescence by which consumer culture operates ensures that many of these discarded items will retain usable features. If in this way much contemporary scrounging is organized around consumer waste, it is also organized by the patterns and rhythms through which this waste is generated, disposed of and distributed. In the cities of the United States and Europe, most consumer trash is disposed of and collected within regular daily or weekly schedules, and so becomes more or less available to trash scroungers according to these schedules. The discarding of edible food follows the rhythms of restaurant kitchens and grocery store restocking; the availability of discarded furniture or appliances increases with the end-of-month termination of apartment leases or end-of-term relocation of university students. The construction of new buildings or remodeling of old ones produces a relatively precise sequence in which lumber, plumbing parts, electrical fixtures and roofing materials are disposed of. For those who scrounge landfills, the arrival of each garbage truck sets in motion a flurry of scrounging activity; for electronics salvagers, the arrival of a container ship defines a new set of dangerous opportunities.

The activities of those scroungers who trade scrounged goods with others are in turn structured by the existence of bartering and exchange networks, both digital and social, and by the viability of second-hand marketplaces, 'flea markets', 'garage sales' and other informal economies. Those wishing to turn scavenged goods into money likewise depend on the dealings and availability of scrap metal companies, commodity brokers and online marketplaces. All of this, from trash scrounging to the barter or sale of scrounged goods, is further structured by the legal environments in which it occurs. In the United States, for example, a recent surge in the theft of relatively valuable metals like copper has led to stringent legal regulations on the conditions under which metal recycling companies can buy scrap metal. More generally, informal trash scrounging by homeless populations and others in the United States and Europe has been increasingly criminalized over the past two decades, often in the context of protecting urban gentrification programs from intrusion by 'undesirable' populations and activities (Brisman, 2010; Ferrell, 2001, 2006; Markusen and Schrock, 2009). In these ways, consumer culture not only generates the waste on which contemporary scrounging depends, but also organizes scrounging around temporal and spatial patterns of waste disposal and distribution, and confines it within the legal categories that accompany ongoing consumerist development.

Aftermaths, off hours and other alternatives

While dynamics of consumer waste set the framework for contemporary scrounging, they do not fully define it. The organization of scrounging as an alternative activity has also been shaped by the cultures and subcultures within which it occurs. Scroungers must, for example, respond to the temporal and spatial patterns of waste disposal and distribution; yet in responding, they create bodies of shared knowledge and codes of conduct that organize the scrounging experience. As regards the temporal aspects of scrounging, scroungers share among themselves an alternative clock and calendar – one that is set to run hours, weeks or months behind the conventional schedules of society. Holidays are not celebrated, but rather the days following them, when holiday gifts or candy will be discarded. Schedules are set not to the beginning of musical concerts or sporting events, but to their aftermaths, when trashed or leftover goods will be made available. The trash bins at construction sites are visited not when plumbers are installing copper pipe and brass fixtures, but when their work is done and their scraps have been discarded. And when scrounging mixed-use neighborhoods, the usual temporal bifurcation of domestic life and work life is reversed: 'work hours' are the time to visit home trash piles, and 'time off' the time to investigate the dumpsters of workplaces. In these ways, communities of scroungers come to organize themselves around alternative temporal rhythms, and to share a distinctly different sense of time (Ferrell, 2006).

This shared temporal reorientation in turn takes on deeper meanings, and spawns broader normative arrangements. Communities of scroungers often construct a sort of collective patience, understanding that goods will be acquired and problems solved not immediately but eventually. As regards grocery stores and food, 'when a new shipment arrives it means out with the old' – and so, a day or week after it is put on sale, 'old' food is regularly and freely available (CrimethInc., 2004: 221). And if successful scrounging means learning to live behind the curve of consumerism, it means learning to live ahead of it as well. Scroungers develop systems to collect, accumulate and store food, clothes, tools, bicycle parts, building supplies and other items so that, when such items are eventually needed, they will be available without having to be purchased. In place of the impulse purchase or the quick run to the store, scroungers typically rely on stockpiles of scrounged goods, shared networks of barter or free exchange and, once again, a value is placed on patience and slow-paced problem-solving. While this approach often relies on the discarded products of consumerism, it also undermines the culture of consumption and so begins to create alternatives to it. It subverts the fast-paced panic of consumerism – the notion that problems can and should be solved immediately, through faster forms of technology and consumption – and replaces this panic with the sort of pace embraced by the slow-foods movement and other progressive subcultures. In terms of money, it begins to erode the very need for it, and so to further undermine contemporary structures of employment, pay and consumption. As the anonymous, unemployed, dumpster-diving author of the book *Evasion* put it: ' "Money?" they ask, the implication being that without money our system was flawed, incomplete. When in fact our lifestyle had stripped money of its value, reduced it to an inefficient and indirect and means of acquiring' (Anonymous, 2003: 80; see Eighner, 1993: 119).

In parallel fashion, collective scrounging reverses the spatial order of the contemporary consumerist city; scroungers remap the city and its meanings in the course of their daily round. Scroungers create informal neighborhood maps that are defined by patterns of trash removal and the availability of trash bins. Individually and collectively, they trace alternative routes through the city – routes that follow back alleys rather than streets; that value the backstage of retail trash disposal rather than the shiny front stage of retail display; and that make landmarks of particularly productive dumpsters or, alternatively, particularly aggressive private security guards or neighbors. Likewise, scroungers define 'desirable' neighborhoods by the quality and availability of their trash, or their proximity to reclamation facilities (Ferrell, 2006). Remapping the city in this way, investing its everyday spaces with alternative meanings, scroungers also organize their own invisibility. Arriving after an event or after a store's closing, easing down back alleys rather than main streets, scroungers achieve the sort of unobtrusive social invisibility necessary for successful trash picking and illicit waste reclamation. By the nature of discarded trash, and by the necessities of reclaiming it, scroungers stand in the shadows of time and space – but standing in these shadows, they create a subterranean world that allows them to sustain their informal economy with a minimum of legal intrusion or public intervention.

Practical and cultural organization of scrounging

The spatial and temporal organization of scrounging is buttressed by shared practical and cultural orientations, both in moments of trash picking and within larger communities of scrounging and reclamation. Among the various dumpster diving subcultures in the United States, for example, a consistent set of normative codes guides the everyday practice of dumpster diving. One account notes that 'I. . .try to leave the dumpster in better condition than I found it', not only because this helps 'the dumpster diver go unseen and unnoticed', but because it respects the work of store employees tasked with taking out the trash (CrimethInc., 2004: 223). Another complains of a case in which inexperienced dumpster divers 'transgressed every law of dumpster diving – "leave the area surrounding the dumpster cleaner than you found it," etc.'; this same account goes on to emphasize the importance of scrounging 'trash for sustenance not profit' (Anonymous, 2003: 68, 71). Expanding on this, the makers of a documentary on reclaiming discarded food urge viewers to 'remember the rules: Never take more than you need, unless you find it a good home. The first one to the dumpster has first dibs, but you always gotta share. Leave it cleaner than you found it' (Seifert, 2010). These informal guidelines reveal two sorts of community organization and affiliation. Even when excluded from or invisible to the larger communities from which they scrounge, trash scroungers still attempt to maintain ties to them, by trash picking in ways that produce minimal intrusion, discord or harm (Ferrell, 2006). Within and among their own scrounging communities, they in turn disseminate codes of conduct that emphasize respect for other trash pickers, the sharing of scrounged resources, and a commitment to dumpster diving as something greater than just another means of material acquisition.

These organizing values are further encoded in the long-term utilization of scrounged goods. For many groups, the environmental benefits of scrounging and reclamation are matched by the social benefits that derive from the sharing of scrounged materials. In the United States, 'libraries' of all sorts – tool libraries, bicycle libraries – lend scrounged and second-hand tools and supplies to those that need them so as to reduce individual consumption and to share knowledge of do-it-yourself repair. In New York City and other cities, clothing recycling programs and 'clothing banks' collect discarded clothing, recycling and reusing some of it (including buttons and zippers), and providing the remainder to various aid programs. Alternative architects like Dan Phillips and Michael Reynolds build low-cost, sustainable homes from scrounged materials, along the way teaching home-building skills and providing housing for the poor in North America, South Asia, and elsewhere (Murphy, 2009; Hodge, 2007). Other groups turn scrounged goods into shared art and collective celebration, thereby reversing the stigma associated with trash scrounging. Trash scroungers in Beverly, Massachusetts, for example, hold an annual Trash Finders' Ball. *Found* magazine – a magazine of lost letters and scrounged photographs – has, since its beginnings in 2001, morphed into a fluid community of books, performances and social events. And across the United States and Europe, communities of artists like the Dumpster Divers of Philadelphia create sculptures, installations and public art from found materials.

Globally, the scrounging of waste often provides an essential economic and cultural foundation for marginalized groups and communities. At times this marginalized reclamation work is integrated with 'legitimate', large-scale economic enterprises, as with the salvaging of decommissioned ships on the beaches of India and Bangladesh (Cairns, 2007), or the massive recycling of global electronic waste in China. At other times this work goes forward as part of smaller communities, or illicit underground economies. In the squatter communities of Baghdad, for example, scrap metal scavenging has created 'an underground economy that sustains and organizes whole neighborhoods', with 'informal turf agreements' and two scavenging shifts per day (Leland, 2011: A10). In the slums outside Dakar, Senegal, residents use garbage scavenged and delivered from the city as building material to shore up streets and houses; in Dharavi, India's largest slum, residents clean, process and repurpose much of the country's discarded plastic. Despite inhabiting an environment that one anthropologist described as 'the worst place I have ever seen in my life', members of the indigenous Warao tribe have, since the early 1990s, scavenged the enormous trash dump outside Ciudad Guayana, Venezuela; their leader declares that 'we've claimed this land and made our life in this dump, and this is where our future rests' (in Romero, 2010: 10). In the impoverished neighborhoods of Kampala, Uganda, self-taught engineers daily turn tonnes of garbage into low-cost fuel for self-employed motorbike taxi drivers; as one of them says, 'we thought we should be part of the solution to the global demand for environmentally beneficial practice' (in Michael, 2010: 46). In Cairo, the *zabbaleen* – unofficial garbage collectors – have for decades served as the city's informal sanitation system, achieving a recycling rate of some 80 percent (Iskander, 2009). These economic and community structures built around collective scrounging provide the basis for further cultural and political organization as well. The *catadores* of Brazil, for example, have over the years organized for improved labor and health conditions; Argentinian *cartoneros* and Mexican trash pickers have formed co-operatives and schools, and staged Somos Todos Cartoneros festivals to publicize their efforts and raise money for medical supplies. Profound economic marginalization regularly lays the foundation on which communities of scroungers must build; just as often, the raw and immediate need for food, clothing and shelter drives marginalized individuals out on daily rounds of scrounging and reclaiming. Yet, out of this marginalization and misery, scroungers many times manage to craft new forms of social and economic organization.

Anarchism, dis-organization and direct action

Among various groups in the United States, Europe, the UK – and, increasingly, worldwide – collective scrounging and reclamation are animated by yet another set of cultural and political dynamics. These dynamics serve to construct scrounging not only as an alternative economic practice, but as a distinctly oppositional practice to legal regulation, mainstream politics and consumerism. They subvert the conventional meanings of informal scrounging, and yet also contribute to its invisibility within conventional media reporting and political discourse. Most interestingly, they serve not so much to organize collective scrounging as to 'dis-organize' it.

These practices are rooted in the long history of anarchist activism, especially as reinvented within the punk and DIY (do-it-yourself) subcultures that emerged in the 1960s and 1970s and that continue today. Essential to this approach is the disavowal of structures of authority or power over others. As anarchists often say, their goal is not to seize power but to destroy it – that is, to undermine the potential for domination and submission in any area of social life. In this context, anarchists battle for autonomy, self-determination and decentralization; they emphasize freedom from top-down social structures, and resistance to the rules and regulations of large-scale organizations. This same ethos shapes relations among anarchists themselves; in place of formal, hierarchical group organization, they work toward leaderless activism, informal consensus-building and 'dis-organization' – that is, a minimal and fluid degree of coordination that is designed only to set further activity in motion. Today, groups ranging from urban liberation movements like Critical Mass and Reclaim the Streets to the Occupy movement embrace this notion of emergent dis-organization as the embodiment of anarchist principles and practice. The associated practice of 'direct action' similarly draws on anarchism's disavowal of legal and political authority, and on its affection for open-ended dis-organization. From the view of anarchists, petitioning those in authority or electing new political leaders only reinforces their power over others; instead, anarchists are determined to take direct action in the situations of everyday life, without asking those in power for permission or aid. These moments of direct action in turn serve to demonstrate that activity can be taken outside usual legal or political structures, and to inaugurate a process of street-level engagement that will set in motion whatever next steps may evolve (Ferrell, 2001).

While this approach at times produces high-profile conflicts with legal authorities unwilling to brook unregulated activity, generally it keeps anarchist activism below the radar of those who are only attuned to conventionally organized political action or highly structured social movements. Furthering contemporary anarchists' public invisibility is their orientation toward work and consumption. Unsurprisingly, anarchists understand the existing system of work, contracts and wages as one of hyper-regulation, risk-management in the interest of predictable profitability, and overall human degradation – and moreover, one set up to enrich and empower the few from the labor of the many. Moreover, they argue, paid work is made a necessity primarily in the interest of consumption – itself a system of false needs and false identities predicated on the annihilation of the earth and its resources. Consequently, anarchists emphasize 'assertive desertion' (Carlsson, 2002: 75–82; Carlsson and Manning, 2010) from both work and consumption – an intentional retreat from the core of contemporary society that at the same time generates a critique and counter-attack against it. After all, as one anarchist publication argues, 'Few people would go to work if they didn't need a paycheck to buy the things they need – so when you consider how to emancipate yourself from wage slavery, the first thing to work out is what you can do without' (CrimethInc., 2004: 577; see also McDonald, this volume).

From the anarchists' perspective, you can do without any and all consumerist creations – and what remain of life's necessities you can find in the trash bin. For anarchists, everyday trash scrounging operates as an autonomous, decentralized process of direct action and assertive desertion that allows its participants to exist outside consumer culture while living an on-the-ground critique and reversal of it. 'Burdens lift and scarcity is averted when the mountains of trash produced by this insane society become supplies and sustenance,' argues

CrimethInc. (2004: 219, 608), a 'decentralized underground' of anarchists. 'Everything that sucks about capitalism is inverted when the dumpster diver scores. Poverty becomes abundance. Loss becomes gain. Despair becomes hope.' For anarchists, dumpster diving also inverts consumer capitalism at the level of status and respectability; dumpster diving his way across America, the anonymous author of *Evasion* wonders

> who the barbarians were, the contemptible. Those operating the machine, enslaving the people, and bleeding the Earth dry. Producing things only to throw them away, digging a hole only to fill it up again. Or those who saw the absurdity of it all, and chose to humbly wait in the shadows of that machine and pick up the crumbs.
>
> *(Anonymous, 2003: 74)*

The material resources produced by daily trash scrounging in turn flow into dis-organized, do-it-yourself anarchist networks of survival and social change. Many anarchist communities host 'free stores' or stage 'really, really free markets'; short on rules but long on scrounged and second-hand goods, these 'stores' and 'markets' operate along lines of voluntary reciprocity and gift-giving, with people from within the community or surrounding neighborhoods taking what they need and bringing in what they don't (see Graeber, 2011). Likewise, Bikes Not Bombs salvages discarded and second-hand bicycles and bicycle parts, teaches biking skills, provides free bicycles to groups in the United States, Central America and Africa, and in general 'uses the bicycle as a vehicle for social change' and community 'self-empowerment' (http://bikesnotbombs.org/about (accessed 2 January 2012)). More broadly, loosely organized networks of anarchist 'gutter punks' predicate their ability to live fluidly and collectively outside the bounds of mainstream society on three forms of scrounging: the picking of food and clothing from trash bins, the scrounging of free transportation by way of freight train hopping, and when necessary, the begging of money from passers-by. From free stores to Bikes Not Bombs and gutter punks, then, contemporary anarchists see trash reclamation as building the basis, materially and culturally, for their resistance to consumer capitalism. To paraphrase the Wobblies, an early American anarcho-syndicalist union often invoked by contemporary anarchists, they endeavor to build a new society within the waste of the old.

Case study: food reclamation

The nature of contemporary scrounging as a form of alternative organization – and in particular, a form of anarchist dis-organization – is especially evident in the case of informal food reclamation. Across a widely dispersed underground of punks, anarchists and direct action activists, food scrounging is understood as a fundamental aspect of autonomy and self-determination, and as a fundamental critique of consumer capitalism's innate wastefulness. From the view of those involved in food scrounging, the manufacture and marketing of food as a commodity (and the movement of this commodified food through global supply chains) defines food by artificial standards of desirability and cosmetic perfection, spawns food products that are unhealthy and unsustainable, and produces vast amounts of everyday food waste (see Seifert, 2010; Varda, 2000). To scrounge and eat discarded food, then, is to confront this system through direct action, and to demonstrate the inequities of its waste. Importantly, it is also to invent a direct, unauthorized and decentralized process for getting food to those left hungry by these inequities.

Within many punk communities the culturally constructed desirability of corporate food products is seen as embodying a host of social harms, from environmental destruction to 'the fetishism of food as a commodity'; consequently, as Clark (2004: 21) puts it, punks prefer food that is by conventional consumer culture standards 'rotten'. In a retail-driven, consumerist society, of course, 'rotten' signifies not so much food's physical spoilage as its exclusion from appropriate consumer channels by way of disposal or theft. For punks, then, there is a 'rotten logic of dumpster diving', as Clark explains:

> By bathing corporate food in a dumpster or by stealing natural foods from an upscale grocery store, punk food is, in a sense, decommodified, stripped of its alienating qualities, and restored to a kind of pure use-value as bodily sustenance.
>
> *(2004: 21)*

For punks, wasted or 'rotten' food is food that has been expelled from the system that produced it – and so scrounging such food serves to redeem something of what food should be.

The emergence of 'freegans' and 'freeganism' over the past decade has revealed a similar inversion by which food trash, when collectively scrounged, can provide a cleansing critique, and with it alternative models for organizing social life. Building both from punk/anarchist traditions and from the do-no-harm food philosophy of veganism, freegans argue that there exists an even more effective mechanism for doing no harm than the vegan model of eating meat-free and dairy-free food: eating only food that has already been wasted. Scrounging discarded food and sharing it with others, freegans argue, lays the foundation for assertive desertion from the entire complex of work and consumption by constructing a cash-free food economy; at the same time, it allows freegans to 'act as a living challenge to waste and over-consumption' (http://freegan.info/what-is-a-freegan/freegan-philosophy/ (accessed 2 January 2012)). This living challenge is in turn sustained by the collective culture of freegans and associated anarchists, who share scrounged food meals, information on scrounged food collection, and other resources. Among these groups are the Radical Cheerleaders, whose remake of the old Wobby organizing song, 'Solidarity Forever', and its stirring 'for the union makes us strong' final verse, includes the following stanzas:

> Is there ought we have in common with the greedy parasites?
> Besides that we eat out of their Dumpsters every night?
> Is there anything left for us? Open the lid and take a bite.
>   For the doughnuts make us strong.
> They have wasted untold millions and they waste more every day.
> While the workers keep producing they keep throwing it away.
>   But the freegans are uniting and we vow never to pay.
>   For the doughnuts make us strong.
>
> *(in Botha, 2004: 100)*

Freegan communities now stretch from North America to Australia and Europe. Even more widespread is an anarchist association that many punks and freegans cite as the model for their informal food reclamation: Food Not Bombs. Since its origins in 1980 among anti-nuclear activists in the United States, Food Not Bombs has salvaged wasted food, cooked it, and served it to the homeless and others in need. Much of this food is reclaimed by arrangement with local food co-ops, bakeries or grocery stores, with Food Not Bombs members hauling away excess food that would otherwise be trashed; other food comes from dumpster diving. Whatever its source, Food Not Bombs participants understand both the reclamation and redistribution of excess food to be an exercise in direct action, and a direct intervention into a system that 'values wasteful consumption over common sense' (CrimethInc., 2004: 248). As the members of the Orlando, Florida, Food Not Bombs group put it,

> our group shares food because people need it and as a means of calling attention to our society's failure to provide food and housing to each of its members. . . . We believe in trying to solve problems such as hunger through direct action as much as possible, and without seeking any permission or assistance from government.
>
> *(https://orlandofoodnotbombs.org/ (accessed 23 December 2011))*

While hundreds of Food Not Bombs chapters are known to operate today in North America, Europe, Africa and around the globe, the actual number and nature of these chapters remains imprecise – due precisely to the nature of Food Not Bombs itself. Variously described as 'an anarchist dis-organization' (Clark, 2004: 28) and 'something between a strategy and an organization' (CrimethInc., 2004: 248), Food Not Bombs promotes only the general principles of consensus, non-violence and vegetarianism, otherwise emphasizing that 'the core of [its] philosophy is that each local group is autonomous' (Butler and McHenry, 2000: 73). Often these local groups quietly go about gleaning food and feeding the hungry in public parks. Other times their public presence, and their commitment to seeking neither the permission nor assistance of the authorities, leads to legal harassment, as with the arrest of hundreds of Food Not Bombs food servers in San Francisco, or the more recent arrest of Orlando Food Not Bombs members, whom the local mayor described as 'food terrorists' (Butler and McHenry, 2004; Ferrell, 2001, 2006; Maxwell, 2011). In either circumstance, and despite the derogations, groups like Food Not Bombs continue their work, and in so doing invent alternative forms of organization and dis-organization amidst the process of everyday scrounging and reclamation.

Conclusions

The contemporary worldwide economic system – perhaps more accurately, the contemporary worldwide economic crisis – goes by any number of names. As used throughout this chapter, 'consumer capitalism' denotes especially the reliance of this economic system on pervasive, profligate consumption. 'Global capitalism' highlights the sheer scale and reach of this current system – a system woven together by multinational corporations, transnational supply chains and migratory labor. 'Late capitalism' carries for many a double meaning, suggesting both a later, consumerist stage that has now supplanted capitalism's early industrial period, and the potential demise of this later capitalism under the weight of its own economic and environmental contradictions.

All of these meanings can be seen intertwined in contemporary scrounging and reclaiming. In fact, the prevalence of scrounging and reclaiming worldwide reveals one of contemporary capitalism's fundamental contradictions: both its successes and its failures spawn waste, and the scrounging of waste at its margins. 'Successful' consumer capitalism is predicated on endless cycles of manufactured need and consumption, and equally as much on the profligate wasting of usable consumer items. 'Failed' capitalism, on the other hand, generates joblessness, homelessness and dislocation, and a growing army of the dispossessed desperately scrounging for survival amidst such consumer waste. In this way, contemporary capitalism produces both the material basis for scrounging and, increasingly, the necessity for scrounging as a strategy of daily survival and alternative organization. It also produces a world in which the successes and failures of capitalism itself are intertwined, and increasingly indistinguishable. Likewise, the growing global gap between rich and poor – another dynamic by which the wins and losses of the contemporary system coincide – comes sharply into relief when encountered amidst impoverished workers reclaiming obsolete iPads in a Chinese electronics dump, or among the hungry scrounging discarded leftovers from behind the high-end restaurants of London or Madrid. The contemporary economic system – the contemporary economic crisis – is stitched together by a grid of international financial institutions, corporate supply chains and global markets; it is also connected by a global network of scroungers and trash pickers.

As regards these scroungers and pickers, it would be difficult to imagine a group more on the margins. Afflicted by poverty, increasingly made illegal, suffering an odd mix of social invisibility and cultural stigma, they interrupt the contemporary flow of waste, immerse themselves in filth (real and imagined) and, against all odds, scrape out a means of survival. Against these odds, and within these most marginal of circumstances, they organize alternative worlds as well. Intervening in the flow of trash from consumer culture to landfill, they confront consumer capitalism's environmental crisis; recycling tonnes of material a day, they suggest the shape that more sustainable practices might take. Creating local communities and larger networks of co-operation and mutual aid, finding shared uses for what is found, they sketch the possibility of alternative economic arrangements organized around something more than markets and manufactured desire. Awash in the waste that now overruns the planet, scroungers show us just how late it is; building alternative forms of social organization from that waste, they offer hope that it is not too late after all. As they remind us of what we are meant to forget, they harbinger a future that others aren't quite ready to imagine.

Resources

DIVE! Living Off America's Waste. Jeremy Seifert, director. Los Angeles: Compeller Pictures, 2010.
An innovative film about confronting and reclaiming food waste.

Empire of Scrounge. Jeff Ferrell, author. New York: New York University Press, 2006.
An overview of contemporary scrounging and reclaiming in the United States, based on the author's own life as a trash scrounger. See relatedly http://empireofscrounge.blogspot.com/

The Gleaners and I [Les Glaneurs et la Glaneuse]. Agnes Varda, director. Paris: Cine' Tamaris, 2010.
A poetic film about gleaning and reclamation, from the acclaimed director Agnes Varda.

Waste Land [Lixo Extraordinario]. Lucy Walker, Joao Jardim and Karen Harley, directors. London: Almega, 2010.
A film that mixes art, trash and hope in showing the organization of the *catadores* (trash pickers) of Brazil's Jardim Gramacho landfill.

References

Anonymous. 2003. *Evasion.* Atlanta: CrimethInc.
Botha, Ted. 2004. *Mongo: Adventures in Trash.* New York: Bloomsbury.
Brisman, Avi. 2010. 'The Indiscriminate Criminalisation of Environmentally Beneficial Activities', in Rob White, ed., *Global Environmental Harm: Criminological Perspectives.* Cullompton, UK: Willan, pp. 161–192.
Butler, C.T. Lawrence and Keith McHenry. 2000. *Food Not Bombs.* Tucson, AZ: See Sharp Press.
Cairns, George. 2007. 'Postcard from Chittagong: Wish You Were Here?' *Critical Perspectives on International Business* 3(3): 266–279.

Carlsson, Chris, ed. 2002. *Critical Mass: Bicycling's Defiant Celebration*. Oakland, CA: AK Press.

Carlsson, Chris and Francesca Manning. 2010. 'Nowtopia: Strategic Exodus?' *Antipode* 42(4): 924–953.

Clark, Dylan. 2004. 'The Raw and the Rotten: Punk Cuisine' *Ethnology* 43(1): 19–31.

CrimethInc. 2004. *Recipes for Disaster*. Olympia, WA: CrimethInc.

Daley, Suzanne. 2012. 'Spain Recoils as Its Hungry Forage Trash Bins for a Next Meal' *The New York Times* (25 September): A1, A6.

Eighner, Lars. 1993. *Travels with Lizbeth*. New York: St. Martins' Press.

Ferrell, Jeff. 2001. *Tearing Down the Streets: Adventures in Urban Anarchy*. New York: Palgrave/Macmillan.

Ferrell, Jeff. 2006. *Empire of Scrounge*. New York: NYU Press.

Ferrell, Jeff. 2007. 'For a Ruthless Cultural Criticism of Everything Existing' *Crime, Media, Culture* 3(1): 91–100.

Gill, Kaveri. 2010. *Of Poverty and Plastic*. New Delhi: Oxford University Press.

Graeber, David. 2011. *Debt: The First 5,000 Years*. New York: Melville House.

Hodge, Oliver. 2007. *Garbage Warrior* (documentary film). UK: Open Eye Media.

Iskander, Mai. 2009. *Garbage Dreams* (documentary film). New York: Iskander Films.

Iwerks, Leslie, 2006. *Recycled Life* (documentary film). New York: Leslie Iwerks Productions.

Leland, John. 2011. 'City Upon a Hill of Scraps: Surviving on Scavenging in Iraq' *The New York Times* (12 January): A10.

Markusen, Ann and Greg Schrock. 2009. 'Consumption-Driven Urban Development' *Urban Geography* 30(4): 344–367.

Maxwell, Scott. 2011. 'Breaking Bread and Breaking the Law' *Orlando Sentinel* (7 June), available online at http://articles.orlandosentinel.com/2011–06–07/news/ (accessed 2 January 2012).

Michael, Wambi. 2010. 'Kampala's Waste Has Surprising Power' *The Guardian Weekly* (3 December): 46.

Moore, Sarah. 2009. 'The Excess of Modernity: Garbage Politics in Oaxaca, Mexico' *The Professional Geographer* 61(4): 426–437.

Murphy, Kate. 2009. 'One Man's Trash . . .' *The New York Times* (3 September): D1, D6–7.

Packard, Vance. 1960. *The Waste Makers*. Harmondsworth, UK: Penguin.

Pellow, David Naguib. 2004. *Garbage Wars: The Struggle for Environmental Justice in Chicago*. Cambridge, MA: MIT Press.

Pritchett, Laura. 2009. *Going Green: True Tales from Gleaners, Scavengers, and Dumpster Divers*. Norman: University of Oklahoma Press.

Romero, Simon. 2010. 'Left Behind in Venezuela To Piece Lives From Scraps' *The New York Times* (19 September): 10.

Seifert, Jeremy. 2010. *DIVE! Living Off America's Waste* (documentary film). Los Angeles: Compeller Pictures.

South, Nigel. 2010. 'The Ecocidal Tendencies of Late Modernity' in Rob White, ed., *Global Environmental Harm: Criminological Perspectives*. Cullompton, UK: Willan, pp. 228–247.

Varda, Agnes. 2000. *The Gleaners and I [Les Glaneurs et la Glaneuse]* (documentary film). Paris: Cine' Tamaris.

Veblen, Thorstein. 1953 (1899). *The Theory of the Leisure Class*. New York: Mentor.

Walker, Lucy, Joao Jardim and Karen Harley. 2010. *Waste Land (Lixo Extraordinario)* (documentary film). London: Almega.

21

Free and open source appropriate technology

Joshua M. Pearce

Introduction

Modern science and engineering has brought a select few the benefits of wondrous technologies at an ever-accelerating rate. Due to this trend, our global industrialized culture (particularly in the US) has come to directly associate high technology with progress (Davies *et al.*, 2008; Kunda, 2006). Our culture makes the sweeping assumption that high-tech solutions are the best solutions and that our lives are better for accepting them. Publications like *Wired* and less-specialized outlets in the mainstream media cheer on the ever-present technological breakthroughs with a breathlessness reserved in the past for the affairs of celebrities and royalty. This widespread belief biases our decision making towards centralized, top-down, 'bigger is better', more complex solutions to both social and technical problems. This bias explains how contemporary society has ended up providing massive subsidies for highly sophisticated, bureaucratically controlled, centralized nuclear power plants, which are inherently so risky that no insurance company is able to indemnify them (Pearce, 2012a). Or why cars have now restructured our cities, relegating bicycles and pedestrians to second-class status.

Nuclear power is notable because it must be heavily government subsidized to survive. Normally the global industrialized culture's love affair with high-tech solutions is closely intertwined with a view that laissez-faire neo-liberalism will enable the free market to provide the best solutions for everyone (Viner, 1960; Dowd, 1996; Miller, 1962; Mirowski and Plehwe, 2009; Overtveldt, 2009). Indeed, this approach has historically provided gains in the understanding of basic science, which has been harnessed to provide spectacular technologies capable of securing mind-boggling profits for the corporations that control them. Thus, the underlying problem is made clear: corporations are no longer organized to secure benefits for the public, simply to gain profit at any expense (Sepp and Frear, 2011). As corporations have grown to wield incredible political power, the state is now often used as a means of profit production for companies at the expense of the best interests of the public (Huffington, 2004). This form of technological bias becomes particularly painful when it is clear that there are sustainable solutions to societal problems. In the example of nuclear power, these profit to expense transfers have occurred by internalizing profit, while externalizing the crippling insurance costs and risks on the public[1] (Zelenika and Pearce, 2011). Without this public insurance subsidy, nuclear power would simply not exist and any number of technically viable distributed sources of renewable power would have long ago taken its place. Such greed and corruption have been common historically, but also provide a hint that conventional society may have a fundamental problem with the way technology is designed and used, no matter how advanced we become.

We are advanced technically and expanding our technical prowess rapidly. It is undeniable that technological development has provided great benefits to humankind in medicine and many other fields, and that technology is indeed developing faster now than ever before. There are more PhDs, scientists and engineers working now than the world has ever seen. More papers are being written and new scientific journals are proliferating at a breath-taking rate. The rate of growth of scholars has been about 3 per cent per year, of scholarly journals 3.25 per cent per year, and the number of articles published in them grows at about 3.5 per cent per year (Mabe, 2003; Ware and Mabe, 2009). Scholarly publishing is exploding and set to take off even faster with the growth of open access (Björk *et al.*, 2008; Phillips, 2010; Tenopir and King, 2009). Legend has it that an ancient Greek named Solon was the last person to know "everything there was to know" at his time. Today, however, the brightest professors struggle to keep up with the burgeoning literature in their own tiny sub-fields. All of this knowledge and all of this technology should have us living in some form of glorious techno-utopia.

Yet something is wrong. Even a superficial review of environmental conditions results in a rather bleak outlook for the sustainability of the world's major ecological systems. On the global front, climate destabilization threatens the world's food supply and economic prosperity is driving an unprecedented number of species to extinction. On the local scale near me in the USA, pregnant women are banned from eating fish out of the Great Lakes because of the risk of birth defects. The long list of increases in bad news (i.e. expanding desertification, drug-resistant bacteria, coral reef bleaching, ozone hole expanding, ocean dead zones, fresh water contamination, etc.) is enough to depress anyone paying attention. Worse yet, billions of people are still mired in dehumanizing poverty and even those in the developed, "rich" countries find their economic situations uncomfortably precarious.

Billions of dollars are spent yearly throughout the world on research and development, and one would expect, from an optimistic point of view, that many of these problems would buckle under the relentless progress of our expanding technological sophistication. Unfortunately, the vast majority of this research and the knowledge created, which is biased towards hi-tech solutions, is not focused on problems related to sustainable development. Surprisingly, even much of it that is, is effectively removed from deployment by intellectual property law (e.g. patents and copyrights) (Pearce and Mushtaq, 2009). The result of this restricted and closed model of technological development primarily for profit is the widespread poverty and environmental desecration seen around the globe. It is our model of technological development that is directly responsible for a morally and ethically unacceptable level of human suffering and death. For example, more than 10 million children under the age of 5 die each year from preventable causes (WHO, 2007). We know how to solve these problems. We have all the tools and more than enough wealth, yet more little kids die every day than the total loss of human life during the 9/11 terrorist attacks. This waste of human life could be prevented by known technologies, many of which are simply not available to those that need it. Availability is restricted by both the cost of access (such as pay-to-view articles on renewable electricity generation under copyright by the IEEE)[2] and by companies wielding patent law to maximize profit at the cost of human lives (e.g. restricting the sale of anti-retroviral drugs to treat HIV in Africa (Shantharam, 2005)). A solution to this general problem of access to critical information for sustainable development is the growth of *open source appropriate technology*.

What is open source appropriate technology?

Open source appropriate technology (OSAT) refers to technologies that provide for sustainable development while being designed in the same fashion as free and open-source software (FOSS)[3] (Buitenhuis et al., 2010; Pearce and Mushtaq, 2009). FOSS is software that is freely licensed to grant users the right to use, copy, study, change and improve its design through the availability of its source code or be "open source". The open-source movement emerged as a fundamentally new, decentralized (Raymond, 1998), participatory and transparent system to develop software in contrast to the closed box, industrial, top-down and proprietary approach (Mockus et al., 2002). The open-source paradigm also normally includes viral components that require users to share improvements with the community under the same open/free terms of the original work (Hansen et al., 2002). These viral qualities are what enable the open-source technologies to develop so quickly as a global team works together. Through these principles of sharing and open access, open source treats users as developers by encouraging contribution, recognizing good work through peer approval, and propagating superior code (Weber, 2000). This philosophy of the open-source movement is described by Levy as the 'hacker ethic' with the following general principles (*Levy, 1984*):

i)   sharing
ii)   openness
iii) decentralization
iv)   free access
v)   world improvement.

This philosophy is enabled by the gift culture of open source, in which recognition of an individual is determined by the amount of knowledge given away (Bergquist and Ljungberg, 2001). The richer you are, the more you give – the more valuable the gift, the more respect you gain (see Rehn, this volume). This type of philosophy should be familiar to many in academia, which has also historically followed a gift culture, which rewards contributors through a process of peer review.

The FOSS movement has produced a community of hackers and computer programmers whose shared goal is to work together to develop better computer software (DiBona et al., 1999). If open-source software such as GNU/Linux is compared against Microsoft's centralized and closed system of software development, a surprising result surfaces. A neutral technical assessment finds that open-source software, developed in the early days mostly by unpaid volunteers, is often of superior quality to the software developed by one of the most powerful companies in the history of the world, employing unquestionably extremely intelligent people (Bonaccorsi and Rossi, 2003). This remarkable result stands against the conventional wisdom that would argue that the profit motive and market forces would enable Microsoft to develop superior software to any random group of volunteers. Microsoft is a large company, with annual revenue of over $40 billion, yet many of its products suffer from technical drawbacks that include bloat, lack of reliability and security holes. Microsoft remains dominant largely because of inertia, but Linux eats up an ever-larger market share (particularly in servers), because open source is simply more efficient and adaptable than closed, hierarchical systems (Kogut and Metiu, 2001). This is due, historically at least, in a large part because a lot more people collaborate on Linux than on Microsoft products. Where Microsoft might utilize a few thousand programmers and software engineers to debug their code, the Linux community has access to hundreds of thousands of programmers debugging, rewriting and submitting code.[4] This type of mass-scale collaboration is driving the success of Web 2.0 applications that emphasize online collaboration and sharing among users (examples include social networking sites and wikis such as Wikipedia). As the Aggroblogger asked several years ago (Aragona, 2005): "Now that Open Source has come of age, the question is not: Is it better than closed software? But rather: To what other systems, outside of software, can we apply the concepts of Open Source and public ownership?"

One area of technology ripe for development of open source is appropriate technologies (AT), which was first popularized by E.F. Schumacher in his classic book *Small is Beautiful: A Study of Economics As If People Mattered* (1973). Although Schumacher did not use the term, he made a powerful argument that simple and small-scale technologies are often both more appropriate and also better solutions to solving our developmental problems. Schumacher advocated demand-led innovation of technologies that are elegant, low energy, economical and designed to match the purpose and needs of those that use it. Thus, "less" can be "more" when introducing appropriate tools and technologies that may seem smaller in scale and complexity, but will be utilized more effectively by the communities (Hazeltine and Bull, 1999). Appropriate technology has since become the term used to describe Schumacher-type elegant solutions. These elegant solutions must take care in the design. McDonough and Braungart argue that design decisions should ensure that we love all of the children of all species for all of time (2002; see Chapter 3, this volume). Appropriate technology is thus defined as those technologies that are easily and economically utilized from readily available resources by local communities to meet their sustainable development needs (Hazeltine and Bull, 2003; Pearce, 2012b). Although much at OSAT is made up of relatively simple and non-complex technologies (e.g. rope pumps[5] as in Figure 21.1), OSAT also encompasses complex and state-of-the-art devices such as solar photovoltaic cells on flexible substrates[6] (Figure 21.2) developed with nanotechnology (Mushtaq and Pearce, 2011). The key to OSAT is that it must meet the boundary conditions set by the environmental, cultural, economic and educational resource constraints of the local community (Buitenhuis *et al.*, 2010; Pearce, 2009). Thus high-technology solutions are often less effective and less elegant than simple technologies, although high-technology devices can be used in new ways. For example, cell phones can be used as a tool to lift rural women out of poverty (e.g. the Grameenphone in Figure 21.3). The national Village Phone programme, which primarily targets women living in remote areas, works as an owner-operated payphone whereby a borrower takes a $200 loan from Grameen Bank to subscribe to Grameenphone and is then trained on how to operate it and how to charge others to use it at a profit. This helps rural residents have access to phone services that would otherwise be impossible for personal or professional use (e.g. a farmer calling to determine the best local city to bring produce to market). Hundreds of thousands of phones are now operating in tens of thousands of villages throughout Bangladesh and expanding to other countries.

As Ian Smillie points out in *Mastering the Machine: Poverty, Aid and Technology*: 'The issue for developing countries is not a trade-off between high and low technologies: it is a trade-off between appropriate and inappropriate technologies' (Smillie, 2000, p. 256). In the same regard, OSAT is not only intended for developing areas, but can and should be applied worldwide, in industrialized regions as well.

There are numerous groups, non-profit organizations, universities, companies and individuals that have embraced the open-source paradigm when working on AT (Zelenika and Pearce, 2011). For example, consider the rapidly growing body of OSAT work done by groups that publish OSAT and encourage open collaboration, including: Appropriate Technology Collaborative (ATC), Appropriate Infrastructure Development Group (AIDG),

Figure 21.1 A manually operated rope pump in a borehole, produced by a local workshop in Mozambique, posted on Akvopedia.org, a website for open water and sanitation resources. As this technology can be sourced and repaired locally, it ensures that it is a long-lasting source of drinking water for the community

Ayzh, Catalytic Communities (CatCom), Compatible Technology International (CTI), Digital Green, International Development Research Center (IDRC), Kopernik, and Practical Action. All of these organizations actively develop and distribute AT through various channels while also making the information about the technologies available.

OSAT in action

The Appropedia Foundation (Figure 21.4) offers one of the best examples of OSAT in action as it harnesses the power of distributed peer review and transparency of process. The Appropedia Foundation hosts Appropedia.org, the primary site for collaborative solutions in sustainability, poverty reduction and international development on the Internet. Appropedia is an advertising-free, Mediawiki-based website like Wikipedia, a website where a large number of participants (including you) are allowed to create and modify the content directly from their web browsers. The use of such OSAT websites has enormous potential to assist in

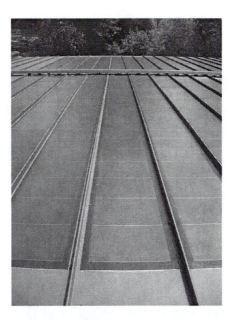

Figure 21.2 Thin-film solar photovoltaic laminates convert sunlight directly into electricity without pollution, on the roof of the Lakota Middle School, WA, USA. The solar cells are laminated directly to the metal roof and are made up of several layers of sophisticated semiconductor layers

sustainable development because it simplifies the administration of collaboratively organizing information, project examples, best practices and "how-to"s (Pearce *et al.*, 2010). OSAT on the Internet is set to expand rapidly as other organizations utilize its information transfer and collaboration capabilities (Buitenhuis *et al.*, 2010; Zelinika-Zovko and Pearce, 2011). Following the open-source paradigm, anyone can both learn how to make and use AT free of IP concerns. At the same time anyone can also add to the collective, open-source knowledge ecosystem or "knowledge commons" (see De Angelis and Harvie, this volume) by contributing ideas, designs, observations, experimental data, deployment logs, etc. The built-in, continuous peer-review should result in better quality, higher reliability and more flexibility than conventional design/patenting of technologies. The free nature of the knowledge also provides lower costs, particularly for those technologies that do not benefit to a large degree from scale of manufacture.

However, it should be noted that an open-source approach is not necessarily an instantaneous panacea for design of anything, including AT. Although, for example, there are many excellent open-source software packages, there are also a notable number of incomplete or poorly coded open-source programs. Thus, there is no implied guarantee that any one specific piece of OSAT will be of high quality. However, with the communities' ability to try out and give feedback on the efficacy of a particular OSAT every day, a swathe of technologies improve. Thus the open-source process tends to create gems that rise to the top and are used alongside many unfinished or less functional concepts and products. These underdeveloped concepts can all be built on by others and improved for the future. This is an advantage of the

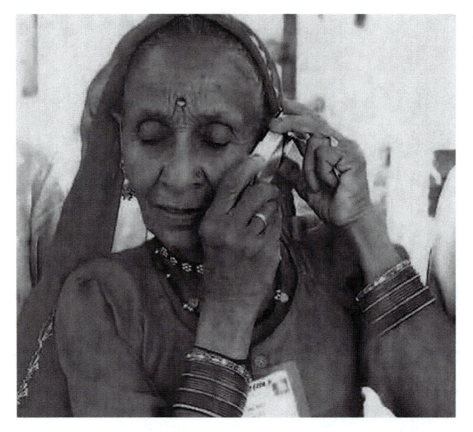

Figure 21.3 Universal mobile phone access throughout Bangladesh, including its rural areas, was made a reality by Grameenphone, which was inspired by the Grameen Bank microcredit model. Originally the Grameenphone was established as a business model where a cell phone could serve as a source of income for rural women. Access to communication at low costs benefits everyone in the community

open-source model. Others have access to truly "stand on the shoulders of giants" and continue with projects where others have left off.

Already the open-source paradigm is gaining momentum in hardware, with such devices as the open-source 3-D printers for both the design, but also the production of OSATs (Pearce *et al.*, 2010). In this case, open-source electronic prototyping platforms (Arduino) can be used to build an open-source, self-replicating 3-D printer (RepRap), capable of manufacturing solid complex pieces without the need for expensive industrial infrastructure (Pearce *et al.*, 2010). RepRap's software and the printer designs are open and available free of charge, while the printer can also make most of its own components. The RepRap project is not only an open hardware project, but it uses open-source software and wiki technology to spread the results in the development community (www.reprap.org).

Work is also underway to utilize post-use "waste" plastic in an open-source hardware project called the RecycleBot (http://www.thingiverse.com/thing:12948) to provide the feedstock filament for the RepRaps (Kreiger *et al.*, 2012; Baechler *et al.*, 2013). A RecycleBot

Figure 21.4 Appropedia.org is the largest OSAT resource available on the Internet. It is a site for collaborative solutions in sustainability, poverty reduction and international development

takes post-consumer plastic, like the HDPE from empty milk jugs, and can transform it into the '3-D ink' used in RepRaps. Twenty milk jugs make about 1 kg of filament, replacing filament on the market that costs between $35 and $50. Already there are several other RecycleBot variants (Filabot Wee: www.thingiverse.com/thing:24583 and Lyman Filament Extruder: www.thingiverse.com/thing:30642) as the evolutionary nature of open-source hardware takes over. The vision for this work is to enable anyone to literally print themselves out of poverty by utilizing a combination of free, Linux-based software, open-source designs on the Internet and Recyclebot and RepRap technologies coupled to local raw materials, such as waste plastic. This technical work is in its infancy, but the potential is clear to a growing number of hackers and researchers assisting on the collaborative projects.

In addition to large, complex prints such as its own parts, the RepRap is also capable of making small, simple components of OSATs. For example, consider the DremelFuge chuck shown in Figure 21.6, which is a printable rotor for centrifuging standard micro centrifuge tubes and miniprep columns (Garvey, 2009). The DremelFuge can be used in the field as an extremely inexpensive centrifuge (costing under $50 – primarily the cost of the

Figure 21.5 A RepRap – a prototype, self-replicating, rapid 3-D printer (about half the components were all printed by another RepRap 3-D printer). The remaining components are either common nuts and bolts or the Arduino-based electronics. Work is underway to be able to print the more sophisticated components such as the electronics

drill – compared to commercial systems, which cost thousands of dollars). It can be used for any application in development needing a micro centrifuge, including medical, biochemistry or education in the sciences (Pearce, 2012c).

With the alternative developmental path of free and open source it is clear that the patent system and closed copyright of information slows dissemination and thus actually hinders the progression of science and technology (Boldrin and Levine, 2008). This is counter to the traditional arguments for intellectual property (IP) as a concept and the historical justification for its existence. In an era of extremely low costs for the sharing of information, the entire concept of IP is increasingly found on the defensive (Boldrin and Levine, 2008) and some authors have argued that IP in the form of patent and copyright law cannot be justified (Kinsella, 2001). Thus, OSAT also enables a path to the end to predatory intellectual property lock-in on the most important technologies for a sustainable society. This is particularly important in the context of technology focused on relieving suffering and saving lives in the developing world. A good example of this is the completely open-source dissemination of

Figure 21.6   The DremelFuge

work done around the solar water disinfection (SODIS) method of water treatment shown in Figure 21.7 (Dawney and Pearce, 2012).

The SODIS method is a solution for purifying drinking water now used by over 5 million people in 24 African, Asian and Latin American countries (www.sodis.ch/projekte/index_ EN). All that it requires is for people to pour their collected water into clear PET bottles and to leave them exposed to sunlight – a source of pathogen-deactivating UV radiation and heat – for six hours. The method has been shown to kill bacteria and protozoan parasites and to inactivate different viruses, and it is reported to significantly reduce the number of children falling victim to diarrhoea (some studies suggesting by up to 70 per cent) and even cholera (by some 86 per cent).[7] The SODIS method is saving lives. This is urgently necessary, as still more than 4,000 children die every day from the consequences of diarrhoea.

Other OSATs can save lives less directly, as, for example, those technologies that help prevent deaths associated with greenhouse gas emissions and climate change. A recent posting of the complete technological design of an open-source wind turbine, including a printable flux generator as shown in Figures 21.8 and 21.9, makes it possible for anyone in the world with sufficient wind resources to provide for their own electrical needs. What is most remarkable is that these designs were posted by a company that sells the devices. This open-source approach is expanding through all areas of technology, from solar photovoltaic cells (Buitenhuis and Pearce, 2012) to microelectronics. Businesses are learning how to share, using open source, while still remaining financially viable. These early successes, perhaps, provide a warning to more conventional, closed firms – that it will be difficult to survive in the future if your business model relies on out-innovating everyone else working together.

As an example of open-source microelectronics, consider the Arduino electronic prototyping platform shown in Figure 21.10. The $20–$30 Arduino is a versatile, yet

Figure 21.7 The SODIS water disinfection method used to clean drinking water with sunlight being used in Indonesia

easy-to-learn microcontroller that can run a number of scientific instruments. For example, Arduinos are used to run radiation detectors, pH meters, oscilloscopes and DNA analysers. However, they can also be used by home owners to automate their heating, ventilation and air conditioning (HVAC) systems to save energy, among numerous other applications, including operating the open-source 3-D printers shown in Figure 21.5. To understand how such OSATs can be used by the public, consider the recent Fukushima nuclear disaster. The public found official reports dubious and government officials appeared to be actively preventing citizens from obtaining data (Brasor, 2012). The US government, for instance, refused to post online whatever radiation levels they were registering as radiation from Fukushima hit the West Coast. Then there were several reports that their proprietary monitors had gone offline or crashed (Washington Post, 2011). In the end, it does not matter if the government monitors suffered from technical failure or some kind of subterfuge on the part of the nuclear industry. Citizens of even relatively non-corrupt countries like Japan and the US can no longer trust that their governments are doing anything in their best interests. A response from citizens in Japan to this misdirection and the outright lies from public officials was to crowd-source radiation Geiger counter readings from across their country, using a collection of both open-source hardware and open-source software (Japan Geigermap, 2012). The results can be seen in Figure 21.12. These developments perhaps provide a warning to those who have historically controlled technology that the technical prowess of the public, combined with advanced networks, is making it increasingly difficult to manage public

Figure 21.8 The plans for this open-source wind turbine are all available free online. It is a wind turbine designed to output 1 kW under optimal conditions and uses a 3-D-printable generator shown in Figure 21.9. http://www.thingiverse.com/thing:28773

Figure 21.9 The 1 kW axial flux generator designed to be printed on a RepRap or similar, with a small build envelope. It features (more-or-less) tool-less assembly. http://www.thingiverse.com/thing:28762

Figure 21.10 The open-source Arduino electronic prototyping platform. This device is used to quickly automate even very complex tasks for low costs

opinion with misinformation. Open-source sharing of technology allows citizens to protect themselves with information.

What all OSATs must have in common is that they are appropriate for the context of the community they are meant for; not all technologies are appropriate for all countries or communities. Although information about radioactive contamination was recently very important and appropriate for Japan, those living in Africa might have more pressing concerns, like food storage. Thus the OSAT to solve this problem might cover very simple, low-cost devices like the Zeer pot-in-pot refrigerator (Figure 21.11). The Zeer pot-in-pot refrigerator can store 12 kg of vegetables, keeping them fresh for up to 20 days while costing less than US$2 to produce (Elkheir, 2002). It is an effective, elegant, low-cost and eminently distributable technology. However, even the operation and engineering optimization of this simple-looking device can be quite complex, necessitating advanced modelling like

Figure 21.11   The Zeer pot-in-pot refrigerator is a refrigeration device invented in Africa which operates through the principle of evaporative cooling

computational fluid dynamics. As one might suspect, resources from the government and corporations in the developed world to apply modern engineering to such devices for the poor are minimal at best. There is a clear and present need for those with the knowledge and tools to help accelerate further the engineering behind OSATs, even those that appear quite simple.

An open path forward

Conventional wisdom again would predict that any type of intellectual property development created using open-source paradigms should not be able to compete with the highly successful and well-demonstrated arguments about freedom and economic incentives deployed by neo-liberals. Surprisingly, the counter-argument comes from the development of science and engineering that underpins the technologies that make up some of the free market's greatest success stories. The vast majority of scientists and engineers are employed by the free market, including those at academic institutions. The science and engineering they do at academic institutions is generally published for everyone else in their particular field to see, if their institution pays the access charges. However, at the time of writing the debate in academia is shifting to favour *open access* journals or open access options for manuscripts, which are available to any reader in the world free of charge.[8] The primary advantage of open access is that the content is available to users everywhere regardless of affiliation with a subscribing library. This benefits:

• authors, as they like to see their papers cited and read more often;

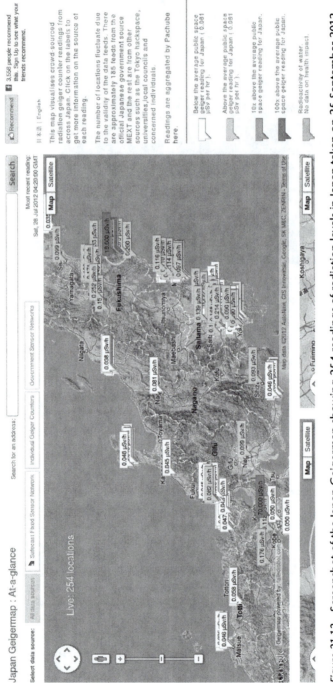

Figure 21.12 Screenshot of the Japan Geigermap showing 254 readings of radiation levels in Japan taken on 25 September 2012

- the development of science and engineering, as it enables academic readers at institutions that cannot afford the journal (as in many developing nations) to participate;
- the general public, as they can more easily see how research affects their lives (e.g. patients can keep up with the latest medical research).

Copyright, patents and trademarks are often lumped together under the term of intellectual property. However, if one person uses information it does not prevent someone else from using it; in fact, if both people use it, it may actually accelerate the development of additional information or innovation. Because of the exclusive monopoly rights governing IP, information is locked up and this often prohibits or slows innovation, which is the exact opposite of the supposed purpose of modern IP laws (Kogut and Metiu, 2001; Boldrin and Levine, 2008). Whereas copyright is automatic, patents must not only be applied for, but also entail a considerable capital investment. This investment is not only to obtain the legal protection of the patent, but also to effectively defend the patent in court. Without this defence the patent is useless. Thus, open sourcing patentable ideas faces unique challenges. In theory, by creating "open access" to ideas, future potential patents lose their viability as one would think the claim to novelty is eradicated.

However, by looking at the current patent literature it is clear that often trivial variations on well-understood technologies are able to gain patents and thus the only real value in patents is in the capacity to defend an idea in court. This again slows technology development. If an innovator has an idea they want to bring to market, they have to invest time and resources into ensuring that their product does not infringe on any patent. In many fields there is a large number of patents with overlapping broad scopes (called patent thickets). Thus our unlucky innovator must seek out and negotiate licences with many patent holders to ensure that the innovator will not be sued for patent infringement. This, of course, is all fairly silly as fundamental concepts in science are increasingly being patented, so innovators run the risk of being sued for ideas long used by nature (or, depending on your perspective, developed by God). Thus, it is not clear that the patent system is anything but a game where those with the largest resources and most lawyers are able to exploit their opponents. For those interested in OSAT, it is similarly unclear how the current patent system would thus be effective enough to protect open-sourced ideas from IP poaching by well-funded individuals or companies. Because of this danger, we could imagine that OSAT could fall within the legal framework of an AT General Public License (GPL), where those plans could be used freely, modified, and republished under the same AT GPL for those in the future all over the world to benefit from.

Currently, the OSAT revolution has not caused enough economic damage to major corporations to be of much concern, but as the sharing of designs and digital manufacturing matures this will no longer be the case. Then IP laws will be used as a club to beat back those that threaten corporate profits regardless of what happens to innovation. This was not the stated reason why IP laws were established initially; IP laws, rewarding innovators for inventions or creative work, were meant to encourage innovation. In some industries this aim may have been achieved in the past with patents,[9] but as technology has advanced this has become less clear and, in other cases, such as software, this claim is highly questionable (Merges and Nelson, 1990). In the case of AT, there is an unavoidable moral and ethical dilemma. Is it acceptable to withhold information that could save the world's poorest people from suffering and death in order to make a profit? For most individuals and academics the answer is obvious.

For companies working in the AT field the answer is more opaque. Although the problems of the global South are given remarkably low support for solutions (as compared to junk food, gaming, makeup, or most any other categories of consumer products) many researchers, companies and academics do work on products meant to assist sustainable development. Companies that do develop and profit from the sale of AT can often deliver affordable, life-affirming products and services to the "bottom of the pyramid" using conventional mass-scale manufacturing and business practices. How can they remain economically sustainable while opening their IP?

Boldrin and Levine (2008) have gone into the detail of both the advantages and the business models that exist to reward innovation in the absence of IP laws. One potential solution to this question comes from an unlikely source: Mrs. T's Pierogies. This is a small Pennsylvanian company that has a very successful business of selling pierogies (filled dough dumplings) and they ship 11.4 million a week (Pearce and Mushtaq, 2009). Recently, they volunteered all of the IP for the making of pierogies in a documentary: they walked the viewer through their plant, and then showed, step by step, how to make a pierogy at home from scratch (that is, they provided the source code for the pierogies). At the end of the documentary, they pointed out that although they showed you exactly how to do it, making pierogies is hard work and many people do not have the time, in which case consider buying Mrs. T's! Thus, even for open-sourced products that are appropriate, and that we want many times, it may be worth it for us to purchase them from a company even if we can do it ourselves. After all, we can easily find out how to make bread, but it is usually easier to buy it. In addition, we usually buy our products from companies that we are familiar with and where we have grown to trust the quality of the product – all of which provide a path for businesses to thrive by innovating without patents.

A similar model is being used by dozens of successful open-source hardware companies, and could be followed for OSAT; the information necessary to provide the basic needs of the world's poorest could be open sourced. There are numerous examples of hardware companies, with over a million in revenue, whose main products are open source; they include Adafruit Industries, Arduino, BeagleBoard, Buglabs, Chumby, Dangerous Prototypes, DIY Drones, Evil Mad Scientist Labs, Liquidware, Maker Shed, Parallax, Seed Studios, Solarbotics and Sparkfun Electronics. Most of these companies support the growing maker community – people that derive value from making things themselves. Phillip Torrone and Limor Fried from Adafruit Industries predict the open-source hardware industry will break $1 billion in revenue by 2015 as it expands rapidly (Torrone and Fried, 2010). These early open-source hardware company pioneers are trying to figure out how to meld old capitalism within a new, open business framework (Buitenhuis et al., 2010). Although there are a lot of options, it is far from clear what the best model is – or even that businesses in the conventional sense are the best solution for providing the things people need for rich, abundant, thriving lives in an era of distributed digital manufacturing.

These models of development are in flux and may or may not work with time. However, for the first time since the industrial age, a new option is open that does not rely on companies. Society has the option to maintain and increase technical prowess at *faster* rates than we observe under the market system, while moving back to self-reliance and peer production using open-source software and hardware – quickly exchanging digital designs and their improvements on the Internet the same way that high school students currently share and mash up mp3s. Digital designs and peer production offer the potential for driving the cost of physical goods down to the cost of the materials and electricity required to make them in home manufacturing systems (Kreiger et al., 2012). These costs are so low that the ability of for-profit corporations to compete is weak at best and thus a new economic paradigm may be emerging. Hubs for this knowledge have already begun to appear, such as Appropedia for

AT-specific information, GitHub or SourceForge for open-source software and Thingiverse for digital (usually printable) designs. It is not clear that the future needs companies or a market-based economy once a gift-based open-knowledge economy is sufficiently mature.[10]

A sustainable future

Throughout the world there exist research institutes, community groups, non-governmental organizations, families and individuals working with different technological innovations to alleviate poverty and mitigate the social and environmental destruction caused by the excesses of consumer-corporate culture. For the most part, they remain disconnected, often re-inventing the proverbial wheel again and again, although their counterparts in another part of the world may have already designed and debugged a similar social solution or technology. Clearly, appropriate technology development could benefit greatly from the application of an open-source model.

Consider the effect of open source appropriate technology taking hold globally – creating a vibrant, virtual community to share OSAT plans and experiences. OSAT venues like Appropedia are enabling designers and field-workers to download plans of water pumps, wind-mills, basic medicines, passive solar, and many other appropriate technologies. Meanwhile, an aggressive group of DIYers are sharing instructions from everything from plumbing and car repair to gardening on sites like Instructables and the 3-D printer users are rapidly expanding their list of printable objects (as of this writing there were more than 140,000 free, printable object designs on Thingiverse). As these communities continue to grow and merge, the design, fabrication and use of all OSATs will become an increasingly low-cost, high-value solution for people throughout the world. In this way, open source appropriate technology will become a true rival to the paradigms of the development of technology and its control by a capitalist class that has dominated civilization since the industrial revolution. A new revolution, built on a dispersed network of innovators, inventors and researchers working together to create a just, sustainable world, will be created.

Join us.

Notes

1 While it is well established that nuclear power is a heavily subsidized industry, one aspect of nuclear subsidization is rarely included in analysis because it is difficult to quantify: the indirect insurance liability subsidy. Currently, in the US, the collective liability cap for the industry is $10 billion. Should an accident exceed that amount, the government (i.e. taxpayers) would step in to cover the excess costs. As such, a cap on insurance liability represents an indirect subsidy, because it reduces the costs of nuclear energy and without it no nuclear power plant could be built. Thus private nuclear power companies are able to profit while the public must suffer both the real physical risk and the insurance cover. A recent analysis clearly showed that even if this relatively small nuclear insurance subsidy were provided at a similar scale of indirect subsidy to the solar industry, more than $5 trillion worth of electricity would be solar generated than we currently obtain from nuclear power (Zelenika and Pearce, 2011).

2 The Institute of Electrical and Electronics Engineers (IEEE) is the world's largest professional association dedicated to advancing technological innovation and excellence for the benefit of humanity. IEEE articles are now available online at http://ieeexplore.ieee.org/Xplore/guesthome.jsp However, even conference proceedings such as Pearce and Mushtaq's (2009) article on OSAT cost US$30 for non-subscribers.

3 Free and open-source software (F/OSS, FOSS) or free/libre/open-source software (FLOSS) is software that is both free and open source. Free software, software libre or libre software is software

that can be used, studied and modified without restriction; it can be copied and redistributed in modified or unmodified form either without restriction, or with restrictions that only ensure that further recipients have the same rights under which it was obtained and that manufacturers of consumer products incorporating free software provide the software as source code. The word "free" in the term refers to freedom (liberty) and is not at all related to monetary cost. Although FOSS is often available without charge, it is not bound to such a restriction.

4 In fact, even Microsoft is now embracing some components of open-source development. A Microsoft representative has recently stated that both SQL Server and the Windows Azure teams are committed to the Hadoop, open-source platform for the long term (Metz, 2011).

5 A rope pump is a simple, inexpensive water pump that uses a loose hanging rope in a pipe, the end of which is placed in a well. As the user pulls the rope out of the bottom of the well, round disks or knots matching the diameter of the pipe pull the water to the surface.

6 Solar photovoltaic cells are solid state devices which convert sunlight directly into electricity. To fabricate such devices normally involves fairly sophisticated technologies. For example, the cells shown in Figure 21.2 were deposited in a plasma-enhanced chemical vapor deposition system under vacuum and the process also included numerous production steps involving laser scribing, metallization and polymer encapsulation.

7 A list of publications showing the efficacy of the SODIS method against different types of disease-causing organisms can be found at www.sodis.ch/methode/forschung/publikationen/index_EN An overview is available at www.sodis.ch/methode/forschung/mikrobio/index_EN

8 For the Directory of Open Access Journals see: www.doaj.org/

9 Even this assertion is highly dubious, as Boldrin and Levine have shown in their book *Against Intellectual Monopoly* (made open access by both authors on their respective websites: http://levine. sscnet.ucla.edu/general/intellectual/against.htm and www.micheleboldrin.com/research/aim. html)

10 The concept of emeritus professorships lends some weight to this potentiality. Appointments to the rank of professor emeritus are normally without salary. Currently, thousands of highly specialized, enormously valuable individuals continue to go back to work at their universities after they have retired – for free. The market system cannot explain such behaviour, but the fact that these professors have essentially evolved above the need for the market economy and have been largely living in a gift-based economy (often for decades) certainly does. These individuals already have enough retirement income to meet their needs and modest luxuries; what they value and what they work for is to continue to be a part of the academic gift economy. With access to the enormous wealth made possible from leveraging open-source technological innovation, perhaps all of humanity will soon have a similar opportunity.

Resources

Appropedia.org

Hazeltine, B. and Bull, C. (2003). *Field Guide to Appropriate Technology*. San Diego: Academic Press.

McDonough, W. and Braungart, M. (2002). *Cradle to Cradle: Remaking the Way we Make Things*. New York: North Point Press.

Raymond, E.S. (1998). The Cathedral and the Bazaar, *First Monday* 3(3).

Schumacher, E.F. (1973). *Small is Beautiful: Economics as if People Mattered*. New York: Harper and Row.

References

Aragona, F. (2005). Open Sourcing Appropriate Technology Part I. *Agricultural Innovations* (17 November 2005). Available online at http://agroinnovations.com/blog/2005/11/17/open-sourcing-appropriate-technology-part-i/ (accessed 19 December 2011).

Baechler, C., DeVuono, M. and Pearce, J.M. (in press, 2013). Distributed Recycling of Waste Polymer into RepRap Feedstock, *Rapid Prototyping Journal* 19(2).

Bergquist, M. and Ljungberg, J. (2001). The Power of Gifts: Organizing Social Relationships in Open Source Communities, *Information Systems Journal* 11, pp. 305–320.

Björk, B., Roos, A. and Lauri, M. (2008). Global Annual Volume of Peer Reviewed Scholarly Articles and the Share Available via Different Open Access Options, *Proceedings of the ELPUB2008 Conference on Electronic Publishing*, Toronto, Canada, June. Available online at http://oacs.shh.fi/publications/elpub-2008.pdf (accessed 19 December 2011).

Boldrin, M. and Levine, D.K. (2008). *Against Intellectual Monopoly*. Cambridge: Cambridge University Press.

Bonaccorsi, A. and Rossi, C. (2003). Why Open Source Software Can Succeed. *Research Policy* 32, pp. 1243–1258.

Brasor, P. (2012). Public Wary of Official Optimism. The Japan Times, Sunday, 11 March. Available online at www.japantimes.co.jp/text/fd20120311pb.html (accessed 11 April 2012).

Buitenhuis, A.J. and Pearce, J.M. (2012). Open-Source Development of Solar Photovoltaic Technology, *Energy for Sustainable Development* 16, pp. 379–388.

Buitenhuis, A.J., Zelenika, I. and Pearce, J.M. (2010). Open Design-Based Strategies to Enhance Appropriate Technology Development. *Proceedings of the 14th Annual National Collegiate Inventors and Innovators Alliance Conference: Open*, pp. 1–12.

Davies, J.B., Sandstrom, S., Shorrocks, A. and Wolff, E.N. (2008). *The World Distribution of Household Wealth* (Working Paper No. DP2008/03). World Institute for Development Economic Research (UNU-WIDER).

Dawney, B. and Pearce, J.M. (2012). Optimizing Solar Water Disinfection (SODIS) Method by Decreasing Turbidity with NaCl, *Journal of Water, Sanitation and Hygiene for Development* 2(2), pp. 87–94.

DiBona, C., Ockman, S. and Stone, M. (1999). *Open Sources: Voices from the Open Source Revolution*. Sebastopol, CA: O'Reilly and Associates.

Dowd, K. (1996). The Case for Financial Laissez-Faire, *The Economic Journal* 106, pp. 679–687.

Elkheir, M. (2002). The Zeer Pot – a Nigerian Invention Keeps Food Fresh Without Electricity, *Science in Africa*.

Garvey, C. (2009). DremelFuge – A One-Piece Centrifuge for Rotary Tools. Thingiverse 1483. Available online at www.thingiverse.com/thing:1483 (accessed 19 December 2011).

Hansen, M., Kohntopp, K. and Pfitzmann, A. (2002). The Open Source Approach – Opportunities and Limitations with Respect to Security and Privacy, *Computers and Security* 21(5), pp. 461–471.

Hazeltine, B. and Bull, C. (1999). *Appropriate Technology: Tools, Choices and Implications*. San Diego: Academic Press.

Hazeltine, B. and Bull, C. (2003). *Field Guide to Appropriate Technology*, San Diego: Academic Press.

Huffington, A. (2004). *Pigs at the Trough: How Corporate Greed and Political Corruption Are Undermining America*. New York: Broadway Books.

Japan Geigermap: At-a-glance. (2012). Available online at http://japan.failedrobot.com/ (accessed 11 April 2012).

Kinsella, N.S. (2001). Against Intellectual Property, *Journal of Libertarian Studies* 15(2), pp. 1–53.

Kogut, B. and Metiu, A. (2001). Open-source Software Development and Distributed Innovation, *Oxford Review of Economic Policy* 17(2), pp. 248–264.

Kreiger, M., Anzalone, G.C., Mulder, M.L., Glover, A. and Pearce, J.M. (13). Distributed Recycling of Post-consumer Plastic Waste in Rural Areas. *Material Research Society*. Online Proceedings Library, 1492, mrsf12-1492-g04-06 doi: 10.1557/opl.2013.258.

Kunda, G. (2006). *Engineering Culture: Control and Commitment in a High-Tech Corporation*. Philadelphia, PA: Temple University Press.

Levy, S. (1984). *Hackers: Heroes of the Computer Revolution*. New York: Doubleday.

Mabe, M. (2003). The Growth and Number of Journals, *Serials: The Journal for the Serials Community* 16, pp. 191–197.

McDonough, W. and Braungart, M. (2002). *Cradle to Cradle: Remaking the Way we Make Things*. New York: North Point Press.

Merges, R.P. and Nelson, R.R. (1990). On the Complex Economics of Patent Scope, *Columbia Law Review* 90(4), pp. 839–916.

Metz, C. (2011). Microsoft Embraces Elephant of Open Source. *Wired*. Available online at www.wired.com/wiredenterprise/2011/10/microsoft-and-hadoop/ (accessed 19 December 2011).

Miller, H.L. (1962). On the "Chicago School of Economics", *Journal of Political Economy* 70, pp. 64–69.

Mirowski, P. and Plehwe, D. (2009). *The Road from Mont Pèlerin: The Making of the Neoliberal Thought Collective*. Cambridge, MA: Harvard University Press.

Mockus, A., Fielding, R.T. and Herbsleb, J.D. (2002). Two Case Studies of Open Source Software Development: Apache and Mozilla, *ACM Transactions on Software Engineering and Methodology* 11(3), pp. 309–346.

Mushtaq, U. and Pearce, J.M. (2012). Open Source Appropriate Nanotechnology. In D. Maclurcan and N. Radywyl (eds), *Nanotechnology and Global Sustainability*. Boca Raton: CRC Press, pp. 191–216.

Overtveldt, J.V. (2009). *The Chicago School: How the University of Chicago Assembled the Thinkers Who Revolutionized Economics and Business*. Chicago: Agate Publishing.

Pearce, J.M. (2009). Appropedia as a Tool for Service Learning in Sustainable Development, *Journal of Education for Sustainable Development* 3(1), pp. 47–55.

Pearce, J.M. (2012a). Limitations of Nuclear Power as a Sustainable Energy Source, *Sustainability* 4(6), pp. 1173–1187.

Pearce, J.M. (2012b). The Case for Open Source Appropriate Technology, *Environment, Development and Sustainability* 14, pp. 425–431.

Pearce, J.M. (2012c). Building Research Equipment with Free, Open-Source Hardware, *Science* 337 (6100), pp. 1303–1304.

Pearce, J.M. and Mushtaq, U. (2009). Overcoming Technical Constraints for Obtaining Sustainable Development with Open Source Appropriate Technology. Science and Technology for Humanity (TIC-STH), *2009 IEEE Toronto International Conference*, pp. 814–820.

Pearce, J.M., Grafman, L., Colledge, T. and Legg, R. (2008). Leveraging Information Technology, Social Entrepreneurship and Global Collaboration for Just Sustainable Development, *Proceedings of the 12th Annual National Collegiate Inventors and Innovators Alliance Conference*, pp. 201–210.

Pearce, J.M., Morris Blair, C., Laciak, K.J., Andrews, R., Nosrat, A. and Zelenika-Zovko, I. (2010). 3-D Printing of Open Source Appropriate Technologies for Self-Directed Sustainable Development, *Journal of Sustainable Development* 3(4), pp. 17–29.

Phillips, A. (2010). Blog to the Future? Journals Publishing in the Twenty-First Century, *Journal of Scholarly Publishing* 42(1), pp. 16–30.

Raymond, E.S. (1998). The Cathedral and the Bazaar, *First Monday* 3(3).

Schumacher, E.F. (1973). *Small is Beautiful: Economics as if People Mattered*. New York: Harper and Row.

Sepp, J. and Frear, D. (2011). *The Economy and Economics After Crisis*. Berlin: BWV Verlag.

Shantharam, Y. (2005). The Cost of Life: Patent Laws, the WTO, and the HIV/AIDS Pandemic, *Undercurrent* 2(2), pp. 48–56.

Smillie, I. (2000). *Mastering the Machine: Poverty, Aid and Technology*. UK: ITDG Publishing.

Tenopir, C.W. and King, D.W. (2009). The Growth of Journals Publishing. In B. Cope and A. Phillips (eds), *The Future of the Academic Journal*. Oxford: Chandos Publishing/Woodhead Publishing. pp. 105–124.

Torrone, P. and Fried, L. (2010). Million Dollar Baby: Businesses Designing and Selling Open Source Hardware, Making Millions. Presented at *Foo Camp East 2010*. Available online at http://vimeo.com/11407341 (accessed 19 December 2011).

Viner, J. (1960). The Intellectual History of Laissez Faire, *Journal of Law and Economics* 3, pp. 45–69.

Ware, M. and Mabe, M. (2009). *The STM Report*. Oxford: International Association of Scientific, Technical and Medical Publishers. Available online at www.stm-assoc.org/2009_10_13_MWC_STM_Report.pdf (accessed 19 December 2011).

Washington Post. (2011). You Can View Official EPA Radiation Readings, *Washington Post*. Available online at www.washingtonsblog.com/2011/03/you-can-view-official-epa-radiation-readings.html (accessed 11 April 2012).

Weber, S. (2000). The Political Economy of Open Source Software. Berkeley Roundtable on the International Economy, Working Paper 140.

World Health Organization (WHO). (2007). *Facts and Figures: Mortality Report*. Available online at www.wpro.who.int/media_centre/fact_sheets/fs_20070801.htm (accessed 19 December 2011).

Zelenika, I. and Pearce, J.M. (2011). Barriers to Appropriate Technology Growth in Sustainable Development, *Journal of Sustainable Development* 4(6), pp. 12–22.

Zelenika-Zovko I. and Pearce, J.M. (2011). Examining Social Barriers to Open Source Appropriate Technology and Innovation through Collaboration with Information and Communication Technology, 17th Annual International Sustainable Development Research Conference, pp. 507–508.

22

Education

By the people, for the people

The Trapese Collective

Introducing popular education

> I was lied to for a long time in our 'traditional' school system. From Columbus to the war of 1812, I only began to learn some of the truth in university. During my 3rd or 4th African History class, I cried, there was so much I didn't know. And since taking my learning into my own hands and into the arms of my community, I have been able to root myself as part of a narrative of cultural creators, activists, nurturers, femmes, as well as Red, Black, Brown, and Yellow people. My story is woven together from the stories we never hear. The moment I began this learning journey, my ability to self-determine drastically transformed. No one could name me, I now had the language and context to name myself. This is radical.
>
> *(Crosby, 2011)*

As this quote underlines, education is a potent tool for transmitting ideological and cultural practices and, as such, has long been a politically contested topic. Precisely because of this potency, there are countless people and projects across the world engaged in a different type of education, a type of teaching and learning which enables people to both understand and get involved in changing the conditions of their lives. Interchangeably known as radical, liberatory, popular, participatory or the 'practice of freedom' (Freire, 1986), this is a collective process of education which can help to build vibrant, active communities and is often entwined with challenging social injustice and inequality. In this chapter, we are interested in how social movements and grass-roots groups are transforming education and being transformed by it. They are realizing that educational activities are not an optional extra when they have spare time, but are fundamental to what they do and how they do it when they try and change their world. Many significant social movements have used education explicitly for social change. There are countless examples, but some important movements for us include the *Mujeres Libres* (Free Women of Spain) in 1930s Barcelona; The Scandinavian Free School Movement; the anti-World Trade Organisation mobilization in Seattle in 1999; the Bolivarian Circles in Venezuela since 2001; radical schools like Summerhill and White Lion in the 1960s; the Nicaraguan Literacy Crusades of the 1960s; the People's Education for People's

Power, South Africa in the 1980s; the Women's Health learning circles in the USA in the 1970s; and the Popular University of the Mothers of the Plaza de Mayo, Argentina since the 1980s. Many excellent guides exist for those who want to find out more (see Freire, 1986; Horton and Freire, 1990; hooks, 1994; Crowther *et al.*, 2005). This chapter does not cover these historical examples, but rather considers how education now can be radically different, and how the commodification of education can be challenged, and even reversed.

The many free schools around the world have been a fertile ground for radical education, and one important example is the Highlander School in the USA. This project emerged from the needs of a variety of social movements in Tennessee, including the lack of political representation. They developed the Citizenship School Programme which taught people how to read using the United Nations Declaration of Human Rights and through which thousands of people from poor black communities were able to register to vote. Their work continues to this day and has adapted to the changing needs of the time as they now describe themselves as a catalyst for grass-roots organizing and movement building (www.highlander-center.org).

One of the key thinkers when exploring popular education is Paulo Freire (1921–1997), a Brazilian educator whose pedagogy continues to provide insights today. Freire was a prolific writer over several decades. While not without his critics, Freire was instrumental in stressing the differences between traditional educational approaches and education for freedom. Freire carried out this analysis in the *Pedagogy of the Oppressed*, a classic of revolutionary education which has had widespread influence. In it he states:

> Education either functions as an instrument which is used to facilitate integration of the younger generation into the logic of the present system and bring about conformity or it becomes the practice of freedom, the means by which men and women deal critically and creatively with reality and discover how to participate in the transformation of their world.
>
> *(Freire, 1986: 34)*

Many have used Freire's ideas to highlight a comparison of formal-state or 'banking' education with popular-participatory-liberatory education. Formal-state education teaches basic skills but also the acceptance of authority in preparation for participation in waged-based work and consumerism. Learners receive knowledge from teachers with an emphasis on end results and rational fact-based information. By contrast, popular education aims to raise critical consciousness by linking education with action. At its core, popular education promotes social justice and solidarity by challenging hierarchies and using a variety of techniques to build collective knowledge, as well as exploring alternatives and valuing emotional, creative responses.

Critiquing the whole schooling system, therefore, has become central for popular educators. The dominant educational system of the global North in the last 200 years emerged around the same time as the Industrial Revolution, and was influenced by ideas about the efficiency of the factory model. Up to the late nineteenth century, education was gifted to poor and working people by religious or philanthropic individuals or organizations. As compulsory, state education developed, it was influenced by the idea that all children were the responsibility of the state and should be educated to be good citizens. The work of Ivan Illich (1971), who denounced the schooling system as an instrumental machine, reproducing social inequalities and an ineffective tool for learning, has been extremely influential. He advocated a more self-directed education, supported by intentional and fluid social relations. Illich's ideas reinforce the idea held by popular educators that school is an institution that reinforces inequality and social stratification. If we are to build a freer, more egalitarian world then replacements need to be sought.

Deep problems remain in the educational philosophies or pedagogies of formal education. In our increasingly complex world, people from across the political spectrum are asking how we can teach in ways that foster creativity better and equip people for the different challenges of the world we live in today. Robinson points out the contradiction that concerns many of us:

> Education is the system that's supposed to develop our natural abilities and enable us to make our way in the world. Instead, it is stifling the individual talents and abilities of too many students and killing their motivation to learn.
>
> *(Robinson, 2009: 5)*

Popular education attempts to break some of the cycles of social privilege and instrumentality associated with the school system. However, it is certainly not within the capacity or intentions of popular educators to reform or replace the entire schooling system. Popular education is the desire to bring about social change and to empower participants to create social change themselves. Although work with children and young people is, of course, important, the explicit aim to foster political action means that most popular education is with adults.

In contrast to the more usual role of a teacher, popular educators take on the responsibility to guide groups beyond 'what is wrong with the world' to explore possible actions that can be taken. Paulo Freire called this process *conscientization* – tapping into, and building on, people's understanding of the world around them. Popular education is a participatory process of action-reflection-action, identifying problems, analysing issues and looking for solutions through common action. In our book *Do It Yourself* (Trapese Collective, 2007), we drew out the following six principles:

- starting from people's daily reality
- learning our own histories not 'his-story'
- learning together as equals
- a commitment to transformation and solidarity
- getting out of formal educational settings
- inspiring social change.

Such an educational approach has the potential to be transformatory at the personal, institutional and societal levels. One of the most exciting, but at times intimidating, characteristics of popular education approaches is that often one has no fixed idea about what these will be.

About Trapese

This chapter is written by the Trapese Popular Education Collective which was established in 2004, in the run-up to the Group of Eight (G8) meeting in the UK. We believed that education, and in particular popular education, was vital in putting forward a different story of the G8. We formed with the aim of doing educational work that hooked a broad range of people into a conversation about capitalism, climate change and global poverty, and attempted to mobilize a response. Our influences included the creative and diverse experiments in horizontal and anti-authoritarian organizing which emerged throughout the 1990s and 2000s through counter-summits, autonomous social centres, anti-capitalist analysis and direct action (see Maeckelbergh, this volume).

So what lessons can we offer from our experiences between 2004 and 2011? Organizationally, we were a small, non-hierarchical group of three that operated with varying degrees of autonomy from each other over the years. We were mostly based in distinct geographical areas and would come together for particular projects and meetings or collaborate online. We worked with many inspirational people over the years, who volunteered their ideas, projects, resources and skills to help Trapese build its radical education activities. We were closely linked to emerging social movements in the UK and so our projects were always entwined with the ebbs and flows of these wider processes. For example, one key theme was climate change and an analysis which located the capitalist system of production and consumption as a root cause. Increasingly, climate justice became an important idea and our work can be seen to follow a trajectory from the topic of climate change on the agenda at the G8 in 2005 through the climate action and climate camps of 2006–2010, the emergence of the Transition Town Movements (see Ganesh and Zoller, this volume), a grass-roots network of communities who work to build resilience in response to peak oil, climate destruction, and economic instability and resistance to the United Nations Conferences of the Parties to the United Nations Framework Convention on Climate Change (known as COP summits).

The success of our collective working rested upon a foundation of shared values, practices and experience that was built up through our shared political analysis and the intense period of mobilization for the G8 counter summit, 2005. Initially our sessions drew heavily on a toolkit produced by a popular education in action collective in Canada who did a similar project. During our successful 'roadshow' in the nine months before the summit, we organized more than 100 events around the UK, Ireland and in mainland Europe. Each session was distinct, but combined participatory information sharing, critical analysis of mainstream discourse and action planning. We attempted to provide a way of looking at the summit, not as global leaders aiming to solve the problem, or for NGOs to 'Make Poverty History' but instead as an opportunity for ordinary people to come together to understand the power the G8 holds within the capitalist system and looking for creative ways to challenge that. One of the greater successes was that we used a wide range of creative activities, from presentations to pub quizzes, and reached many people who would not necessarily come to a political meeting. A downside in terms of popular education methodology was that we were not able to work with groups over a longer period of time.

Bringing together our individual perspectives was a strength that led us to work on the fertile edges between grass-roots activist spaces, the academy, the creative arts and NGO/ voluntary sector organizations. Over time, our focus turned to projects to build capacity, such as skill sharing or training, producing written resources and critiques and working on longer term projects. These included co-editing *Do It Yourself: A handbook for changing our world* (Trapese Collective, 2007) and the MA in Activism and Social Change at the University of Leeds, which reflected a desire to try and embed radical popular education within formal education settings. Two key moments in developing our practice were the week-long Popular Education gatherings that we organized in Spain in 2006 and in England in 2008, opportunities to work through debates and try out ideas with other educationalists. Following the publication of our handbook in 2007, we tried to bring the resources to life – through workshops at gatherings, conferences and counter summits. These ranged from interventions on topical debates, to weekend-long, site-specific workshops and a series of events in a modern arts gallery. We also organized two week-long residential courses called 'Tools for

Social Change', that combined critiquing and discussing political issues such as democracy, education and sustainability and then exploring tools for action to put alternatives into practice; for example, learning skills for consensus decision making, popular education toolkits and campaign planning.

Running through Trapese's work was a commitment to experimentation and 'learning from doing' ourselves. We were driven by passion for our subjects but did not pretend to be experts or to have all the answers. Instead we facilitated spaces where people from different backgrounds could share their perspectives and this created a rich mix of knowledge and, at times, inspiration. As we built up a toolkit and experience over the years, we could pull out relevant pieces as required and were able to respond to diverse requests. Ultimately, things have moved on, both personally and politically, but through our commitment to sharing resources and open source knowledge, we hope that these resources will continue to be adapted and re-experimented with, as we have done ourselves.

Lessons from popular educators today

This chapter argues that popular education methods are still relevant today, especially for those trying to build educational alternatives. We now turn to consider some characteristics of education done through, and with, social movements that have transformative ambitions. The groups we discuss here may not all call themselves popular educators, but we have chosen initiatives that, for us, help to illuminate the power of this type of educational work.

Making links through critical literacy

Literacy was a key motivating factor in the work of Freire, working in one of the poorest areas of the world, and explicitly linking people's inability to read and write to their lack of agency in changing the conditions of their oppression. Put simply, he linked reading the word and the world. Adult illiteracy continues to affect many people, but literacy is much broader than being able to read and write. As anyone who has ever learned another language will know, there are many layers to any text. There are subtleties and contextual clues, choices of vocabulary or cultural references that can be mined for meaning. Critical thinking is the idea that as we read we are constantly questioning, exposing the power relations beneath. From this we come to see that there is no one, static, view of the world. The role of the educator is to ask 'problem-posing' questions, to dig deeper into people's reading of a situation: what context does this situation come from; why is it like this; who holds the power here; how could we change it?

Herman and Chomsky's ideas are useful here concerning corporate control and bias in the media by asking who is the author, where do they come from, who is paying for the publication? Who was consulted, who wasn't? (Herman and Chomsky, 1988). There are many independent media projects, that exist globally, which aim to expose and challenge corporate control. Spoof newspapers are a good example, presenting alternative views in the guise of a mainstream paper. In London in 2010, *The Metr0* was produced as part of an action that targeted the mainstream press. By telling a familiar story but subverting the political agenda, this action attempted to call attention to the often hidden positions of the press. Given its direct attack on the circulation of free daily newspapers, it also attracted a court injunction (Greenslade, 2010).

Another contemporary example is the Reflect ESOL project which worked with the campaign group 'Justice 4 Domestic Workers' linked with the union Unite. Justice 4 Domestic

Workers (J4DW) is run by and for migrant workers and most of the campaign members are domestic workers forced to work abroad because of extreme poverty in their home countries. They campaign to improve conditions in this country, including visa rights, employment rights and exposing abuse from employers. The Reflect UK team worked with the campaign group, with particular focus on developing English language and literacy skills as key tools for their campaigning work. They used aspects of participatory and critical pedagogical methods to explore issues of importance to the group. The participants, who mostly had low levels of written English, wrote a short article for publication that expressed their collective situation of feeling trapped. This was reflected in their lack of freedom of movement and the conditions of their employment. Marissa Begonia from J4DW said, 'At first, it was a very big question mark, can we do it? But they worked together, contributed ideas and they have in the end a very good article, that is very important to them, to raise their issues and problem' (Reflect ESOL, 2011).

Drawing attention to the root causes and structural linkages between individual cases of oppression is the core work of popular educators. In the 'spiral model' of reflective learning (see Figure 22.1), linking the individual case to their broader picture is central and many groups try and emphasize these links.

For example, working with unemployed people we might ask for alternative explanations that look beyond individual failure, lack of motivation, inadequate grades, and instead explore the historical and socio-political reasons that mean that there are few jobs in a given locality. Making these kinds of links is beautifully illustrated by Gihan Perera from the Miami Worker's Centre:

> We have a clear analysis of how the destruction of public and subsidized housing is directly related to neoliberalism. We don't assume that our base comes in with that analysis, and we don't try to impose that analysis on our base. But we think that the point of the Workers Center is to create a space to have that dialogue. And our responsibility is not just to fight around local issues. Instead, we want to fight around housing and ask how that turns into global lessons for global issues. How do lessons in terms of power and power dynamics lead to lessons in terms of how housing is connected to neoliberalism? We felt like the point of organizing is to create that space.
>
> *(Center for Justice, Tolerance and Community, 2006)*

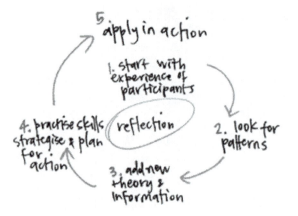

Figure 22.1 'Spiral model' of learning (based on Arnold *et al.*, 1991: 38)

Exploring links also means linking wider issues to local reality. How do the decisions made by transnational institutions filter down and impact on us? Are there direct ways that we can influence their decisions? The KLEAR project in Kilbrarrack, just outside of Dublin, Ireland is an inspirational example from the early 1980s. Originally publicized simply as a chance for young mothers in a working-class area to 'Get out of the house', the classes became an important part of forming relationships and taking action. The classes were led by what the students wanted and their experiences – of claiming unemployment benefit, or of their children's experiences at school – became the material for writing classes. The project was linked to the consciousness-raising of the time and led to women speaking out about recession and the way it impacted upon them. They organized demonstrations, wrote letters and got involved with running the building and the classes, from interviewing the teachers to planning the curricula. One learner said, 'It gave us permission to become activists, and out of that we got a sense of our own power and how good we could be starting other groups in other areas and linking up, they could do it too' (Beyond the Classroom, 2010).

Space for dialogue and direct democracy

We live in a society where adversarial politics are the norm. Political parties are pitted against each other and, although the differences between their actual policies are often limited, opponents argue over who is right. This competitive nature filters across our society. Conflict between competing points of view is endemic, from aggressive international trading to violent conflict over apparent ethnic difference or resources. While conflict can be an important catalyst for change, and is not always negative if well managed, popular education aims to bring different types of knowledge and of experiences into a shared place of learning, where emerging issues or contradictions can be exposed and explored and common ground is established.

Dialogue is a key tool here that involves listening to what someone is saying and responding. It is a collective journey, where each speaker will influence the direction of the conversation. Paulo Freire called this 'dialogic learning'. So, while you have your opinions, ideas and conceptions of the world, they are not fixed. You cannot understand this reality separately from the reality of those around you. You must therefore listen and attempt to understand what is being said about other perspectives in order to fully understand your own.

In contrast, the orthodox or didactic approach to education places the teacher as a fountain of knowledge and the learner as an empty vessel, waiting to be filled. Popular education aims to be much more equal – the experiences and knowledge of the learner are valued and the teacher is assumed to develop too. This collective knowledge is built through dialogue. In this sense, education is not about teaching someone the right answer, but developing possible solutions together. For example, if we value emotional and sensory knowledge we can build up a very different picture from that which emerges from 'hard' facts.

A further principle is that all voices are equally heard. Positions of power influence who is listened to. Race, gender, religion, sexuality, class, nationality, profession, accent, education, first language, literacy, access to technology, physical ability and health are just some of the many factors that can impact upon our ability to be heard. These factors do not render people 'voiceless' but can often make it more difficult for voices to be heard. Popular educators work to create spaces where many different voices can be heard, but also recognize and challenge long-standing and often invisible power relations inside groups. So, for example, people explicitly involved in anti-oppression work need to continually reflect on their own behaviour and attitudes. As we saw above, this is the 'spiral of learning' (Arnold *et al.*, 1991: 38) approach of popular education, where undertaking action and reflection at the same time encourages us to go beyond our comfort zones, to places that can challenge our underlying assumptions, and make real change.

One innovative approach to building dialogue and communication is Community Resolve who work with young people from different areas of inner city Bristol in the UK. There have been long-standing and often violent conflicts between 'gangs' and Community Resolve facilitators have made creative interventions at various levels – individual, group, intergroup and institutional – to unpick the issues of power, identity and structural causes that underlie and perpetuate the conflict in this area. A photography project working with primary school-children visiting and making friends across the different areas allowed stereotypes to be challenged and common ground to be found. This slow, but multi-layered, approach appears to be having profound effects and leaves people feeling more confident '[w]hen they are equipped with the skills to understand and deal with conflict' (Community Resolve, 2012).

Many groups and events have been putting these kinds of actions into practice. The counter summit has become a key activity of global social movements – from World Social Forums and the KlimaForum at the Copenhagen COP summit, to teach-ins and People's Assemblies – making spaces for creating radical, alternative and open discourses are fundamentally linked to building movements, informing campaigns and challenging the status quo. Within these events, forms of consensus decision making, such as large-scale spokes-councils, are fundamental to determining that frames of discourse are not held by the few but, instead, open up spaces which allow for all voices to be heard. It is hard to quantify the impact that these different examples have had on the individuals involved, or overall. However, these spaces for dialogue consciously aim to develop the communication skills which are so important to people who are speaking out, working together and challenging oppression.

Tackling consumerism

Our lives are saturated with stuff, goods and services produced for profit and sold in the marketplace (see Ferrell, this volume). Our global economy, our workplaces, our communities and transport systems are geared up towards producing and distributing all these things. It is increasingly clear that this is causing multiple problems – from crippling personal debt, to rising carbon emissions from resource use and transportation, and to transforming our identity from citizens to consumers. The humble commodity has come to shape almost every aspect of our lives. This commodification has extended beyond simply consuming more goods and services; whole areas of our lives can be valued and then traded in the marketplace. Beyond the basic things that we need for a decent life, our public services, resources, land, and even our air and water, now carry a price tag. This privatization is part of a great enclosure (see De Angelis and Harvie, this volume) that limits public access to the things we depend on and goes against the long, historical struggles for the creation of publicly, nationally and commonly owned assets.

How can the penetration of the market economy into many aspects of our lives be resisted? First, we can rethink the assumption that the work we do in our lives is only done for profit or a wage (see Williams, this volume). It is useful to think about the difference between the labour we do to enrich ourselves as humans and the work we do to earn a wage. John Holloway (2010) calls this the difference between 'doing' and 'done', and Chris Carlsson (2008) talks about this in terms of the 'nowtopians' who are experimenting with ways of living and activity based on free exchange. Second, it means building a commons, not just in terms of land, but also in terms of social relations between commoners who can manage these resources for the common good. There are many examples here such as barter markets, local exchange trading systems, community orchards and a whole raft of self-provisioning, from bee keeping to beer making.

Education is a fundamental area in the struggle against commodification. State-run education, in both rich Western nations as well as poorer low-income countries, represents one of the last, relatively untouched public commons – ripe for a great sell-off to the private sector. In universities, academic labour is increasingly instrumentalized through metric-based publishing and performance reviews and monitoring systems such as the Research Excellence Framework in the UK, turning teachers and lecturers into instructors for the market. At the same time, students are now more akin to consumers, with educational experiences geared towards meeting the needs of the corporate business world and preparing them for a life as a debt-burdened consumer. In the UK in 2012, university entrance fees tripled to £9,000 annually, and prestigious global universities are selling degree courses through World Bank-funded franchise models to universities in poorer countries who do not have the resources to develop their own curricula.

In response, there has been resistance on the streets – such as in Chile where there have been riots in a long struggle over access to the nation's elite university system – but we have also seen the creation of projects that are putting into practice a radically different notion of education. Free schools and free universities have been springing up, including The People's University in New York, which took inspiration from the Occupy Wall Street movement; the collectively run Social Science Centre which is part of the 'University of Utopia', a loose collective of anti-capitalist scholar activists originating from Lincoln, UK (http://blog. universityofutopia.org); and The AnarchistU in Toronto, Canada, a collective committed to offering free education in a radically democratic way.

The Really Open University (ROU), based in the UK, describes its vision:

> Imagine an education system where participants teach what inspires them, and learn what they are passionate about – a space where people share and develop their skills and knowledge not in the individual quest for jobs and profit but in a mutual attempt to create a more equitable and sustainable world.

ROU defines itself through three ideas: strike, occupy, transform. They are committed to abandoning spaces of paid education, creating new spaces to develop an alternative, free education and, through this, transforming participants. They call for three reforms: the Abolition of all Fees and the Institution of a Living Wage for students, a debt jubilee for all past students, and the abolition of the Research Excellence Framework and performance management. They hold workshops, have been involved in occupations and sit-ins, and publish an occasional newsletter called the 'Sausage factory' inspired by the words of Karl Marx (1867):

> [A]school master is a productive labourer, when, in addition to belabouring the heads of his scholars, he works like a horse to enrich the school proprietor. That the latter has laid out his capital in a teaching factory, instead of a sausage factory, does not alter the relation.

ROU held a week-long free university during the national day of action in March 2010, where students, teachers and members of the public offered free workshops and sessions on a range of issues – from understanding capitalism to bike workshops. Lecture halls were occupied and participants joined in the rallies that were held as part of a national day of strike action. Their activities show how they are committed to transformation on a number of different levels – the personal, the institutional and the societal.

Organizing ourselves

Surely we could manage our lives more, not to create more work, but to have more fulfilling communities, personal relationships and leisure time. We are surrounded by ordinary people and groups who are experts in how to do things better, but their skills and abilities are overlooked because of bureaucracy and centralization. It's not just that it is more empowering to manage our own lives, but more collective forms of self-management are often better at dealing with the problems our current societies face such as climate change, political dependency, poverty and debt.

In the era of austerity which followed the financial crisis, how to organize and to act collectively, as opportunities opened up, were important questions for popular education. Let's be clear. We are not talking about self-management in the liberal-individual legalistic sense, where individuals are cut adrift from responsibility and focused on maximizing profits in the market. Rather, this is self-management that undermines the logic of private ownership and recognizes that the individual thrives when our needs are met collectively (see Chapter 3 in this volume). It is about challenging the role of the expert – the architect, the planner, the teacher, the politician. Collective self-management builds a common ownership and management of spaces and services, and erodes the logic of individual gain. This is much more than simply trying to be more self-reliant. It is about self-determination – the ability to own and control resources and land.

Learning to manage our own lives is crucial for a number of reasons. It is empowering, rather than waiting for politicians, planners, or local business elites to make change on our behalf. A brief glance at any city shows us the real outcome of an estranged system, over which we have little control: bleak outer estates, choking motorways, peanuts from planning gain, handing over swathes of cities to modern-day corporate robber barons (pension companies, corporate banks, entertainment multinationals). Haven't they had their turn? If the powerful could have made our cities great they would have. Groups of ordinary people, self-organized and empowered, can do a much better job. Countless micro examples of self-management are flourishing, such as eco-villages, workers and housing co-operatives, syndicalist unions, self-build housing, workplace organizing and strikes. All this involves education, but not the buying of credentials which characterizes the modern university.

Feeling the power of collectives comes through our daily encounters and activities with others. Learning collectively, and undertaking useful, life-affirming activity as part of it, allows us to revalue education not just as a means of securing employment, but of developing meaningful relationships with others. A priority is to find ways out of education as a route to demoralizing and low-wage jobs and to develop ways of living which meet our own needs, not those of the money economy. Radical collective learning, combining manual and intellectual labour, allows us to appreciate the importance of stimulating our minds and ideas, but also of learning practical skills to enable greater self-reliance. Mutual aid, developing an ethic of care for others and creating voluntaristic and free support structures, is both individually empowering and also provides incredibly useful social networks.

The Camps for Climate Action were illuminating examples of self-management and a living laboratory for testing new skills for a world beyond fossil-fuel dependency. An annual cycle of summer Climate Camps began in the UK in 2006 focusing on different sources of carbon emissions: Drax power station in 2006, as the UK's single biggest point source of CO_2; Heathrow airport in 2007, due to expansion plans of terminal 5; Kingsnorth power station in 2008, due to the controversies surrounding plans for the first carbon capture and storage site; Blackheath in London in 2009, which focused on the role of the city of London; and Royal Bank of Scotland in 2010, which focused on the company's role in fossil-fuel investments known as the 'Oil and Gas Bank'. The Camps had four principal aims of movement building, education, direct action and sustainable living. The week-long Camps aimed to create a convergence space through which these four aims could be realized. The Climate Camp became so successful as a model that, by 2009, it had been replicated in Wales, France, New Zealand, Switzerland, Ecuador, India and Ghana.

The Camps were organized through neighbourhoods, each based around a region or city of the UK. The neighbourhoods had daily meetings using consensus decision making with rotating facilitators. These fed into a site-wide plenary which made larger decisions of strategic and site-wide importance related to issues of media, actions and community relations. The Camps usually culminated in a day of action focusing on a mass trespass event based around decentralized actions organized through autonomous affinity groups. Through self-organizing, the Camps' participants become their own educators as they experimented with organizing everything from local energy generation, to mass cooking and medics providing autonomous healthcare. New skills were learned, shared and spread which could help with dealing with potential future social ecological crises. There were also bases, platforms and safe spaces for training, forming and taking direct action and collective learning on the root causes of climate change, using the location as a live context for the learning experience.

Clearly there are many limits to education that is more self-managed and empowering. How do we make the potential of truly liberatory education seem feasible and necessary in an age when many of us have come to expect everything to be done for us, or that problems can be solved by buying in solutions? Why should we do it ourselves, when we are so used to the institutionalization of schooling and delegated authority? These are tough questions, and ones that need addressing. But as responses from politicians, institutions, universities and schools fail to live up to the scale of the problems we face, the desire for self-management and self-empowerment through more liberatory forms of education will only grow larger. We must never forget that processes of radical and popular education are crucial building blocks of an anti-capitalist and less hierarchical world.

Revisioning: make the impossible possible

Corrupt financial and political systems, a rapidly changing climate, dwindling natural resources, and cuts to public services can add up to a fairly bleak picture of the coming years. There is an influential school of thought that argues that without constructing a positive vision for the future it is very easy to become disillusioned and certainly impossible to know what path or paths to take to get there. The Transition movement (see Ganesh and Zoller, this volume) is an example of a wide network of people who are organizing for a brighter future, as Transition founder Rob Hopkins states:

> By shifting our mind-set we can actually recognise the coming post-cheap oil era as an opportunity rather than a threat, and design the future low carbon age to be thriving,

resilient and abundant – somewhere much better to live than our current alienated consumer culture based on greed, war and the myth of perpetual growth.

(Hopkins, 2008)

Dealing with these issues will not be achieved by councils, governments, corporations or small groups of experts introducing new legislation, but by resilient and empowered communities who are able to work together. Thirty years of neo-liberal policies, increasing use of information technology and increased migration have severely eroded locally rooted communities. In the face of these challenges it is vital that there is ongoing educational development work to bring people together, in a way that fosters co-operation, mutual aid and solidarity. Building resilience can take many forms – environmental, economic, social and cultural. Ultimately it is about developing good communication, and having the flexibility to deal with the challenges we face.

A critical part of building community resilience and enhancing well-being is exploring and developing connections between groups and reciprocity. Popular education methodology has a huge role to play in doing this. Through creating good processes within a group, it is possible to transform a passive or questioning level of awareness around an issue to one where the participant is actively engaged and empowered to take action. Dealing with subjects such as climate change can leave us despairing; it is therefore important to try and turn those feelings into practical steps for action and ultimately turn dreams into realities.

Revisioning is a process in which a group maps their current situation based on the daily reality of participants and then facilitators lead the group towards other possible scenarios. This is the 'dream element', the opportunity to allow imaginations to flow and creativity to abound. These revisioning exercises can take many different forms depending on the group; from small group discussions, to drawing pictures of a group's desired future, to acting out scenarios. Forum theatre, as practised by Augusto Boal (1985), allows a group to imagine transforming a scenario of oppression, by acting out different ends to a familiar situation. All these activities use creative methods to bring about a shared vision of the future which participants would be willing to work towards.

Revisioning in the case of Transition rejects the dominant idea of a fossil fuel dependent society and instead works towards a low carbon future. This common agreement by 'transitioners' in turn leads to action planning to work towards building that low carbon vision. The Transition Movement calls this the 'great re-skilling'; in other words, relearning skills that have been forgotten, such as how to mend clothing, grow and preserve food, fix bikes, and build low impact houses. A facilitator's role, therefore, is to ensure that there is ample time and energy within a group to allow participants to identify what they need to make the future a reality.

It is important to provide support and peer-to-peer learning when engaging in such work. Communities of practice such as Fiery Spirits, who have over 1,000 members across the UK and Ireland, link up rural activists and practitioners. Fiery Spirits practitioners set out to accelerate learning by activists, professionals and policy makers who are working to build resilient and sustainable communities. It does this by enabling practitioners to connect, challenge and learn from each other both at face-to-face events and virtually, via a social networking website. Projects range from community broadband and social entrepreneurs working with council staff to sustain local services, to unlikely alliances of retired servicemen, ethical bankers and land campaigners who are creating community land trusts to deliver affordable local housing. They are all united by principles of participation and inclusion by communities and groups into the process.

An example of a revisioning at the global scale can be found in the work of the worldwide Occupy movement. Since it began in late 2011, in Zuccotti Park in New York City's Wall Street financial district, Occupy has provided an alternative vision for a more equal world using its slogan 'we are the 99%'. Occupy groups all over the world have organized camps with workshops, lectures and skill-shares. Like many smaller movements and mobilizations before, their general assemblies are innovative and inclusive processes for decision making that explicitly counter marginalization and foster active listening. The Global May manifesto of the International Occupy Assembly states, "We want another world, and such a world is possible" and goes on to make a series of demands to transform political and economic systems to the service of people's welfare, and to support and serve the environment, not private profit. Many have found this collectively written and endlessly debated statement helpful in mobilizing action at a local level around a global set of demands.

Some problems that we have experienced

Just like any participatory process, there is no magic formula that can avoid the at times messy reality of human social interaction. Of course, it is possible to learn a great deal from mistakes if situations are reviewed honestly and openly.

Common ground?

What happens when participants in an educational workshop or process hold views that are diametrically opposed? Although conflicting views can provide fertile ground, there are inevitably times when one or more people seem to be irreconcilably at odds. Exposing these deep-rooted differences of opinion risks splitting the group or otherwise disrupting what had been a functioning, if somewhat superficial, working relationship. While this is not necessarily a bad thing in the long run, it can be a difficult thing to manage well. Popular educators should anticipate these kinds of issues and be aware that they will not necessarily be able to resolve them.

Barriers to action

While popular education explicitly attempts to build capacity towards social action, it cannot necessarily overcome significant hurdles. Through exploring an issue, it is quite possible that a group takes the decision that there is no appropriate course of action, or that there are not people who are able or willing to do what is deemed necessary. This could range from operating in a repressive environment where risks are seen as too high, to a simple lack of belief that anything will change. The role of the facilitator when a group is choosing an appropriate course of action can be very challenging and it takes sensitivity, tact and strategic awareness to guide a group, while at the same time constantly attempting to let the wishes of the group emerge. At the same time, education is by no means a prerequisite to taking action, and of course millions of examples exist of spontaneous and effective actions that do not emerge from lengthy processes. Some have argued that rather than facilitating action, such educational processes can actually get in the way (Scathach, 2011).

Who is the educator?

Although some excellent training, support and resources do exist, the popular educator is largely self-taught, self-appointed and self-directed. This lack of a formal role can be both liberating and also problematic. Although the power to determine the place, time and content of any educational programme will be ideally not held by the educator alone, it is difficult to eradicate the ingrained power dynamic of hierarchy between the 'learner' and the 'teacher'. Some individuals will navigate this better than others, but it has certainly left popular educators open to the criticism that:

> [Popular education] can replicate the very same social relations it attempts to expose. . . . In a group dynamic, it also allows the loudest voices to dominate, and these usually reflect the relational privileges in the group. The abiding struggle of educators is to facilitate without leading. In trying to create space for horizontal learning, popular education practitioners risk exposing themselves and learners to the tyranny of structurelessness [for more, see Jo Freeman's seminal 1972 text *The Tyranny of Structurelessness*] – whereby hierarchies become established via the attempted negation of their very existence.
>
> *(Scathach, 2011)*

It is important to recognize that participatory methods are also increasingly the norm in mainstream pedagogy and that there is nothing inherently radical about methodologies unless combined with a political position.

This kind of educational work can only be done step by step, identifying cracks for action and organizing that can be built slowly and patiently in communities from the bottom up. At some point, new institutions need to be built which represent stable bases for organizing alternatives outside the marketplace. But resources and capacities are needed to establish and maintain these. A key area for vigilance is how to ensure that these do not become co-opted or commodified slowly without noticing. Such action will also always include compromises and playing the system at its own game and using its own resources against it in creative ways.

Final reflections: putting popular education into everything we do

In this chapter we have considered a variety of projects that are engaged in some kind of popular education, the word popular meaning here 'of and from the people'. The examples are therefore as diverse as the local realities from which they have emerged. For us, the potency of popular education emerges from combining content, methods, context and values. For example, critical analyses from voices that are normally ignored can be combined with methods that enable meaningful participation and ownership, at the same time as promoting values such as co-operation and solidarity and breaking learning out of the classroom and taking it to the streets, workplaces and public parks. We hope to see an increase in the kinds of popular education highlighted in this chapter as people respond to the changing economic and social landscape of the twenty-first century. These initiatives represent a radical kind of popular action learning which poses a huge challenge to conventional education in a number of ways: it is focused on how we manage and respond to big issues such as climate change and the attack on free public services, it rejects working in disconnected silos and instead embraces holistic working, it embraces uncertainty and risk rather than reinforcing the status quo, it insists that knowledge must be created collaboratively that goes hand in hand with creating practical skills and resources. Clearly, with the profusion of web-based information there has been an explosion of peer-to-peer communication that is more participatory and collaborative, and events such as the TED lectures in the USA and the Do lectures in the UK have showcased alternative knowledge and understanding to a broad audience. Popular education that attempts to build egalitarian relationships not based on profit must learn from these without losing its radical spirit.

What we want to stress is that popular education is much more than a toolkit or an approach to teaching. It is more a philosophy that informs all our social change activities. As Gihan Perera states when talking about the groups who have been using popular education at the Miami Workers Centre:

> Witnessing the success of these organizations is proof that popular education methodologies could be more than an organizing technique; it has the potential to be the fabric that runs through everything the Center does.
>
> *(Center for Justice, Tolerance, and Community, 2006)*

In this sense, the approach informs our campaigning, our texts, our events, our mobilizations; always trying to link the present to its historical roots, creating space for dialogue and collective learning and challenging fixed ideas. For anyone interested in challenging conventional education, placing a central emphasis on this kind of radical and popular educational work and committing to doing education differently (whether it is with employees, volunteers or members of the public) should be seen as a central part of their efforts of working towards social change. Rather than understanding in detail the theories of popular education, what really matters is the way that the social change agents approach their work. Examining honestly one's own position and the motivations for what you are doing is crucial. Unlocking this self-reflection is also fundamental to breaking down the division between teacher and learner, activist and public. For activists, academics and community leaders it can be hard to balance the urgency of their organizing efforts with the humility to realize that we truly need to work in a way that puts people at the centre of the process. As Jerome Scott, director of Project South, says, we need 'to develop thousands of leaders, not just two or three or four, but thousands of leaders if we were going to be able to ensure that once the movement breaks out and takes a leap, that it moves in the correct direction, and that we win.'

Resources

Amsler, S., Canaan, J.E., Cowden, S., Motta, S. and Singh, G. (2010). *Why Critical Pedagogy and Popular Education Matter Today*. Nottingham: C-SAP: Higher Education Academy Subject Network for Sociology, Anthropology, Politics.

GlobalLocalPopEd.org: http://cjtc.ucsc.edu/globallocalpoped/index.html

Horton, M. and Freire, P. (1990). *We Make the Road by Walking: Conversations on education and social change*. Philadelphia, PA: Temple University Press.

Popular Education News: www.popednews.org/resources.html

Reflect ESOL participatory approaches to language learning: www.youtube.com/watch?v=ZWBvNhNHww0

Trapese Collective. (2007). *Do It Yourself: A handbook for changing our world*. London: Pluto Press. Available online at http://site.ebrary.com/id/10479950

References

Amsler, S., Canaan, J.E., Cowden, S., Motta, S. and Singh, G. (2010). *Why Critical Pedagogy and Popular Education Matter Today*. Nottingham: C-SAP: Higher Education Academy Subject Network for Sociology, Anthropology, Politics.

Arnold, R. and Burke, B. (1983). *A Popular Education Handbook: An educational experience taken from Central America and adapted to the Canadian context*. Ontario: CUSO Development Education.

Arnold, R., Burke, B., James, C., D'Arcy, M. and Thomas, B. (1991). *Educating for a Change*. Toronto, Canada: Between the Lines and the Doris Marshall Institute for Education and Action.

Beyond the Classroom. (2010). *DCTV » Community Education Series*. Available online at www.dctv.ie/main/?p=1788 (accessed 28 December 2012).

Boal, A. (1985). *Theatre of the Oppressed*. New York: Theatre Communication Group.

Brookfield, S. and Holst, J.D. (2011). *Radicalizing Learning: Adult education for a just world*. San Francisco, CA: John Wiley.

Carlsson, C. (2008). *Nowtopia: How pirate programmers, outlaw bicyclists and vacant-lot gardeners are inventing the future today*. Oakland, CA: AK Press.

Center for Justice, Tolerance, and Community. (2006). *Bringing Globalization Home: Portraits of popular education at the global-local junction* (report). Santa Cruz, CA: Center for Justice, Tolerance, and Community.

Community Resolve. (2012). Available online at www.communityresolve.org.uk/about-us/ (accessed 28 December 2012).

Crosby, K. (2011). *Queer, Gifted & Black: Radical education*. Available online at http://queergiftedblack.blogspot.co.uk/2011/05/radical-education.html (accessed 28 December 2012).

Crowther, C., Galloway, V. and Martin, I. (2005). Introduction: Radicalising intellectual work, in C. Crowther, V. Galloway and I. Martin (eds), *Popular Education Engaging the Academy*. Leicester: NIACE.

Freeman, J. (1972). The Tyranny of Structurelessness. *Berkeley Journal of Sociology*, Vol. 17: 151–165.

Friere, P. (1986). *Pedagogy of the Oppressed*. New York: Continuum.

Greenslade, R. (2010). METRO publishers go to court over spoof issue. *The Guardian*, July.

Herman, E.S. and Chomsky, N. (1988). *Manufacturing Consent: The political economy of the mass media*. New York: Pantheon Books.

Historyisaweapon.com (n.d.). *History Is A Weapon*. Available online at http://www.historyisaweapon.com (Accessed 28 December 2012).

Holloway, J. (2010). *Crack Capitalism*. London: Pluto Press.

hooks, b. (1994). *Teaching to Transgress: Education as the practice of freedom*. New York: Routledge.

Hopkins, R. (2008). *The Transition Handbook: From oil dependency to local resilience*. Totnes, UK: Green Books.

Horton, M. and Freire, P. (1990). *We Make the Road by Walking: Conversations on education and social change*. Philadelphia, PA: Temple University Press.

Illich, I. (1971). *Deschooling Society*. New York: Harper & Row.

Kane, L. (2001). *Popular Education and Social Change in Latin America*. London: Latin American Bureau. Available online at http://catalog.hathitrust.org/api/volumes/oclc/45952761.html

Marx, K. (1867). *Capital*, Volume 1. New York: International Publishers.

Reflect ESOL. (2011). *Participatory Approaches to Language Learning*. Available online at www.youtube.com/watch?v=ZWBvNhNHww0 (accessed 2 January 2013).

Robinson, K. and Aronica, L. (2010). *The Element: How finding your passion changes everything*. London: Penguin Books.

Scathach, I. (2011). *Popular Education as a Doomed Project?* Available online at http://shiftmag.co.uk/?p=457 (accessed 2 January 2013).

Trapese Collective. (2007). *Do It Yourself: A handbook for changing our world*. London: Pluto Press. Available online at http://site.ebrary.com/id/10479950

23

Social movements and global governance

Marianne Maeckelbergh

Introduction

This chapter explores the decision-making practices within global social movement networks to describe alternative forms of organization that these movement actors are creating through their practices. These emerging practices are of analytical significance because they represent an alternative model of global governance being developed within the everyday organizational practices of these movements. These practices are far from perfect, and the leap from movement practice to global governance is a large one, but this in no way diminishes the importance of developing a deeper understanding of both the potentials and limitations of such alternative modes of organization.

The global social movement at the heart of this discussion is the alterglobalization movement, which first became visible on a global scale when tens of thousands of activists descended on the 1999 WTO ministerial meeting in Seattle, Washington, USA. The protests blockaded all access to the conference centre and succeeded in forcing the cancellation of the first day of the WTO meetings and, in the long run, derailing WTO negotiations entirely. Due to clashes between police and protestors, downtown Seattle became a battle-zone, the National Guard was called in and images of police brutality travelled worldwide. The media began to speak of an 'anti-globalization' movement, which activists themselves later re-dubbed more accurately the alterglobalization movement, the Global Justice Movement or the movement of movements. In the years that followed Seattle, alterglobalization activists spread all over the world, turning up en masse to protest at nearly every gathering of multilateral organizations – such as the WTO, the IMF/WB and the G8 – and organizing annual gatherings of up to 200,000 people from all over the world in the form of World and Regional Social Forums. Their critiques of the dominant system bridged the economic and the political by simultaneously bringing into question the legitimacy of representative democracy and of 'neo-liberal' and/or 'capitalist' economics.[1]

The alterglobalization movement arose in the context of a deep gap between the ideal and the real of democracy. As multilateral organizations increasingly became sites of power for decisions affecting national policy and economic development, systems of representative democracy became incapable or unwilling to answer citizens' concerns. The emerging scale of 'global governance' exposed a more fundamental problem with representative democracy, however, which, as many movement actors argued, was that it treats human diversity as a political 'problem' to be erased – an erasure presumed necessary for political stability and the creation of a governable polity. Representation as the structure through which to channel public opinion within democracy presumes that the diversity of interests held by the body politic can be fully understood and given voice to by one or a few political actors and that those few actors are capable of, and are justified in, reconciling conflicting interests, in theory, on behalf of the public. What movement actors were increasingly realizing, over the course of the 1990s and 2000s, was that structures of representation tend to reconcile conflicting interests not on behalf of a diverse and global public, but on behalf of particular capitalist interests. This was a complex argument in the early years of the alterglobalization movement, but today, after the 2008 ongoing economic crisis, the argument that governments rule in the interest of capital over people has become far easier to understand as an unprecedented number of people internationally are losing their homes (renters and owners) to banks, while their governments hand trillions of dollars to these same banks. And then, to add insult to injury, the government claims there is no money available for social safety nets. The alterglobalization movement slogan 'people not profit' has become a defining terrain of struggle in the early twenty-first century with continuous street battles, strikes and occupations around the world.

The decision-making practices that I describe in this chapter have to be understood against the backdrop of these larger political and economic processes. The contemporary structure of nation-state-based representative democracy has emerged hand in hand with the capitalist economic system and today it is becoming increasingly clear that the centralized and hierarchical power embodied in the nation-state, legitimized through structures of representative democracy, serves primarily to facilitate the smooth running of exploitative economic relations through which a small number of people profit at the literal expense of billions of other people worldwide. The mechanisms through which capitalist profit are generated have been elaborately described elsewhere in this volume (see Chapters 1 and 19 in particular). These descriptions help to frame the reasons why social movements have been growing over the past decades and why they erupted internationally in 2011. The ongoing economic crisis has made it clear to millions of people (whether they understand it in these terms or not) that the free market economy, and capitalism in general, is an economic model that can only survive through the appropriation and enclosure of property, through precarious and flexibilized waged labour systems, through mechanisms of surveillance and control, and by placing the means of production in increasingly fewer hands (even as the actual production process is distributed across the globe). The crisis has also made it easier to see that this set of economic relationships depends on defining democracy as a political system in which the only form of political participation available to citizens and non-citizens is through representation. This representation, in turn, usually means that their political input is mediated and framed by the very people who profit from this system of appropriation. This mediated form of political participation serves to disempower the public and distance them from defending their own interests in the public sphere. The larger aim, therefore, of many of those involved in the alterglobalization movement and contemporary movements responding to the economic crisis, is to reclaim this political power – to reclaim the ability to determine for themselves the decisions that most affect their everyday lives, their ability to survive and their ability to determine their political future.

Such an elaborate process of collective self-determination, however, requires elaborate structures of organization – and it is these structures of organization, emerging imperfectly and slowly from the decision-making processes developed by social movements, that are the subject of this chapter. In the first section I explore the practices of consensus decision-making and horizontality, including the key principles of democratic decision-making found within the alterglobalization movement, and argue that implicit in consensus decision-making and horizontality is the assumption that if there is a clear and highly structured procedure in place for *how* to decide, then there need not be an agreement on *who* decides. Movement actors therefore displace one of the central questions of democratic theory – the classic question of '*who* rules?' – and develop instead a set of principles for *how* to rule that challenge both the individualism and the homogeneity of liberal representative democracy. In so doing, movement actors open up the possibility for a much more diverse democracy in which conflicting identities and opinions flourish. In the second section, I delve deeper into the implications of this alternative democratic practice for how we think about global governance. Here I bring insights from ethnography on movement practices into dialogue with democratic theory on pluralism, liberty and authority to show how the movement's emphasis on diversity and horizontality transforms the way democratic values take shape. Finally, I explore some of the main critiques of these decision-making practices by bringing them into the current historical moment, drawing on ethnography of the 15 May and Occupy movements which have used versions of the decision-making processes described here, based on similar political values of horizontality, inclusion and diversity.

The findings presented in this chapter are drawn from years of working within the organizing processes of five anti-G8 mobilizations (2003, 2004, 2005, 2007 and 2008), two European Social Forums (2003 and 2004), one World Social Forum (2004) and short research stints in Barcelona, Madrid, Athens, Cairo, New York, Oakland and London in 2011 and 2012 during a period of intensified political upheaval internationally. Over the past ten years, I have attended hundreds of movement decision-making meetings in fifteen different countries. Sometimes I attend the meetings as an observer, but at other times I take on more active roles, including acting as chair or facilitator of the meetings or as a trainer in consensus decision-making. This more active role has granted me insight not only into what is said at meetings and how interests are publicly negotiated, but also into how meetings are prepared, how agendas are set, and how meetings are structured before they even begin.

Decision-making in the alterglobalization movement

Rather than practising democracy through the nation-state or geographically defined constituencies, movement actors develop decentralized and open-ended network structures which they use as a basis for decision-making on an international scale. This fluid organizational structure makes it possible, at least in principle, for decisions with a global impact to be taken at the local level and fed back to supra-local levels through a complex network of meetings and discussions with temporary representatives communicating back and forth between various levels of decision-making.

Within the alterglobalization movement, decisions are taken, in principle, by consensus – even when the meetings are attended by hundreds or thousands of people. Although not every space of collective decision-making within the alterglobalization movement is equally good at implementing consensus, when the actors diverge too far from the implicitly agreed-upon procedures for consensus, other movement actors will immediately point this out and critique the 'process' for not fulfilling the principles of democratic decision-making of the movement. The autonomous strands of the movement, those that have less affiliation with political parties or traditional left ideologies, tend to be better at implementing consensus-based decision-making. Within the European and World Social Forum, organizing processes which attempt consensus decision-making tend to yield more controversy due to the involvement of local government officials, political parties and trade union leaders.

In this section I will focus primarily on the practices found within the Dissent! Network in the UK during the 2005 anti-G8 mobilization, which can be taken as an example of how the more autonomous networks implement the democratic decision-making model at the heart of the alterglobalization movement, and, more recently, the 15 May and Occupy movements. The key concept that opens the door to understanding how decision-making within the movement works is the word 'process', which arises with astounding frequency in the alterglobalization movement and Occupy movements. But it is not primarily the frequency with which this term is invoked that makes it important, it is the context in which the term is used – namely as a referent for the values for which the movement stands. As such, conflicts about *process* expose some of the key values of the movement, namely the importance of consensus, prefiguration and horizontality. In this section I attempt to explain briefly these principles and how they work within the more autonomous strands of the alterglobalization movement.

Consensus

> Consensus decision making is a creative and dynamic way of reaching agreement between all members of a group. Instead of simply voting for an item and having the majority of the group getting their way, a group using consensus is committed to finding solutions that everyone actively supports, or at least can live with. This ensures that all opinions, ideas and concerns are taken into account.
>
> *(Seeds for Change, n.d.)*

The above description is taken from the website of Seeds for Change, a training group based in the UK that was actively involved in facilitating the decision-making process during the 2005 anti-G8 mobilization in the UK. The handouts they produce were circulated across Europe prior to the G8 summit by the Action Trainer's Collective of the Dissent! Network, which was the umbrella network that coordinated the anti-G8 camp/alternative village and the blockades and actions against the G8. All of Dissent!'s meetings were run by consensus and the procedure was more or less as follows.

The participants (sometimes hundreds of people) sit around a room or tent in a circle. One or two people, sometimes more depending on the size and type of meeting, will take on the role of 'facilitator'. The facilitators are responsible for making sure the 'process' runs smoothly. Although all participants are expected to 'respect the process' and self-manage their behaviour accordingly, the facilitator's *only* role in the meeting is to manage the process – ideally they have no stake in the decision being made.

At the beginning of the meeting, the facilitator usually checks first to make sure everyone is happy to have him or her facilitate the meeting. The next step is to approve a proposed agenda and possibly a group agreement about how the meeting will be run. Agenda items are usually determined ahead of time by a facilitation working group that compiles agenda items from the other working groups. The network as a whole is divided into many different working groups organized around topics such as actions, logistics, budget, kitchens, trainings, content, transport, communications, media, toilets, etc. These groups meet before the larger network meetings and prepare proposals or important points of information that everyone should know and then they bring these items to the larger meeting. Those participating in the larger meeting then get to approve or amend the proposed agenda and add items to the agenda at the beginning of the meeting.

Decision-making can take several different formats. The facilitator or the person/group making the proposal will first introduce the proposal. Then the facilitator takes questions for clarification about the content of the proposal. These clarifying questions are then followed by points for and/or against the proposal. If the meeting is very large, these discussions often take place in smaller groups so that everyone has the chance to voice their opinion without everyone having to listen to each person's point of view. One person from each smaller group is then asked to present all the concerns and ideas that arose within their small group discussion to the larger group. This group of temporary representatives will discuss for five to ten minutes how to improve the proposal, usually in the same room, so that everyone else can follow the discussion, and then they will take a new version of the proposal back to their smaller groups and discuss concerns again for another five to ten minutes. This process is repeated as needed until the proposal has taken all or most of the concerns into account and until those with concerns that cannot be taken into account are satisfied.

In order to aid the discussion, the participants often use 'hand signals'. The practice of hand signals is introduced at the beginning of the meeting as part of the group agreement. An example of a basic group agreement might include the following five points: (1) make sure everyone is heard, (2) respect each other's opinions, (3) practise active agreement, (4) use hand signals, and (5) help keep to time. There is usually a sixth point, an anti-oppression clause, added at the start of the meeting that involves everyone in the meeting agreeing to refrain from exhibiting behaviour or using language that is sexist, racist or oppressive in any way.

There are many different hand signals, but the basic set includes: two hands up, fingers waving in the air, which means 'yes, I agree'; two hands down, fingers waving, which means 'I disagree'; one index finger in the air means 'I have a comment I would like to make'; two index fingers in the air means I have a 'direct response' to the person speaking right now, please let me jump the queue and speak next. Finally, there is one fist in the air (or nowadays an X made by crossing one's forearms in the air), which is called a 'block' and means that the person wants to keep the whole group from carrying out the decision. In practice, when someone uses the block it tends to result in more discussion and amendments to the proposal or to the person just 'standing aside' (i.e. not taking part in the proposed course of action) rather than an actual block, but the ability to block is an important part of the 'process' because it allows for minority voices to be heard and respected, even in very large meetings.

These hand signals help the flow of discussion by allowing for non-verbal communication. In the same way that splitting up into smaller groups allows for everyone to speak without everyone having to listen to each and every person, hand signals make it possible for everyone to express at least agreement or disagreement without having to break the flow of discussion to let everyone say 'yes' or 'no', one at a time. It is also more effective than clapping or booing because it makes no noise and therefore causes less interruption and less influence on the mood of the discussion. The distinction between one finger raised and two index fingers raised also helps to keep the conversation on topic because the facilitator can call on those with two raised index fingers first. The direct response, however, is often used as a way to merely jump the queue and the question of how 'directly' related a person's comment has to be remains unclear.

All of these procedures, however, are only the tip of the iceberg and cover only the practical question of how the 'process' works. The more interesting question has to do with the principles that underpin the movement's choice for this decision-making process. First, underlying the importance of process is the assumption that the way in which the movement organizes itself reflects how the world should and could be organized more democratically. This assumption invokes a prefigurative strategy for social change that is partly responsible for why 'process' is so heavily contested and so essential to the actors involved: the decision-making process represents an important part of the alternative world for which they are struggling. Second, this prefigurative strategy rests on values of non-hierarchy and of diversity that are embodied in structures and practices that movement actors refer to as 'horizontality'. Horizontality as a guiding organizational principle invokes a notion of organization as a continuous process rather than a set of institutions, and therefore allows for a more fluid and open approach to politics than the idea of organization as a structure, or a set of structures, allows.

Prefiguring horizontality

Prefiguration is a practice through which movement actors create a conflation of their ends with their means (see Chapter 3). It is an enactment of the ultimate values of an ideal society within the very means of struggle. As Nomadlab (2002) writes:

> Prefigurative politics is based on the notion that the 'future society' is how we act in the present, what kinds of interactions, processes, structures, institutions, and associations we create right now, and how we live our lives.

If prefiguration is about 'how we act' then prefiguration is, importantly, something people do, not something people demand from a centralized authority empowered to act on their behalf. Heavily influenced by DIY tendencies and squatter movements in the US and Europe, and by autogestion and land rights movements elsewhere (see Corr 1999, 2005; Atzeni and Vieta, this volume), the alterglobalization movement stems from many movements who have a common practice of constructing the world, community or project they desire without the intermediary of a government or corporate representative. Prefigurative movements are:

> movements that are creating the future in their present social relationships . . . social change isn't deferred to a later date by demanding reforms from the state, or by taking state power and eventually instituting these reforms.
>
> *(Sitrin 2006: 4)*

The particular form of prefiguration that lies at the heart of the democratic praxis in the alterglobalization movement is based on a practice called 'horizontality'.

Horizontality (or, *horizontalidad*) is a term used by movement actors to refer to less hierarchical, networked relationships of decision-making and the creation of organizing structures that actively attempt to limit power inequalities. Due to the assumption on the part of movement actors that power always centralizes – that people, groups and ideas will always intentionally or unintentionally accrue power – horizontality is a set of practices that continuously challenge these power hierarchies as they arise. It is therefore necessarily a continuously changing process. As Sitrin (2006: 3) argues, '*horizontalidad* is a living world that reflects an ever-changing experience'. Through decision-making principles of horizontality, the movement creates a collective dynamic that is responsive to changing circumstances as it moves from one country to the next, or from one moment to the next. This continuous refusal of rigidity in decision-making structures results in a remarkable capacity to incorporate diversity among participants and in the outcomes of the decisions reached.

Implications for global governance

The increased awareness of, and openness to, diversity within the decision-making practice of alterglobalization activists is one of the key contributions of the movement to improving the way we conceptualize and enact democracy in the twenty-first century. In this section I examine three shifts in democratic values and structures that occur when diversity instead of unity becomes the guiding principle of democratic decision-making.

First, accepting diversity as a normative principle means that conflict resolution is transformed to allow for not only multiple inputs, but also multiple outcomes to decision-making. Second, this diversity of outcomes is linked to the movement's rejection of the assumption that free and equal individuals can exist, leading the movement to take as its starting point the active and continuous creation of equality through horizontality. Third, the authority of 'process' in the decision-making practices of the alterglobalization movement in shaping the range of acceptable behaviours of the participants invokes a definition of 'liberty' in which movement actors are expected to accept limitations to their own actions in order to enhance the 'liberty' of all those involved. In closing, I reflect on these transformations in the meanings of diversity, equality and liberty in order to show how creating space for differences to coexist without any forced unity breaks with most democratic theories and practices, even deliberative democratic models which maintain univocity as the normative ideal.

Diversity not unity: creating constructive conflict

The network structure of the alterglobalization movement allows the movement to reject unity as a guiding principle in favour of diversity. Networks have no start, no end, and no identifiable membership (at least, global social movement networks do not have these), making universal suffrage impossible. Instead, within the network, groups align and realign themselves as their political positions and aims shift, but the network as a whole remains intact. In contrast to organizations or institutions, whenever an irreconcilable conflict arises among participants, as it inevitably does, the network can split without breaking the ties between the conflicting groups. In this way, even contradictory and irreconcilable differences do not necessarily threaten the network as a whole. For example, when the more autonomous actors in the European Social Forum came into irreconcilable conflict with the more traditional left actors over 'process', the network split and the autonomous groups set up several parallel Social Forums that took place outside of, but alongside, the official forum, which despite concerns about the distribution of resources after the split, served overall to add to the diversity of the ESF.[2]

Diversity in the alterglobalization movement, therefore, is not the same thing as 'pluralism' in democratic theory. The movement's use of the term diversity not only understands 'the people' to be diverse and complex, but also incorporates the notion that in a democratic system this diversity in 'the people' needs to be translated into a diversity of outcomes. Pluralism, by contrast, refers to creating channels of input from multiple, reified groups into a singular, political process, usually with an element of competition between these groups as they each attempt to defend their interests. The focus on competition between actors already distinguishes pluralism considerably from the notion of diversity within the alterglobalization movement, but the differences go much deeper.

While many democratic theories acknowledge the irreducible plurality of 'the people' and their interests, the significance of this movement's focus on diversity is not that it understands 'the people' to be diverse and complex, although it does, but that it allows this diversity in 'the people' to be translated into a diversity of outcomes – thereby removing the element of competition between groups. Rather than a focus on giving each person or group of people an ability to have equal input into the decision-making process, regardless of whether anyone takes their input seriously, the movement emphasizes the idea that equal inputs are impossible and that therefore the emphasis should be on outcomes and how well they reflect the concerns of all those involved. If the inequality of inputs has been acknowledged and challenged, then this will be visible in the outcome. In horizontal organizing, therefore, 'diversity' becomes more than the acceptance of Rawls' 'fact of reasonable pluralism' (see Cohen 1993) because on the one hand it acknowledges the inevitable inequality of inputs and, on the other hand, it stresses the outcomes of decisions over the inputs, thereby bringing the political back into a 'pluralism that misses the dimension of the *political*' (Mouffe 1996: 247).

Outcomes that incorporate a diversity of perspectives are often multiple outcomes; this model of democracy is distinguished considerably from most democratic theory because democracy is no longer aimed at the pursuit of unanimity. Many forms of democracy understand political decisions to be collective and that the need for democracy is 'premised on the fact of disagreement' (Cohen 1996: 101), but nearly all mainstream and alternative democratic theories, including deliberative democracy, assume 'that the pursuit of agreement is the only way forward, [and] that conflict must be resolved through mechanisms of collective deliberation' (Knowles 2001: 334). However, when equality and inclusion become key political values for a global polity, it is safe to say that a single outcome that unifies all people, all over the world, for any decision (other than perhaps some very abstract notions), is impossible to reach at any given moment, and becomes even harder over time as circumstances and interests shift.

This emphasis on diversity as a way to avoid exclusion is of great political importance to most actors within global movement networks, many of whom have been subjected to violent forms of exclusion at the hands of the contemporary nation-state and capitalist system – especially in the 'global South'. Horizontality can be viewed as a direct challenge to these forms of governance. As Hogden (1973: 26) has argued, colonialism was based on a Judaeo-Christian perspective in which civilization by definition necessitated the homogenization of diversity. For many movement actors, therefore, unity, as a political value, is perceived to be inextricably linked to the 'western imperial programme' (Inden 2001) where the 'Indians' or 'natives' were deemed to have no values merely because their values were different from those of the colonialists (Todorov 1985; Pagden 1982; de Certeau 1988). The nation-state as the current organizing principle and structure for democracy is predicated on creating unity within a given geographical area, while the capitalist system results in a uniformity of economic policy regardless of who is elected. The current historical moment is characterized by the creation of literal walls in order to enforce the ideology of spatially segregated homogeneity, from the scale of urban geography (see Davis 1990; Caldeira 1996) to the scale of nation-state borders.

Equality and liberty

Shifting the emphasis of diversity from inputs to outputs is the result of the implicit assumption in movement actors' decision-making processes: namely, that equality cannot be declared by an authority, cannot be established and forgotten about, but rather has to be continuously created and recreated. Horizontality as a movement practice is based on the assumption that power will centralize if given the chance and that power will always be distributed unequally between participants whether it be along the lines of gender, race, education, skills or other personal characteristics.

This starting assumption about equality has several consequences for the way democracy is practised, the most important of which is the rejection of voting as a decision-making method. Voting is a system based on an input-oriented principle of equality based on 'one man, one vote' and, movement actors believe, it cannot lead to equality because it *always* results in unequal outcomes – outcomes which favour one group (the larger) over others. When the starting assumption is that an equality of inputs is impossible (due to inevitable power inequalities), the outcomes of decision-making become doubly important because the outcomes and the degree to which the outcomes take into account the interests of all those involved becomes the key measure of equality. This, as we saw above, is only possible when the outcomes are allowed to be diverse.

In order for consensus decision-making to function smoothly, strict guidelines have to be adhered to by at least most participants. The group agreement mentioned above, whether explicitly or implicitly present, demands not only that participants refrain from certain types of behaviour, but also that they display continuous active engagement with the process. This is an obligation-oriented approach to liberty that undermines the classic opposition between liberty and restrictions to behaviour (Wolff 1996: 116). Instead it assumes that liberty is a collective construct for which everyone is responsible and not an individual possession or unqualified right to 'act as you like, so long as you do not harm the interests of another person' (Mill 1962: 136).

These euphemistically labelled 'guidelines' create a form of authority, but rather than placing authority in specific people, horizontal organization places authority within a process. R.S. Peters (1958: 221) argues that social systems 'can only be maintained if there is general acceptance of procedural rules which lay down who is to originate rules, who is to decide about their concrete application to concrete cases, and who is entitled to introduce changes.' However, it is precisely this idea – that some people should have the right to command and all the others have the obligation to obey – that is being brought into question through horizontal organization. Nevertheless, meetings are structured according to a series of procedural rules for decision-making. However, because the authority that is making decisions about restrictions is the meeting itself, there is no external actor that is imposing restrictions. Consequently, the assembly creates a collective authority out of all those in attendance.

Liberty in the alterglobalization movement is not a passive liberty to be consumed by the individual but, just like equality, it needs to be built and actively worked on by those involved so that authority, if we can still call it that, becomes a collectively held and fluid form of power. There are many rules that limit the range of acceptable behaviours, but these rules are fluid and they shift from meeting to meeting, depending on the people involved and the topics to be discussed. Because the rules are fluid, they can be brought into question, discussed and confirmed or rejected by the actors whenever necessary. The real liberty here lies not in being totally free from restrictions on behaviour, but in being able to influence what the restrictions are and to change them if needed. When the 'rules' that guide horizontality become too rigid, however, a form of authority is created that can no longer be influenced by those participating and new forms of inequality emerge.

Limits and potentials of horizontal decision-making

The decision-making practices developed within the alterglobalization movement were the legacy of centuries of social movement organizing, with a crucial turning point in the 1960s. While egalitarian and inclusive forms of decision-making are as old as time, the 1960s were an historical moment when this prefigurative strategy of social change, in which developing alternative models of organization was so important, became a central priority for social movements internationally. These experiments were widely regarded as failures, the most classic critique being Freeman's (1970) constructive essay on the 'tyranny of structurelessness'. But in recent years several attempts have been made to reclaim the history of participatory democracy as one of the key innovations of the 1960s period (see Horn 2007; Polletta 2002; Maeckelbergh 2011), and with the benefit of hindsight, a more realistic assessment of the 1960s would be that the experiments with participatory democracy initiated in the 1960s required time to develop and are today still an imperfect but important work in progress.

Throughout the 1970s, 1980s and 1990s, social movements continued experiments with participatory and consensus-based models of organization, slowly improving many but not all of the problems of structurelessness and informal hierarchy. In the 1990s, these experiments were rejuvenated through the rise of Zapatista-inspired practices of the *encuentro* and the Argentinian experiments with *horizontalidad* in the aftermath of the 2001 crisis (see Atzeni and Vieta, this volume). The structure of the *encuentro* took on global significance through the networks of the alterglobalization movement, and is important still today in social movements that are challenging the enclosure and appropriation of property in the aftermath of the housing crisis. As the Movement for Justice in El Barrio, an East Harlem-based community movement fighting for decent housing and self-determination in New York City argues:

> An Encuentro is not a meeting, a panel or a conference, it is a way of sharing developed by the Zapatistas as another form of doing politics: from below and to the left. It is a place where we can all speak, we will all listen, and we can all learn. It is a place where we can share the many different struggles that make us one.
>
> *(MJB 2009)*

The long history of experiments with horizontal forms of democracy has led today to an unprecedented proliferation of horizontal organizational methods internationally embodied in the 15 May and Occupy movements. The decision-making practices that were carried out by an international, mobile group of alterglobalization movement actors are now the main organizational structure for many social movements that have swept across the world since 2011, occupying public space, reopening public imagination and involving, for the first time, millions of people worldwide in local movements that were organized along the principles of horizontal decision-making, demonstrating that horizontal organization can be at least as effective as other forms of organization, and perhaps even more so, for coordinating global days of action in a way that ensures even internationally coordinated actions emerge from below, grounded in the diverse realities of specific places.

These most recent, large-scale, open and public experiments with democracy have also highlighted some of the limitations and areas in need of improvement if horizontal decision-making is ever to be the alternative to representative democracy that many movement actors would like it to be. The limitations are, however, not those most commonly levelled against these movements from the outside. The theory of social change that is implicit in horizontal prefiguration is one that aims to re-invent all of society by developing new political and economic structures that decentralize and de-hierarchize power continuously and change the way power operates. It is by definition anti-systemic — at least towards the current system of the nation-state and capitalism, which only function when there is centralization and hierarchy.

From this perspective, the fact that both the alterglobalization movement and the 15 May/ Occupy movements have no clearly articulated demands should rather be seen as a strength than a critique, because the refusal to frame political conflict in terms of demands is a rejection of centralized and external sources of authority. It is a recognition of the impossibility of achieving equality and meaningful political participation as long as a few members of society are granted the power to respond to demands, especially when those people also have the power to enclose on the commons and to reap profit from doing so (see De Angelis and Harvie, this volume). As one of the participants active in Occupy Wall Street (OWS) put it:

> For people that think that economic, political and social justice is reducible to a set of demands, they're just wrong. This is a structural issue that is happening globally and it is a crisis of capitalism. We want to ask better questions and be in dialogue about what the answers are going to be but we're in no rush.
>
> *(interview, 15 September 2012)*

The growing awareness that the problems are structural has led to even more emphasis on horizontal decision-making as a 'better' structure through which to realize democratic values such as equality, participation and liberty. This has also led to an intensification of movement attention to the limitations of horizontal decision-making.

Even before people occupied and set up camp in Zuccotti Park near Wall Street on 17 September 2011, thereby becoming 'Occupy Wall Street', there were continuous discussions about the role of structure and structurelessness in decision-making within OWS. After they were evicted from the park on 17 November 2011, the discussions about structure were heated. Most of the participants' critiques were not about a lack of structure, but about too much structure, about the rigidity with which the structure was carried out – described as too 'bureaucratic'. Whole discussions were being organized on the theme of bureaucracy within Occupy. It seems that what people were learning was that structures of horizontality need to remain open and fluid, malleable to changing circumstances and multiple interests if they are to be as inclusive as possible to a diversity of actors. The question which is thus far unresolved is how malleable? How inclusive is too inclusive for the process to work, given that the existing structures are not always equally capable of being both inclusive and empowering? Answers to these questions will only emerge from practice and further experimentation.

The limitations that became most apparent through the grounding of horizontal decision-making in local contexts were connected to capitalist relations. Horizontality was suddenly faced with questions about the distribution of vast and essential resources and many participants responded with attitudes of competition based on the idea that resources are limited (a problem that was common in the Social Forum process too, but not in the autonomous strands of the alterglobalization movement). The tendency to resort to competition, combined with a habitus of proprietary attitudes towards tasks, skills and knowledge, made communication between the working groups – which were the basis for the network structure – more difficult. Communication between the nodes of the network is essential to keep horizontal organizational structures functioning with as little hierarchy as possible, and it seems that capitalist relations to property and resources make it considerably harder for horizontal organizational structures to challenge the tendency towards centralization and hierarchy.

Horizontality, however, is a learning process. 'Walking we ask questions' is the famous Zapatista slogan, and it is an attitude that stays open to the input of all those participating as they collectively search for answers. Much like the horizontalized labour process of self-managed worker's movements, the process of horizontal organization within global social movement networks is not perfect and faces many limitations when practised within the logic of capitalism. However, the process is based on a collective praxis of learning through doing that is built, step by step, from the bottom up (see Chapter 22 on education) and as participants become aware of these contradictions, horizontality has at least the potential to become a political practice that fundamentally unsettles not only prevailing structures of democracy, but also those of capitalism.

Conclusion: decentralized network democracy

> Globalization is in essence a crisis of representative democracy . . . what is the solution? To articulate an alternative participatory democracy.
>
> *(Klein 2005: 225)*

The alternative model of democracy that the alterglobalization, 15 May and Occupy movements are developing is based on a decentralized network structure. This, at least in theory, allows for a form of democracy to emerge that has a greater capacity for the incorporation of diversity and minority concerns by giving everyone more avenues for meaningful participation, as well as an active role in shaping structures of governance. This represents a considerable break from contemporary democratic theory and practice, even from 'alternative' democratic theories, such as those of deliberative democracy, because even these alternative models of democracy maintain 'univocity' as the ultimate aim of the democratic process (Honig 1996). In the dominant paradigm of democracy and governance today, democracy is the process through which the many interests of 'the people' become represented by one idea, one conclusion, one voice (based on a Hobbesian notion of social stability). But the reality of this drive for unity, as noble as it may seem, is that it leads to the exclusion of all those who do not fit within the particular construct of unity as determined by those in power. Within governing systems based on representative democracy, this perceived need for uniformity is expressed in the form of elections and majority rule. Majority rule, however, has long been criticized for excluding minority voices or, worse, for forcing these voices to concede by threat or use of violence (Graeber 2008). The value of 'the vote' as the primary symbol of democracy under these circumstances is rightly questioned by contemporary social movements. But these movements do much more than merely question existing structures of democratic governance; they are also slowly building alternative structures and procedures in order to replace these less participatory and less egalitarian systems.

One of the main accomplishments of the alterglobalization movement has been to create participatory models of decision-making that can be enacted on a large scale through locally and globally interconnected network structures, in which, at least in principle, decisions taken at the local level can be communicated and coordinated across vast distances – from the local, to the regional, to the global level through the building of connections and communication between the 'hubs' within the network. This development challenges and undermines the common argument that participatory forms of democracy are only possible in 'small, decentralized, self-sufficient units' (Young 2000: 124; Dahl 1989; see Rossiter and Zehle, this volume). The 15 May and Occupy movements were the first experiments in grounding these transnational decision-making processes in the day-to-day organizing of social life. This new step in the development of horizontal democracy has brought participants into a more direct confrontation with everyday relations of capital in the form of their own subjectivities as the consumers and producers of goods and services (see Chapter 1, this volume). It will likely require many more years of experimentation to develop more horizontal, collective and collaborative subjectivities, but the first step has been taken and the experiments continue.

As these structures for decentralized, participatory democracy spread on a global scale, these global movement networks are turning the relationship between scale and representation on its head. Representation as a political structure was originally intended as a way to make democratic participation possible for everyone, even at the larger scale of the nation-state (larger compared to the city-republic of Athens or Rome). Hardt and Negri (2004: 238) point out that the task of the French revolutionaries was partially aimed 'at addressing the question of scale, was to reinvent the concept [of democracy] and create new institutional forms and practices. Representation . . . was central to the modern attempt to address the crisis of democracy.' Today, it is precisely the problem of scale that underlies this movement's *aversion* to representative structures. Representation functions on the assumption that a certain portion of the constituency will have identical interests and creates a circumstance in which only these *shared* interests get expressed, but these shared interests become fewer and farther between as communities become more diverse and the scale of decision-making more global. By developing a participatory, network-based model of democracy, global social movement networks have taken an important step towards creating more inclusive structures of democracy for an era of globally integrated governance.

Notes

1 Not all movement actors are explicitly anti-capitalist. Some perceive themselves to be only against certain forms of neo-liberal or free market policies and others are explicitly anti-capitalist.
2 For a more in-depth discussion of the role of the circumstances under which splits occur in the functioning of the network and the question of resources associated with this example, see Maeckelbergh (2009: 183–186).

Resources

Seeds for Change: www.seedsforchange.org.uk/resources
A series of excellent guides for consensus decision-making, facilitation and meetings in small and large groups.

A quick guide on group dynamics in people's assemblies: http://takethesquare.net/2011/07/31/quick-guide-on-group-dynamics-in-peoples-assemblies/
Reflections and suggestions from the Group Dynamics Commission of the Assemblies of the Puerta del Sol Protest Camp, 15 May Movement, Spain.

The New Anarchists. David Graeber, author. *New Left Review*, 2002.
One of the first texts to identify and concisely present the key analytical insights to be gained from the alterglobalization movement.

The Will of the Many: How the Alterglobalization Movement is Changing the Face of Democracy. Marianne Maeckelbergh, author. London: Pluto Press, 2009.
An analysis of horizontal decision-making and prefigurative politics as an alternative form of global democracy.

Horizontalism: Voices of Popular Power in Argentina. Marina Sitrin, editor. Oakland: AK Press, 2006.
A book of interviews about the popular rebellion in Argentina in 2001 that describes the philosophy and practice behind forms of horizontal organization.

The Occupy Movement in Žižek's hometown: Direct democracy and a politics of becoming. Maple Razsa and Andrej Kurnik, authors. *American Ethnologist*, 2012.
An article that explores the philosophical importance of horizontal, minoritarian decision-making in the Occupy movement in Slovenia.

References

Caldeira, T. 1996. Fortified Enclaves: The New Urban Segregation, *Public Culture* 8(2): 303–328.

Certeau, M. de. 1988. *The Writing of History*. New York: Colombia University Press.

Cohen, J. 1993. Moral Pluralism and Political Consensus, in D.J. Copp, J. Hampton and J. Roemer (eds), *The Idea of Democracy*. Cambridge: Cambridge University Press.

Cohen, J. 1996. Procedure and Substance in Deliberative Democracy, in S. Benhabib (ed.), *Democracy and Difference*. Princeton, NJ: Princeton University Press.

Corr, A. 1999. *No Trespassing!: Squatting, Rent Strikes, and Land Struggles Worldwide*. Boston, MA: South End Press.

Corr, A. 2005. Anarchist Squatting and Land Use in the West: Direct Action and the Critique of Real Estate. Available online at http://squat.net/archiv/anders/anarchist_squatting.html (accessed 11 October 2012).

Dahl, R. 1989. *Democracy and its Critics*. New Haven, CT: Yale University Press.

Davis, M. 1990. *City Of Quartz: Excavating The Future In Los Angeles*. London: Verso.

Freeman, J. 1970. The Tyranny of Structurelessness. Available online at http://struggle.ws/pdfs/tyranny.pdf (accessed 7 October 2012).

Graeber, D. 2008. There Never was a West: Or, Democracy Emerges from the Spaces in Between, in *Possibilities: Essays on Hierarchy Rebellion and Desire*. Oakland, CA: AK Press.

Hardt, M. and Negri, A. 2004. *Multitude*. London: Hamilton.

Hogden, M. 1973. *Early Anthropology in the Sixteenth and Seventeenth Century*. Philadelphia: Pennsylvania University Press.

Honig, B. 1996. Difference, Dilemmas and the Politics of Home, in S. Benhabib (ed.), *Democracy and Difference*. Princeton, NJ: Princeton University Press.

Horn, G-R. 2007. *The Spirit of '68: Rebellion in Western Europe and North America 1956–1976*. Oxford: Oxford University Press.

Inden, R. 2001. *Imagining India*. London: Hurst & Company.

Klein, N. 2005. Reclaiming the Commons, in T. Mertes (ed.), *The Movement of Movements: Is Another World Really Possible?* London: Verso.

Knowles, D. 2001. *Political Philosophy*. London: Routledge.

Maeckelbergh, M. 2009. *The Will of the Many: How the Alterglobalization Movement is Changing the Face of Democracy*. London: Pluto Press.

Maeckelbergh, M. 2011. The Road to Democracy: The Political Legacy of '1968', *International Review of Social History* 56(2): 301–332.

Mill, J.S. 1962[1859]. On Liberty, in M. Warnock (ed.), *Utilitarianism: On Liberty*. London: Collins.

MJB (Movement for Justice in El Barrio). 2009. An invitation to the second NYC *encuentro* for dignity and against displacement. Email, sent to nyc@ e-list on 24 May 2009.

Mouffe, C. 1996. Democracy, Power and the 'Political', in S. Benhabib (ed.), *Democracy and Difference*. Princeton, NJ: Princeton University Press.

Nomadlab. 2002. Breaking Free of the Protest Mentality. Available online at www.indymedia.org.uk/en/2002/07/36374.html?style=handheld (accessed 7 October 2012).

Pagden, A. 1982. *The Fall of Natural Man: The American Indian and the Origin of Comparative Ethnography*. Cambridge: Cambridge University Press.

Peters, R.S. 1958. Symposium: 'Authority', in *Proceedings of the Aristotelian Society* 32.

Polletta, F. 2002. *Freedom is an Endless Meeting*. Chicago, IL: University of Chicago Press.

Scheper-Hughes, N. 1995. The Primacy of the Ethical: Propositions for a Militant Anthropology, *Current Anthropology* 36(3): 409–420.

Seeds for Change. n.d. Available online at www.seedsforchange.org.uk/free/consensus (accessed 7 October 2012).

Sitrin, M. 2006. *Horizontalism: Voices of Popular Power in Argentina*. Oakland, CA: AK Press.

Todorov, T. 1985. *The Conquest of America and the Question of the Other*. New York: Harper Perennial.

Wolff, J. 1996. *An Introduction to Political Philosophy*. Oxford: Oxford University Press.

Young, I.M. 2000. *Inclusion and Democracy*. Oxford: Oxford University Press.

24

Horizons of possibility

Challenge, co-optation and transformation

But perhaps our starting point for a politics of meaning should not be a monolithic category of hegemony or domination countered by a grand, utopian space of pure resistance, especially if the forms of that hegemony or resistance become foundational categories which can always be known in advance. The indulgence in nostalgic desire for 'authentic resistance' might blind us to the multiple, mobile points of potential resistance moving through the regime of power. Rather than positing these categories as foundational and thus invoking a metaphysics of closure and presence, we might examine the unexpected, subtle, and paradoxical twists in actors' discursive strategies, following out the ways meanings are re-appropriated and launched again in continuous struggles over meaning.

(Kondo, 1990, p. 225)

Localization is a solution multiplier.

(Norberg-Hodge, July 2011)

How far have we come in imagining and pursuing alternatives?

In 2007, on the brink of what would become the biggest global financial meltdown since the Great Depression, the *Financial Times* launched a new look to the newspaper with the strap line 'We Live in Financial Times' on a series of advertisements. One of the most prominent of these was the face of Virgin founder and entrepreneur Richard Branson, superimposed on the iconic image of Che Guevara and rendered in a simple black on red, reflecting the original image that has adorned the T-shirts of thousands of young radicals the world over in the last five decades.[1] The dramatically recast image was accompanied by the words 'Business revolutionaries. Past, present and future.'

In 2005 the English translation of Boltanski and Chiapello's *The New Spirit of Capitalism* was published by Verso, rapidly gaining a wide readership both within and outside academia. Their basic thesis was that the counter-cultural movement of the 1960s, with its radical critique of bureaucratic power relations and alienation, and its demand for greater autonomy and creativity in work – what they call the 'artistic critique' – had been largely incorporated into the 'new spirit of capitalism'. Reviewing a corpus of writings by popular management theorists and consultants published in the 1990s, Boltanski and Chiapello concluded that the demands of the *soixante-huitards* for more autonomous, creative and humanistic work, and alternative organizational forms, had been met by a new ideology, or spirit, of capitalism. This discursive re-articulation of capitalism's values did not, however, change the fundamental drive toward unlimited accumulation and growth and, in fact, came at the cost of the traditional demands of labour for job security, pay and collective representation (Boltanski and Chiapello, 2005).

These two examples demonstrate the melding of resistance and the popular insurrectionary imagination with power and corporate PR. They point to the enormity of the theoretical and practical political challenges facing alternative expressions and projects of what we might call a 'New Economy' if that term hadn't already been consigned to the dustbin of recent history along with the neo-liberal illusion of inevitable, perpetual growth that it came to stand for (Cock *et al.*, 2005). Indeed, if Boltanski and Chiapello (2005) are correct, then the dynamism so often accorded to capitalism itself is illusory. Instead, it is dependent upon the creativity of its resistant subjects for novelty and change, at least at the level of its imaginary. As a system of economic production and accumulation, consumption and expropriation, capitalism lacks an essential spirit that can motivate the active engagement that it needs from its subjects. Without a 'spirit' to animate it, capitalism is literally pointless.

This insight can be developed in two directions. While Boltanski and Chiapello (2005) focus on the spirit of capitalism that motivates managers and entrepreneurs, or at least that moves students to want to become managers and entrepreneurs rather than, say, environmental activists, capitalism also needs an outside to drive consumption. This can readily be seen in the extravagant lifestyle, well-being and spiritual claims made on behalf of 'the super brands' (Klein, 2009). The levels of consumption found in the so-called 'advanced' capitalist economies cannot be explained by our basic human needs, any more than commodity consumption can actually fulfil the lack that we still feel in these most affluent of societies (James, 2007). In promising authenticity, community and spiritual fulfilment, brands claim to transcend mere consumption and, in the process, draw upon a promise of an outside in order to drive more of the same. In this way consumption is dependent upon something *outside* the commodity form in order to reproduce that very form. At the same time, capitalism is expansive not only in increasing production and market reach, but also in capturing and incorporating new domains of activity, including, for example, the reorientation of nearly every public holiday toward an opportunity to consume goods and services and the absorption of formerly fringe musical genres and their accompanying counter-cultural lyrics (Heath and Potter, 2004; Rehn and Sköld, 2005).

The other direction is in the appropriation of new organizational forms. Drawing upon organizational forms and practices from outside of business – for example, teams, participation, decentralization, or even leaderlessness – private enterprises and management theorists have regularly sought to take insights from other disciplines and areas of human activity and rebrand them for managerial consumption. For example, the last three decades have seen seemingly revolutionary calls for organizations to focus on *becoming* cultures (Peters and Waterman, 1981), to enter the 'new age of the flat organization' (McLagan and Nel, 1997), or embrace empowerment (Hardy and Leiba-O'Sullivan, 1998) and participation (Cooke and Kothari, 2001).

So where does this leave a book like this one, a question that we broached in the first three chapters? Having laid out a series of alter-capitalist organizational forms and mapped the full circuit of production from the mobilization of resources through production, to consumption and social reproduction, have we perhaps succeeded in little more than laying out the terrain for capitalism to capture these diverse movements and leave them devoid of any real transformative capability? Many of the contributors to this collection, and the editors, work in universities teaching a new generation of employees and managers about business ethics, cooperative forms, environmental sustainability, consensus decision making, etc., but when our students graduate, we assume that most of them will follow the path of least resistance into conventional corporate employment of one form or another. Can a book like this, and the organizational forms and practices found within its pages, offer a real and significant challenge to contemporary corporate-consumer capitalism? To address this question it is worth reviewing some of the shared features of the 'alternatives' reviewed in this collection.

What 'family resemblances' do we see in today's alternatives to conventional ways of doing work, commerce and organizing?

We have tried to bring together a great diversity of alternative organizational forms, including the usual suspects like cooperatives and intentional communities, as well as some less visible movements and networks that are gaining ground, even if not widespread attention. These examples of new business practices, economic models and networks for social change have diverse relationships to capitalism and globalization. All of them share, however, a spirit of critical questioning as well as a critical optimism with respect to social betterment. Many of these forms, again such as many cooperatives, are somewhat institutionalized; but even in those cases, their visibility is by no means universal. Practically all the alternatives discussed here must also, however deliberately or semi-consciously, negotiate their own boundaries vis-à-vis the status quo. Within the course of such navigation, many of these forms can end up being more like tweaks of 'the system' than radical departures from it. Indeed, the relationship between any so-called alternative and what we commonly refer to as the 'mainstream' is likely to be dynamic. We now consider several ways in which the alternatives profiled in this volume challenge conventional organizational typologies, and urge us to reconsider organizational types even as we reconsider the mainstream of contemporary corporate-consumer capitalism.

We have before us diverse organizational and quasi-organizational categories

This volume has presented a remarkable variety of alternatives and for that diversity, as well as many lovely surprises on these pages, we are grateful to all of our contributors. Perhaps the most 'underground' of these alternatives are networks of the dispossessed, such as scroungers and international refugees (see Chapters 20 and 9, this volume, respectively). At the same time, we have included within the reach of the discussion the household, the symbolism and materiality of the commons, consumption and simplicity, and the global environment. In other words, the principles and models offered here consider both dimensions and instances of contemporary economic life.

Some alternatives are more easily recognized as organizational forms; others are not

Some of these alternatives are more easily recognized as formal organizations; others are not and therefore offer important challenges to theorizing (see Chapter 10, this volume). The age of the network is now almost a hackneyed expression; however, it means in practice that organizational boundaries today are fluid, contested, and in many cases unable to be discerned (see Castells, 2010: *The Network Society*; Rainie and Wellman, 2012). The possibilities for non-commodified labour, as practised both historically and today, do not usually employ the vehicles of organizational forms although they may find a degree of institutionalization in a community (see Chapter 7, this volume). Gift relations and economies are often pursued with suspicion toward institutionalized organizations and sectors, yet there are important examples of their quasi-organized status in communities and metropolitan areas throughout the global South (see Chapter 13, this volume).

Some alternatives are wide in reach; some are small and localized in influence

Some of these alternatives are, by their very nature, more extensive; others are locally grounded. Indeed some communes, collectives and cooperatives rise out of a very particular place and are explicitly opposed to their own expansion, and perhaps to the very idea of growth. This can be a matter of organizational integrity and value fidelity as well as local commitment; however, it can mean, in practical terms, non-continuance, even in some instances 'organizational suicide' (see Rothschild and Whitt, 1986; cf. Cheney, 2002). The fear of extinction has, in fact, led many cooperatives to adopt more expansionist policies as they confront regional and even international markets (on this logic, see especially Chapters 4 and 5, this volume). But, even in cases such as the Mondragon cooperatives which have in some ways pursued conventional multinational strategies, the question of 'selling out or not?' needs to be reformulated in more nuanced terms, such as 'What lessons can we carry forth?' (Azkarraga *et al.*, 2012).

Some alternatives are positioned more within the mainstream; some are outsiders

Some of these alternatives presented within this volume are positioned on the banks of the mainstream; others are seemingly in different currents altogether. Recuperated enterprises, cooperatives and intentional communities (see Chapters 3, 4, 5 and 6, this volume, respectively) do not necessarily take an anti-capitalist standpoint but are advanced in ways to make the locality and the group pre-eminent in the line of control over organization and capital. Similarly, advocacy of Fair Trade, social accounting practices and appropriate technologies (see Chapters 11, 18 and 21, this volume, respectively) need not try to upend the capitalist boat but do seem intended to change its course.

Consider the case of the John Lewis stores in the UK. Widely touted as a model for employee partnership that can succeed, it has bucked the recession by growing over the last few years when other stores are struggling or even going out of business. It would be hard to argue that a high-street department store that sells high-end branded goods to affluent middle-class consumers is a viable alternative to mainstream capitalism. On the other hand, it is owned by a trust; it has a sophisticated structure of employee representation throughout the management structure; and profits are distributed to employees in the form of an annual bonus, rather than as a dividend to external shareholders. While there is clearly something in the argument that workers' participation, within a wider capitalist economy at least, is merely a form of self-exploitation (Hyman *et al.*, 2005), it would be a rather short-sighted analysis that denied any difference at all between the John Lewis partnership model and a familiar transnational like Microsoft, for example. As Cathcart has argued (2013a, 2013b), the very fact that there is a debate about democracy in John Lewis is impressive in itself, though the representation that does exist needs to be continually defended against the encroachments of hierarchical managerialism and ideas about what 'the market' needs.

Thus, we are reminded of the nuances within cases as well as across the spectrum of possibilities. The black and white 'sell out or not' question makes for lively debate and quotable quotes, but is not well adapted to the complex realities of a dynamic global economy with changing relations between players and, as we hope, the appearance of new ones on the stage. (Even the much-pilloried Wal-Mart has been making significant commitments toward environmental sustainability in its Chinese operations.)

Some alternatives hold with broader movement goals, while others seek only specific and perhaps even just temporary change

Some of these alternatives embrace broader social movement goals; others are more modest in their ambitions. Most community currencies are not pursued with wider social movement goals in mind but rather as a contribution to the autonomy of a locale and its citizens (see Chapter 12, this volume). Most LETS systems are intensely local although pursued with an evangelical hope for the diffusion of their practices more widely. To the extent that radically democratic forms of education and governance are embraced (as discussed in Chapters 22 and 23, this volume, respectively) the potential for global social change is certainly implied, even if not pursued. The same is true with respect to re-engagement of the debate over the decentralizing capacity versus the centralizing forces of the internet (as discussed in Chapter 10, this volume), in which a 'global consciousness' is so much a part of affairs that at times the networks may well appear to be as placeless and rootless as they are, in a certain sense, leaderless.

However, the manifestations of social movement goals are perhaps more complex and nuanced today than in the past, in large part because of the recognition of the global implications of local activities. Some forms of self-provisioning and bioregionalism, along with transition towns (see Chapters 14, 15 and 16, this volume, respectively) are examples of practices that are, on the surface, necessarily local; yet they are often practised with a strong global ethic and frequently involve wider networking of local interests. This is especially the case where environmental sustainability and stewardship are part of the pantheon of values for an organization or movement.

Challenges

Of course, the traditional response to these issues from the political left is to point to the challenges of scale and coalition building across situations, cultures and issues. Books like Sharzer's (2012) *No Local* and Harvey's (2012) *Rebel Cities* point to the difficulties of bringing a diverse, motley collection of small-scale, often local initiatives together to form a coherent alternative to a politically, economically and culturally institutionalized system like capitalism. This is a worthwhile criticism to put forth against the collection of alternatives presented in this volume, and it's one we want to address.

Many would legitimately ask: Doesn't there have to be a global alternative to challenge the global domination of supra-national, multi-lateral institutions like the IMF, World Bank, WTO, various free trade agreements, etc.? Doesn't the scale of resistance need to match the scale of the problem? Indeed, this is a question posed in some segments of the political right as well as by some brands of the political left, given a shared suspicion of global control, although linked to rather different ideologies. Without a truly global alternative – in vision and in practice – perhaps the best we can hope for is to become management gurus in the new, or even newer, capitalism. In other words, is the best we can hope for is to become somewhat more 'social' entrepreneurs? As a system, and to the extent that it represents a matrix of forces, perhaps capitalism will simply find a way to incorporate the demands we laid out in our Chapter 3 into its imaginary and thereby captivate a new generation of aspiring managers and willing workers, while leaving its basic structures of ownership, accumulation and exploitation intact?

We think this means that the relationships between, as well as within, organizations must be considered in examining the 'alternativeness' of any particular case. Organizational dependency, as opposed to true interdependency, is often in question. As long recognized in resource-dependency models of organizations, and in the experiences of many organizations in the so-called 'independent', third or non-profit sector, true organizational islands are rare. In this regard, the sociology of religion is instructive, with its primary categories of cult, sect and denomination, ranging on a continuum from severance from the larger society to coextensiveness with it (Troeltsch, 1956). Not all alternatives are 'against' everything, or 'against' the same things. The degree to which an organization 'leans on' and becomes part of the system it defines itself against is a point at which the alternative 'pivots', as well as perhaps achieves leverage in terms of effecting significant change.

In the cases of the examples presented in this volume, many alternatives rely heavily on existing, capitalist institutions and their supporting political frameworks: Fair Trade movements rely upon global as well and local markets; social movements use established networks of communication and information; voluntary simplicity may be enabled by accumulated capital; and even scroungers depend on the excesses and waste of the contemporary consumer (see Chapters 11, 10, 14 and 20, this volume, respectively).

An alternative future for capitalism?

This final chapter considers the relationship between 'alternatives' and social change. On the one hand, mainstream, capitalist organizations have adopted and assimilated alternatives like participation, green consumption, voluntary work and decentralized forms of organization, suggesting that 'alternatives' like those contained in the volume are too readily absorbed and routinized to generate widespread social-structural change. A good example is the ambivalent outcomes of micro-finance institutions, as discussed by Lightfoot in Chapter 3, this volume. On the other hand, the persistence of alternatives, and their actualization of radical, alternative organizational principles, suggests a more positive potential for fundamental change in our ways of 'being and doing the economy'.

Maybe the dialectical relations between capitalism and its alternatives can be illustrated by getting back to the idea of this book as a capitalist product which we started with in Chapter 1. This book is a good example of an explicitly articulated 'alternative' being re-inscribed within the circuit of traditional capital. While the managers at Routledge, Taylor and Francis or Informa plc may not be hoping for great profit directly from the sales of this book, their primary interest in the alternatives represented here is, directly or indirectly, the creation of shareholder value rather than the promotion of alternatives to capitalism. We want this book to do one thing; they want it to do another. We readily acknowledge, then, the fuzzy boundary between reformist activities within the system and efforts positioned more clearly outside of it (see Schor, 2004).

We could even go further. As Rehn notes in Chapter 13 on gift economies, the academic labour of research and writing sits in an ambiguous relationship with economic value. On the one hand, the direct financial rewards from writing journal articles or book chapters rarely recompense the long hours spent researching, analysing, writing, editing, reviewing and rewriting. Indeed, many academics would consider themselves lucky to receive any direct remuneration for their writing. At least formally, such work is undertaken as a gift to the wider academic community, if not to the sum of general human knowledge, rather than through a narrowly instrumental, calculative rationality. On the other hand, however, academics are not by any means the worst-paid workers in the world and can benefit from the cultural capital accrued by publishing, leveraging this capital to gain promotions and to aid their employers – the universities – to rise up in the rankings, recruit students, and ultimately earn a salary. In this way, academics are remunerated for research and writing, only not by the publishers who own the copyright, or at least reproduction rights, for their work. Instead their pay comes from a combination of student fees, public funding and philanthropic giving. The publishers, like Routledge, profit by acting to distribute and market the products of academic knowledge-work and so can profit from it, regardless of its content. They can make money from selling criticism of how they make money.

This book and the diverse alternatives presented in it may not look like a great challenge to global capitalism. Global capital is probably more likely to implode through its own contradictions – in particular through environmental constraints – than through the threat of opposition within the covers of a book like this. Capitalism is certainly a substantial force, but as we have seen it is neither omnipotent nor uniform. There always remains some space, some level of choice we can exercise, sometimes in the wake of shuttered factories or impoverished communities, sometimes in the spaces which consumerist culture has not yet invaded. In these cracks of capitalism, alternatives remain essential laboratories for post/non-/modified capitalist practices. There are times and spaces within the cracks of capitalism which allow for partial autonomy (Shukaitis, 2010) where, while not standing outside capitalist relations, we are not 'governed quite so much' (Foucault, 2001) by them. The alternatives presented in this book prefigure ways in which we could, and may have to, reconstruct our lives in ways that are not 'governed quite so much' by capitalism. And we find this Great Recession an especially apt time to consider alternatives, especially because experimentation clearly seems to be flourishing in many parts of the world (as we have learned and observed through many of our own contacts).

How does hegemony look in the light of the Great Recession?

There are many terms and metaphors for the relationships between major forces of society and their potential for influence. These include reform, irony, parody, subversion, co-optation, recuperation, equifinality, incrementalism, transformation, and revolution. We also recognize the unintended consequences that may accompany any change or movement, as shown so powerfully in the history of technology (Wright, 2005). Needless to say, even the relationship between two forces or movements can be extremely complex and, in terms of 'alternative organizing', a great deal of activity may be going on under the surface. Networks of scroungers and their associated centres for distribution and sharing are but one of the most telling types of 'extra-economic' activity today. But there are discursive as well as material moves that may not be readily apparent. For example, consider the widening appeal of employee ownership to segments of the political spectrum not previously inclined toward such a set of options (Alperowitz and Dubb, 2013), or the ways in which arguments for 'markets' might be separated from a celebration of capitalism (Chartier and Johnson, 2011).

Is imagining, practising and writing about alternatives futile?

Some forms of protest and alternative have existed for as long as capitalism, and hardly seem to have made a dent in it. The corporate social responsibility movement, widely apparent since the late 1970s, has yielded the Global Compact (1999) underwritten by many transnational corporations and yet has also lost its potential edge because its goals and practices are so easily adopted, promoted and contained (Christensen *et al.*, 2011; Zorn and Collins, 2007).

In response we would argue that recuperation or appropriation is not a frictionless, unilateral process. Appropriation is not total; it can never be. It is in many cases precisely the transgressive and distinctive nature of alternatives, of their oppositional nature, that constitutes their appeal to capitalism, that enables capitalist appropriators to extract a rent value out of them. For example, Harvey (2011) argues that capitalism can only cash in on oppositional, transgressive practices to the extent that they remain transgressive, that they can be branded and sold as 'distinctive'; but in order to have exchange value, their uniqueness also needs to be translated into a system of tradable equivalents that undermines their very distinctiveness. Capitalism's commodification and capture of everything is not a smooth process; it is full of contradictions, as suggested by the claim that 'The spaces for transformational politics are there because capitalism can never afford to close them down' (Harvey, 2011: 111). Similarly, as De Angelis and Harvie discuss in this volume (see Chapter 19), capitalism relies on the continuing existence of the commons, it cannot destroy them. These dialectical relations between capitalism and its others create spaces of potentially productive tension.

Alternatives are not passive, static entities any more than is contemporary capitalism, but rather are fluid, dynamic movements that have the ability to shift, disband and reconstitute. For example, the fact that capitalism empties organic agriculture or micro-finance of certain values or practices doesn't mean that these values or practices no longer exist, or that they are prevented from resurfacing elsewhere. Thus a handbook of alternatives written three decades ago would have looked very different from what we ended up with here, or from the sorts of alternatives that would be included in such a handbook three decades hence. Moreover, we hope that we are correct in assuming that even the list of types of alternative organizations we imagine now will be augmented by the imagination and practices of the future.

So, what sort of stance should we take toward social change?

General pessimism in the face of the self-destructive tendencies around us would seem to be at least as rational as the commonplace argument of the inevitability of the further exploitation of fossil fuels at the extremes of the earth. We each and together have our good days and bad ones, of course, in terms of keeping hope alive amidst dire predictions for where our civilization and its home are headed. But, pessimism can also yield self-fulfilling prophecies of a disastrous sort, even by sheer neglect. A reasonable degree of pessimism of the intellect is necessary for analysis and for informed choice. But strategy that is absent of some measure of hope and passion isn't fully a choice – that is, not one that can be embraced and pursued in a thorough or sustained manner. In this sense, it is as important to consider the emotional tenor of a position as it is its ethical position.

A compelling and well-articulated treatment of these issues comes to us from J.K. Gibson-Graham (2006) in *A Postcapitalist Politics*. Unlike most critical accounts of social and economic change, it explicitly brings in the psychological dimensions of work within and toward the transformation of economy and society. It tries to correct for the overly cognitive, rational and somewhat problematic way in which 'realism' is often deployed. We use the term realism here in the sense of buying into the argument of inevitability of current forces and even of seeing them as monolithic. The kind of 'stance ' that Gibson-Graham advocates embraces ethical and strategic positions but is deeply tied to place and people and is acutely sensitive to the motivational tone of any project or proposal. The 'imaginary' in this way must be fully activated at the individual and group levels, and this also involves a different kind of realism that sees avenues of genuine possibility without the preoccupation that those can necessarily lead toward broader movements. Gibson-Graham's argument resists seeing the status quo as monolithic, as univocal, or as unchangeable. But, it also rejecst the notion that local projects, like many discussed in this volume, should be dismissed as limited in scope, escapist, or destined to be short-lived. Thus, Gibson-Graham offers critical-ethical enterprises a much-needed social psychology of emotion, a sense of the strength and fragility of a belief that the world might be different.

Too often, of course, alternatives to the status quo are dismissed as fantasy or as threat and, either way, not taken for what they could mean in terms of reorganizing. Local currencies, time banks and alternative trade organizations (see Chapter 12, this volume) have been laughingly dismissed by corporate powers; worker cooperatives have been treated as isolated cases (and are still framed that way in the mainstream press; see Chapter 5, this volume); the assertive attempts of the dispossessed to claim voice and unity have in many parts of the world been quashed (as can be seen in responses to some protests and organizing activities in response to corporate control of water and water systems; Callister, 2013).

The point is not that we seek some pure form of resistance or transformation any more than we can seek pure democracy. But we can hold out ideals of autonomy, solidarity and responsibility (as articulated in Chapter 3, this volume) as beacons for practice, however imperfectly realized, because we do have before us, in both history and the present, extraordinary examples of human cooperation. This means moving from individual practices outward. Just as there can be conscientious consumption (see Kendall *et al.*, 2007), so there can be deliberate, even if contingent, organizing. To repeat what we said in Chapter 3, organizing is politics made durable, and we must always see it like that; otherwise we risk assuming that the world has to be, must always be, like this.

Toward insurgent entrepreneurship

Perhaps the key here is 'imagine', but part of this process of making new social relations is actually recognizing the openings and possibilities that already exist, many of which have already been tested. This is difficult to accomplish, of course, when points of leverage for social change and many of the current experiments around the world receive scant attention in the mainstream media, or within the business and management parts of university education. As many of the contributors to this volume have suggested, working at the group, neighbourhood or community level while networking more broadly can allow for the kind of social support and resource access needed for sustaining projects as well as individual motivation to work on them. This is certainly one of the lessons of Occupy, where many participants observed the power of their dual experiences: in face-to-face democracy and work, and in networked collaboration (Taylor and Gesen, 2011).

Throughout this book we have examined a range of practices that, in some sense, offer an alternative to the capitalist mainstream. If we understand capitalism in the most minimal sense as accumulation for its own sake, these alternative practices might be considered inadequate, for they can too easily be re-inscribed within conventional capitalist dynamics.

For example, faced with mountains of waste, it doesn't take a great leap of imagination to move from living through scavenging to creating a large recycling business to appease consumers' eco-consciences and make a lot of money. If it is structured through conventional share ownership, CEO-controlled hierarchies, with minimum wage employees and a main eye for the bottom line, this would be little more than another capitalist enterprise exploiting a new market niche (Rogers, 2005). On the other hand, if scavenging offers a space for an existence that is independent of waged labour and oriented toward the subsistence of the scavengers, however organized, then this could hardly be considered capitalism by any recognized definition. Not only is such scavenging not, in Ferrell's account (see Chapter 20, this volume), oriented toward the accumulation of a surplus for reinvestment, but it does not involve waged labour, a key feature of capitalism.

A more ambiguous example could be termed a hybrid. Imagine a worker's cooperative, with strictly egalitarian profit sharing, consensus-based, participative decision making, operating as a social enterprise to reduce waste and landfill in a city. Would this be capitalism as we know it, in the absence of hierarchy, a surplus/profit to productively reinvest, and a separation of employees from ownership? If, as we suggested in Chapter 2, capitalism is itself more varied and less monolithic than we often assume, then asking questions about capitalism's ability to recuperate these alternatives is perhaps asking the wrong question. In order to have a plurality of non-capitalisms, we must have a plurality of capitalisms: 'By analogy here, the specificity of capitalism – its plural identity, if you like – becomes a condition of the existence of a discourse of noncapitalism as a set of positive and differentiated economic forms' (Gibson-Graham, 1996: 14).

At the centre of these questions is how we imagine not only alternatives, but also the capitalism that they are alternative to. The omnipotence projected onto capitalism – reinforced by its own refrain of inevitability (Aune, 2002; Fisher, 2009) – becomes disempowering and depresses any possibility of active, positive engagement in making worlds. Thus what we need is a radical, insurgent form of entrepreneurship, perhaps of the sort envisaged by Hjorth and. Steyaert (2004: 3), when they write about entrepreneurship as 'forms of social creativity, taking place primarily in societal rather than in business contexts. Entrepreneurship is a societal force: it changes our daily practices and the way we live; it invents futures in populating histories of the present, here and now.' From this perspective, entrepreneurship is not an essentially capitalist practice, encroaching into the 'social' as a force of capitalist commodification and strictly performative rationality. Instead, entrepreneurship, like capitalism, is understood as unstable and contested: a set of potentially transformative practices of invention for communities as well as for individuals. Rather than bemoaning the recuperation of alternatives by a hegemonic capitalism, from this perspective we would be better to examine the lines of variation and difference that organizational entrepreneurs – whether scavengers, anti-capitalist social movements, or worker co-operators – set in motion.

For a critical social theorist, it may be more comfortable and reassuring to spot the recuperation, and thereby demonstrate one's cleverness and intellectual mastery of capitalism, but this is a very limited strategy if the real goal is social transformation. It leads to a cynical distance from the activity of organizing and world making, a resistance to commitment or even a statement of preference. What is required is a more open, active and experimental form of positive critique which brings new things into the world.

To return for a moment to Boltanski and Chiapello's (2005) insightful and sweeping analysis of capitalism and its discontents, we find one significant risk with critical projects explaining (away) all forms of resistance is that they unintentionally construct closed circuits. 'There appears to be nothing "external" to the explanation which could cause it to fail because everything is included' (Parker, 2013: 126). In this way, critical scepticism bordering on certainty, however informed by data and examples, can ironically mirror or, worse, support the 'inevitability' posture of apologists for the status quo. Social imagination is ultimately the loser in such a match of predominant system with domineering critique, or with an endless discovery of reasons why change is always flawed.

Perhaps the stance of Vandana Shiva (2000, 2011, 2012), Indian scientist and activist, writer and leader in global solidarity economics, is instructive. Her model is one of unflinching investigation and critique, yet with a consistent vision of hope and possibility, grounded in basic human needs and connections with one another and the earth. Her position is at once deeply rooted in local experience and yet infused with awareness of, and connection to, global conditions and trends. Within this wide horizontal channel for action are a multitude of streams and confluences.

An exceptionally powerful documentary, *The Economics of Happiness* (Norberg-Hodge, 2011), features Shiva and a number of other leaders in social, economic and environmental change. Even more importantly, the film shows how local activities and projects can be connected to larger movements: how, for example, farmers' markets and bioregional food strategies can be interlinked, not only in a broader social consciousness but also in terms of networking for social change. Ranging across topics from studies of happiness to individual identity and consumption to international regulation of multinational corporations to alternative GDPs, the documentary makes vivid the local in the global and vice versa. The same ethos is manifest in outlets like *Yes!* magazine and indeed at the annual World Social Forum itself. These, and thousands of little-known but vibrant initiatives around the world, are precisely the types of projects and messages that offer motivational power as well as some capacity for transformative change.

There is tremendous potential for the appropriation and transformation of entrepreneurship, a master trope of our times. This is not the 'social entrepreneurship' which simply moves state functions to the private sector, but an 'organizational entrepreneurship' which politicizes and reorients organizing. We need to shift entrepreneurship to the group level, infusing it with an element of insurgency, while recognizing also the contingent opportunities for change. This can involve as much a revival of virtue ethics, reinvigorating the economy with the very virtues like compassion and empathy that Adam Smith (1976a, 1976b) featured in his oft-misunderstood account of the market (see Werhane, 1991) and reaching and preaching beyond the choir of left-leaning activists. There is no substantive reason that any of the alternatives discussed here should have limited appeal across the political spectrum. Indeed, witness new alliances in many parts of the world today, grounded in commitments to local communities and with the recognition of the dysfunctions of government as well as megacorporations. There are signs that the cooperative movement, for example, is now embracing a much wider audience and cast of participants, ranging from labour unions to high-tech entrepreneurs. So, we are reminded to be careful with reliance on traditional classifications and presumptions about the bases for group coalescence and loyalties.

A new spirit of insurgent entrepreneurship, complete with sensibilities of autonomy, solidarity and responsibility, offers qualified hope, even though the outcomes of our collective actions, on any level or location, must remain uncertain. Dr Martin Luther King, Jr. observed that at the front end of any movement, there is always great uncertainty; it is only in retrospect that we know what worked. But failing to experiment, to be both critical of and playful with the socio-economic order, is to accept a kind of inevitability, and this is something that we ought to avoid. If this book provides resources to avoid inevitability, then we will be happy.

Notes

1 At the time of writing, the full set of images for this advertising campaign could be viewed at: http://theinspirationroom.com/daily/2007/we-live-in-financial-times/ A Google image search for 'Branson Che' should turn up several sites with the image if this link is no longer functioning when you come to read this (and assuming that Google is still around and global capitalism hasn't collapsed, taking the internet with it). When we asked the FT if we could reproduce the image in this book we were refused permission as the syndication team was 'advised by legal that FT cannot syndicate this particular advertisement'. While quite happy to appropriate images of radical critique and revolution for the purpose of promoting entrepreneurship and selling newspapers, something that we can only assume Che Guevara would have had a few issues with, they are uncomfortable about their images appearing in an academic text. Given that the advertisements appeared in numerous public spaces, for example, on the walls of the London subway, this raises interesting questions concerning the enclosure of culture and the foreclosure of public debate in the quasi-privatized spaces of copyright and advertising billboards. There are some parallels with the discussion of the commons and enclosure found in Chapter 19.

Resources

Each chapter has had its own resources, but this is our collection, which stands as our resources for Chapters 1, 2, 3 and 24.

Alperowitz, G. (2013). *What Then Must We Do?* White River Junction, VI: Chelsea Green Publishing.
A political economist and journalist describes what he thinks a new American economy might look like in the future.

Benhabib, S. (1996). *Democracy and Difference*. Princeton, NJ: Princeton University Press.
A book by a political theorist about the tensions between democracy and the politics of identity and difference.

Carlsson, C. (2008). *Nowtopia: How Pirate Programmers, Outlaw Bicyclists and Vacant-lot Gardeners Are Inventing the Future Today*. Oakland, CA: AK Press.
Not an academic book but very engaging and readable and presents a nice review of radical organizational practices today, at least in the US.

Chang, H-J. (2011). *23 Things They Don't Tell You About Capitalism*. London: Penguin.
A book which exposes the myths of capitalism, and the truths about inequality, free markets, regulation and globalization.

Fisher, M. (2009). *Capitalist Realism: Is There No Alternative?* Winchester: Zero Books.
Using examples from film, fiction and education, Fisher argues that capitalist realism exercises a powerful grip on our imagination. He goes on to suggest that there are tensions and contradictions within capitalism that make it anything but realist.

Gibson-Graham, J.K. (2006). *A Post-capitalist Politics*. Minneapolis: Minnesota University Press.
Two academics show how capitalism can be put in its place, and what sorts of theoretical and practical strategies are needed to do so.

Guin, U. Le. (1974). *The Dispossessed*. New York: Harper and Row.
A celebrated science fiction novel which explores the practicalities of an anarchist society.

Harvey, D. (2011). *The Enigma of Capital and the Crisis of Capitalism*. London: Profile Books.
Harvey, a Marxist geographer, explains what capitalism is by describing the various ways in which it seeks to accumulate money; he also argues that capitalism is endemically prone to crisis.

Michaels, F.S. (2011). *Monoculture: How One Story is Changing Everything*. Kamloops, BC: Red Clover Press.
This book suggests that we live in a monoculture dominated by economic values that shape all areas of our lives: from our work, to our relationships with others or the environment, to our health.

Patel, R. (2009). *The Value of Nothing*. London: Portobello Books.
In this book, Patel asks why things cost what they do, and explains the failures of the market in accounting for real costs.

Reed, D. and McMurty, J.J. (eds). (2009). *Co-operatives in a Global Economy: The Challenge of Co-operation Across Borders*. Newcastle upon Tyne, UK: Cambridge Scholars Publishing.
A comprehensive and global review of cooperative methods of organization for production and consumption.

Rowe, J. (2013). *Our Common Wealth: The Hidden Economy That Makes Everything Else Work*. San Francisco, CA Berrett-Koehler.
Shows how capitalism relies on all sorts of environmental, social and informational commons, and just how important it is to reclaim the idea of collective resources.

Worldwatch Institute. (2013). *Is Sustainability Still Possible*? Washington, DC: Island Press.
Presents the latest thinking on the challenges of a sustainable economy, and the social prospects if we do not manage to create one.

References

Alperowitz, G. and Dubb, S. (2013). *The New Alliance: Organizing for Economic Justice, Building a New Economy*. Working paper. College Park: Democracy Collaborative, The University of Maryland.
Aune, J.A. (2002). *The Selling of the Free Market*. New York: Guilford Press.
Azkarraga, J., Cheney, G. and Udaondo, A. (2012). Workers' participation in a globalized market: Reflections on and from Mondragon. In M. Atzeni (ed.), *Alternative Work Organizations* (pp. 76–102). New York: Palgrave Macmillan.
Boltanski, L. and Chiapello, E. (2005). *The New Spirit of Capitalism*. London: Verso.
Callister, D.C. (2013). *Immersed in Water Conflict: Humor and Process Literacy as Rhetorical Strategies in Internal Coalition Maintenance*. Unpublished PhD dissertation. Salt Lake City: The University of Utah.
Castells, M. (2000). *The Rise of the Network Society*, 2nd edn. Malden, MA: Wiley-Blackwell.
Cathcart, A. (2013a). Paradoxes of participation: Non-union workplace partnership in John Lewis, *International Journal of Human Resource Management*.
Cathcart, A. (2013b). Directing democracy: Competing interests and contested terrain in the John Lewis partnership, *Industrial Relations Journal*.
Chartier, G. and Johnson, C. (eds). (2011). *Markets not Capitalism*. Brooklyn, NY: Autonomedia.
Cheney, G. (2002). *Values at Work: Employee Participation Meets Market Pressure at Mondragon*. Ithaca, NY: Cornell University Press.
Christensen, L.T., Morsing, M. and Thyssen, O. (2011). The polyphony of corporate social responsibility: Deconstructing accountability and transparency in the context of identity and hypocrisy. In G. Cheney, S. May and D. Munshi (eds). *Handbook of Communication Ethics* (pp. 457–474). Princeton, NJ: Lawrence Erlbaum Associates, Incorporated.
Cock, C. de, Fitchett, J. and Volkmann, C. (2005). Constructing the new economy: A Discursive perspective, *British Journal of Management*, 16(1): 37–49.
Cooke, B. and Kothari, U. (2001). *Participation: The New Tyranny*? London: Zed Books.
Fisher, M. (2009). *Capitalist Realism: Is There No Alternative*? Ropley: Zero Books.
Foucault, M. (2001). *Fearless Speech* (J. Pearson, ed.). New York: Semiotext(e).
Gibson-Graham, J.K. (1996). *The End of Capitalism (As We Knew It): A Feminist Critique of Political Economy*. Oxford: Blackwell.
Gibson-Graham, J.K. (2006). *A Postcapitalist Politics*. Minneapolis: University of Minnesota Press.
Hardy, C. and Leiba-O'Sullivan, S. (1998). The power behind empowerment: Implications for research and practice, *Human Relations*, 51(4): 451–483.
Harvey, D. (2011). *The Enigma of Capital and the Crisis of Capitalism*. London: Profile Books.
Harvey, D. (2012). *Rebel Cities: From the Right to the City to the Urban Revolution*. London: Verso.
Heath, J. and Potter, A. (2004). *The Rebel Sell: Why the Culture Can't be Jammed*. Minnesota: Capstone.
Hjorth, D. and Steyaert, C. (eds). (2004). *Narrative and Discursive Approaches in Entrepreneurship: A Second Movements in Entrepreneurship Book*. Cheltenham: Edward Elgar.

Hyman, J., Thompson, P. and Harley, B. (2005). *Participation and Democracy at Work*. London: Palgrave Macmillan.

James, O. (2007). *Affluenza: How to Be Successful and Stay Sane*. London: Vermillion.

Kendall, B.E., Gill, R. and Cheney, G. (2007). Consumer activism and corporate social responsibility: How strong a connection? In S.K. May, G. Cheney, and J. Roper (eds), *The Debate over Corporate Social Responsibility* (pp. 241–266). New York: Oxford University Press.

Klein, N. (2009). *No Logo*, tenth anniversary edition. New York: St Martin's Press.

McLagan, P. and Nel, C. (1997). *The Age of Participation*. San Francisco, CA: Berrett-Koehler.

Norberg-Hodge, H. (2011, July). The economics of happiness (lecture). Christchurch, NZ: Tedx. Available online at www.theeconomicsofhappiness.org/helena-on-tedx

Norberg-Hodge, H. (2011). *The Economics of Happiness* (film). Available online at www.theeconomicsofhappiness.org

Parker, M. (2013). Beyond justification: Dietrologic and the sociology of critique. In P. Du Gay and G. Morgan (eds), *New Spirits of Capitalism* (pp. 124–141). Oxford: Oxford University Press.

Peters, T. and Waterman, R. (1981). *In Search of Excellence*. New York: Harper & Row.

Rainie, L. and Wellman, B. (2012). *Networked*. Cambridge, MA: MIT Press.

Rehn, A. and Sköld, D. (2005). 'I Love The Dough': Rap Lyrics as a Minor Economic Literature, *Culture and Organization*, 11(1): 17–31.

Rogers, H. (2005). *Gone Tomorrow: The Hidden Life of Garbage*. New York: New Press.

Rothschild, J. and Whitt, J.A. (1986). *The Cooperative Workplace: Potentials and Dilemmas of Organizational Democracy and Participation*. New York: Cambridge University Press.

Schor, J. (2004, 15 August). Lecture on the global economy. Whidbey Island, WA.

Sharzer, G. (2012). *No Local: Why Small-scale Alternatives Won't Change the World*. Arlesford, UK: Zero Books.

Shiva, V. (2000). *Stolen Harvest: The Hijacking of the Global Food Supply*. Cambridge, MA: South End Press.

Shiva, V. (2011). *The Corporate Control of Life: 100 Notes, 100 Thoughts*. Kassel, Germany: Hatje Cantz.

Shiva, V. (2012). *Making Peace with the Earth: Beyond Resource, Land and Food Wars*. Columbia, MO: South Asia Books.

Shukaitis, S. (2010). Sisyphus and the labour of imagination: Autonomy, cultural production, and the antinomies of worker self-management, *Affinities: A Journal of Radical Theory, Culture, and Action*, 4(1): 57–82.

Smith, A. (1976a, 1759). *The Theory of Moral Sentiments*. A.L. Macfie and D.D. Raphael (eds). Oxford: Oxford University Press.

Smith, A. (1976b, 1776). *The Wealth of Nations*. R.H. Campbell and A.S. Skinner (eds). Oxford: Oxford University Press.

Taylor, A., Gessen, K. *et al.* (2011). *Occupy! Scenes from Occupied America*. London: Verso.

Troeltsch, E. (1956, 1912). *The Social Teachings of the Christian Churches*. London: Allen & Unwin.

Werhane, P. (1991). *Adam Smith and his Legacy for Modern Capitalism*. New York: Oxford University Press.

Wright, R. (2005). *A Short History of Progress*. New York: Carroll & Graf.

Zorn, T.E. and Collins, E. (2007). Is sustainability sustainable? Corporate social responsibility, sustainable business, and management fashion. In S.K. May, G. Cheney and J. Roper (eds), *The Debate over Corporate Social Responsibility* (pp. 405–416). New York: Oxford University Press.

Index